Race and the Rise of the Republican Party, 1848-1865

Race and the Rise of the Republican Party, 1848-1865

James D. Bilotta

This book was printed in the United States of America.

To order additional copies of this book, contact:

Xlibris Corporation

1-888-795-4274

www.Xlibris.com

Orders@Xlibris.com

15393

CONTENTS

TO MY WIFE AND CHILDREN

Acknowledgement

To my friend John D. Milligan for all his help

INTRODUCTION

During the antebellum period, and in particular in the 1840's and 1850's, the antislavery movement in the Northeastern and Western sections of the United States became increasingly politicized. Rather than remaining the almost exclusive domain of a handful of abolitionists, the antislavery cause became popular with a large number of Eastern and Western politicians, newspaper editors and popular writers. Beginning with the formation of the Liberty Party in 1839 and, more importantly for the purpose of this study, with that amorphous mass known as the Free Soil movement in the 1840's, and its outgrowth, the Free Soil Party in 1848 and the Republican Party in 1854, the antislavery cause achieved political significance. This work demonstrates that racial considerations formed a crucial element in Free Soil and Republican antislavery thought and action. At the same time, it will show that not all Free Soilers and Republicans were consistently swayed by racist dogma, that a small but significant minority at times expressed opinions on the Negro race and its place in American society that were contrary to those held by the majority in their parties.

Relatively large numbers of Free Soilers and Republicans endorsed ideas on race currently held by many of those associated with the scientific and learned communities of the period, ideas which viewed the Negro as racially, that is, as biologically, inferior to the Caucasian and the Caucasian race as superior to all others. Numerous learned writers, physicians and scientists, including some founding members of the Free Soil and Republican Parties, claimed that differences among the races, not simply physical but mental, were innate and hence permanent.

Contrary to the belief in environmental causation held by many of the rationalist philosophers of the eighteenth century enlightenment and by the radical abolitionists and some intellectuals and scientists of the antebellum period, a belief which stressed the essential unity of all mankind, these writers maintained that environmental factors were inconsequential in influencing a person's development and ultimate worth. Race was the key determinant. In fact, each race had its own distinct and inborn characteristics. In essence, physical appearance alone was the key to correctly anticipating an individual's physical and mental capacities. More pointedly, all one had to do to judge an individual's abilities was to determine his or her skin color.

Since Southern slavery meant the presence in the United States of large numbers of allegedly inferior, black-skinned people, questions touching the future status of that institution, such as whether slavery should be allowed to expand into the West or whether the black race should continue in bondage or be freed, were to many antislavery politicians and writers racial questions as well as sectional or economic ones. Ironically, the same racist ideas promulgated by some Southerners to defend slavery were used quite effectively by some Northerners to attack it. It is no coincidence that with the rise of racialist theories also came the rise of a strident, political antislavery movement. Many of the policies adopted by both Free Soilers and Republicans were influenced by racial considerations, which had for their central core the belief in the inferiority of the black man. For example, the policies of containing slavery in the Southern states, perhaps best exemplified by the Wilmot Proviso, or of colonizing the black man out of the country, were in part predicated on the theory that black people represented an inferior race, not fit to associate and, in particular, copulate or intermarry with the superior Caucasian race, lest they dilute the purity and therefore the superior qualities of the latter race. It was deemed to be in the white man's best interests that the two races should ultimately be separated, even to the extent that blacks be deported out of the country thereby leaving an homogeneous white population in control of the country to develop and enjoy the fruits of its material wealth.

Hence, with some important exceptions, mainly among those who at times embraced environmental causation with its concept of universal man, this writer finds that most members of the Free Soil and Republican Parties manifested little of the moral or reforming zeal existing among radical abolitionists who demanded an immediate end to slavery. Rather, the antislavery stance of these parties was basically conservative and racial in nature, for the most part limited to preventing the expansion of slavery and the black man, and often addressed to pragmatic concerns which would win the support of white voters. A good portion of the Free Soil antislavery argument can be translated into a plea for a soil free of black people. In this context antislavery can be viewed as anti-black. The incessant use of the adjective 'white' by Free Soil and Republican politicians lends strong credence to this view. White skin connoted something good, whereas black skin symbolized evil. Reduced to its lowest common denominator, the campaign against the expansion of slavery had as much, if not more to do with the question of race, as it did with the issues of the relative merits of opposing systems of labor. In the process Free Soilers and Republicans often subordinated purely class interests to racial considerations, by dividing workers along a color line. The Free Soil movement was narrowly defined, white in complexion, and antagonistic to the interests of black Americans both in and out of slavery. At times Free Soilers and later Republicans displayed an obsessive, almost pathological fear and hatred of black people. Whereas Southerners sought to dominate black people, Northerners would have nothing whatsoever to do with them. In the final analysis racialist arguments were used far more effectively to attack than defend slavery.

Historiographically, however, this view of the Free Soil and Republican Parties as basically conservative and racist was not emphasized until relatively recent times, and in particular until the advent of the black civil rights movement of the 1960's. Prior to the sixties, many historians tended to equate these parties and their policies with abolitionism. They stated, implicitly if not explicitly, that antislavery politicians and writers were engaged in a moral crusade to end slavery, and often they pictured these politicians and writers as being aided by an abolitionized North. Some of these historians went so far as to depict Free Soil and Republican politicians as abolitionists- 'higher law' radicals-whose goal, the destruction of slavery, was merely a means to achieve the social and political equality of all people, black and white. With the exception of chroniclers who explained the Civil War either as an economic confrontation or a needless conflict, historians usually viewed antislavery politicians and writers as men of principle fighting the evil influences of slavery for the good of the nation and its citizens. Most historians, however, virtually ignored black people themselves and white racial prejudice against blacks.

The view of a Republican and abolitionized North battling against the immorality of Southern slavery was particularly prevalent among Northern writers who, as soldiers and politicians during the Civil War, declared that war to be the result of a conspiracy of Southern slaveholders. This group included such writers as James G. Blaine, Henry Wilson and John A. Logan who, not just coincidentally, belonged to the founding generation of the Republican Party. Blaine describes the Republican Party as one which "stood upon principle and shunned expediency." Wilson draws a closer connection between political antislavery and radical abolitionism, when he writes that the "Republican cause" represented the "highest plane of antislavery thought and purpose," because it was "inspired by freedom." So much was this the case, declares Logan in his aptly titled book, *The Great Conspiracy*, that the major issue for Abraham Lincoln and the Republicans in the 1860 presidential campaign was that of "human freedom."[1]

Later writers who, as Nationalists or Neo-Nationalists, saw the War as an 'irrepressible conflict' between the North and South, also tended to equate Republicanism with abolitionism. Although not as vindictive toward the South as the Northern writers who emphasized a slaveholders' conspiracy, such historians usually depicted the Republican Party as having morally regenerated the nation through a successful battle with slavery. The Nationalist historian James Ford Rhodes clearly depicts the Republicans' indebtedness to political antislavery on the part of the radical abolitionists: the "Republican Party . . . ," he flatly asserts, "could not have succeeded without the backing of a multitude of men and women who . . . believed slavery to be a cruel wrong, opposed to the law of God and to the best interests of humanity." In keeping with this idea, James

Schouler writes of the spirit of "splendid moral reform" which motivated the party. Perhaps for these historians the best embodiment of the reform spirit was Lincoln, who, John W. Burgess told his readers, was noted for his "absence of prejudice" and, therefore, "founded policy upon morality." According to this school of historical thought, other Republicans joined Lincoln in refusing to endorse the Crittenden Compromise proposals because such an agreement would be the equivalent of "moral suicide." Some Nationalist writers carried this concept of Republican idealism even further by depicting Lincoln as a radical, revolutionary hero. "Lincoln's election," noted Arthur C. Cole in *The Irrepressible Conflict*, "inaugurated a revolution" against Southern slavery. The Neo-Nationalist, Dwight L. Dumond, believes that the political antislavery movement "was an intellectual and religious crusade for moral reform," which "abolitionized" the North and, under Lincoln's Republican leadership, ultimately freed the slaves. Arthur Schlesinger, Jr., another Neo-Nationalist, draws a parallel between the extension of Southern slavery during the antebellum period and the extension of fascism preceding World War Two. Both were acts of "aggression," but for Republican politicians, the former "made a moral choice inescapable."[2]

Other earlier historians in search of the causes of the Civil War also described that war as an 'irrepressible conflict,' but not so much over the moral issue of slavery as between two competing systems of labor and capital. Yet, even these writers, the 'Economic' school, and their pro-Southern contemporaries of the Nashville or Agrarian school still managed at times to identify free soilism and republicanism with abolitionism. Charles A. and Mary R. Beard were perhaps the best example of those who subscribed to economic causation. In several instances the Beards write of "abolitionists and free-soilers" as though they were one and the same group of people, while Republican politicians were the chief spirits behind "the anti-slavery agitation." Writers from the Southern or Agrarian school, such as Arthur Young Lloyd and Ulrich B. Phillips held similar views. Like the Beards, Lloyd perceives "a direct connection between the abolition propaganda and the agitation of the slavery issue," and links both to "the formation of a major sectional [Republican] Party." Phillips writes as if he really believes that "Republicans were abolitionists in disguise."[3]

Even Revisionist historians who, although not as strongly as the Agrarian writers, tended to sympathize with the Southern cause by advancing the 'repressible conflict' thesis to counter the interpretation of the Nationalists did, at times, portray the Republican Party as abolitionized. "The Republican Party," according to Avery O. Craven, was "a professed defender of Christianity, democracy and progress" which drew "on the moral assumptions of the [abolitionist] reformers" for its strength. James G. Randall writes of the "moral indignation" which the Republicans in general felt toward slavery, and, in particular, of Lincoln's "moral indignation and reforming zeal." In describing the 1860 presidential campaign, Randall notes the "representation of Lincoln as a 'black Republican' and an enemy of the South" by the Southern Democratic press, "with no public effort on Lincoln's part to correct the impression." One is left with the conclusion that Lincoln was either unwilling or unable to refute this characterization of himself. Kenneth Stampp, too, writes as if the Republican Party was created around the ideal of abolition. He refers to the "intense degree of moral fervor" which "antislavery radicals" brought into the Republican Party, and concludes that "in a very real sense it was this group which gave the Republicans their raison d'etre, their driving force." Another Revisionist historian, George Fort Milton, not only links abolitionism with republicanism but, pointing to David Wilmot, among others, states that "Radical anti-slavery men were in the saddle when the Republican [presidential] Convention met . . . in Philadelphia [in 1856]." This same party, he goes on, was "an Abolition party, under the name and disguise of a Republican Party."[4]

Generally, then, it can be seen that although historians among different schools disagreed in their interpretations of the causes of the Civil War, they nevertheless connected free soilism and republicanism with abolitionism, and many wrote as if moral considerations significantly contributed to the Republican opposition to Southern slavery. Further, the writers in these various schools usually ignored black interests and rights as well as the white racialism which permeated much of the political antislavery movement during the antebellum period.

Beginning with the modern civil rights movement of the 1960's, a number of historians concerned with the Free Soil and Republican Parties, such as Frederick J. Blue, James A. Rawley and Chaplain W. Morrison, became conscious of these omissions in the works of previous writers and initiated a more critical/ skeptical examination of the "moral imperatives" which supposedly propelled antislavery politicians. What they argue hardly comports with the picture that "Republicans were abolitionists in disguise." On the contrary, far from being morally driven, antislavery politicians based much of their opposition to slavery expansion on their belief in the inferiority of the black man, and often defended their policies by appeals to white racial prejudice and open attacks upon the black man. Moreover, far from identifying themselves with the abolitionists, Free Soilers and Republicans denounced the radicals as "useless agitators" and refused to associate with them. Whereas a number of earlier historians wrote about an abolitionized North, this newer school of historians challenges that idea. When writing about the Wilmot Proviso, Blue notes that it "was . . . devised as a means to shift the issue from opposition to slavery per se, to the more practical . . . matter of opposition to the expansion of slavery." Blue concludes that "on the issue of race, almost all Free Soilers demonstrated how similar they were to Democrats and Whigs." By "sharing the racism of northern society" they indicated that they, too, wanted "to avoid any contact with the black population." Rawley holds a similar view. He notes that "antiextension came to be endowed with morality, but it was a morality shaped by ethnic preconceptions." Rather than being exclusively a battle for "human freedom," the "ordeal of the Union," as Rawley states it, "was, among other matters, a racial ordeal." Writing about the opposition to the extension of slavery as embodied in the Wilmot Proviso, Morrison finds that this Proviso was "commonly called the 'White Man's Resolution' by free soilers." He adds that "if the desire for white supremacy was the strongest emotional force behind the Southern opposition to the Wilmot Proviso," then, "it seems likewise to have been one of the strongest emotional forces for the movement for the Proviso in the North."[5]

Allan Peskin also questions the older idea of an abolitionized North. He writes that "although the Northern states had rejected Negro slavery, they did not embrace the Negro." Indeed, Peskin believes that "in most Northern states the Negro was regarded as a nuisance at best, and at worst a menace to the prosperity of white working men." Therefore, Eugene H. Berwanger concludes, Northern whites feared the increase of the black population in the United States. Much of this "Negrophobia" was rooted in worry about miscegenation and the demand by free blacks for socio-economic equality, both of which were seen as a threat to white dominance. Concurring with this thesis, Ronald G. Walters emphasizes that "before the decade [1840's] was out, a portion of the Liberty Party men drifted off into the Free Soil movement," and made their political appeal "to the self-interest, rather than the spirituality of whites."[6]

Larry Gara, another student of free soilism, states that "when Northern Negroes asked Free Soilers what they thought should be done for them or what course they should follow, the recommendation was always the same: separation and usually colonization in some other country." Gara goes further and draws a significant distinction between the Free Soilers' attack on slavery, as an immoral institution, and their attack on the extension of slavery and the slave power. Gara, like Blue and Walters, discovers little of the radical abolitionist element or concern for the black man as a human being within either the Free Soil or later Republican Parties. He thinks that the "combination of anti-slave power and anti-Negro sentiment was a powerful attraction in both the Free Soil and Republican programs."[7]

Although Eric Foner argues that Republicans were ideologically driven by a free labor philosophy, yet he credits this critical interpretation when he deals with the 'Barnburners' or Democratic defectors to the Free Soil Party in New York state. He writes that "they made it clear that their support of the [Wilmot] Proviso was based as much on repugnance to the prospect of a Negro population, free or slave, in the territories, as on an opposition to the spread of the institution of slavery." Contrary to the view of earlier historians, Foner notes that "theirs was no moral opposition to the slave system," because the "Barnburners were concerned for the fate of the free white laborer of the North." Free white laborers, for their part, "would never migrate to an area of slavery, both because of their animosity to the Negro, and because they could not compete with slave labor." Gerald Sorin agrees with Foner's analysis, and adds that the New York Barnburners "wanted to write a general non-extension platform, that could attract some abolitionist votes, as well as the votes of whites who wanted to keep blacks out of the West." "The Barnburners," Sorin finds, "had a long history of Negrophobia."[8]

In summing up the views of this newer school of historians, George M. Fredrickson notes that "most Northern opponents of the extension of slavery, carefully disassociated themselves from the abolitionists, and their ideal of racial fraternity," but rather campaigned on the premise that "theirs was exclusively a white man's cause." Skin color was as important to them as it was for the ethnologists of the scientific community. Fredrickson sees deeper implications in this hostile racial attitude among Free Soilers and Republicans toward black Americans, implications that were to make necessary the later civil rights struggle of the 1960's. He believes that the "fact that Northerners could oppose slavery without a commitment to racial equality, helps explain why the Civil War resulted in the emancipation of the Negro from slavery, but not from caste discrimination and the ravages of racism."[9] In fine, Fredrickson calls for an extensive reexamination of the intellectual roots of the political antislavery movement.

The object of this study will be to carry forward the work of these newer historians by relating Free Soil and Republican antislavery policies more closely to the racial theories in vogue in the intellectual and scientific communities of the period. At the same time, however, the research leads the present writer to disagree with some of the more recent scholarship. First, this study disagrees with those writers who hold that the Free Soil and Republican Parties became racially conservative only as they matured.[10] It will provide evidence that from the start both parties were racist. Second, this study will endeavor to show that the newer historians may have moved the balance too far in the direction of painting all Free Soilers and Republicans with the same racialist brush. There were a small number of antebellum intellectuals, antislavery politicians and writers who, at least part of the time, and quite strongly, endorsed environmental causation rather than genealogy as a determinant of human activity. People sometimes change their views over time, and given the period under consideration, approximately 1848-1865, and the extraordinary geopolitical events associated with this period, change is understandable.

It is important to indicate these changes and inconsistencies in the hope of presenting a more balanced account.

It might be objected that most recently some historians have already begun to reemphasize the racially egalitarian ideas of certain antebellum Republican leaders, including Lincoln. By and large, however, these scholars have not as yet considered whether such ideas were disseminated by Republican writers and journalists. Nor have they thoroughly traced the antecedents of these ideas back through the Free Soil movement to the scientists and intellectuals of that day. Moreover, to this writer, it appears that these historians may be on their way simply to restoring the old balance which favored the Nationalistic and Neo-Nationalistic view that the Republican Party was after all essentially abolitionist in its philosophy and motivation.[11] In other words, research for this study indicates that the facts lie somewhat between a conclusion of the latter type and a conclusion which only stresses negative white racial attitudes.

Finally, this study will be done on a large scale, scrutinizing the words and ideas of many politicians, editors and writers. It is hoped that a kind of synthesis on the topic can be achieved. In order better to achieve this synthesis and because this interpretation departs from older interpretations, it will be necessary to quote many of the antislavery politicians and writers. In this way the reader is permitted the opportunity not only to go back in time and judge precisely Northern opinions concerning blacks, but also the emotional depth of these opinions.

By examining the works of prominent ethnologists, scientists, physicians, and numerous dilettanti who produced monographs, pamphlets, and articles for medical journals, magazines and newspaper publication, all of which are usually located in university libraries; by perusing the speeches of antislavery Congressmen published in the *Congressional Globe*, and the speeches made by campaigning politicians at the local level and reprinted in community newspapers; by reading the collections of letters and manuscript material left by politicians, which are found in state and local historical societies, in university libraries, and in the Library of Congress; by going through the pages of leading Free Soil and Republican newspapers, which are also found in state and local collections; and by studying the campaign pamphlets and books of those popular writers who were formulating a political antislavery philosophy for the Free Soil and Republican Parties, and whose works are located in state and university libraries, the present writer through many years of labor was able to garner the racial attitudes of a relatively large number of antislavery politicians and compare them to those of the intelligentsia. These sources were supplemented by a wealth of biographical material, party histories, and state and local histories and articles which deal with various facets of the growth of the political antislavery movement. Also, by way of contrast, the views of some white radical abolitionists were gathered from newspapers, biographies, or autobiographies to be juxtaposed to those of the Free Soil and Republican persuasion.

Lastly, the attitudes of black Americans, mainly those free blacks residing in the antebellum Northeast and West who were in a position to express their feelings on free soilism and the Republican Party are also examined. Much of this material was gleaned from speeches delivered by black abolitionists and printed in radical abolitionist newspapers, such as the *Liberator*; from articles and editorials in black owned and operated presses; from pamphlets which recorded speeches and resolutions passed at black political gatherings; and, occasionally, from autobiographies and secondary accounts by black historians. These data allow even more light to be shed on the racial attitudes harbored by many Free Soilers and Republicans.

In the final analysis, it is the wish of this writer that the reader will come away from this work with a greater appreciation of the importance of white racialism in the growth and development of the political antislavery movement from the inception of the Free Soil Party to the end of the Civil War.

CHAPTER 1

THE GREAT ZOOLOGICAL CHAIN: THE INTELLIGENTSIA LOOK AT THE BLACK MAN

The most noticeable of all physical differences between human beings, is the difference between a very dark skin and a very light one. How dark a person's skin will be is determined by a biochemical called melanin. The more tiny particles of melanin per square inch of skin, the darker the skin.

Robert Froman, 1972

When the United States accelerated its drive for Western lands during the 1840's and 1850's, political leaders quickly discovered the appeal which the concept of manifest destiny had for their constituents.[1] Manifest destiny- the idea that white Americans were destined, by divine or higher law, to control and rule over the land mass between the Atlantic and Pacific Oceans- was built upon a given set of racial assumptions. These assumptions, in turn, rested upon a base of well-respected 'scientific' theory.

Although the early nineteenth century had no monopoly on racial theorists or racial theories, certain naturalists, ethnologists and learned writers in that period, who were themselves Caucasians, did make a major contribution to the development and popularization of a racial ideology. Seen in the context of manifest destiny, there appeared to be a national need, a national demand, for a racist doctrine in the antebellum period, a doctrine which became more popular as the Civil War approached. This doctrine served as a rationale for the expropriation of Native American lands, or worse, the extermination of Native American peoples. More importantly, as concerns this study, it served as an excuse to either contain black people in the South or remove them altogether from the country. This ideology held that just as different 'races' were characterized innately by different physical traits, so too, were they characterized innately by different mental and temperamental traits. Most advocates who subscribed to this creed sought to prove, moreover, that the Caucasian race was superior on both counts. It was physically superior and it was mentally, that is, intellectually and morally, superior to the darker skinned races, and in particular the black race. These writers described the Negro as having been separately created by God Himself as a permanently distinct and genetically inferior being. For them race became the most important determinant of culture. The vicious and in many cases contradictory and nonsensical nature of the intelligentsia's attack on the black man is painfully obvious.

This is not to conclude, however, that all white intellectuals who pondered the subject of race accepted the negative appraisal of the black man; some of them openly denied black inferiority. However, these people, who constituted a distinct minority of whom perhaps half a dozen were important politicians, were themselves divided in their thinking. One group, in attempting to defend blacks against the charge of innate inferiority, went to the opposite extreme and declared that in certain respects they were innately superior to whites. It professed the precept that all men were of a single creation by God, and voiced a sympathetic, even romantic, attitude toward blacks which was itself biologically based. The second and even smaller group of thinkers rejected all biological determinism. While accepting the concept of a single creation, it accounted for differences between the races by citing environmental factors.

In sum, the learned community, with some exceptions, pictured blacks as sub-human, and in doing so laid a foundation for those who sought to maintain the 'purity' of the Caucasian race or who believed they could profit by the easy political or economic exploitation of a people defined as an inferior breed. Furthermore, by providing Southern slaveholders with a scientific rationale for their peculiar institution, antebellum racial theorists helped reinforce sentiment for the exploitation of most of America's black and mulatto populations.

The scientific grounding for a racial ideology developed with the beginnings of modern anthropology, zoology, physiology and ethnology shortly after the American Revolution. During this period there was an urge within the intellectual community to classify newly discovered plant and animal life. The idea of a zoological chain was developed, a hierarchical chain with no gaps, that connected one form of animal life to another. Organisms were ranked from the lowest, least complicated form of animal life to the highest, mankind. For many, however, the need to classify and rank did not stop with human beings, as distinctions, based on skin color and covering virtually every aspect of life, were created among men. This racialist movement continued to gain momentum during the antebellum period. Both native and foreign 'naturalists' played a role in this development as it affected the United States.[2]

If there was one person at the end of the eighteenth and beginning of the nineteenth centuries who helped to focus America's attention on racial theories, that person was Thomas Jefferson. This did not mean that Jefferson's major concern was with racial ideology; rather, that from that time forward, when the question of slavery and the future role of the black man in the country was being discussed in Congress, Jefferson's name was frequently invoked. It was particularly introduced to support various schemes for separating the races by colonizing black people abroad.[3] Given the politicians penchant for pointing with pride to him as a Founding Father, Jefferson was apparently looked upon as an oracle with the last word on the question of race. In fact, the impact of the racial ideas which Jefferson presented in his *Notes on the State of Virginia*, first published in 1787, was felt in both the scientific and political communities. Jefferson, after all, was probably the most prominent scientist and political philosopher in the United States at the beginning of the nineteenth century.[4]

In emphasizing the physical differences between the black and white races, such as skin color, anatomical features and hair texture, Jefferson set the stage for other racial theorists of the nineteenth century. He noted that the "first difference which strikes us is that of colour." He wondered "whether the black of the Negro resides in the reticular membrane between the skin and scarfskin, or in the scarfskin itself; whether it proceeds from the colour of the blood, [or] the colour of the bile?" In either case he concluded that the "difference [in skin color] is fixed in nature." Jefferson believed this difference was important in measuring and determining the relative beauty of the white and black races. He asked his readers if the "fine mixtures of red and white, the expressions of every passion by greater or less suffusions of colour in the one [are not] preferable to that external monotony, which reigns in the countenances, that immovable veil of black, which covers all the emotions of the other race?" Obviously Jefferson believed they were. Furthermore, Jefferson observed, blacks "have less hair on the face and body. They secrete less by the kidnies and more by the glands of the skin, which gives them a very strong and disagreeable ordour. This greater degree of transpiration, renders them more tolerant of heat, less so of cold than the whites." In sum, Jefferson found that the "flowing hair, a more elegant symmetry of form, [and] their [the blacks'] own judgment in favour of the whites," was evidence enough in support of white physical superiority.[5]

Given the superior physique and beauty of the Caucasoid in comparison to the Negroid race, Jefferson early suggested the application of eugenics to insure that miscegenation did not compromise the aesthetically "superior" white race. If the "circumstance of superior beauty is thought worthy [of] attention in the propagation of our horses, dogs, and other domestic animals, why not," Jefferson asked, "in that of man?"[6]

Jefferson followed his physical description by contending that in mental and temperamental characteristics blacks were also different and inferior to the Caucasian. "Never yet," he noted, "could I find that a black had uttered a thought above the level of plain narration; never seen even an elementary trait of painting or sculpture." Rather than being intellectually inclined, black people were more emotionally oriented. Jefferson stated that "their existence appears to participate more of sensation than reflection." When it came to the musical talents of blacks, an area which itself appealed more to the emotions than to the mind, Jefferson maintained that "they are more generally gifted than the whites." He seemed to suggest blacks were more sensual than whites when he observed that black people "seem to require less sleep" than whites and, apparently lacking sexual restraint, "they are more ardent after their female." Even "their griefs" were described by Jefferson as merely "transient."[7] The import of this whole passage in Jefferson's *Notes* was to convince the reader that mental and personal characteristics were transferrable through the biological act of procreation. Mental differences, just as physical differences, were viewed as innate. The critical conclusion to his argument, given the fact that Jefferson considered himself a product of the eighteenth century enlightenment, was the inability of the black man to reason. Actually, by setting up the white man as the standard of excellence by which to measure all other racial groups, Jefferson seemed to fly in the face of many eighteenth century rationalists and their belief in environmental causation and the essential equality at birth of all mankind.

Jefferson believed environmental causation could help explain the successes and failures of white citizens, yet when investigating the behavior of black people he found biological factors to be the probable determinants. "The improvement of the blacks in body and mind, in the first instance of their [racial] mixture with the whites," he wrote, "has been observed by everyone and proves that their inferiority is not the effect merely of their condition of life [i.e., slavery]." It was not their environment, "but nature which has produced the distinction [in abilities]." In effect, Jefferson strongly suspected "that the blacks, whether originally a distinct race or made distinct by time . . . are inferior to the whites in the endowments both of body and mind."[8]

In thinking blacks to be more sensual and unreasoning, physically and mentally inferior to whites, Jefferson seemed to be placing blacks closer to the animal world, than to the human order. In fact, he apparently was likening blacks to the apes when he wrote that the male "oran ootan" preferred to copulate with black women over females of his own species. It was because he believed blacks had animal-like characteristics that Jefferson feared the possibility of a racially mongrel society developing within the United States.[9]

One way to avoid the threat of such a society was to avoid the perpetuation of Negro slavery. The fact that Jefferson was a Virginia slaveholder did not prevent him from attacking the continuance of the peculiar institution. For example, he wrote that "there must doubtless be an unhappy influence on the manners of our people produced by the existence of slavery among us. The whole commerce between master and slave is a perpetual exercise of the most boisterous passions, the most unremitting despotism on the one part, and degrading submissions on the other."[10] Slavery was hardly an acceptable situation, but neither, however, was emancipation. In query fourteen of his *Notes on Virginia*, entitled "The Administration of Justice and the Description of the Laws," Jefferson dealt at some length with the twin questions of race and slavery. One problem posed by the immediate abolition of slavery would be that of racial warfare and future civil discord, the inevitable consequence, he believed, of two distinct races living within the same society. On the question of emancipating the slaves and permitting them to live in the same political community as the whites, Jefferson objected on the grounds that "deep rooted prejudices entertained by the whites; ten thousand recollections by the blacks of the injuries they have sustained; the real distinctions which nature has made; and many other circumstances will divide us into parties and produce convulsions, which will probably never end but in the extermination of the one or the other race."[11] Jefferson was one of the first American statesmen to hold before the public the specter of racial warfare.

Another and perhaps more important factor mitigating against the immediate destruction of the peculiar institution was the dreaded prospect of miscegenation. With his low opinion of the black race, Jefferson feared racial amalgamation. As he wrote in 1814 to Edward Coles of Virginia, who was then private secretary to President James Madison, "amalgamation with the other color, produces a degradation to which no lover of his country, no lover of excellence in the human character, can innocently consent."[12]

To avoid both the prospects of a race war and the equally fearful possibility of a "mongrelized" society of mulattoes, Jefferson proposed that, when emancipation came, the black people should be separated by colonizing or deporting them to a different country. Colonization would allow the South to get rid of both slavery and its black population. To Jefferson's mind, distinctions in race were critical, and drastic political steps had to be commenced to preserve the country for the white race. "When freed, he [the black slave] is to be removed beyond the reach of mixture." Six months before he died on July 4, 1826, Jefferson wrote about the advisability of colonizing black Americans in the West Indies.[13] For him, America's 'manifest destiny' did not include the black man.

I

Jefferson's opinions were echoed and elaborated upon by others within the learned community both abroad and at home. Even though most Southern intellectuals and men of science used the same racialist arguments as their Northern counterparts, they, unlike Jefferson, did so in defense of slavery, rather than to justify colonization. Nevertheless, irrespective of their location, most of the white intellectuals whose racial theories seemed to find a receptive audience among America's learned population found, as did Jefferson, that skin color was the most obvious physical distinction between the respective races. When Dr. Herman Burmeister, a German professor of zoology at the University of Halle, observed the Negro, he wrote about the "peculiarity" of the "black color of his skin."[14] Arthur DeGobineau of France, perhaps the dean of nineteenth century racial theorists, described the black man's color as anything but beautiful, and was somewhat horrified because the "flesh is black on a foundation of grey."[15] Dr. James Hunt, an eminent British physician and president of the Anthropological Society of London, even carried the thought of skin color to the black man's brain, and argued that both were of the same dark hue. Hunt insisted that the "grey substance of the brain of a Negro is of a darker color than that of the European; that the whole [Negro] brain is of a smoky tint."[16]

Another set of physical characteristics, which these writers condemned, had to do with the black man's body. According to white critics, various parts of the black's physique were either over or underdeveloped, and thus out of proportion with the rest of his anatomy.

A number of the learned community claimed that his arms, legs, hands and even his fingernails were unusual in their dimensions and were, in fact, ugly and animal-like when compared to those of the Caucasian. Marvin T. Wheat, an apologist for slavery from Louisville, Kentucky who wrote under the pseudonym, Alonzo Alvarez, believed that the black man's "forearm is longer in proportion to the humerus" than that of the white man. Likewise the Negro's hand, when contrasted to that of the Caucasian's, was "more bony and tendinous and less muscular." Wheat described the fingers of the black as "longer, [more] slender and less fleshy" than the white man's. His "nails project more over the ends of his fingers," and in that regard bore a strong "resemblance to claws." Wheat went on in great detail to point out differences in the thighs and legs of the respective races and thought that the "muscles of the [Negro's] leg are also very different . . . [which] gives to the limb a very unsightly form."[17] To Burmeister, the unusual dimensions of parts of the Negro's anatomy meant that the whole body was disproportional in shape. He began by noting that the "first glance shows the Negro to be a peculiar type. The most striking marks of peculiarity are in the relative dimensions of the various parts of his body." Burmeister pointed to the "short neck of the African" and the "great length of his arms." The black man also had a "much shorter body and longer legs," which physical characteristics, in Burmeister's mind, served to "increase the difference between him and the European."[18] DeGobineau described these disproportionate parts as "absolutely hideous," especially the "size of the [black man's] head" and the "extreme thinness of the limbs."[19]

Because of his supposed ungainly physique, some writers thought that the black man's posture was faulty when compared to that of the white man. Wheat did not believe that the black man's head was "equally well balanced on the spinal column."[20] Well-known medical practitioners, such as the American, Dr. John Van Evrie, and the Englishman, Dr. James Hunt, agreed with Wheat. While Hunt claimed that the Negro "rarely stands quite upright,"[21] Van Evrie, a physician and publisher from New York City, called attention to the "tout ensemble of the [black man's] anatomical formation," which was "incapable of an erect or direct perpendicular posture."[22]

There was hardly a part of the black man's outward physical makeup that was not described by the learned community as unusual or peculiar in some respect. For example, the Negro's hair was a popular item for study and comment. Like his fingernails, it was sometimes linked to the animal world. The "hair of the Negro . . . present[ed] many peculiarities," stated Burmeister. He thought it resembled lamb's wool, and referred to it as a "curly head of wool."[23] DeGobineau made similar claims. He depicted the Negro's hair as "flat or wavy, and generally woolly."[24] Van Evrie described it as a shield from the sun; it was "such a complete mat or network, as to be wholly impenetrable to the rays of a vertical sun." Not only did the black man's hair protect him from the climate, but apparently it served the role of a helmet, to shield the head from physical harm. Van Evrie wrote about a "common practice among them [blacks] of butting each other with their heads." Even though the practice resulted in "knocking them off their feet," with a "concussion heard at considerable distances," such head butting "never results in injury, for the dense mat of semi-wool that covers the head protects it from mischief."[25]

While other parts of the black man's body did not attract as great attention as did his hair, there were still those who claimed that his teeth, ears and genitals were 'abnormal.' Wheat, for instance, insisted that the black man's teeth naturally "point obliquely outward," while those of the Caucasian's were "nearly perpendicular." The Negro's teeth were also "larger, stronger, sharper [and] farther apart." In fact they were very similar to those of animals, because the "cuspidati are more truly canine" than those of the white man.[26] Burmeister claimed that the "small ear of the Negro cannot . . . be called handsome."[27] And, while few writers of that period dealt specifically with the genitals of the respective races, Wheat on one occasion, argued that those of the Negroid and Caucasoid races were different because "in the African the penis is larger and the testes smaller" in comparison to the Caucasian.[28]

Less visible physically than the hair or the teeth of the black man but no less important in the minds of the learned community, were the allegedly tangible differences in blood. Apparently the color and the consistency of the black man's blood differed from the Caucasian's. Both Dr. Samuel Cartwright and Wheat spoke, in comparison to that of the Caucasian, of the "darker blood" of the Negro. Cartwright, a New Orleans physician and advocate of slavery, stated that the white race abounded "with red blood," while the black race had "molasses blood, sluggishly circulating and scarcely penetrating the capillaries."[29] According to Wheat, not only was the skin of the Negro darker and hence peculiar, but also his "blood" was "of a darker color than in the Caucasian race."[30]

The Negro's skull was also assumed to be thicker and more dense than that of the Caucasian; like hair, it acted to protect the brain from injury. When Wheat commented on the black man's skull, he maintained that the "bones of the head are thicker, more compact, and therefore stronger and heavier than in the Caucasian."[31] Likewise, Mrs. Henry Schoolcraft, wife of the federal Indian Commissioner and herself known in congressional circles, noted in her book on the South, that it was impossible for a white master to knock out a slave with a blow from his fists because the skull of the black man was so thick and hence impervious to injury.[32] Some thought, besides serving as a source of protection, the Negro's skull functioned as a tool. James Hunt argued that the blacks' "skull is very hard and unusually thick, enabling the Negroes to . . . carry heavy weights on their heads with pleasure."[33]

Another factor which presumably indicated that blacks were physically distinct from whites was the Negro's voice. It was alleged that the black man's voice had certain feminine characteristics, such as a high pitch. The "larynx in the Negro is not much developed, and the voice resembles sometimes the alto of an eunuch," claimed James Hunt. The physician reasoned that from the "peculiarity in the Negro voice . . . he can always be distinguished" from the Caucasian.[34] Burmeister referred to the black man's voice as a "sort of shrieking falsetto," in contrast to the deeper, more manly tone of the Caucasian.[35]

Just as scientists thought blacks to be physically distinct from whites in so many areas, a number of leading physicians assumed that blacks were distinct in that they were not affected by certain diseases which affected whites. James Hunt stated that "occupations and diseases which are fatal to the Europeans are quite harmless to the Negro."[36] This was especially the case with yellow fever. Dr. Josiah C. Nott, an acclaimed surgeon and writer from Mobile, Alabama, who, like Cartwright also defended slavery, wrote about the yellow fever epidemics which periodically struck New Orleans and noted that the "Negroes, under all circumstances, enjoy an almost perfect exemption from this disease."[37] Dr. Daniel Drake, from Cincinnati, Ohio, who was one of the most respected physicians in the West and also a founder of the Free Soil Party, believed that "blacks seldom suffer from yellow fever" although whites regularly contracted and died from the disease.[38]

The possibility that immunity from disease might just as easily have been construed as evidence of racial superiority apparently escaped these writers. Or, perhaps, they saw the black's immunity to certain diseases as evidence that he, as a slave, could safely toil in environments that would be unhealthy for the white man.

Because the black man's teeth were "pointed" or his blood was "darker" may have been proof enough for some people to believe that he was intellectually inferior to the Caucasian. Others, however, insisted that the black man was physically unique in specific ways directly related to intelligence. Certain members of the scientific community thought that they could determine intelligence by measuring a person's brain size or cranial capacity. Craniology, due to the work of various naturalists who unearthed and collected ancient skulls of the respective races, enjoyed a rising popularity among the learned community in the 1830's and 1840's. When scientific investigators measured the dimensions of human skulls, they found what they believed to be a marked distinction between those of the Caucasoid and Negroid races. Craniologists claimed that the black man's cranial capacity was smaller than the white man's. They assumed a smaller skull capacity meant a smaller brain and, therefore, the less the degree of intelligence. They concluded, in effect, that black people were less intelligent than whites because blacks had smaller skulls.

One of the earliest members of the American scientific community to work in the field of craniology was Dr. Samuel George Morton, a famous physician from Philadelphia. Morton amassed a collection of skulls from various parts of the world. Sealing off the openings, he poured white pepper seed into the skulls to gage their capacity. As a result of his investigations Morton claimed that the average Caucasian skull was seven cubic inches greater in size than the average Negro skull. He concluded on the basis of his research findings that, intellectually, some Ethiopians represented the lowest quality of humanity, therefore seeming to imply a connection between blacks and the highest quality of life in the animal world. His book, *Crania Americana*, published in 1839 made a deep impression on the disciplines of ethnology and anthropology.[39]

Morton's theory enjoyed the support of many physicians, including Van Evrie and Nott. Van Evrie, in fact, claimed that the absolute difference in cranial capacity between whites and blacks was greater than Morton believed; he insisted that the average "Caucasian brain measures 92 cubic inches [while] . . . the [average] Negro brain measures from 65 to 75 cubic inches." From his observations he concluded that the black race was intellectually stagnate.[40] Nott, who was familiar with Morton's studies, claimed that black people had less brain matter than white people, and from that assertion deduced that those with the "largest brains," have the "most powerful intellect." Moreover, "brains below a certain size are always indicative of idiocy."[41]

Leading European ethnologists and physicians whose works were influential within the American scientific community, concurred with the beliefs of Van Evrie and Nott. James Hunt referred to the "arrested development of the [Negro] brain," as proof enough that the black man was intellectually deficient.[42] Burmeister stated that the "brain of the Negro is relatively smaller than that of the European."[43]

Even those intellectuals not directly involved in the work of the scientific community readily accepted the conclusions of the craniologists and equated brain size or cranial capacity with intelligence. Sidney George Fisher, a Free Soiler, Republican, and a constitutional lawyer from Philadelphia, wrote that the average brain of the white man was "92 cubic inches," while that of the black man was only "83 [cubic inches]." On that basis, he concluded that intellectually the "white is the highest in the scale, the black the lowest."[44] Wheat agreed with Fisher about the white man's capacity but, arguing that the black man's cranial capacity was smaller than Fisher believed, surmised that it was only "seventy-five cubic inches." Blacks, according to Wheat, possessed even less intelligence than Fisher gave them credit for.[45]

Closely related to the field of craniology was the newly developing 'science' of phrenology. In fact a number of craniologists also doubled as phrenologists. Both were interested in the skulls or heads of people. Although phrenologists believed that by examining the shape and contours of the head one could make deductions concerning peoples' intelligence and mental characteristics, they did not thereby discount brain or head size as a determining factor. George Combe, a Philadelphia phrenologist and close friend and associate of Samuel Morton, appended an essay to *Crania Americana* entitled, "Phrenological Remarks." In this essay Combe declared that the average size of the brain of the black man was smaller than the average brain of the Anglo-Saxon. Besides contributing to the new field of phrenology, Combe's essay tended to confirm the popular nineteenth century belief that the larger the size of the head, the greater the intellectual capability.[46] Arriving at the same conclusion, Nott, who also dealt with phrenology, claimed that the "Negro and other unintellectual types, have been shown . . . to possess heads much smaller . . . than the white races[sic]," and that "men of distinguished mental faculties have large heads."[47]

Strictly speaking, however, most of those who wrote on the subject of phrenology were more interested in the shape of the head or facial configurations of the respective races. When phrenologists examined the shape of the black man's head, they found what they said was further evidence of the Negro's supposed mental inferiority. James Hunt, for example, observed that the peculiar shape of the black man's skull, might "give a clue to much of the mental inferiority, which is seen in the Negro race."[48]

Perhaps the conclusion drawn by phrenologists which most influenced general white attitudes toward black people was the theory of facial angle.[49] The facial angle was a measure taken at the juncture of two lines, one drawn vertically from the anterior edge of the upper jaw to the most prominent part of the forehead, and another drawn horizontally through the external opening of the ear to the base of the nostrils. The ideal angle was assumed by white phrenologists to be almost a right angle, of between ninety or even ninety-five degrees; that is, a very large facial angle. Ethnologists, when speaking of Caucasians, applied the term 'frontal races' when describing such characteristics. According to phrenology, the front part of the skull or brain contained the intellectual functions, while the back part contained the emotional or so-called animal functions. People who belonged to the frontal races had a broad or large forehead, and these features were correlated by many nineteenth century American thinkers with a large brain and hence greater mental prowess. Biographers often pictured their favorite statesmen and politicians with such heads. On the other hand, because their measurements averaged only sixty to eighty degrees, blacks were described as having a smaller facial angle. The black man's chin or mouth was projected forward of the top of the skull. This 'projected muzzle' and its corresponding receding forehead, along with the overdeveloped back of the head, purportedly proved that the black man was an intellectually dull creature and, hence, he was more closely related to the animal world than to that of human beings. His projected muzzle or smaller facial angle was used to relate the black man directly to the monkey or ape.

In 1857 Cartwright helped to popularize the expression "prognathous man" which a number of ethnologists used to describe the black man with his smaller facial angle. In his essay, entitled "Natural History of the Prognathous Species of Mankind," Cartwright wrote that "prognathous is a technical term, derived from pro, before, and gnathous, the jaws, indicating that the muzzle or mouth is anterior to the brain." Because of this facial angle, Cartwright stated explicitly what Jefferson had only implied: the black man, he insisted, was "more like the monkey tribes and the lower order of animals, than any other species of the genus man." Cartwright declared that although "young monkeys and young Negroes . . . are not prognathous like their parents," they "become so as they grow older." As a result of his observations, he believed that the "Negro approximates the monkey anatomically more than he does the true Caucasian."[50] Dr. J. Aitken Meigs, a professor of medicine at the Philadelphia College of Medicine, also believed that the skulls of black men were considerably smaller than those of the European race, and that the "narrow, low and slanting forehead" of the Negro's skull, and the "elongation of the jaws into a kind of muzzle, give to this head an animal character." Like Cartwright, he claimed that the "Negro [head] structure approximates unequivocally to that of the monkey." Meigs left no doubt in his readers' minds that the black man was a member of the "inferior races, the so-called prognathous [races], characterized by a narrow skull, receding forehead, and enormous anterior development of the maxillae." The "intellectual part [of the black man's brain] is lessened." As a result of these "findings," Meigs concluded that the "mental faculty" of the black man "is in entire abeyance to the animal."[51]

Others, such as Nott, James Hunt, Van Evrie and Wheat, lent support to the work of Cartwright and Meigs. Hunt referred to the black man's "flattened forehead, which is low and compressed," because the Negro had a "facial angle generally between 70 and 75 degrees, occasionally only 65 degrees." This "proved" that the "brain of the Negro . . . approaches the ape far more than the European, while the Negress approaches still nearer to the ape."[52] The "narrow forehead and small cerebrum, the centre of the intellectual powers, and the projection of the posterior portion, the centre of the animal functions," Van Evrie held, "render[ed] the Negro head radically and widely different from that of the white man." He went on to state that "there is a certain resemblance between the Negro and the ourang-outang."[53] Wheat believed the Negro's forehead to be "narrower and more retreating" than that of the Caucasian because the "sincipital region is inferior in its capacity in proportion to that of the occipital."[54] Dr. Johann J. J. Von Tschudi, a well-known German naturalist whose works were translated into English and distributed in the United States, declared that "negroes, in respect to capability for mental improvement, are far behind the Europeans . . . because the structure of the negro skull, on which depends the development of the brain, approximates closely to the animal form."[55] A student of phrenology from New York, Richard H. Colfax, was repulsed by the physical features of the black man: "His jaws [are] large and projecting; his chin retreating; his forehead low, flat and slanting, and . . . his eyeballs are very prominent." These "peculiarities" contributed to "reduce his facial angle almost to a level with that of the brute." Colfax asked his readers if "any such man [could] become great or elevated" intellectually.[56]

To confirm their belief that the black man was more emotional than rational, and hence more closely associated with the animal world than with humans, ethnologists uncovered other physical oddities. Many writers assumed that Negroes had "larger nerves" and sense organs than Caucasians and that, therefore, like animals, they were more keenly aware of outside forces affecting their bodies. For example, like animals, blacks were said to have a more highly developed sense of smell. Moreover, their eyesight was keener than that of the Caucasian. Nott, for one, maintained that blacks had larger nerves, and in fact considered their physical features "organically inferior" to those of the Caucasian.[57] Colfax laid down the axiom that in "proportion as the nerves are largely developed, so do the animal attributes exceed the powers of [the] intellect." He went on to note that the "portion of the brain which presides over the organic or animal functions, and from which the nerves have their more immediate origin, will, in the same ratio, exceed in size the superior or thinking portion."[58] Cartwright insisted that the "typical Negro's nervous system is modeled a little differently from the Caucasian, and somewhat like the ourang outang," because the "nerves of organic life are larger in the prognathous species of mankind than in the Caucasian." The "nostrils of the prognathous species of mankind open higher up than they do in the white." Hence, Cartwright concluded, the "Negro approximates the lower animals in his sense of smell, and can detect snakes by that sense alone."[59] Holding that the "nerves of the Negro are large compared with the brain," Van Evrie proclaimed that the "periphery of the nervous system . . . dominates over the centre." He further concluded that the basic animal senses of the black man were much sharper and better developed than those of the white man.[60] Wheat declared that the spinal cord of the Negro was larger than that of the Caucasian and, therefore, the "motor nerves of the African generally are larger in proportion to his brain, than those of the Caucasian. In this he resembles the inferior animals." Especially was this the case in his sense of smell and acuteness of vision. To Wheat the fact that the black man's "nose is short and depressed," merely meant that "its cavities are more capacious, and the olfactory nerves are spread over a more extensive surface than in the Caucasian." When referring to the Negro's eyesight, he asserted that the "orbiter cavities are wider and deeper" than those of the white man, giving the Negro larger eyes and hence, animal-like, better peripheral vision.[61]

Others, such as James Hunt, also claimed that the black man's "nasal cavities . . . are spacious" and that the "senses of the Negro are very acute, especially the smell and taste."[62] Von Tschudi added that "sensuality is the impulse which controls the . . . whole existence of the negroes."[63] DeGobineau thought that the Negro's "senses, especially taste and smell, are developed to an extent unknown to the other . . . races." From these "facts," he concluded that the "very strength of his [black man's] sensations is the most striking proof of his inferiority."[64] Meigs captured the attitude of many in the learned community when he referred to the black man's nerves as "animal" organs which, when compared to those of the Caucasian, were described as "enlarged." Like animals, the blacks' "sensuality is only equalled by their stupidity, as one might readily infer from the ample accommodations for the organs of the senses."[65]

In effect, the black man, in almost every way conceivable, was viewed as physically distinct from the white man. He was seen as a 'freak of nature,' and depicted as 'ugly' when compared to the Caucasian. More importantly, he was sometimes pictured as being more closely related to the animal world than to the human. When DeGobineau viewed the black man, he was "involuntarily reminded of the structure of the monkey."[66] Blacks were clearly believed to be physically inferior to whites. Wheat summed up the attitude of many ethnological writers when he wrote that the black men's "organs, their brains, their eyes, their faces, their foreheads, their skulls, their skins, their colors, their hair, their flesh, and their blood, are all different from ours, and bear, in most respects, a strong resemblance to the lower order of animals."[67]

Given its claims concerning the Negro's physical deformities and inferiority, it comes as no surprise that the learned community went further and concluded he was mentally and temperamentally deficient as well. In 1854, with the publication of the *Types of Mankind*, the work and themes of such scientific leaders as Dr. Morton and Dr. Nott came to a climax. This work, a recapitulation of many of the theories already expounded upon by Morton and Nott, represented a combined effort on the part of Nott, George R. Gliddon and others, such as Dr. Henry S. Patterson and Dr. William Usher. When describing *Types*, historian Thomas Gossett notes that the "idea which appears over and over again . . . is that the non-white races are incapable of taking the first step toward civilization, when they are of unmixed blood."[68] This is not to say that these scientists recommended miscegenation to improve the so-called inferior races. On the contrary, as will be noted, they believed that the Caucasian race must be kept as pure as possible by preventing any mixture with allegedly inferior racial stocks. *Types of Mankind*, which coincidentally was dedicated and addressed to the "statesmen of the country," contributed to the belief that, when contrasted with Caucasians, black people were mentally and temperamentally inferior. And, even though at $7.50 it was an expensive volume for the 1850's, it went through ten editions and was well received.[69]

One of the best known scientists in the country, and a major contributor to the *Types of Mankind*, was the Harvard professor Louis Agassiz. A Republican, he was a close friend of many party leaders. His extensive work in zoology led him to the conclusion that basic personal characteristics were innate and racially determined. He noted that "nations and races, like individuals, have each an especial destiny: some are born to rule and others to be ruled . . . such has ever been the history of mankind." Agassiz was a firm believer in both scientific classification and ranking of racial groups and in the inferiority of the black man. He first met a black person face to face in Philadelphia in the early 1840's. While visiting Dr. Morton, Agassiz was repulsed by the physical appearance of Negroes, and recorded his impressions of what he perceived as their peculiar anatomical features. He compared the shape of their limbs, skin color, hair and lips with those of the white men, and convinced himself that blacks represented both a different and an inferior variety of human being. More importantly, Agassiz, as had other ethnologists of the period, deduced from these physical properties a series of temperamental or psychological characteristics. While some writers viewed blacks as violent and aggressive people, most saw them as passive and imitative. At times, then, the black man was described as both a placid coward and a violent incendiary. In either case black behavior was linked to animal characteristics. For his part Agassiz depicted blacks as passive creatures when compared to the more aggressive Caucasians. He stated that black people were "indolent, playful . . . subservient . . . [and] unsteady in their purpose."[70] These opinions, coming from a scientist of Agassiz's stature, were bound to exert an influence on American thinking.

For example, however much the idea seemed to contradict its theory that blacks had an acute nervous and sensory system, the learned community of the antebellum period also commonly insisted that blacks were indolent, apathetic and lazy. While Morton thought the white man was distinguished by vigorous intellectual and physical activity, the Ethiopian was "noted for indolence."[71] DeGobineau believed the Negro was destined to occupy the lowest and weakest position in the "scale of race" because of the "innate laziness of the race."[72] Cartwright insisted that black people needed less oxygen than whites, and this was "proved by their motions being proverbially much slower, and their want of muscular and mental activity."[73] And, in spite of his contention that the black man's nervous system was overdeveloped, Van Evrie maintained that the Negro's brain was "so sluggish, his whole nervous organism so incomplete" that the "tendency to somnolency" was "irresistible."[74] Burmeister declared that the "highest enjoyment of the Negro generally consists in idle lounging,"[75] while Colfax claimed that there "never existed a tribe of whites who were characterized by as much . . . listless apathy, sluggishness, and want of national and personal pride, as even the most refined Africans."[76]

Having depicted the black man as inherently lazy, learned writers naturally concluded that he was a poor worker who was unwilling to labor because of a lack of ambition. Burmeister wrote that "however easy labor may be to the blacks, they seldom enjoy it."[77] Cartwright compared the black man to an "animal in a state of hibernation, waiting for the external aid of spring to warm it into life and power." Since blacks supposedly lacked the will to utilize their muscles, Cartwright equated their life style with a "vegeto-animal existence." The "white men of America," he stated, "have performed many prodigies, but they have never yet been able to make a Negro over work himself."[78] Mrs. Henry Schoolcraft, too, believed that because of their physical makeup, black people could not be overworked;[79] and Van Evrie averred that the black man, when "left to his own volition . . . never can be a producer or laborer proper" because "indolence is a positive enjoyment to the Negro."[80] Fisher declared the Negro was "by nature indolent and improvident;" the "motives which stimulate other races to industry, have weak influence over him."[81] Drake concurred in Fisher's assessment by pointing to what he believed to be the black man's "love of ease and conviviality" and his "inferiority in . . . ambition."[82]

In point of fact, the scientific community pictured the black man as so lazy as virtually to prefer starvation to searching out food for himself. The "negretian," insisted Cartwright, "has such little command over his own muscles, from the weakness of his will, as almost to starve, when a little exertion and forethought would procure him an abundance [of food]."[83] James Hunt held that the innate laziness and "natural improvidence" of the black man was proved by the fact that Negroes were a "half-starved and therefore half-developed race." If the food were procured for the black man, however, that was a different matter. According to Burmeister the Negro "becomes like a well trained animal and cares for no other enjoyment in life than being . . . abundantly fed."[84] But, Hunt added, "his tardy death is hastened by those who no longer care to find him food."[85]

Commensurate with his laziness the Negro was assumed to be an easygoing, contented fellow who was by nature docile and submissive. One of the reasons the 'sambo' stereotype-which depicted the black man as an apathetic, irresponsible, abject, and humble fool-had such a strong hold on American writers of fiction during the antebellum period was because its foundation rested on 'scientific' evidence.[86] Morton, for instance, referred to the "pliant Negro, yielding to his fate and accommodating himself to his condition." Moreover, black people were playful, carefree types, who were "proverbially fond of their amusements."[87] Although Burmeister saw black people as "docile, few of them are judicious." Compared to the Caucasian, the "black man is more disposed to be submissive."[88] Drake, too, thought Negroes to be "docile." He referred to the black man's "intrinsic servility" and "unwonted deference . . . in their intercourse with us [whites]."[89] Combe believed that the smaller brain of the Negro accounted for his greater docility in comparison to the white man.[90]

The 'cringing' character of the sambo personality was also manifested in the pretended superstitious nature of the Negro. Blacks were people who were easily frightened or spooked. Therefore Negroes, in the eyes of James Hunt, were "given to the crudest superstition," while Morton described black people as "not unfrequently characterised by superstition."[91]

Some scientists and medical practitioners, such as Cartwright and Van Evrie, for example, found a solution to the black man's supposed docility in the institution of Southern slavery. To them slavery apparently represented a haven for the weaker-willed Negroes. Cartwright stated that since blacks had "an instinctive feeling of obedience to the stronger will of the white man," then slavery was good for black people because the "subordination of the inferior race to the superior is a normal . . . condition."[92] Van Evrie carried this thought further when he asserted that a "peculiar system [slavery] adapted to its [black race's] specific nature, and which provides for that eternal subordination to the Caucasian man . . . is not merely a necessity of human existence, but an imperative duty devolving on the superior race."[93]

Along with being described as indolent and docile creatures, blacks were often characterized as people who were indifferent to the finer things of life. One example of this indifference was ostensibly manifested in the types of food they consumed. Blacks, like animals, did not care what they ate and drank as long as they ate and drank. James Hunt noted that due to the black man's alleged indifference, the "most detestable odors delight him, and he eats everything."[94] DeGobineau, like Hunt, maintained that "all food is good in his eyes; nothing disgusts or repels him. What he desires is to eat furiously and to excess; no carrion is too revolting to be swallowed by him."[95] Burmeister referred to the black man's "eating and drinking in quantity, rather than in quality" as proof of black indifference.[96]

That black people were apathetic and even indifferent to life was 'proved' by their attitude toward punishment, pain and death itself. The black man had masochistic tendencies, it was claimed. He was not only insensitive to punishment and pain, as animals were thought to be, but he actually seemed to enjoy being beaten. DeGobineau insisted that the black man was "equally careless of his own life and that of others." When the Negro became endangered, he demonstrated "a monstrous indifference" toward his own life.[97] Without indicating to what lower species he referred, James Hunt noted that "like certain animals, the Negro seems apathetic under pain."[98] Van Evrie likewise pointed to what he believed to be the black man's "organic insensibility . . . to physical pain," which caused the Negro to be "indifferent to the approach of death."[99] Cartwright thought he had discovered a "remarkable ethnological peculiarity of the prognathous race," when he observed that "any deserved punishment, inflicted on them with a switch, a cowhide or whip, puts them into good humor with themselves and the executioner of the punishment."[100] Straining credulity to its breaking point, one physician claimed that he had "amputated the legs of many Negroes, who have held the upper part of the limb themselves," without any visible sign of pain on their part.[101]

While the learned community usually characterized the black personality as passive, indifferent and sambo-like, these writers sometimes depicted it as aggressive and daring. Apparently a number of them were unable to make up their minds about the black man's temperament or, possibly, they were unaware of the contradictory nature of their own arguments. Be that as it may, the Negro was sometimes pictured as a passionate individual with intense drives and desires. This opinion, at least, seemed more congruent with the view that he had overdeveloped nerves and animal-like senses. Moreover, blacks were assumed to be revengeful and given to fits of anger to the point of being blood-thirsty killers. Like animals, they were depicted as unstable and unpredictable, capable of striking when least expected. In this regard David Turnbull, an English traveller and writer who held a Masters degree from Cambridge University, characterized black people as "half-savage."[102] DeGobineau wrote about the capricious and violent black character, and claimed that the black man "has an intensity of desire . . . which may be called terrible." His passions were such, that he "pursues the object that has aroused his senses and inflamed his desires," yet, the "desires being soon satisfied . . . the object [is] forgotten." The Negro, in DeGobineau's mind, "kills willingly for the sake of killing."[103] Because blacks were given to "explosions of passion," Dr. James Hunt described their temperament as "choleric." Moreover, they were a "revengeful" people, who were fond of "sowing discord."[104]

Another negative characteristic attributed to the black personality was immorality. Blacks, for example, were believed to be natural thieves. They were also cowardly people, who would rather run than fight, or, because of intense fear, even commit suicide. Without honor and, in fact, without cleanliness, they were a sinful and physically-dirty people who, like animals, gave off offensive odors. In a word, because of the personal habits attributed to them, blacks were considered ungodly.

A number of writers, such as Mary L. Booth, James Hunt and Van Evrie, claimed that the black man was immoral. Booth, a well-known Irish-Catholic novelist from Brooklyn, New York, used the concept of "sin" to describe the development of races, and insisted that the Negroid race was the most sinful. She stated that "there is the fact of human degeneracy, called by theologians original sin . . . . Taken as simple degeneracy, as a simple fact in man's natural history, it has various degrees, and from these various degrees spring what we call races." In correlating "sin" with natural history, Booth thought that the "least degenerated variety [race] is that commonly called the Caucasian; the most degenerated is the African. The African is the lowest variety and stands farthest removed from the true ideal of typical man."[105] Apparently, completely unaware of the role of faith in their lives, James Hunt held that black people were "void of any religious feeling." Obviously attributing this negative characteristic to that part of their ancestry which was African, he pointed to the "intense immorality which exists among the Mulattoes," and stated that their only purpose in life seemed to be "drunkenness, gambling, sexual gratification and ornamentation of the body."[106] Turnbull, too, asserted that black people had no concern for religion, and referred to the "malignity of the African race" to describe this alleged immorality.[107] In a statement reminiscent of Jefferson's view of the black's transient grief, Van Evrie called attention to what he believed to be the "feeble moral nature and superficial and capricious affections of the Negro, [which] lead him to regard . . . separations of wives and husbands, of parents and children, with indifference."[108]

Part of the black man's reputed immorality, said the intellectuals, was demonstrated in his tendency to steal. They depicted the Negro as a sneaky character who performed his nefarious work at night. James Hunt believed he was naturally "thievish," while Drake compared the black man to an "animal of the night" and, like such animals, prone to "petty thefts . . . from a habit of pilfering." While Turnbull also described blacks as thieves, Morton claimed that they were known for their "deception and falsehood." Cartwright simply referred to them as "dishonest."[109]

Along with being sinful and thievish, blacks were also described as notorious cowards. They were a people without a sense of honor and were unable, because of their aforementioned passivity and docility, to defend themselves. Evidently overlooking his attribution of violence to blacks, DeGobineau held that when the black man's life was in danger, he demonstrated "either a monstrous indifference, or a cowardice, that seeks a voluntary refuge in death."[110] From the fact that the black man "feels and silently recognizes the superiority of the white man," Burmeister concluded, " . . . comes that cowardice of the Negro, which all observers have remarked."[111] James Hunt likened the black man to a coward who "has no love for war ∴ . . but prefers to die in a state of apathy, or he commits suicide."[112] Cartwright, conveniently ignoring or perhaps unaware of the Haitian Revolution and other slave uprisings, maintained that blacks were a spineless race because "there never has been an insurrection of the prognathous race against their masters, and from the nature of the ethnical elements of that race, there never can be."[113]

Personal cleanliness for the middle class was also considered a sign of morality in the nineteenth century; since the black man was believed to be dirty and slovenly in his dress and appearance, he was considered immoral. To Burmeister, for instance, the Negro was "not only unclean, but untidy in his dress, and will at any time prefer some worthless rag to a whole shirt or an entire pair of breeches."[114] Cartwright, like Jefferson, depicted black people as foul smelling creatures. The Negro "emits the strongest odor when the body is warmed by exercise," he wrote.[115]

The learned community found further evidence confirming the passive nature of the Negro's personality in his imitativeness. Said to be both lazy and intellectually inferior to the Caucasian, the black race was supposedly incapable by itself of creating or producing anything of value. However, since there were black writers, mathematicians, inventors and statesmen in the world, these racial theorists developed an argument to explain away the discrepancy: they insisted that 'talented' Negroes were not really creative or original, but simply imitative. Like trained dogs or horses, they could learn only by mimicking their masters. The ability to mimic or imitate, in fact, may have been one of the few faculties in which black people were superior to whites. DeGobineau noted that "we often hear of Negroes who have learnt music, who are clerks in banking houses, and who know how to read, write, count, dance and speak like white men . . . . The solution is simple. There is a great difference between imitation and conviction . . . . Let us see our Negro . . . creating for himself . . . putting ideas into practice . . . taking foreign notions and moulding them to his purpose. I will wait long for the work to be finished; I merely ask that it may be begun."[116] Negroes were "not without talents," Burmeister averred, "but they are limited to imitation . . . . He [the Negro] has neither invention nor judgment." Furthermore, Burmeister claimed that the "imitative faculty presupposes the power of observation, which is possessed in a high degree by the Negro."[117] Concurring, Morton wrote that "Negroes have little invention, but strong powers of imitation."[118] To Van Evrie, black people were "like children, like the inferior animals" because they "naturally imitate the superior being;" he proclaimed that God gave the Negro "his imitative capacity."[119] Linking the black man to the Simian family, Von Tschudi maintained that the "imitative faculty of the monkey is highly developed in the negro . . . . "[120] Drake also emphasized the black man's "imitativeness," while James Hunt insisted that the "domestic Negro is improved in intelligence . . . from the imitation of the sayings and doings of the superior race."[121]

All of the above character traits attributed to black people have two qualities in common; they are negative and they connote white repudiation of blacks. In sum, the Negro was depicted as sub-human because he was assumed to be the intellectual inferior of the Caucasian. "I am," Burmeister noted, "defining with justice the Negro mental capacity, when I state that the Negro has the creative powers of mind in an inferior . . . degree to the European."[122] From an examination of the physical "deformities" of the Negro, DeGobineau deduced that the black man's "mental faculties are dull or even non-existent."[123] Van Evrie agreed; he declared that the Negro suffered from "limited intellectual power."[124] Wheat said that if God "had intended all races to be possessed of the same understandings; their progress, their refinement and enlightenment the same, it would have been as easy to have molded all after himself." However, when one observed the black man, Wheat stated, "it is evident that it [understanding] was not" equally divided among the races.[125]

As a result of the black man's pretended mental and psychological inadequacies, the intelligentsia articulated the assertion of a black people incapable of producing a refined civilization or culture. Black people were considered a biologically backward race totally deficient in the arts and technology and incapable of any scientific progress exhibited by the advanced Caucasian world. The black man was being defined as uncivilized, ostensibly because his culture was different from the white man's culture. James Hunt, for instance, viewed the black race as uncivilized, and claimed that "there are races existing, which have no history, and that the Negro is one of these races." Echoing Jefferson, he wanted to know the "name of one pure Negro, who has ever distinguished himself as a man of science, as an author, a stateman, a warrior, a poet, an artist."[126] Francis Pulszky, a well-known Hungarian archaeologist who, along with his wife, Theresa, published his work in America, charged that black people were so backward culturally, that they "never had any art of their own."[127] As far as Drake, too, was concerned, black people had no "property, learning, science, arts, enterprise, or aspiration, which our own people do not possess and display in a much higher degree."[128] Renowned German geographer and naturalist, Dr. Henry Barth, who detested slavery and whose works were known in the United States, attributed this backwardness to the "ignorance and simplicity of the black races [sic]."[129] Even after four thousand years in Africa, "with every advantage that liberty and their proximity to refined nations could bestow," Colfax stated, "they have never even attempted to raise themselves above their present equivocal station, in the great zoological chain."[130] Dr. Julian M. Sturtevant, professor of mathematics and natural sciences at Illinois College and one of the founders of the Illinois Republican Party, asserted that the "Negro is to a great extent a barbarian in the midst of civilization."[131] DeGobineau confidently concluded that the "European cannot hope to civilize the Negro," because the "lesson of history . . . shows us that all civilizations derive from the white race."[132]

In conclusion, the learned community generally and, particularly, ethnologists, believed that, both physically and mentally, the black man was closer to the animal world than to the human. Physically, his hair was likened to that of animals; his head reminded writers of an ape's head; his arms, legs, and feet were said to be ungainly, disproportional to other parts of his body, and similar to those of the ape; even his teeth were "canine," while his fingernails were compared to claws. Moreover, when these writers examined the black man's sense organs, they claimed to have found further evidence linking the Negro to the animal kingdom. Like an animal, the Negro's eyes were large, affording him acute peripheral vision. His nasal cavities were larger than those of the Caucasian, which enabled him, animal-like, to pick up scents, including those of other animals, at great distances. In fact, his nerves were believed to be larger than the Caucasian's, adding to his ability to feel, more keenly than the Caucasian, outward stimuli effecting his body.

However, in presenting the black man's mental temperament, the intelligentsia contradicted themselves by claiming that the Negro, presumably like an animal, was insensitive to punishment and pain. If, as they stated, the black man possessed larger nerves and was more sensitive to the forces of the outside world, then one would think he would be more sensitive to pain. Furthermore, there were other negative mental traits, such as his alleged indolence, which led some writers to compare the Negro to an animal in a state of hibernation. The Negro was also likened to a docile animal, who appeared to be indifferent to life, and who therefore lacked strong feelings or attachments to his kin. Again, however, the intelligentsia contradicted themselves by describing the black man as an aggressive character with strong drives and passions similar to that of animals. And, like an animal, the Negro was a member of a 'dirty' race, a race which preferred at times to go naked. To clinch their arguments, the learned community viewed the black race as innately unintelligent and, therefore, permanently uncivilized. Blacks were biologically incapable of founding or, for that matter, participating and contributing to an 'advanced' civilization; they were simply without culture. The closest the black man could aspire to civilization, as defined by these Caucasian writers, was to mimic or imitate the white man. But even this supposed imitative ability of the Negro was cited as further evidence that the black man was connected to the animal world. Given this constant barrage of negatives it's no wonder that some blacks could become Uncle Toms.

Because the black man was considered so radically different from and inferior to the white man, a number of writers believed that he could not possibly have come from the same creation as the Caucasian. This group, including such learned people as Morton, Agassiz, Colfax, Hunt, Wheat and DeGobineau, in effect challenged the biblical interpretation of a single creation as set forth in Genesis.[133] This belief, known as the polygenic theory of creation, held that God created distinct races whose characteristics remained unchanged. No physical or environmental factors could account for the tremendous racial differences; no outside environmental forces could transform a white man into a black man or a black man into a white. Van Evrie stated the case concisely when he noted that the "Negro . . . could no more originate from the same parentage with us, than could the owl from the eagle."[134] The polygenic theory of distinct races was accepted by most of those who believed that there was no hope for the improvement or assimilation of the Negro in a predominantly white society. The belief in distinct races from separate creations formed the background for racialist thought in the United States during the antebellum period.

In opposition to the polygenic theory of creation was the monogenic theory. The latter held that all races of man descended from common ancestors, but, due to environmental factors-ranging from climate and diet to one's political state (slavery)-physical and mental differences began to emerge along racial lines. This school of thought, which will be examined below, constituted a minority view in antebellum America.[135]

II

Whether or not they believed in polygenism, it has been seen that most learned writers proclaimed both physical and mental superiority for whites. Indeed, each time they assessed a black trait or ability, they applied a white standard which, they insisted, approximated perfection. Physically the white man was beautiful. To illustrate, DeGobineau described the European as "superior in beauty, in just proportion of limb and regularity of feature." Only "those who are most akin to us," he asserted, "come nearest to beauty."[136] After criticizing the poor posture of the black man, Van Evrie portrayed the white man as "perfectly erect, with the eyes on a plane with the horizon." And such appealing features did not stop there; the Caucasian's "broad forehead, distinct features, and full and flowing beard," Van Evrie added in a moment of extreme racial pride, "stamp him with a superiority and even majesty denied to all other creatures."[137]

Mentally and temperamentally, said these extollers of the white race, the Caucasian's superiority was even more pronounced. While they decreed black people as ignorant, brutish, sensual, animal-like creatures, they praised white people as clever, practical, reasoning beings, able fully to develop their intellectual powers. Whites, wrote DeGobineau, were "gifted, with reflective energy . . . with an energetic intelligence." This intelligence gave them "a feeling for utility . . . a perseverance that takes account of obstacles and ultimately finds a means of overcoming them." It also gave them an "extraordinary instinct for order." At the same time this "immense superiority . . . in the whole field of intellect" was, in the white man, as contrasted to the more animal-like races, "balanced by an inferiority in the intensity of their sensations."[138] It was, Fisher claimed, this "intellectual and moral energy," which had enabled the white man alone to create "that development of free government, industry, science, literature and the arts, which we call civilization."[139]

To the learned community the Caucasian was the pinnacle of refined culture and technological progress; the Negro, the antithesis of civilization. Even the Reverend Mr. Theodore Parker, for all his contacts with both the Garrisonian abolitionists and the militant abolitionists who aided John Brown in his Harper's Ferry raid, affirmed that the Caucasian was far superior in this respect. Compared to the African, who was much "inferior . . . in general intellectual power" and to other darker "inferior races, which have always borne the same ignoble relation to the rest of men and always will," the "Caucasian," he wrote, "differs . . . ; he is humane; he is civilized, and progresses. He conquers with his head as well as with his hand."[140] Wheat was in full agreement. "All the great sciences are of Caucasian origin," he avowed; "all inventions are Caucasian; literature and romance come of the same stock; all the great poets are of Caucasian origin." In fine, "no other race can bring up to memory such celebrated names as the Caucasian race."[141]

Perhaps more than anything else, these writers attributed the civilizing abilities of the Caucasians to their peculiar affinity for 'liberty.' DeGobineau maintained that white people were unique in their "extreme love of liberty .... They know better how to use it and ... set a greater price on it."[142] Parker said he had "no doubt" that the "African race is greatly inferior to the Caucasian ... in that instinct for liberty which is so strong in the Teutonic family."[143] Because of this special aptitude, Nott thought that the Caucasian race had the "mission of extending and perfecting civilization," particularly since whites were "by nature, ambitious, daring [and] domineering."[144]

The belief among the intelligentsia in the vast superiority of the Caucasian and his civilization over other races, in particular the Negro, and their cultures, was often conjoined in the United States by its belief in the supremacy of the Anglo-Saxon or Teutonic branch of the Caucasian race over other branches of that race. This ethnocentrisim seemed to be an ever present element in Free Soil and Republican thinking. If the Caucasian stood at the top of the racial ladder, the Anglo-Saxons, as an ethnic group, occupied its highest rung. Social Darwinists in the 1870's-1900's period would repeat the same litany, depicting the Anglo-Saxon as the pinnacle of the evolutionary process. The famous Free Soil physician, Daniel Drake, viewed the Anglo-Saxons as the highest developed of all racial and ethnic groups. Horace Bushnell, and Parker, both New England ministers identified with the political antislavery movement in the East, expressed similar views. Parker, who as noted described Caucasians in terms of a "master race," claimed the Anglo-Saxons to be the most developed and progressive ethnic branch of the Caucasian race.[145] Ralph Waldo Emerson, another New England antislavery advocate and one of the originators of New England transcendentalism, depicted the Anglo-Saxon as belonging to a "race with a future." This "fair Saxon man, with open front and honest meaning, domestic, affectionate, is not the wood out of which cannibal or inquisitor, or assassin is made." No, the Saxon belongs to the highest order of civilization and was made for "law, lawful trade, civility, marriage ... colleges, churches, charities and colonies."[146]

To these Anglo-Saxon supremacists other white ethnic groups were obviously inferior. Some writers saw them so even in their affinity for liberty and freedom. Louis K. Klipstein, a well-known philologist and author, pointed out that while the "institutions of the Anglo-Saxon were always characterized by popular freedom," the Spanish were "indolent" and the French known more for their "easy amiability." Both latter groups were "incapable of holding any rational idea of liberty."[147] Cultural refinement, too, as manifested in literature, was evidently an Anglo-Saxon monopoly. "No nation but the English," Parker declared, "could have produced a Hobbes, a Hume, a Paley, or a Bentham. They are all instantial and not exceptional men in the race."[148]

Emerson argued that the English as examples of Anglo-Saxon superiority were, specifically, examples of the destiny of that branch of the Caucasian race to dominate inferior peoples. "It is race, is it not," he asked, "that puts the hundred millions of India under the dominion of a remote island in the north of Europe?"[149] If one accepted the premise, the conclusion of course, followed. If the Anglo-Saxons, or at most the Caucasians, were indeed a proud, strong, intelligent, incorruptible race, with an innate love for liberty and freedom; if their institutions were models for 'lesser breeds' who aspired but somehow were never able to achieve democracy; if all this were true, then was it not inevitable that the white people would one day overspread the world? Bushnell viewed this as a process by which "to people the world with better and finer material." He claimed that Caucasians were increasing in population at a faster rate than other races, and as a result were spreading themselves over broader areas of the world. By the same token the native races of foreign lands were disappearing, thereby making room for the superior people.[150]

More specifically, in the New World, the Anglo-Saxons or Caucasians had their manifest destiny to overrun North America from coast to coast, and eventually Central and South America, too. Standing in their way, however, were those inferior races who were not up to the intellectual and moral level of the white man. In North America was the large black population centered in the Southern states. "Race avails much," warned Emerson, " . . . [and] race in the negro is of appalling importance."[151] Black men, said Bushnell were, "physically speaking, animals and nothing less."[152] A principle factor in the learned community's (at least that portion of the learned community which did not actively defend slavery) fear of the blacks, was that their presence, as Jefferson had cautioned, might lead to miscegenation and miscegenation, or to use the nineteenth century term, amalgamation, could, by leading to the eventual deterioration of the purity of the Caucasian race in America, prevent that race from realizing its destiny.

This gloomy prophesy was based on a theory, widely accepted in the antebellum period, that racial characteristics were conveyed in the blood. Heredity was not, as we believe today, a matter of genes and chromosomes, but rather a matter of blood. Instead of the belief in standard blood types, which cross racial lines, antebellum scientists claimed that each race had a uniquely different blood type by which that race was perpetuated. Intellectual ability and character traits, attributed to a particular race, such as indolence or cowardice, were supposedly carried in the blood of that race. Parker, for one, openly avowed this to be true, while Drake referred to "white" and "black blood" to distinguish such characteristics.[153] DeGobineau was one of the first ethnologists to popularize such a theory. When DeGobineau spoke about blood, he invariably used the term either in conjunction with the word race, or to mean race itself. He ascribed degeneration "to the quantity and quality of the new blood," which degenerate peoples had received, "in consequence of the various admixtures of blood." This deterioration would be most acute, DeGobineau maintained, when one mixed the blood of the most superior, or Caucasoid race, with that of the most inferior, or Negroid race.[154] The result of such a union, the mulatto, he considered a racial pariah, whose very presence symbolized the downfall of Caucasian supremacy.

In light of the then current views on the subject of blood, it is not surprising that most of the learned writers who considered the matter were opposed to miscegenation, or the mixing of the blood of the white and black races. Southern writers generally believed that slavery would prevent such mixing. Northern writers, on the contrary, usually believed that slavery fostered miscegenation. In any case another contradiction can be detected in the thinking of both groups. While they seemed to believe that a natural repulsion or separation, even an aversion, perhaps abetted by labor competition between whites and slaves or free blacks, would work to inhibit or prevent interracial copulation, they at the same time worried that miscegenation just might occur notwithstanding, with disastrous results for the white race.

Fisher was one of those who subscribed with Agassiz to the polygenic theory of creation. He noted that the "types of races, at least in their primary classification, are permanent." Physically and mentally, the "division between white and black is more strictly maintained" than between other races. Therefore, Fisher stated flatly, "the two races can never amalgamate and form a new species of man."[155] Booth discussed the "intervals" among races in general, and between the black and white races specifically. She declared that "between one variety [race] and another, there is an interval. This interval is greatest between the Negro and the Caucasian." The result was that the "two varieties do not easily amalgamate. Their amalgamation is in some sense irrational and violent, and the amalgamation is a deterioration."[156] Wheat was one of the few among the learned community who elevated sexual antipathy between the Caucasoid and Negroid races to a physical law. He believed that such antipathy was so strong, that miscegenation would automatically be precluded. Physiologically, he wrote that "with reference to the coloring fluid contained in the rete mucosum, under the cuticle of the human being . . . we see that of the white race bears an affinity for the white race." From there he concluded that the "affinity in coloring causes the affinity for generating with each other, in contradistinction with those not of the same color . . . and this natural law of preference . . . pervades the whole creation."[157] Apparently on similar grounds Booth thought it impossible to have a society where "persons . . . have a mutually instinctive aversion to intermarriage, for marriage is the basis of the family, and the family is the basis of general society."[158]

More commonly, however, the white writers described the aversion to interracial mating as principally a white aversion to black. One of the major reasons behind the tremendous power and progress exhibited by the Anglo-Saxon race, when compared to the Spanish and their racially mixed colonies, claimed Parker, was the refusal of the Saxon to "mix his proud blood . . . with that of another race." The Saxons, he said, had an "antipathy" to racial mixing that was "almost peculiar to this remarkable tribe."[159] Klipstein, too, thought that an important reason why Anglo-

Saxon nations remained supreme, when compared to Latin powers, was because of their ability to hold themselves aloof from amalgamation with inferior breeds.[160] Sturtevant, along with Parker and Klipstein, was convinced that a society of mixed races could not possibly be perpetuated because white males and females would not intermarry with black partners. "Prejudice against color," he claimed, was "one of the most remarkable and one of the most respectable features" of the Anglo-Saxon people.[161]

This process of white exclusivity was evidently at work within the United States, or at least it was more obvious in the Northern United States. Drake, for example, refused to believe that "any portion of the people of the North, a few abolitionists excepted, do or ever will desire to mingle with the Anglo-Saxon blood of Newton, Shakespeare, and Milton, that of even the greatest 'Kings' which reign in Guinea."[162] And Elias H. Derby, a New England lawyer and author, confidently described the desire of the Western states, "to perpetuate in its purity the Anglo-Saxon blood."[163]

At times, however, those who studied the problem did not seem all that confident that prejudice or natural factors would keep the races apart sexually. After all there were many slaves, and a growing number of free blacks, of mixed racial ancestry in the South. True, Van Evrie maintained that "unless there were some moral or physical cause, some disease of body or mind, which rendered her incapable of self-guidance, it can hardly be supposed that an American born [white] woman, ever committed such an indecent outrage upon her own womanhood, and sin against God, as to mate with a Negro." True, too, that to Van Evrie such an act would be a "sin against God;" because God had created separate races, one superior and one inferior. Yet notwithstanding all of his assurances, the medical doctor apparently still felt it necessary to warn his readers that it was the duty of the superior race to keep itself separate from the inferior order.[164] Nott's warning was just as pointed. Since to him the white race represented the closest example of a pure racial group, while the black race represented inferior beings, the former simply must not interbreed with the latter. Nott wrote that "those races of men most separated in physical organization, such as the blacks and the whites, do not amalgamate perfectly."[165] Agassiz's advice went so far as to hint that, if need be, the two races should be kept apart forcibly. In a letter to Samuel Gridley Howe, a Harvard medical graduate and Free Soiler, he wrote that "from a physiological point of view it is sound policy to put every possible obstacle to the crossing of the races and the increase of half-breeds."[166]

The reason why these intellectuals were so opposed to miscegenation was, of course, not far to seek. Black blood was, Dr. Drake declared, simply incapable of bringing anything of value to the union of the two races. Indeed, quite the reverse; "in proportion as the black race should be elevated, the white race would be depressed."[167] Nott and Agassiz were in complete agreement with Drake.[168] Miscegenation could only mean the deterioration of the white or superior racial stock, until the proud Saxon people would lose their identity and, in Klipstein's words, "harmonize with those among whom they dwell."[169] Why should whites wish to amalgamate with the black man when, according to Sturtevant, he was so weak, physically and mentally, that a "large portion of his children die in infancy,"[170] or when, according to Fisher, the "animal predominates in his character over the intellectual and moral; his mind is weak, his passions are strong?"[171] Richard Colfax was incensed with the radical abolitionists because, he claimed, they "proposed that the two races should . . . amalgamate with each other." Would it "not be as reasonable," he asked his readers, "to expect the Negroes to amalgamate with that equally valuable race of inferiors, the orang-outang?"[172]

To bolster their opposition to miscegenation, Booth, Parker and Klipstein all pointed to the alleged breakdown in Spanish society as an example of what happened when races mixed.[173] "In all countries where the mingling of the two races [black and white] has gone on to any considerable extent," Booth asserted, "we find a great deterioration in the white race." She warned her readers that precisely the same kind of "marked deterioration would result in our [American] Southern society were intermarriages between them to become frequent."[174] "Wherever it is practiced," Agassiz told Howe, "amalgamation among different races produces shades of population, the social position of which can never be regular or settled." Therefore, "the idea of amalgamation is most repugnant to my feelings."[175] Von Tschudi seconded Agassiz's opinion on the results of amalgamation, adding that mulattoes, "as members of society . . . are the worst class of citizens."[176]

Not merely could miscegenation lead to social breakdown, it could also, said those who argued against it, lead to biological breakdown. The proof was found in the product of miscegenation, the mulatto. The latter, besides representing the destruction of pure Caucasian racial lines, was considered by the intelligentsia to represent a sickly, weak and degenerate variety. Nott, in 1842, wrote an article for the *American Journal of the Medical Sciences*, entitled "The Mulatto a Hybrid—Probable Extermination of the Two Races, if the Whites and Blacks are Allowed to Inter-marry." Here he argued that mulattoes were less intelligent than whites, but more intelligent than pure blacks.[177] Booth also declared that, because of the infusion of superior white blood, mulattoes represented an improvement, intellectually, over the pure black.[178] The problem with mulattoes, as Nott saw it in his article, however, was that they tended to be delicate creatures, who were susceptible to chronic diseases. Because mulattoes "obey the laws of hybridity," they died off more quickly than either of their parent branches. Therefore, he concluded, they were "less prolific than the parent stock."[179] Fisher agreed: mulattoes were "weak in constitution and unfruitful with each other."[180] Van Evrie added that the "Mulatto or Hybrid of the fourth generation, is as sterile as the mule or most animal hybrids are in the first generation."[181]

Most writers, however, thought that the mulatto was actually more defective in both the mental and physical senses, than the pure Negro. According to DeGobineau, blood became "adulterated and impoverished," when it was mixed across racial lines. So, any propagation between races was bound to deteriorate the "purity" of the varieties involved.[182] Klipstein believed it to be a "well established fact, that . . . amalgamation of widely differing races, like the Negro or Indian with the Caucasian, produces a short-lived progeny, not possessed of the best qualities of either race."[183] The "population arising from the amalgamation of two races," Agassiz asserted, "is always degenerate," because "it loses the excellences of both primitive stocks, to retain the vices or defects of both."[184] Concurring with Agassiz, Von Tschudi claimed that mulattoes "unite in themselves all the faults, without any of the virtues, of their progenitors. As men they are greatly inferior to the pure races . . . ." He then prepared an elaborate chart naming the degenerative offspring of such unions.[185] In effect, these intellectuals were arguing that it was better for both races, but in particular for the 'superior' Caucasian, that miscegenation be avoided.

Besides the threat it posed to racial purity, a second reason a large body of blacks caused the intelligentsia, particularly those in the North, to be apprehensive, was that its very presence in a society which was predominately white, would eventually bring on racial warfare. Most white writers, especially those who had little personal contact with black people, seemed to believe that it was natural for distinct races, specifically the Caucasoid and the Negroid, to despise each other to the point of open conflict and bloodshed. Jefferson had warned of such an eventuality when he wrote of the "fire bell in the night."[186] The fear of a possible black insurrection was not only manifested by some Southern slaveholders, such as Jefferson, but more importantly by those writers living in the free states. Agassiz, Parker and Fisher all expressed fear over the possibility of a race war, if blacks and whites continued to live together.[187] Drake captured this feeling, claiming that if the black population continued to increase, then eventually "rebellions, amounting to local civil wars, will carry dismay throughout our cities and drench their streets with blood."[188] Apparently black people threatened not only the blood lines of the Caucasian, but his very life as well.

III

Most of the learned community who wrote or spoke on the subject of the black man in the United States insisted that solutions must be found to avert the twin dangers which his very presence supposedly fostered-miscegenation and racial warfare. Although a few occasionally argued that nature had already provided the means, in that physiological forces were preventing miscegenation by keeping the races apart, this conclusion, it has been noted, was evidently not generally accepted by the intelligentsia, especially by those living in the North. The many mulattoes in America proved it wrong. Besides, might not racial or sexual antipathy, rather than prevent a race war, promote it?

In contrast to Southern apologists for slavery, such as the well-known editor and publisher, J.D.B. DeBow,[189] most Northern thinkers on the subject proposed two specific remedies-containment and colonization. The first concern of these writers was to prevent any further dispersion of the black race within the United States. Northern intellectuals believed that as long as blacks resided in America, they should be confined to the South. Containment would enhance the purity of the Caucasian race and prevent racial conflict elsewhere in the nation. Slavery, some thought, provided the surest method of containment. Others held that, on the contrary, slavery would lead to a further dispersion of blacks because the slaveholders would insist on extending their peculiar institution westwardly. An end to slavery, said these writers, was the answer. That solution/resolve, however, must not be precipitous, lest it, too, invite further dispersion. The elimination of slavery must be gradual, and it must be accompanied, first, by legislating a uniform code of Northern state laws for restricting blacks to the South by prohibiting their migration into the North; and, secondly, a national program to remove eventually, all blacks from the country through colonization.

To be sure, as will be seen, a few writers deviated from these precepts. Some said neither containment nor colonization would be necessary since newly freed blacks, no longer sheltered by the fostering care and paternalistic protection of slavery and unable to compete with superior white workers in the free labor market, would in time become extinct. And some said containment and colonization would not be necessary because newly freed blacks, unshackled and free to seek their 'natural' habitate in warmer climatic zones would, of their own accord, migrate southward and out of the United States. Most Northern intellectuals, even if the processes operated as predicted, seemed unwilling to rely upon either such slow-moving proposals. Consequently, they embraced both containment and colonization to eliminate the dangers of miscegenation and racial conflict to the future of the Caucasian race in America.

A number of Northern writers concerned with the twin dangers of miscegenation and racial warfare were unwilling to disturb slavery, at least in the short run, because, with the overwhelming majority of black people living under slavery, these problems remained in the South. This perspective received a favorable response by most Southern writers, since slavery itself provided the proper method for regulating the black man's associations with whites. This Northern view was advocated within the learned community by those who also believed they were antislavery in sentiment, but who, in fact, merely opposed the further extension of slavery. Charles Eliot Norton, a Harvard professor and an antislavery author for the prestigious *Atlantic Monthly*, claimed that the "black is, in many of his endowments, inferior to the white," and accordingly, he suggested the creation of a "new Africa" around the "Gulf of Mexico." He worried about the "inevitable increase of the slaves," yet thought that "where the black race is now settled, it will stay, but it must be confined within its present limits." Norton asked his readers if this new Africa "shall . . . push its boundaries beyond their present limits; shall more territory be yielded to the already widespread African race? It is not the question whether the unoccupied space of the South and West shall be settled by Northern white emigrants . . . or by Southern white emigrants . . . but it is the question whether New England or New Africa shall extend her limits; whether the country shall be occupied a century hence by a civilized or by a barbarous race."[190]

By contrast, Sturtevant and Parker believed that both 'problems' could be solved simply by abolishing slavery and throwing the black man into an economic grinding wheel. Whereas radical abolitionists, such as William Lloyd Garrison and Wendell Phillips, held that immediate emancipation should be the first step in the elevation of the black man, Sturtevant and Parker seemed to hold that it should be the first step in his destruction. The Republican physician Sturtevant, a strong supporter of emancipation, pointed a finger of guilt at the South for helping to perpetuate the black race in the United States. "There is," he stated, "great reason to doubt whether our colored population has ever increased at all, except in slavery . . . . It is slavery and slavery alone, which has swelled their numbers." Moreover, he noted that "there is no reason to suppose that the increase of the free colored population would be in a greater ratio, if all were emancipated;" on the contrary, he insisted, "it would be in a much smaller ratio." Once the black man becomes a free laborer, "he is brought into direct competition with the white man; that competition he is unable to endure and he soon finds his place in that lower stratum . . . where he . . . cannot support a family." As a result of this enforced poverty, the black man "will either never marry, or he will, in the attempt to support a family, struggle in vain against the laws of nature, and his children will, many of them at least, die in infancy."[191]

Parker concurred with Sturtevant. The "Anglo-Saxon," he noted, "does not like the Africanization of America," occurring under Southern slavery. The solution, he insisted, was emancipation, because the white laboring man was both physically and mentally superior to the black. The results: the "white man kills out the . . . black man. When slavery is abolished, the African population will decline in the United States, and die out of the South." As proof he made a prediction concerning the statuses of the working classes of the two races in the Northern states; after only "two generations, what a change there will be in the condition and character of the Irish in New England. But in twenty generations, the Negroes will stand just where they are now [at the bottom of the socio-economic ladder], that is if they have not disappeared."[192] Sturtevant, sounding much like later nineteenth century Social Darwinists, concluded that the "welfare of society . . . requires that it should be propagated from the strong, the sound, the healthy, both in body and mind; from the . . . most vigorous and noblest specimens of the race, and not from the diseased, the weak, the vicious, the degraded."[193]

Some writers, including Drake, Booth and Colfax, did not believe that emancipation in itself would obviate the problems which, they insisted, blacks posed for Caucasian Americans. Drake especially feared that free blacks would migrate northward if slavery were immediately abolished. Therefore, he urged, the "states of the North should, by a uniform system of legislation, shut out all emancipated and fugitive slaves, and the states of the South, with equal uniformity, should forbid all emancipation, except under guarantees that the liberated should not be permitted to seek an asylum in the North." How the Southern states would guarantee such an eventuality he did not say. He went on to detail the specific form of his exclusionist legislation. He recommended the "registration of all the colored people of the free states," so that these states "might inflict and re-inflict, as long as they [blacks] remained, such penalties, to be discharged by labor on public works, as would bring them into a slavery worse than that from which they had been emancipated or had escaped." Further, Drake suggested, Northern blacks should not be allowed to hold real estate or have access to the courts of law.[194]

Booth and Colfax also thought that any solution of the 'black problem' required drastic steps. They opted for a program of total separation of the races through colonization. Booth, while attacking the radical abolitionists who opposed colonization, believed that the best method of preventing amalgamation was to colonize all newly emancipated blacks abroad. At one point she stated that "we have no scruples and believe the government might forcibly remove them from its territory to another . . . in a community by themselves." Her proposal, she claimed, would, a la Parker, "avert . . . the Africanization of free [white] American society." Besides, she reasoned, "we can see only degradation and oppression for the black race, so long as it inhabits the same territory with the white." Free blacks would be "outcasts" and "pariahs" because no one would either associate or hire them. But if they were colonized, "such migration or exode will be the beginning of the uprising of their race." In particular, she and other colonizationists claimed, whites would be doing the black man two favors. By sending the Negro out of the country, they would be protecting him (1) from the further humiliation and oppression produced by white prejudice, and (2) from the fate/calamity prophesied by Parker and Sturtevant, that is, from ultimate ruin and destruction at the hands of the white laboring classes in the economic struggle for survival. However, as she admitted, Booth's primary concern was not "liberty for the black race, so much as for the white race."[195]

Richard Colfax, too, worried about the effects of an immediate end to slavery: "if their [blacks'] physical organization will continually prevent them from attaining a level with the whites," then it was "unreasonable . . . in [sic] those enemies to our country, called abolitionists, to unloose within the bosom of this now happy community, a body of such people." Rather than free the slaves immediately as the radical abolitionists proposed to do, and thereby contribute to the amalgamation of whites with an inferior race, Colfax recommended gradual emancipation coupled with colonization abroad.[196]

Drake, together with Norton and Derby, supported a combination of the containment of most blacks in slavery, and the colonization of some blacks out of the country, or, as in Derby's case, their segregation within a separate community in the South. Drake wanted some blacks colonized specifically to Liberia. The "slave territory," he maintained, "is a fixed quantity, while the slave population is an increasing quantity, and it requires no resort to mathematics to prove that the time will come when the former must be extended, or the latter arrested in its increase, by sending from the slave states a number equal to what are born [annually]. Deportation will then be the only remedy."[197] While Norton believed that the black race "must be confined within its present limits [the South]" as far as the immediate future was concerned, he insisted that in the long view "there is no room in the United States, or in any of their unsettled territory, for . . . this transatlantic Africa."[198] Derby, by contrast, cast doubts as to the merits of an external or foreign scheme of black colonization. Instead he recommended an internal program of colonization which envisaged the containment of the Southern black population on the Eastern seaboard, while adding to their numbers blacks from other parts of the country. He noted that there was "a belt of territory from the Dismal Swamp [of Virginia] to the Capes of Florida . . . of the average width of nearly one hundred miles," and with an "area at least two hundred millions of acres, competent to sustain forty millions of Negroes." Rhetorically, Derby wanted to know, had "not nature designed a black fringe for this coast?" "Here," he declared, was a "climate often fatal to the whites, but suited to the Negro" because there were "no harsh winters or chilling snows."[199]

Derby's view of the suitability of blacks for warmer climes was not singular. While some form of colonization probably expressed the most popular option among the intelligentsia and, of course, those in the American Colonization Society, there were others, like Agassiz and Van Evrie who, while not opposed to colonization per se, thought that this process would occur naturally following emancipation. They developed a natural migration or drainage theory which, in turn, was based upon a theory of racial/climatic stratification.

Because the black man was viewed as physically different from the Caucasian, the learned community concluded that the Negro adapted better than the white race to certain environmental or geographical zones. The scheme to colonize blacks back to Africa was itself an expression of this thesis. Ethnologists developed climatic charts and maps to match the various races to particular topographical areas. For the racial theorist subscribing to biological determinism, the environment was not something that changed or acted upon individuals. For them it was not the sum total of political, social and economic forces and ideas that affected an individual's mental behavior and physical development or influenced a person's social or economic status. Rather, it was merely the passive or tangible force of climate. In this narrow sense 'the environment' was a predetermined or constant factor, even as races were assumed to be. Just as racial theorists reasoned that there was a hierarchy, or scale, of races, so too they reasoned that there was a hierarchy or stratification of climate zones to which God, by separate creations, had neatly assigned the different races. Actually, since these ethnologists were white and since they believed that warmer or tropical climates were injurious to the Caucasian, whereas temperate or cooler climatic zones were salutary, it is difficult to avoid the thought that they used the polygenetic theory to justify assigning black people to the more southerly or tropical regions.

Nott proclaimed the black man to be a "native of the hottest region on the globe, where he goes naked in the scorching rays of the sun, and can lie down and sleep on the ground in a temperature of at least 150 degrees of fahrenheit." In the same heat, the white man "would die in a few hours." By contrast, Nott declared, white people were "regenerated by transportation to cold parallels of the temperate zone," while the black man "steadily deteriorates and becomes exterminated north of about 40 degrees north latitude."[200] It has been noted that in support of this view some ethnologists claimed that blacks were immune to certain tropical diseases. Drake, on the other hand, while admitting that "in the sugar and cotton states, the chief diseases of the latter [black] class are intermittent and remittent fevers," went on to insist that "as we rise into colder climates, their disorders multiply, and great numbers die from scrofula, consumption, and inflammation of the lungs. All this shows that the constitution of the black man, born in the United States, is not adapted to the North."[201] The "climate in which the Negro can work and thrive," Fisher insisted, "repels the white, whilst the Negro is excluded from the North . . . by the climate."[202] Connecting allegedly black physiological characteristics to climatic factors, Wheat asserted that the "skin of the African generates less heat than that of the Caucasian, and its temperature is therefore lower." Consequently, "it more powerfully and successfully resists the action of heat from without." However, the black man's skin "resists a low temperature with less power. Hence the superior fitness of the former [Negro] for hot climates and of the latter [Caucasian] for cold ones." Even the black man's foot was "more easily chilled and injured by the frost, than the foot of the Caucasian," because of its "scantier supply of blood. It is fitted, like the African hand, to a warm climate."[203]

Agassiz and Van Evrie built on this climatic thesis to posit a natural theory of colonization. Agassiz became a strong supporter of Lincoln's Emancipation Proclamation; he believed emancipation would cause a natural separation of the races without any need for the government to finance deportation. His "reason for believing that the colored population of the North will gradually vanish, is founded in great degree upon the fact that that population does not increase where it exists now" in a cold climate. Agassiz hoped that "as soon as the condition of the Negro in the warmer parts of our states has been regulated according to the laws of freedom, the colored population in the more northern parts of the country will diminish." He saw this as a "natural consequence of unconquerable affinities; the colored people in whom the Negro nature prevails, will tend toward the South, while the weaker and lighter ones will remain and die out among us." Even though the process was theoretically dictated by nature, to the point where he referred specifically to "thermal laws," Agassiz wanted this process supplemented by man. The Northern states should pass exclusionist legislation. Such laws would "accelerate their [black people's] disappearance," thereby maintaining the purity of the Caucasian race in the North. The result of these processes would "tend to diminish this unnatural amalgamation and lessen everywhere the number of these unfortunate half-breeds." Freeing the slaves, according to Agassiz, would start a great southward migration of black people out of the United States. This theory of migration coincided perfectly with his stated conviction that "no two distinctly marked races can dwell together on equal terms." While black people were drifting southward, lighter skinned peoples would be moving northward.[204]

Van Evrie, styling himself an humanitarian and fearful of the possibility of racial warfare, or worse, mulattoism, propounded a theory similar to that of Agassiz's, whereby the "Negro element constantly tends southward, a black column ever on the march for its own centre of existence." This, or what might be called a drainage theory of migration, allowed Agassiz and Van Evrie to be humane-by advocating the emancipation of the slaves, while at the same time predicting the eventual migration of black people, and with it the preclusion of racial corruption or conflict.[205] It was all part of the scientific thesis of the period, which viewed races as completely distinct-even down to the geographical areas they were to occupy.

IV

While so many of the intelligentsia exhibited an openly hostile racial attitude toward black Americans, there were some who took the opposite extreme and advocated what historian George M. Fredrickson has called "romantic racialism."[206] These people, fewer in numbers, enjoyed much less influence. The romantic racialist also believed in racial or biological determinism, but unlike the hostile racialist, he cited what he claimed to be innately derived characteristics to show that in certain respects blacks were superior to whites. The distinction lay in the fact that the romantic racialist attributed some positive innate qualities to blacks, while the hostile racialist saw virtually all their qualities as inferior. In this way romantic racialism represented a step away from the hostility manifested by the typical white supremacist.

For instance Jefferson, in one sense, might be considered a romantic racialist. He depicted the typical Negro as ignorant, ugly and sensual; but when it came to talents in certain types of music, he believed, as noted, that black people were superior to Caucasians.[207]

Some romantic racialists believed that whites were stronger intellectually, while blacks were stronger physically. More commonly romantic racialists claimed that the Negro was morally of a higher order than the Caucasian. Moncure Daniel Conway, a one-time Virginia slaveholder turned radical abolitionist lecturer and author, who subscribed to the theory of monogenism, insisted that "blacks are morally very much superior to the whites." Black people, he said, made faithful and unselfish friends, who were motivated by a sense of honor.[208] Likewise James Russell Lowell, the celebrated New England writer and poet, astutely observed that throughout history the "oppressor has always endeavored to justify his sin by casting reproach upon the moral or intellectual qualities of the oppressed." Lowell then went on to maintain that the "Caucasian mind . . . can never come to so beautiful or Christian a height of civilization, as with a mixture of those seemingly humbler, but truly more noble [moral] qualities" which the black man possessed.[209] Doubtless the best known proponent of the romantic view of the black race was the antebellum, antislavery writer Harriet Beecher Stowe. In her most famous tome she declared that "for moral traits of honesty, kindness, tenderness of feeling, for heroic efforts and self-denials . . . they [black people] have been remarkable, to a degree that . . . is surprising."[210]

From such premises some romantic racialists arrived at the conclusion that miscegenation was good by fusing together, in one person, the superior qualities of each race. Mulattoes, rather than being a sickly and degenerate race, were depicted as physically stronger and healthier, intellectually brighter and spiritually and morally superior than either of the parent stocks. Conway and Lowell were among those who maintained that miscegenation would result in an improvement over the 'pure' Caucasian. Benjamin Hunt, a Philadelphia businessman who spent seventeen years living in Haiti, supported the idea of miscegenation for the purpose of both eradicating slavery and racial prejudice. Arguing that blacks were physically stronger than whites, while whites were mentally stronger than blacks, he proposed that amalgamation would create a perfect race which could expand into and economically exploit the areas south of the United States. When he spoke about creating a colony of American settlers in Haiti, Hunt was, therefore, not thinking of separating the races. Rather, he hoped that white and black Americans would go to Haiti together. These settlers would combine the "strength and soberness of the Negro" with the "grace of form and intelligence of the whites." Hunt insisted that "neither the white race nor the black race will do any ultimate good in these Southern latitudes by itself . . . . " By uniting the superior Caucasian intellect with the superior physique of the Negro, Hunt wrote, the "head and the hand are thus placed on the same person" and the "problem of Negro slavery will be solved." Miscegenation would develop a superior laboring class for the American tropics. Hunt sincerely believed that the "Anglo-Americans, with the Africans, whom a part of the former now hold in bondage, will one day unite to form this race for the tropics." Nor was Hunt opposed to the extension of miscegenation in the warmer or Southern United States. He argued that "should there . . . prove to be any part of the Union where the climate or the culture really requires the labor of the black man, then there he will remain, and eventually be absorbed by the dominant race." Hunt observed that "from that point, the complexion of our population will begin to shade off into that of the dark belt of Anglo-Africans, which will then extend across the northern tropics."[211]

To Hunt, the mulatto, instead of representing the worst of both races or some kind of infertile hybrid, represented the ideal human being. He was "capable of succeeding in all the liberal and mechanical arts, and some of them have proved this . . . the people of color in general are good, and susceptible of elevation of mind." The mulatto, if found within a suitable climate, was one of the "longest lived . . . of all the human beings."[212] Conway also accepted the idea of miscegenation. He was "firmly persuaded that the mixture of the blacks and whites is good; that the person so produced is, under ordinarily favorable circumstances, healthy, handsome and intelligent." He spoke at times of combining the "Saxon mind with the African temperament" to produce a more perfect individual.[213] Lowell wrote that "we have never had any doubt, that the African race was intended to introduce a new element of civilization, and that the Caucasian would be benefited greatly by an infusion of its gentler and less selfish qualities."[214]

In short, romantic racialists also recommended eugenics, not to make man better by keeping the races pure, but to make man better by crossing the races. Lowell and some romantic racialists, however, were apt, as were some hostile racialists, to contradict themselves. Lowell, at times, pictured black men with admirable qualities, so much so that whites would do well to fuse with them. At other times, as when he attacked the institution of Southern slavery in *The Biglow Papers*, he expressed a very hostile racialism by comparing black people with swine.[215]

Moncure Conway and Benjamin Hunt also contradicted themselves, to an extent, by sometimes expressing a belief in environmental rather than biological causation. Their digression, unlike Lowell's, did not connote hostility toward blacks. The idea of environmentalism represented the antithesis of theories based on race. It stemmed from the philosophy of the eighteenth century enlightenment carried into the early nineteenth century. To the eighteenth century rationalist, the environment was more broadly conceived than by those who believed in biological determinism. The environment was more than just the climate. It represented a whole range of outside forces which operated on and affected people's lives. For example, besides climate, the environment might include such factors as educational opportunities and natural resources; the presence or absence of epidemic diseases; soil conditions and methods of cultivation; and the religious practices and political system under which people lived. Rationalists believed that differences among nations or races in physical strength, intelligence, population size or whatever could be explained by such environmental factors. In origin, then, man was universal; there were no real innate or biological distinctions in mental or physical abilities among groups of people. Moreover, rationalists viewed man as a sensible creature who, with his intellectual faculties and free will could, to some extent, alter and improve his condition and life style. Rationalism, with its corollary of environmental causation, was, in sum, a philosophy which offered man hope.[216]

Since the environmentalists adhered to the concept of universal man, the idea of men belonging to specific races was not important in their scheme of things. They did not accept the concept of a hierarchy of races, by which assumption one could supposedly rank the quality of each racial group. In fact their philosophy represented a direct refutation of the belief in fixed and permanent differences among racial groups. They supported the monogenic theory of creation, as opposed to the polygenic thesis; physical characteristics cut across racial lines and were due largely to climatic factors. Nevertheless, the environmentalists did not use the climatic argument to assign races to permanent geographical zones. More importantly, they did not consider physical differences as significant in determining mental ability; intellectual traits also cut across racial lines, and the races were basically equal in mental endowments. Somewhat like the romantic racialists, although for a different reason, a number of environmentalists saw nothing wrong with miscegenation.

The belief that physical characteristics, such as skin color, facial angle, hair and limbs, cut across racial lines was held by a number of environmentalists, among whom were Dr. Johann Friedrich Blumenbach, the Reverend Dr. Samuel Stanhope Smith, Dr. James Cowles Prichard and Dr. Benjamin Rush.

Blumenbach, a German anthropologist, exerted considerable worldwide influence on the development of ethnological studies in the eighteenth and early nineteenth centuries. He, with Georges-Louis Buffon of France, is considered one of the founders of modern anthropology. Earlier than Morton, he collected skulls and observed variations in skin color; he arrived at different conclusions than Morton. From the variations in skulls and skin color, Blumenbach formulated a system of racial classification. He divided human beings into the basic five-group racial format-Caucasian, Mongolian, Ethiopian, American and Malayan-which anthropologists still use. The term Caucasian was supposedly coined by him. Blumenbach, however, never tried to classify or rank races on a superior to inferior scale. Nor did he subscribe to the theory of polygenism, or its concomitant, innate or biologically inherited character traits. Instead, he subscribed to the theory of environmental causation; consequently, when explaining differences in skin color, he noted that "warm climates invariably predispose men . . . to a redundancy of the bilious secretion, and the smallest surcharge of this secretion imparts to the skin a yellow appearance, which, by remaining long in contact with the atmosphere, assumes a darker hue, and if exposed . . . to the immediate influence of the sun, approaches . . . towards the black."[217]

The Reverend Dr. Samuel Stanhope Smith, president of the College of New Jersey at Princeton, and deeply influenced by the work of Blumenbach, held an analogous view regarding skin color. In almost the exact words he wrote of the "bilious secretion," and thought that the climate was one of the determining factors in accounting for differences in skin color. He utilized, as did other antebellum ethnologists, the concept of color gradations as determined by latitude; by going from North to

South (or from a colder to a warmer climate), one also went from lighter to darker skinned peoples. Smith stated that "each parallel of latitude is . . . distinctly marked with its characteristic complexion."[218] Lowell, too, believed climate had an influence "upon complexion."[219]

Not all environmentalists relied upon a climatic explanation to explain skin color. Dr. Benjamin Rush, a prominent physician from Philadelphia, claimed that the color of black people was due to "endemic leprosy." Rush warned white people not to intermarry with blacks, since their children would be infected. He thought black people could be cured of their color. He spoke of "attempts to dislodge the color in Negroes" and, in this way, make them happier since, according to him, even blacks preferred the color white.[220]

Environmentalists also held common views regarding the origins of such physical characteristics as facial angle, cranial capacity, texture of hair and contour of the limbs. These, too, were dependent on climatic and dietary factors and crossed racial lines. Lowell posited that "changes . . . in the shape of the skull, in the length and general characteristics of the limbs, and in the development and tissue of the muscular system, are brought about by the habits and diet of a race."[221] Samuel Smith wrote about the "effects of climate and other physical influences, in diversifying the figure of the head." People who lived in colder climates had broader foreheads than those, like the Negro, whose facial "depression" was caused by the "torrid zone" in which he lived. "The color of the hair" of the black person, Smith wrote, also "is . . . affected by the temperature of the climate." Its "sparseness and coarseness . . . is analogous to effects which we have already seen to be produced by the temperature of arid climates . . . by the excessive heat of a vertical sun." Lowell agreed that the "color and texture of the black man's hair" were "dependent upon the climate, or some other circumstances of local condition."[222]

Diet apparently could influence physical characteristics. Although most of the environmentalists seemed to shy away from attributing these characteristics to such socio-economic factors as employment conditions and living quarters, Samuel Smith may have by implication. He claimed that the "poor and laboring part of the community in every country, are usually more dark in their complexion . . . more coarse and ill formed in their limbs, than persons of better rank."[223] Another environmentalist was much more explicit. Dr. James Cowles Prichard, a well-known English physician whose influence extended to America, noted that "slender, lean and elongated limbs are generally found in races who are badly fed, and in those whose food is chiefly or entirely of vegetables."[224]

No race had a monopoly on special physical characteristics. Moreover, Blumenbach found no significant evidence to indicate that particular facial angles were associated exclusively with particular races. Rather, there was as great a variation in facial angles among the skulls of Negroes as among the skulls of Caucasians. While certain skull characteristics may have been dominant among certain racial groups, those characteristics could also be found in all racial groups.[225] Prichard also pointed out that there were no unique physical features peculiar to any one race. He attacked the idea that black people were more like apes than human beings. He found that the "difference between adult apes and men in the length of the extremities is so great as to render all such comparisons very remote, and of very doubtful importance with respect to any ulterior conclusion." The reason for the misconception, Prichard thought, was that the differences among the black and white races, which polygenists pointed to as evidence, were simply based on averages, and averages could be very deceiving. He went on to note that "there are many Europeans whose forearms are as long as those of Negroes, and there are Negroes who resemble Europeans." In short, "individuals among other races are frequently seen who strongly resemble the more characteristic form of the African," and "all the peculiarities of the Negro countenance are discernible in the persons of Europeans."[226]

A number of environmentalists attributed not only physical, but mental and temperamental characteristics to outside, or environmental, factors. If both races were born with the same average mental and psychological makeup, then the ignorance or immorality which racial theorists attributed to blacks must be due, said some environmentalists, to the influence of Southern slavery or were simply figments of the propagandists of the institution. Prichard, who subscribed to the concept of universal man, wrote that all races "have common affections, sympathies, and are subjected to precisely analogous laws of feeling and action, and partake, in short, of a common psychical nature, and are therefore proved . . . to belong to one species of lineage." He poked a damaging hole into the argument of the polygenists by noting that "Negro children do not appear in any respect inferior to white children in their faculties." "On the contrary," he continued, "they seem to be generally more forward as infants."[227] Blumenbach, who avoided deducing mental or personal characteristics from his observations of physical characteristics, castigated pro-slavery racialists when he "attacked all political or social abuses of anthropological ideas, in particular the notion that black men were on a lower level of humanity than white men."[228]

Rush, like Blumenbach, did not believe in an intellectual hierarchy of races or that outward physical appearances were a clue to mental abilities. Contrary to the polygenists, Rush thought that all people were created the same, in the sense that they had equal intelligence at birth. On a number of occasions he brought Negro men of science before the public and was happy to consider them his associates. Rush was involved in the early antislavery movement, and noted that if anything acted to debase the black man, it was the institution of Southern slavery.[229] Another monogenist, Moncure Conway, apparently forgetting his romantic racialist ideas, stated in his book, *Testimonies Concerning Slavery*, that black people had the same ability to learn and benefit from education as white people. This fact would only become more obvious, he argued, when slavery was destroyed. He gave examples of famous black thinkers; he found that intellectual abilities crossed racial lines, for they were not the exclusive property of the Caucasian race. "My observation leads me to believe," Conway noted, when speaking of black people, "that so far from [their] being a poor or inferior set, we might, under proper training, have . . . some of the first men of the world."[230]

Wilson Armistead, an English antislavery writer who also believed in the unity and equality of all men, published, in 1848, a 560-page book entitled, *A Tribute For the Negro*. Armistead's work, which sold in the United States-and in which he acknowledged his indebtedness to Dr. Prichard and to the New York abolitionist Gerrit Smith-is essentially a collective biography of world famous black men. Attacking slavery, he wrote that the "hapless victims of this revolting system are men of the same origin as ourselves, of similar form and delineation of feature, though with a darker skin." Armistead was convinced that black men were "endowed with minds equal in dignity, equal in capacity" to those of Caucasians. Black people, moreover, had the "same social dispositions and affections" as white people. He believed that much of the "prejudice and misinformation" directed against black people had "been fostered with unremitting assiduity by those interested in upholding the slave system." If slavery were abolished, and if blacks were permitted to participate in society on an equal basis, Armistead was certain that they would demonstrate that they were "not inferior in natural capacity, or deficient of the intellectual and amiable qualities which adorn and dignify human nature."[231]

Another environmentalist who argued that mental differences were affected by social and cultural conditions, as well as by climate, was Samuel Smith. Having no appreciation or understanding of African cultures, he thought that the black man was a dull and violent creature, not only because of slavery, but because of the savage nature of African society. However, if the black man could be brought to America as a free man, rather than a slave, he, given the country's more temperate climate, would begin to show improvement, and to look and act more like the white man. Although Smith had no particular love for the black man, he hoped that if the black man would not go away, he would at least become a white man.[232]

In light of their belief in the physical and mental similarities between the races environmentalists, as a group, did not fear miscegenation, as did the racial theorists who were hostile to the black man. They held that the mulatto was not an inferior or degenerate creature simply because the Negro was not. Samuel Smith, for example, was not averse to the idea of racial intermarriage, if that was what it took to "lighten up" the black countenance.[233] Prichard, who wrote that the "black . . . inhabitants of Africa have frequently beautiful features, and scarcely differ in form from [inhabitants of] the European nations," did not believe mulattoes were weaker beings. He observed that because they could reproduce themselves they could not possibly be infertile hybrids, unable to perpetuate themselves, as some ethnologists and popular writers insisted. Indeed, Prichard pictured them as healthy and very prolific.[234]

In short, the environmentalist put forth a belief in universal man. People were basically the same at birth, and differences which later appeared among groups were not, for the most part, the result of innate or biological processes, but rather could be traced to outside forces or circumstances affecting those groups. Conway summed up the concept of the brotherhood of mankind when he stated that the "evening-star of the epoch of separate races is the morning-star of Human Unity . . . . Nations are great in proportion as they are of mixed races."[235]

V

Notwithstanding the work of the romantic racialists and the environmentalists, those who preached a hostile racialism enjoyed an increasing popularity among the reading public within the United States.[236] There were many more of such writers, and most of their works were published in America in fairly large editions. As leading scientists, physicians and literati, they gave strong support to the polygenic theory of creation. Whether from Europe or the United States, they argued that, by being different, the black man was inferior.

The racist ideas to which they gave currency embodied such concepts as his innate physical and mental inferiority; the black' fitness for life only in the warmer or tropical climatic zones. In addition to the persons already mentioned, there were many other writers and intellectuals who contributed to the development and perpetuation of this antebellum racial ideology. The cumulative effect of this racialist literature was bound to exert a powerful impact on the political community. Men of learning from both the Northern and Southern United States agreed in this pejorative estimation of the black man.[237] Where the writers from the two sections parted company was in the conclusions they drew from this estimation. Southerners, with exceptions, employed racist theories to buttress their institution of slavery; if black men were inferior, they should be kept in slavery and made to serve the superior white man. Northerners, with exceptions, employed these racist theories to obstruct the expansion of the institution of slavery; if black men were inferior, they should be contained in the South to prevent miscegenation and racial conflict and, in time, be removed from the country, leaving the nation to the superior white man.

CHAPTER 2

EARLY FREE SOILERS AND THE BLACK PRESENCE

So the Negro is free [in the North], but he cannot share the rights, pleasures, labors, griefs, or even the tomb of him whose equal he has been declared; there is nowhere, where he can meet him, neither in life nor in death. In the South, where slavery still exists, less trouble is taken to keep the Negro apart: they sometimes share the labors and the pleasures of the white men; people are prepared to mix with them to some extent.

Alexis DeTocqueville, 1848

If racial theorizing in the first half of the nineteenth century had remained the concern only of the naturalists and ethnologists of the scientific community, its impact on American society would have been considerably less. Contemporaneous with the development of racial theories by the scientists of the antebellum period, however, was their public adoption by both Southern slaveholders in defense of their peculiar institution and by many of those Northern politicians, political writers and newspaper editors in support of the Free Soil doctrine to exclude slavery from the Western territories. While one group-Southerners-wanted to maintain their complete dominance over black people, the other group-Northerners-had a total aversion toward blacks and therefore wanted nothing to do with them. The use that the former group made of racial theories is not the subject of this work; however, the use that the latter group made is. Free Soilers fell victim to the same gaps in logic, the same contradictions, which plagued the intelligentsia.

These Northern Free Soilers helped to disseminate among their constituents and readers scientific theories regarding the inferiority of black people and these racist theories conveniently dovetailed with the particular antislavery rationale that they were promoting. In other words, given the fact that all slaves were black, the effect of repeating the scientific litany that black people were racially inferior and a threat to the white race was to strengthen the argument that slavery must be excluded from the territories. The Free Soil leaders, in fact, came to put so much emphasis on the racial reasons for keeping slavery out of the West that they seemed at times to be arguing that the struggle for supremacy in the territories was not so much a struggle between the North and the South, or even between slavery and freedom, as one between the black race and the white race. In the process they evinced a deep, almost pathological fear and hatred of black people. In particular, many Free Soilers appeared unhappy, tortured, over miscegenation, over the prospect of a mixed race peopling the United States. Perhaps one reason for fearing miscegenation was tied to the idea of identifying people by skin color. This idea was used by members of the dominant white group to protect their leading position in society. Numerous whites sought to persuade their own and subordinate group members that whatever alleged differences existed between the two were fixed and permanent. The expression 'race' denoted these differences. But, a problem arose which threatened this simple method of ranking people by appearance; that problem was the mulatto. In the latter case outward appearance could be deceptive, as many Free Soil and later Republican politicians noted. It was becoming increasingly more difficult to distinguish whites from blacks, or superior from inferior peoples. Biologically, race was becoming irrelevant. In effect, miscegenation was breaking down the barriers which the scientific community had erected and which many whites stood behind to safeguard their socio-economic dominance in society.

Following still further the reasoning of the scientific community, Free Soilers reached the conclusion that if the white race was to realize its destiny in North America, the black race must not merely be contained in the South but ultimately removed from the continent altogether. Again, this suggests a psychological insecurity in the presence of black people, an insecurity manifested by the Free Soilers' constant need to identify with the dominant white race. Yet even among Free Soilers, as among members of the learned community, there were some who were ambivalent in their views toward black Americans, for, at times, they countered the polygenists' idea of a permanently distinct and innately inferior black race with an idea advanced by environmentalists, namely, that all men were the same at birth and were all members of one race, the human race.

I

The political antecedents of this Free Soil doctrine may, of course, be traced back at least to Thomas Jefferson, who was a politician as well as a scientist. After Jefferson, the two politicians who were probably the most influential in propagating the reasoning which led from the premise of black inferiority to the conclusions of containment and removal or colonization, were Henry Clay of Kentucky and David Wilmot of Pennsylvania. The example that Clay set for his fellow Whigs and the example that Wilmot set for his fellow Democrats were soon taken up by the leaders of new political coalitions-first, within the Free Soil Party and then the Republican Party-as their own.

Henry Clay, like Jefferson and many of the learned classes, endorsed, as fact, the physical and mental inferiority of the black race. Also like Jefferson, in whose rejected Ordinance of 1784 and adopted Ordinance of 1787 can be discerned the seeds of the idea, Clay adopted the policy of containment. The Compromises of 1820 and 1850, in which he played such an important part, restricted, in certain ways, the extension of slavery and slaves. More than Jefferson, however, Clay attempted to put into practice colonization as the final solution of America's race problem. Nevertheless, Clay's policies on slavery and race were throughout, influenced as Jefferson's had been, by his affection for the Union. The roles which he assumed in framing the legislation of 1820 and 1850 left him secure in his title as the 'Great Compromiser.' Henceforth, the term 'Clay Whig' would define one who worked to preserve the Union by making concessions on the issues of slavery and race.

Before tracing the details of Clay's ideas on these subjects, a distinction should be drawn between a radical antislavery person, or abolitionist, and a political antislavery person of the Clay persuasion. Where the former had no wish to preserve the Union if its preservation required a prolongation of slavery, the latter would preserve the Union even if its preservation precluded an immediate end to slavery. This is by way of saying that any reform impulses generated by the Whig Party, and those later political groupings and parties which looked to Clay's example, would be conservative, pragmatic and, in so far as possible, dedicated to maintaining the political status quo. It is not without significance that, subsequently, Abraham Lincoln and his political allies were commonly referred to as 'Clay Whigs.'

That Clay's policies respecting the Union and slavery were circumscribed by his views on race has been suggested. It remains to be shown that this was indeed the case. As one of the most prominent Border state politicians of his time, as the acknowledged father and leader of the Whig Party, and as the only politician with sufficient influence to mold that party into an effective political opposition to the Democracy of Andrew Jackson, Clay, by lending his prestige to current racial theories, would be bound to exert a profound influence on conservative political antislavery thought.

Clay commented publicly and negatively on the physique and mentality of the black person. As had Jefferson and many students of ethnology, he depicted the "physical structure" of blacks as totally different and distinctly inferior to Caucasians. He also described black people as "ignorant, uneducated and incapable of appreciating the value or enjoying the privileges of freedom." Black slaves, Clay declared, were "kept in subjection only by the superior intelligence and superior power of the predominant race." By implication, he seemed to impute immorality to black Americans generally, when he claimed that "of all classes of our population, the most vicious is that of the free coloured . . . . Contaminated themselves, they extend their vices to all around them." In general, blacks were "a suspicious race of another complexion." In short, like the hostile racialists within the scientific community, Clay argued that blacks constituted a distinct and separate race.[1]

Apparently accepting the polygenic theory of creation, Clay maintained that blacks were a people "for . . . whom He [God], by their physical properties, had made unlike and put asunder" from Caucasians. "It has been His divine pleasure to make the black man black, and the white man white, and to distinguish them [the blacks] by other repulsive constitutional differences."[2]

Clay said that he feared the presence of this inferior and distinct black race. Opposed to granting blacks political, social or economic equality within the United States, he was particularly concerned with the growing number of free blacks in American society. He held that in those slave states where blacks outnumbered whites, the "blacks could not be emancipated and invested with all the rights of freemen, without becoming the governing race." Given his avowedly low estimate of their talents, it is difficult to comprehend Clay's prediction that blacks could become "the governing race;" yet he failed to resolve this apparent contradiction in this thinking.[3]

Troubled over this increase in the free black population, Clay was unsympathetic to the radical abolitionists of the variety of William Lloyd Garrison and Wendell Phillips for advocating the immediate abolition of slavery. In fact he publicly attacked and castigated them for being disloyal to the white race. "They proclaim," Clay declared, "that color is nothing; that the organic and characteristic differences between the two races ought to be entirely overlooked and disregarded."[4]

Clay's opposition to the further expansion of the free black population, he claimed, was based on a number of racial concerns. First, and perhaps most salient, he was deeply distressed over miscegenation and its ultimate effect on the superior race, "if this promiscuous residence of whites and blacks, of freemen and slaves, is forever to continue." He raised the fear so often voiced by members of the scientific community when he asked "what would be the condition of the two races . . . upon the supposition of an immediate emancipation?" Since the "abolitionists oppose all colonization . . . it irresistibly follows," Clay warned, "that they are in favor of amalgamation." Clearly hinting they were hypocritical in their call for racial equality, he issued a challenge to the radical abolitionists to start the process of total integration. "I have heard of none of these ultra-abolitionists furnishing in their own families or persons examples of intermarriage." Invoking the support of the Almighty, Clay evidently felt secure in asking the question: "Does any man recommend amalgamation, that revolting admixture, alike offensive to God and man?" "We may, without presumptuousness suppose" that blacks and whites "were never intended to be joined together."[5]

Clay also expressed concern about the future of white laborers if slavery suddenly vanished. For one thing, he worried about the competition that free black laborers would provide for whites. In 1843 he wrote to his friend, the Reverend Calvin Colton, a fellow antislavery conservative who resided in Washington, D.C. and edited the *True Whig*, regarding a pamphlet Colton was writing. Clay advised that its "great aim and object . . . should be to arouse the laboring classes in the free states against abolition." Clay wanted Colton to "depict the consequences to them of immediate abolition. The slaves being free, would be dispersed throughout the Union; they would enter into competition with the free laborer; with the American, the Irish, the German, [and] reduce his wages." In this way Clay divided the working classes along a color line. Apparently again forgetting his low opinion of the abilities of blacks, Clay was not as sanguine as Dr. Julian Sturtevant or the Reverend Theodore Parker that whites would emerge triumphant in this competition. Furthermore, Clay predicted dire social consequences for white laborers should the radical abolitionists gain political leverage. The freed black man would "be confounded with him [the white laborer] and affect his moral and social standing . . . . Their [radical abolitionists'] object is to unite in marriage the laboring white man and the laboring black man and to reduce the white laboring man to the despised and degraded condition of the black man." Why the abolitionists wanted to degrade the white laborer Clay never explained. He was only interested in pointing out that abolitionists were the true enemies of white labor because they wanted "to keep the blacks here, that they may interfere with, degrade and debase the laboring whites."[6]

A third racial concern evinced by Clay had also been already brooded about. Like Jefferson and the learned writers of the antebellum period, Clay warned of the possibility of racial warfare if Caucasians and Negroes, whether slave or free, continued to reside in the same society. He warned that "color, passions and prejudices would forever prevent the two races from living together in a state of cordial union." If this bi-racial society was maintained "who," Clay asked, "can imagine the servile wars, the carnage and the crimes which will be its probable consequences?"[7]

To cope with these perceived difficulties and to counter abolitionist demands for immediate emancipation, Clay proposed several solutions to the general problem of slavery in America which, to his mind, was synonymous with the problem of the black man in America. Ranging from the mild to the extreme, from a policy of non-extension and containment, to one of colonizing blacks abroad, the solutions offered by this former slaveholder constituted the essence of the conservative, Free Soil approach to the alleged black problem.

In keeping with his philosophy of the supremacy of white labor, Clay desired to preserve the greater part of the free Western territories for white European laborers. According to his grandson, Thomas H. Clay, it was Henry's recommendation, while Speaker of the House during the debates over the Missouri Compromise of 1820, to establish 36 degrees, 30 minutes as the northern most line of demarcation for prohibiting the introduction of slavery into the territories. Again, during the debates over the annexation of Texas and the subsequent Mexican War, Clay remained hostile to the expansion of Southern slavery and supported the principle of non-extension.[8]

Clay's most important work, the Compromise of 1850, was itself a fairly effective way of keeping slavery and black people out of the newly acquired Mexican Cession. He said he believed in the "natural limits thesis," a perspective which claimed slavery to be geographically and climatically incompatible with the new territories, since the products which could be grown profitably by slave labor could not be raised outside the South. Clay, indirectly and directly, put forward the case for a limited popular sovereignty. Excepting California, he thought it "inexpedient" for Congress to legislate either for or against slavery in the remaining territories acquired from Mexico. Therefore, the territorial governments in New Mexico and Utah would be organized without mention of slavery. California, the key prize in this sectional dispute should, he noted, be admitted according to the wishes of its people, i.e. as a free state. Clay was therefore willing to leave the slavery question up to the territorial legislatures. Free states readily endorsed this argument, since they had been attracting a large immigrant population of white laborers from Europe who, by becoming Western settlers, could act through their legislatures to keep slavery and black people out of the territories. The South not only lacked this advantage, but the overwhelming majority of Southerners who moved to the new territories or to the free states were non-slaveholders, many of whom detested slavery and black people. Consequently it might not, in Clay's estimation, be necessary to secure national legislation specifically framed to exclude slavery from the territories. Such laws would only antagonize the South further and lead to unnecessary sectional discord. Historian Samuel M. Schmucker believes that Clay's "immediate purpose" in proposing the Compromise of 1850, "was to exclude slavery from all the territories acquired by the United States, by the treaty [of Guadalupe Hidalgo] with Mexico, and also to exclude it from New Mexico."[9]

The containment of slavery and blacks in the South was not, however, Clay's ultimate plan; he called for a program of gradual emancipation by which slaveholders would be compensated, presumably by the state and federal governments, for the loss of their property. Central to this scheme was the colonization out of the country of the emancipated blacks. As it had been for Jefferson and other intellectuals, Clay relied upon colonization, or the separation of the races, as his final solution to the problem of the black man's presence.

Clay's involvement in the antislavery movement officially began on December 21, 1816 when he and several prominent political leaders met at the Davis Hotel in Washington, D.C. to found the American Colonization Society. Ostensibly the Society was simply a group of benevolent social reformers, but the policy of sending, usually voluntarily but in some cases forcibly, black Americans out of the country, which the Society adopted, represented a conservative approach to the issues of race and slavery. This was so because, as conceived by colonizationists, the objective was not so much to ameliorate the burden of slavery or to change the hostile racial environment in which the black man lived, but rather to get rid of the black man and, thereby, keep America white. In an important sense supporters of colonization acted to increase white racism by continually stressing the pretended dangers that blacks represented to white Americans. Clay became the single most influential political crusader for the idea of colonizing black Americans back to their "native lands."[10]

For all of its conservatism, however, the American Colonization Society still embodied the first major attempt at institutionalized antislavery. As such, the Society did not fail to draw in Congress the criticism of powerful pro-slavery forces, under such leaders as South Carolina's Robert Y. Hayne and John C. Calhoun. At the same time because the Society seemed to some to represent a form of protest against slavery it, at least in its early stages, attracted many genuinely antislavery people, some of whom were later to become radical abolitionists strongly opposed to the whole idea of colonization. William Lloyd Garrison, Gerrit Smith and Theodore Dwight Weld started their antislavery careers as colonizationists but eventually repudiated its objectives and, by the mid-1830's, they left the Society.[11]

Unlike Jefferson, who mainly confined himself to theorizing about the presence of black people in America, Clay helped found the Colonization Society and, as an example to other slaveholders, manumitted his own slaves and settled them in Liberia. He argued that blacks themselves would benefit from colonization. Freed from slavery but left in the United States, they would still have to contend with white prejudice and discrimination. Clay, like Mary Booth, maintained that, under such circumstances, the result would be the "social, moral and political degradation . . . of the colored race." Freedom and resettlement to Africa, said Clay, would avail blacks of opportunities unavailable to them in North America. Former slaves would also, Clay insisted, "carry back to their native soil the rich fruits of religion, civilization, law and liberty," which they, presumably, acquired while in slavery.[12]

Clay's commitment to the welfare of the black people may, of course, be questioned. If he really believed that slavery introduced blacks to the bounties of white culture, why would he want to terminate its purportedly positive influence through gradual emancipation and colonization? It is difficult to escape the impression that Clay's rationale was merely a convenience which rested upon those racial beliefs which he had expounded at other times. Indeed, in seeking support for his program, he at times argued the necessity of deporting the black man, because that step, first of all, would end amalgamation and its "revolting admixture," the mulatto, and preserve the alleged superiority of the white race. "Nowhere in the United States," Clay stated, "are amalgamation and equality between the two races possible." Therefore, "it is better that there should be a separation, and that the African descendants should be returned to the native land of their fathers."[13]

Deportation would also eliminate a source of competition for the white laboring classes. For the last time before his death, in January of 1851, Clay addressed the annual meeting of the American Colonization Society at Washington, D.C. He pointed out the socio-economic advantages which he believed would accrue to white laborers by giving support to black colonization. "Will not the white laborers of the North be benefitted, essentially benefitted, if the black portion of the laboring community is sent to Africa and they are relieved from all competition with them?" Clay advised his listeners to "go to the cities and in all of them you will see the struggles which exist there between white and black labor." In what could be construed as an appeal to the racial prejudices of the white workers in the country, Clay gave assurances that "even in labor itself, there is an indisposition on the part of the white man to mix and mingle with the black." In effect, Clay found that by adopting colonization, the "white man of the North will be benefitted" and likewise the "white man of the South will be benefitted."[14]

Finally deportation, according to Clay, would remove the possibility of racial war. He agreed with Doctors John Van Evrie and Julian Sturtevant: the races were so dissimilar that they could not live together on a basis of equality and peace. Separation was the only remedy to prevent them from killing each other.[15]

That Clay's principle concern was with the welfare of the white race becomes ever more evident when one studies his detailed plans, put forward publicly as early as 1827, for colonization and for preventing what he called the "enslavement of the white race." Specifically, the proposals were meant to allay white consternation over the growing number of black people in the United States. With the "population of the United States being at this time estimated at about ten millions of the European race and two of the African," Clay reasoned that the "annual colonization of a number of both of its [black] classes (bond and free) . . . would accomplish more than to keep the parent stock stationary." He calculated that black Americans were increasing at the rate of fifty-two thousand per year. If, however, this many blacks were sent out of the country annually, by the end of thirty years, or approximately 1860, given the natural mortality rate of many in the older generations, very few black people would be left within the United States. At the same time, as blacks left the country, whites would enter and "there would be annual space created for an equal number of the white race." He even estimated the annual shipping tonnage required for such an undertaking and its costs.[16]

The major expenses for the project would, according to Clay, be borne by black emigrants themselves. Clay's plan called for a gradual emancipating of slaves so they could pay their passage to Africa by working on public or state projects for three years. He also made provision for the slaveholders to receive compensation for their colonized slaves from the state and federal governments, along with aid from the American Colonization Society. All details for the actual transportation of black emigrants would be handled by the Society.[17]

The scheme envisioned by Clay, however, never seriously got beyond the planning stage, as neither black people nor slaveholders gave it their endorsement; nor the United States Congress its long-term financial backing.[18]

Clay's own objective, nevertheless, did not appear to be in doubt; he summed up his argument for colonization with a powerful appeal to white racial pride. His major interest, he said, was to "render us one homogeneous people," and he concluded by noting: "I prefer . . . the liberty of my own race to that of any other race . . . . To make the black man free . . . would virtually enslave the white man."[19]

If Henry Clay set the example for the involvement of Whigs in the Free Soil movement, Representative David Wilmot of Pennsylvania set the example for the involvement of Democrats. However, whereas Clay took several decades to develop fully his example, Wilmot made his known at one dramatic session before the House of Representatives. On August 8, 1846, during an evening meeting of the House, Wilmot introduced his famous 'Proviso,' or amendment, to President James K. Polk's Two Million Dollar Bill. By this bill, the administration sought congressional funding to conduct negotiations with Mexico for the purchase of Mexican land. Though simple in its intention, Wilmot's Proviso carried profound implications; it stated that Congress would exclude slavery from any territory that in the future might be acquired from Mexico. Soon referred to by its supporters as the "cornerstone resolution," the Proviso, while initially defeated, came to epitomize the fundamental ingredient of the political antislavery appeal, that is, of the political position later assumed by the Free Soil and Republican Parties; slavery must not extend into the free and open territories.[20]

Wilmot never hid his objective while proposing his Proviso. He frankly admitted he desired to keep slavery and black people in the South in order to reserve the territories solely for white people. Racial factors manifestly played a part in his thinking. Like the scientists and writers of the learned community, Wilmot described black people as inferior to Caucasians. Blacks constituted, he insisted, a totally distinct group; in fact, he compared blacks to a disease, "overshadowing the country" with the "germ . . . of evil." Wilmot's main concern apparently was with the competition that black people, as slaves entering the territories, would pose for white laborers. While describing the slaveholder he maintained that the "unproductive tillage of his human cattle [takes] that which of right belongs to free labor, and which is necessary for the support and happiness of our own race." As was true of Clay, Wilmot did not explain how the "unproductive tillage" of black laborers, whom he depicted as lazy and indolent, could compete successfully with the productive tillage of white laborers, whom he said were known for "their enterprise, their diligence, their economy," which "builds up new empires in the West." Negro slavery, as he put it, could only bring "dishonor and degradation upon the poor white man" because the latter would be "brought in close contact with the servile labor of the black."[21]

That Wilmot opposed the extension of slavery into the territories did not imply his support for an immediate end to slavery. While he hoped that "we might by a mighty effort, solve peacefully and without blood, the problem of slavery," nonetheless, if racial conflict should occur he, speaking for the North, stood "ready, at all times, to sustain the institutions of the South as they exist with our money and with our blood . . . ." Even so, Wilmot seemed convinced that by containing slavery in the South, the size of the black population would also be contained and, presumably, the threat of racial strife would be lessened. As proof, he cited Cuba. "There is," he asserted, "no increase of slaves in Cuba, although . . . the foreign slave trade is carried on . . . with that island." The reason for this demographic stability, according to Wilmot, was that "there is no room for them [blacks] to spread, and the market is fully supplied with laborers." Black slaves "are like any other stock of which merchandise is made. Widen the market for their sale and you stimulate the production." By restricting the expansion of slavery one also restricted the growth of the black population. Here Wilmot drew a parallel that later Free Soilers and Republicans would also draw: the "extension of slavery and the increase of slaves are identical and inseparably one and the same thing."[22]

To sum up, Wilmot, suggestive of Daniel Drake and Louis Agassiz, supported Northern exclusion of black slaves from the territories and their containment within the South. Far from eschewing a racial approach to sectional politics, he appealed directly to skin color; the major motivation behind his proviso, he declared, was to preserve the Western territories for the white laboring man. "I would," he told Congress, "plead the cause of the rights of white freemen. I would preserve for free white labor a fair country."[23]

However, for Wilmot, as for Clay, containment was only the first step to insure American's white racial destiny. Speaking before Congress in 1850, the Pennsylvanian stated that "notwithstanding the vast increase of slavery in the last sixty years, I entertain the hope so ardently cherished by our fathers, of its ultimate extinction." Specifically, Wilmot noted that the "negro race already occupy enough of this fair continent," and he

wanted to "keep what remains for ourselves . . . for the free white laborer."
Wilmot, among other Free Soilers, believed that containing and restricting
black slavery in the South would eventuate in an end to the institution and
freedom for the slaves. Wilmot said that the freed black man, however, would
have to find a new home, outside of the United States, and he recommended
colonization as the means to this end. Wilmot looked "forward to someday,
remote it may be, when the South, in its own way and by its own voluntary
action, will set about the great work of emancipation and the separation of
the two races." To help the South in its efforts to colonize black people, he
hoped that the North would "cooperate to the full extent of its resources and
power." Wilmot did not want the "evil to grow beyond our control . . . with
ten millions of blacks [both free and slave]."[24]

In spite of the need he saw for a nationally sponsored program to
deport blacks, Wilmot nevertheless subscribed, as did Agassiz and Van
Evrie, to the drainage theory of natural migration. Believing that white
laboring people were distinct from black laboring people, he hoped that
someday the "black population, as it shall increase and press upon the
country, can pass off and become mingled up with the mixed races of
Mexico and South America."[25] But more immediately, Wilmot wanted
such a population kept out of the Western territories.

Wilmot, in his attitude toward radical abolitionism, followed Drake,
Van Evrie and Clay. Discussing his feelings on the small number of
radicals who wanted slavery abolished immediately and without black
expatriation, Wilmot noted that "I stood up at home and battled time and
again against the abolitionists of the North. I have assailed them publicly."
Unlike these abolitionists, Wilmot claimed that he had "no squeamish
sensitiveness upon the subject of slavery, nor morbid sympathy for the
slave." Indeed, his only concern seemed to be for "Northern men, who
dared to vindicate the rights of free labor, to speak and vote in favor of the
white man and his children."[26] In the final analysis Wilmot believed his
views on race and the extension of slavery were identical to those of
Thomas Jefferson, the "great apostle of our [Free Soilers'] faith." Wilmot
averred that he "had followed in the footsteps of Jefferson," in "his efforts
. . . to circumscribe slavery within state limits," and thereby eventually
preserving for the Caucasian race the vast lands of the West.[27]

II

Many of the racial arguments of the intellectuals were first made popular at the national level by disgruntled Democratic and Whig politicians from the Northeast who, with David Wilmot, had strongly disagreed with the Polk administration over the slavery expansion issue. Although their numbers would eventually be eclipsed by Democratic defectors in the Mid-western states, these Easterners took the lead in forming the Free Democracy or Free Soil Party, which later dovetailed into the Republican Party. In New England the Free Democracy was represented by a number of national politicians, four of whom were Julius Rockwell, Chauncey F. Cleveland, Ephraim K. Smart and John M. Niles. All of these Congressmen expressed the racial sentiments made prevalent by the scientists and writers of their day. What is remarkable is the consistency, the constancy of these ideas. They seem to have been accepted by some politicians like the laws of thermodynamics were accepted by physicists.

Representative Rockwell of Massachusetts viewed blacks as both physically and mentally inferior to Caucasians. When debating an 1848 bill for organizing the territorial government of Oregon, Rockwell supported the exclusion of free blacks from the territory. "To suppose," Rockwell noted, "that the free Negroes would assist in peopling the Territory of Oregon, is to suppose that they are endued with the intelligence, enterprise and energy of the Anglo-Saxon race. The colored race will never be there in any great numbers, unless the institution of slavery carries them there." Believing that the westward extension of that institution would mean a growth in the size of the free black population, and being sympathetic to efforts to exclude the latter, he asked his fellow Congressmen: "What kind of a population is this, against which our new states are fencing themselves, and what kind of a population is it, which you are about to inflict upon the territories?" Being, like many whites exercised by the question of race, and apparently convinced that whites and blacks could not live together without warfare erupting, Rockwell also asked his audience: "Shall the two races unnecessarily be planted together, be compelled to remain together for all time, or the one to exterminate the other?"[28]

Some of these Free Democrats opted for the same solutions proposed by the intelligentsia. Representative Cleveland of Connecticut strongly backed both the containment and colonization of blacks. He did so because of the same fear that troubled Rockwell, i.e. of future black insurrection. In fact, when addressing the House, Cleveland predicted the " . . . ultimate extinction of the white race by the blacks," if slavery were allowed to expand and the black population grow.[29]

At least one dissatisfied Democrat from New England came out for containment and colonization for essentially selfish, economic reasons. During the debates over the admittance of New Mexico and California, Representative Smart of Maine told fellow Congressmen that keeping slavery out of the Western territories was tantamount to "providing free territory for . . . men of our own race." Regarding blacks, they should be colonized because they were a "troublesome population," which blocked European immigration. Smart conjectured that economically Missouri "would be the New York of the West" if it had entered the Union as a free state, a state free of black people.[30]

Another Free Democrat, Senator Niles of Connecticut, took an extreme position and argued against the admission of any of the Mexican Cession territories. Because of his overriding fear of miscegenation Niles opposed the acquisition of the Great Southwest, which acquisition would bring into the Union the "lesser" or mixed breeds of Mexico. He pointed to Dr. Johann "Tschudi, a distinguished German naturalist" and his book, "Travels in Peru," to prove that this population "possess[ed] the basest and most barbarous qualities." In short, mestizos stood as a prime example of the "evils of race." As further evidence of the presumed dangers of miscegenation to Caucasian America, Niles presented to fellow Senators Tschudi's chart naming the results of various crossings and concluded by asking the following respecting the Union: "What kind of blood will you infuse into it."[31]

Part of Niles' fear of miscegenation was connected to this belief in climatic determinism. The Connecticut Senator noted how the "temperate zones or cold climates are most conducive to energy of character, physical and moral." That being the premise, he naturally deduced that the Anglo-Saxon was the "superior race," while people of darker complexion, from warmer climes, were inferior beings.[32]

Another group of dissidents who, although perhaps more slowly than their Free Democratic counterparts, moved into the Free Soil and later Republican Parties, were the New England Conscience Whigs. Politicians and writers, such as Horace Mann, Richard Henry Dana Jr. and Daniel Webster, subscribed to the same racist imperatives that motivated many members of the intelligentsia and Free Democracy. Mann is just another example of an individual who, like Agassiz, Sturtevant, Fisher and so many others, wore two coats, i.e. intellectual and Free Soiler/ Republican. The pioneer educator from Massachusetts had been involved with Ralph Waldo Emerson and Theodore Parker in the development of New England transcendentalism and antislavery attitudes. At times he, also with them, expressed ideas inimical to black interests.

Mann, who served in both the Massachusetts and national legislatures, viewed blacks as mental and temperamental inferiors. When calling attention to how the white children of the South were educated, he declared that the "children of the South, more or less, and generally more, are tended and nurtured by slaves. Ignorance, superstition, vulgarity, passion and perhaps impurity, are the breasts at which they nurse." Blacks could not have been too passionate or vulgar, however, for on another occasion he described them as a "docile, peaceable people, not aggressive and predatory." Despite this obvious contradiction, Mann dwelt upon what seemed his favorite theme, black ignorance. In fact, he asserted, the blacks' "language proclaims their ignorance. If you have occasion to send them on an errand, they cannot read the direction of a note . . . . Their ideas are limited within the narrowest range." Doubtless influenced by the conclusions of scientists such as Samuel Morton, James Hunt and George Combe, Mann attributed part of this ignorance to the fact that blacks had a smaller brain, an "African brain," whereas white workers were of superior intelligence because they had a larger brain, an "'Anglo-Saxon brain.'" Obviously this assumed black ignorance adversely affected their ability to perform skilled labor. Mann amended to a speech he made before Congress a pamphlet, in which the Reverend Henry Ruffner of Virginia argued exactly that. Evidently attributing the absence of a shipbuilding industry in Virginia to the inability of black workers, Mann stated: "we do not blame our Southern people for abstaining from all employment of this kind. What could they do? Set their negroes to building ships?" In the same speech he referred to Negroes as "black work animals," and found that "one black drudge cannot support one white gentleman."[33]

Mann seemed to blame England for originally transporting black slaves to North America, and declared that "if their descendants had never been propagated here . . . their places would have been supplied by white laborers, by men of the Caucasian race, by freemen." And, even though the South "might not have had so gaudy and ostentatious a civilization as at present . . . it would have had one infinitely more pure and [economically] sound," consisting of at least "three million [more] white . . . citizens, adding to the real prosperity of the country."[34]

Like Wilmot, Mann appealed to the interests of "white labor." "Slavery," he maintained, "drives free laborers . . . out of the country, and fills their places with negroes." Nevertheless, in terms similar to Sturtevant's, Mann described blacks as a "doomed race," a "savage population," whom he did not wish to see "multiply." Like Wilmot again, Mann used symbolism, a metaphor based on color, in depicting blacks as something evil or bad; he referred to the "three millions of slaves, that now darken our Southern horizon." For Mann, however, this darkening process was more than just a figure of speech. He declared that slavery meant the "corruption of [white] blood," which corruption "does not stop with the first, nor with the second generation . . . but . . . goes on forever," even, he hinted, in the halls of Congress. He chided Southern representatives: "I have seen members of this House to whom I have been disposed to give a friendly caution to keep their 'free papers' about their persons, lest . . . they should be seized and sold for runaway slaves." Over and above the corruption of Caucasian blood, the rapid growth of the South's black population held a more ominous prospect for Mann. He also warned his colleagues of "poison . . . murder and conflagration," and of a particularly sensitive topic for white Americans-"black violation . . . of our daughters and our wives"-if the black population continued to grow.[35]

Fellow Massachusetts Conscience Whig, Richard Henry Dana Jr. could, like Mann, easily double as both intellectual and Free Soiler. Dana was a lawyer, famous writer and newspaper journalist, as well as an early follower of Henry Clay. He was also a member of the Saturday Club, or as it was dubbed, "Agassiz's Club," a weekly gathering of Cambridge, Massachusetts intellectuals, and a personal friend of Agassiz. As had other Free Soilers, Dana held a low opinion of black people. According to Dana, who in 1848 became involved in the Free Soil Party almost at its inception, blacks were both physically and mentally deficient. When describing two black abolitionists whom he had recently heard speak, he referred to their characteristic black "facial angle," and wrote that these "two conceited, shallow-pated Negro youths, named [Charles] Remond and [Frederick] Douglass, were among the chief speakers. They . . . evidently had but little strength of mind by nature." Black people, Dana believed, had been "marked for persecution, servitude and contempt for centuries. The judgment has reached beyond the color [of] the skin, and extended to the physical and intellectual function." Just as Marvin Wheat and Herman Burmeister had compared black people to animals, so did Dana. The life of one white man, he assured himself, was worth a "whole zoo" of lesser breeds. It followed naturally from his opinions that Dana would fear the results of miscegenation. He wrote in his journal that he had a nightmare, in which he attended a party given by the abolitionist, Wendell Phillips, "at which blacks and whites were mixed together . . . [and] that there was one fellow there who was disposed to make fun of the whole affair, and took up a saucer of black currant jelly and asked `whose ice cream is this?'" On another occasion Dana seemed to echo Wilmot. Indicating his concern over a possible black insurrection in the future, Dana stated that "when I consider what the white race is, and what the black race is and always had been, I confess that in case of a slave uprising, I . . . would go with my own race." Indeed, at times his only interest seemed to be for his own race. Consequently he acquiesced in the discriminatory legislation which segregated black people in the public places of Massachusetts. And, although Dana had been a counselor for the defense in a number of fugitive slave cases in the early 1850's, he had a particular dislike for the radical objectives of abolitionists such as Wendell Phillips and William Lloyd Garrison.[36]

Two other Massachusetts anti-extension Whigs who served in Congress, Senator Daniel Webster and Representative Orin Fowler, worried over the South's increasing black population. Although Webster was at first reluctant to follow the Conscience Whigs, he endorsed the Wilmot Proviso and spoke out in the Senate against slavery moving west. Using the same symbolism as Mann, the famous attorney referred to the "darkening cloud" overspreading the West and demanded that Congress pass legislation to halt the westward expansion of slavery.[37] Fowler was confident that the movement of black slaves into the West would be contained "by the clear-headed, strong-hand, [and] lion-hearted power of the American Anglo-Saxon people."[38] A third Conscience Whig and later Free Soiler and Republican, Representative Jacob Collamer of Vermont, expressed the same anxiety over the acquisition of the Mexican Cession territories as had John Niles. Collamer despised the mestizo population of the Southwest because it was "in no way homogeneous" with the "Saxon race."[39]

Another New England writer, journalist, and Free Soiler, James Shepherd Pike of Maine, was opposed on racist grounds to increasing the black population of the United States, whether by annexing new lands already inhabited by them, or by allowing slavery to spread into the Western territories. Therefore, he stood against the annexation of Cuba when, as a correspondent for Horace Greeley's *New York Tribune*, he protested in 1852, that "if we take Cuba . . . we must take . . . half a million of very black and very ignorant persons, who would by the process [of annexation] become our fellow citizens." They would, he warned, "choose a black governor, black judges, black representatives to Congress, black everything. Now our impression is very decided that a large majority of the [white] people in this country consider that a great avalanche of black voters upon us is not a thing to be coveted." Pike held that the "predominate black population" in the Caribbean Islands, "constitutes an insuperable bar to their incorporation into our system." In apparent agreement with Louis Klipstein, he added that additional "populous territory filled with black, mixed, degraded and ignorant or inferior races [was something] we do not want," because "blacks and mulattoes and quadroons and mestizos we have enough of, and more than enough."[40]

Pike was equally opposed to admitting such people to the free Western territories. It would, he said, be tantamount to admitting a "leprous intruder." In early 1854, when the Kansas and Nebraska bill was being debated, Pike saw the measure as a "comprehensive plan of Africanizing the whole of the American hemisphere." With other Free Soilers, he viewed the battle over slavery in the territories as a racial conflict between the South, representing the black race, and the North, representing the Caucasian race.[41]

Even liberal Free Soilers from New England, such as Representative John Palfrey of Massachusetts, who sometimes advocated political rights for black Americans, at other times expressed views which were inimical to black interests. For example, in 1848, Palfrey refused in Congress to "discuss the question whether the negro inferiority is to be traced to a congenital incapacity, or to the . . . low culture of many generations."[42] In either case, of course, blacks were assumed to be inferior.

While Wilmot, Rockwell, Mann and others were battling in Congress and Dana and Pike in the press against the extension of slavery, a powerful Free Soil following from New York state was, for a time, lending its support to their efforts. Historian William O. Lynch emphasizes the importance of these dissident New York Democrats to the organization and growth of conservative political antislavery thought. Lynch believes, in point of fact, that New York can be considered the center for the creation of early free soilism.[43] Between 1846 and 1848 the Free Democracy or 'Barnburners' of that state, under the leadership of Martin Van Buren and his son, John, took up the task of forming an antislavery political party. The first national Free Soil Party presidential convention was held in Buffalo in 1848. It chose ex-president of the United States, ex-administration Democratic leader of the state, Martin Van Buren, as the party's presidential candidate.

Some of the platform resolutions passed at this Buffalo convention were indicative of the conservative bent of the new party; these Free Soilers were mainly dedicated to securing rights for white men, not blacks. For instance, resolution two recognized the inviolability of slavery in the South, by stating that "slavery in the several states . . . depends upon the state laws alone, which can not be repealed or modified by the Federal government." The Free Soil Party, resolution two continued, "propose[s] no interference by Congress with slavery within the limits of any state." However, in its next resolution, the Party came to its raison d'etre and, invoking the name of Thomas Jefferson and the Ordinance of 1787, promised its followers "to limit, localize and discourage slavery . . . in all the territories of the United States." While black people were to remain in the South as slaves, at least in the foreseeable future, the free territories of the West, according to resolution eight, should be occupied by white settlers, both native and European born. "Let the soil of our extensive domain be kept free for the hardy pioneers of our own land, and the oppressed and banished of other lands, seeking homes of comfort and fields of enterprise in the new world." And, while it is true that most of the platform resolutions dealt with some aspect of the slavery question, Free Soilers did not eschew a pragmatic appeal, and included several resolutions dealing with internal improvements, tariffs, and homestead legislation. Hardly the work of one-idea abolitionists, the 1848 Free Soil platform was rather that of practical politicians. Far from wishing to dissolve the Union over the issue of the continuance of slavery, as some radical abolitionists had proposed, Free Soilers at the Buffalo convention seemed willing to let the peculiar institution be, as long as it remained in the South. In fact, one delegate from New York gave some advice to any Southerners, who might want to break away from the Union because they felt the federal government was not doing enough to protect their slave interests: remain in the Union, he said, because you need the North to help prevent black insurrections.[44]

The New York Free Soil Party represented a conglomerate of diverse groups-Conscience Whigs, ex-Liberty Party men, but mainly Free Democrats. However, because it was partially based on disaffection within regular Democratic Party ranks, the Free Soil movement was relatively short-lived in New York. There it never gained the prominence and cohesiveness that it later would in the territories and states of the Northwest. Nevertheless a number of leading Free Democrats from New York, including John Van Buren, John A. Dix and Preston King, gained national attention. They openly set forth racial views similar to those expressed by Henry Clay, David Wilmot, and the ethnological and scientific community. Historian John Mayfield argues that the New York Free Soilers, "like most northerners . . . shared an indifference bordering on contempt for black rights that proceeded from a deeply ingrained racism." As proof of this he writes that "they hesitated to endorse political equality for black New Yorkers."[45]

In an address delivered to the 1847 Democratic Free Soil Convention at Herkimer, New York, John Van Buren linked Free Soil opposition to slavery expansion to racial factors. Van Buren had blamed slavery for the continued presence of blacks in the United States. He charged that the "doctrine of Jefferson . . . that slavery is a great social evil, which should be gradually but certainly eradicated . . . has been discarded by a school of modern politicians of the South." He expressed concern over social contact between the races, within a slave society, and hinted that this contact could lead to miscegenation. Slavery, Van Buren noted with dismay, was the "sole means for the continued associated existence of the black and white race[s]." Referring to miscegenation directly, he declared that "this ominous and repugnant theory is now sought [by Southern politicians] to be carried out in practice by the conquests of free territory and the establishment of slavery therein." Van Buren ended his plea by playing on white racial fears: "In behalf of the free white laborers of the North and South, in behalf of the emigrant from abroad . . . we protest against the extension . . . of an institution, whose inevitable concomitant is the social and political degradation of the white laborer." He said nothing about slavery's degrading effects upon black people, nor did he evince any concern about the future of free black laborers. Instead, Van Buren acted to divide working people by putting forward a resolution to preserve the free territories for the future welfare of the white working classes.[46]

Although in language less racially provocative, John Van Buren's father, Martin, also spoke against the admittance of black people into the free territories of the West. After winning the 1848 Free Soil presidential nomination, he stated in his acceptance speech that "if a slaveholder desires to remove there [to the Western territories], he must dispose of his slaves, and employ free labor, as his countrymen and neighbors did."[47]

United States Senator Dix was another politician who expressed the wish to keep black people out of the territories. He apparently based much of his opposition to the expansion of slavery on racial factors. Similar to Wilmot, Dix, in a speech to the Senate, insisted that "an enlargement of the surface over which slavery is spread, carries with it by force of invincible laws, a multiplication of the race held in bondage; in other words a substantial increase of the number of slaves." Dix expressed alarm over this probable increase, especially if slavery were allowed to move into the free West. If "extension in respect to surface is multiplication in point of number . . . [then] one of the most interesting and important problems, both for the American statesman and philosopher, is to determine of what race or races this vast population shall consist."[48]

John Dix, of course, knew precisely of what race he wanted this population to consist. Believing that black people were much inferior to Caucasians, he warned that their "additions to our numbers are in the highest degree undesirable;" because "they add nothing to our strength, moral or physical." Rather, he said, recalling Arthur DeGobineau and other nineteenth century scientists, it was most important that the United States "be peopled by the same race which had overspread Europe, and made it what it is in science, in art, in civilization and in morals," spheres of accomplishment in which Dix obviously found black people wanting. He thought the number of European immigrants coming into the country should be increased, because only they "constitute an element of no inconsiderable force in the ratio of our progression," representing as they did, the "highest race in the order of intellectual and physical endowment." The "nearer the great body of our people, those especially who till the earth, approach the same standard in intelligence and political importance, the more likely we shall . . . maintain internal tranquility." In keeping with this objective, Dix called for an homogeneous white population to fill the Western territories. The latter, he insisted, by right belonged "to our own descendants, as well as the oppressed and needy Caucasian multitudes of the world . . . . I hold it to be our sacred duty to consecrate these spaces to the multiplication of the white race."[49]

One thing, however, could stand in the way of the occupation of the American West by the free race of superior whites and that, according to Dix, was the enslaved race of inferior blacks. To him the key to this threat to white hegemony lay in the word 'enslaved.' If both the white and black races could enter the territories as free peoples, Dix would have been confident of the ultimate outcome. He, with Sturtevant and Parker, was convinced that freedom for the black man would eventuate in his extinction; being inferior to the white man the black, as a free laborer, would simply not be able to compete on equal terms with the superior European laborer. The proof, Dix declared, was found in the Northern states: There, "it may be satisfactorily shown that the free black population . . . does not increase by its own inherent force," and that "it will not be reproduced and in a few generations the process of extinction is performed." The problem, as Dix saw it, was that most blacks in the United States were slaves, a huge capital investment for slaveholders, not free people, and it was as slaves/chattel that Southerners wanted to take them into the Western territories. Only under slavery, Dix was convinced, could these people thrive and multiply and impede European immigration by reducing the demand for white laborers. Therefore blacks, as slaves, were undesirable in the West, because "their tendency is to exclude whites to the extent that they contribute to supply the demand for labor."[50]

New York Free Democrat, Representative Henry C. Murphy, wanted to not only contain black people in, for the most part their native South, but eventually hoped to colonize them out of the country. He told the House that the people of the free states did not want a black population among them, because "we were taught by our mothers to avoid all communication with them," especially sexual liaisons. Despite what Murphy called the "natural" antipathy of race, he felt constrained to warn his congressional colleagues of the "commingling of the blood of the races." Like Dix, he believed that white labor competition would keep blacks out of the free states, where "they are driven from the employment of the whites" and "not allowed to associate with the whites." However, if neither the fear of miscegenation on the part of Caucasians nor the fear of unemployment on the part of Negroes failed to keep the latter out of the North then, in obvious reference to the Northern black laws, he "would go for enacting laws of a most penal character" to keep them out.[51]

Another member of the New York Free Democracy, United States Representative Preston King, held views similar to those of Dix and Murphy. During the Mexican War King asked Congress whether the "territory now free, which shall come to our jurisdiction, be free territory, open to settlement by the laboring man of the free states, or shall it be slave territory, given up to slave labor?" The Wilmot Proviso, King argued, in answer to his own question, should be adopted by Congress because it was "just to the white men who fight our battles and who constitute the strength of the country in peace or war." King castigated those representatives in Congress who supported the extension of slavery, and tied his opposition to such extension to racial considerations.[52]

Van Evrie and Agassiz had preached that the white and black races were totally distinct, and therefore could not live and work together under the same government. King agreed. He insisted that the "labor of the free white men and women, and of their children, cannot and will not eat and drink, lie down and rise up, with the black . . . . " "Free white labor," he said, "will not be degraded by such association." "False and recreant to his race and to his constituency," King charged, "would be any representative of free white men and women, who should, by his vote, place free white labor upon a condition of social equality with the . . . black." Like many other Free Soilers, King equated the Northwest Ordinance of 1787 with the Free Soil philosophy of the non-extension of slavery. Nowhere did King express any concern over the fate of the laboring black man. In fact, he referred to those radical abolitionists who did, as a "small squad of ignorant fanatics."[53]

When New York Free Democrats, such as Representative William Collins did address the issue of the laboring black man, they usually did so in a pejorative sense. Collins who, like practically all of these defectors would soon join in creating the Republican Party, asked the House to help restrain black labor in the South, because he believed it "negligent," and as such it "exhausted" the soil where employed. By definition, the same concerns motivated Collins as motivated other Free Democrats, i.e. the increasing black population and the fate of white labor in the Western territories. His speech, like that of many Eastern Free Soilers, was riddled with the adjective "white."[54] Once again skin color overrode class interests.

Martin Grover, a member of the Free Soil Party from Alleghany, New York, was also more concerned about white rights, than black rights. He, along with New York Free Democrat, Representative Timothy Jenkins, regarded the issue of slavery expansion "as a question not [of] whether blacks or slaves are to be free, but [of] whether we whites are to be free ourselves," free of the contagion of black people. Speaking frankly, Jenkins asked Congress the same question: "What is its effect upon the white race?"[55]

It was this anxiety over blacks, slavery and their impact on the welfare of the white race that was slowly tearing apart the Democratic Party.

George O. Rathbun of Auburn, New York, was another dissident who broke with administration Democrats because of their opposition to the Wilmot Proviso. Serving in the United States House of Representatives between 1843 and 1847, he agreed with Wilmot that Jefferson was the original architect of the policy of the non-extension of slavery into the territories, and that Wilmot had merely resurrected that policy. "This Wilmot Proviso," declared Rathbun, " . . . was a proviso drawn by Thomas Jefferson himself and was one of the provisions of the Ordinance of 1787, for the regulation of the Northwest territory." Rathbun was ready to castigate especially those Northerners who stood in the way of the passage of the Proviso. Senator Lewis Cass of Michigan, he charged, "was preparing to desert, to turn traitor to the North . . . and to become a soldier under the black banner of aggressive slavery." Rathbun made it plain that his major interest in backing the Proviso was racial, not humanitarian. "I speak not of the condition of the slave," he wrote, "whether the effect of slavery is beneficial or injurious to him. I am looking to its effects upon the white man."[56]

Rathbun's reference to the "black banner" was also an indication of the prominence he gave to race in his support of the Proviso. This New Yorker, like Wilmot and Pike, viewed the black man and the South as symbols of evil and as dangerous to the Caucasian race. Regular Northern Democrats, such as Cass, were simply "tools in the hands of Southern men, to aid in extending this curse of the white man [black slavery] to territory now free." The expansion of slavery into the territories would not merely cover these areas with black slaves, it would, Rathbun seemed convinced, result in a general influx of free blacks into both the territories and the Northern states. To forestall such an eventuality, Rathbun backed Northern efforts to exclude free blacks. In 1847, while addressing Congress in support of the Wilmot Proviso, he attacked the Governor of Virginia who, he charged, had "set forth with great care and no small ability, a plain, simple proposition to drive out the forty-nine thousand free blacks in that state, into the territory of the free states." Rathbun went on to note that "as far as New York is concerned, should the refuse part of the population of Virginia reach our territory, we will carry them back to Virginia."[57]

As noted, not all of those who sympathized with the early New York Free Soilers, belonged to the Democratic Party. Conscience Whigs, along with ex-Liberty Party men, also played a role. Four such Whigs from New York were Washington Hunt, Lewis Henry Morgan, William Henry Seward and Charles E. Clarke. Representative Hunt of Lockport, New York, feared that the acquisition of the Great Southwest would bring into the Union an "incongruous mass of Spaniards, Indians and mongrel Mexicans," people of mixed blood who were dangerous not only to the gene pool of white Americans, but to the safety and internal security of the United States.[58]

Morgan, a founder of the American School of Anthropology, also considered himself an antislavery or Conscience Whig who, following Henry Clay, opposed the expansion of slavery for racial reasons. He wished to preserve the purity of white America because he believed, with DeGobineau, that the "Aryan race . . . represents the central stream of human progress, because it produced the highest type of mankind, and because it has proved its intrinsic superiority, by gradually assuming the control of the earth." When writing to Senator John C. Calhoun of South Carolina on the question of slavery expansion into the territories, Morgan therefore, insisted that "we [Northerners] are afraid of the indefinite propagation of the colored race, upon which the South [by extending slavery] seems determined." Morgan found that the "feeling towards that race in the North, is decidedly that of hostility. There is no respect for them; no wish for their elevation, but on the contrary a strong desire to prevent the multiplication of the [black] race so far as it is possible to do so."[59]

New York Representatives, Seward and Clarke, told the House that they too were worried over the "multiplication" of the Negro population. When debating the Compromise of 1850 Seward, who was soon to be a powerful figure in the new Republican Party, pronounced the "African race . . . distinct" from the Caucasian. To this New Yorker black people represented "inferior masses," and as such a "disturbing" political element within the Union. Similar to Collins, Seward declared that blacks did not fit into the American political equation because they were "docile," hence they were "less productive than free white labor," which he defined even further as "this vigorous Saxon race of ours."[60] During the same debates Clarke indicated his very low opinion of black people. He echoed the views of numerous ethnologists, claiming that the black man was "dull . . . he adds nothing to our stock of knowledge . . . he makes no inventions," and it was because of this professed mental lethargy that he was enslaved. Clarke contrasted his picture of a backward black race to that of the "superiority of the American Anglo-Saxon race," superior, he declared, because of its "useful inventions . . . [and] labor saving machines." Moreover he, as had a number of the intelligentsia, claimed that the black man was a coward, because "he is not useful either in offensive or defensive war." Despite this supposed cowardice, however, Clarke feared that blacks could revolt at any moment and that therefore Caucasians were "sleeping in a [powder] magazine, on the crater of a volcano."[61]

In neighboring New Jersey, United States Senator William L. Dayton, also a Conscience Whig who later helped found the Republican Party and in fact ran as its first Vice Presidential candidate, expressed dismay over the rapidly growing mulatto population in the South. In doing so he was voicing the same concerns as any number of the intelligentsia, including Drake and Agassiz. Dayton asked the Senate to provide a detailed description of the various shades of population when taking the 1850 federal census. With this information Dayton assumed that "important physiological facts" on the health, longevity and fertility of mulattoes could be established. Worried over the dangers of miscegenation and wishing to test the theory of a separate creationism, he pointed to "Professor Agassiz . . . and others," who held blacks to be of "an originally different race." Agassiz's name and works were well-known in Congress.[62]

Dayton's fellow Senator and Conscience Whig, Jacob W. Miller, also suggested that black people were members of a distinct creation, or as he put it, a people among the "lowest grades of humanity." To Miller the black man did not belong in the United States, because the "negro is a timid creature . . . an inferior being," when juxtaposed to the allegedly superior Caucasian. However, this New Jersey Senator declared that in spite of this inferiority, and apparently contrary to his own argument, the black race was capable of improvement and had, in fact, demonstrated such improvement under American slavery.[63]

It has been seen, then, that important Eastern politicians factored the spectre of race into their reasons for opposing the extension of slavery onto the public lands of the West. So, too, did certain newspaper editors and contemporary writers.

III

The fight against the extension of slavery enjoyed the early support of a number of leading journalists and pamphleteers in New York state. Since the written word was the most important means of mass communication at this time, these writers were bound to exert a tremendous influence on the reading public. One such was Oliver C. Gardiner of New York city who, in 1848, edited and published one of the first major Free Soil Party pamphlets. Gardiner, a Free Democrat, attacked Lewis Cass of Michigan and the regular Democratic Party on the issue of slavery expansion which, according to the pamphlet's title, was *The Great Issue* in that year's presidential election. Gardiner charged that Cass and a number of regular Democrats believed that if, instead of being concentrated in the South, slavery were spread over a greater geographical area, i.e. if slaves were dispersed, the institution would eventually disappear.[64] In criticizing Cass' nomination for the presidency by the Democratic Party, and when speaking directly of Northern white laborers, Gardiner asked: "are they so blind as not to see that if slavery were planted on the shores of the Pacific, it would rapidly extend by importation and speculation, in spite of all laws to the contrary?" When Gardiner used the word slavery, he also meant black people. He inquired if these same laboring whites "overlook what he [Cass] conceals, that by diffusion, the ratio of increase [of black people] would be trebled . . . . " With this increase and diffusion of slavery, Gardiner proclaimed, would "be found that most abhorrent of all forms of increase by the mixture of the races." Gardiner's pamphlet asked the white workers of the North if they could vote for a presidential candidate who supported amalgamation of the races through the expansion of Southern slavery.[65]

Another Free Soil pamphleteer from New York state, Russell Jarvis, also desired to keep the Caucasian race "pure," especially the Anglo-Saxon portion of that race. Jarvis, as did many Free Soilers, wallowed in ethnocentrism by promulgating the idea of "Anglo-Saxon superiority," which assumed superiority could only be maintained if the Anglo-Saxon refrained from sexual unions with blacks and what he called the lesser breeds. Reminiscent of Klipstein and Bushnell, he claimed that "according to natural laws . . . the Anglo-American race, stronger in mind and body than the feeble Indian or the degenerate Spanish Creole, will finally overrun, overpower . . . and extirpate the Mexican, even without force." Darker skinned people were simply no match for the superior Anglo-Saxons who, according to Jarvis, were destined to rule the whole of the North American continent from East to West.[66]

David Dudley Field, a well-known constitutional lawyer and writer from New York city, also subscribed to the notion of Anglo-Saxon supremacy. Field belonged to the Barnburner faction of the Democratic Party, and introduced the "cornerstone resolution" at the state Democratic Party Convention at Syracuse, in 1847. This resolution, which was adopted by the convention and was simply the Wilmot Proviso in another guise, declared against the extension of slavery into the free Western territories. However, like Free Soilers in general, Field was, at least for the time being, willing to let slavery live in the South. At the same convention, therefore, he supported another resolution which declared that radical abolitionists, or those who wanted the immediate emancipation of the black man without restrictions, were "dangerous people." In 1848, when addressing a meeting of the New York Free Democracy, Field noted that the "true Democracy [was] careful for the rights of all, esteeming slavery a local institution, [to] which the federal arm does not extend." But, he continued, "where there is freedom now slavery shall not intrude." He prophesied that "our vast Pacific domain shall be consecrated to free labor." The Western territories "shall not be covered with Negro cabins . . . but shall smile with villages raised by free [white] immigrants from our own and other lands." He seemed concerned over "whether the dignity of free and honest labor shall be maintained or cast down by a degrading companionship with [black] servitude."[67]   .

Two of the most significant and best known newspaper editors in New York city, one a Democrat, William Cullen Bryant, and one a Whig, Horace Greeley, gave their early support to the cause of free soilism.

Bryant, the editor of the *New York Evening Post* and a personal acquaintance of Louis Agassiz, was particularly incensed at the regular Democrats because of what he perceived to be their roles in the controversies over the Mexican War and the extension of slavery. And, if his editorial statements are indicative, his opposition to their objectives was strongly influenced by his racial attitudes.

In his columns Bryant joined the members of the learned community, such as Cartwright, Klipstein and Parker, in emphasizing the important part blood played in determining the qualities of the various races. As a strong proponent of the manifest destiny of the superior white race in North America, he opposed any policy that threatened to compromise the purity of the Anglo-Saxon blood line. Consequently he worried that war with Mexico would lead not simply to Americans annexing the lightly settled Mexican territories of the Southwest, but that the United States might seek to incorporate the state of Mexico itself, with its "bastard civilization" of people of mixed blood. "The infusion of European blood," which, he implied, was inferior because it was only Spanish, and "that, too, infused in a highly illegitimate way," had not been sufficient to improve the "character of the Mexican people. They do not possess the elements of an independent national existence" as did people possessed of Anglo-Saxon blood. Mexicans, Bryant concluded, were still nothing more than "aboriginal Indians," fated to "share the destiny of their race," and Caucasians should avoid association with them.[68]

If Bryant was troubled that an infusion of Mexican blood might compromise the superior qualities of the Caucasian race in North America, he seemed even more distraught about the effects of an infusion of black blood. Again agreeing with the scientists of his time, he warned his readers that the black man was mentally and morally inferior to the white. He was, Bryant declared, known for "his ignorance and his improvidence." Describing an incident in which a slave named Toby had delivered a speech, Bryant, following DeGobineau and Burmeister, pointed to the so-called "imitative instinct" peculiar to black people. During a visit to the Barnwell District of South Carolina, he noted that the "blacks of this region are a cheerful, careless, dirty race, not hard worked and in many respects indulgently treated." He believed that it was the determination of the black slave, "to lead as easy a life as he can." On another occasion Bryant seemed to imply that a comparison could be made between the black man and the monkey. After observing a group of black slaves at work, he noted that they began to sing the "monkey-song, probably of African origin, in which the principal singer personated a monkey, with all sorts of odd gesticulations."[69]

Given his predilections, it is not surprising that when the issue of the annexation of Texas came before Congress in 1844, Bryant, a firm believer in manifest destiny for the white man, seemed concerned lest the expansion of slavery would lead to an inundation of the Western territories by black men. To Bryant blacks not only posed a threat to Caucasian blood lines, but also to the economic well-being of white laborers. After Texas was annexed, he wrote that "we gave up the whole of it to slavery . . . from every part of which the free laborer is shut out . . . by gangs of black workmen."[70]

Bryant's belief in free soilism rested, he said, on the welfare of "the [white] laborer . . . who on coming from over-peopled Europe, may transport himself thither [West] and procure a thrifty and happy home." If the black man was taken to the free territories, on the other hand, "his touch pollutes the soil, and it is no longer a fit place for the [white] laborer." Therefore, the possibility of black workers competing with white laborers in the territories must be assiduously avoided. Bryant, much as Hinton Rowan Helper later on, purported to sympathize also with the white working men of the South. He declared that their "interest . . . is of course, against the extension of slavery, an institution" that "not only competes with their labor, but degrades it." "At any time in the South," he told his subscribers, "you see white mechanics forced to work side by side with slave mechanics," and what was even worse, "sometimes under the control of a Negro 'boss.'" Whatever the real feeling of the "poor [Southern] white working men," Bryant was convinced that "in the estimation of the slave owners," racial "mixture and authority of this sort are good enough," for lower class whites. By contrast, Bryant claimed, Northern white laborers would never stand for such a system, where they were placed in close association and contact, and sometimes under the direct supervision of blacks.[71]

Bryant also appealed to race to gain political backing for the candidates he favored. In 1848, while campaigning for Martin Van Buren and the Free Democracy, he ran the following advertisement in the *Evening Post*: "Free Soil, Free Labor, Free Men, Forever . . . the soil for the white man and not for the Negro . . . this is a movement [free soilism] to exclude a gentleman of the South with his Negroes from these territories, and to admit the Irish, Scotch, Germans and Dutch . . . . Who shall have it [the West], white men or slaves?" The titles which Bryant used for his editorials, when discussing the issue of the expansion of slavery, are again suggestive of his racial views. Under one such title, "What shall be done for the White Man?" he continued to equate the word slave with black man, thereby ignoring the interests of the growing free black population. He wrote that the "question involved in the restriction of slavery in the new territories, is . . . not one which particularly concerns the slave, but one which concerns the white man." Indeed Bryant, like Wilmot and other Free Soilers, showed little or no compassion for the black man, whether free or slave. He left no doubt in his readers' minds that the question of slavery expansion was very much a question of skin color as well as labor philosophy.[72]

As a result of his beliefs, Bryant was anxious to disassociate free soilism from radical abolitionism. He declared that "there are some who call this doctrine [free soilism] abolitionism, but they call it by a false name." Bryant defined free soilism as "simply a claim in favor of the rights of the white man."[73] Bryant and any number of radical abolitionists could probably have agreed that free soilism and abolitionism were quite distinct.

Horace Greeley, the prominent Whig editor of the *New York Tribune* and longtime backer of Henry Clay, viewed the issue of slavery in the territories much as his Democratic counterpart, Bryant. Although, as will be noted below, his expressed opinions on racial matters were not always consistent, Greeley seemed at times also to endorse the hostile racialism exhibited by the scientific and learned community. He ran lengthy articles, in serial form, under titles such as "Interesting Scientific Intelligence," in which he presented the latest findings of well-known ethnologists. One of these articles reprinted an essay by Dr. Samuel Morton of Philadelphia who, according to Greeley, was "perhaps the most skillful and learned craniologist of the present day." Greeley concluded from Morton's essay, that "among the facts elicited by this investigation are . . . [that] the Teutonic or German race, embracing as it does the Anglo-Saxons, Anglo-Americans [and] Anglo-Irish, etc., possess the largest brain of any other [sic] people." Black people, however, were near the bottom of the list in brain size. If Morton's measurements were correct, then, given the current phrenological doctrine, that the larger the brain the greater the intelligence, it followed that black people were less intelligent than whites. Moreover, Greeley had great personal respect for Louis Agassiz and published all his lectures on modern zoology in the *Tribune*, and even issued a separate edition of such because of popular demand. In fine, under Greeley the *Tribune* frequently acted as a conduit for popularizing the racial theories of the scientific community and, enjoying the largest circulation of any newspaper of that era, it was no wonder why these theories gained credence.[74]

Greeley himself at times seemed to have had no qualms in stating that the black race suffered from "natural disabilities" and "intellectual deficiencies" and hence was an "inferior race." On these occasions, sounding very much like Burmeister and James Hunt, Greeley depicted blacks as sambos, as "ignorant, indolent, and devoid of history," a people whose only aspirations in life were the "easy filling of their stomachs and the stylish covering of their bodies." At the same time blacks were also members of that "race, which is content with cast-off clothes and cold vituals, so that they come easy and require no forecast." The *Tribune*'s editor further described blacks as a race that "too generally love idleness and low sensual gratifications." Greeley strongly implied that the black man was so weak, that one reason he remained in slavery was his own lack of energy and will power. In 1850, while describing the United States, Greeley stated that "here is a black race of three to four millions, living among a [free] white race of some twenty million . . . . The former are all the descendants of slaves, and a good part of them are still slaves." In short, blacks were inherently members of "the servile race." So much was this so, that Greeley sometimes expressed dismay that if these slaves were freed immediately, "many . . . would be personally the worse for their freedom, being enabled thereby to indulge those pro-pensities for idleness, dissipation and vice," which he associated with their race.[75]

When Greeley wrote about the Caucasian, and in particular what he and others mistakenly called the "Anglo-Saxon race," however, he was, like Parker and Emerson, inevitably full of praise. In a public address Greeley described the laboring people of New York city, who were overwhelmingly white, as a separate race. This "laboring race" was none other than the "Anglo-Saxon race, [which] produces . . . a most intense impression upon the world of business and of politics." While blacks were ignorant, indolent and immoral, Anglo-Saxons were creative, diligent and prosperous, altogether "remarkably energetic, intelligent and progressive; full of daring and adventure."[76] Accordingly, laborers were not only divided along racial lines, but ethnic ones as well.

Given his often expressed low opinion of black people, Greeley evinced misgivings over the increase in their numbers in the United States. Blaming the slave states for this increase, and utilizing the symbolism and metaphor of color made popular by other Free Soilers, he referred to the South as the "black power," because it was the "Negro-growing and negro dealing interest."[77]

As had numerous Free Soilers, Greeley too insisted that he based his political opposition to slavery expansion on the ideas of Thomas Jefferson and the Northwest Ordinance. In doing so he also, albeit obliquely, raised the issue of miscegenation. When describing a hypothetical situation in which a Southern planter and his slaves had just arrived in the new territories, Greeley conjectured that "by and by the planter undertakes to sell one of his help, which may be his own child and may not."[78]

Congruent with Bryant, Greeley was worried that if slavery were allowed to expand into the free territories, blacks would provide labor competition for whites. Indeed Greeley believed that white laborers generally would avoid the Western territories altogether, if black people were working there as slaves. He felt that "slave labor always did and always must degrade and discourage free labor, where the two are brought fairly in contact." He asked his readers, "why is it that a giant stream of foreign immigrants sets so steadily toward the free states and territories of the Northwest?" Greeley, anxious that the West be preserved for white

European immigrants, answered his own question: recent immigrants avoided the South because of the presence of black slaves. Soon after the Wilmot Proviso was brought before Congress in 1846, Greeley became one of its most enthusiastic backers. For Greeley, as for other Eastern Free Soilers, the Wilmot Proviso was the "White Man's Resolution," and conversely he referred to the whole question of slavery expansion as the "Negro question."[79]

Since to Greeley's way of thinking opposition to slavery expansion was a matter of protecting white rights, he often appeared unconcerned about the welfare of the slaves and on occasion seemed ready to support the institution of Southern slavery where it already existed. For example, even though he objected to the stringent provisions of the Fugitive Slave Law of 1850, Greeley evinced no moral scruples about citizens of the free states turning over fugitive slaves from the South to the proper federal authorities. Here Greeley's anxiety for the preservation of the federal Union was an important influence. He noted that "in a special case and for a special end, we have agreed to recognize the master's dominion over his slave, and to that extent we must respect our engagement, or repudiate the Union altogether." He reasoned that "if a human being, found in one of the free states, is duly found to have been by law a slave in one of the slave states, and to have escaped thence without his master's permission, then he must be delivered up whenever the master shall in due form claim and identify him." It is hard to conceive of a fugitive's stopping first to ask his master's permission to escape. Logic aside, however, Greeley did not seem particularly concerned about the overall moral implications of returning a fellow human being to slavery. His main worry, Clay Whig that he was, centered on whether the proper legal formalities were being observed.[80]

Greeley manifested much the same attitude when he discussed the black codes of the Southern states. Since the black codes of the Northern states were very similar, both in purpose and form, to those of the Southern states, and since Greeley at times was apparently critical of those of the Northern states, it is difficult to understand how he could defend what he himself once referred to as the "barbarous laws of the Southern states in reference to free Negroes . . . . " Yet he allowed that they "may be justified by the plea of necessity." The black laws may have been inhuman, but because they were deemed necessary by the South, they should remain on the statute books lest the South take exception and dissolve the Union. Also, when the Free Soil Party platform of 1855 excluded a call for citizenship for free blacks, Greeley refused to complain, but, was satisfied, as long as slavery was interdicted in the free territories. When comparing Greeley's attitudes on slaveholding in the South, or the fugitive slave law, or the black codes, to those of a radical abolitionist, Greeley's antislavery posture appears to be that of a political pragmatist, rather than of a moralist.[81]

Similar to Bryant, Greeley disliked radical abolitionists and, at times, stigmatized them as "men of one idea," who did more harm than good to the Free Soil cause. On one occasion, when defending Henry Clay from abolitionist attacks, he declared that "we cannot assent to the assumption that every slaveholder is necessarily hostile to the [economic] interests of Northern free labor. How can we, knowing, as we do, Henry Clay?" Greeley refused to rule out voting for a candidate, "simply because he is a slaveholder." In fact, the editor of the *Tribune* never tired in his support of Henry Clay. Greeley stated that "for our part, we would gladly avoid intestine convulsions and the danger of disunion, by committing the whole subject of slavery extension unreservedly into the hands of . . . Mr. Clay." Probably with that in mind Greeley, after some initial doubts, defended the Compromise of 1850 as a great victory for Northern white laborers and antislavery interests. As for the interests of black men Greeley, in an article entitled "The Blacks and the Tribune," noted that "we profess no peculiar friendship for them." Greeley readily admitted that "we have known very little of them personally" yet, he insisted, "so far as we have any partialities, they are of course against the African blood and hue."[82]

Though the *New York Tribune* and the *New York Evening Post* were the two most influential journals in the cause of free soilism in the Northeast, other prominent Eastern newspapers were important to the cause. One was the *National Era*, edited by Gamaliel Bailey and published in Washington, D.C. As did Bryant, Greeley and other Free Soil writers and politicians, Bailey pronounced blacks physically and mentally inferior to whites. Blacks, said Bailey, were people who had an "animal constitution." And, while he described the "American people (whites we mean)", as "generally enlightened," black people were "incapable of equality in civil and social relations," because of their "natural [mental] incapacity," their lack of "native energy and tact." Therefore, as did most ethnologists, Bailey concluded that black people were generally "indolent, unenterprising, thriftless, [and] improvident." Apparently disturbed by the numerous blacks living around Washington, D.C., Bailey asserted that "not being very enterprising, they naturally linger on the borders of the states they have left." These blacks were simply sambos, because they were marked by "passive submission to contumely and wrong."[83]

On the other hand when Bailey examined the Caucasian, and especially the Anglo-Saxon, he, in keeping with Greeley and most other white commentators, was full of adulation. He "wish[ed] that the colored people had more of that spirit of enterprise which animates the Anglo-Saxon race, making it the great . . . civilizer of the world." It was this superior Anglo-Saxon, Bailey noted paternalistically, which the indolent black man should model himself after, if he ever hoped "to command a respectable position anywhere." In fact blacks "must become possessed with the same spirit of self-relying enterprise," demanded Bailey, and this they could only do by learning to "emulate the . . . Anglo-Saxon race."[84]

Other newspapers in the Northeast with smaller circulations also supported the Free Soil movement and used racial arguments to advance it. For instance, both the *Ithaca Journal* and the *Buffalo Daily Republic* seemed to echo the racial views of the *National Era*, the *Tribune* and the *Evening Post*. The *Ithaca Journal* expressed fear over the increase and diffusion of the black slave population, and castigated Southern "slave breeders." The *Journal* was proud to note that the "land of the North gives no increase to slaves [blacks]."[85] In 1848, while covering the first national Free Soil convention, the *Buffalo Daily Republic* attacked Democratic Party regulars by noting in bold letters: "Behold the Traitors to the White Man and to Freedom." Likewise, the *Republic* considered the "American white laborer," to have proprietary rights to the free territories of the West.[86] The *American Free Soil Almanac*, which was published in Boston, asked its readers if "honest, independent, free labor, shall be kept out of it [the territories], as if it were planted with the pestiferous Bohan Upas [a poisonous tree found in tropical Africa]?"[87] Several other Free Soil newspapers from Boston, the *Boston Post* and the *Boston Times*, came out for "Van Buren and freedom," while attacking the "black flag of the slaves."[88]

Perhaps the most well-known Free Soil newspaper published in Boston was the *Emancipator and Republican*, edited by Henry Wilson. Wilson would later become a leading Republican United States Senator from Massachusetts, and after the Civil War the Vice President under Ulysses S. Grant. Wilson, who was a close personal friend of both Theodore Parker and Louis Agassiz and, in fact, in 1863 nominated the latter to the Board of Regents of the Smithsonian, also disseminated some of Agassiz's racist opinions. To illustrate, Wilson cited Agassiz's name when describing the polygenic theory, noting that people "were not made to differ as they now do merely by the influence of climate and other external circumstances, but were originally created substantially as they now appear . . . . " Wilson also described the work of an English physician and ethnologist, Dr. Charles Pickering, in which the Free Soil editor wrote of the "physical peculiarities" of the blacks. Temperamentally Wilson depicted black people as sambos, as "happy people," because of their "fondness for dance music." Morally, black men were described as licentious animals, because they had many wives and supported "themselves by robbery . . . . " Therefore, when Henry Wilson referred pejoratively to the South as the "Black Power," he did not do so in the interests of black people.[89]

Another Free Soil newspaper in the Northeast, *The Liberty Press*, published in Utica, New York, depicted black people as evil and immoral. Metaphorically this journal referred to the South as the "dark slave power," which was "polluted," because it had "insisted on the right to spread over that young and fertile soil [the free West] the curse which has cursed the whole South and is fast sinking the nation." *The Liberty Press* attacked the idea of annexing new territory in the Southwest, because such territory was "for the purpose of providing places for the superabundant slave population of the South." "The South," it continued, was "demanding more territory for the propagation of this rank and overgrown evil." Anxious over the growing black population in the slave states, *The Liberty Press* published statistics comparing the rates of increase of the black and white populations in the North and South, and was happy to report that "at least four-fifths of the immigrants from foreign countries, all white persons . . . go into the Free states." Viewing Mexicans and other darker skinned peoples as inferior breeds, this newspaper, echoing Bryant's, "oppose[d] the incorporation of any considerable portion of Mexico" into the Union, "from an unwillingness to commit the destiny of the country to such inhabitants as Mexico is at present composed of." As it was for most members of the learned community, racial mixing was anathema to *The Liberty Press*, which referred to Maryland and Virginia as a "shame" and a "disgrace," because they were "slave breeding states," and many of these offspring were "often the children of the masters or their sons."[90]

IV

From the above sampling it is evident that the leaders of the anti-expansionist movement in the Northeast employed the theme of race to secure support for their Free Soil philosophy. Reiterating the premise of the scientists and intellectuals of their day, they described blacks as a race distinct and inferior to the Caucasians. From this premise followed their other statements on the subject. These politicians, writers and editors went on to express concern that, if slavery were allowed to expand into the Western territories, the results could be disastrous for white Americans: the inferior black people would increase in numbers not only in the West but in the country at large; white immigrants from Europe, for whom the territories should be reserved, might not be able to compete with the slave labor of blacks; black slaves would eventually become free blacks, posing further economic and political competition; social contact between the races could lead to miscegenation or to racial conflict; at the very least working beside blacks would degrade and debase the European laborer and he, consequently, might rather stay out of the territories altogether. At times, indeed, the letters, speeches and publications of the Eastern Free Soilers seemed to make the issue of slavery expansion into a struggle between the Caucasoid and Negroid peoples over which race would control the future of the Western territories and possibly of the nation.

The question of whether the Free Soil disseminators of these racial theories really believed them is difficult to answer. Those who publicized such ideas can, of course, be seen as opportunists who, being aware of and taking advantage of the teaching of the intellectuals about the desirability of an homogeneous white America, were simply pursuing political and economic gain. Or they can be seen as people who were genuinely influenced by the teaching of the intellectuals. In the latter case, after all, they would simply have been adopting the ideas of many of the most prominent thinkers of their times. Could it be an earnest of their sincerity that the advocates of Free Soil doctrine actually sought to implement the solutions recommended by these thinkers for the problems that blacks supposedly posed for America? Whatever the answer, one thing must not be forgotten. Whether the Free Soil leaders were opportunists or true believers or a bit of both, the basic racial assumption of the scientists was clearly an element in their actions. Taking the lead from intellectuals, such as Daniel Drake, Louis Agassiz, and Mary Booth, and from political leaders, such as Henry Clay and David Wilmot, Northeastern Free Soilers turned to the solutions of containment of black people in the South and their eventual colonization or deportation out of the country.

For most Free Soilers, containment seemed to have meant no more than keeping the slaves in the South and preventing additional free blacks from coming into the North. Julius Rockwell, the Massachusetts Free Soiler, counseled that "wherever the African race exists out of Africa, it is best that it should be in a state of slavery, and that in that condition the colored race enjoy more than in another state." Similar to Jacob Miller of New Jersey, Rockwell claimed that slavery represented a civilizing or educational institution for the backward African; but, he warned, it must be confined to the South lest the Africans be dispersed over the North and West and thereby bring on racial mixing and conflict.[91] Gamaliel Bailey wrote about keeping back the "dark and insidious tide of slavery." "Slavery is local," he declared, and it should "remain so." And, even though Bailey had no particular love for slavery and wanted to see it eventually ended, he too, as had Rockwell and Miller, viewed it as a school for the lowly black man, because it brought him into contact with the superior Caucasian. "No one will deny that American slaves have advanced in all respects far beyond their ancestors [in Africa] who," Bailey noted, "were mere uncivilized pagans of brutish ignorance and loathsome practices." But, as a consequence of Southern slavery, native blacks were "less puerile and barbarous in their tastes; not so strongly marked by ridiculous pretensions," as Africans were assumed to be. Even so, Bailey admitted that American blacks were still far below the white man in ability.[92] John Dix agreed with Rockwell and Bailey, that the blacks should remain in the South. Apparently influenced by Agassiz and certain ethnologists, however, he maintained that climatic factors might work to constrain blacks from leaving that section. If they were restricted to the South, whether by force or climate, Dix believed that, over time, the numbers of blacks would slowly decrease. It was the expansion of slavery into new territory which led to the growth of the black population.[93]

New York city's two influential newspaper editors-Bryant and Greeley-also lent their support to containment. Bryant insisted that the "champions of free soil for free labor raise no controversy" with the slaveholder over the issue of slavery in the South. They "only demand that he shall not take them [slaves] into the territories to expel the free laborer by the repulsion of their presence." Actually Bryant doubted the "possibility of perpetuating the black race . . . upon a soil which is tilled by the white man." Once whites reached the territories in sufficient numbers, they would keep the blacks out. Until that day, however, slavery must be excluded by the federal government.[94] Greeley made the same qualification that Bryant and other conservative antislavery Free Soilers made: slaveholders for the time being had the right to keep slaves in the South but not to take them into the West. The "distinction between slaveholding and seeking to wield the power of the federal government for the extension of slavery," Greeley declared, "is a vital one . . . . " He found nothing wrong with slavery in the short run if it remained in the slave states. If it were to expand westward, however, it would be "blackening with slavery a domain larger than all the old free states" and, if it expanded as far as California, it would be "to blacken its soil by the commission of [a] useless crime."[95]

Some Free Soilers, however, such as Bailey, were willing to support a program of gradual emancipation. Given his belief that slavery was a paternalistic institution, which acted to perpetuate the black race in America, then freeing the slaves would throw black men on their own resources, which resources Bailey held in low esteem. In effect he had no fear of gradual emancipation because of his belief in the total superiority of white labor. This superiority was especially evident in the Northern states, Bailey remarked, where he described white labor as "formidable competition" for free blacks. It was so formidable, he thought, that "labor is monopolized to a great extent by the white race" in those states. Like Parker and Sturtevant, Bailey believed that the free black man would never survive this competition. "Turn him [the black man] free into the field of civilized competition," Bailey insisted, "and it will not be necessary to take from him anything that he has."[96]

Although some Free Soilers, Rockwell for instance, looked no further than the containment of blacks as slaves in the South, others saw containment as no more than a temporary expedient. And, even though Bailey believed that the result of a gradual emancipation would be disastrous to black Americans, he still maintained that these newly freed blacks should leave the country, preferably settling in Mexico or the Caribbean. In effect many Free Soilers believed that if white people were ultimately to realize their manifest destiny in North America, black people would have to be removed. Colonization, as Henry Clay envisaged it, seemed to be the one sure way of accomplishing that end. Historian Charles Foster comes to the nub of the matter when he writes that "beneath all of the attractive arguments which embellished colonization, was race prejudice . . . [;] the object [of the colonizationists] was not to remove the prejudice, but to remove the Negro."[97]

Free Soil pamphleteer Russell Jarvis argued that to be successful containment and colonization had to be implemented together. In answer to those who held that the diffusion of slavery throughout the country would eventually lead to its demise, Jarvis claimed that "a shorter, safer, surer mode of destroying it is fencing it round with an impassable wall, excepting an outlet for foreign and free colonization." The wall, presumably, was to be erected by passage of the Wilmot Proviso and

Northern state laws to exclude free blacks. Therefore, the "remedy for slavery would be found in a vigorous prosecution of foreign colonization," providing that the North, by virtue of its black laws, also closed "all domestic drains" and thereby "force the slave states to this vigorous prosecution."[98]

Although not every proselytizer for Free Soil saw containment and colonization interacting as closely as Jarvis did, most who supported one supported the other. While containment held slavery and the black people in check, colonization must be encouraged to guarantee the eventual termination of both slavery and the black presence in America. Dix, who worried that the South might after all succeed in expanding its peculiar institution and with it the number of black people, concurred that containment must be coupled with colonization. Actually Dix seems to have believed that containment by itself was already failing. At odds with his own view that free blacks in the North would soon die out, he argued that colonization was needed not simply to rid the South of its blacks, but to rid his own and other Northern states of this undesirable population. "If fifty thousand free blacks in New York were to be withdrawn," he predicted, "their places would be filled by an equal supply of white [immigrant] laborers."[99]

Colonization was backed by others who subscribed to free soilism, such as Washington Hunt, Daniel Webster, Jacob Miller and John P. Hale. Both Hunt and Webster were vice-presidents of the American Colonization Society, and demanded that the federal government use any means to effect the removal of black people from the country.[100] Because Miller believed slavery functioned as a school for barbaric blacks, he concluded that black Americans should be sent to Liberia, to aid in the "civilization" of black Africans. Besides uplifting Africans, colonization offered white Americans a means to exert economic and political influence on that continent. He noted that American "commerce shall expose to the eye of the world the rich mines of natural wealth which now lie hidden in the dark forest of that neglected continent." Miller depicted colonization in terms of satisfying a nascent American imperialism, which idea was picked up by other Free Soil and later Republican politicians, politicians who would in a few decades adopt the philosophy of Social Darwinism as a perfect excuse to expand United States influence abroad. In fine, African colonization would rid the United States of an unwanted race, while at the same time open up an economic bonanza for American investors.[101] Even antislavery politicians with a liberal reputation, such as Senator John P. Hale of New Hampshire, a one-time Free Democratic presidential candidate in 1852, proposed to colonize this supposedly inferior population out of the country. In 1850 Hale was not above having a laugh in Congress at the expense of darker skinned people. At the same time he presented a petition to the Senate asking it "to pass a bill to remove from the country all that portion of the African race who are both willing and ready to emigrate to Africa."[102]

Bryant was another who, like Dix and Webster, worried about the "accumulation of the black population." He wrote articles lauding the work of the American Colonization Society. To him colonization appeared, moreover, to be the only alternative for black Americans. Similarly to Henry Clay, he asserted that "it is a sad but indisputable truth, that in this country the colored man has no future." Africa or the tropics, however, were the "natural home and the obvious asylum of the Negro." They were "mostly peopled by his race [and] the climate is most indulgent to his constitution." The "perennial and abundant productions of their soils, protect him from the distress and privation, which in colder climates are the natural consequences of his ignorance and his improvidence." Apparently not as sanguine as Clay about the civilizing influence of American slavery on blacks, Bryant concluded that only in the tropics "can the Negro hope to take those primary lessons in civilization, which his race have never yet mastered."[103] Sounding both humane and selfish, Bailey added that the "colored people should go precisely where they can live most comfortably." "Were we [sic] a colored man," he proclaimed, "we [sic] would never rest from our [sic] wanderings," in search of a new home. Colonization, as he envisaged it, however, would involve a two-way flow, with white immigrants coming into the country, while native born blacks were leaving. "While the white population of Europe is colonizing the United States," Bailey demanded, "why should not the colored population of the United States colonize Mexico and the West Indies?" Specifically he had Haiti in mind where, he claimed, the once lazy and ignorant black man would suddenly undergo a complete transformation. Once out of the United States, he declared, "their industry, their acquaintance with the arts of civilization, their energy, would give them a decided ascendancy in that island."[104]

Greeley also supported colonization of blacks abroad. He did so on two grounds. There was, of course, his stated racial reason, deriving from his various concerns about miscegenation, labor competition and black inferiority. As early as 1834 Greeley expressed grave doubts about whether it was possible for the white and black races to live together within the United States. Later, in a letter to a Mr. W.C. Cowan of Albany, Missouri, he wrote that the "mixture of whites and blacks in the same community, society, household . . . is not favorable to the moral purity or social advancement of either caste." Greeley concluded, therefore, that the best policy was to "let the two races form separate communities."[105]

Greeley's second expressed reason for endorsing colonization followed from his first. He promoted the project because, he said, there was little hope for socio-economic improvement of blacks within the United States. As Bailey had prophesied, so too Greeley believed that only by emigrating elsewhere could blacks ever hope to become more "civilized." "It does seem to us," he noted condescendingly in 1850, "that this idea of colonizing is a work to which the black race among us are called and which it is cowardice, is baseness on their part to shrink from." Obviously full of advice for black people, Greeley insisted that "something of this they must do, if they do not choose to form a degraded and despised caste forever."[106]

To advance colonization Greeley endorsed the exact plan that his political idol, Henry Clay, had proposed back in 1827. "The Tribune earnestly favors the idea of extending national aid to the speedy and final extirpation of the slave trade, by colonizing the slave coast of Africa." The "world knows . . . [that] the free blacks of America ought to consecrate their lives to the work of regenerating and civilizing the land of their forefathers." Greeley went on to provide optimum annual figures: "We believe that emigrants to Africa would do better if they were fifty thousand a year, than they can while they are but a few hundreds."[107]

Although "Africa was the proper arena in which to develop the talents and capacities of the black race, for . . . social elevation," Greeley was willing to consider other possible places for black settlement. The important thing to him was that blacks should leave the United States. "Whether the black race sees fit to colonize Africa or not," he stated, "we insist that they ought to colonize somewhere." He too, as had Bailey, suggested Haiti as an alternative site for colonization, because he, along with the ethnological community, believed black people especially created for warmer, tropical climates. Apparently carried away with the idea to the point that he forgot his conviction relative to the innate inferiority of blacks, Greeley enthused over Haiti as follows: "Why not make that a black California; people it, subdue it, improve it, beautify it, and demonstrate . . . to the confusion of all . . . the capacity of the race for freedom, civilization and continuous improvement?"[108]

V

This inconsistency in Greeley's thinking, when he considered matters of race, was, as has been seen, not uncommon among the literati and politicians when they thought about that subject. Whether they claimed to have the welfare of black people in mind, as did Clay or Greeley, or whether they were openly hostile to the blacks, as were Van Evrie and Dix, consistency in logic was not their strong hand. To emphasize this point it may be instructive to study Greeley's inconsistencies more closely because, as with the learned people and Free Soil leaders, Greeley, himself, did not seem to recognize the ambiguities, contradictions or ambivalences that were manifest in his statements about black people in the United States. Despite his oft expressed opinions that blacks were racially inferior, the editor of the *Tribune* wrote that he supported their local efforts toward self-improvement and socio-economic uplift. And, notwithstanding his advocacy of the colonizing of blacks abroad, he backed their efforts to achieve equal legal and political rights within the Untied States.

More specifically, while castigating black people for being naturally lazy and ignorant and essentially incapable of any advancement, Greeley hinted that, if they would only apply themselves, they could become efficient laborers and raise themselves on the scale of social and economic values. In 1850, in answering a black reader and critic of the American Colonization Society, Greeley wrote that "so long as the free blacks persist in sticking to the whites, mixing up with them, serving their tables, currying their horses, sawing their wood and blacking their boots," they were merely "confirming the current impression of the whites, that they were intended for servitude and are intrinsically good for nothing." At another time, when answering criticisms which the black abolitionist Frederick Douglass had directed at his newspaper's support for colonization, Greeley stated that "such men as [Samuel] Ward, [Henry Highland] Garnett [sic], and [Henry] Bibb convince us that their race was not made merely to scour knives . . . we wish their example would be equally convincing to their own people" who, Greeley believed, were not up to the standards of their leaders. Nevertheless, Greeley thought that emancipated slaves would pose no labor problems because, while remaining in the South, they "would keep quietly at work, receiving wages from their present master and earning twice as much as ever before." Sounding very much like a radical abolitionist, he predicted that "when our people shall have become really hostile to slavery, there will be no need of exporting the emancipated Negroes," because "they will all be needed here, and will be a more healthy, cheerful, [and] tractable body of laborers than the planters can find [elsewhere]." Even in this scenario, free blacks would still be confined to the South. Contrary to the polygenists, Greeley professed to believe "Negroes to be men descended from Adam and Eve, and as capable of higher and higher development as whites are." In their present condition, however, blacks were "good for nothing, because they have no rights, no social position, no hope, no friends."[109] In effect, similar to the environmentalists, Greeley thought the black man capable of improvement, just as the white man. All the black man needed to better himself was the same opportunities which society offered the white man. In taking this view, he was implying that the black man's problems were not innate or racially derived, but rather external, a by-product of the hostile environment in which he found himself.

If deprivation of their rights was one reason Greeley believed that black people were "good for nothing," then it might be supposed that he would call for the United States to bestow political and legal rights on them. As a matter of fact he did exactly that; but his ambiguity of thought about blacks was further illustrated in his also calling for them to be colonized abroad, which policy can only be construed as a total denial of their civil rights within the United States. A closer look at Greeley's specific demands for black rights would seem to reveal only more confusion. For example, his belief that the fugitive slave laws should be enforced to preserve the Union was apparently qualified by his expressed conviction that equal protection of the laws should be extended to blacks charged as fugitives. "The law [of 1850]," he wrote, "ought to provide for a fair trial and an indisputably just decision as to the fact that the person claimed is really the slave of the claimant." Or again, Greeley's sometime opposition to citizenship for blacks conflicted with his other time support for equal suffrage rights for free blacks in New York state. While criticizing the work of the Democratic controlled New York state convention which was considering the elective franchise, Greeley stated that, "being Democratically settled, we entreat them to withdraw all opposition [250.00 dollar property qualification] to extending to poor Negroes the right so justly conceded to rich ones." He wanted all males to vote, because that was only "just, equal, liberal and according to the Declaration of Independence." Yet after chiding the Democrats on exactly how they were going to determine who was white enough to qualify as a voter, Greeley apparently was willing to accept limited black suffrage as better than no suffrage at all: "As to the 'separate submission' of the right of colored men to vote [250.00 dollar property qualification] we must take what we can get." Commenting sarcastically on a black suffrage referendum in the neighboring state of Connecticut, Greeley said that the white voters of that state "are called [upon] . . . to say whether they hold that a man has a right to a voice in making the laws which are to govern him because he is a man or because he is of a particular line or complexion." Greeley hoped Connecticut would not continue to deny a portion of her citizens the franchise, "merely because their distant ancestors were inhabitants of Africa and were darkened by its fervid sun."[110]

Seemingly also at odds with his stated opposition to general citizenship for blacks was Greeley's attack on the black laws of Ohio. In 1849 Ohio was in the process of repealing part of its legal code which discriminated against its free black population. Greeley encouraged Ohio Whigs to support the repeal. He asked them "who and what are they who in your state have upheld and gloried in the atrocious black laws" and have "studiously denied to our African population the rights, the treatment and even the name of men?"[111]

Continuing to agitate for political rights for blacks Greeley, at the same time, never lost an opportunity to inject partisan politics into the issue and to flay the administration Democrats. "When poor blacks are to be hunted from their hard won homes as unfit to live free among white men," he asked, were not regular Democrats often "found ready and eager actors in the business?" Greeley identified these Democrats with those "who mainly boot down and vote down every proposition to extend the right of suffrage to colored men." In 1849 Greeley also attacked the U.S. State Department as being sympathetic to such Democratic sentiments. When addressing its recent decision to deny passports to black people, he noted that this action "was based expressly on the fact that by immemorial proscription, colored persons had not been deemed entitled to passports, as American citizens." Greeley believed this policy to be "flagrantly wrong," because "no Secretary of State . . . has a right to deny to one citizen what he is ready to accord to another, merely on account of a difference in color." Greeley found the cause for such rejection in the "counterfeit Democracy that effected that decision, by the lowest appeals to the prejudices of the baser sort of whites." When addressing his fellow Whigs from Connecticut, Greeley stated that "this clamor against 'Niggers' is naturally Loco Foco [Democratic], and is just on a par with the usual devices of that party." Many voters were won over to the Democratic side, he averred, "through its abuse of 'Niggers.'"[112]

Whatever uncertainty existed in Greeley's mind when he contemplated the position of blacks in America seemed to disappear when he addressed himself to white prejudice against blacks. On that subject his writing was usually consistent. In an article entitled "Colorphobia," he described numerous cases in which free blacks, riding on steamboats in the North, were forced out of dining rooms and ordered to ride above decks. He also castigated the prejudice he saw in an incident in which a black man, who was attempting to pay his fare, was forced off a New York city streetcar by the driver. Greeley cited such examples "to hold up to notice and to the increasing contempt of the reflecting, the absurd prejudice against color, which is so strong in the minds of a large proportion of Northern persons." Interestingly he then compared racial attitudes in the North, to those in the South and in Europe, and found, similarly to DeTocqueville, that "at the South no one feels himself injured by riding in the same carriage with a colored man." In Europe, "color is no bar to admission to the best society."[113]

Respecting the South and its lack of "colorphobia," perhaps Greeley overlooked the fact that because the races were in close contact with each other, social tensions were reduced. After all, black workers, whether unskilled or skilled, slave or free, formed the backbone of the Southern economy. Little or nothing could be done without them. And, since most slaveholders were small operators, owning between two and four slaves, it was not unusual to find master and slaves working together. In the North, on the other hand, blacks were peripheral players economically, usually living in segregated areas and doing what menial labor was available. Southern black workers, and in particular servants, often lived in the same house with the master, cooked and ate the same food, nursed his children, and black and white children grew up and played together. More importantly, interracial sexual unions were quite common which, in itself, would indicate some form of physical attraction, or put another way, recognition of a common humanity. It would seem, then, that all of these associations, and in particular the latter, would tend to dissipate that "colorphobia" which both Greeley and DeTocqueville found in the North.

By demonstrating the extent to which white racial prejudice pervaded everyday Northern life, and how the resulting behavior was irrational, the editor of the *Tribune* clearly saw himself as pointing out a moral lesson to his Caucasian readers. Perhaps Greeley should have taken his own lesson to heart when expressing his opinions about black people. While he condemned the North in general and the Democratic Party in particular for contributing to white racial prejudice he still, at times, contributed to such prejudice himself.

Unlike Greeley or Clay, however, most Free Soil leaders appeared consistent in their prejudice against black people. Where they evinced inconsistency was not in manifesting the prejudice but rather, like the scientists they emulated, in striving in spite of inconsistencies to hold on to that prejudice even if it flew in the face of evidence to the contrary. By maintaining their prejudice, it has been seen that they lent support to the Free Soil doctrine that the territories must be reserved for free white people. Perhaps no better summary of the details of this alliance between white racial attitudes and the Free Soil doctrine can be found than that given by the Free Soil lawyer and author, Sidney George Fisher. Fisher began by saying that he did not object to slavery, so long as it was confined to the South. He claimed that, in the short run at least, black people "are better off here in slavery than in Africa in freedom," because mere contact with the omnipotent Caucasian left them "far superior intellectually and morally . . . [to] native Negroes" though, of course, still far inferior to the white man. Nevertheless, his tolerance of slavery in the South did not mean that Fisher was prepared to tolerate its expansion into the West. He was not, and his reasoning was not far to seek. Fisher was opposed to any extension of slavery because he was opposed to any extension of black people.[114]

The question of who should settle the open territories of the West, wrote Fisher, was not primarily one of whether the area should be slave or free. It was, more importantly, a question of whether the area should be settled by black people or by white people. "The opinions of the North, in relation to slavery," he stated emphatically, "are the result of the laws of race" which, in turn, were derived from the "science of ethnology." What was being called the issue of slavery in the free Western territories was in reality a racial issue "between the Saxon of the North and the Negro of the South, as to which shall possess and cultivate vast regions of unoccupied fertile land." In fine, the issue involved a racial contest "between the white and the dark, the superior and inferior races of mankind."[115]

In this contest for supremacy in the Western territories it was imperative, Fisher told his readers, that the white race emerge triumphant. "Is it not . . . the obvious duty of the nation which holds the Negro in subjection, to prevent the growth of a race which is incapable of liberty or civilization, which is just so much heathenism and barbarism wherever it exists?" Fisher feared that the "increase of the Negro[es]" was, in fact, "already far too numerous [sic] for safety." In the short run the containment of slavery through non-extension was primarily a means of "restraining the growth of the Negro race, within those limits of climate, where he [sic] alone can work." Ultimately Fisher viewed containment as the only means to "check the growth of Africa in America."[116]

Fisher was convinced that the white person of the North was rising to the racial challenge. "True to his instincts of conqueror, colonizer, founder, the Saxon of the North claims this [Western] land for himself. He claims that he, and not the Negro, shall occupy and till it." As far as the white person of the South was concerned, Fisher was willing to "let the Southern Saxon go . . . to the territories, if he will, but [he must] leave his Negroes behind him, or take them to regions where the white man cannot work." "The North," Fisher insisted, "claims the right to exclude slavery, in other words the Negro race, from those territories, but at the same time declares that it will respect and maintain slavery in the states where it already exists."[117]

The fact that Northern whites recognized the dangers attending a spreading black race augured well, Fisher was convinced, for the eventual triumph of their race in the West. So, too, did the inability of the free black laborer to compete with the free white laborer. It was axiomatic: If whites could keep black slaves out of the territories, they would never have to worry about free black laborers in the territories. With Drake and Agassiz, Fisher argued that the "climate in which the Negro can work and thrive repels the white, whilst the Negro is excluded from the North both by the climate and the competition of the more intellectual and energetic race." Fisher believed that the identical process was then being replicated in the Western territories. The "Negro is not only disappearing from those [Northern] states where he is free," but likewise from those other areas "where the climate allows the white man to obtain a footing as a laborer."[118]

Fisher's final conclusion was obvious and congruent with that of Free Soilers in general. Since the free black man could not compete in the open market with the free white man, the latter, by excluding slavery from the territories, could guarantee that they would become a Saxon domain.[119]

VI

To put into proper perspective the conservative/racist character of the Free Soil philosophy, as it was being defined by Clay, Wilmot, Fisher and others, it may be instructive to note what the more radical supporters of political antislavery were doing. While the conservative Free Soilers did not found the Free Soil Party until 1848, others, desiring more fundamental change, had already taken political action. Almost a decade earlier the Liberty Party had been founded at Warsaw, Wyoming County, New York. This party's original platform was solely concerned with attacking slavery. It called for an end to the interstate slave trade, an end to the Fugitive Slave Law of 1793, and an end to slavery in the District of Columbia. Although it did not call for general emancipation, it has usually been portrayed by historians as the most radical political expression of the antislavery movement and, certainly, its program was considerably more radical than that supported by Free Soilers of the Clay-Wilmot-Fisher variety.[120] Furthermore, when Liberty Party men defended the rights of working people they did not make distinctions among the latter based on skin color; and, when Liberty Party men discussed the future of black people in America, they did not advocate colonization.

Perhaps the best example of a Liberty Party man was Gerrit Smith of New York state who, rather than support the Free Soil Party's candidates and principles in 1848, ran separately as the Liberty Party's nominee for president. Smith had some interesting points to make about the Free Soilers who confined their antislavery activities to supporting Wilmot's Proviso. "Who," he asked, "is the Wilmot Proviso man? He is the man, who, under the most favorable representation of him, is willing to let slavery live, where it now lives, but no where else." In reality, Smith observed, "a license to slavery to live any where, is a license to it to live every where. Call you the Wilmot Proviso man an anti-slavery man? He is a pro-slavery man." Smith went on to draw a clear and crucial distinction between other antislavery politicians and Liberty Party followers. "The Liberty Party," Smith explained, "actually takes the ground of the political and social equality of all men. He is not a Liberty Party man, who makes political rights turn on physical peculiarities; and he is not a Liberty

Party man, who does not as warmly welcome a colored man as a white man to his dinner table." On the other hand, those antislavery people who "exclude colored men both from political and social equality . . . thereby stamp with hypocrisy their professed devotion to the doctrine of equal rights."[121] Quite early then, there were those within the political antislavery movement, such as Gerrit Smith, who recognized the conservative and racist bent of Wilmot's and the Free Soil Party's political appeal. This recognition, of course, did nothing to prevent the growth of that party.

During the 1852 presidential campaign Smith was not remiss in directing a political attack at the Free Soil or Free Democratic Party. Smith asked his followers to vote for the Liberty Party candidate, William Goodell, in lieu of John Hale. Being an abolitionist committed to the higher law doctrine, Smith stated the reasons for his decision:

> The Free soil parties flatter themselves that God denounces but the slave-holder. No less, however, does He denounce them, who suffer the slave to be held. The Free Soil parties flatter themselves, that God denounces but the slave-catcher. But, no less certain and fearful are His denunciations against them, who suffer the slave to be caught.

In that same year Smith was elected to Congress as an Ultra-Abolitionist from New York, but resigned before his term expired. In Congress he blamed all Caucasian Americans, North and South, for the existence of slavery, and recommended "its unconditional, entire and immediate abolition."[122]

Perhaps more telling than Smith's opposition was the fact that leading black abolitionists were also critical of the Free Soil Party. Why shouldn't they be? Given that party's endorsement of Southern slavery, the vituperative attitude of many of its members toward black people, the fact that many Free Soilers saw nothing immoral in returning blacks to slavery-nor with Northern black laws-there was little reason for blacks to support such a party. When Samuel R. Ward addressed the black voters of New York state, he urged them not to vote for Martin Van Buren and the Free Soil Party. " . . . [C]an the colored voters of New York State support that nominee and join in that movement?" Ward asked, and then answered with a resounding "No!" Instead, he advised black voters to remain loyal to the smaller but more radical and morally sound Liberty Party, and to vote for the " . . . outspoken, uncompromising, impartial and truly practical philanthropist, Gerrit Smith."[123] Martin R. Delany likewise refused to endorse the Free Soil Party in 1848, and when speaking before a black convention in Cleveland, Ohio, recommended that blacks " . . . support such persons and parties alone as have a tendency to enhance the liberty of the colored people of the United States."[124] In 1852 Frederick Douglass, who equivocated at times, wrote that he was "a 'Liberty Party' man and think I can give a more direct vote against slavery by acting with that Party, than by voting with any other."[125] Obviously important black leaders were not enthused with the Free Soil Party and, as had Gerrit Smith, held strong reservations about the party's commitment to the war on slavery.

VII

Applying the distinction, made by historians Larry Gara and George M. Fredrickson, between a follower of political antislavery and an abolitionist, and using this distinction as a basis for evaluating the Free Soilers, few would qualify as abolitionists. Quite the contrary; most of the above examined Free Soilers viewed the black man in much the same light as did the learned community, i.e. as a racial inferior, and they were usually harsh critics of the radical abolitionists. Such abolitionists were generally written off as 'useless agitators.' Accepting historian Robert P. Ludlum's major characterization of a radical as one who is motivated by a "rigorous persistence in attempting to compel the acceptance of an ideal" and who is also the "stubborn foe of compromise," then, it would be difficult to find a radical reformer among the Free Soilers of the East. Their attitude, for the most part, was that black slavery was alright for the time being, as long as it remained confined within the Southern states.[126]

Between 1850 and 1854 political antislavery and free soilism seemed to lose some of its intensity in the Northeastern United States, and especially in New York state. This may have been due to a number of factors, such as the pacifying effect of the Compromise of 1850; the partial reconciliation among the warring factions within the Democratic Party; or the fact that, in an effort to keep their party whole, a number of antislavery Whigs were trying to avoid the extension issue. While this was occurring in the East, however, the situation in the West was quite different. There free soilism took strong root and blossomed forth into a viable antislavery, political coalition. It was also in the West where the potential for the spread of slavery and the black man was perceived by white politicians as a real socio-economic threat to their white constituents. In short, it was in the West where an alliance between political antislavery and white racism became particularly pronounced.

CHAPTER 3

FREE SOILISM IN THE WEST

The exclusion of slavery from the territories is only an incidental part of a general policy of which colonization is the cornerstone.

H. C. Trinne, 1859

Since the Republic's beginning, the issue of the expansion of slavery into the Western territories had never been far below the surface of American politics; and when the annexation of Texas and of additional Mexican territories in the West was being hotly debated in Congress, in the 1840's, the subject became a catalyst for sectional political alignments. To many Southerners the West seemed a logical area into which to expand their peculiar institution and out of which to create new slave states. By contrast, many Northerners, especially those living in the states of the old Northwest, were unwilling to let pro-slavery forces gain a political foothold in the new territories. As a result, during the late 1840's the latter began to organize into a Free Soil Party. Together with their counterparts in the East, and in particular the Free Democracy of New York state, Western Free Democrats, antislavery Whigs, and Liberty Party men created the new antislavery coalition.

Certainly one of the most important reasons for Western opposition to slavery expansion was the fear that as a result of the spread of slavery, the Western territories might someday be overrun by black people. As was true in the Eastern Free Soil movement, many in the Western Free Soil movement who perceived themselves as antislavery in sentiment were, in truth, less concerned about immediately ending slavery where it existed in the Southern states, than about stopping the expansion of slavery and the black race into the Western territories. In a word, in the West, too, Free Soilers perceived the battle against the expansion of slavery as also a battle for racial dominance, to ensure that the territories would be white and free, and not black and slave.[1]

Although other factors, such as the acquisition of Western homesteads were important, that the factor of race was tied to the homestead issue and played a still more important part in their opposition to slavery expansion was manifested in the arguments that Western politicians, newspaper editors and other Free Soil leaders employed in support of the Free Soil objective. Emulating Henry Clay, himself a son of the Western border, and David Wilmot, they appropriated the racial arguments developed by the scientific and intellectual communities and depicted the Negroid race as inferior to the Caucasoid. As proof, they reiterated the familiar litany: intellectually blacks were no match for the whites. They were patently stupid, sensual, immoral, docile, indolent and lazy. Physically, being closer to the lower animals, they were repellent. Racial amalgamation had, therefore, to be avoided. To mingle what was called black blood with white blood would lead to the decline of the white race and violate God's plan for separate races of men. The idea, dignified by scientists, that in the beginning He had created distinct races for distinct climates, found a ready following in Western free soilism. Many Western Free Soil adherents, like those in the East, viewed America as destined, racially and climatically, to be the exclusive home of the Caucasian race, which they often defined more narrowly using the misnomer, the Anglo-Saxon race. Mexicans, Native Americans, but more especially Negroes were characterized as the 'lesser breeds,' people who somehow fell outside the protection of Anglo-Saxon law, who did not count and who, therefore, were to be displaced.

As did the arguments of the ethnologists and of the Eastern Free Soilers, at this point the arguments of the Western Free Soilers became somewhat confused. Some prophesied that as black people came into contact with Anglo-Saxon settlers, they would inevitably be destroyed by competition with what was assumed to be the superior white race. Other Free Soilers, however, worried that despite their racial inferiority, blacks, as slaves being forced to labor without wages, or as free laborers receiving wages too low to be acceptable to white laborers, would be able to compete successfully. To these Free Soilers, hope for an homogeneous white United States lay either in the intelligentsia's theory of natural migration, or in colonization to transport blacks out of the country. In the meantime slavery, the breeding ground for an inferior race, and hence an ultimate threat to Anglo-Saxon dominance, must be contained within an already bastardized and blackened South. Contradictions aside, the final conclusion on which the great majority of Free Soilers could agree was that the soil of the West should remain free of slavery and black people to guarantee a pure white population in the new free states which would be carved from the area.

That this was the conclusion of most Free Soilers did not mean it was the conclusion of all. A small number of party members were much less willing to accept the increasingly popular theories of the intellectuals that the black race was inferior and incapable of improvement. In defending the rights of black people, in fact, these Free Soilers at times approached the standards of the radical abolitionists, in the sense that they repudiated the polygenists' assumption of distinct and permanently different races, and instead subscribed to the environmentalist belief in universal man. When defending the rights of black people, they were defending the rights of white people as well, since both were members of the same human race. If these more enlightened people were only a minority within the Free Soil movement, they were an important minority.

I

Although in the Eastern United States the racial tenets of the scientific establishment had been espoused by enough leaders of the Free Soil movement to give them currency, they never generally received the political attention in that section of the country that they did in the West.

Obviously the threat of a black inundation of the West was more real and immediate than an invasion of the Northeast. Therefore in the West, prominent Free Soilers, embracing the racial credo with apparent relish, went to considerable lengths to articulate the idea that black people were inferior to white people. Here too, the use of more violent language and statements, for instance the frequent reference to 'niggers,' appeared to be more acceptable.

Perhaps the most telling aspect of the argument held that blacks were intellectually inferior. This view, reminiscent of the teachings of Doctors Josiah Nott and Samuel Morton and other scholars, found expression among a number of leading Western Free Soilers. For example, speaking to the lower house of Congress, Representative John Pettit of Indiana emphasized that he was "not one of those who believe that [the black man] is the [intellectual] equal of the Northern European, or his descendent . . . the Anglo-Saxon." The proof of the black's mental inferiority, said Pettit, could be found in two facts: in the size of his brain, which was "but little over one half the volume of brain, that attaches to the Northern European race;" and in the uncivilized state of wild Africa, his ancestral homeland.[2] The idea that Africa was a barbarous place and that its barbarism was owing to the intellectual inferiority of its inhabitants had, of course, been emphasized by the intellectuals; and Western Free Soilers, along with their Eastern friends, accepted the cue. While white people had "been steadily advancing in civilization," declared Michigan Representative Jacob M. Howard, black people had "continued barbarism in their own country for thousands of years." The reason, according to Howard, was simple: "blacks . . . [were] an inferior race, unequal in intellect to the white race . . . ."[3]

Howard argued, in fact, that the mental handicap under which blacks labored helped explain why they had been unable to extricate themselves from slavery in the American South.[4] Senator Thomas Corwin of Ohio agreed. Describing blacks as colossal fools, he professed to believe that they had volunteered to become slaves to the white man. Had anyone, he asked his fellow senators, "found out on the face of the earth, a man fool enough to give himself up to another and beg him to make him his slave? . . . Not one man of our complexion of the Caucasian race could be found quite willing to do that."[5] Not satisfied with keeping Africa barbaric, these people were, according to United States Representative Edward Wade of Ohio, now in the process of reducing America to barbarism. Blacks in slavery, he charged, were "reversing the onward movement of civilization" by "turning us back to the barbarism of Africa."[6]

When Western Free Soilers identified the areas in which blacks were intellectually deficient, they could range from the general to the particular. Temporary Missouri resident George Pattison, previously of Indiana and a Free Soil friend and admirer of influential United States Representative George Julian of that state, broadly expressed a low opinion of the "fund of intelligence" of the average "nigger."[7] George T. Brown of Illinois, editor of the *Alton Weekly Courier*, wrote that black children "are . . . utterly destitute of all knowledge that tends to elevation." Brown's publication also carried an article from a New Orleans newspaper which had reassured its Southern readers that they had no reason to fear a slave insurrection because blacks were so ignorant that "not one in twenty has the slightest knowledge of the use of arms."[8] Sounding much like the respected physicians, James Hunt and Daniel Drake, Representative Pettit insisted that blacks, as compared to whites, were "far more incapable in the arts, sciences, letters, philosophy, sound judgment and common sense."[9] Implying that blacks were ignorant even in simple arithmetic, newspaper publisher and later Congressman, John Wentworth of Illinois, declared that "if there is anything that the average Southern Negro does not know, it is his own age."[10]

Not only did black people allegedly lack ability in the refined disciplines and, even more basically, lack common sense, they apparently fell far short in moral decency as well. Some Western Free Soilers depicted them as petty thieves. Wentworth told of how when he was a Congressman living in the District of Columbia he awoke one morning to find missing both his boots and his black servant who cared for them.[11] Other Western Free Soilers in characterizing the moral turpitude of the black people went much further, even perhaps than their Eastern counterparts. Pettit affirmed that blacks were more sensual beings than whites, with "more of the animal and less of the mental."[12] As if to confirm Pettit's assessment, one Free Soil and later Republican newspaper from his own state, the

Evansville Daily Journal, described black people as drunken rowdies, who were only interested in cheap "entertainments" and "fisticuffs."[13] Newspaperman George Brown described them as "creatures lost to every sense but their own degraded necessities and passions;"[14] while Cassius M. Clay, the well-known Free Soil writer, reformer and politician from Kentucky, called them "house-breakers, poisoners, rogues, perpetrators of rapes and mid-night murders."[15] Another Free Soiler and the editor of the early *Chicago Tribune*, Thomas A. Stewart, claimed that, because they were a morally weaker race, blacks living in the Northern states were dying off. Although their physical weakness partly explained their high mortality rate, so too did their moral corruption, especially, wrote Stewart, the "indifference among our colored population to marriage."[16]

An important aspect of the stereotype of the black man's mental attributes, and one which found favor with Western Free Soilers, was that which portrayed him as innately lazy and shiftless, with no care for the morrow. Free Soiler and Protestant minister, the Reverend Mr. Henry B. Whipple of Minnesota, spoke to this point. He maintained that the blacks' mental and moral deficiencies were of such a gross order that they inevitably led to "idleness, lies, [and] ignorance," as well as "lack of forethought and prudence."[17] Free Democrat and later Republican David K. Cartter of Ohio referred to free blacks as a "worthless" race, and warned that any area of the country which accepted them would soon "become a common alms-house."[18] Congressman John A. Kasson of Iowa concurred with Whipple's and Cartter's views. While visiting in Virginia, Kasson wrote to his brother that the "niggers, although uniformly treated with kindness, are as lazy as the land is lean."[19] Kasson's Iowa protege, Governor James Grimes, held a similar opinion. Black slaves were, he avowed, a shiftless lot. Should the free territory, he asked, be the future home of a people, who were "weary," and who would drag their "indolent limbs over the state, or shall it be thrown open to the hardy and adventurous freemen of our own country?"[20]

The innate lassitude which they attributed to blacks naturally led Free Soilers to conclude that, whether free or slave, these people were irresponsible and had no aims, no desire to succeed. In an editorial in his *Alton Weekly Courier*, George Brown complained that "it is too much the case, that Negroes in the free states have no worthy ambition or aspirations for education, responsibility and wealth."[21] Claiming to have "studied the Negro character," Cassius Clay concluded that "above all, [Negroes] have not the stimulus of self-interest, as the whites." The result was that blacks made inefficient, if not inert workers. Clay described them as "not so skillful, so energetic . . . . They waste as much . . . through carelessness and design." Since they "lack self-reliance, we can make nothing out of them."[22] Brown's newspaper published an article by a Northern reporter who described a conversation with a slaveholder. The latter told him that blacks were "monstrous lazy; they won't do nay work, you know, untils you are close to em all the time."[23]

Free Soilers simply could not comprehend why slaveholders continued to support such innately inefficient laborers. While Congressman Benjamin Wade of Ohio did not consider slavery an economically viable institution, he implied that part of the problem rested with black people. Agreeing with Whipple, slavery and its component black labor force were not only immersed in "ignorance [and] sin," but also in "idleness." Benjamin, the older brother of Edward, asked a close friend the following: "What farmer in Ohio would bind himself to keep a drove of niggers to cultivate his farm, he engaging to feed and clothe . . . such."[24] Apparently, black workers were such an economic deficit that they were not able to pay even for their own keep. Corwin told his Southern congressional colleagues that "your lands are worn out, because the slave has turned pale the land, wherever he has set down his black foot."[25] Cassius Clay maintained that blacks were as useless as a tribe of monkeys, because, rather than for work, "God has made them for the sun and the banana."[26]

This description of the black mind as immoral, lazy and indolent, was but part of the stereotype commonly known even then as 'sambo.' Sambo was a simple, abject creature, who seemed to enjoy life in the worst of circumstances. Whipple, travelling in the deep South in the 1840's, drew a picture of the typical black as a carefree, happy-go-lucky character. "Some of the funniest beings I have ever seen," he wrote when describing Southern free blacks, "are of the Negro dandy species. So much gas and wind and smoke, with a little charcoal, is seldom seen. They are decided bloods, as may be seen by the dashy dress and foppish air . . . . Some of these free Negroes make quite a show in their fine carriages and look quite like nabobs . . . ." To assume that the Reverend was kindly disposed toward these people, even in a patronizing way, would be a mistake. "Aside from their property and selfish powers of acquisition," he added, "they have but little mind." How they were ever able to acquire property, given Whipple's previous description of them, he never explained. Nor did this Northerner exempt destitute free blacks from the stereotype. "Your real drunken loafer negroes," along with the dandy, constituted "a happy race of beings."[27] Other Free Soilers, such as Congressman Robert C. Schenck of Ohio, likewise held, in referring to free blacks, that the "greater portion seem happy and contented."[28]

Whipple and Schenck were describing free blacks, but Free Soilers were just as apt to attribute the same characteristics to black slaves. In 1841, after witnessing the breakup of a Kentucky slave family along the Mississippi River, state legislator Abraham Lincoln of Illinois commented, albeit sympathetically, that "amid all these distressing circumstances, as we would think them, they [blacks] were the most cheerful and apparently happy creatures on board. One played the fiddle almost continually and others danced, sang, cracked jokes and played various games with cards."[29] George Pattison, who had lived in the slave state of Missouri for two years, wrote that black slaves "appear to be the happiest of mortals." In fact, Pattison was convinced that they "are happier, far happier, than the poor whites of Indiana, Ohio, or Illinois."[30]

Though sambo seemed to enjoy life, he was also supposedly easily frightened when confronted by his pretended Caucasian superior. Cassius Clay spoke of the "mental subserviency of the black slave," while George Brown reprinted an article in his newspaper, in which a slave, under arrest, was depicted as "thoroughly scared, negro-like." At the same time this particular black man was typical of "drunken negroes . . . overflowing with potvalor [sic] and as great a liar and coward."[31]

Even those within the Free Soil movement who sometimes supported the cause of equal political rights for black people, such as Ohioans Benjamin and Edward Wade, and Joshua R. Giddings, the latter a Free Democrat and one of the most liberal members of Congress, expressed doubts about the intelligence of black Americans. In 1854 Benjamin

Wade, who believed that blacks belonged to a naturally docile race, apparently felt it necessary to clarify to other Congressmen what he had meant, when he had spoken about political equality for black people. In what sense, he asked, were "they . . . created equal? . . . Not in physical power, certainly not. Not in point of intellect; nobody pretends." They were created equal in one sense only; the legal sense, that is, as persons entitled to political rights equal to those enjoyed by white Americans. Simply "because a man is weak, because he is ignorant, because he is [an] imbecile, does not confer the right upon the first man who is wiser or stronger than he, to subject [him] to minister entirely to the wishes of the stronger man."[32]

Brother Edward voiced similar views. While calling in Congress for equal political treatment of the few free blacks who were already in the Western territories he, like Benjamin, argued condescendingly that they should be extended equal considerations precisely because they were inferior. "Are not idiots your inferiors? Are not minor children your inferiors? . . . Why then not treat the black at least with equal kindness."[33] The Wade brothers may have argued for political equality for blacks, but certainly not on the grounds that they were intellectually equal to whites. Even Giddings seemed to have misgivings about the intellectual ability of blacks. Although at times he spoke as if he really believed blacks were capable of intellectual improvement, on other occasions he seemed to adopt essentially the same attitude toward blacks as the Wade brothers. For instance, he proclaimed "it . . . our duty as statesmen . . . to raise up the bowed down, to exalt the humble, [and] to inform the ignorant."[34] However, there were other Free Soilers who openly expressed the belief that blacks could never rise on the intellectual scale for the simple reason, in the words of Robert C. Schenck to his daughters, that they were "mere animals, little above the brutes."[35] Grimes of Iowa compared Southern black people to "cattle and horses," while John Wentworth likened them to the "cattle" he had seen in the Chicago stockyards.[36]

In comparing blacks to the lower species, Western Free Soilers sought to demonstrate that blacks were not merely mentally inferior to whites and therefore closer to animals, but that blacks were also physically inferior to whites and therefore closer to animals. In fact, if these Free Soil critics declared the mental capacity of blacks little above that of an animal, on occasion they declared his physical capacity virtually identical to that of an animal with, as Cassius Clay, quoting Montesquieu put it, an "ugly body" that was altogether repulsive.[37]

Following the example of the learned community, and in particular the ideas of Doctors Herman Burmeister and Samuel Cartwright, Free Soilers depicted the black man in animal terms, both implied and explicit. He was dirty, had a foul odor and breath, and bred with frightening rapidity. By linking blacks to the animal world, Free Soilers were acting as the precursors for what would later become known as evolutionary sociology, or Social Darwinism. Black people were somehow locked in time, and had failed to evolve to the level of the Caucasians. Free Soilers could pose as good Christians and still retain their belief in black inequality. If, in Christian theology, all men are brothers and therefore equal, then one way to deny blacks equality-and still remain a good Christian-would be to deny that blacks were men. Schenck of Ohio described blacks as "very dirty and often nearly naked."[38] Congressman Kinsley S. Bingham of Michigan asked why the free soil of the territories should "be polluted with the sweat of the slave?"[39] Some Free Soilers, the Wade brothers for instance, maintained that black people had an animal-like odor. Edward Wade wrote to his friend, Representative Albert Gallatin Riddle of Ohio, that he could probably smell out a Whig newspaper, "as quick as . . . Cuban-blood hounds could a Seminole, or a Dough Face Dandy could a nigger."[40] Benjamin Wade, in an 1851 letter to his wife written just after he had arrived in Washington, D.C., complained of the monotonous food "everyday cooked by niggers, until I can smell and taste the niggers." The city itself he described as a "mean, God forsaken nigger . . . place, of which the nigger smell I cannot bear."[41] George Pattison thought that if Northern white laborers had to work in the South, "many of them would be placed alongside of a big odoriferous buck Negro."[42] Less frequently cited as offensive was the breath of the black man, although Thomas Corwin called it "tainted."[43]

Like animals, too, blacks apparently multiplied at an alarming rate. Schenck and Edward Wade both drew analogies between the slave economy of the South, with its increasing number of black slaves and, in

Wade's phrase, an "animal economy." Schenck said the increase in slaves was like the increase "of cattle or other animals."[44] Wade elaborated: In both slavery and the "animal economy, the fecundity is inversely as the lowness of organization . . . ; that is, the lower the organization the more rapidly may they be multiplied."[45] The Reverend Mr. John Kirk of Illinois, an antislavery Whig, charged that slaveholding Virginians, in particular, were guilty of engaging "in the flesh mongering market, growing human cattle" and that Virginia "hatches out more young slaves every night, than they have removed in the past year by colonization."[46] Cassius Clay warned that the general increase in slaves was reaching the point where white workers would be "overrun" by black men, as if by a swarm of "black rats."[47]

Although the mental and physical characteristics which Free Soilers attributed to the black man have here been considered separately, it is important to remember that they were inseparable in the minds of these people. As noted, it was in the first place the black man's different appearance which had enabled white intellectuals to declare him a distinct species, inferior in both the physical and mental senses. Put another way, the intellectuals and the Free Soilers who accepted their ideas were, in effect, first labelling the black man's different physical traits as inferior and then claiming to deduce from his pretended physical inferiority his mental inferiority. The Free Democratic newspaper editor and later Republican Senator, B. Gratz Brown, carried in his influential St. Louis *Missouri Democrat* an article which made the connection. It reported the execution of a slave. After describing him as of "gingerbread complexion, and strongly marked with negro features, having a large mouth [and] thick lips," the writer pointedly concluded that his "physiognomy [was] indicative of great stupidity."[48]

All of this denigrating of the black man as being mentally and physically similar to the lower animals carried with it, of course, the implication that the white man was far above both him and the animals. Eastern and Western Free Soil leaders, and the intelligentsia of the era, portrayed the Caucasian race, and especially its Anglo-Saxon branch, as representing, in all of its purity, the highest form of civilized man. Here again, Social Darwinists of the 1870's-1900's period, many of whom were themselves Anglo-Saxons, such as Herbert Spencer and William Graham

Sumner, said exactly the same thing, i.e. that evolution had culminated in the Anglo-Saxon. Pettit claimed that the Caucasoid and the Negroid were "two races distinct in their [physical] organization; in the volume of intellect, of mind, of brain; different in the rapidity of the coursing of the blood through their veins."[49] Such words echoed those of any number of the scientists of the period, including Samuel Cartwright, Samuel Morton, Daniel Drake and Josiah Nott. Thomas Hart Benton, a Free Democrat from Missouri, followed the scientific argument to its ultimate conclusion when he expressed belief in the conception of a "scale of races." Similarly to Eastern Free Soilers Theodore Parker and Horace Bushnell, he described the whites as the most advanced race because of their "moral and intellectual superiority," and the blacks as the most backward. Benton also placed the yellow race below the white, but nevertheless "far above the Ethiopian or black, above the Malay or brown (if we must admit five races), and above the American Indian or Red."[50]

If other races stood above the Negroid, however, they still could not approach the Caucasians. As proof, Western Free Soilers recapitulated the elaborate exegesis laid down by the intelligentsia. The Caucasian race, and its Anglo-Saxon variety in particular, was superior to other races because among its innate qualities were such sterling characteristics as industry, perseverance, pride, and love of freedom. These qualities destined the white man soon to rule the continent from coast to coast and eventually to rule the earth. Cassius Clay spoke of the "vaunted Saxon blood, which no dangers can appal, no obstacles obstruct." Obviously influenced by the work of scientists such as George Gliddon, Clay continued: "Modern discoveries prove that the builders of the Pyramids and the Egyptian founders of science and letters were whites." This was evidence enough for him that the "Caucasian race" was the "first in civilization through all past time."[51] "Civilization," added Benton, had always been the "preference of the whites . . . ."[52]

In the same way that the industry and enterprise of the white race had accounted for past civilization, so, said the Free Soilers, it was accounting for civilization in the Northern United States. To make this point they compared the economic achievements of white laborers in the North to those of black slaves in the South. Disregarding the fact that class differences crossed racial lines, many of these Western Free Soilers ignored or deprecated the achievements of black labor. Significantly referring to free workers as a "race," Congressman Richard Yates of Illinois told a Georgian that if his state had "relied upon the hardy arms of free white labor," instead of the lesser energy of black slave labor, then "where now she [Georgia] grows her one bushel of wheat, she would grow her two bushels." The white laborer, according to Yates, was simply more efficient and diligent than the black. "It is the energizing power of free [white] labor, which has built our railroads, set the wheels of machinery in motion . . . and laid the solid foundation of our permanent prosperity."[53] Corwin was thinking along the same lines, when he asked his Southern colleagues in Congress: Is "not Massachusetts more productive today, than when the foot of the white man was first impressed upon the soil?"[54] He obviously did not believe that the same could be said for states which relied on black labor. Free Soilers who expressed such sentiments seemed to deny that black slaves had made any contribution to the Southern or national economy.

Other Free Soilers, including Corwin, Joseph K.C. Forrest, who wrote the antislavery editorials for John Wentworth's *Chicago Democrat*, and Congressman Joseph Wright of Indiana, believed the Anglo-Saxon to be unique in his love of democracy and freedom, and at least part of that uniqueness was accounted for by the blood of his race. According to Corwin, the reason that the free Negro could not "start all at once into a free Anglo-Saxon," was because he did not have the "blood of liberty flowing in every vein."[55] Wright declared that the reverence for freedom of petition was something peculiar to the liberty-loving Saxon. Referring to the framers of the United States Constitution, he maintained that "they were conscious that Anglo-Saxon blood was in their veins, and we find this true Saxon feeling exhibiting itself long before the adoption of a written constitution."[56] Forrest, too, referred to Caucasians as a "liberty loving race."[57]

According to the crusading Free Soil editor of Chicago's *Western Citizen* (and later the *Free West*), Zebina Eastman, the liberty-loving Caucasian, especially the "wonderful Anglo-Saxon race," was assigned the "position of leadership in the great world drama." As had numerous Free Soilers and later Republicans, Eastman confused ethnicity with race. The Chicago editor then declared that "now," the Anglo-Saxon, "controlled the destinies of the world . . . [and] the population of the earth is fast becoming Anglo-Saxonized."[58] Benton elaborated on Eastman's point, when he noted that "it would seem that the white [Anglo-Saxon] race alone received the divine command, to subdue and replenish the earth, for it is the only race that has obeyed it."[59] United States Representative and newspaper editor Schuyler Colfax of Indiana, thinking of the American West in particular, seconded Eastman's and Benton's opinions; he wrote of how the "vanguard of Anglo-Saxon civilization pushes forward," and would soon take "possession of the wide-spread territories of the West."[60] In essence the darker skinned races, or 'lesser breeds,' as these Free Soil politicians and journalists sometimes referred to Native Americans and Mexicans, but in particular black people, would have no place in the future development of the West. This Free Soil belief in the 'manifest destiny' of the Caucasian, or what they termed the Anglo-Saxon 'race' flew, of course, in the face of climatic determinism, by ignoring the fact that much of the West was arid and hot, quite unlike the temperate and cooler climates for which the Caucasian was supposedly adapted.

Professing to believe that the white race was, as the progenitor of civilization, far above the black in both mental and physical attributes, Western Free Soilers not surprisingly came to the same conclusion as Eastern Free Soilers: interracial breeding between whites and blacks must be avoided. Like DeGobineau, they often posed the problem as one of mixing the blood. For whites to mix their blood with the blood of blacks, would be to dilute their innately superior racial qualities. Corwin told fellow Congressmen that such contact between the races would be tantamount to the white party's contracting a disease. Would "I," he asked, be anymore "obliged to receive into my family a man with the smallpox or the leprosy, that they may be infected?"[61] Pettit wanted white people to avoid any sexual contact with the "degraded" and "degenerate" black race.[62] Representative Joseph Root of Ohio seemed to imply that the purity of the blood of the Anglo-Saxon may have been already threatened. He asked Congress if "we have improved on the Anglo-Saxon blood, or . . . have less of it than we claim?"[63]

Some Free Soilers, Cassius Clay for example, referred to amalgamation as "illicit commerce with the Negro," and predicted that "our morals are to be still more corrupted with more mulattoes to stand as eternal curses . . . most damning monuments of our self-abasement and crime, diluting the boasted purity of our Saxon blood."[64] Similarly, Reverend Whipple stated that "I do not like to see such an amalgamation of colour . . . . As cooly as some may talk of amalgamation, I for one can never be reconciled to this heterogeneous mingling of colours. Give me either the blood of the white, or that of the black." To Whipple, mulattoes were a "sickly" and "jaundiced" race.[65] It was for reasons such as these that some Free Soil editors, Eastman for instance, argued the "futility of all attempts . . . to amalgamate [the] races."[66]

White opposition to amalgamation can, perhaps, be reduced to three basic fears. One, of course, was the fear that the white race would be weakened biologically. In addition, there were political and social fears. Giddings referred to the "descendants of Mr. Jefferson and of Martha Washington, who were well known throughout the country to be [no] more than half white." He then asked fellow Congressmen the rhetorical question: did "such mixture improve or deteriorate a man?"[67] Another liberal Free Soiler from Ohio, Salmon P. Chase, sometimes expressed concern over the threat to the purity of the Caucasian population. On one occasion, when speaking of mulattoes, Chase stated that "Ohio desires a homogeneous [white] population and does not desire a population of varied character."[68] Lincoln put his finger on the nub of the political fear. For a society to be truly democratic, and for all its members to enjoy the full blessings of citizenship, it must, he insisted, be racially homogeneous, by which he meant, all white. Black people, to Lincoln's thinking, represented an inferior population, and hence a threat to the total dominance of the white race.[69] George Brown's *Alton Weekly Courier* raised what was perhaps the white man's ultimate social fear; it warned its readers that miscegenation might lead to social equality for black males, which many Free Soilers further extrapolated into sexual equality. His newspaper presented an article signed by "Yeoman," in which a Southern slaveholder asked a Northern reporter: "how would you like to hev a nigger feelin just as good as a white man? How'd you like to hev a nigger steppin up to yer darter?"[70]

As the capstone to their argument against amalgamation, Western Free Soilers turned to a familiar theme. Racial mixing, they averred, was no part of God's plan for either Caucasians or Negroes; He had created the races separately and intended for them to remain separate. Agreeing with Louis Agassiz and John Van Evrie, a number of Free Soilers—among them Cassius Clay, Salmon Chase, Thomas Stewart, Eastman and Corwin—insisted that God had destined black people for life in the hotter, tropical zones. Clay spoke about the "incapability of the Negro's constitution to stand cold." Rather, blacks were "designed" by nature for a "hot climate."[71] Chase seemed convinced that the cooler temperatures of his state of Ohio would keep blacks from migrating there in any numbers.[72] Part of Stewart's contention that blacks were becoming "extinct" in the Northern United States was based on the colder climate of that region, when compared to that of the Southern United States.[73] And, one of the reasons Corwin opposed his country's acquiring New Mexico, was because he equated that area with the "hottest climate on the earth." Why, he asked, annex a region "where the white man could not work," but where the black man could and was presumably destined to?[74] Still, one must not forget the contradiction: despite their professed belief in climatic determinism, Free Soilers continued to express fears about racial amalgamation.

These, then, were the fundamental racial tenets of the Free Soil movement: blacks were inferior beings, whites were superior beings, and the latter, to maintain their superiority, should, above all, not copulate with the former. From these presumptions-elaborated by scientists and writers and adopted by politicians-followed the rest of the Free Soil doctrine, not, it must be added, without plenty of further contradictions.

II

Since the Caucasian or Anglo-Saxon was the most advanced race, said Free Soilers, it was destined in North America to rule the continent from sea to sea. And, since the Negro was the most retarded race, said Free Soilers, it must not be permitted to stand in the way of this process. In fact, God had already insured that it would not. He had, they said, given the black race an affinity for climates warmer than that of most or all of North America. The trouble was that this God-given remedy for separating the races was being thwarted in the American South by a system of labor which held the two races together. Slavery in that region was already leading to increases in the black population, to the kind of racial amalgamation which polluted the pure white blood with inferior black blood, and to the danger of racial conflict. Worse still, Southern slaveholders were pressing to take their chattels into the Western territories. Once blacks were in the territories, not only would increased amalgamation and the deterioration of the white race continue apace, but other unhappy consequences would follow. Here Western Free Soilers placed special emphasis on the degrading effects of mere association with blacks, the competition which black laborers would provide for white laborers, and the direct relationship between the spread of slavery and the still further growth of the black population.

As if to illustrate the point that slavery was preventing God's climatic solution for precluding amalgamation from operating, Western Free Soilers depicted the slave South, with its large black population, in allegorical terms, as a dark or black region, a region which bred mulattoes and which, therefore, posed a threat to the dream of an homogeneous, purely white United States. Kinsley Bingham, while describing the North and its predominately white population as Anglo-Saxonized, put the South and its black population beyond the pale of the superior race.[75] Kentuckian Cassius Clay, an admirer, he said, of the free North, stated that the "ratio of the increase of the blacks upon a given basis, diminishes [in the North] compared with the increase in slavery," under which there was "amalgamation of the two races . . . . "[76] Giddings expressed a concern that the swollen black population of the South could spill into the North. If the "slaves [in the South] . . . are to increase," he warned, the "number of fugitives [coming North] will of course increase more rapidly." This Ohio Congressman on several occasions ridiculed the South because of the racial mixture of its population. He asked: Was the "genealogy of the slave" important "in estimating his value? If he have descended in the paternal line from one of the best families in the 'Old Dominion,' shall he be deemed of greater value than though he were of pure African blood?"[77] Whipple expressed dismay at the range of racial hues among Southerners; "I have not seen a place . . . where there is such an endless variety of shades and colours."[78] Chase seemed to consider the South a separate racial region. Writing to a colleague about the growth of antislavery politics in the North, he asked if it were "not about time to carry the war [against slavery] into Africa?"[79] Joseph Forrest nicely summed up such opinions when he labelled the South, the "Sable Republic."[80]

As well as seeing the South as a darkening region where the races amalgamated, Western Free Soilers saw it as a tinder box which could easily ignite with slave insurrections and racial conflict. The danger, they declared, was directly proportional to the increasing number of slaves. Bingham wrote to his wife that "this is really the safest country in the world, and yet this vast Negro population of the Southern states may make us trouble and produce civil commotion."[81] Thomas Corwin of Ohio called slavery a "troublesome institution," because "it requires too much law, too much force, to keep up social and domestic security." The slave, he feared, would someday revolt and "upturn the order of society."[82] Cassius Clay, speaking directly to the slaveholders of his state, asked them: "What right [do you have] to keep powder in your houses, which may blow up the 600,000 free whites of our unhappy country [Kentucky]?" Clay admitted that, given its present rate of growth, he was "forced . . . to the conclusion that the slave population must increase till there is no retreat but in the extermination of the whites."[83] Corwin's fellow Ohioan, Joshua Giddings, painted a picture almost as bleak as Clay's. In 1852 he warned Congress that if it allowed the number of black slaves to increase, especially by annexing Cuba, "with its present slave population . . . you and I may live to see our slave states devastated by a servile war . . . . Fire and sword will be carried by the infuriated slaves of the plantations and villages." Giddings further prophesied that some "eight hundred thousand free colored people in the neighboring [Caribbean] islands will sympathize with them [and] some [Frederick] Douglass, some [Charles] Remond, some [Samuel] Ward, or other hero, will be found to plan and conduct insurrections."[84]

To Free Soilers the South was not satisfied merely to people itself with inferior blacks; it was intent on peopling the Western territories with them. There the latter would be anathema to free white labor, according to Free Soilers. Congressman Jesse Olds Norton of Illinois said that the very idea of personal contact with the black man was enough to cause revulsion in the blood of the proud Anglo-Saxon worker. "It is idle," he declared, when speaking of white laborers, "that these men can be placed alongside of the Negro . . . . The blood of every freeman, be he Saxon or Celt, recoils from such a degrading equality."[85] When addressing Congress in 1845 on the subject of the annexation of Texas, Jacob Brinkerhoff, Representative from Ohio, claimed that laborers from the North would simply "not go and plough, and dig, and chop and grub by the side of the Negroes of the South."[86]

Perhaps not; yet Free Soil politicians still railed against the competitive threat that black workers would supposedly pose for white workers, if slavery were to expand westward; because, notwithstanding their statements made on other occasions that, given his indolence and inefficiency, the black worker would be unable to compete successfully with the white worker, as a slave he could be forced to work. Forrest proclaimed that "poor white boys want some of the new territory, where they can go and mend their fortunes, without coming into competition . . . with the slave." Applying the same thought to California, he stated that "our white boys say that God had given every man two hands, and that he has a right to pick or dig gold with them. But, when a man undertakes to bring [to California] a whole drove of slaves and pick and dig gold away from freemen, they will not stand it."[87] Benjamin Wade also maintained that the presence of blacks in the territories would destroy a labor preserve meant for whites. On one occasion, when addressing Senator Archibald Dixon of Kentucky, he charged that "your statesmanship is Africanized and you want to Africanize this whole [Western] territory." On another occasion, Wade ridiculed a Southern Congressman because, he said, the latter was upset that he could not take into the free territories to work for him "his old 'mammy' . . . who nursed and brought him up to manhood."[88] Lincoln held a similar view on the future of the territories as a white labor sanctuary. "We want them," he said at Peoria, Illinois, in 1854, "for the homes of white people. This they cannot be . . . if slavery shall be planted within them."[89]

Many Western Free Soilers expressed another concern, one also being expressed by Eastern Free Soilers. If slavery were allowed to expand into the free territories, not only would the black man be diffused over a wider geographical area, but the size of the general black population would increase more rapidly. Such an increase would directly threaten the dream of an homogeneous white population in the West and in the country as a whole.

Schenck declared that "whenever you open up new fields to be occupied by slave labor . . . you establish new markets for slave property, and increase its value in the states where it now exists." By increasing the monetary value of slaves, slavery expansion would, he concluded, also "promote an increase of the number of slaves. Early marriages among them will be encouraged, [and] . . . by all the laws of population and subsistence, add to their number."[90] James Grimes of Iowa expressed consternation over the growing number of black people in neighboring Missouri. He asserted that since Missouri's entrance into the Union as a slave state, "they have increased from that time to the present, at the rate of three thousand a year, and Missouri now contains more than a hundred thousand slaves."[91] Likewise Representative Caleb B. Smith of Indiana, when quoting Jefferson, pointed out to his congressional colleagues, that "'under the mild treatment our slaves experience . . . this blot in our country increases as fast or faster than the whites.'"[92] Referring to this same expansion, Brinkerhoff asked fellow Congressmen if they were ready to "expand and multiply . . . human shambles?"[93] Representative Owen Lovejoy of Illinois likened the expansion of the Southern black population to that of a "fantastic ape,"[94] while Schuyler Colfax described it as a "cancer," an "unmitigated curse" and, utilizing the metaphor of race so popular among Free Soilers, urged that it not "be allowed to darken that great basin of our country, between our present frontier and the Rocky Mountains, soon to be densely peopled with all the accessories of Anglo-Saxon civilization."[95] Could "any man believe," Bingham of Michigan asked, "that this unexampled increase in population, whether of slave or free [blacks]," would have occurred, "if they [black slaves] had been confined to the original slave states?"[96]

Lastly, Free Soilers were apprehensive that black slaves taken into the territories would not only increase in number but would one day become free blacks. According to this view, Western Caucasians would then be faced with a vast free black population in their midst. Pettit, in addressing this supposedly potential problem averred that the "idea that Negroes, if they are to go there, are [eventually] to be free and freemen, is to my mind preposterous." Why was it preposterous? Because, said Pettit, "all history and all experience have shown that two distinct and separate races cannot live upon the same territory, under the same government, on an equality."[97]

III

It is obvious, then, that the involvement of Western Free Soilers in antislavery politics was in the main motivated by their concern for the welfare of white people—a welfare they saw threatened by slavery and black people. They prided themselves on being identified with the dominant race, or politically with a "white man's party;" and, no more than Eastern Free Soilers, did they manifest interest in the welfare of blacks, whether slave or free. As noted above, many of the public statements made by Free Soil politicians point to this conclusion, but it can be instructive to emphasize that these people could establish their priorities with great clarity. When Thomas Hart Benton spoke in St. Louis against the expansion of slavery he reasoned as follows: "I look at white people and not at black ones; I look to the peace and reputation of the race to which I belong."[98] Cassius Clay on one occasion put it this way: "Every feeling of association and instinctive sentiment of self-elevation, lead me to seek the highest welfare of the white, whatever may be the consequences of liberation to the African." Perhaps indicative of the Free Soilers' fear and hatred of black people, on another occasion he said, still more pointedly, that if they sought an end to slavery it was "not because we love the black man best, for we do not love him as well; we confess we are full of prejudice."[99] Schenck openly avowed that his major reason for opposing the expansion of slavery was "in justice to the rights of the whites."[100]

Much of the Free Soil opposition to the Kansas and Nebraska bill was based on the grounds of white interest. Richard Yates announced that "if slaveholders are permitted to take their slaves into Nebraska and Kansas, the inequality and injury are to the free white men of the North and South." He said nothing about the greater "inequality and injury" suffered by the black slave.[101] Nor did James M. Morgan, the Iowa editor of the antislavery *Burlington Telegraph*, when he warned that passage of the bill would mean that "Negroes [slaves] may go there but foreigners [European immigrants] cannot . . . . "[102] Another Free Soiler, Congressman Lewis D. Campbell of Ohio, was angered at his Southern colleagues because they wanted black slaves admitted into new territories, but still more because they wanted them counted for purposes of congressional apportionment. Campbell was adamant on the point: "a nigger shall not be regarded [as] an inhabitant."[103]

If by "inhabitant," Campbell meant 'citizen,' he was revealing a tender nerve among Free Soilers. Troubled that the expansion of black people as slaves could compromise the welfare of whites, they were also worried about what an end to slavery might do. Lincoln expressed anxiety over what would happen to the rights of whites if the slaves were suddenly freed. Speaking in Peoria, Illinois, he asked his white audience whether it would be right to "free them, and make them politically and socially our equals? My own feelings will not admit of this . . . [and] we well know that those of the great mass of white people will not." In keeping with this sentiment Lincoln, during his early political career, had opposed suffrage for free blacks.[104]

Following such logic, most Free Soilers denounced the handful of radical abolitionists of the Garrisonian and Phillipsian persuasion who, regardless of consequences, sought the immediate end of Southern slavery and equal social and political rights for black people. Caleb B. Smith insisted that "there was a vast difference between advocating the principle of free soil and advocating these ultra notions, which would place the black race on the same social platform with the whites." He had "never believed, that those who desired the free soil principle . . . would advance these propositions, looking as they did rather to the disorganization of society."[105] Fellow Indiana Free Soiler Pettit held American blacks in such low esteem, that he declared it "utterly impossible that a Negro can become a citizen."[106] Brinkerhoff, who supported the Wilmot Proviso as the "Thomas Jefferson Proviso," also wanted to disassociate the Free Soil movement from radical abolitionism. The adoption of the Proviso, he predicted, would "prevent any question of abolitionism arising hereafter."[107]

One problem with the abolitionists, according to Cassius Clay and Pettit, was that their creed was based on the false premise that there was a higher law and the Declaration of Independence was its expression. Clay, who described himself as a "practical abolitionist," called the advocates of such notions "incendiaries."[108] Addressing Congress, Pettit stated that "as to ultra, extreme abolitionism, I hope there is not much of it here," and attacked the higher law doctrine head-on. "It is alleged [by abolitionists] that all men are created equal, and the Declaration of Independence is referred to, to sustain that position." That position, Pettit proclaimed, "is not true in fact; it is not true in law; it is not true physically, mentally, or morally . . . . I hold it to be a self-evident lie." Only a sentimental fool, Pettit added, could believe such nonsense. He, for one, had "no sickly sympathy with the Negro. I am not one of that class of men who are constantly harping upon the wrongs of the degraded or degenerate blacks."[109]

Another problem with the abolitionists, according to Free Soilers Wright, Benton and Colfax, was that the cure which they proposed was worse than the disease. Wright observed that although "he regarded slavery as an evil . . . he looked upon the proceedings of those miserable abolitionists as far worse."[110] "Reckless fanatic" and "wicked incendiary" were the words Thomas Benton used to dub the radical abolitionist. Such people, he averred, formed societies that "had already perpetrated more mischief than the joint remainder of all their lives spent in prayers of contrition and in works of retribution could ever atone for." Specifically, he charged, these radicals published tracts which did nothing to contribute "to the understandings of the slaves, but to their passions . . . inspiring vague hopes and stimulating abortive and fatal insurrections."[111] When writing to William H. Seward, Colfax, after flatly denying he was an abolitionist, deprecated the abolitionists' "agitation for agitation's sake" which, he held, was threatening the very continuance of the Union.[112] As an earnest of their opposition to the objectives of the abolitionists Lincoln, together with Illinois legislator Dan Stone, introduced into the Illinois General Assembly in 1837 a series of resolutions. These stated that the United States Congress had no constitutional right to interfere with slavery in the individual states. One of the resolutions admitted that the "institution of slavery is founded on both injustice and bad policy, but that the promulgation of abolition doctrines tends rather to increase than abate its evils."[113]

Other Free Soilers, such as Benjamin Wade, Schenck, Chase, Representatives Henry Smith Lane of Indiana and Orville H. Browning of Illinois, and Senator James R. Doolittle of Wisconsin all, at one time or another, expressed hostility toward radical abolitionism, and several stated that they would have no qualms in voting for a Southern slaveholder for President of the United States.[114] Whipple captured the position of many

Western Free Soilers on radical abolitionism, when he stated that "if to be opposed to the immediate emancipation of the slave is to be a proslavery man, I am one."[115]

IV

In light of the double threat that, on the one hand, the 'black' South, and its objective of expanding slavery and, on the other hand, abolitionism, and its objective of immediately freeing the slaves, allegedly posed to the welfare of their race and to their dream of an homogeneous white America, Western Free Soilers joined Eastern Free Soilers in endorsing various remedies espoused by the learned and scientific people. These remedies, which Free Soilers usually proposed under the rubric of antislavery, had one thing in common; whether opposing further annexation of territory, supporting containment, or calling for colonization, all of them had as their purpose ultimately to segregate white Americans from contacts with or economic competition from blacks, or those with an admixture of black ancestry, and other so-called inferior breeds, or darker skinned peoples.

Since a number of Free Soilers equated warmer climates with 'inferior breeds' and racial amalgamation, one way to avoid these racial contacts would be to prevent the annexation of more territory containing such undesirable populations. Accordingly, many Western Free Soilers opposed the acquisition by the United States of territories, such as the Great Southwest or Cuba, with their Mexican or mestizo elements. When addressing Congress during the lengthy debates over the Mexican War, Representative Joseph Root of Ohio referred to Mexicans as "greasers," a "debased people," who were "descendants of the old Spaniards, with a pretty considerable dash of the Negro and the Indian in them." He opposed the annexation of Mexican territories because it would mean that their people, who "were all, white, black or yellow, without distinction of color, [would be] adopted as citizens of the United States, with us." Instead, Root's "sympathies were first, in favor of the white race . . . . "[116] Pettit likened Mexicans to a "bastard race," and noted that an "attempt was made in Mexico . . . to harmonize and cultivate . . . two separate and distinct races. I need not stop to tell . . . the result, and how signally that attempt has failed." The lesson to be learned from Mexico, Pettit observed, was that "men who are constituted physically and mentally different, cannot enjoy, on an equality, one commonwealth together. One must be the superior [race] and the other the inferior."[117] Forrest's misgivings were similar. He opposed the acquisition of Mexican territory in southern California because the people there were "chiefly a mixture of Indians and Negroes." He stated that "all this population in the U.S . . . . would be counted Negro, and consequently inadmissable to the rights of the white races [sic]." Forrest seemed concerned for the interests of Southern whites, in the event of these territorial acquisitions. He believed that the "colored population [within these territories] will be the people who are to decide upon the question of slavery. Their decision will be for liberty . . . and what then is to become of the Southern states, with ten or twenty states of colored freemen flanking them?"[118]

When discussing the issue of the possible annexation of Cuba in 1852, Giddings, likewise took a negative view of the local inhabitants. The Cubans, whom he described as black, should not be "brought into full political association with our people," because they were "desperate" and "degraded minions," who had "little regard for human life." Would such a people be "equal in moral[s]," Giddings asked, and should they have "political influences" equal to that of "our free citizens of the North?"[119] He obviously believed not.

If they opposed their country's annexing warmer lands inhabited by supposedly lesser peoples, Western Free Soilers seemed still more opposed to letting slavery, with the 'lesser' people it held enthralled, expand into the Western territories. In this respect their opposition seemed even stronger than that of their Eastern brethren. They themselves, after all, lived adjacent to or wished to move into these territories, which the very term 'free soil' meant must be kept free of slavery and slaves. And the way to do that was to contain the institution and its chattels within the Southern states. True, Free Soilers, generally, worried that the 'black' South would itself thwart their final goal of achieving an all-white America, and they were convinced that sooner or later they would have to address this problem. For the present, however, containment would be the stopgap to restrict the diffusion of black people and slow the increase in their numbers. Browning of Illinois expressed an attitude typical among Western Free Soilers. "I can," he asserted, "have no doubt of the abstract injustice of human slavery, and as little doubt that whilst the Negroes remain in the country, the good of whites and blacks is alike consulted, by preserving the present relations between them."[120] Fellow Illinoian Richard Yates, "would not disturb slavery in its present limits."[121] Cassius Clay declared that if slavery were not restricted, the black population would increase "in physical power, while the whites is [sic] retrograding in the same respect."[122] Others, such as Joshua Giddings, John Wentworth, Henry Smith Lane and Schuyler Colfax expressed similar opinions.[123]

Western free soilism already had a legal foundation upon which to construct a policy to contain black people in the South: both the Northwest Ordinance and the so-called Northern black codes had been in force for some time before the expansion of slavery became an important sectional issue. During the period of the Confederation, Jefferson had propagated the idea of preventing the spread of slavery into the Old Northwest. In response, the Congress of the Confederation had embodied this principle in its Northwest Ordinance of 1787, which also provided for the political organization of the area under territorial governments. Henceforth black people, held as slaves, were not to be brought into the Northwest territories. The Northwest Ordinance, however, had said nothing about free blacks migrating into the area in question. So the legislatures, initially of the territories and subsequently of the new states formed from these territories, adopted, either by legislative statute or constitutional provision, the black codes.

These codes were manifestly based on the assumption that it was the duty of the territorial legislatures and state governments to protect their white citizens from a black incursion. By severely discriminating in various ways against free blacks, they were designed to encourage to leave the area those who were already there, and to discourage from coming into the area those who might have been newly manumitted in the South, or emancipated in those Northeastern states which were in the process of abolishing slavery.

Those states in the Northwest which were closest geographically to the Southern slave states, namely Ohio, Indiana and Illinois, passed some of the most stringent black codes. To illustrate, in January 1804 Ohio passed "An Act to Regulate Black and Mulatto Persons," which provided that such people, upon entering the state, had to produce a "certificate of freedom," from "some court within the United States;" that blacks who were already in the state, had to be "registered" in the clerk's office of the county in which they resided, and pay a registration fee; and that white Ohioans employing black people who did not have a "certificate of freedom," were themselves guilty of a crime punishable by a fine of from $10.00 to $50.00 for each offense. In 1807 this Act was amended, so that no black or mulatto could settle in Ohio, unless that person posted, within twenty days after his or her arrival, a $500.00 property bond "before the clerk of the court of common pleas of the county in which such Negro or mulatto may wish to reside." Moreover, no black or mulatto was to be allowed to testify in a court case, "where either party to the same is a white person." The original Ohio State Constitution of 1802 excluded black people from voting, and as late as 1861 Ohio passed a law prohibiting intermarriage between Negroes and Caucasians within the state. While these acts were aimed at free blacks, Ohio, as early as 1807, had its own fugitive slave law, imposing heavy fines ($100.00) on white Ohioans caught within the state aiding or harboring escaping black fugitives.[124] One black man expressed his disappointment in verse:

> Ohio's not the place for me
> For I was much surprised
> So many of her sons to see
> In garments of disguise
> Her name has gone throughout the world
> Free Labor, Soil and men
> But slaves had better far be hurled
> Into the lion's den
> Farewell, Ohio
> I cannot stop in thee
> I'll travel on to Canada
> Where colored men are free[125]

Having earlier adopted general black codes of their own, Indiana in 1852 and Illinois in 1853, passed legislation making it altogether illegal for black people to settle within their borders. In fact between 1840 and 1860, as the debates over the expansion of slavery heated up, discriminatory legislation against black people became more severe generally in the states of the Northwest. This was reflective of increasing white racialism. Characteristically, these black laws either provided for outright exclusion, or for the posting of a high property bond by migrating blacks. Since most newly manumitted blacks lacked the financial resources to cover such a bond, the intent of this legislation was tantamount to exclusion. Also, in most of the states of the Northwest, blacks were forbidden to vote, testify in court, possess weapons or serve in the state militias. Securing employment was made difficult for them, because white employers who hired black people were subject to fines. Intermarriage between blacks and whites was prohibited and, despite the fact that some black property owners were assessed school taxes, little or no provision was made for the public education of black children. Some of these restrictions remained in force until after the Civil War. Whenever black codes were submitted to popular referenda, they usually received strong public sanction from white voters.[126]

Laws against miscegenation and intermarriage are especially indicative of the Free Soilers' fear of mixed races. Almost every Northern state had such laws. Clearly, legislators would not pass an act against miscegenation, unless they thought it occurred. The passage of this legislation would itself tend to contradict the argument that blacks and whites were naturally repellent and antagonistic to the point where sexual unions between them would never occur by choice. Perhaps more than any other factor, the large mulatto population in the South would contradict such an assumption.

While support for the black laws came from the many whites who had previously migrated into the Northwest from the slaveholding states, support also came from Yankee migrants and those residents associated with the Free Soil movement and party. Such Free Soilers, later to become Republicans, as Jacob Brinkerhoff, Cassius Clay, Oliver P. Morton, Caleb

B. Smith and Abraham Lincoln, backed the codes. Referring to black people, Pettit of Indiana once told a group of Southern Congressmen, that they should "just take care of them . . . in your own states, but keep them out of mine." Corwin stated that the "citizens of Ohio cannot accept these black men."[127] However, as will be noted, some leading Free Soilers, such as George W. Julian and Salmon P. Chase, opposed the black laws, but they were in a minority. Most Free Soilers either openly upheld legislation to enforce civil disabilities on blacks, or were at best indifferent to the effects of such legislation. The general impact of the black laws was, of course, to keep both Negro slavery and the black man in the South.

Besides the black laws, the principle device by which Free Soilers hoped to keep black slaves in the South was the Wilmot Proviso. As did Eastern Free Soilers, Forrest, when supporting containment, and advocating its application to the Oregon territory, called it the "White man's resolution." It was, he said, the basis for guaranteeing the "vacant territory of the continent, to be acquired by our blood . . . as a sacred trust for the millions of free white laborers who are to be its inhabitants."[128] To Ohio Representative Cartter, the Proviso was the only means for white Oregonians "to guard themselves against the intrusion of blacks into that territory."[129] Others from Ohio and Indiana would agree. Corwin, too, thought of protecting future white interests in Oregon. He feared that if Congress failed to apply the Proviso, with its principle of non-extension, and allowed slavery to gain a foothold there, and if, eventually "slavery be abolished there, [the black man] will be free . . . and any attempt to exercise power over him . . . will be nugatory."[130] In partial answer to Corwin's fears, fellow Ohioan and future Republican, Representative Samuel F. Vinton, would discourage free blacks from either settling or remaining in Oregon, by restricting the suffrage to "white" males.[131] Caleb B. Smith would apply a similar disability in California. While noting that "he had been as ardent and as consistent an advocate of free soil . . . as any gentleman," Smith just as proudly proclaimed that "he had voted against extending the right of suffrage to negroes in California."[132] If legal proscriptions failed, Brinkerhoff, in a letter to Chase, also supported the Proviso, but opted for force, if necessary, to exclude all black people from the West. "I have," he wrote, "selfishness enough, greatly to prefer the welfare of my own race, to that of any other, and vindictiveness enough to wish to leave and to keep upon the shoulders of the South the burden of the curse which they have themselves created."[133]

Implied in their endorsement of the Wilmot Proviso and their opposition to the expansion of slavery and black people was, of course, the Free Soilers' willingness to coexist, at least for a time, with slavery and black people, providing both stayed in the South. Indeed, some Free Soilers openly described slavery as the instrument for keeping blacks in the South. Notwithstanding their reservations about the character of the institution and the dangers it presented even in the South, they saw that if slavery were restricted to the South, so too, would be the vast majority of blacks. On the other hand, if slavery were to be abolished, the black people would seemingly be free to move where they chose; and despite the professed 'scientific' belief that their natural movement would be still further to the south, Free Soilers were apprehensive that their movement just might be in the other direction. In short, the containment of slavery offered a temporary respite from a possible black invasion. True, it flew in the face of the ultimate objective of a Caucasian North America, but until remedies for achieving that result could be affected, slavery in the South would at least keep the rest of the country virtually white.

At the same time slavery, whatever its faults, might provide a more salutary environment for black people than they had experienced in the so-called dark continent. Like the Southern defenders of slavery, some Western Free Soilers joined certain Eastern Free Soilers in arguing that the institution was acting as a school which brought the barbaric African into contact with the superior civilization of the white man. One must remember that at this time it's doubtful if any politician ever questioned the belief in the superiority of Western civilization.

Reverend Whipple became convinced that slavery was the best condition for the black, who was "at present unfitted for freedom. He is not prepared to exercise that noble perogative."[134] Browning believed that, until such time as the black was so prepared, Southern slavery was the "civilizing process," by which the "African savage" would be elevated intellectually.[135] Cassius Clay claimed that the "true African is far lower in intelligence . . . than the American negro," and that even the "dullest eye can also see that the African [slave], by association with the white race, has improved in intellect."[136] Pettit went so far as to pronounce as a "blessing to the entire . . . black race . . . that they have been and are enslaved in this country." The Congressman stated "unhesitatingly and unreservedly . . . that the advantage [of slavery] was a positive one to the black man . . . . Who does not know," he asked his fellow legislators, "that the Negro in this country . . . is infinitely . . . more improved and in a better condition than his ancestors were, or his relatives now are, in the wilds and burning sands of Africa? Has he not commenced receiving civilization?" However, Pettit at another time seemed to change his mind. On that occasion he held the black man's mental abilities in such low esteem, that he doubted whether black people were "capable of receiving [this] blessing at all . . . ."[137]

Yet, the Western Free Soilers who saw slavery as an aid to containment and a means of civilizing the black race were usually not prepared to accept the institution as a permanent proposition. They, as Eastern Free Soilers, looked to the eventual end of both the slave labor system and the black presence in the United States. The question was, how to affect these objectives? The answers that Western Free Soilers propounded were analogous to those being advocated by their Eastern cohorts. Some claimed that it was really only necessary to achieve the first objective; the second would follow as a matter of course. However, there were different views on how this would come about. One group thought that the mere freeing of the black man from bondage, would start in motion a black exodus toward the warmer climatic zones south of the United States. Blacks were thought to be creatures of warmer or tropical climates who, if given the opportunity, would magnetically be drawn to such areas. In effect, this drainage theory of natural migration would eliminate any need for colonizing or transporting blacks out of the country.

Another and larger group of Western Free Soilers arrived at the same conclusion, but by different means. They believed that since slavery contributed to the well-being of black people, its demise would mean their demise. In other words the inferior blacks, once set free, would die out, because they would not be able to compete economically in the real world of free competition. As Dr. Sturtevant and other members of the scientific community were predicting, the black people would be overcome by the superior intelligence and physical prowess of the free white laboring class. This kind of thinking, fostering as it did the premise that after it was freed the black race would, in time, be eliminated altogether, allowed a number of Free Soilers both to advocate a conservative program of gradual emancipation, usually coupled with compensation for the slaveholders, and to claim that any supplemental policy to restrict free blacks to the South would not be necessary.

Zebina Eastman, for instance, as had Agassiz and Van Evrie, seemed, at times, to subscribe to the theory of natural migration. "Colored people," he insisted, "are driven by laws which govern society and nations to the torrid regions of the continent." Give blacks their freedom, he continued, and "they will form and control this empire," south of the United States.[138]

Those who argued that free competition in the job market would spell the doom of the black man, cited the example of the free labor market of the North where, according to them, the black population was decreasing in size. Pettit "refer[red] to Boston and to New England, to show . . . that the negroes of the Southern states, in slavery, live longer, than in the Northern states in freedom." He went on to add that the "Northern states . . . actually have a diminution of black men among them."[139] According to Cassius Clay, the "day you strike off the bonds of slavery, experience and statistics prove the prophecy of Thomas Jefferson, that the ratio of the increase of the blacks upon a given basis, diminishes, compared with the increase in slavery." The reason, said Clay, was that in the labor society of the North, the "influx of white immigration swallows up the great mass of the African race, in the progress and civilization of the more energetic white." The Kentucky politician predicted a definite "decrease of the blacks . . . in a state of freedom."[140] One of the reasons George Brown advanced for attacking the Illinois black law of 1853, was that the black population of the state was already decreasing and, therefore, the law was not necessary. He brought forth county-by-county statistics which, he said, proved his point, and prophesied that "if the negroes continue to decrease in a ratio equal to that between 1845 and 1850, it would only take a few years more to extinguish the entire race in Southern

Illinois."[141] Benton asserted that in a free labor economy, the "white race will take the ascendant, elevating what is susceptible of improvement, [and] wearing out what is not [the blacks]."[142] And, in spite of his professed belief in the theory of natural migration, Eastman, too, claimed that the greater enterprise of the Northern white worker would act to keep black people out of Illinois. Therefore, he did not fear the "advent of a few poor, ignorant, friendless Negroes . . . ."[143]

V

While some Western Free Soil proponents sometimes argued that gradual emancipation, together with the natural working of an economically determined free labor market, or perhaps a climatically determined migration, could be relied upon to rid the United States of both slavery and its black population, most Western Free Soilers, as many Eastern Free Soilers, apparently were not convinced. To them gradual emancipation could better be paired with colonization to offer a more immediate and lasting solution to the 'black problem.' A program, specifically designed to encourage slaveholders to free their slaves by removing the latter and their free brothers from the country, seemed a surer means of separating the races and thereby preserving the well-being and racial integrity of America's dominant Caucasian society.

Various of the specific reasons why colonization appealed to Western Free Soilers have been mentioned, but it may be instructive to review them in the present context. Some Free Soilers favored colonization for the same reason that they favored containment; they feared the threat of the labor competition which the black man purportedly posed to the white laborer. Francis Preston Blair Jr., his cousin B. Gratz Brown, and Edward Bates, all leaders in the Missouri Free Soil movement, expressed this view. These Missourians wanted to preserve the Western territories for an homogeneous and prosperous white working population, and one way to do so was gradually to emancipate black men from slavery and to colonize them abroad. Bates, who was later to become Lincoln's Attorney General, had been a member of the American Colonization Society since the 1830's, and was a one-time president of the Missouri Colonization

Society.[144] Likewise Thomas Corwin of Ohio, a vice-president of the American Colonization Society, thought that it was imperative that the races be separated. He stated that "if you bring slave labor into competition with the white, it degrades the latter. I believe the nigger will destroy the white man in his home [the United States], if let alone."[145] Jacob Howard of Michigan also supported black colonization. He agonized over the future of the white laboring classes and believed that slavery, "united with the private interest of the [slave] owners, form[s] a barrier not easily to be overcome. How to overcome it; how to restore the African to freedom and still preserve the ascendency, the integrity, the rights and the liberties of the white race, is how to achieve a wonderful event in the history of this nation." Howard saw colonization as the answer to this dilemma.[146] In an article, entitled simply "Colonization," Thomas Stewart claimed that the labor of the black man was not wanted in America, because America was destined to be peopled and developed by white European laborers. He thought that American blacks should go "back" to Africa, to help in the economic development of that continent.[147]

Coupled with the fear of labor competition was the ever present dread among Free Soilers of amalgamation, if blacks remained in the United States. Colonization seemed to offer a sure means of avoiding racial mixing. Lincoln, for example, warned of the possible increase of amalgamation, and noted that such racial mixing was all too common in the South. In order to ameliorate this problem, he became a manager of the Illinois State Colonization Society, and remained a strong and consistent supporter of black colonization.[148] Also seeing the deportation of blacks as an answer to amalgamation, Cassius Clay became a life member of the Colonization Society. He insisted that the "difference of color is an . . . impassable barrier between the two races." Removal of blacks would be a step toward the "unity of the white race," but Clay was disappointed at the hitherto "slow progress of colonization."[149] Lyman Trumbull of Illinois, too, believed that because the white and black races were physically distinct, especially in point of skin color, there was no way the two could ever be assimilated. Consequently, the blacks would have to leave.[150] In neighboring Indiana, the Free Soil constituents of both Elisha Embree, an antislavery Whig, and George W. Julian, a former

Whig turned Free Soiler, expressed similar concerns. Embree received a letter in 1849 from one L. Kintner, in which the writer, when attacking Senator John P. Hale of New Hampshire, noted that "Mr. Hale refuse[d] to give of the publick [sic] treasure, to cary [sic] that evil [black people] from amongst us, the ony [sic] way that the evil can be lessened. It certainly will increase the evil to free them amongst us and mix them with our children's blood." Kintner, who opposed immediate abolition without colonization, went on to compare radical abolitionists with the Tories of the American Revolutionary period: "I consider the abolitionist the worst of the two, for the Tory wanted a white King, but the abolitionist wants to make a baboon his equal."[151]

Julian received a letter in 1852 from one of his election campaign workers, A.L. Robinson of Evansville, Indiana, in which Robinson noted remarks made by several of Julian's followers on the need to separate the races and preserve the purity of the Caucasian race. One constituent told Robinson that "'his [Julian's] speech [on the need to end slavery] is every word true, but it won't do to set the niggers free in this country among white folks.'" Another noted that "'I agree to everything he [Julian] says, if he can find any way to get rid of them [the blacks].'"[152] Even more liberal Free Soilers, such as Salmon P. Chase, seemed anxious to preserve a pure white population. In Congress he obliquely expressed worry over Southern miscegenation, noting that some persons held in slavery were almost white. In effect, skin color wasn't always a good criterion for judging who was and was not a slave. However, Chase had a solution to the dilemma posed by racial mixing. As a member of the Ohio Colonization Society, he advised black leaders that their emigration was desirable. Writing to Frederick Douglass, Chase asserted that "I have always looked forward to the separation of the races." In 1850 he opted for a system of domestic colonization to achieve this separation.[153]

Along with eliminating labor competition and miscegenation, Free Soilers believed colonization would prevent the insurrection and civil discord fomented by the presence of what they claimed was a distinct and inferior race. Cassius Clay dramatically called for colonization "in the name of our wives, our children, our daughters and sons, our friends and relations, our homes and our country," because "this nuisance [black slaves]" was "utterly intolerable and dangerous to our peace and safety."[154] Trumbull thought that, because the growing black population of the United States presented a threat of future racial warfare, there was really no alternative but to emancipate and colonize it to a different country.[155] Trumbull's colleague, Abraham Lincoln, like most Free Soilers a supporter of colonizing both slaves and free blacks, spoke about "freeing our land from the dangerous presence of slavery, and at the same time . . . restoring a captive people to their long-lost fatherland." However, he did recommend that this be done gradually, so that neither race would be injured by the change.[156] In 1849 Andrew M. Carnahan, an antislavery Whig who headed a select committee of the Indiana Legislature meant to deal with the black presence, asked for state funds to carry out black colonization. If the races remained living together, he predicted, "there must be a fusion or explosion, and to mingle the Anglo-Saxon with the African blood, is as much to be deprecated as the alternative evil." Carnahan went on to state that the "bloody scenes of St. Domingo affirms the fact . . . [that] a servile war is more to be apprehended, should the colored race still be permitted to multiply so rapidly in our midst, than is a dissolution of our Union."[157]

A final reason offered by Free Soilers in support of colonization, was that the process would somehow both uplift those blacks being colonized from America to Africa and civilize the native Africans. First of all, Free Soilers said that the mere separation of American blacks from whites would free the former from the competition of the latter. Benjamin Wade held that colonization would give the blacks the opportunity to form their own communities away from the influence of the dominant race. Able to withdraw from the menial service occupations which were their lot in America and to learn useful trades in Africa, they could better themselves economically. At the same time, Wade prophesied, the colonists would, by earning the respect and gratitude of white Americans, reduce the latter's prejudice. Lastly, the emigrating blacks would bring to the Africans the rudiments of a more advanced civilization.[158]

As has been pointed out, a number of Free Soilers likened American slavery to a learning process, whereby originally ignorant and barbaric black people had been put in contact with the superior intelligence and more advanced civilization of white America. By colonizing ex-slaves in

Africa, the American Colonization Society would, through them, be sending the elements of white civilization to their benighted brethren of the so-called 'dark continent.' Granted that their inferior intelligence had enabled blacks in America to imbibe only the essentials of the white culture; yet, even these would be far superior to anything the Africans had known. In point of fact, in their eagerness to extol the benefits that would accrue to blacks in Africa, the Free Soilers sometimes seemed to forget the intellectual limitations they attributed to blacks in America. Cassius Clay endorsed black colonization because he thought it a means to "civilize Africa."[159] If American blacks were repatriated to Africa, Lincoln enthused, "they will carry back to their native soil the rich fruits of religion, civilization, law and liberty."[160] Pettit supported a congressional appropriation for the American Colonization Society with the glowing forecast that the Society would "settle it [the West Coast of Africa] with civilized communities," would, in fact, "put civilization as a wall along the Coast of Africa, where these creatures [black slaves] are [presently being] brought from the interior."[161]

An obvious place for the Free Soilers to agitate the cause of colonization was in the old American Northwest. In that section of the country, in contrast to the South, white people could see no benefit deriving to them from the local black population. In reality, as noted, their anti-Negro sentiment was rapidly increasing. So the legislators of the region began to consider various schemes for implementing colonization. Notwithstanding the lip service they paid to the benefits which the latter supposedly offered both races, when these schemes are studied in the light of the black codes which the lawmakers were already putting on the books, they simply provide more evidence as to which race the whites really meant to benefit. Together, the black codes and colonization could rid the Northwest of black people: the codes would work to prevent the migration of more free blacks into the area; colonization, supplemented by the codes, would clear the area of those free blacks already in residence. As perhaps an appropriate indicator of white prejudice in the Northwest and the attitudes of the Free Soilers in the region toward free blacks, one may quote Zebina Eastman, the Chicago newspaper editor. "Political hostility to them is so great, and the prejudice so deep rooted" that they had no chance of bettering themselves. Lest his own feelings on the subject be misunderstood, Eastman recommended draconian measures. There were, he said, only two alternatives for white Americans when dealing with black people: "to hunt down and destroy" them, or, ignoring his statements on their natural migration, "to send them out of the country, to Africa or any other convenient place."[162] In the event, it was the latter of Eastman's alternatives which the local state legislators sought to implement.

Accordingly, in the late 1820's the Ohio Legislature, under the impetus of Governor Allen Trimble, developed the "Ohio Plan" of colonization. Implicitly recognizing, at least temporarily, the continuance of the institution of slavery in the Southern states, the plan provided that Northern free blacks would be colonized out of the country. It envisaged the cooperation of all the free states in ridding the North of Negroes. The problem was that many of the newer Northwestern states, including Ohio itself, lacked the financial resources to carry out a viable colonization effort. Nevertheless, the plan continued to be popular with many Ohio legislators, and in the late 1840's and early 1850's efforts were again under way to implement it. In these years the Ohio Legislature voiced approval of the project and appointed a state agent of colonization, David Christy; but again, due to a lack of funds, Ohio was unable to get the movement off the ground.[163]

In neighboring Indiana, however, some steps were taken in the 1850's to colonize blacks abroad. Under the auspices of Governor Joseph Wright, who would become a strong backer of the Lincoln administration, and aided by the state appointed commissioner of colonization, the Reverend James Mitchell, later Lincoln's Commissioner of Emigration, the Indiana Legislature began making small appropriations for the colonization of Indiana's free black population. Governor Wright, when speaking of this population before that body in 1850, clearly tied the black codes to colonization. He declared that "we in the North are adopting extraordinary means for removing them, by prohibiting them from holding property, excluding them from the protection of the laws, and denying them any rights whatever." Wright fully endorsed colonization by telling the legislature that "in this great struggle for the separation of the black man from the white, let Indiana take her stand . . . other states in this Union have their own settlements in Liberia. Let Indiana have hers." In concluding, he called for a "bold and decided movement on the part of the general government, which will look directly toward the separation of the colored race from the white race."[164]

Likewise in Illinois, Judge David Davis, who would later manage Lincoln's first presidential campaign, headed the drive for black colonization, and himself was one of the elected officers, along with Lincoln, of the Illinois State Colonization Society.[165] Orville Browning, another Illinoian who would wield much influence in the Lincoln administration and served on a committee of the Illinois Legislature, whose function it was to investigate as subversive abolitionism within the state, delivered the committee's 1834 report. It recommended the colonization of Illinois' black population. In 1845 Browning became vice-president of the Illinois State Colonization Society.[166]

For many Free Soilers, such as Zebina Eastman, it did not matter where the black man was to be colonized. The major consideration was that he be separated from the white race. Eastman himself suggested several possible sites. "Let the black man go to Africa, Canada, the West Indies, and he will be likely to benefit himself by the change." On one occasion Eastman recommended Jamaica as a proper place, because black people were believed to be created by nature for warmer climates. On another occasion he backed a scheme, under consideration by the Ohio Legislature in 1849, which would colonize Ohio blacks in the newly acquired Mexican Cession territories. On the other hand, if climate stood in the way of ridding the country of blacks, it could just as conveniently be ignored; Eastman reversed himself when he advised "all the colored people living in the [free] states . . . to emigrate to Canada," because the "law of Canada respects them as men."[167] Free Soilers Giddings, Browning and Lovejoy, also were adamant that some place must be found to relocate blacks. Lovejoy, like Eastman, suggested a plan to colonize black Americans in Canada.[168]

Although Free Soilers usually envisaged an all-white America for the future, a few, George Brown, Chase, Doolittle and Joseph Root among them, backed a scheme of internal colonization, i.e., to set black Americans off by themselves, in separate communities within the United States. It's significant to note that most of these projected black settlements were in the South, far from their own homes in the overwhelmingly white North. Root wanted to give "our people of African blood . . . homesteads and territorial governments in the far South, and invite . . . them to go there and be the dominant race under the national government."[169] Brown stated that "should they [blacks] in time to come, form into separate states or communities in this country, the intelligence and morality [acquired from whites] will certainly render them worthier citizens."[170] Most colonizationists, however, wanted blacks removed from the United States.

VI

In spite of the policies, hostile to black people and abolitionism, which the Free Soil Party commonly supported, there were associated with that organization some people who more than occasionally disagreed with these policies and some who quite consistently did so. Perhaps it goes without saying that those who most consistently disagreed were themselves black. Frederick Douglass and a number of other influential black men had good reason to be suspicious of the objectives of the Free Soil movement. They opposed the Free Soil policies of colonization and of excluding free blacks both from the territories and the states of the Northwest. Nor did they perceive the Free Soil Party as a true abolitionist party. Most Free Soilers seemed to them more interested in containing the institution of slavery than in immediately abolishing it. In this regard Douglass noted that a large number of Western Free Soilers were willing, openly, to support slavery in the Southern states, as long as it remained there. Moreover, recognizing the appeals to race which often accompanied Free Soil rhetoric, Douglass was convinced that the "cry of 'free men' was raised not for the extension of liberty to the black man, but for the protection of the liberty of the white."[171]

Nevertheless, Douglass and some black leaders realized that however imperfect and racially oriented the Free Soil Party might be, there was no other viable political organization to which the black man could turn in his quest for basic political equality. The Liberty Party, in the few areas in the North where it did gain a following, was considered much too radical by most whites. More importantly, neither of the two major parties offered any hope. The national Democratic Party, with the exception of the growing number of Free Democrats, seemed committed to supporting the expansion of Southern slavery, while the Whig Party, unwilling or unable to face the issue of slavery was, between 1850 and 1852, in the process of disintegrating. Consequently, with grave reservations, a small number of Northern black political leaders, best represented by Douglass, slowly turned to this new third party. Additionally, if the Free Soil Party was beset within by anti-abolition sentiment, it still encompassed some white politicians who, although inconsistent in this respect, came at times as close to representing abolitionism in both state and national politics, as any white politicians would.

It has been noted that the subject of race was one on which an Eastern Free Soiler such as Horace Greeley was given to self-contradiction. Western Free Soilers, too, often seemed equally confused; at times their various statements on black people were irreconcilable. Perhaps the reason lay in the dilemma Free Soilers confronted. On the one hand was their political desire to develop an effective new party, broad in appeal, yet distinct in its program from the established parties. On the other hand was the balance that they sought to strike not merely between their opposition to the extension of slavery and their support for the preservation of the Union, but between the various opinions which they themselves held on black people.

It was in respect to this last point that a small number of Western Free Soilers departed markedly from the sentiment of many of their fellow party people and, it is important to note, from sentiments that they themselves sometimes expressed. While other Free Soilers gave voice to racial feelings, these members of the party on occasion spoke out against the stereotype of the inferior black and such well-known vehicles of white racialism as the black codes, the fugitive slave laws and Southern slavery itself. Though it is easy to exaggerate the impact that these more enlightened whites had on American racial thought, it is important to explain their actions in some detail, if only to emphasize that not all white politicians were negative in their attitudes toward black people. Further, these liberal politicians were, in effect, helping to mount a limited attack upon antebellum white racial prejudice and its effects. The mere recognition of such prejudice was, in a sense, a step in that direction, but some of them did more than recognize the source of the problem. They called for the equal protection of the laws for black people and aided black fugitives directly in their quest for freedom. Like the radical abolitionists, whom they sometimes openly defended and with whom they sometimes associated themselves, they, in their efforts to upgrade life for the oppressed black American, appealed to a higher law and its corollary, the concept of universal man. Contrary to the polygenists, they believed that all men were born essentially the same, physically, mentally and temperamentally, and that the environment in which each individual found him or herself explained any differences which later appeared among such individuals. Given the right environment all men would show improvement. Since being enslaved was hardly conducive to such advancement, and therefore unacceptable to white men, neither should blacks be forced to accept it. At such times these Free Soilers seemed less concerned than most in their party with compromising their position on slavery to preserve the Union, and more concerned with challenging the popular racial theories propounded by the scientists of their day and the final conclusion to which those theories led: that the races must be separated. Among this group, which gave some hope to black leaders, were the politicians George W. Julian, Owen Lovejoy, Elihu B. Washburne, Joshua R. Giddings, Salmon P. Chase, and Edward and Benjamin Wade, and the newspaper editors, Zebina Eastman and Joseph Forrest. But again, the fact that the names of most of these men have already been associated in this text with racial views and schemes, only proves that even some of the most broad-minded of Free Soilers were not immune to being contradictory on these controversial matters.

To begin, these Western liberals questioned the stereotype of the improvident, ignorant black. For instance, when Giddings addressed himself to the status of black fugitives then living as free men within the Northern states, he optimistically stressed their initiative. He insisted that "most of them had acquired, or were in the way of obtaining, sufficient real and personal property . . . and even many of the luxuries of life. They were educating their children, and becoming intelligent and useful members of communities." In slavery, too, blacks, to Giddings, manifested intelligence. While visiting Mount Vernon, he wrote to his daughter that "we were politely waited upon by the colored woman, of whom I spoke, who, although a slave, certainly possessed more intelligence and good breeding, than many white ladies."[172]

Liberal Western Free Soilers, such as Julian, Eastman and Chase, were also cognizant of the prevailing white prejudice against color manifested in American society. Quoting positive opinions, such as those of Giddings himself, and of that rather untypical scientist, Dr. James Cowles Prichard, which refuted the dominant racial stereotype of blacks, liberal Free Soilers recognized the irrationality of white prejudice. The "American people," Julian wrote to a group of free blacks in Chicago, "are emphatically a Negro hating people. By their actions politically, socially and ecclesiastically, they declare that the Negro is not a man. In illustration of this feeling, I might refer to the legislation of your state, particularly to that most atrocious enactment known as the 'Illinois slave [black] law.'"[173] Like Julian, Eastman was quick to acknowledge that the "naked prejudice of color may have had something to do with the action of the Illinois majority," in passing more stringent black codes.[174] In 1843, in a letter to Daniel O'Connell, the Irish freedom fighter, Chase delved to the root of the racial problem, by noting the "cruel and wicked prejudice against persons of color, which . . . too generally characterizes the American people."[175]

Not only did these liberal Free Soilers recognize white prejudice in American society as a whole, they were not remiss in pointing the finger of guilt at racial prejudice within their own party. Julian thought that "our [Free Soilers'] abhorrence of the institution [of slavery] is from the lips, and not from the heart. We do not hate it with an earnest and robust hatred that goes out into deeds." Instead, "we hate the Negro with a practical vengeance. It is no counterfeit, no mere disguise, but a blighting, scathing, ever-present hatred, under which the colored race withers and is consumed in our midst." Julian was critical of fellow Free Soilers like Wilmot, whose only wish was to confine slavery and the black man within the Southern states. Non-extension ideas of the Wilmot variety did not go far enough for Julian. He thought that this "cheap and popular method of hating slavery . . . may accord with the frigid temper and technical ethics of the politician . . . but it will not satisfy the fervent, uncompromising spirit of the abolitionist."[176] Chase, in 1844, and again in 1849, came out against all politicians-those who claimed to be antislavery and otherwise—"who issued the most disgusting appeals to the lowest prejudices against the blacks." Chase seemed fully aware of the political appeal which Negro-baiting had among Northern white voters.[177]

Having recognized the existence and irrationality of white racial prejudice, liberal Free Soilers were not hesitant in assailing such prejudice, especially as it was manifested in the Northern exclusionist black laws. Julian, for example, attacked the Indiana black laws, by linking them with the backers of slavery in his native state. He told his legislative colleagues that if they were to "ask the people of Indiana if they hate slavery . . . [the latter] will point you to their constitution and laws forbidding colored men from coming into the state; denying those who are in the right of suffrage; taxing them to support the government, whilst refusing them any share in the school fund; forbidding them to testify in our courts and even questioning their right to travel on our railways." Julian went on to castigate Northern black laws in general. He noted that "our hatred of the Negro has cropped out in black codes in the free states, which rival in villainy the worst features of the slave laws of the South."[178]

If Julian recognized racial prejudice in the North, he still put much of the blame for its existence on the South. Northern prejudice, he said, was the creation of Southern slaveholders and their Northern friends, who were "instilling into the general mind a deeper and deeper hatred of the colored race; cramming down our throats that most wicked and gigantic lie, that our American prejudices are unconquerable."[179]

Liberal Free Soilers in Ohio were particularly active in attacking their state's black laws. Benjamin Wade was one of the initiators in the Ohio Senate of a movement in the late 1830's to repeal these statutes; and to this end he presented on behalf of black Ohioans petitions pleading their case. Giddings and Chase joined Wade in this fight. All three seemed appalled at the consequences which flowed from the fact that under the black laws black residents were not considered citizens of the state. Wade was especially interested in seeking legal means to protect free blacks from Southern bounty hunters who, allowed to enter the state to recapture fugitive slaves, sometimes made off with free blacks instead. As non-citizens the latter, of course, could not avail themselves of the state's legal machinery for protection against kidnappers. For his part, Chase regarded the "exclusion of colored children from [Ohio] schools" as "a clear infringement of the [state] constitution and a palpable breach of trust." Wade wanted the state to establish schools, separate ones if necessary, for these children.[180]

Chase seems to have played an important role in securing a partial repeal of the Ohio black laws in 1849. The amendment for repeal, as he drew it up, stated that free black persons could enter Ohio without having to produce 'freedom papers,' or register at the county clerk's office. Blacks could also be employed without a 'certificate of freedom' and could testify in court cases against whites. Moreover, blacks were to be provided with schools, albeit separate. Although Ohio blacks would still be unable to vote, hold public office, sit on juries, or obtain poor relief, Chase, through political bargaining for his United States Senate seat in 1849, was able to make life a little easier for them and for those who emigrated there. He apparently had no consuming fear of black people moving into his home state.[181]

Criticizing his state's black laws, Eastman charged that "Illinois bowed herself very low to [the neighboring slave state of] Missouri, when she voted to authorize the legislature to make a law which would effectively prohibit colored people from coming into this state as residents." As stated in the prospectus of his newspaper, one of the reasons that Eastman became an editor, had been "to lead off in a thorough system of organization, for the repeal of the late slave [black] law of the state [of Illinois]." Eastman also assailed the black laws of Ohio, Indiana and Delaware. Apparently he, like Chase, unworried that black Americans might settle in his home state, based his opposition to the black codes mainly on humanitarian and moralistic grounds. He viewed discriminatory legislation as a penalty imposed on those of a different color. On one occasion, when a black man was lynched in Mobile, Alabama, for allegedly raping a white woman, Eastman angrily asked his readers if "they ever hang a white man for committing a like outrage on a colored woman?"[182] In this way he exposed in his newspaper the double legal standards involved, and the cruelty and immorality associated with a racially discriminatory system of justice.

Liberal Free Soilers also spoke out against the exclusion of free blacks from the territories, and the economic and political deprivation they suffered as a consequence. In 1849, when debating against the clause in the proposed Oregon homestead bill which would have excluded blacks from any benefits, Giddings dubbed it no more than proof of prejudice against color. In a letter to his daughter, the Congressman wrote that "I spoke again on Wednesday in regard to restricting our lands to settlers in Oregon to white persons. I had sixteen minutes only to speak, but think I killed the bill." At one point in his political career, as the result of defending the legal rights of blacks in the ship *Creole* case, Giddings had been censured by Congress and forced to resign his seat in the House of Representatives.[183] Analogous views on exclusionist legislation were held by Forrest. He, too, attacked the Oregon bill, but did so in broader terms, in terms of a class conflict between labor and capital. The "real question [in the territories]," he maintained, "is between free labor and the slaveholding capitalist." Forrest, recognizing that many with racial views saw the struggle out there as one between the races, sought to supply a corrective, and warned his readers that "he who mystifies this question, so as to represent that the issue is between the white and black races, instead of free labor and the slaveholding oligarchy, has too little information."[184] In this case Forrest was one of a few Free Soilers to recognize that free black labor had the same interests-and therefore was entitled to the same rights-as white labor.

Another Western Free Soiler, Edward Wade, joined Forrest by utilizing the debates over the Kansas and Nebraska bill to issue a call for equal socio-economic rights for free blacks in the territories. According to Wade this bill was not only racial in intent, but was a piece of class legislation. He claimed that the bill "donates large tracts of land to the rich. The white man with millions is the object of your [Congress'] bounty, while the poor black man is insultingly denied this simple gratuity." The Kansas and Nebraska bill was a measure, "which thus outrages every sense of right . . . [and] which had for its object the oppression of the poor black man."[185]

In that same session of Congress a proposed homestead bill was introduced, which specifically excluded black people from its advantages. During the ensuing debate Giddings indicated his willingness to at least allow mulattoes the benefits of the proposed bill. He suggested an amendment, "inserting before the word 'white' the words 'more than one half,'" and went on to note the contributions made to both the nation and his own state by "men who have colored blood in their veins."[186] Representative Washburne of Illinois told Congress that he wished to secure for every male citizen the benefits of homestead legislation, "without regard to the color of his skin."[187] Chase refused to support the proffered bill, because "it is unjust to deprive Negroes of holding property in the territories." When Chase "moved to strike out the word white" in the bill, however, the Senate overwhelmingly rejected his proposal. Chase's reaction was to imply that in this regard even some slave states treated free blacks more fairly. "To extend to them the full benefits of this bill," he declared, "would only recognize in them that capacity to hold real estate which is secured to them by the laws of North Carolina and of Virginia."[188]

In 1854 Giddings indicated his support for immediate political rights for the free black population of the District of Columbia. On that occasion he moved to amend the District's Charter bill, so as to grant habeas corpus to free blacks living within the city, and thereby enable them to protect themselves from Southern bounty hunters and kidnappers.[189]

Some liberal Free Soilers carried the argument for equal political rights for free blacks further. In 1854 Edward Wade, for example, asked Congress to provide equal suffrage for blacks in the territories.[190] Chase, however, as early as 1845, was supporting the national enfranchisement of free blacks.[191] Zebina Eastman was one of a few journalists before the Civil War to come out openly for general suffrage for free blacks.[192]

Free Soilers, such as Edward Wade and Eastman, thought that free blacks should be equal before the law; because, they said, the Constitution, and the government it spawned, had been created colorblind. Wade, recognizing no distinctions in color before the law, told his congressional colleagues that "it has been said here by gentlemen, that they understood that this was a white government. Well, I did not suppose that the government had any particular color." The younger Wade maintained that the "Constitution says nothing about any tribe or race of men; it speaks of persons and whoever bears that character is a member of the government if born within its territories."[193] Eastman concurred in arguing that "citizenship does not depend upon color, and the free black man has therefore, pledged to him by the bond of our Union, an indefeasible right of going to and settling in any part of our common country, with no restrictions which are not imposed upon other citizens." Because Eastman believed that true democracy meant "equal laws for all people," he attacked politicians who continually played upon racial differences. "We hate the distinctions of sects and races," he stated, when in 1849 he addressed the issue of political reform. "In our social and political arrangements they should be entirely unknown."[194]

In calling for equal political rights for black Americans, liberal Free Soilers utilized both secular and religious appeals. In the best tradition of the eighteenth century enlightenment, Giddings fought legal discrimination against free blacks on the basis of the Declaration of Independence and the dictum that all men, regardless of their complexions, were equal before the law. Whenever he was given an opportunity to draw up an antislavery party platform, Giddings maintained that the principle of the Declaration should be included in it. He carried the idea of equal political rights still another step when, to defend this principle he, like the radical abolitionists, invoked a 'higher law' than the Constitution or man-made law. The "barbarous doctrine that white men were not bound to respect the right of black men to live," was, he insisted, "revolting to Christianity."[195]

That liberal Free Soilers in the West expressed dissatisfaction and moral disgust with the injustices experienced by free black people is, then, manifest. But what opinions did they express respecting the deeper injustices experienced by blacks who were chattels to the Southern system of slavery? A few, Chase and Eastman among them, sometimes did condemn that system publicly. To Chase it represented an unnatural relationship between one man and another and was, as a consequence, a violation of God's "higher law," which "invests every human being with an inalienable title to freedom."[196] Sounding very much like a Garrisonian abolitionist, Eastman declared point blank that the aim of his *Western Citizen* was "not merely for the restriction" of slavery, "but the extinction of slavery wherever it exists."[197]

Few liberal Free Soil adherents, however, openly attacked the treatment of black slaves in the South. On the other hand most did defend the interests of black slaves when the institution which held them enthralled seemed to encroach on the rights of the free states. Accordingly, these liberal Free Soilers publicly censured the national fugitive slave laws and worked to end the enslavement of blacks in the nation's capital. A few also labored on the Northern routes of the Underground Railroad to aid black fugitives in their escape to freedom.

Owen Lovejoy, while attacking the Illinois black laws, was at the same time critical of the federal fugitive slave laws. As a Congregational minister defending black fugitives, he appealed to the 'higher law' doctrine. Man-made fugitive slave laws, he charged, contradicted the law of God, that all men are equal before Him and, "if there is any part of the [United States] Constitution or any law of Illinois, that requires us to break the laws of God, then I call on you . . . to come and help me trample them in the dust."[198] Julian acted as defense counsel in several cases on behalf of black fugitives.[199] Chase, because of his legal services to escaping fugitives, earned the nickname, sometimes applied opprobriously, the "attorney general for runaway Negroes." In 1837, in arguing the defense for the "colored woman Matilda," Chase based his case both on constitutional grounds, and on the supposition that color, per se, was no crime. He asserted that "color . . . affords no presumption against anybody. It is no cause of detention or imprisonment. The time has not yet arrived in Ohio, when color implies either crime or bondage." Several years later, in 1841, Chase unsuccessfully defended an Ohio Quaker, John Van Zandt, when the latter was arrested for aiding and harboring escaped fugitive slaves. In 1850 Chase attacked the Fugitive Slave bill in Congress. He likened the measure to a form of legalized kidnapping, and condemned it on the grounds that once a black fugitive passed beyond the jurisdiction of slavery, he became a free man. Blacks were still men, according to Chase and, congruent with his position on the fugitive slave laws, he backed, as had a number of Free Soilers, the passage of Northern personal liberty laws, which granted due process to escaped fugitives.[200]

During the controversy which arose over the 1851 riot in Christiana, Pennsylvania, Eastman placed the blame for the riot on the Fugitive Slave law of 1850. He noted that "liberty is as sweet to the Negro, as it is to the white man; slavery as bitter." Contrary to Senator Thomas Corwin's belief, Eastman wrote that "there is no man so dull as to prefer the latter to the former, and low as the Negro race is said to be by pro-slavery advocates, we do not believe there is a slave from Mason and Dixon's line to Florida, who would not undergo hunger, thirst and severe privations to realize the glorious boon of freedom." One of Eastman's major reasons for helping to organize and support both the Illinois Liberty Party and later the Illinois Free Democratic Party, was to attack the fugitive slave laws as a "gross outrage upon human liberty." This editor, on numerous occasions, expressed in his journal concern over the fate of black fugitives.[201] Edward Wade, with Lovejoy, Chase and Eastman, was also a staunch defender of escaping fugitives; while his Ohio colleague, Joshua Giddings, called for the repeal of the 1850 Fugitive Slave law, and publicly "advised fugitives to arm themselves and to shoot down those who should attempt to rob them of their God-given right to freedom."[202]

Several Western Free Soilers went further than assailing the fugitive slave laws in public forums, or defending black fugitives in Northern courts; they actively helped to hide such fugitives in their escape efforts. Owen Lovejoy, for instance, was a member of the Underground Railroad in Illinois, and he was arrested in 1843, and tried-and later released-for harboring a fugitive slave.[203] Edward Wade and Zebina Eastman were also members of the Railroad and did their part, by aiding and abetting the concealment of black fugitives who were escaping from slavery.[204]

In the late 1840's liberal Free Soilers mounted a drive in Congress to end slavery in Washington, D.C. A few of them wanted an end to slavery in the country altogether. Both Chase and Giddings fought for the immediate abolition of slavery in the District of Columbia. Chase believed that slavery in the District was immoral and, being a constitutional lawyer, that it also was illegal and unconstitutional.[205] To abolish slavery in the District, Giddings drew up a bill in 1849 that included a provision for the free black population of the city to vote on the question. The Ohioan wrote that "I talked with Mr. Willmot [sic] today. He was evidently alarmed at my course on the subject of slavery in the D. of C. [?] Linart of Maine also expressed his perfect horror at the thought that I would permit [former] slaves to say whether they desired freedom [for their enslaved brothers]. I pity these men."[206]

Whereas most Free Soilers at various times endorsed the policy of separating the races through a program of black colonization, liberal

Free Soilers sometimes reversed themselves and attacked both the policy and those conservatives within their party who thought colonization necessary for the survival of the Caucasian race in America. Eastman, for instance, denounced Henry Clay's efforts in behalf of the colonization cause and, referring to Clay's plan of colonization, wrote sarcastically that if the Declaration of Independence were modified to fit the purposes of the colonizationists, it would have to read that "all the black people are endowed by their creator with inalienable rights at the age of twenty-five, to be enjoyed by them in Africa, on the indispensable condition that they shall emigrate to that country at their own expense, after having worked until that time for others for naught." On another occasion Eastman objected to colonizationists "styling themselves . . . the friends of the colored race." Apparently forgetting his own sometimes support for the program, Eastman, at this point, seemed to view colonization as a reactionary idea, a tool of Southern slaveholders to rid the country of its free black population. The constitution of the Illinois Antislavery Society, in the framing of which Eastman played a leading role, stated that the "objects of this society shall be the entire abolition of slavery in the United States, without expatriation, and [with] the elevation and improvement of the people of color."[207]

Julian, at least during the 1840's and 1850's, outrightly opposed colonization, and told the free blacks of Chicago that "especially should the free colored man rebel against the policy that would exile him from the land of his birth." Julian was incensed at the idea that white Americans should "get up an `Ebony' line of steamers for the purpose of transporting our 'debased and degraded' free black to Africa, to Christianize that continent." Julian was quick to point out the inherent contradiction in the arguments of the colonizationists. On the one hand, colonizationists were depicting the black man as sub-human, "too indolent to take care of himself, and too hopelessly stupid to exercise the rights of citizenship." On the other had, once the black man was in Africa, the colonizationists "talk to us about the 'improvability' of the Negro race. They deny its inferiority to the Anglo-Saxon." To Julian's way of thinking, "if the African is a man, and the natural equal of the white man, only wanting equal opportunities, he should be free, whether in America or Liberia."[208] Like the radical abolitionists who attacked the inherent racial basis of the colonization movement and therefore opposed colonization, Julian believed that black Americans should be offered equal opportunities and rights within their own country.

While most Free Soilers wished to avoid the charge of defending abolitionism and, in fact, often assailed the radical abolitionists in speech and print, a small number of Western Free Soilers were sometimes willing to hazard the charge. Occasionally they even seemed proud to be associated with the abolitionist movement. In 1843 Chase, albeit in a private letter, defended William Lloyd Garrison and his *Liberator*.[209] Both Eastman and Julian were more open in their defense of this unpopular minority. In 1854 Eastman asked his readers: "who . . . should be ashamed to be called an abolitionist? We glory in the name, as one significant of the noblest attributes of the heart." Like the radical abolitionists and, according to him, contrary to Schuyler Colfax's ideas, Eastman claimed that "agitation is the purifier of morals, as well as nature . . . let us rejoice then in agitation. It is the hope of the world."[210] Similarly, rather than condemn the agitation of the radical abolitionists, Julian, who had Quaker antecedents, praised it. He denied in Congress that the radical abolitionists "are guilty of inciting or of wishing to incite servile insurrections . . . these abolitionists are generally the friends of peace, non-resistants, the enemies of violence and blood." When writing to William Lloyd Garrison, he noted that "nothing could afford me more heart felt gratification, than to imbibe afresh, the resolute purpose and martyr's spirit, of our great movement, by a friendly communion with its heroes." Far from shirking such an association, wrote Julian, he wished to maintain an "unfaltering faith in our continued labors for the oppressed."[211]

An important philosophical factor that, in their more enlightened moments, set these liberal Free Soilers apart from fellow party members, was their belief in the concept of universal man: all men, of whatever color or race, had the same basic needs and wants and, modified only by outside circumstances and fortune, the same basic abilities to meet those needs. Like an equally small number of environmentalists, such as Doctors James Cowles Prichard, Benjamin Rush, and the Reverend Moncure Daniel Conway from the scientific and learned community, Julian, Giddings and Chase confronted directly the popular antebellum belief in pre-determined behavioral characteristics based on race. Julian admired the radical abolitionists precisely because they "evinced so strong, so steadfast and so vital a faith in the fatherhood of God and the brotherhood of man." At one point, in stating what he believed to be the objective of true radicals, Julian said that "we are to rescue the doctrine of a common brotherhood from the limbo of unmeaning abstractions and make it incarnate in the popular heart. One God, one humanity, one love from all for all. This is the platform of the abolitionist, and this is the platform of the Christian." Julian characterized those, like himself, who supported radical abolitionism, as the enemies of "caste, bigotry and proscription." Instead, they wished to replace these worn out prejudices with the "brotherhood of all men, without regard to race, color, religion or birthplace."[212]

With similar fervor Giddings stated that "if the spirit of justice does not find its place in the heart of the American people, in doing justice to free colored persons, they never can do justice to the white man. The spirit of humanity is universal." The Ohioan frequently referred to the brotherhood of "all mankind," and to the worth of anyone who bears the "image of his creator." He spoke of the democratic goals to which Free Soilers should direct themselves, and declared that the "Free Democracy believe[s] that governments were constituted to protect, elevate and render our race, our whole race, more happy."[213] Giddings made no distinctions here, on the basis of skin color; when speaking of 'race,' he clearly meant the human race. Chase and Benjamin Wade expressed kindred views. Chase, on hearing Jefferson Davis of Mississippi refer to slaves as "cattle," was disturbed by such callousness. Although he may not have fully accepted the notion that black men were in every respect equal to white men, Chase at least viewed them as men, who were entitled to basic political rights, and not as sub-humans with no rights.[214] Wade, in response to the query of a Southern Congressman about whether blacks were the equals of whites, asked: "do they [blacks and whites] not all have their life from almighty God? . . . I say, in the language of the Declaration of Independence, that they [black people] were 'created equal,' and you have trampled them underfoot, and made them apparently unequal by your own wrong."[215] Eastman was a staunch backer of the Quaker Elihu

Burritts' "League of Universal Brotherhood." At the top of the front page of the *Western Citizen,* he carried its logo and its motto; "God hath made of one blood all nations of men." It would be difficult to find a stronger statement on behalf of the concept of universal man. Eastman applied the League's principle to all laboring people, the black slave, the free black worker, and the white laborer. All belonged to the same working class, to the same "brotherhood of man."[216]

Yet, in spite of such protestations on behalf of the concept of universal man, these Free Soilers, though more tolerant and broad-minded than the majority, continued to manifest ambivalent attitudes toward the black man. This equivocation became evident in the condescending manner they sometimes assumed toward him. When addressing the free blacks of Chicago, Julian told them that they should raise themselves up, by demonstrating their "industry, sobriety and uprightness . . . by embarking generally in agricultural and mechanical employments and abandoning those which depress you." As if blacks were not aware of the fact, their destiny, he counselled, was in their own hands, and added that the "Anglo-Saxon must be met in something of the same bold spirit by which he himself is actuated."[217] The task for the black man who hoped to raise himself socially and economically, was essentially one of emulating the Anglo-Saxon. In a sense, and indicative of the double standard inherent in American racialism, the black man had to constantly prove his right to receive equal treatment. As newspaper editor George T. Brown put it: blacks, "like all other races . . . must strive for self-improvement and elevation, to be respected." Before they could be accorded equal treatment, they had to first demonstrate and prove to the satisfaction of white Americans "how independent and respectable they can be."[218]

Some Free Soilers demanded more. Eastman, for example, once implied that to be accepted, blacks must even exceed whites in their achievements. He told a black audience at the African Methodist Episcopal Church in Chicago, that "[your] enemies charge . . . that you are ignorant, lazy, thriftless and vicious, and the state, therefore, looses no good citizens by your expulsion. I am not going to repell [sic] this charge here to your faces. A defense may be more profitably made somewhere else, if it could be made." Nevertheless, he went on to tell his listeners that they "must be the reverse of this [negative stereotype] in every respect. You must be perfect men and women. You must be the best specimen of all that men respect in manhood . . . you must excell [sic] in all things." If that were not enough, Eastman exhorted them to "take possession of the money power of the country," so as to gain the respect of the white man.[219]

Those Free Soilers who viewed black people in this condescending manner were, however, at the least assuming that blacks were capable of improvement. This opinion was an advancement over the opinion of most Free Soilers, who held that, because of innate factors, blacks could never progress and that therefore the only solution to the black presence was to make certain that blacks left the country, either by removing any barriers to their natural migration to warmer climates, or through colonization. In the same way, although politicians, such as Giddings, Chase and Julian, were mainly concerned with defending black political rights, they, in expressing belief in the oneness or universality of mankind, were also chopping away at the foundation of antebellum racial theory, with its basic theme, the creation of separate or distinct races. Even though these Free Soilers were not always consistent in their stated attitudes toward black Americans, they were able to recognize racial prejudice when they saw it, and at times pointed accusingly at their fellow Free Soilers as racists. Also important, this meant that the cause of equal rights for black Americans was not completely ignored within the white political community. There were a few white politicians around who would battle against the continued political oppression of black people. These politicians, however, were the exception. For the most part blacks, like Frederick Douglass, had to fight their own battles.

VII

In sum, it has been seen that, broadly speaking, the Free Soil movement in the West, even more than in the East, was buttressed by racial assumptions which, in turn, were strongly influenced by current theories developed and propagated by the scientific community. The major tenet of Western Free Soilers, opposition to the extension of slavery, was itself heavily freighted with racial implications. To be sure, the issue was often presented as one of preventing the extension of slave labor for the benefit of free labor; but, as noted, its presentation was so frequently couched in racial terms that this fact cannot be ignored. Because they viewed black people to be an inferior race-degraded intellectually, morally and physically-Free Soilers, generally, insisted that their presence in the territories, whether as slaves or as free men, would pose a threat to the safety, economic well-being and racial purity of superior white Americans.

If further proof of the racial content of the Free Soil philosophy were needed, it was again present in the frequency with which irrational contradictions were inherent in the arguments the Western Free Soilers employed. Perhaps the most glaring contradiction can be found in their ambivalence about the relative competitive abilities of the white laborer vis-a-vis the black. Did the Free Soilers really believe that the black laborer was genetically the inferior worker? If so, why did most insist that the competition he would provide, either as chattel or free man, must be excluded from the West? At least those Free Soilers, who avowed that white competition would drive the black worker to extinction or that, if the black worker went West, the application of his inferior abilities, to the territories, would preclude their full economic development, were in their arguments consistent, if no less racial.

But there were other inconsistencies in Western Free Soil thought. Was not the black man, once freed from slavery, supposed to migrate naturally to the warmer zones for which God had molded him? Why, then, did Free Soilers believe it necessary to pass Northern exclusion laws to contain him in the South? For that matter, was not much of the American West hot and arid and, therefore, according to climatic determinism, a natural habitat for the black man? Why, then, did Free Soilers hope to preserve it for the white man? Or again, was not the civilizing influence of slavery in white America supposedly preparing the black man for eventual freedom? Why, then, did Free Soilers support colonizing him outside the country, rather than letting him enjoy his newly inculcated freedom right here? The only way to explain such apparent inconsistencies is to recognize that, running through all of them after all, was one consistency: the idea that race made a difference.

As has been noted, however, not all Western Free Soilers subscribed to this idea. Giddings, Julian, Chase, and a few others fought against the stereotyping of blacks as inferior, and were, at least part of the time, opposed to the black laws and the idea of black colonization. Politicians such as they, were sometimes capable of showing a real interest in the welfare of America's black population, but even they were not always consistent in this respect.

Western Free Soilers, whether of Whig or Democratic antecedents, were to form the basis of the newly created Republican Party. The West became the birthplace of the new party, and almost all of the Free Soilers noted to this point had leading roles in its formation. The major premise of the new party, the non-extension of slavery, was something on which all Western antislavery politicians could agree. Many, whether as state governors, such as Richard Yates or Oliver Morton, or as cabinet officers, such as Edward Bates, Caleb B. Smith, Montgomery Blair or Salmon P. Chase, or as confidential advisors and legislative leaders, such as Frank Blair, James R. Doolittle, Lyman Trumbull or Orville H. Browning, or newspaper editors, such as B. Gratz Brown and Zebina Eastman, would, to the end of the Civil War, continue to exert political power within the Republican Party. The Republican Party represented Free Soil thought come of political age, and with its maturation many of the current racial ideas seemed to find a more secure home in antebellum American politics. Implementing a solution to the so-called black problem appeared to Free Soilers ever more urgent, as the debate over slavery expansion heated up, and the nation drew closer to civil war.

CHAPTER 4

FROM FREE SOILERS TO REPUBLICANS

> There are, however, physical differences. The skin of one is
> black-of the other, white: the hair of one, fine and knotted-of
> the other, coarse and straight; the lips of the one, thick and
> protruding-of the other, thin and compressed; and the
> perspiratory exhalations of the one are said to be more odorous
> than of the other.

James Harlan, 1856

With the passage of the Kansas and Nebraska Act on May 30, 1854,
political antislavery moved from the loose coalition exemplified by the
Free Soil Party, to a sectionally more unified and powerful third party
that quickly came to political dominance in the free states of the North
and West. This new Republican Party, a direct outgrowth of the Free Soil
movement, was born and nurtured in the Western states which previously
had been heavily Democratic. Conservatism on the slavery issue had
formed a part of the politics of this area when Democratic, and it did so
when Republican. Although, as will be noted in chapters five and seven,
a small but important group of Republicans seemed at times committed

to supporting rights for black people, most Republican politicians appeared opposed to what were termed 'ultra' notions, and prided themselves on belonging to a conservative party, one that could, for the time being at least, live with slavery in the South. Instead, they championed the rights of the white man, and all but ignored the rights of the black. When, therefore, a handful of radical abolitionists wanted the black man emancipated immediately and, with full political, social and economic rights, to live in the same society as white Americans, they were openly criticized by most leaders of the Republican Party.

And, just as racial ideas had played an important role in the Free Soil Party, so did they among these Republican politicians. Republican racialists characterized the black man in the same manner as they had previously, when Free Soilers. Again, there was an almost pathological fear and hatred of black people, which was manifested in the same determination to avoid all contact and association with them. The time period had changed, the political issues were couched in different terms, but the views of these antislavery politicians on the black race remained virtually static.

Physically, blacks were still described as repulsive and closer to the animal world. Mentally and morally, they were once more depicted as members of an ignorant, licentious and backward race, sub-human creatures with whom the white race should avoid any connection, especially sexual union. Perhaps more than either the ethnologists or Free Soilers, Republicans emphasized the obstacles which blacks, mulattoes and, indeed, all darker skinned people allegedly represented to the civilization and economic progress of white Americans. In keeping with this view, the long-term objective of most Republicans followed that of the Free Soilers: eventually to transform the country into a white preserve. But the fact was that, according to Republican perception, the Southern states, with their growing black slave population and their seeming insatiable appetite for more territory into which to expand that population, and the Democratic Party, with its increasing support for the expansion of slavery and for Southern interests in general, were part and parcel of the black threat to that objective. Nevertheless, as will be described in chapter five, Republicans seemed optimistic that the application of certain tactics could surmount even such formidable obstacles.

I

Essentially, the origins of the Republican Party can be traced to the growth of the Western Free Democrats. These Free or Independent Democrats felt that Democratic Party regulars were too closely identified with the protection and promotion of Southern slave interests. They began to desert the regular Democrats over the Mexican War and the resulting Wilmot Proviso controversy, and by doing so came to form one nucleus of the Western Free Soil Party. The Compromise of 1850, but in particular the fugitive slave law which constituted a part of that compromise, was another factor which irritated the Free or antislavery Democrats. While not passed under a Democratic administration, the Compromise enjoyed the support of many Democratic regulars who, in fact, had been largely responsible for its passage; and their role in its passage was viewed critically by the antislavery Democrats.[1]

The final affront to the Independent Democrats was provided by the Kansas and Nebraska bill. Sponsored by the administration Democrat, Senator Stephen A. Douglas of Illinois, this measure was passed under a Democratic administration. In fact, the beginning of the Republican Party can be traced directly to the "Appeal of the Independent Democrats in Congress," a document written by Ohio Free Democrat, Salmon P. Chase, and signed by Edward Wade, Joshua R. Giddings, Gerrit Smith, Alexander Smith and Charles Sumner, in protest against the offensive bill which organized the territories of Kansas and Nebraska. Chase, among others, was particularly incensed at section thirty-two of the bill, which repealed the Missouri Compromise of 1820, and with it the geographical line of 36 degrees, 30 minutes latitude, north of which lay that part of the West from which the Compromise had excluded slavery. This Compromise had been described by Western Free Soilers as a sacred trust forever inviolate from political tampering. The "Appeal" called attention to the fact that this trust had been again "solemnly declared in the very compromise acts [of 1850] 'that nothing herein contained shall be construed to impair or qualify' the prohibition of slavery north of 36 degrees 30 minutes; and yet, in the face of this declaration, that sacred prohibition is said to be overthrown." To the signers of the "Appeal" the role of the "slave power" in violating the trust was clear. "We shall go home to our constituents . . . ," they declared, and "call on the people to come to the rescue of the country from the domination of slavery."[2] Obviously the signers thought that a new and more unified political front was needed to stem the threat of slavery expansion, and the Republican Party came to represent that front.

Accordingly, the nascent Republicans of 1854 saw the Kansas and Nebraska Act as a direct attack on the principle of the non-extension of slavery, the basis of Western free soilism. The act threatened to diffuse slavery, and with it the black man, into territories which these Western Free Soilers hoped to preserve for the growth and development of an homogeneous white laboring population. Moreover, once the Republican Party became a viable political organization, other events and issues, such as the Dred Scott decision and the questions of acquiring Cuba for the United States and of reopening the African slave trade, were viewed by its members not merely as political or economic attacks on Northern Americans by the slave South, but as racial attacks on white Americans as well. Given their low opinion, their fear and dislike of both the black man and Southern slavery, the utilization of a racial ideology by most Western Republicans followed as a natural consequence. From their Free Soil antecedents, they came proudly to identify themselves as members of a "white man's party."

To be sure, racial ideology was hardly a monopoly of the Republican Party, but that party expressed it in a different way. Whereas the racism of the Democratic Party was pro-slavery, in that it supported the expansion of black people so long as they were slaves, the racism of the Republican Party was antislavery, in that it opposed the expansion of black people whether they were slaves or free. In other words, the pro-slavery expansion of the Democratic Party looked to the peopling of the West with blacks, while the antislavery position of the Republican Party looked to reserving the West for whites. Arguing the latter point, Republicans could appeal to all of like mind. They could, for example, appeal to those Western farmers, whose desire for land, being apparently insatiable, feared not only the aggrandizement of that land by a few large slaveholders, but also the eventual liberation of their black slaves and the competition for that land that the freed blacks would represent. Moreover, by appealing to Caucasian homogeneity, the new party could also appeal to a broader political spectrum, including recent European immigrants, many of whom lived in urban areas and were concerned about labor competition from free blacks. In essence, armed and imbued with the racial ideology which had been developed by the intellectual community and nurtured and popularized by numerous Eastern and Western Free Soilers, Republicans had a ready made arsenal with which to assault the black man, the South, and what they derisively called the "Nigger Democracy."

II

The Republican Party, and in particular the Western wing of that party, was dominated by politicians who were conservative on the issue of race and who evinced small concern for the enslaved black man. For instance, most Republican politicians, like Free Soil politicians, were reluctant to interfere with the institution of slavery in the slave states. Most wished the party to nominate only moderate or conservative candidates whose policies would be far removed from the objectives of the radical abolitionists. Indeed, Republican leaders attacked the handful of radical abolitionists, who were concerned more with slavery's effects on the black man than its threat to the white.

Republicans went out of their way to reassure Southerners that they had no immediate designs to abolish their peculiar institution, as long as it remained in the South. Wilmot, as a Republican, assumed the same position on slavery in the South, as he had as a Free Soiler. Referring to the slaveholder, he said: "we neither assail nor defend his asserted right to hold this peculiar kind of property. We simply affirm that we have nothing to do with it, and propose to let him and his slaves alone."[3] Fellow Pennsylvania Republican, Representative Samuel S. Blair, said that he had "never known a Republican" who would not resist any attempt to interfere with slavery in the South.[4] When speaking about slavery at Alton, Illinois in 1858, Senator Lyman Trumbull of that state denied that the Republicans had "any intention to interfere with that institution in the states." A year later he assured Southern Congressmen directly that his party would not touch their "domestic institutions."[5]

Statements by other Republican leaders reiterated the point. Representative John Sherman of Ohio asserted that he was "opposed to any interference by the northern people with slavery in the slave states."[6] Congressman Dewitt Clinton Leach of Michigan declared similarly: "with slavery in the states where it exists, we do not propose to interfere."[7] Indianians, Lieutenant Governor Oliver P. Morton and Congressman Henry Smith Lane, announced in identical words that "we have nothing to do" with slavery in the states.[8] No Republican, Jesse K. Dubois of Illinois proclaimed, "undertakes to muddle" with slavery in the South.[9] Using the strongest possible language, Senator Henry Wilson joined Dubois in reassuring Southerners that he and his fellow Republicans had never "expressed," never even "entertained . . . the opinion that the Congress of the United States has the power to abolish slavery in the States of this Union."[10] In sum, Republican policy in regard to slavery, said former Senator, former Jacksonian Democrat, Thomas Hart Benton of Missouri, rested on "non-intervention in the states."[11] For the present numerous Republicans seemed willing enough to guarantee to the Southern states their right to maintain slavery.

Even those Republicans, such as Benjamin Wade, Owen Lovejoy and Salmon Chase, who tended to be identified with the more liberal elements within the party, appeared, by 1860, to fall over each other in their desire to assure the South of their conservative intentions concerning slavery. It would seem that the immediate threat of secession and the desire to preserve the Union interrupted, for the time being, the program of these people for the eventual elimination of slavery and the removal of blacks from America. Wade told his Southern colleagues in Congress that there was no reason for them to leave the Union, because the Republican Party did not intend to tamper with the institution of slavery. "There is no convention of Republicans; there is no paper that speaks for them; there is no orator that sets forth their doctrines, who ever pretends to interfere with your peculiar institution."[12] Representative Lovejoy of Illinois was just as reassuring, when he insisted that the "Republican party do not believe, there is not a man who voted for Lincoln who believes, that we have the constitutional power to abolish slavery in the states where it now exists."[13]

Chase, fearing the breakup of the union, carried his reassurances further. Sounding rather like John C. Calhoun, he was willing to guarantee the South congressional protection for slavery because, as he noted in November of 1860, "disunion . . . [would mean] abolition . . . and abolition through civil and servile war, which God forbid." In effect, the South needed Northern protection against possible slave uprisings. Chase went on to state that "if I were President, the question of slavery should not be permitted to influence my action one way or the other." A month later, when writing to Henry Wilson of Massachusetts, Chase called for "unaffected good will toward the slave states and their people, by every concession consistent with adhesion to principle." While he was apparently unwilling to breach the basic Republican principle of non-extension, Chase nevertheless noted that "under this last head of concession may be included such legislation as will provide compensation [to slaveholders] for escaping fugitives."[14] These views may sound strange coming from liberal Republicans, and particularly from Chase who, as previously noted, opposed slavery on moral grounds. Yet, when considered in the light of practical politics, they do not.

That Republicans viewed themselves as politically conservative and pragmatic is apparent. When Illinois Republican J. McKibben wrote to Trumbull he noted that the "Republicans are surely the conservative party [and] I am proud of it."[15] Jeff L. Drigger, another of Trumbull's constituents, talked about maintaining within the Republican Party a "respectable [and] commanding conservatism."[16] In a letter to Lincoln, Caleb B. Smith hoped that the "whole Northwest" would be placed on "conservative Republican ground."[17] John A. Kasson's biographer calls the Iowan "a moderate . . . who considered a conservative candidate and conservative platform indispensable to victory" for the party in 1860.[18]

Even in its early years the party was dominated by conservative politicians. The first national Republican convention to choose a presidential candidate in 1856 was presided over by conservative members, such as Lane of Indiana and William Dennison of Ohio. David Wilmot was chairman of the platform committee at this Philadelphia convention.[19] More indicative, perhaps, of the conservative makeup of the early party, was the presence of the old Jacksonian Democrat turned

Republican, Francis Preston Blair of Maryland, father of Frank, James, and Montgomery. In 1856 he was made permanent chairman of the party at a national gathering in Pittsburgh.[20]

By 1860 the senior Blair was opposed to Chase's nomination by the party, because he thought him too radical.[21] Instead, father and sons backed their conservative cohort, Edward Bates of Missouri.[22] Orville H. Browning of Illinois, Schuyler Colfax, Kasson and others, including Lincoln, at one time gave their support to Bates for the nomination.[23] At the same time Caleb B. Smith was behind the equally conservative Cassius M. Clay for the vice-presidential slot.[24] In the end they settled for Lincoln to head the ticket; he, as a moderate conservative, would not, they were convinced, disappoint them in the future. Paul Selby, a close friend of Lincoln and one of the founders of the Illinois Republican Party, saw little of the abolitionist in Lincoln.[25]

Given the racially conservative nature of their party and their assurances to the South that slavery, at least for the immediate future, was inviolable in the states where it already existed, it was consistent for most Republicans to disassociate themselves from the doctrines of the radical abolitionists. They were convinced, moreover, that such a tactic was a sine qua non for building a winning political organization. In Indiana and Pennsylvania, for example, Republicans were emphatic that for them to win elections, the voters "must be convinced that the party was not as 'radical' as its opponents alleged. It was imperative to refute the charges of 'abolitionism.'"[26] One of Trumbull constituents, J. C. Sloe, counselled similarly. To succeed politically it was absolutely essential for Republicans to stay "clear of abolitionism and fanaticism."[27]

Following this logic, Republican politicians seldom missed an opportunity to pledge that neither the party nor its membership subscribed to radical thought. After becoming a Republican, Lovejoy rejected the idea that he was an abolitionist, and when speaking before the party's 1855 national convention, he called not for an end to slavery, but merely for more understanding on territorial policies by the Democratic administration in Washington.[28] In stronger terms Maine Republican, Representative Ephraim W. Farley, told House members that he found himself "differing on most every point" with the "Abolitionists."[29]

Republican Representative John J. Pearce of Pennsylvania assured that same body that his party had "no sympathy with . . . abolition mad-caps."[30] "It is an audacious libel to state that the Republican party is an abolition party," declared Frank Blair at a Republican rally in Maryland in 1856;[31] and a New Jersey party member stated that same year that the "party is no abolition, no Radical, no Revolutionary party."[32]

To emphasize the point, Republican leaders further denied that they had the least intention of uplifting blacks. In Oregon, for example, they not only "disclaimed any connection with abolitionism" but "denounced the idea of racial equality."[33] And Congressman Cydnor Bailey Thompkins of Ohio offered as proof "that the Republican party is not an Abolitionist party" the fact that "we have never at any time, made any attempt to raise the black man to an equality with the whites."[34] Thomas Corwin attacked those in the North who, in any way, favored Negro equality, and in particular "Wendell Phillips" and the "Garrison[ian] Abolitionists." Utilizing the flip side of this argument, he then noted that these same abolitionists "denounce the Republican Party everywhere that they can . . . . "[35] Therefore, the basic appeal of Republicanism was conservative, not radical. Republicanism was not to be confused with abolitionism, and this continued to be the party's theme through the latter 1850's and into the next decade. In 1860 Senator James Grimes of Iowa announced that in the unlikely event any abolition ideas might find there way into the party, he would take "the lead" in rooting them out.[36]

As noted, to further disassociate themselves, Republican politicians sometimes assaulted the perpetrators of radical abolitionism by name. Especially vilified were people like John Brown who, to many Republicans, represented the end result of radical abolitionist thinking. In truth, of course, there was only one John Brown; but conservative Republicans liked to stereotype all abolitionists as John Brown's. Wisconsin Senator James Doolittle, when defending a Republican sponsored homestead bill, classified the radical abolitionists with Brown because, he said, they wished the "unconditional emancipation of the four million slaves by force." Worse, they wished these freedman "to remain upon a footing of equality in all respects, side by side with the white race." He called this solution of what he termed the Negro problem, the "John Brown solution."[37] Many Republicans made "repeated statements that John Brown was not a member of the Republican Party."[38] "Abolitionists" of whatever stripe, declared Thomas Corwin, "are not Republicans . . . ."[39] If he had a choice, John Sherman said, he "would not have one single political abolitionist in the Northern states."[40] Although Congressman Eli Thayer of Massachusetts admitted that people like Brown and Phillips had "good motives . . . their judgement was invariably bad. Their methods were everywhere condemned. They never attained to the dignity or influence of a party, or even a faction."[41] Lane was more pithy. He denounced them as simple "fanatics," with no respect "for law, order . . . and the old standard of the Constitution."[42] Lincoln and David Davis of Illinois also described the radicals as dangerous, and "deplored as incendiary" any attempts by such people to repeal the Fugitive Slave law of 1850, or abolish slavery in the District of Columbia.[43]

What all of this meant, naturally, was that the party must at all costs avoid identification with abolitionists such as Brown, William Lloyd Garrison or Wendell Phillips. They were, said Greeley, narrow minded; visionaries, according to Thayer, who "never saw anything as it was."[44] In short, their approach was far too constricted to attract voters in the white community, especially among recent European immigrants, a group that Republican politicians felt it necessary to capture to achieve political success. To the contrary, the Republican appeal must be broad enough to attract the generality of white voters.

Like the Free Soilers, therefore, Republicans emphasized that their party was the party of white people. It would cater to their desires and not those of black people. The Republican politicos spoke of the imperative of defending the Caucasian race, with especial emphasis on its free laboring classes. Governor William Bissell of Illinois called for the "renewed vigilance" of those "who seek to promote the happiness and elevation of the white race."[45] Fellow Illinois Republicans insisted that the United States "government was made for white and free people, and should be wielded for their benefit."[46] These Republican leaders noted that white laborers were particularly worthy of their attention. Edward Bates indicated his support for them by describing himself as first and foremost the "friend of the white man and the cause of free labor."[47] One of Lincoln's most influential political advisors, Francis Preston Blair, applying the same thinking, proclaimed that he would "fight the battle for the rights of the white cultivator of the soil and the white mechanics."[48]

The inference of such statements was clearly that the defense of white men and white laborers could only flourish at the expense of the black man and black laborers; other Republicans explicitly said so. In effect, a dichotomy was created among working people, one which was based on skin color. When Lyman Trumbull addressed the 1856 Republican National Convention, he stated that "it is not so much in reference to the welfare of the negro that we are here, but it is for the protection of the rights of the laboring whites."[49] In the same vein, when Cassius Clay spoke to a political rally in Kentucky, he declared that he was "an emanicpationist . . . [who was] in favor of defending the rights of the white [laboring] man, and not of slave labor and the black man."[50] Writing to the Reverend James S. Davis of his home state, Clay added: "I am for my own, the white race and against all other races on earth."[51] New York Republicans Reuben E. Fenton in the House and William H. Seward in the Senate indicated, in Fenton's words, their overriding concern for "free white laborers over that of the bondsmen . . . . " Seward left no doubt in anyone's mind as to which race he championed, when he told Congress that " . . . the equality which our [Republican] system of labor works out is the equality of the white man."[52] And, David Wilmot let it be know that he too was only interested in the welfare of his own race and color, and not in that of the black race.[53]

Even liberal Republicans, such as Senator John P. Hale of New Hampshire, expressed the same sentiment. While debating the issue of Kansas statehood, Hale told his colleagues that he spoke "for the white race . . . for my own kith and kin, for the white Saxon . . . and not for the colored race . . . . "[54]

When Illinois and Indiana Republicans said that the national government must be "wielded" for the benefit of white people, they meant, of course, that the Republican Party should be the wielder; because, they said, it was "emphatically the white man's party, owing its first and highest fealty to him."[55] Trumbull and Representative William Cumback of Indiana used identical words — "we, the Republican party, are the white man's party," Trumbull adding the following: "We are for free white men, and for making white labor respectable."[56] William H. Herndon, Illinois politician and law partner and close friend of Lincoln, confirmed that once in office Republicans would legislate "for the action of the white people . . . . "[57] And Lincoln himself, doubtless, spoke for the party when he held out the promise that it would ensure that the "superior [economic and political] position [was] assigned to the white race."[58] As a portend of the approaching civil war, Seward went one step further, noting that white interests demanded the "ultimate emancipation of all men."[59]

III

Promising, at least for a time, to leave slavery in the South inviolate, choosing mainly conservative leaders, rejecting abolitionist ideals and idealists, wooing white voters by explicitly denying the concerns and interests of black people—all testified to the conservative nature of the Republican organization. Even more indicative of that nature was the manner in which many Republican stalwarts mimicked the scientists and the ethnologists of their day by publicly charging that black people were racially inferior to Caucasians, and that, consequently, the spread of blacks and the institution of slavery of which they were the cornerstone, represented an evil influence for white Americans.

Republican political leaders depicted the black man as physically distinct and inferior when compared to the Caucasian. Cassius Clay, who was familiar with the work of the ethnologists, averred that there were "physical differences in structure" between the two races, and as an example declared that black people had thicker skulls.[60] When debating Stephen A. Douglas at Charleston, Illinois in 1858, Lincoln used almost identical terms, claiming that "there is a physical difference between the white and black races" which was so prominent, that it would "forever forbid the two races living together on terms of social and political equality."[61] Other Republicans, such as Senator Trumbull, Representative Alfred Wells of New York, Senator James Harlan of Iowa and Representative Edward Wade were more specific, as they emphasized the black man's physical differences in skin color, facial features, hair texture and physique. Trumbull, when speaking at a Republican gathering at Chicago in 1858, observed that the Dred Scott decision would permit Southern slaveholders to carry into the free territories Negro slaves, whose skin color was as "black as the African, with flat noses, thick lips and woolly heads."[62] Wells referred to the black man's skin as "inky" in color, and in terms reminiscent of Jefferson, an "unchanging ebony," while his hair was a "compact twist."[63] James Harlan described these same physical differences, and also noted that the black man's body was "less symmetrical, his face less beautiful," than that of the white man.[64] In condemning the idea of reopening the slave trade in 1860, Wade alluded to the black man as a "thick-lipped and repulsive African."[65] Wade's argument is typical of that of any number of Republicans. He could assail as morally reprehensible the illegal slave trade, but in doing so he reached even lower by denigrating the basic humanity of black people.

Not only did Republicans describe the black man as physically distinct and ugly, when contrasted to the Caucasian but, just as had Wheat, Burmeister and Van Evrie, a number of them emphasized these differences in order to link the Negro to the lower biological orders, in particular to the ape. Michigan Senator Zachariah Chandler drew an analogy between fugitive slaves and "horses, sheep, cattle, mules, etc., escaping from one state into another."[66] Representative Frank Blair of Missouri likened blacks to "horses and other stock," for which the slaveholders had to provide.[67] One of the free state men in Kansas "didn't believe niggers to be human any more than a horse or a dog." He claimed that a "nigger . . . was an animal, a cross between the baboon and the man." This free stater based his conclusions on physical differences, and he asked his audience if "they [blacks] look like a white man? Was not their hair woolly, lips thick, nose flat, skull thick, and couldn't any anatomist tell the bones of a nigger from those of a human being?"[68] In fact, during the debates over the admission of Kansas, Republican Senator LaFayette S. Foster of Connecticut argued that "certain naturalists have traced men down into the race of ourang-outangs."[69] Harlan argued that the black man was directly related to the ape. He referred to blacks as a "species of the monkey race," and insisted that the "negro will be healthy and vigorous in any country that produces the Chimpanzee."[70]

In apparent agreement with Josiah Nott and Samuel Morton, Republicans also described the Negro as inferior to the Caucasian both mentally and temperamentally. In 1860 Senator Henry Wilson set forth his claim about the mental inferiority of the Negro. He stated unequivocally that he did "not believe in the mental or the intellectual equality of the African race . . . ."[71] Seward seconded Wilson's opinion by asserting that blacks were intellectual "inferiors," while Republican Representative William Stewart of Pennsylvania stated point blank that "they lack intelligence." Adding to this Republican barrage, Representative William A. Gilbert of New York referred to the "dark and benighted mind" of the black man.[72] Lovejoy, on several occasions, also drew attention to what he said was the mental "inferiority of the enslaved race. We may concede it as a matter of fact that it is inferior."[73] When arguing against the admission of Kansas as a slave state in 1856, Harlan, citing the writings of the "traveler . . . the historian . . . [and] physiologists" described exactly in what areas the black man was mentally deficient: His "perceptions [were] less acute; his conceptions less clear; his memory, consciousness, belief, powers of reasoning and will more feeble," than those of the Caucasian.[74]

Seward excluded labor skills from the black man's mental abilities. He exclaimed that "it is no longer the ignorant labor of black barbarians [that is needed], but labor perfected by knowledge and skill."[75] In almost identical language Republican Congressman Eliakim P. Walton of Vermont made the same point. He referred to black people as an "incompetent [labor] force . . . of barbarian Africans."[76] And, Seward and a number of other Republicans said, the black man was incapable of being educated or taught technical skills. Representative Philemon Bliss of Ohio declared that black mental deficiencies were of such a gross order, that they prohibited any "natural aptitude of the negro to improvement."[77] Frank Blair agreed. He said that the possibility of improving or educating the black man, even in basic mechanical skills, was so remote, that "a [white] man might as well attempt to educate his negro for the legal profession, as to attempt to put him at a mechanical trade, in competition with the [white] mechanics of my district."[78] "[Y]ou cannot give it [black labor] skill, you cannot instil into it the force of enterprise or the power of productiveness," claimed a group of Iowa Republicans.[79] That was because black people were "deluded [and] helpless creatures," according to Republican Representative John F. Farnsworth of Illinois.[80] Senator James Dixon of Connecticut pictured black labor as uneconomical and wasteful, and basing his conclusions on "David Turnbull's" writings, declared that "scientific improvements and new modes of manufacture" would preclude the future use of black workers. Quoting directly from Turnbull, Dixon told fellow Congressmen that one white worker could perform the labor of "'any two of the most robust of the African race.'"[81]

Like the ethnologists and Free Soilers, one of the reasons Republican politicians advanced to explain the black man's immunity to education and resultant lack of labor skills was that, since his emotional attributes outweighed his reasoning faculties, he lacked the necessary self-discipline. Harlan, for instance, spoke about the Negro's "appetites, passions, instincts, and desires" as being "less manageable" than those of the more rational Caucasian.[82]

This purported lack of mental energy of the black was also partly attributed to what was believed to be the natural laziness of the Negro. He had, insisted those Iowa Republicans, "no aspirations."[83] During the long, drawn-out contest for Speaker of the House in late 1859, Benjamin Wade read a letter before that body from Hinton Rowan Helper, the foremost Republican political and economic philosopher of the time. In his missive, Helper pictured Virginia's black population as a large bloodsucker or parasite which, because of its innate indolence, lived off the labor of the state's white workers. The letter noted how Virginia's "black children have sucked her . . . dry."[84]

This portrait of the black man as mentally slow and lethargic, a person without will or enterprise who loved ease, fit nicely into the picture of a servile race of sambos. Congressman Lewis D. Campbell of Ohio placed some of the blame for the South's alleged economic backwardness on just such a race. Campbell described a case of a Congressman from Georgia returning home. "One of this head darkies escorted him out to the cornfield. The grass was higher than the corn, and he [the Congressman] charged the boy with having neglected the crop. Sambo readily replied 'not much corn massa, but mighty nice crop of grass.'"[85] A Republican leader from Wisconsin, Carl Schurz, when attacking the South in a speech at the Cooper Institute of New York city in 1860, stereotyped black people as "Sambo[s]" and added that if they were permitted into the Western territories, they would soon create "thriftless communities." This influential German immigrant seemed to assume that blacks remained in slavery of their own volition, and told one Southern slaveholder that his "laboring man must be a brute, in order to remain . . . a slave."[86] Trumbull subscribed to the sambo stereotype and described blacks as a "servile race."[87] Harlan, too, referred to blacks collectively as a "servile population," and captured the feelings of many Republicans on the black man's personality, when he maintained that "negroes are an inferior race; that they are far below the white in [mental] capacity . . . and [that] the highest position of which they are capable is that of menials."[88]

Part of this sambo stereotype was ostensibly manifested in the black man's cowardice. Just as had the intelligentsia and Free Soilers, Republican leaders claimed that blacks were natural cowards. Accordingly Trumbull and Congressman David Kilgore of Indiana viewed blacks as a people without honor or courage. Trumbull, by referring to fugitive slaves as merely "runaway niggers,"[89] implied that blacks were people who naturally ran from danger. Kilgore asserted that a Negro could be frightened by his master's simply "threaten[ing] to take him to Indiana and sell him to an abolitionist, and that the very threat causes the poor negro to almost cry his eyes out."[90] One Ohio Republican leader, Louis Krouskopf, was more blunt than either Trumbull or Kilgore; he depicted black people in general as simply "cowardly niggers."[91]

At the same time that blacks were being described by Republicans as a servile, cowardly race, they were also being pictured as having quite different characteristics, those of a savage and aggressive race. David Kilgore hinted at the aggressive tendencies of blacks when noting that sometimes "a negro becomes a little overbearing."[92] Using stronger terms, Seward viewed the black man as barbaric, and tied this trait to his supposed ignorance.[93] Harlan feared that if the black man remained in the United States, he "would remit . . . to his original condition of barbarism."[94] When attacking the idea of reopening the slave trade, Edward Wade referred to Negroes as "black barbarians;"[95] while, when calling for the restriction of slavery, Wilmot stated that "slavery gives to the state an ignorant savage."[96] During the heated debates over the admission of Kansas, Bliss of Ohio, citing "Dr. [Henry] Barth" as his authority, used identical language, describing black people as "savages."[97] In 1859 Governor Bissell labelled all black people as "savage Africans,"[98] and a Kansas free stater asserted that he "did not want nigger traders to have the opportunity to bring here [into Kansas] all the vicious . . . niggers, with which the South was overrun."[99]

That nothing be left from their indictment of blacks, Republicans also described them as immoral, licentious and lewd people. Moreover, blacks were supposed to lack basic affections for their families and country, and were ungodly liars, who had no sense of fairness and justice. Benjamin Wade depicted black women as natural prostitutes, and quoting from Helper before Congress referred to them collectively as "'black sluts.'"[100] Harlan claimed that the black man's "love of parents, of offspring, of man, of country, of truth, of honor, of justice and of God, [were] less reliable" than that of the white man.[101] Senators Wilson of Massachusetts and Doolittle of Wisconsin used the same terms in summing up the attitude of many Republicans on the assumed inferiority of the Negro, when Doolittle stated that he did "not believe that . . . the negro was mentally, and physically, and morally . . . the equal of the white man."[102]

Since many Republicans professed to believe that black people were racially inferior to Caucasians, it was not difficult for them to follow the example of members of the learned community, such as Samuel Cartwright and Daniel Drake, and declare that blacks were a totally distinct race, or species, as they sometimes used the term, from whites. Wanting to place themselves as far from the black man as possible, a number of Republicans adopted the polygenic theory of creation. In 1860 Thomas Corwin told his fellow Congressmen that nothing more was necessary than simply to "look at the black man as he is, and the white man as he is," to determine whether blacks and whites sprang from the same parentage. Obviously Corwin did not admit that they did.[103] Another Ohioan, Representative John A. Bingham, left no doubt in anyone's mind, claiming it "impossible for men to establish" the "physical or mental equality" of the two races.[104] Republican Representative Thomas Williams of Pennsylvania believed blacks distinct, but was willing to "leave the negro . . . and his place in . . . the social scale to the ethnologists . . . ."[105] Because of "his strong conviction of the inequality of whites and blacks," Edward Bates averred that the two races were totally distinct.[106] Illinois Republicans Trumbull and A. Ballinger said that they agreed. Trumbull, going to the highest authority, told the Senate in 1859 that "I know that there is a distinction between these two races, because the Almighty himself has marked it upon their very faces." Ballinger added that "they [blacks] are a distinct race [and] we want them to remain so."[107]

Other Republicans subscribed to polygenism, some invoking the names of the leading scientists. Analogous to writer Mary Booth, Frank Blair referred to what he termed the "ineradicable antipathies of race," and added that this "antipathy between the races is as enduring and deep seated as the conflict between the systems of free and slave labor." He concluded that the black man is "a being . . . alien to our nature."[108] Harlan declared that the two races were proved distinct right down to the diseases each was susceptible to. Addressing the Senate, Harlan cited "Dr. [Samuel] Morton" and "Professor [Louis] Agassiz" to prove it as "settled, that the negro is less liable to the yellow and other fevers, than the white race." Drawing further inferences from this line of argument, Harlan declared that other well-known intelligentsia, such as "[Josiah] Nott and [George] Gliddon say . . . that each race probably had a distinct origin . . . ." The Iowa Senator then went on to note that the scientific "authorities are equally harmonious in asserting that the negro is more liable to other diseases, among which I mention the 'elephant leg' and the 'yaws.'"[109]

Some Republican politicians wanted to make sure that all white Americans were aware of such 'differences.' For example, Congressman James Ashley of Ohio said that there was an absolute need for whites, North and South, to recognize the distinctiveness of the black race, and he was therefore incensed at the South because "no distinction of races or color is made here." Fellow Ohioan Benjamin Wade also was angered by the fact that the two races lived and worked together in the South. He maintained that two such different races must live apart from each other.

"It is perfectly impossible," Wade insisted, "that these two races can inhabit the same place."[110]

A number of Republicans carried the polygenist idea of the black race as a distinct and different race which should not be permitted to reside with whites even further. Indicative of their all consuming fear of the black man, they compared Negroes and the slavery of which most were an integral part to a disease which, like cancer, ate away at the vitals of the nation. One Kansas Republican described black people point blank as "diseased niggers."[111] In 1859 Bates of Missouri referred to the issue of slavery expansion as a "Negro question," as a "pestilent question," which Southern politicians should not agitate.[112] Henry Wilson metaphorically called attention to the "polluting footsteps of the bondsman," which resulted in the "land [being] stained."[113] Others, like Frank Blair, drew an analogy between the expansion of black slaves into the West and a "virus," which "has penetrated and is spreading through the veins of this nation, and unless speedy relief is found, we shall be fatally infected."[114] Both Owen Lovejoy of Illinois and Jacob M. Howard of Michigan were more specific when describing this disease. Reminiscent of a number of Free Soilers, Lovejoy, while addressing Congress, personified black slavery as "a man . . . [that] is leprous, dripping with a contagious disease."[115] In almost the same language, Howard added that if the Western territories should be opened to Negro slaves, they would become "cursed with . . . 'leprosy.'"[116] The "idea that the presence of blacks in the virgin land of the West was pollution of holy ground," notes historian Klaus J. Hansen, "was not entirely metaphysical."[117]

Frequently, in equating the spread of black people with that of a dangerous disease, Republicans, wallowing in the metaphor of race, simply reduced the contagion to the color black. One Republican campaign song for 1856, entitled "Suffering Kansas," called on the country's voters to "rescue the nation from Slav'ry's dark chain."[118] Congressman William Kellogg of Illinois referred to the "dark form of slavery, in its hideous deformity . . . demanding Kansas as its own."[119] Bliss spoke about Southern slavery in Kansas as "blackening the continent with African social organizations," while Republican Representative Thomas J. D. Fuller of Maine simplified this metaphor when he referred to the eventual inundation of Kansas by a "black tide."[120] When reading from Helper's letter in Congress, Benjamin Wade pointed to the evil effects of Negro slavery in Virginia, and warned that if slavery were allowed to spread to the West, Western whites would inherit "this lovely land, blackened with a negro population."[121] Worse, Western whites, declared Walton of Vermont, would be "wholly buried beneath" a "black flood."[122] In 1858, in referring to the Dred Scott decision, Frank Blair claimed that "if the decision of 1857 had been made in 1847, so that slaves could have been removed to California . . . the busy marts of trade and the gold mines of that country would have been blackened with slaves." Blair was particularly graphic in 1860, when campaigning for the Republican Party in Philadelphia. He asked his audience: "must this black vomit remain always upon our stomachs, turning to yellow fever upon our skins?"[123]

IV

Just as many Republican leaders viewed the black man in much the same light as racialists in general, they, like the latter, also viewed the Caucasian in quite a different light: as a being physically, mentally and morally superior to the black man. Similar to a number of learned writers and many Free Soilers, they saw this superiority as particularly evident in the Anglo-Saxon portion of the Caucasian race.[124] In fact, for many Republicans, as for many in the other two groups, the Caucasian race was synonymous with that Anglo-Saxon portion. Presumably, in this ethnocentric scheme, other Caucasoid peoples ranked below the Anglo-Saxon, but at the same time far above the Native American or African. To Harlan, white meant Anglo-Saxon, and on several occasions he spoke about what he called the "admitted inferiority of the African to the Anglo-Saxon."[125] Frank Blair declared that the white man was physically superior to any race on earth, especially the Negroid race. He discussed the "beauty of that fair and glorious line which we believe to be in form and soul the noblest development of mankind."[126] Harlan, too, referred to the superior beauty of the latter, and facetiously asked his fellow Congressmen if anyone had "proposed to make the negro, by law, as beautiful as the Anglo-Saxon; as symmetrical in his proportions?"[127]

Morally and mentally the same contrast between the races held true. Suggestive of Samuel Morton, Frank Blair pronounced the white race the most moral in the world. Harlan wanted to know if any Congressman "proposed to make him [the black man] his [the Anglo-Saxon's] equal in intellectual development, or in moral sensibilities?"[128] The "vigor of industry and enterprise," Howard claimed, were exclusively "inherited in the white man."[129] In 1858, when Republican Senator Preston King of New York spoke about the successful laying of the Atlantic cable he, too, dwelt on the superior intellectual and physical powers of the Anglo-Saxons, and gave credit to the same factor emphasized by DeGobineau; "this [feat] had been accomplished by the blood of the race. It is the strong Caucasian blood, in which there is not a bad drop, that has done it. It is the brain, the blood, and the vital force of the Anglo-Saxon race that has placed the cable at the bottom of the ocean."[130]

This fascination with the blood of the Caucasian affected a number of Republicans besides King. They too, consistent with Parker, DeGobineau and the ethnologists, viewed the Anglo-Saxon's alleged superiority as a biological product of that blood. When Ashley of Ohio spoke of white blood, he described it as the "best blood of the dominant race," meaning, of course, what he and other politicians erroneously called the Anglo-Saxon race.[131] In neighboring Pennsylvania Republican Representative James H. Campbell said so specifically, glorifying the "unconquerable blood of the Anglo-Saxon race."[132] The Reverend James Mitchell of Indiana declared that the Anglo-Saxon's superior qualities were a direct product of his blood.[133] Carl Schurz seemed enthused when noting that the Anglo-Saxons "pride themselves on their unadulterated Anglo-Saxondom" and their ability to remain pure blooded "without absolutely absorbing the other national elements."[134] In 1858 fellow Wisconsin Republicans referred to the Anglo-Saxons as a race possessing "free blood,"[135] apparently meaning that Anglo-Saxons had a biological monopoly on the desire to be free.

The idea that Anglo-Saxons were a uniquely freedom-loving people found support among Republicans, as it had among Free Soilers. Some politicians made a direct connection between physical features and political preference. To illustrate, when Representative Samuel G.

Andrews of New York spoke of the Anglo-Saxons, he told Congress that "their sympathies for freedom" were "as irradicable as" their "blue eyes and flaxen hair . . . ."[136] Benjamin Wade talked of the "old guarantees of liberty" which, he insisted, the "Anglo-Saxon race everywhere have considered sacred."[137] "Anglo-Saxon justice, civilization and Christianity have prevailed," Frank Blair boasted, whenever they have come into contact with the cultures of other races.[138] Trumbull dealt with what he said was the strong spirit of self-determination among the Anglo-Saxons and noted how the "Anglo-Saxon race struggled hard against the encroachment of government."[139] There was a proud, defiant, independent spirit described here, which the so-called inferior, darker skinned races supposedly lacked.

This claim among Republicans that the Caucasians, and in particular the Anglo-Saxons, were a strong, spirited and persevering people, who had an abundance of courage, was widespread. Frank Blair described the Caucasian race as no less than an "heroic and indomitable race," while Vermont Representative Justin S. Morrill noted that the Anglo-Saxons were possessed of "inherent energy." John Sherman, in affirmation of Blair's statement, called attention to the "cool, determined courage and resolution, which forms the striking characteristic of the Anglo-Saxon race."[140] In 1856 Eli Thayer of Massachusetts, who headed, among other things, an emigrant aid company to settle Kansas with white immigrants, glorified the Anglo-Saxons while assailing Democratic policies in Kansas. The "Saxon spirit, so long dormant, and forbearing under insult and persecution . . . ," he stated at Worcester, Massachusetts, "could not brook this willful outrage." Thayer insisted that "deep in the nature of this race is found that untamable ferocity, which fears nothing, but can endure everything."[141] Republican Senator Hannibal Hamlin of Maine, soon to be the party's first Vice-President under Lincoln, drew an analogy between Republican resistance to the Lecompton Constitution and the heroic "blood of the Anglo-Saxon race," which race apparently opposed this pro-slavery document.[142] Harlan asserted that there was no race on earth "as capable of enduring fatigue or enduring toil." In fact he claimed that the Anglo-Saxons represented the most powerful race on earth.[143]

Anglo-Saxon ethnocentrism even found expression among recent

German immigrants. In 1859 Schurz spoke for many Republicans, when he declared that the Anglo-Saxon was the natural "leader" of all the other peoples, being the most "practical . . . with his spirit of independence, of daring enterprise, and of indomitable perseverance." Ignoring the toil and important economic contributions of generations of black workers, he argued that the "Anglo-Saxon may justly be proud of the growth and development of this country" and this was due to the "undaunted spirit of his race . . . the enviable talent of acting when others only think . . . the stubborn steadfastness necessary to the final execution of great designs." In short, the "Anglo-Saxon spirit," Schurz maintained, "has been the locomotive of progress," throughout the civilized world.[144]

For many Republicans, as for many Free Soilers, the alleged superiority of the Caucasian race and Anglo-Saxon people readily translated itself into the concept that it was the manifest destiny of that race to control the North American continent from coast to coast. As a corollary to this argument Indians, but more importantly black people, were sometimes seen as only minor obstacles to white continental expansion. Although Doolittle perceived the black population of the South as a barrier to the expansion of the Northern white population into the Southwest, he confidently predicted that "within the next thirty years there shall be a free white population of more than fifty millions, with an identity of interest in the commerce of the Mississippi and the Gulf of Mexico," and they would not, he insisted, allow their expansion to be blocked, "on account of negroes held in slavery." On a number of occasions Doolittle referred to what he termed the "ultimate destiny of the Anglo-American and the Africo-American races in this new world," and, within the United States this destiny did not include the latter group.[145]

Territorial expansion was also clearly a question of race for Seward, who, because of his stated belief in the mental and physical superiority of the Caucasoid over the Negroid race, proclaimed that the white laborer "must and will have" the whole continent from ocean to ocean. "To secure it, he will oblige the government of the United States to abandon intervention in favor of slave labor." This "expansion of the empire of free white men is to be conducted," Seward asserted, "through the process of admitting new states . . . [and] the white man, whether you [Congress] consent or not, will make the states to be admitted, and he will make them all free states."[146] Other Republicans viewed the issue in the same light. Representative Matthias H. Nichols of Ohio saw the extension issue as virtually synonymous with the "negro question."[147] Although Frank Blair wanted to save the West for the Anglo-Saxon, he saw this process as predestined in any case.[148] Another Republican, W. D. Haley, also viewing the Anglo-Saxons as the "chosen people" for occupying the North American continent, wrote that "if we [Republicans] are true to the purpose for which God has reserved this continent to the Anglo-Saxon race, we shall inaugurate a career of human freedom."[149] Thayer carried this logic to its conclusion when he prophesied that the Anglo-Saxons would not only conquer the North American continent, but the world as well, because of their "sublime endurance . . . proud defiance . . . [and] unvarying courage." The "Saxons will make law and language for the world," Thayer averred, and in its own way his emigrant aid company would help to achieve these results.[150] Harlan was sure that the Anglo-Saxon would go beyond making laws for other peoples and converting them to the English tongue. He, as had Theodore Parker, proclaimed that the "Anglo-Saxon must proceed to enslave the world, for he is now, doubtless, the strongest race on the globe."[151]

V

While Republicans sometimes spoke as if any obstacles to the white man's destiny would swiftly be swept aside, they more frequently claimed that the South and its growing black population posed a very serious threat to the dream that America would soon be Caucasian from ocean to ocean. No better proof of the form which the threatening image of the South assumed in the Republican mind can be discerned than the name which party members applied to that region-'the black power.' The epithet implied a political and economic area which favored black interests at the expense of white interests. Frequently, Republicans simplified the picture further by reducing the South to the color black, in contrast to the North which they naturally described as white. At times they could even wax allegorically; the South was the "Black Horse," the North the "White Horse."[152] Pearce of Pennsylvania was also fond of allegory, noting that the "difference between free labor and slave labor is as the difference between the light of day and the darkness of the night."[153] During the debates over the Kansas and Nebraska bill one Ohio Congressman presented a map in the House; on which the slave states were colored black and the free states white.[154] Once more, the implication was unmistakable: The South was regressive, morally impure and black; the North was progressive, morally pure and white, and for Republicans therein lay the problem.

As a sign of this more progressive and advanced North, Senator Henry Wilson, a personal friend of Louis Agassiz, maintained that the "names associated with American science," such as "Agassiz," made "their homes in the free states of the North," rather than in the slave states of the South.[155] Since it was widely claimed that a white skin per se represented advancement and intelligence, any policy that encouraged an increase in white people was progressive. The appeal to white power was not lost to party members. As opposed to the black South, stated J. S. Cole of Illinois in a letter to Trumbull, the Republican North represented the "white man's cause. I say the white man's cause, for it has come to that pass."[156] Alfred Wells seemed to confirm Cole's assessment, when this New Yorker drew a distinction between Northern and Southern societies in terms of the "Anglo-Saxons" in the North and the "swart descendants of Africans" in the South.[157] Again, as opposed to the South, where the "gates are thrown open to the African," Illinois Governor Bissell noted that his state had "interdicted" only "one race . . . [from] entering her territory, the negro race. Illinois," he proudly stated, "invites the European and repels the African."[158] Williams of Pennsylvania reduced the political struggle between the North and South to merely a "question of ethnology," a question of the white race versus the black.[159] The struggle, wrote John Sherman of Ohio, in words reminiscent of Michigan Free Soiler Kinsley Scott Bingham, was between the black South and the white, or Anglo-Saxon, North. Sherman expressed assurance, however, that in this struggle the Anglo-Saxons, whom he referred to as "our race," would eventually triumph under Republican leadership.[160]

To substantiate their judgement against the South as the black power, Republicans levelled a number of charges. Slavery, or as Illinois Republican F. W. Jones phrased it, the South's worship of the "Black God of Slavery"[161] was, of course, part and parcel of these charges. More particularly the allegations held that the South promoted a rapid growth of its slave population by fostering both intraracial breeding among blacks and interracial breeding between blacks and whites. Echoes of the scientific and Free Soil communities were obviously present in these allegations.

Some Republicans seemed convinced that the South was mad with its program to breed more black slaves. While campaigning for his party in 1854, Frank Blair declared in Brooklyn, New York, that the South needed no more blacks. It was already black enough; "there was nothing but niggers and blackberries" there now.[162] Six years later Krouskopf described the Southern states as no more than "breeders of Negroes and Mulattoes."[163] Harlan noted that that section had a much larger Negro population than all the other states combined. He claimed that this "servile population . . . would so far predominate, as to enable them to degrade the white people to the condition of the negro,"[164] something he and other Republicans seemed anxious to avoid.

While speaking at Bloomington, Illinois in 1858, Lincoln also referred to the problem posed by the increasing numbers of blacks in the South.[165] Giddings and his Ohio colleague, Republican Representative Benjamin F. Leiter, exemplified this concern when they referred to the South respectively as either the "American Africa" or simply "'Africa.'"[166] Doolittle spoke of the "immense and constantly increasing weight and growing preponderance" of the South's black population. He asked Southern Congressmen "what will you do with them?" And then, quoting Jefferson almost verbatim, he added: "You are holding the wolf by the ears." His Southern colleagues, he said, "must make an outlet for these people, or you must be Africanized in those states where they [blacks] are increasing in such a ratio" as to eventually overwhelm the "whites."[167]

In condemning the South's preoccupation with its black population, Republicans at times seemed almost to say that the South was having an amorous affair with black people. Virtually every facet of the Southerner's life, from birth to adulthood, was marked by close contact with black people, to the point where blacks became an accepted part of the slaveholder's household, i.e. to the point where racial distinctions became blurred, became, in effect, meaningless. Time after time Republican politicians emphasized, invariably derisively, that section's apparent fixation and intimate association with black people. At a Republican rally in Kalamazoo, Michigan in 1856, Zachariah Chandler replied to the South's charge, that the North was endangering the Union by not enforcing the Fugitive Slave law of 1850, with these words: "what was the terrible danger of the Union," that the North threatened? "There was a Negro lost," he answered sarcastically, and "lo, the Union was in danger."[168] Owen Lovejoy best summed up this amorous affair of Southerners and blacks when making the following comments about a hypothetical Southerner:

> [W]ould you believe it! The vary first service rendered him on earth is preformed by a nigger; as an infant, he draws the milk which makes his flesh and blood and bones from the breast of a nigger . . . he is undressed and put to bed by a nigger, and nestles, during the slumbers of infancy, in the bosom of a nigger; he is washed, dressed, and taken to the table by a nigger, to eat food prepared by a nigger; he is led to and from school by a nigger; every service that childhood demands is preformed by a nigger . . . and when he reaches manhood, he invades the nigger quarters to place himself in the endearing relation of paternity to half-niggers.[169]

The acid test which for most Republicans testified to the South's strange relationship with black people and proved conclusively that it was indeed the black power, was the evidence supplied by the many mulattoes in Southern society; miscegenation was clearly a widespread practice, a practice that deeply troubled many Republicans. Bliss of Ohio expressed his disgust over Southern miscegenation. Speaking of the black man he came to the nub of the issue for many Republicans, noting that "slavery brings him into an unnatural contact with the white man," which contact "is visible . . . in the parti-colored complexion of the denizens of kitchen, plantation and slave pen."[170]

The most common form of miscegenation involved the union of white men with Negro women, but there were also numerous cases of the opposite, i.e. white women and Negro men. In fact, there were cases of intermarriage between black men and white women in the antebellum South.[171] No matter what form, the issue of such interracial copulation was, of course, the mulatto, the increasing numbers of whom Republicans feared and loathed. Viewing miscegenation as a crime against the white race, Republicans sometimes likened the South to a criminal, a traitor to white America and in particular to the North with its supposedly pure Caucasian blood lines.

Obviously the antebellum South produced the overwhelming majority of mulattoes in American society. Consequently, there is more than a germ of truth in Republican accusations that the South didn't seem to care, get into a collective dither, over the growing mulatto population in its midst. Numerous Republican politicians attacked Southerners for promoting the most basic form of black-white equality. There was, no doubt, more sexual freedom and license in the South, vis a vis the North, and given that one might argue that there was an element, a recognition of a common humanity present due to the prevalence of interracial copulation. Certainly there were numerous white Southerners, mainly males, but females as well, who could not have despised black people physically if they were willing to have sexual intercourse with them. One would have to assume that some level of attraction existed. In effect, Southern society had important components of a cultural pluralism that was present in French Canada, with its metis population, and Spanish America, with its mestizo population. In fact, along with the Five-Civilized tribes of the South, members of whom had intermarried with various Caucasian groups from the early 1600's on, there were large elements of both French and Spanish settlers in the South before Anglo-Saxons settled there en masse. All these groups had been mixing for years, and this mixture was particularly evident in the states of Texas, Louisiana and Florida. Free Soilers and later Republicans attacked incessantly racially mixed societies, and it's no coincidence that the areas where these parties were strongest were the same areas with a more nearly homogeneous Caucasian population. Therefore, it is hard to escape the conclusion that Anglo-Saxon society, as it developed in the Northern United States and of which the Republicans were the foremost political manifestation, feared and rejected cultural pluralism.

So, in the tradition of the intellectuals and the Free Soilers, Republicans constantly spoke out against miscegenation. A. Ballinger proclaimed that in the first place the major reason he and his family had joined the Republican Party was because its adherents "loathe the idea of Negro amalgamation."[172] A number of Republicans stated their opposition to miscegenation in formal position papers. For instance, in 1857 a meeting of Illinois Republicans, chaired by Gustave Koener, set forth the objectives of the new party in a series of resolutions, one of which explicitly said, "we abhor an amalgamation of the black and white races."[173] Sometimes Republican aversion to miscegenation took the form of opposition to marriage between black and white partners. Cassius Clay opposed "alliances between whites and blacks as involve progeny . . . ."[174] James Ashley's strong objection to miscegenation was manifested in a "distaste for interracial marriage."[175] In attacking Stephen A. Douglas' efforts to link the Republican Party to a policy of miscegenation, Abraham Lincoln asserted that he was "against the counterfeit logic which concludes that because I do not want a black woman for a slave, I must necessarily want her for a wife. I can just leave her alone." Later, while stump speaking in Columbus, Ohio in 1859, Lincoln joked that here he was "fifty years of age and . . . had never had a black person for a slave, nor yet for a wife."[176]

And yet, joining their scientific contemporaries in apparently ignoring sexual attraction across racial lines, the politicians in opposing miscegenation managed to present contradictory arguments. On the one hand, they insisted that white people were inherently revolted by interracial amalgamation; on the other hand, they insisted that white people must be kept apart from black people to prevent amalgamation. Speaking before the Illinois Legislature in 1857, Lincoln claimed that there was a "natural disgust in the minds of nearly all white people, to the idea of an indiscriminate amalgamation of the white and black races."[177] Frank Blair, harking back to Louis Agassiz and Josiah Nott, maintained that nature had "put a badge [of inferiority] upon the African, making amalgamation revolting to our race." On several occasions Blair announced that "amalgamation between the races" was "abhorrent" to white Americans.[178] It was abhorrent, Republican Judge William Kitchell of Illinois declared, because the Almighty had willed it so; "amalgamation with them [blacks] . . . would be a sin against God."[179] This divinely inspired abhorrence notwithstanding, however, the races had apparently to be separated to prevent miscegenation; and, said Blair, the South with its institution of slavery was thwarting this separation. The "inferiority" of black men, said the influential Missouri Congressman, was "conclusive argument against blending them in the same community, to deteriorate the superior by admixture or contact with the inferior races." The South, by encouraging the "unnatural juxtaposition . . . of the races," was perpetuating the major cause of miscegenation and was therefore "tainting the morals and corrupting the blood of our race."[180]

The allegedly dire consequences which racial amalgamation would bring to white people had already been spelled out by scientific and Free Soil groups; and Republican politicians seemed to accept their conclusions. Racial mixing would ruin the pure blood lines of the Anglo-Saxon and Caucasian; and, if, as was assumed by many Republicans, the black man was genetically backward, uncivilized and barbaric, then would not the mixing of his blood with the white man's cause these same racial characteristics to appear among the offspring? Congressman John Hutchins of Ohio charged that "there is in the slave states 'a visible admixture' of Anglo-Saxon with African blood;"[181] and Owen Lovejoy claimed it was "well known" that under slavery the "Saxon blood is being infiltrated into the blood of the enslaved."[182] While Kitchell had called miscegenation a sin against God, Ashley called it a sin against white civilization, and predicted that "if slavery continues, it [miscegenation] must become universal, blighting and corroding [to] the life-blood of the nation." Indeed, in words almost identical to Frank Blair's, he asked his fellow Congressmen, "has not slavery already corrupted the blood, to say nothing of the morals of millions" of white people?[183]

Republican orators warned that this process could in time lead to the complete disappearance of pure white American blood. A popular way of emphasizing this point was for them to speak of how blacks were becoming whiter. Representative Francis Kellogg of Michigan warned his colleagues that the "African race was bleaching out rapidly at the South, and the returns of the census confirm the statement."[184] Philemon Bliss made reference on several occasions to the "amalgamation tendencies of slavery" as "constantly bleaching out the African."[185] Trumbull remarked that in the South the "black race is fast bleaching,"[186] while Alfred Wells spoke of the dangers of "bleaching" with an "abject race," which process was growing with a "terrible rapidity" in the slave states.[187] Ashley, invoking the memory and thoughts of Henry Clay, insisted that at the present rate, "a hundred years will not elapse . . . before the last unmixed African slave will have disappeared before the bleaching process of Southern amalgamation."[188] At that time, presumably, the corrupting black blood would be completely hidden behind a white skin. Distinctions based on race would be meaningless. Speaking specifically of Virginia, Benjamin Wade, quoting from Helper, put it a bit differently. If slavery should continue in that state, its white population "'shall be as motley as Joseph's coat, of many colors, as ring-streaked and specked as father Jacob's flock was in Padanaram.'"[189]

For Republican political figures, as for the literati and Free Soil people, nothing symbolized the possibility of an end of pure Caucasianism more than the product of Southern miscegenation, the mulatto, including, as Ashley put it, the "octoroons, the quadroons, and the myriads who are tinged with the blood of the dominant race, in every Southern state."[190] These people were depicted as belonging to an inferior mongrel race. Even though Trumbull noted that "some of them [mulattoes] are so white, you can hardly distinguish the negro blood in them," he was still opposed to their presence.[191] Frank Blair proclaimed that "by long contact, their [blacks' and whites'] blood will become so mingled, that they will merge into a mongrel race." Evidently in contradiction to the idea that the 'bleaching process' would continue until the black race in America disappeared, this conception held that the result of miscegenation would be a grotesque, inferior hybrid, incapable of reproduction. "This . . . commingling . . . process," according to Blair, was, at least in the South, "already far advanced [and] threatens to make us a race of hybrids," in which the physical beauty, strength, and moral and intellectual leadership of the white race would be permanently destroyed. Like Nott, he charged that mulattoes were not able to reproduce their kind and that such "hybrid races carry degradation alike into government as into communities. Indeed, they cannot perpetuate themselves . . . [and] where the line is confined to this color for a few generations, it fails." Blair averred that this "mulatto caste" was destined to occupy the lowest economic stratum in the country.[192]

Cassius Clay, like Blair and other Republicans, played on the fears of his white constituents. While speaking in Kentucky, he asked his listeners if they would not rather have "manufacturers built up, and love to see the prosperity of the white race, instead of building up a degenerate mulatto race, as is now going on in the slave states?"[193]

Lincoln turned to hard statistical evidence to make the point. He used the 1850 federal census to compare the number of mulattoes in a Northern state, New Hampshire, with the number in a Southern state, Virginia. He stated that the number of people of mixed racial ancestry in the "Republican, slavery-hating State of New Hampshire . . . amounts to just one hundred and eight-four. In the Old Dominion," however, "there were a few more mulattoes . . . seventy-nine thousand seven hundred and seventy-five, twenty-three thousand more than there were in all the free states." Moreover, Lincoln declared that in all the slave states there were "three hundred and forty-eight thousand mulattoes," but "in the free states there were less than sixty thousand mulattoes, and a large number of them were imported from the South." Therefore, Lincoln concluded, amalgamation was a product of Southern society, because the "virtue of the [black] female was as much at the disposal of the master, as was her body."[194] Representative Harrison G. O. Blake of Ohio was also concerned, but where Lincoln had given the figure for all mulattoes in the South, free and slave, Blake focused on those in slavery. "According to the Census of 1850," he said, "there were . . . in the slave states two hundred and forty-six thousand, six hundred and thirty-five mulatto slaves."[195]

If Republicans, as did other white Americans, defined anyone with identifiable Negro ancestry as black, this fact did not prevent them from complaining loudly about Southern enslavement of the "white blood" that flowed in the veins of mulatto slaves. In some cases the tables were reversed, the master being much darker than the slave. Republicans evidently lost sight of the fact that the main ingredient in becoming a slaveholder was capital. It didn't matter if you were black or white and, in fact, there were black slaveholders. Blake observed that, as a result of miscegenation the South now held as slaves people who appeared to be white. He declared that "slavery in this country is not based upon the theory that the white man has a natural right to hold the negro in bondage. If it were, a man in whom the white blood largely predominated would not be held as a slave."[196] Hutchins agreed. It was, he said, "quite likely there is as much Anglo-Saxon as African blood enslaved there" in the South.[197] Having charged that Southerners held "a man in slavery . . . without reference to the amount of negro blood in his veins," Blake accused them of something that he considered worse yet: Southerners would "permit a man of negro blood and even a full-blooded negro, if free himself, to hold slaves. In some instances the master has a much larger proportion of negro blood in his veins than some of those he holds in slavery."[198] As newspaper editor William Cullen Bryant had warned, in the South black people could actually be placed above whites. In fine, the South, at the very least, was promoting equality between the races.

Republican politicians, indeed, often seemed to equate sexual relations between the races in the South with the white South's intention of encouraging racial equality, a charge which, as already noted, was not entirely fatuous. Congressman John Hutchins, while assailing miscegenation in the slave states, said that he was opposed to any idea of Negro or mulatto equality.[199] Owen Lovejoy implied that white Southern men were, in effect, taking both white and black women as their wives, and thereby elevating the latter to equality with the former. He spoke about the "offensive and brutal lusts of polygamy" which, he said, were an accepted part of life in the South.[200] And Ashley referred to "criminal negro equality." "It is in the land of slavery," he told a Southern colleague, "[where] you must look for amalgamation and the terrible degrading negro equality which is inseparable from such amalgamation."[201]

Another indication, and the principle bone of contention, which seemed for most Republicans to prove that the South was committed to black power, was that section's desire to extend Negro slavery, not only into the free West, but into areas south of the United States, such as the Caribbean and Central America. Many Republicans already concerned about the increase of black people and mulattoes in the South, said that such an expansion of slavery's domain would have two effects: 1) it would increase the number of black people and mulattoes in new areas, and 2) it would bring the undesirable mixed populations of Latin America into the Union, and hence into contact with Caucasian Americans.

Congressman Timothy Crane Day of Ohio, in assailing the Kansas and Nebraska Act, noted how that act had wrecked the Missouri Compromise of 1820 and disturbed the "order of nature" which had kept "an equilibrium" between the slave states and the free states. Under the Missouri Compromise, he continued allegorically, "twins, one black and one white, were placed into the arms of the Republic, at each accouchement of the territories."[202] Now, apparently as a result of the Kansas and Nebraska Act, more black slave states would be added to the Union. To Thayer, the act simply proved that the South was a "triumphant tyranny of . . . black power."[203] Kilgore of Indiana asserted that Southerners would not be interested in the admission of Kansas at all, if there was not a "negro in the question."[204] Speaking out against the South and the Kansas and Nebraska Act, Fenton of New York urged fellow Northerners to carry the political battle into the South, or as he referred to it, "into the very camp of Africa."[205] Using equally strong language, Frank Blair described slavery expansionists as a people "who wish to seize the territories for themselves and negroes, and throw out the poor white men."[206]

As far as slavery expansion was concerned, many Republicans acted as if Southern slaveholders had combined to form a conspiracy to deny the white man his interests and rights in the West. When Carl Schurz spoke at St. Louis in 1860, he referred to a hypothetical dialogue between a Southern slaveholder and a Republican, in which the slaveholder charged: "We want the negro in the territories. You [Republicans] give us the foreign [European] immigrant" instead.[207] When writing to his father in that same year, Henry Doolittle mentioned the radicalism of Wendell Phillips and his violation of the laws, but added that "his crime is white, compared with that of those who are forcing slavery into free territory."[208] The latter's crime evidently was black.

The South's crime was black, in the sense that many Republican leaders, already, as noted, exercised over miscegenation and the growth of the black population, seemed convinced that with the expansion of slavery would come a still speedier increase in the country's mulatto and black populations. Like the scientists and Free Soilers before them, they predicted that this more rapid increase would further threaten the racial purity of white America and the economic interests of white laborers. On numerous occasions, Republicans made clear their thoughts about such an eventuality. For instance, Ohioan James Ashley expressed deep concern over the danger of an increase of the mulatto population in the country as a whole. He referred specifically to this increase as the "crime of Southern amalgamation," and added that the "Republican party are opposed to amalgamation." He prophesied that, if slavery continued to expand, "five million will . . . be of the mixed race," but in fifty more years, twenty million "of these slaves will be so white, that they cannot be distinguished from white persons." Ashley concluded that "no lover of his country and the human race can contemplate this picture without a shudder."[209] "There are hundreds of thousands of mulattoes, quadroons and octoroons" in the United States, declared Francis Kellogg, all a product of Southern society, but what was worse, the "number is rapidly increasing."[210]

Governor Samuel Kirkwood of Iowa also expressed alarm over how the expansion of slavery would lead to a "large and rapidly increasing [black] population" in the Unites States.[211] While campaigning for Lincoln in 1860, Schurz too connected the "fearful increase of the negro population" with the spread of slavery.[212] Bates seemed especially worried over the "growing numbers of our free black population," which he argued resulted from the extension of slavery.[213] Frank Blair feared the "multiplication of [both] slaves and freed men," and proclaimed that the black man, "whether as a slave or free man . . . is found to be fatal to the interests of our race." If slavery expansion were not halted, he predicted that "in a half century the four millions of slaves now in the slave states will become twenty-five millions."[214] Addressing the question of the relative increase of blacks to whites in the country, Benjamin Wade warned of slavery's diffusion leading to an increase in "negro slaves, instead of white freemen," and reduced the entire slavery expansion controversy to simply "this nigger question."[215] Thomas Corwin expressed the apprehension of many of his Republican cohorts, when he asked Southerners derisively, "how many million negroes have you now?" If slavery were allowed to spread into the West, Corwin claimed, "you shall have in the ordinary increase of negroes in this country, fifteen million working hands in Texas [and] you will have [in total] forty-five million slaves there." Eventually, Corwin maintained, "you will want nearly twenty million working hands, which would give you a negro population of about sixty million." He then asked his Southern colleagues if this increase in black people was not the "very madness of the moon? You have four million negroes now, and you must increase the number to sixty million . . . you seem not to care for the suffocation of white men."[216] While the statistical predictions made by Republicans to warn of increases in the black and mulatto populations varied rather widely, they were, nevertheless, significant in one respect: all of them were obviously indicative of the deep racial fears and prejudices of the prognosticators.

The idea that the South was unconcerned with so-called white interests was also encouraged by that section's seeming determination to acquire Cuba and areas in Central America for future slave territory. For years Cuba had been a major base for the illegal Southern slave trade. Why not recognize the reality by acquiring it and creating another slave state? Various Southern filibustering expeditions, such as that of Narcisco Lopez, had tried to do just that. The problem here, however, as many Republicans saw it, was that those areas were inhabited by Latin American peoples whom, as has been noted, they equated with mulattoes and 'lesser breeds,' that is, darker skinned people, who, they said, were also the product of interracial copulation and who, they claimed, were responsible for the impotence of Mexico and the Central American states. When Thayer of Massachusetts compared the Latin and the Saxon, he implied such impotence, by stating that the "Latin races claim that their founders were nursed by a wolf." However, "Saxons," said Thayer, without citing his sources, "have a higher origin. Their founder was nursed by a polar bear," the latter, apparently, a tougher, more virile and more courageous animal, and one that was pure white in color.[217] Congressman Thomas Williams declared that "ethnological differences" between the Anglo-Saxons and the Latin "races" accounted for the superiority of the former. These "differences" stemmed from miscegenation, because the Latins south of the United States crossed "readily with the black man," while this was "rarely" the case with the Anglo-Saxons in North America.[218] Williams was apparently ignorant of the 'bleaching process' occurring in the Southern states, a process which many of his Republican colleagues railed against incessantly. Bates was more blunt when, in 1859, he referred to these same Latin peoples as simply "mongrel populations" who, he declared, were "wholly unfit to be our equals."[219]

Both Owen Lovejoy and John Sherman held Mexicans in low esteem, although for entirely different reasons. Lovejoy spoke about the "barbarism" of the "State of Mexico," while Sherman labelled Mexicans "a feeble and distracted people."[220] Mexicans, according to Frank Blair, were only a "semi-barbarous people;" and he also called attention to what he termed the "effete state of the Spanish race in Honduras and the other Central American states," as a by-product of interracial unions.[221]

Feeling this way, Republicans rejected the idea of bringing these peoples under American aegis. For example, Edward Bates was not "inclined to see absorbed into our system . . . the various and mixed races . . . which inhabit the continent and islands south of our present border. I am not willing to inoculate our body politic with the virus of their diseases, political and social disease[s] which, with them, are chronic and hereditary."[222] Indicating what he considered to be the expansionist objective of the South's 1860 movement for independence, Judge Kitchell, a constituent of Trumbull's, wrote the following: "A Southern confederacy, what an insane idea. If they had all Cuba and all Mexico it would only increase the black power and terminate in a black despotism of government."[223] This fear of an increasing black population, and hence eventual black rule, was shared by Republican Representative John J. Perry of Maine, who stated that the annexation of Cuba would not only add more slaves to the present black population, but "would add . . . a large number of free blacks" as well.[224] And for what purpose? The South, answered Doolittle, was attempting to politically counterbalance the "growing power . . . of the great Caucasian race in the North" by "bringing into this Union millions upon millions of the mixed races . . . . "[225]

Senators Dixon of Connecticut and Chandler of Michigan were more specific when assailing plans to acquire Cuba. Dixon, citing "David Turnbull" as a source, told fellow Senators that it would be impossible for Cubans to come into the same Union with the superior Anglo-Saxon race, not only because they were of "different habits" but more importantly because of the "character of the [Latin] race." To Dixon's mind this Latin "race" was a mongrel creation, one which was incapable of "self-government."[226] When Chandler compared Cubans to Anglo-Saxons, he labelled the former "lesser breeds." Addressing Senator John Slidell of Louisiana, where sentiment and support for acquisition was particularly strong, Chandler asked rhetorically: "You propose to pay $200,000,000 for what? For the right to govern one million of the refuse of the earth." He called Cubans an "ignorant, vicious and priest-ridden" people. Cubans were "superstitious" and, he added, obviously oblivious of the irony, "they are bigots as well," because "they are devout Catholics." Worse still, Cubans did not even make good slave masters, because they were so "utterly indolent themselves", presumably like their Negroes whom "they allowed . . . to do pretty much what they please." The Anglo-American master, on the other hand, Chandler critically described as "energetic; he drives, he works his negroes." "Is not this a beautiful population," Chandler asked Congress sardonically, "to bring into the Union as a state . . . do you want these people in your Union? Are you prepared to pay . . . to bring such a set of criminals into the Union?" This Senator was convinced that "there was not a crime on the calendar which had not its fixed value in the Island."[227]

VI

In addition to heaping scorn on the South and its promotion of the black man, Republican political leaders spent a good deal of time in castigating the Democratic Party—and the feelings they voiced expressed more than simply partisan politics. Republicans viewed the Democracy as the very vehicle by which the South went about achieving its nefarious goals relative to the black man. After all, did not Democrats in general support the expansion and multiplication of black slaves in both the

Western territories and areas south of the United States; and, after all, had not Democrats been instrumental in securing passage of the two most vicious pieces of legislation yet promoted by the black power—the Fugitive Slave law of 1850 and the Kansas and Nebraska Act of 1854? To most Republicans the Democracy and the South were all but synonymous, and the charges that Republicans made against their oppositional party were in many ways similar to the charges they made against the section.

For example, Republican officeholders expressed the conviction that Democrats were behind a plot that, by increasing the number of blacks in the country—through diffusing them into the free territories, or reopening the African slave trade, or breeding slaves, or pushing the American political sphere south of the slave states—would increase their party's base of political support in Congress and the country at large. Respecting the West, Indiana Republican George B. Currey voiced misgivings about the "aims that [the] Black Democracy have in this our [white] territory."[228] According to Harlan, Democrats were going out of their way to plant the black man in the West: "although it is manifest that negroes cannot or will not emigrate from their old homes to new countries in large numbers, the Democratic Party . . . proposes to secure their rapid occupancy of all that part of the continent."[229] The final goal of this policy, warned the 1859 Iowa Republican Party platform, was to "Africanize" the territories.[230] Legalizing the importation of African slaves was also part of the Democratic plot, charged Congressmen John Farnsworth and Edward Wade. Wade warned that if the Democrats were successful, the "shores of the American continent" would be "made to swarm with vast multitudes of . . . imbruted barbarians imported from Africa."[231] In keeping with Edward Wade's theme of importing blacks from Africa, Republican Representative James B. McKean of New York singled out Southern Democrats and attacked them for belonging to the "Anglo-Congo school of oratory . . . ."[232]

Breeding more blacks and acquiring Cuba were two more means to Democratic ends. To Uriah Mills of Illinois, Democrats were nothing more than "Negro breeders."[233] Lincoln's good friend Herndon pointed to racial and pecuniary interests as the motivations behind such breeding. The "Nigger Democracy is no democracy," he proclaimed, "but is most emphatically an aristocracy, first of race and secondly of money, as embodied in Niggers."[234] Attacking the idea of acquiring Cuba, Benjamin Wade and Frank Blair expressed views common among Republicans. The "whole purpose of the Democratic party," Wade claimed, was to "go through the earth hunting for niggers. That is all there is of Democracy; and when you cannot raise niggers enough for the market, then you must go abroad fishing for niggers through the whole world."[235] Blair concluded that Democrats belonged to the party, that "run after the negroes."[236]

If all this were not enough, according to Republicans, Democrats were additionally increasing the number of black people by encouraging miscegenation and therefore an increase in mulattoes. The charge was levelled at Southern Democrats who, presumably, were in a better position to contribute to the mulatto population than their Northern counterparts. Francis Kellogg put a political twist on the familiar theme. The "whole African race at the South are growing whiter and whiter everyday," he insisted; and, "as there are no Republicans in these states, this [mulattoism] must be considered Democratic."[237] This blatant phenomenon, said Republican politicians, put the lie to the Democratic accusation that it was the Republican Party which favored amalgamation. Actually, amalgamation was common in the South, averred Frank Blair, because the Democrats "resist the Republican doctrine of a separation of the races, and insist upon maintaining the white and black races in contact with each other."[238] The Democratic charge of amalgamation, declared Henry Wilson, "proceeds from men who have the oder of amalgamation strong upon them."[239]

Northern Democrats, and especially Senator Stephen A. Douglas of Illinois, also came in for their share of abuse on the subject of amalgamation. Republicans accused them of joining their Southern fellows to promote it in the territories. According to Lyman Trumbull, "Douglas is unfortunate in sowing troubles, wars, desolations, amalgamation and polygamy in his territorial bills." This Republican Senator seemed particularly bitter when asserting that under Douglas' leadership "amalgamation is continually in the head of the bogus Democracy . . . [and] the Democracy think of nothing but amalgamation, [and] probably do nothing but amalgamate."[240] Schurz added that Douglas "insists that there must be a little variety . . . of white and black labor, and that seems to be his favorite mixture . . . [and] the more slaves, the more variety."[241] When deriding blacks and the Douglas Democrats, Representative Israel Washburn of Maine drew a round of laughter in Congress when he exclaimed, "long may they bleach."[242] Interfusion apparently was popular with the opposition, as William Kitchell labelled the pro-slavery Democracy the "Mongrels and Mulatto Party."[243]

Some Republicans, in addition to attacking the Democrats for encouraging miscegenation, hinted that they favored interracial marriage. In 1856, while describing Republican policies concerning slavery, Congressman George Julian stated that "we were decidedly opposed to marrying the negro,"[244] implying that Democrats were not. Republican Representative Henry L. Dawes of Massachusetts did more than imply. When describing his own state he told fellow Congressmen, much to the chagrin of congressional Democrats, that "we had a Democratic Legislature one year . . . and it was in that year that the law was repealed prohibiting the intermarriage of blacks and whites."[245] After denying a story about a white girl from Michigan who married a black man, Francis Kellogg of that state "venture[d] the assertion that where one white woman marries a negro in a Republican state, a hundred white men can be found in Democratic states who sell their own children because they are tainted with African blood."[246] John Farnsworth carried this idea further, when chiding congressional Democrats for wishing to marry black people. He proclaimed that "in regard to social equality, we leave that to the taste of people. Republicans are not at all afraid that they will marry negroes. It requires no restraining laws to prevent that." However, Farnsworth continued facetiously, "if my Democratic friends are afraid that they will be tempted to intermarry with colored people, I will very cheerfully join in voting them a restraining law to prevent it."[247]

Apart from accusing the Democrats of working to increase the black population and the frequency of miscegenation, Republicans charged that in their enthusiasm to promote black interests Democrats were quite neglecting white interests. Indeed, according to the 1859 accusation of Congressman William Windom of Minnesota, "until they blow off all their gas about the 'eternal nigger,'" there would be no hope of Democrats supporting measures beneficial to the white man.[248] J. B. Turner of Illinois provided a case in point; while congressional Democrats were always ready to vote for legislation to apprehend runaway Negroes, they were equally consistent in voting against legislation "for the protection of free white citizens."[249] Frank Blair, Calvin C. Chaffee and Henry Wilson portrayed the white laborer as the particular victim of the Democratic preoccupation with blacks and slavery. Democrats, declared Blair, "appear in their true colors, as enemies of the free white laborer and as preferring their negro slaves to white men."[250] Republican Representative Chaffee of Massachusetts expressed alarm over the future of white labor, maintaining that the "policy" of the Democratic Party was to "Africanize the productive industry of the country."[251] "The Party that upholds slavery in America," concluded fellow Massachusetts Congressman Wilson, "that would extend its boundaries, increase its influence and its power, is the mortal enemy of the free white laboring-men of the United States."[252]

It was in the territories especially that Democrats were supposedly working to aid and abet black interests at the expense of white. "I protest," exclaimed Indiana Republican C. W. Gibson, "against giving the land we fought [Mexico] for . . . that cost the lives of some of the best men of the nation, to people of color."[253] As Republican John Kasson of Iowa put it, in its zeal to foster non-white benefits, one Democratic administration after another had "intervened in the territories to disturb [the status quo] and resist the will of the free white man there."[254] This policy, said Republicans, was rapidly alienating white people.

If Democratic policy in the territories prevailed, Republicans, such as the Illinoian Owen Lovejoy were convinced that free white laborers would stay away from them.[255] Blacks in the territories, said Lane of Indiana, would mean that the "free white emigrant is cut off."[256] Putting slavery in the territories, Senator Foster of Connecticut asserted, would be the same thing as putting the white population there "under the incubus of a black population, either slave or free,"[257] would guarantee, Trumbull told a St. Louis audience, that the "inalienable rights of the whole white race are trampled down and hand-cuffed."[258]

Of all Northern Democrats who allegedly ignored the interests of white people in the territories, Senator Douglas was the target of the sharpest Republican barbs. Frank Blair accused him with being no less than the "arch enemy of our race."[259] Rather than looking to white concerns, claimed Chicago Republicans, Douglas preached "negro equality" wherever he spoke.[260] And even changing his position on the Lecompton Constitution could not redeem Douglas: speaking for the Republicans of Sangamon County, Illinois, J. T. Knox noted that "we have no confidence in his new zeal for the white man."[261]

It was indeed respecting Douglas, the Lecompton Constitution and the issue of Kansas statehood, that Republicans seemed particularly adept at picturing the Democrats as partial to black interests over white. Schuyler Colfax of Indiana insisted that under Democratically adopted legal codes for that territory black people were actually treated better than whites. "[W]hile a white man is compelled to serve out the penalty of his crime at hard labor," the black slave, for the same offense, was not, because his master had prior rights to his labor. "Here is the [culpable] section," he continued, pointing to the Lecompton document. The question for its Democratic authors, "is not a question [of] whether Africans are to be slaves, but whether freemen of your own race and color, are to be made the serfs of the Lecompton usurpers."[262] Tompkins, who could not have agreed more with Colfax, asserted that he opposed the Democratic promotion of slavery in Kansas, "because of the great wrong that it does to the white race."[263] Concurring with Tompkins and Colfax were Republican Congressmen Ephraim W. Farley and James Doolittle. Doolittle insisted that his only concern in this controversy was for the "free white laboring men of Kansas," and Farley used the same expression.[264] In the estimation of the self-styled Democracy, concluded Trumbull, the "recapture of a single negro . . . is of more consequence than the protection of hundreds of white men" in Kansas.[265]

Given the Democratic majority on the Supreme Court, it was probably inevitable that many Republican politicians would view the Dred Scott decision of 1857 as simply another gambit by the black Democracy to expand slavery and the black man into the Western territories. Few Republicans assailed the decision on the moral grounds that it was deleterious to the interests and well-being of the black man, and that, in the final analysis, it rested on racial arguments; most attacked it because they perceived it as a Democratic ruling, dangerous to the interests of the white laborer. Although some went to the other extreme and appeared to defend the decision, obviously they did so to further their assault upon the black man.

Even though he was not directly involved in the case, Bates, soon to be Attorney General under Lincoln, regarded the pronouncements of the Democratic Court as obiter dicta. Since Scott was not a citizen of Missouri, Bates held that he was not a citizen of the United States, and therefore Chief Justice Roger B. Taney should have refused to hear his case on that ground.[266] Iowa Republican leaders Samuel J. Kirkwood, James F. Wilson and Josiah B. Grinnell were critical of the ruling not because it discriminated against blacks by denying them citizenship, but because, they feared, it would, by judicially overturning the Missouri Compromise, further encourage Democrats to expand slavery and the black man into the West.[267] Another Iowan, Senator James Harlan, predicted that this decision by the "Democratic members of the Supreme Court would . . . fill the virgin territories with negroes," a course anathema to Republican policy.[268] Other members, including F. S. Rutherford of Illinois, also thought that the decision would allow black people to overrun the white settlers in Kansas. [269] Connecticut Republican, Representative Sidney Dean, was blunt concerning the ruling. The Democrats, he told the House, "mean a 'nigger' in Kansas, or no Kansas in the Union."[270]

Numerous Republicans viewed the Dred Scott decision as a pro-slavery Democratic plot. The typical Democrat, Trumbull claimed, was "one of those who believe in the Dred Scott doctrine, [and] you see him with the woolly heads around him."[271] Frank Blair expanded this thought when remarking that the decision indicated that the Democrats were "willing to see the free white men of the country excluded from every territory."[272] Henry Smith Lane concluded that the decision, in effect, wrecked the basic non-extensionist doctrine of the Republican Party; "there is not this day, if that decision is to stand, one inch of free soil in the United States."[273]

Some Republicans read more threatening omens into what, like Trumbull, they called the "Dred Scott doctrine." Doolittle joined Lane in holding that the Democratic Court's decision would allow "slavery into every state in the Union."[274] Some Iowa Republicans worried that if slavery were allowed everywhere, the increased demand for slaves would bring success to the Democratic campaign to reopen the African slave trade and thereby bring still more blacks into the country.[275] Trumbull expanded upon this apprehension: he noted that because of the Court's action an increased number of black people would be settled in the West to augment the danger of miscegenation. "I shall enter into no argument with Judge Taney or anyone else," Trumbull stated sarcastically, "as to . . . their [blacks] amalgamation with the whites, by allowing intermarriage between the races, nor as to placing negroes, whether bond or free, socially or politically on a level with the white race."[276]

Lincoln agreed with Trumbull's assessment: declaring that the "Dred Scott case affords a strong test as to which party most favors amalgamation . . . . [W]e [Republicans] desired the court to have held that they [Dred Scott, his wife and two daughters] were citizens . . . that they were, in fact and in law really free. Could we have had our way, the chances of these black girls ever mixing their blood with that of white people would have been diminished, at least to the extent that it could not have been without their consent." However, even though Lincoln, notwithstanding the decision, believed that legally, the "different states have the power to make a negro a citizen under the Constitution of the United States if they choose," he personally was "not in favor of negro citizenship," and "if the State of Illinois had that power, I should be opposed to the exercise of it."[277]

Other Republicans, however, appeared to endorse the decision for the same racially inspired reasons that Trumbull and Lincoln condemned it. A Republican judge, Randolph Manning of Michigan, citing the Dred Scott decision, denied a black man equal rights to accommodations on a steamboat because the black man was not "'a component part of the [white] community.'"[278]

The Republican charge that the Democrats pandered to the interests of the black power and the black man was also meant to counter the Democratic charge that the Republicans, with their reservations about the character of slavery and their opposition to the expansion of that institution, were the real supporters of the interests of the black man. In fine, each party seemed determined to prove itself innocent of any concern for the rights of black people at the expense of white people. And in this exchange, the 'Black Republicans,' as the Democrats called them, were, if anything, more vigorously on the offensive. In your attempts to link the members of the new Republican Party to the black man, Cassius Clay told the Democrats, "you have cried 'nigger, nigger' in Pennsylvania, in New York, in Minnesota, and all these states have decried against you. The cry has returned back upon you, and you have been discovered to be the party disposed to sacrifice the rights of the white man for the nigger." Because of this racial backlash, Clay confidently predicted that the "Republican party is going into power in 1860."[279] Perry of Maine implored congressional Democrats to examine their own party first, a "party whose very existence is shrouded by the 'black' pall of Egyptian night," before casting aspersions and insults on congressional Republicans.[280] While speaking in Chicago in 1858, Trumbull who, as had been noted, believed with Lincoln that the Dred Scott decision defined precisely which party was really biased against white people, assailed the "African Democracy." Any member of that party, he stated, is "in the habit of calling out 'nigger' to everybody else, while he is hugging a nigger under each arm." In St. Louis he continued: The Democrats may "call the Republican party the nigger party, but," he added, striking a tender nerve in the political opposition, "it [the race issue] never split up our party as it has the Democratic party."[281]

No, the name calling of the Democrats could not pierce the Republican armor. Never mind that they "apply to us opprobrious epithets . . . 'Black Republicans,' 'negro-worshippers,'" cried Cumback of Indiana when addressing the House on the Kansas question in 1856. "I say to them today, that we are the only white man's party in this country; we are the only party who look to the interests of the great mass . . . of the free white laborers."[282]

Republicans in general took up the cry. During the 1856 presidential campaign the "Circular of the National Committee" of the Republican Party labelled slavery the "black institution," and the Democratic Party which supported it, the "Black Oligarchy."[283] Again and again, and especially in the West, the same shout was heard. A number of Republicans in Michigan charged that Democrats generally, like Southerners specifically, "'worshipped niggers.'"[284] One Republican Congressman from New York alluded to the opposition party as the "Black South American Party."[285] California Republicans variously referred to Democratic Party regulars as constituting the "'African Democracy,'" the "'nigger-driving Democracy,'" or simply the "'Black Democracy.'" [286] Illinois Republican George P. Eisenmayer called them "Nebraska Niggers;"[287] another Illinoian, S. T. Glover, pictured them as the "negro Democracy in their native colors;"[288] and yet a third son of that state, Lincoln's close associate, Herndon, who said that he "hate[d] and dread[ed]" the "Nigger Power," constantly referred to the Democrats as the "nigger drivers" who, he said, would always be known as the "nigger Democracy."[289] Democrats "can no more run their party without niggers" declared Ohioan Benjamin Wade, "than you can run a steam engine without fuel."[290] A Wisconsin Republican, Charles Billinghurst, broadened his attack by appealing to nativist sentiments as well; Democrats in his state made up the "latter day Saint Democracy . . . founded upon niggerology, liquor and Romanism." They were, Billinghurst added, but part of the "African party" of which Stephen A. Douglas was the presidential candidate.[291]

The conclusion from this kind of thinking seemed clear enough. If the Democrats were indeed the party of black interests; if they posed in fact a danger to white interests; if, as Trumbull charged in St. Louis, the answer to the question "what is their policy in the territories" could be answered by the single word, "nigger," then asked many Republicans, was not the Democratic Party a growing danger to the commonwealth? Chandler spoke to this concern by drawing an analogy between the Democratic Party and a sinking ship. The implication here was that if the Democratic Party continued to rule the country, the country would sink under the unproductive weight of the black man. He stated that "niggers crowded her deck, and niggers crowded the hold, niggers in the cabin, niggers in the forecastle. In fact, wherever you looked . . . nothing but niggers."[292]

VII

Republican attacks on the 'black' South and the 'black' Democracy consequently went well beyond mere name calling. Many party members made dire predictions about what would happen if these so-called black forces continued to rule the country, continued to seek the expansion of slavery into the Western territories and thereby contribute to the ever increasing size of America's black population. It may be instructive to examine more closely the exact reasons that Republican politicians cited to bolster their claims. As noted, this black population was depicted as a threat to the economic interests of white laboring people. Class interests were sacrificed for racial ones. Specifically, many Republicans assumed that even though black workers could not, in the long run, survive the economic competition of skilled white laborers, they, being both unproductive and unskilled and therefore unable to fit into the labor force of a technologically advanced and sophisticated industrial economy, would, in the short run at least, retard the progress and destiny of white America's economic growth. Others believed that white workers could not compete with black workers, because the latter would always work for lower wages, if free, or no wages at all, if they remained in slavery. Also, many Republicans insisted that the very presence of a large black population could 1) jeopardize by the process of miscegenation the racial purity of Caucasian society and 2) threaten through slave insurrections and racial conflicts the peace and security of that society. From these considerations evolved much of the Republican racial appeal in the presidential campaign of 1860.

Since many Republicans considered the black race a weak or worthless race, in the words of James Grimes a "degraded race,"[293] they believed that it fell short in the attributes which spelled success in the competitive world of the superior white man, that it was, in truth, an obstacle to the white man's economic progress. Seward, when campaigning for his party in Detroit in 1860, sought to give credence to such a belief, claiming that in the United States the "African race . . . is a foreign and feeble element, like the Indians." This Republican comparison with Native Americans would have significance both during and after the Civil War as the Western tribes came under increasing military attack directed by Republican administrations. He went on to describe the black man as a "pitiful exotic, unwisely and unnecessarily transplanted into our fields."[294] Because they were so weak and feeble, Trumbull stated, black people could not "take care of themselves." Therefore, whites would have to provide for them.[295] Pennsylvania's William Stewart and Ohio's Benjamin Wade agreed almost verbatim with Trumbull's assessment, Wade calling blacks a "race of men who are poor, weak, uninfluential, [and] incapable of taking care of themselves."[296]

In keeping with this idea of black men as economically worthless, Frank Blair picture them as an obstacle to the economic progress of white America. He was certain that the black man represented a "burden and obstruction to our progress." He likened Negroes to a "superincumbent weight" on the American people. Furthermore, when stumping for the party in St. Joseph, Missouri in 1859, Blair charged that "one negro is more in the way of a railroad, than three mountains," and described free blacks as a "class of men who are worse than useless to us."[297] Henry Wilson insisted that because this unproductive black labor was being used in the South, "thousands of square miles, millions of acres of the best soil of the western world, have been blighted, blasted, [and] desolated."[298] Massachusetts colleague Chaffee attempted to quantify the assumed "unproductiveness" of black labor, claiming that white labor "is more than twice as productive."[299] And, as had Wilson, Representative Edward Ball of Ohio, when opposing the Kansas and Nebraska bill, invoked the argument of soil exhaustion. Depicting Northern agriculture as superior to Southern, Ball seemed to blame the black man for the difference, maintaining that the "sweat of the negro is the poison of the soil . . . . "[300] Some Iowa Republicans explained the blacks' alleged lack of material progress by referring to the scale of races. They concluded that since blacks were a weak and worthless race, "they were a people without laws and without a history" who have "ever, and will ever, fall far, far in the rear, in the race for ascendancy."[301]

The contrasting belief that the white laborer was mentally, physically and morally superior to the black laborer and hence more productive, was no more than a specific application of the general Republican belief in the racial superiority of whites. For them, skin color was an important factor in measuring a person's aptitude for labor. Carl Schurz, as had William Kellogg, identified the white laborer with "progressive humanity,"[302] thereby implying that black laborers were not progressive. Republican Representative Thomas McKey Edwards of New Hampshire referred to white laborers, specifically to "Anglo-Saxon" laborers, as an "industrious and intelligent population," with the same implication.[303] Insisting that he spoke for the white Northern mechanic classes, Lovejoy proclaimed that if the South "had more white laborers and fewer black ones . . . labor in the South would be more respectable."[304] Frank Blair "believed in the supremacy of free white labor" and that "keeping these [Western] territories for free white men," was the only way "to build up rich states west of us." He insisted that a progressive community required "skillful and intelligent free [white] labor to supply its wants," rather than black laborers who presumably could not.[305]

Clearly if by a progressive community Blair meant one that was dominated by mechanical and manufacturing enterprises, then Minnesota Republican, Representative Alexander H. Rice agreed completely with Blair and removed any doubts on the subject. Rice did not believe that the "African can compete with the white laborer in the competitions of mechanical industry . . . ."[306] In the North, Thayer added, "we can buy . . . negro power, in a steam-engine, for ten dollars," and run this engine "for one year for five dollars." Why then, he asked his congressional colleagues, should we pay "$1000 for an African . . . and $150 a year to feed and clothe him," when the steam engine was more cost effective and efficient?[307] The Free Soil territorial governor of Kansas, John W. Geary, was still more explicit, when he spoke about the laboring "white man, with his intellectual energy, far reaching science and indomitable perseverance," as the "peculiar object of my sympathy."[308]

Politically, Republicans were able to tie many of their attacks on the South and the Democratic Party to pragmatic, economic issues, such as the presumed threat of competition from black labor. Therefore, while on the one hand they could argue that the black man would not be competitive enough with the superior white laborer to fit into the economic mainstream, on the other, they could reverse themselves and argue that the black man was indeed a competitive menace to white labor. The latter position lent to their arguments a plausibility which Democratic arguments apparently lacked. Never mind that they exaggerated the threat of black labor competition. It was just such fear tactics which appealed to Northern whites and won the Republicans their first presidential election. Seward who, in one case, described black labor as weak and worthless, hence of little concern to the superior white laborer, nevertheless on another occasion warned Congress that the "European immigrant . . . avoids the African [laborer] as if his skin exhaled [a] contagion." Why was this? Because, Seward said, black labor competition would "sink," would lower the wages of white workers "down to the level of the African . . . ."[309] One Illinois Republican, F. R. Payne, wrote about the "competition and abominations of nigger spreading Democrats" in the territories.[310] Benjamin Wade claimed that black slavery drove "free [white] laborers, farmers, mechanics, and all . . . out of the country, and fill[ed] their places with Negroes."[311] Benjamin's brother, Edward, saw the extension of Southern slavery "as a means of supplanting our white population and filling their places with blacks." Black workers, or what he called "these barbarian Negroes," would act "as substitutes" and thereby "take the place of intelligent and highly civilized white laborers." This substitution, in turn, would presumably lower the economic productiveness and progress of the entire nation.[312]

Frank Blair felt as strongly as Edward Wade about such competition and its ultimate effect on the country's economy. He insisted that the "friends of the free white laborers object to the acquisition of new California, for their [blacks'] occupation and employment. It is clear that the two races cannot occupy the same states without mutual [economic] injury." Blair noted that the continuance of Negro slavery was dangerous to the welfare of "free labor, cities, and the [white] race." Furthermore, he maintained that the very juxtaposition of blacks and whites in the same society was a "contact odious and revolting to the entire mass of laboring white men." This "strong repugnance of the free white laborer to be yoked with the negro refugee," only "breeds an enmity between races, which must end in the expulsion of the latter [blacks]."[313] Agreeing with Blair, William Kellogg observed that the white "freemen of the North will not, cannot, in their natures, in their pride of manhood, labor with and beside slaves." One of the differences between these two laboring populations which would preclude their working together, Kellogg asserted, was that "free [white] labor thinks, acts, progresses and improves." On the other hand, the black slave laborer apparently was not capable of thinking or improving, because he had to be "driven." The conclusion: Black labor only "corrupts and retrogrades," wherever it was introduced.[314]

A second threat which blacks purportedly posed to white Americans entering the Western territories was the threat to Caucasian racial purity. Republican Philemon Bliss hinted at this danger. The expansion of slavery into the territories, he warned, would bring the black man "into unnatural contact with the white man."[315] David Wilmot came closer to the point. Keeping blacks out of the territories would prevent them from commingling with white people, an eventuality which he said would be a "social disgrace."[316] Trumbull, who referred to the whole matter of the extension of slavery into the territories as no more than a "nigger question," sarcastically labeled his Democratic opponents those people "who are endeavoring to prevent amalgamation by extending . . . slavery and all of its temptations and opportunities."[317] Zeroing in on the issue of miscegenation in Kansas territory, Lincoln averred that "if white and black people never get together in Kansas, they will never mix blood in Kansas. That is at least one self-evident truth,"[318] one that Republicans seemed acutely aware of.

Besides the threats to the professed purity of the white race and of possible economic competition, the growing number of blacks were seen by a number of Republicans as a threat to the peace and security of the dominant white society. As had their Free Soil predecessors, Republicans appeared to be in constant dread of black insurrections and racial conflicts. This attitude seemed strange, in the sense that the overwhelming majority of black people lived in the South, far from their own families and constituents. In any event when New Yorker James McKean compared the slave society of the South with the free society of the North, he referred to the "insecurity of the one [and] the safety and stability of the other."[319] Seward stated allegorically that it was "unprofitable to cultivate [blacks] at the cost of the desolation of the native vineyard." He dwelt on the "evils of discontent and the dangers of domestic faction" that would result if slavery were permitted to grow.[320] Pinpointing the problem, Frank Blair proclaimed that the "increase of slaves will ultimately lead to an explosion and a bloody issue," quite possibly another "St. Domingo."[321] Doolittle likewise warned Southern Congressmen that if such an increase continued, "other calamities the most to be dreaded," such as the "scenes of San Domingo [would be] reenacted within the Gulf states."[322] James Ashley drew an identical analogy, while fellow Ohioan Cyndor Bailey Tompkins likened the situation to the "recital of the butcheries of Nat Turner . . . because the white inhabitants where it [slavery] exists, live in constant dread and alarm," in fact they live "with horror."[323] When referring to the growing black population, Lovejoy metaphorically noted that "it is better to remove the [powder] magazine, than to be kept evermore in dread of a lighted match."[324] Nor were Iowa Republicans reticent when they described this black population as the "most dangerous element that now threatens the peace of the nation."[325] Illinoian William Kitchell charged that racial antipathy within the United States was so great that "there is an irrepressible conflict between the black and white races."[326] Trumbull, like Jefferson and Henry Clay, warned of "consequences which we shudder to contemplate," if the black population continued to increase at its present rate. He then offered the Republican Party as the answer to the problem of the peace and well-being of Caucasian Americans. He "contended that the safety of the country depended on the success of that party, and its defeat would be a blow aimed at the rights of free white men."[327]

Republicans, therefore, acted on the premise that they were the white man's party. This reasoning became particularly evident when they set forth the solutions with which they proposed to deal with the problems, of labor competition, miscegenation and racial conflict, which blacks supposedly posed for white Americans. In short their solutions, like the problems they identified, were based on racial assumptions and were essentially identical to those of the intelligentsia and Free Soilers.

CHAPTER 5

EARLY REPUBLICANS AND THE BLACK PRESENCE

> But some people say that slavery is a curse to the white man.
> They abandon the idea that it is a curse to the negro.

> Alexander H. Stephens, 1854

Believing as they did that the black man was racially inferior to the Caucasian, Republican politicians sought ways to keep the races apart. In this respect Republican solutions to the alleged problems presented by blacks in the United States followed very closely those of their Free Soil predecessors. Seeking to guard against the racial 'corruption' posed by an expanding mulatto population and wanting to protect the so-called racial purity, economic interests, and peace and security of the white laboring classes, virtually all Republican politicians, like Free Soil politicians previously, supported the policy of containment of blacks in the South.

Containment, however, was, for these Republicans as it had been for Free Soilers, only the immediate remedy since the latter also bequeathed to their successors the rest of their racialist legacy. Therefore, which policy a Republican recommended as the follow-up to containment-whether to rely on the drainage theory of natural migration, or the competition of white laborers, or a program of colonization, or on some combination of these proposals as the final means of disposing of the black population-depended upon which aspect of that legacy he found most convincing. Ultimately, it was colonization which came to be viewed by the majority of antebellum Republicans as the most effective means by which to separate the races and ensure that eventually the United States would be populated by one homogeneous white people.

That a majority of Republican leaders felt a need to create an all-white America did not mean that all Republican leaders felt the same way. Ironically, even some conservative Republicans who championed black colonization at times spoke paternalistically about uplifting the black race within the United States. Analogous to latter day Social Darwinists, some Republicans anticipated the idea of the 'white man's burden.' On the other hand, a small but significant group of the more radical Republicans sometimes expressed the view that the black race could not only remain in the country, but should be given some measure of equal justice. Consequently Republicans, like Free Soilers, were not always consistent in their views toward Negro people.

I

When addressing Congress about the future of the black man within the United States, Senator Doolittle of Wisconsin implied that blacks could not be accepted as citizens of the United States and asked quite frankly: "what are you going to do with these men?"[1]

One thing that Republicans could do would be to continue the Free Soil policy of containment by seeking to keep black people out of the Western states and territories and thereby confining them to the South where, together with their kinfolk in slavery, they could be more easily dealt with in the future. In truth, most Republican politicos, as most Free Soil, believed that the real stumbling block to the creation of an homogeneous white population in the United States was the institution of slavery itself, which they saw as encouraging the growth of a black population, both slave and free. Slavery had, of course, been ended in the

Northern states by constitutional or legislative means, but Republicans insisted that two problems previously identified by the Free Soilers continued to be potentially dangerous. First, notwithstanding old laws which discriminated against them, some free blacks still lived in the states of the Northwest, or what was then considered the West, and more might be coming. Secondly, and more critical, the South was still adamantly seeking to expand slavery into the territories.

To deal with free blacks who were resident in these free states and to discourage the migration of more free blacks into them, Republicans supported policies which continued to discriminate against the former and exclude the latter. The process of discrimination could take various forms. It could, for example, deprive blacks of the right of suffrage. Given the opportunity, most Republican politicians expressed their negative opinion on this subject. Republican Iowa and Wisconsin both defeated legislative proposals to grant blacks the franchise.[2] In Minnesota, Republicans joined Democrats in eliminating black suffrage from the state's 1858 constitution.[3] In 1856 Michigan's Attorney General, Republican Jacob M. Howard, declared that election inspectors "could determine a voter's color," in order to deny him the franchise on the basis of race.[4]

Or, more broadly, Republicans could simply deny that free blacks were citizens in any sense. During the Minnesota state constitutional convention of 1860, Republicans joined Democrats in defeating "a proposal to strike out the word 'white,' where it appeared before [the word] 'citizens' . . . . "[5] William Herndon of Illinois strongly criticized a reapportionment bill sponsored by the Democrats in that state's 1857 legislative session. The bill would have provided for the counting of both white and black people which, said Herndon, was contrary to the apportionment section of the Illinois constitution. The latter, he pointed out, said that only "'white' shall be the basis of the law . . . . "[6]

In general, however, both major parties resisted black political equality, and Republican Representative James Wilson of Indiana said so explicitly. When discussing the franchise, Wilson declared that the "Republican party is as much opposed to negro equality as the Democratic Party."[7] Another Republican wrote to Doolittle that the Negro, being "inferior to our race in all respects . . . is not to participate in governing the white race."[8] They were not to participate, insisted LaFayette Foster of Connecticut, because they were themselves "incapable of self-government."[9] Although Representative John J. Farnsworth of Illinois did not support the total exclusion of blacks from Oregon, as provided for in its constitution for admission to the Union, he was nevertheless willing to leave to Oregonians the question of "who shall sit upon juries" or "who shall be allowed to vote."[10] Fellow Illinoians Abraham Lincoln, William W. Orme and Lyman Trumbull, and Missourian Edward Bates all expressed strong sentiments when agreeing with Senator James Harlan of Iowa, when the latter declared that blacks "can never become fit for citizens of the states or Union; that they cannot be intrusted with a participation in public affairs, or to engage in the public defense; that they can never become members of society." In 1858 Lincoln said that he was "not [now] nor ever . . . in favor of bringing about in any way the social and political equality of the white and black races"[11] Even Giddings, one of the most liberal Republicans, equivocated at times and joined his more conservative cohorts. Speaking for the party he noted the following: "We do not say the black man is, or shall be, the equal of the white man; or that he shall vote or hold office . . . ."[12]

Another means by which Republicans sought to reserve the Western states for white people was by advocating the exclusion of free black people from them. Congressman George Julian of Indiana set the tone when he stated that he "opposed setting them [blacks] free among us."[13] Senators Preston King of New York and Benjamin Wade of Ohio were of like mind. King fully supported the wishes of the people of Oregon " . . . to be free from the settlement of blacks among them."[14] Declaring that "free negroes are despised by all [and] repudiated by all," and that white prejudice against them was "immovable," Wade called for the exclusion of Negroes from all the free states; because "we [Republicans] have objections to them." Forgetting for the moment that the South was the 'black power,' he proclaimed that "this species of population are just as abhorrent to the Southern states," as "to the North."[15]

In various Western states Republican heirs to the Free Soil philosophy continued to support exclusionist legislation. In Iowa, for instance, "stringent bonding, registration and prohibitions against free Negroes" were maintained, and Republican support for these measures was clearly indicative of Republican determination to keep blacks out.[16] In Indiana, too, Republican racial feeling ran strongly. Republicans there "continued to uphold Indiana's laws for the exclusion of Negroes." When the state's black leaders called on the Indiana Republicans to aid their movement to repeal that state's black laws, they were ignored.[17] Albert G. Porter of Indiana candidly told his congressional colleagues his reasons for supporting the black laws: "It is not probable . . . with the prejudices of my early education, that I would be likely to have too great [a] sympathy for Negroes. In Indiana we have adopted a constitutional provision that no negro, whether he be bond or free, shall be allowed to come within its limits." Porter was satisfied that exclusion was the correct course to follow; otherwise white laborers would have to compete with blacks. "[We] Republicans in Indiana," he concluded, "put our advocacy of the exclusion of negroes upon the same ground which it was put in our state constitution."[18] In neighboring Illinois, Republicans spoke similarly. A. Ballinger of that state insisted that "we [Republicans] don't want them, slave or free." In particular, he averred, the "free ones are obnoxious."[19] Another Illinois Republican, fearing the spread of miscegenation, called for the strict enforcement of black exclusionist legislation in his state.[20] A third son of Illinois, Senator Lyman Trumbull, stated emphatically that "our policy is to have nothing to do with them [blacks]." By "them," Trumbull, of course, meant free blacks as well as slaves. Not only were Republicans in the Western states willing to exclude free blacks from their presence but, according to Trumbull, the "North [in general] does not want a free negro population."[21]

Representative Frank Blair of Missouri agreed with Trumbull that the North would exclude free blacks. Although he believed that the "North may receive an absconding [black] straggler here and there . . . what states," he asked, "would receive five million" blacks? The "Northern states will not receive them," he proclaimed. Blair expressed relief because the "law of the North has put its ban upon immigration of negroes into the free states." But, if the legal barriers were not enough, Blair insisted that whites, North and South, were prepared to go one step further. Picturing blacks as dangerous to the safety and welfare of white Americans, he claimed that "there is not a state in the Union, that would not fly to arms, to resist the intrusion of 100,000 free negroes within its limits."[22] Said Congressman Thomas Corwin of Ohio: "I am for the white man;" free blacks, if not excluded, would "destroy" white interests in the free states.[23] The assumption continued: white interests and black interests were mutually exclusive.

While all of the states of the West and Northwest had excluded blacks as slaves and most of them subsequently acted to exclude blacks as free persons, the threat of the extension of slavery and with it a free black population into the Western territories remained. Excluding slavery from these territories was for Republicans, as for Free Soilers, another means of containing the black population within the slave states. Just as they had when Free Soilers, Republican politicians adopted the Wilmot Proviso as the linchpin of their party's position on slavery in the territories. Although prominent Western Republicans might voice ostensible respect for the inviolability of slavery in the South, they were openly adamant that it must be contained there. The party might have no legal right to touch slavery in the states where it existed, admitted Congressman Henry Smith Lane of Indiana, but "in the territories," he insisted, "we have." The immediate "mission of the Republican Party," he announced, while campaigning in Indiana in 1859, "is to restrict slavery to its present limits."[24] Other important Republicans, including Oliver Morton, Edward Bates, Montgomery Blair, William Dennison and the longtime former Democrat, Thomas Hart Benton, agreed. Blair acted as defense counsel for Dred Scott in the historic case, and in his lengthy arguments laid down the Republican axiom that Congress did indeed have the authority to interdict slavery in the territories.[25] The immediate priority of the party, said Ohio Governor Dennison, should be "repressing the invasion of slavery," by "keeping it within its own boundaries."[26] "Prohibition [of slavery] in the territories," declared the retired Senator from Missouri, Thomas Benton, was a central doctrine of the party.[27] As Congressman Dewitt Clinton Leach of Michigan put it: "we say to slavery 'thus far and no further.'"[28]

The fact that the subject of excluding slavery from the territories never strayed far from the subject of excluding black people from the territories merely served one more time to prove that racial concern was a prime chemical in the formula of containment. If Free Soilers had monotonously intoned race to justify their policy in the territories, so too would Republicans. One Illinois party organizer, William R. Wilkinson, wrote during the 1860 presidential campaign that he was not only appealing to the voters on the basis of "free speech" and a "free press," but also for the enactment of legislation to protect the "free territories for free white men."[29] Foster of Connecticut made the same demand in the Senate.[30] David Kilgore of Indiana plead with his Southern congressional colleagues "to keep the negroes to themselves, and not thrust them into our faces . . . ."[31] In neighboring Illinois Republican A. Ballinger wrote likewise that the South could "keep her negroes if they wish them, . . . if they will only keep them to themselves, and not intrude them upon us."[32] As noted in chapter four, the Republicans often pictured the Democratic Party as the surrogate of the slave states and therefore of the black man. As James Harlan saw it, the slavery extension controversy was simply a question of racial preference, and the "policy of the Republican Party would people our vast public domain with the white race . . . ." Harlan, therefore, asked Democrats, "Why not adopt the Republican policy [of exclusion]?"[33]

Trumbull, while attacking the Dred Scott decision, was not so conciliatory. The Illinois Senator was quick to point out that this Democratic decision to expand slavery into the West was "certainly no part of the Republican creed, which seeks to preserve the free white laborer and white man from contamination with negro slaves by keeping it [sic] out of the free territories." Indeed, this creed was for the benefit of "free white men, who do not want anything to do with negroes . . . ."[34] Republican Jesse K. Dubois, one of Trumbull's constituents, added that "when they [Democrats] undertake to make the Negro national, we beg to be excused and say stop."[35]

Preventing the expansion of slavery into the territories would also discourage the continued growth of the black population and all the evils that Republicans associated with that growth. To illustrate, when Wisconsin Republican, Representative Cadwallader C. Washburn spoke for the party respecting black people and the expansion issue, he did so as follows: " . . . [W]e propose to prevent their increase as much as possible, by refusing to open new territories to be despoiled by them . . . ."[36]

Excluding slavery from the territories would prevent the calamities which, it has been seen, Republicans had forecast if action were not taken. For example they said it would eliminate labor competition, an issue which, in their minds, was intimately connected to one of racial preference. By ignoring the interests of black workers, class interests were subordinated to racial ones. Speaking for the party, Senator Hannibal Hamlin of Maine opposed black labor moving into the territories. "If we have no feeling whatever for other races we may be pardoned," said the Senator, because "we would honestly incorporate and advance in our government that system [of labor] which will elevate our own race."[37] Iowa Republicans, in supporting exclusion, demonstrated "clear evidence of their determination to brook no competition from Negro labor under any condition" either in Iowa or in the Western territories.[38] Concurring with that determination, Porter of Indiana "believed that negro labor [free or slave] ought not to be suffered to come into competition with white labor in Indiana," or "in the territories."[39] Keeping blacks out of the territories, stated Frank Blair, would release the "free white laborer from a competition that now excludes him from nearly all employments."[40] "There should be no slave labor where the white man can work," Thomas Corwin insisted.[41]

Exclusion would also avoid that other, often prophesied calamity, miscegenation. Republican Orville Leston of Illinois asserted that the "only remedy to prevent the amalgamation of the white and black race[s] . . . is to separate and consequently prohibit the blacks, free or slave, from immigrating to the free states or territories."[42] Lincoln was in agreement: "[I]f we do not let them [blacks and whites] get together in the territories, they won't mix there." Separating the races was the objective, he told Stephen A. Douglas in their 1858 Chicago debate; "but as an immediate separation [in the South] is impossible, the next best thing is to keep them apart where they are not already together," that is, in the territories. While Lincoln said that he hesitated to speak for the entire Republican Party on this issue, he expressed confidence that "a very large proportion of its members are for it, and that the chief plank in their platform, opposition to the spread of slavery, is most favorable to that separation." During their Carlinville debate Lincoln seized the offensive and referring specifically to the Kansas controversy asked his audience the following: "Douglas pretends to be horrified at amalgamation, yet had he not opened the way for slavery in Kansas, could there have been any amalgamation there?" Whose policies were more favorable to miscegenation, Lincoln queried rhetorically, those of his opponent, who would vote to extend slavery, or his, which relied on legal sanctions to block its expansion?[43] Corwin was less circumspect. Apparently forgetting his earlier insistence that nature could be relied on to assign whites to certain climatic zones and blacks to others, he warned an audience of Southerners that Republicans "will keep out the Negro . . . I care not whether the territory be at the north pole or near the equator, they will go there and will keep your negroes out."[44]

As Lincoln intimated, nowhere was the relevance of race to containment more pointedly made than in 'bleeding Kansas.' Trumbull proclaimed himself "for the government of free white men," whereas under the Lecompton Constitution "they have no right to determine the institutions for the government of white men." That constitution "amounts simply to giving the free white people of Kansas a right to determine the condition of a few negroes."[45] In arguing for a renewal of exclusion, Congressman David Ritchie of Pennsylvania reasoned that if "a free white population is superior to a black slave population . . . in founding a state . . . it follows that the law [Missouri Compromise of 1820] prohibiting the introduction of the inferior race into Kansas . . . ought not to have been repealed."[46] As Robert J. Walker, the territorial governor, formerly from Mississippi, astutely noted, "those who oppose slavery in Kansas do not base their opposition upon any philanthropic principles, or any sympathy for the African race, for in their so-called constitution, framed at Topeka, they deem that entire race so inferior and degraded, as to exclude them all forever from Kansas, whether they be bond or free."[47]

Indeed, if any doubt existed that the Topeka Constitution reflected the will of the Republican Party, it was dispelled by Republican Party leaders. Doolittle pictured the struggle in Kansas as being in the nature of a contest to see which race got there first and excluded the other. The contest, however, had a happy ending: "we [Republicans] drove slavery out of Kansas, by free white men first taking possession and holding it."[48]

The party, said Maine Republican Israel Washburn, would keep Negro slavery out of Kansas, so that " . . . one white man could stand on a position of equality with another."[49] Speaking in Chicago in 1858, Trumbull related how the slaveholder "marches up to Kansas and when he gets up to the [territorial] line, the white men of Kansas meet him and say 'we do not want you to bring these niggers here; we don't want that population here.'"[50]

In view of such sentiments, it is not surprising that Republicans saw the struggle in Kansas as crucial. Should slavery not be contained by exclusion from that territory, Benjamin Wade had predicted in 1856, it would "not only be established in Kansas, but in every territory, if not every state in the Union."[51]

There was no question, then, that Republicans were as equally determined as Free Soilers that slavery must not be permitted to spread to the territories, or the new states that would be carved from them; and Republican leaders, like Free Soil leaders, assured their followers that precedents had already been established. The Founding Fathers, maintained Frank Blair, had been crystal clear on this point. Their creed had included the "policy of [the] non-extension of slavery," and the "standard of Republicanism must be advanced to embrace the whole [of that] creed . . . . "[52] Henry Smith Lane pointed specifically to Jefferson as an exponent of containment. His Northwest Ordinance of 1787 was a fine example of that Father's determination to prevent the expansion of slavery into the territories. This policy, Lane added, had also been the "doctrine of the Whig platform as laid down by Mr. [Henry] Clay."[53] Lincoln, too, rang in Clay's name. He cited that statesman's "speeches [as] showing him in favor . . . of excluding it [slavery] in the formation of new states where it did not exist."[54] More recently, the Compromise of 1850 had, according to Frank Blair's father, Francis Preston, offered a means of restricting slavery to the South.[55]

By adhering to these precedents and, above all, by overcoming the South's resistance to the Wilmot Proviso, the Republican Party would exclude the slave system from the territories; and, when this exclusion was combined with the exclusion of slavery and black people from the Western states, the effect would be to isolate the 'black South' from the rest of the nation. Accordingly, Eli Thayer's "Emigrant Aid Association announced its purpose to form a cordon of free states around the slave territory."[56] Thinking of a permanent and impregnable wall, Congressman Cydnor Bailey Tompkins of Ohio wanted to "draw an impassable line around slavery, and confine it within its present limits."[57] Other party members urged that white settlers be "posted in all the West," so that "they would hem in slavery in the Southern states, surround it . . . and contribute to the final destruction of the system."[58] Only when it was "completely hemmed in," predicted Wisconsin Republican Edward E. Dunbar, " . . . and not till then, will the South become conscious of the enormity of the evil she is fostering." In other words, only after the Republican Party had succeeded in containing slavery would the South take a serious introspective look at its peculiar institution, would, in Dunbar's words, the "South begin to cast about and inquire 'what shall we do to rid ourselves of four or five millions of blacks?'"[59]

II

As noted, Republican support for confining slavery and the black man to the South was predicated on the assumed benefits that policy would bring to the Caucasian population of the country. When Republican Senator Jacob Collamer of Vermont opposed the extension of slavery, he did so on the premise that "this Government was [created] for [the benefit of] the white race."[60] In the words of Senator Seward of New York: Far from having "an unnatural sympathy with the negro," Republicans "who have protested against the extension of slavery" were really evincing "concern for the welfare of the white man."[61] "It is not the rights of [the] black man that the Republicans are contending for," declared Hawkins Taylor, Republican leader of Keokuk County, Iowa, "but for the freedom of the white man."[62] Respecting the territories specifically, the Republican Party, by excluding slavery and blacks from them, would not only be eliminating the twin threats of economic competition and miscegenation but would be reserving them for white settlement. This policy, Harlan told Congress, was in marked contrast to the policy of the Democratic Party. The effect of the latter policy, too, would be exclusion, but exclusion of the wrong people, "exclusion of millions of our own blood," exclusion of the "superior by the inferior race."[63]

No, cried King of New York; the "territories of this country must be preserved for the white man."[64] Others concurred with King. "I am for sustaining the rights of free white labor in the territories," declared fellow New York Republican, Jonas A. Hughston.[65] "All of the national territories," echoed James Doolittle, "shall be held for white men." And, indicative of his faith in the white man's manifest destiny, the Wisconsin Senator claimed that the West was reserved for the Caucasian by a higher law, because it was "that zone where he was placed by the God of Heaven."[66] Republican territorial Representative, Marcus J. Parrott of Kansas, referred specifically to the white man's "'manifest destiny,'" when asserting before Congress that the "black race and the red race are fated to fade and be scattered before the advancing whites."[67] "It is for the interests of this great country, for the interests of the people who are to settle our territories," Trumbull stated emphatically, that "they should be settled by a free white people."[68] Congressman Henry Waldron of Michigan said that he was looking to a time in which the "white laborer would carve out his own future on the prairies of the West."[69] And when Frank Blair and Edward Bates, stumping for the party in 1860, called for the territories to be occupied by an "homogeneous people," no one doubted by which color they defined homogeneity.[70] It was the Caucasian race which would ultimately people the West, and when it did so, Tompkins of Ohio assured Congress, it would be "surpassing in power and glory anything the world has ever seen."[71] None of these sentiments augured well for the future of darker skinned people, and in particular blacks and Native Americans, the latter soon to be the victims of a series of Great Plains Wars under a succession of Republican presidents.

The political instrument which would effect this wonderful conclusion in the territories, said Republicans, was, to be sure, their party. From the beginning of its national existence, that party had made clear its racial preferences. The "Appeal of the Independent Democrats," indeed had at the outset called for a free West preserved for a "free, industrious and enlightened population . . . freedom-loving emigrants [sic] from Europe, and energetic and intelligent laborers from our own land," who would not "work beside slaves."[72] In its first presidential campaign in 1856, the Republican National Committee had declared that Republicans were a people "who would make a constellation of free, bright republics [from the Western territories], constituted of the white race alone."[73] By reserving the territories for the white race, Republicans, in the promise of David Wilmot, would defend the "independence, dignity and rights of the free white laboring man and his posterity."[74] "[O]ur policy," wrote one of Trumbull's constituents, Republican J. M. Palmer, "is . . . to throw ourselves . . . in front of the movement [of slavery into the territories], to make it a contest for free homes for free white men."[75]

Palmer's emphasis on "free homes" pointed the way. In fine, Republicans believed it imperative that their policy of excluding the black man from the territories be coupled with a program that, by providing free homesteads, would attract the white man to the territories. The first section of one homestead bill introduced into Congress in 1854 restricted its benefits to "any free white person." Moreover, since the expression "citizen of the United States" was usually included as a qualifier in most of these bills, and since most states did not recognize black citizenship, blacks found themselves doubly excluded.[76] Shortly after Lincoln's election in 1860 Doolittle wrote to Trumbull that the party should continue to press its "homestead policy for free whites in our territories." The Wisconsin Senator frankly supported homestead legislation, "because opening our territories to free white men will, in my opinion, tend to prevent their Africanization."[77] Michigan Republicans endorsed homestead legislation because, they said, they desired the benefits of free land to go to white and not black people. In 1860 the chairman of the Republican Central Committee of Michigan presented a homestead resolution which proclaimed that the "permanent welfare of our country must rest upon free white labor . . . . "[78] With similar intent the Adair County Republicans of Missouri passed a resolution which supported homestead legislation and declared that they were "in favor of preserving the territorial domain for homes for free white laborers."[79]

When Republicans came to draw up homestead bills to present to Congress, they designed them to appeal not only to Western farmers, who had long been clamoring for free land, but also to white workers in the

East and in particular to new immigrant workers from Europe. Recognizing the fear of white workers, native-born and immigrant, of labor competition from black workers, writes one historian, Republicans adopted a "free-homestead plank, in an attempt to lure working men into the party."[80] Actually, both Western farmers and Eastern workers could agree on the point. By 1860 the homestead bill of Republican Congressman Galusha Grow of Pennsylvania was endorsed by Wisconsin Republicans, precisely because its passage would ensure that in the future the territories would be occupied by free white laboring men and not by Africans;[81] earlier, the immigrant Hungarian archaeologists, Francis and Theresa Pulszky, had written that the objective of attracting immigrants by homestead legislation was to cause a "dense white population [in the West] which can and will displace slavery."[82] Harlan concurred, and in 1860 asked fellow Congressmen to accept the Republican homestead policy and by doing so "people the continent with the most . . . intellectual and powerful people," by which he meant, of course, Caucasians.[83]

The trouble, however, Benjamin Wade insisted, was that Northern and Southern Democrats did not appreciate this objective. Instead of backing homestead legislation so that white laborers, immigrants and farmers could establish themselves in the free territories of the West, they were more interested in increasing the size of the black population in the country. According to Wade, the homestead question between the two parties came down to this: "shall we give niggers to the niggerless, or land to the landless?"[84] When Iowa Republicans called for homestead legislation, they quoted Wade almost verbatim: Their appeal was based on "land for the landless versus Niggers for the Niggerless."[85] In 1859, while campaigning in St. Joseph, Missouri, Frank Blair castigated the slave states, because the "South demanded . . . opposition to the homestead bill, fearing . . . the throwing open of the public lands to the poor white men of the North."[86] James Harlan, when speaking of the Western territories, captured the sentiment and position of many party members, when he declared that the "policy of the Republican Party invites the Anglo-Saxon, the Celt, the Gaul, and others of Caucasian blood, by its proposed preemption and homestead laws, to enter and occupy them, and by the exclusion of slavery, it will practically exclude the negro and kindred races."[87]

III

While Republican leaders followed the intelligentsia and Free Soilers in adopting the short run policies of exclusion and containment, they also followed them in adopting long run policies. Some Republicans believed that merely emancipating the slaves over a period of time, with compensation to their masters, would eliminate the pretended black problem, because freed blacks would not survive in the competitive labor market of their white superiors. Others espoused a belief in natural migration, and thought that, once emancipated, blacks would move of their own volition toward the tropical regions of Central and South America. Finally there were many party members who believed that, to clear the nation of the black presence, emancipation must be accompanied by what was termed voluntary colonization, or even, if necessary, outright deportation. Although the belief in climatic determination was just as important for the second group of Republicans, as it had been for the learned community of Agassiz, Van Evrie, and others, it was not, as will be seen, without significance for the last group. Furthermore, some Republican colonizationists saw black emigration as an opportunity for American imperial ventures in Central and South America, while others advocated what could be termed white colonization, whereby Caucasian settlers, usually laborers from what were described as the more advanced Northern states, would supplant black laborers in the South and elsewhere. In any event the ultimate objective was to create an homogeneous white population for the United States.

A number of Republicans favored a program of gradual, compensated emancipation. The liberal and later Radical Republican, Charles Sumner, for example, "'expressed a willingness to compensate slaveowners at national expense,'" if they would emancipate their chattel.[88] Owen Lovejoy was also willing to support such a policy, even if emancipation were only very gradual. "We shall not push you," he assured Southern slaveholders. "If you say that you want a quarter of a century, you can have it; if you want half a century, you can have it. But I insist that this system [slavery] must ultimately be extinguished."[89] Apparently, neither Sumner nor Lovejoy saw such a scheme as posing a danger to the economic interests of the white laboring classes. Other party members who supported gradual emancipation obviously did not. Isaac Lea and Dr. Julian M. Sturtevant of Illinois, both Republican organizers in that state, were among those who believed that once freed, the black man would die out. With his innately inferior labor skills, he simply lacked the wherewithal to compete with the superior white laborer for the necessities of life.[90] John Pettit predicted that if blacks came North in large numbers, they would eventually "starve," because they could only gain a "scanty subsistence from a scanty employment." Simply stated, this Indianan surmised that blacks would be "overpowered and annihilated" by Northern white labor.[91] Using the "free people of color . . . at the North" as an example, Congressman John Thompson of New York put it this way: "a fearful diminution has taken place in their numbers" as a result of "poverty" caused "by the social pressure of the white upon the negro, of the superior upon the inferior [race]."[92]

Like the ethnologists and Free Soilers, many Republicans seemed convinced that climate was paramount in determining the habitat of the different races. Commonly, party members located the white man's 'natural' domain as being in North America, while they located the black man's as being further south. Connecticut Republican, Representative Alfred A. Burnham, claimed that the tropical regions near the equator were congenial to the black man, implying that they were not so for the white man.[93] Politically, climatic determinism came into play when attacking the idea of annexing Cuba. Senator Zachariah Chandler of Michigan told his fellow Congressmen that white "people cannot live there," because "tropical diseases always rage there at certain seasons of the year." By contrast, the Senator averred, black people were obviously living on the island, presumably immune to such diseases.[94]

Other Republicans opined that much of Central and South America, although by climate inhospitable to white people, was ideally suited to black people. Governor Samuel J. Kirkwood of Iowa claimed that the Negro was "peculiarly adapted by climate" to those regions.[95] Benjamin Wade agreed that those equatorial "tropics . . . [provide] a climate perfectly congenial to . . . the negro . . . where his nature seems to be improved . . . and where the white man degenerates in the same proportion as the black man prospers."[96] In fact, according to Frank Blair, blacks were the only people "capable of exertion in that climate." "[W]hile the white man degenerates and withers in the glare of all its splendor," Blair asserted, the "black man, by virtue of that mysterious quality of organism conferred by race," finds this region "an elixir for body and mind." Black people, the Missourian concluded, were "children of the sun."[97] James Doolittle, too, called blacks "children of the tropics." Sounding much like the Philadelphia businessman and amateur ethnologist, Benjamin Hunt, Doolittle insisted that the areas south of the United States were simply "too hot to be occupied by free white laborers," but were perfect for "colored men of African descent." In fact, blacks were "superior to the white man there, physically at least."[98]

By the same token Republicans declared that the Northern Hemisphere was ideally suited for the white man's habitation but quite unsuited for the black man's. In sum, where the black man supposedly thrived, that is in the tropical zones, the white man wilted, and where the white man supposedly thrived, that is in the colder zones, the black man succumbed to the harsh climate. To the Republicans who accepted this line of reasoning the final result seemed ordained. "In the solution of these great [racial] questions," prophesied Doolittle, "the men of our own race, from the temperate zones of the Old World . . . will hold, in the end, exclusive possession of the temperate zones of the New, while the descendants of the men of the tropics of the Old World, now among us, will find their homes in the tropics of the New." Hence, "is [each man] adapted by the laws of his constitution," for a specific geographical zone, namely the "zone of his fathers [sic]."[99]

Obviously, some Republicans believed that geographical determinism would at the least help rid the United States of its black population. They assumed that, once freed from slavery, the black man would naturally gravitate to his optimum habitat, the warmer, tropical regions, and conveniently leave the Caucasian in sole possession of his optimum habitat, the temperate United States. When Missouri Congressman Frank Blair talked about the "immense accession to her [Missouri's] white population from the East," he also described the anticipated exodus of the black man as a "mass of another hue," which would inexorably pass "toward the South." This movement, Blair believed, would, in turn, encourage more whites to enter his home state. Waxing poetically, he predicted that "more light will pursue this dark, retreating body, as it follows the shadow of a cloud passing from our fields."[100] Similar to Agassiz and various Free Soilers, Doolittle thought that only the institution of slavery prevented this natural draining away of America's black population, and he told his Southern colleagues that they "must make an outlet for these people." He referred to this process as a "resistless current in human affairs," which "is flowing onward to the tropics with this race." Claiming that the "colored race will go further and further south, and by a system of gradual amelioration and emancipation, be removed at last," he noted that, "for one, I would not undertake to resist it. I would aid it onward and onward." Also like Agassiz and these Free Soilers, Doolittle was convinced that this migration southward of the "colored race" was destined "by the very force of climate." At the same time, the "white race [would] become so enfeebled in the tropics, by the operation of the same laws," that it must move back to its more temperate zone.[101]

Just in case these so-called natural laws failed to do their duty, however, and providing Southern slaveholders would accept a program of gradual, compensated emancipation, many Republican political leaders, including Frank Blair and James Doolittle, were willing to help the process along; they would actively encourage the colonization of America's black population to warmer climates in Africa, or the Caribbean and Central and South America. When campaigning in Philadelphia in 1860 Blair asked his audience rhetorically: "why not [by supporting black colonization] conform to the laws of nature, by which we see the different races of men planted in the different [geographical] zones?" Only in this way, Blair insisted, would the two races be "each . . . [in] the climate for which he [sic] is adapted." In fact, Blair put the party on the side of God when he stated that the "Republicans favor the colonization of the negroes, providing them homes in a region that the Almighty intended for them."[102] In similar fashion Trumbull also equated the Republican policy of colonization with some master plan of God, claiming "a distinction between the white and black races," which was a product of the "Omnipotence Himself."[103] While Blair was campaigning in Philadelphia, Benjamin Wade spoke before Congress on the subject of freed blacks, maintaining that Congress should endorse colonization because it "owes it to itself and to the free white population of the nation to provide a means whereby this class . . . may emigrate to some congenial clime."[104]

Congress evidently also owed such a policy to the originators and leading national heroes of the country. To illustrate, many Republicans proudly pointed to Jefferson and the Founding Fathers, or to Henry Clay, the great Whig leader, as their predecessors in supporting the idea of black colonization. Benjamin Wade, for one, spoke about the "far-reaching sagacity of Thomas Jefferson," who had suggested colonization years ago.[105] James Ashley noted that the Republicans "favor, as Jefferson did, the emancipation and separation of the races."[106] Bates' biographer writes that "in all matters Bates was a moderate, a great admirer of both Jefferson and Clay," and one who favored Henry Clay's doctrine of black deportation "as the only way to preserve a country of white men." Bates, like Clay, "envisioned a program of gradual, compensated emancipation and colonization" for blacks.[107]

Trumbull likewise invoked the names of both Jefferson and Clay when he endorsed the "idea of the deportation of the free negro population from this country." The Illinois Senator said that he "agree[d] with the sentiment of Mr. Jefferson, that two races which are marked by distinctive features cannot live peacefully together."[108] "Jefferson," Doolittle, too, asserted, "foresaw that the races could not dwell securely and happily together." When writing to Governor Kirkwood of Iowa, he proclaimed colonization the "great Jeffersonian plan for the solution of the negro question." In public, too, Doolittle's solution to this supposed problem was that "proposed by Jefferson [and] concurred in and sustained by . . . Clay;" it was the "only wise and practical one," in that it called for the "colonization and deportation of the emancipated race."[109]

The "time has ripened for the execution of Mr. Jefferson's plan," Frank Blair maintained. Jefferson, he continued, "favored the separation of the races for the sake of the negro, but still more for the sake of his own race," because Jefferson "knew full well that the chief evils of slavery do not fall on the slave." Citing Jefferson for his inspiration, Blair wrote to Governor Kirkwood asking that his state "take the first step in the great scheme [colonization]." By doing this Iowans would be "carrying into practice the long cherished plans of Mr. Jefferson . . . to provide an outlet."[110]

Undoubtedly in the view of Republicans the most important beneficiary of black colonization would be the white man. Iowa Republicans were convinced that colonization would be a boon to the white race. Although they claimed that "both races suffer from being together . . . of the two, the white race are the greatest [sic] sufferers."[111] Republicans were not reticent in lauding the ways in which black colonization would serve Caucasian America. Explicitly, it would accomplish several objectives. In relieving the country of black people, colonization would end worry or concern among Republicans over the increasing size of the black population within the United States. In 1860 the Adair County Republicans of Missouri adopted a colonization resolution which stressed the "great importance of separating the two races" because "of the rapidly increasing free colored population of the several states."[112] Appealing for congressional acceptance of colonization and alarmed at the "increasing . . . ratio [of black people in the South], compared with the increase of the whites," Doolittle averred that colonization offered the "southern slave states the only possible escape from Africanization."[113]

As envisaged by Republicans, merely beginning a government sponsored program of black colonization would encourage the extinction of slavery within the United States. Frank Blair's older brother James, declared colonization a prelude to emancipation and, contingent upon Southern acceptance of such a program, predicted that "not far distant in the future, I can behold the extinction of negro slavery."[114] Frank Blair called on the South to start the process of colonization: "to begin the movement for emancipation." To Blair's mind the solution to the problem of slavery was simple; all that was required was land for colonization: "whenever a region is acquired . . . to make a permanent home for our American freedman, emancipation will take place rapidly."[115] The "final end" of slavery, said Edward Bates, "would come with the adoption of colonization."[116] A fourth Missouri Republican and friend of the Blair family, James B. Gardenhire, stated point blank that colonization "will free us of slavery . . . without leaving free negroes among us."[117]

With the end of slavery and the black man within the United States would also come the end of worry over future slave insurrections and racial confrontations. Colonization, it was thought, would result in the peaceful separation of the races. Kirkwood claimed blacks threatened white tranquility, but he viewed colonization "as a means for relieving our country of the vast numbers of these [black] people among us."[118] One Connecticut Republican, Representative Orris S. Ferry, would, a la Henry Clay, gladly use federal revenues to colonize black Americans, because of what he labelled their "irritating contact" with the "prouder [white] race."[119] Congressman Charles B. Sedgwick of neighboring New York insisted that "free blacks had become . . . a dangerous element in their [white] society," but such an element could be eliminated by the "policy of their colonization."[120]

Most Republicans seemed optimistic and viewed colonization as a feasible national program, therefore assuming a cooperative South. Evidently they believed that Southern whites were as paranoid over black people as they were. Frank Blair maintained that the Northern states, like the Southern states, feared a large free black population within their midst and when speaking at St. Paul, Minnesota he told the South that "unless you provide an outlet for the negroes . . . and then . . . go for a separation of the races," the North would not consider emancipation, even if the South should decide on such a course.[121] Colonization, Benjamin Wade asserted confidently, "will insure a separation of the races," and by doing so prevent racial conflicts from developing, because it was "impossible" for the black and the white races to live together and "be prosperous and happy." Besides, Wade conjectured, such a scheme would be "easy" to accomplish.[122] The Secretary of the Indiana State Board of Colonization, the Reverend James Mitchell, who otherwise predicted "a struggle between the black and the white race which, within the next one or two hundred years must sweep over this nation," called for a "state supported program of colonization" as a necessary component in achieving a "well digested separation policy," which would avert the impending conflict.[123] Doolittle agreed with Mitchell, but insisted that a nationally sponsored program of colonization was necessary so that "we [the North and the South] shall effect the ultimate, peaceful separation of the races."[124]

Other Republicans pointed to what they thought was the major benefit which would accrue to the white race through black colonization; the purity of the white race would be preserved. Republican concern here seemed indefatigable, and implicit in this concern was the belief in the racial incompatibility of blacks and whites. For instance, when speaking at Springfield, Illinois, Lincoln stated that what he "would most desire, would be the separation of the white and black races." This desire was born of the knowledge that "a separation of the races is the only perfect preventive of amalgamation," and this separation "must be effected by colonization."[125] Fellow Illinoian, Judge William Kitchell, reiterated Lincoln's point, demanding that the blacks be colonized, "or the white race will amalgamate with them."[126] Ashley of Ohio also viewed colonization as the ultimate answer to the presumed problem of miscegenation in the United States.[127] All Caucasians, Frank Blair wrote, "who believe that the negroes are an inferior race, will rejoice in a complete separation of the races," because this separation was the only way to "avoid that contact which deteriorates our own [race]." Since Blair depicted miscegenation as the "pollution" of the blood of the superior race, for him nothing could stop this deterioration, but a "complete separation" of the two races. Like Lincoln, Kitchell and Ashley, he insisted that colonization "will save us from amalgamation."[128] A group of Indiana Republicans suggested a more direct approach to achieve this separation and end the black problem: If "miscegenation was an inevitable result of the system of slavery in the South . . . the way to stop it was to put an end to slavery," by deporting the black man out of the country.[129]

Some Republicans conjectured that colonization would lead to an expansion of the white population in the country. To illustrate, James Blair prophesied that the "fresh footprints of the departing slave will be blotted out by the advancing steps of thousands of white freeman." While campaigning for the party in Missouri, he told his listeners that the state would soon overflow with white men, would, in essence, become a "white man's state" and "it will be the brightest day in your history, when he [the black man] is . . . removed from your soil," so that white settlers could claim sole possession of it.[130]

Black colonization, however, was perceived as more than just a solution to the so-called race problem. For a number of Republicans it represented an opportunity for American economic and commercial expansion into the areas south of the United States. Acquiring settlement lands in Central and South America, could also mean acquiring economic and political control over those lands. A well-monitored policy could ensure that these lands, as protectorates established for the habitation of the deported blacks, would be under the control of the United States government. And given that sponsorship, the black colonists would be a spearhead for American economic penetration into these areas and for American commerce with indigenous peoples. Imperialistic overtones, therefore, accompanied much of the rhetoric of Republican colonizationists. It's hard to escape the thought that this incipient Republican imperialism would later bear fruit under future Republican administrations, such as those of William McKinley and Theodore Roosevelt. During the heyday of Social Darwinism, the racist ideology, the party, and the main areas of interest, i.e. the Caribbean, Central and South America, were all the same. There is a nice continuity here between black colonization and the later quest for empire.

When Frank Blair described the tropical area of the New World, he described it as a promised land, where "all that is required to develop its untold wealth, is a race of men capable of enduring the climate." He had no doubt that it would be by the "negro race . . . alone,.that those regions are to be regenerated." There was, of course, again the contradiction. As long as the black man was in their midst, Blair and most Republicans, as had their Free Soil predecessors, depicted him as an ignorant and useless sambo; however, once in the tropics he would suddenly, they seemed to argue, become something of a superman. A miraculous metamorphosis would take place. Negro emigrants, Blair proclaimed, would "bear with them a knowledge of our civilization and government; they would carry habits of industry acquired among us, and a morality and religion not possessed by any of the people of those countries." In the end he was certain that colonization "will give us the commerce of the richest tropics on the globe," by giving the superior Anglo-American race control over the "feebler races within the reach of its influence," and thereby help the United States "establish a great national power" in the Western hemisphere.[131]

Blair was joined by other Republican leaders, such as Eli Thayer, no stranger to emigration schemes and commercial endeavors, who spoke of forming "a number of companies, which can control the [black] emigration of this country" to Central America. These emigration companies, declared the Massachusetts Congressman, would act as "bands of steel" by which "we [can] bind the people of Central America to us and to our interests." Thayer, who spoke of this process as the "Americanizing of Central America," was particularly interested in the "profit of the thing [black emigration]," which would accrue to white Americans like himself.[132] Ohio Governor Dennison pictured American black colonists as "building up a new domain, pregnant with political and commercial advantage" for white businessmen.[133] One result of black colonization in the Latin republics, Doolittle stated succinctly, would be "the opening of an empire at our feet."[134]

Also of importance to the new party was what it hoped would be the appeal of colonization to the conservative Border slave states, states in which the Republicans wanted to make political inroads. Doolittle believed that colonization would offer "a measure of policy, by which our friends in Missouri, Maryland, Delaware, Kentucky and Virginia, who are emancipationists, can fight the battle and win the victory there."[135]

Not only would colonization serve the white man, Republicans argued it would presumably serve the black man as well, by placing him in his 'predestined' or 'natural' climatic zone. Republicans also averred that by removing him from the prejudice, dominance and competition of the white man, the Negro would be additionally benefitted. Perhaps this claim was an attempt to lure blacks into accepting their scheme. Ironically, Republicans seemed to be adding daily to the growing prejudice against black people. At any rate Representative William McKee Dunn of Indiana proposed black colonization "for the benefit of such free persons of African descent" who would be gradually emancipated from slavery.[136] Iowa Republicans referred to what they called the white man's "prejudice of centuries" against blacks, as sufficient reason for promoting colonization.[137] Lyman Trumbull dressed his arguments in humanitarian garb, insisting that such a scheme would benefit blacks, because "there shall be no superior race to domineer over them."[138]

One area in which blacks were supposedly dominated by whites was that of labor skills. But with the adoption of colonization, free blacks would have the opportunity, according to Doolittle, "to seek elsewhere a more favorable field for their labor." Indeed, Doolittle viewed colonization as a form of black homesteading. When addressing the Senate he elaborated. He stated that the Republicans "propose to the people of this country, a policy which looks towards opening the . . . whole of Central America, the whole of the inter-tropical regions of this continent, as homesteads for the free colored population of the United States." Furthermore, the Wisconsin Senator described colonization as the only means to give "civil and social equality to the free colored men who are among us."[139] As others, before and after him, Doolittle failed to see the inherent contradiction in his proposition; that, in fact, colonization was a complete denial of black civil rights. Harlan maintained that colonization would allow the black man to "flourish and prosper" and to "demonstrate to the world his capacity for self-government," things which he ostensibly could not do while in the white society of the United States.[140] Echoing Doolittle and Harlan, Frank Blair observed that only by leaving the country and setting up a government of his own, away from the influence of the superior white man, could the black man hope to achieve his civil liberties.[141] Bates of Missouri captured the arguments of Republicans who thought colonization would benefit black Americans, when he depicted such a program as "humane," in the sense that colonization would protect the weaker black race from aggressive whites.[142]

A few Republicans also saw colonization as aiding the black race in general by both propagating Christianity in and excluding slavery from areas outside the United States; they predicted that colonization would end the perpetuation of slavery and help prevent the spread of it to the areas being colonized. In keeping with the idea that American slavery was a school, a learning experience for black people that, according to Corwin, "enlightened" them, he then argued that ex-slaves, by being colonized in Africa, would "accomplish the great work of Christianizing and civilizing the African race."[143] As had Harriet Beecher Stowe, Corwin apparently viewed Christianity and slavery as incompatible institutions. Doolittle put it this way: "Plant hundreds of thousands [of free blacks] in all these states [in Central and South America], and slavery and the slave trade can no more go there than they could go through a wall of fire." Colonization, he continued, "pre-occupies the ground with free colored colonies."[144]

Whether speaking within Congress, or corresponding without, Republican political leaders invoked colonization as the remedy for the black problem. In 1857 Lincoln wanted his party to take the lead in adopting a colonization program, because the Democrats would not. Pointing to the Democratic administration in Washington, he stated that "no political party . . . is now doing anything directly for colonization."[145] When he became president he would correct that omission. In 1859 Montgomery Blair wrote to James Doolittle that colonization "would . . . define accurately our [Republican] objects and disabuse the minds of the great body of the Southern people . . . that the Republicans wish to set Negroes free among them to be their equals."[146] Doolittle also wrote a letter that same year to a fellow Republican Senator and backer of colonization, Hannibal Hamlin. The Wisconsin politician called on all Republicans to adopt the following program: "Let our cry in 1860 be down with the slave trade, down with filibustering, down with amalgamation; we are for a separation of the races."[147]

Perhaps the most enthusiastic advocate of black colonization was Frank Blair. Blair made several major speeches around the country lauding colonization. Between 1858 and 1860 he spoke in such places as St. Paul, Philadelphia, St. Louis, Boston and Cincinnati. In these speeches the Missouri Congressman took Roger B. Taney's ruling in the Dred Scott decision to its logical conclusion. Referring to the Chief Justice's ruling that a black man has "no rights which we [whites] are bound to respect . . . that he is not included . . . in the great Declaration of the rights of humanity . . . that he has no soul," Blair called for black colonization.[148] Instead of denouncing the Court's decision on ethical and moral grounds and calling for citizenship for blacks and the removal of their legal disabilities, the Missourian, by calling instead for the removal of black people, seemed to lend substance to Taney's arguments that blacks were not citizens, that they did not belong in the predominantly white society of the United States. Frank Blair's strenuous efforts on behalf of colonization were probably spurred by the fact that his father, the aged patriarch, Francis Preston Blair, strongly recommended the same policy.[149]

Republican constituents applauded the efforts of party politicians on behalf of colonization. For instance, a number of Trumbull's Illinois constituents wrote to him heartily endorsing his commitment to black colonization. One of them, D. C. Phillips, noted that he was "exceedingly pleased" with Trumbull's course, because "it shows the right spirit and has the proper end in view, colonization of the Negro population." This program, Phillips was convinced, would "be hailed with delight throughout the West."[150] Another, J. McKibben, wrote that black colonization "meets not only my views, but the views of this part of the state."[151]

Even those Republicans who were associated with the liberal wing of the party and at times questioned the morality of black colonization, such as Charles Sumner and Salmon P. Chase, seemed at other times to subscribe to the idea. Sumner "'expressed a willingness . . . to examine plans for colonizing freedman in the tropics.'"[152] Chase was more specific on the future area of tropical settlement; prophetically he spoke of finding a "means of settling them in Hayti."[153]

Like James Blair, some Republicans went beyond the concept of voluntary colonization, by calling for the forceful eviction of the black man from the country. Few would accuse Trumbull of being self-effacing in this matter after he promised fellow Senators that the "idea of the deportation of the free negro population from this country" would become a "part of the creed of the Republican Party."[154] One of Trumbull's constituents, Judge Kitchell, echoed that Senator's feelings when he wrote that it was "vain to talk of emancipation without a corralitive [sic] rule of deportation," and he called for a Republican "plan for the colonization of all the now free Negroes and all others, as fast as their masters may please to free them." He insisted that the "blacks must be deported . . . . "[155]

As an adjunct to black colonization, a few Republicans supported a scheme of white colonization, or the homesteading of white men to replace the black laborers who, under colonization, were to be deported.

Albeit in a limited way, this idea was put into effect through the efforts of Congressman Eli Thayer of Massachusetts, who sent white immigrants into Kansas, and planted a white settlement in Virginia. He described the result as a Caucasian "invasion," by a "great Army of industry" which brought with it "intelligence, refinement and moral progress." In fact, Thayer referred to this "Army" as the "Yankee race, [which] has at least an octave more compass than any other," and said that Congress "should colonize the northern border slave states" with this race, and thereby "exterminate slavery."[156] Montgomery Blair endorsed Thayer's Emigrant Aid Association, especially in its work in planting white settlers in Kansas.[157] Similarly, Benjamin Wade supported a program for homesteading the South with white workers.[158] Also from Ohio, Republican Louis Krouskopf maintained that through black colonization the South would lose its worthless Negro population, but that through white colonization, they "will soon be replaced by [the] immigration of free men . . . 7 million of white free non-slaveholders" from the North.[159] One Republican, after hearing of Thayer's plans for Kansas and the South, wrote enthusiastically that "some such plan as this is the only means whereby the efforts of the nigger-drivers . . . can be effectually thwarted." Apparently disagreeing with theories of climatically determined racial zones, however, he predicted that this project would prove conclusively "that a white man can work wherever a black one can, as far as heat is concerned," and "if this scheme is successful, slavery extension . . . is at an end."[160] In spite of Thayer's work, the major efforts of the Republican Party nevertheless remained directed at black colonization.

Having decided upon the policy of colonization, Republicans needed to find a suitable location to which to deport black people. For some Republicans, any place would do, as long as blacks were removed from the country. In Indiana and Pennsylvania, Republicans simply "advocated[d] a policy of colonizing the free Negroes outside the United States."[161] However, since most party members believed in the theory of geographic determinism, they assumed that blacks belonged in a warmer or tropical climate. To illustrate, while opting for black colonization before Congress, Harlan declared that his party sought "to procure for the negro a home and an abiding place, outside of the United States, within the tropics."[162]

Several Republicans were more specific than James Harlan as to where this warmer or tropical location should be, and taking their cue from the American Colonization Society, which had been instrumental in the establishment of Liberia, a number of party members recommended Liberia or simply Africa as a possible site. Some of Kirkwood's Iowa constituents thought it a good idea to set up for this purpose "a line of Governmental Mail Steamers . . . between this country and Liberia."[163] Henry Smith Lane and Charles Sedgwick, on the other hand, did not care where in Africa blacks were colonized, believing only that if they were emancipated from slavery, they should be colonized on that continent.[164]

Ultimately most Republican leaders came to favor a warmer location closer to home, such as Central or South America, or the Caribbean islands. Logistically this made more sense to them because transportation costs would be cheaper and the actual operation easier to carry out. Bates, for one, stated that "Africa is distant and presents so many obstacles to rapid settlement, that we cannot indulge the hope of draining off in that direction, the . . . free black population" of the United States. Instead, the "tropical regions of America . . . offer a far better prospect" and, considering cost, a more "practical plan of colonization."[165] Trumbull was of similar mind: "I myself am very much inclined to favor . . . a plan for colonizing our free Negroes . . . somewhere in Central America." He, too, believed "it . . . impracticable to transport this great population to Africa."[166] Kirkwood joined Trumbull and Bates and strongly recommended "colonization in Central or South America" because, in a pragmatic vein, it "would be much less expensive" than colonization in Africa.[167]

In Ohio, Governor William Dennison thought that the federal government should start the process by looking to the "acquisition of some rich region in Central or South America, as a province for our native blacks."[168] The Republicans of Adair County, Missouri passed a resolution which declared that they were also "in favor of the general government procuring by treaty or purchase, in Central or South America, the rights of settlement and citizenship for the free colored men in the United States."[169] Having on numerous occasions expressed a willingness to "give the white laboring man the temperate latitudes" and the "free colored races the tropical latitudes," Doolittle, purporting to speak for the party, said Republicans would use the government "to secure in Central and tropical America, homes for the negro population." Specifically, the Wisconsin Senator named "Hayti, Jamaica, [and] Honduras" as potential sites. One major problem for Republicans, however, which would later become apparent, was to "induce those tropical states which are already in possession of the colored races . . . to open wide their territories for the surplus population of the United States of African descent."[170] Frank Blair, as did other Republicans at this time, joined Doolittle to back a governmental program that envisioned the "gradual transfer of four million of our freedmen to the vacant regions of Central and South America." By vacant regions Blair obviously meant someone else's land. Evidently this 'abandoned' land which Blair had in mind belonged to the Haitians, because, he asserted, "Jefferson . . . designated the Island of Hayti as the proper place for the colonization of our blacks."[171]

That colonization was an integral and logical part of the antislavery policy that Republicans set forth before Congress was clear. Politicians like Benjamin Wade and Governor Dennison of Ohio saw such a logical consistency in the party's adoption of colonization. Dennison wrote to Wade, that he was "thinking about saying something [in his inaugural address] . . . favorable to Frank Blair's colonization scheme," and he wanted Wade's endorsement for his stand. "I have the impression that you like it [colonization]," he continued, "and may not be unwilling to advocate it in the Senate." Moreover, since Wade had "given the subject some thought," and "in view of the logical sequence of the Republican argument against slavery [and in order] . . . to have something affirmative before the territories on this slavery subject from the Republican Party," Dennison believed that " . . . we may do our cause well to favor this colonization scheme." Wade carried out his part of the plan when speaking before Congress in 1860. He stated that "we [Republicans] shall be as glad to rid ourselves of these people [blacks] . . . as anybody else . . . . We will not drive them out, but we will use every inducement to persuade these unfortunate men to find a home there [in the tropics]. I hope," Wade continued, that "this great principle [colonization] will be engrafted into our platform as a fundamental article of our faith."[172]

Other Republicans saw the same continuity in argument. "I trust," Trumbull asserted before Congress, "that the Republican party will make it part of its creed, that this government should procure some region of country, not far distant, to which our free negro population may be taken."[173] According to James Ashley, by May of 1860 colonization was already an accepted part of Republican policy. Unequivocally Ashley proclaimed to Congress that the "policy of the Republican Party is . . . an ultimate separation of the two races . . . ."[174] James Harlan also opted before Congress for black colonization, declaring that the "Republicans will urge the adoption of the [colonization] proposition introduced by my friend [James R. Doolittle] . . . ." The Iowa Senator reasoned that this Republican position on the supposed race problem was much more logically consistent with general white racial attitudes than the Democratic one, which would lead to the diffusion and increase of black Americans, with all that that portended.[175]

Practically all Republican politicians in Congress supported black colonization. Even those Republicans, such as Doolittle and Frank Blair, who subscribed to the theory of natural migration, introduced various resolutions to accomplish colonization. In June of 1858 and again in March of 1859 Doolittle submitted a resolution into the Senate which, with the backing of numerous other Senate Republicans, was ordered printed for consideration by that body. This resolution called upon the Committee on Foreign Relations to inquire into the "expediency of acquiring, by treaty, in Yucatan, Central or South America, the rights and privileges of settlement" for "such persons of color of African descent, as may voluntarily desire to emigrate."[176] Trumbull added that this program should be a national endeavor, "and to show the sympathy of the North for the South . . . we will contribute liberally of our means to relieve the country of the free negro . . . and of all slaves who may be voluntarily emancipated." How the North would raise the funds for such a contribution he didn't say. Nevertheless, there was no doubt in the mind of the Illinois Senator that Republicans "would colonize them. We colonize Indians on our Western frontier, why can't we colonize the negro as well."[177]

In January 1858 Frank Blair introduced into the House of Representatives one of a number of Republican resolutions calling for black colonization. This one asked that a select committee be formed "to inquire into the expediency of providing for the acquisition of territory either in the Central or South American States, to be colonized with colored persons from the United States who are now free, or who may hereafter become free." Like Doolittle's, Blair's resolution enjoyed wide Republican support and was ordered printed for further consideration by the House.[178] William McKee Dunn of Indiana offered a similar resolution in May 1860, this one specifically calling for the Committee on Foreign Relations to inquire into the feasibility of acquiring land for a black settlement "on the adjacent islands south of the United States." Dunn's resolution was ruled out of order, however, after Jabez L. M. Curry, a states rights Democrat from Alabama, had registered his strong objections.[179] Apparently most of these early Republican colonization resolutions wound up in the Committee on Foreign Relations, where they remained. Perhaps party congressional leaders realized that their efforts were a bit premature. Between 1858 and 1860 Democratic opposition to colonization was too strong to overcome. Republican leaders would have to put off implementation of their program until they assumed power.

IV

While most Republicans seemed to subscribe to the racial beliefs that gave rise to the policies of exclusion, containment and colonization, some of them, even among the conservatives, also voiced sentiments which seemed to acknowledge a certain responsibility, albeit paternalistic, for uplifting the black race from the slough to which its purported moral and in particular mental weakness had reduced it. More important, a small but significant number of Republican political leaders manifested mixed feelings about both the racial beliefs of their party and the paternalism its members sometimes revealed. Just as had a few Free Soilers, a few Republicans (including those who as Free Soilers had once expressed similar thoughts) occasionally expressed the wish that black people should receive some measure of justice within the United States. These Republicans at times openly attacked slavery and the fugitive slave laws which lent it support; criticized the racial conservatism within their own party; and inveighed against the discriminatory policies of the Northern states and territorial governments.

Two things must be emphasized respecting these latter, more radical Republicans, however. First, they were themselves by no means innocent of racial bias. Even while speaking out on these subjects, they, too, could evince a certain paternalism and could continue to support black colonization. Secondly, although they exerted an effort to secure some justice for black Americans, most of that effort was never translated into political reality.

White paternalism, as it would later under the shibbolith, the white man's burden, may have acted to reaffirm the white man's belief in his own superiority and goodness. As an expression of this paternalism, the Illinois Republicans stated in 1857 that they "consider that [black] race . . . [more] entitled to sympathy, than . . . [to] constant and unrelenting oppression."[180] Congressman Philemon Bliss of Ohio spoke of how the white man "who seeks the elevation of the low, himself is elevated; while he who would keep them down, himself sinks."[181] Even though fellow Ohioan Edward Wade accepted the idea of white superiority, he ridiculed the ideas of "Rabbi Agassiz, Rabbi Gliddon, and . . . others" on distinct races, not only because such views contradicted the Bible, but more importantly because they were used to enslave fellow men.[182] Although Henry Wilson "refused to defend the Negro as a racial equal," he declared that "if the African race is inferior," it should be "educated" and "elevated."[183] Given the fact that the black man was a weak creature, William Seward insisted, he was "not the less therefore, entitled to such care and protection as the weak everywhere may require from the strong."[184] Frank Blair cautioned similarly that "even if the superiority of one race is established," that did not mean that the "inferior races are made for its service. On the contrary," he continued, "it is the true mission of a superior and enlightened race to protect . . . the feebler races."[185] Lovejoy expanded on this idea when he asserted that just because the black man was naturally "weak" or "inferior in intellect and position" did not mean that whites should "take advantage of him." He believed that even the "poorest and the lowest human being . . . the most degraded type of humanity . . . has a right to liberty."[186]

Perhaps James Harlan best captured the feelings of these Republicans;

if the black man's "body is weak, his mind feeble, his moral sensibilities obtuse, does that," he asked his fellow Congressmen, "confer the right on the man of strong body, of vigorous intellect and of acute moral sensibilities, to seize, overawe and enslave him?" When Harlan called for "separate schools . . . for the education of the colored children of the District [of Columbia]" he argued that it was only in this way, that "we [whites] can provide for the education of this degraded class of the community." Harlan wanted to know "what law of nature is there that prevents the strong from taking care of the weak; that prevents the powerful, the rich, those who are able, from providing for the education of the ignorant, the poor, the weak, the feeble?" Since, he proclaimed, the Anglo-Saxon was the greatest race, it was its especial mission to be "just to the weak, as well as the strong."[187]

Unfortunately, most Republicans who uttered such sentiments did little or nothing to implement them. A few party members, however, who appeared to be more enlightened than most, did seek to achieve some justice for black Americans. One way they did this was by helping black fugitives who were escaping from slavery. Both Joshua R. Giddings and Owen Lovejoy at times were able to rise above the rhetoric of paternalism by secretly continuing to give aid to escaping fugitives. Giddings kept a spare room in his Ashtabula, Ohio home, to hide them.[188] Lovejoy also harbored fugitives and even boasted of the fact. "There is no human being, black or white," he claimed, "that ever comes to my door and asks for food when hungry, or shelter, when houseless, but receives it."[189] In 1855 Governor James Grimes, one of the founders of the Republican Party in Iowa and the first Republican governor of that state, was confronted with his first case involving a fugitive slave who had escaped to his state. He wrote to his wife that he would "furnish no aid to the manstealers, and it has been determined that the negro shall have able counsel and a resort to all legal means for release;" but, he added, "I am sorry I am Governor." Three days later Grimes again wrote to his wife, this time expressing relief that his ordeal was over; that "negro is free, and is on his way to Canada."[190]

Some Republicans called for legal action to aid such fugitives. Hoping to secure due process for accused fugitive slaves found on Michigan soil, one of the more radical Michigan Republicans, Austin

Blair, backed a strong personal liberty law for his state in 1855.[191] James A. Garfield, an Ohio Republican, wanted his state to reenact the personal liberty law of April 1857, which would at least ameliorate the effects of the Fugitive Slave law of 1850 and give blacks a semblance of justice.[192] In the same vein Salmon P. Chase called for the reenactment of that same law (which was, in fact, reenacted, but for only ten months before it was again rescinded), so as to prevent "peaceful [free black] inhabitants," from being "cruelly kidnapped" by Southern slave bounty hunters.[193] It was just such activity on the part of these bounty hunters which prompted Schuyler Colfax in 1856 to protest against the Kansas slave codes' suspension of the writ of habeas corpus for accused black fugitives.[194]

A number of the more radical party members also assailed the inequity of the black codes. Chase had done so as a Free Soiler and he continued to do so. While Republican governor of Ohio he unsuccessfully recommended the repeal of that state's "Visible Admixture law," which allowed local judges to deny the franchise to anyone "'whenever it shall appear to such judge or judges, that the person so offering to vote has a distinct and visible admixture of African blood.'" Chase did not believe that free blacks should be discriminated against, since they were "guilty of no crime but color."[195]

In combatting racial discrimination, George Julian was critical of his fellow Indianans. Equating exclusionist legislation in the Northern states with that in the Southern slave states, he noted the "sad truth . . . that Indiana is the most pro-slavery of all our Northern states. Her black codes, branded upon her recreant forehead by a majority of nearly one hundred thousand of her voters, tells her humiliating pedigree far more forcibly than any words I could employ."[196]

In keeping with Julian's concern, Republican Representative Thomas M. Howe of Pennsylvania assailed the plan to exclude blacks from the benefits of Western homesteads. During one debate Howe moved an amendment to strike out the adjective "white," thereby allowing free blacks equal rights to these lands. Skin color, proclaimed Howe, was not grounds for denying a family a right to acquire a home.[197] Maine Republican, Representative Charles H. Gilman, not only protested against the exclusion of blacks, as provided for in the Oregon Constitution, but also their exclusion as witnesses in Oregon's courts. In fact, he carried his protest to the national level, noting that "By our naturalization laws, 'free white aliens' can only become citizens of the United States." To Gilman this limitation on citizenship was clearly wrong, and as a model he pointed to his own state, where the black man "is a citizen" and one who can "compare favorably with those whose skin is whiter."[198] From neighboring Massachusetts, Republican Senator Daniel Clark denounced the Kansas Constitution because it "excludes the free negro from the state." As had Gilman, Clark carried his defense of the black man to the national level, and held that the "free negro is as much entitled to live in one part of the country as another."[199] Schuyler Colfax attacked the idea that before they could even be employed in Kansas territory, blacks and mulattoes had to supply freedom papers to prospective employers to prove that they were free persons.[200]

Even the more conservative Doolittle at times expressed in Congress strong reservations about the exclusion of free blacks. In 1858, referring to exclusion in Kansas, he noted that "one provision in this [Topeka] constitution, declares that 'free negroes shall not be permitted to live in Kansas, under any circumstances.'" He wanted to know how in Kansas the black man could "assert his freedom" under such regulations? "Can he go into any court in Kansas and assert it? If he apply for a [writ of] habeas corpus, if he bring a suit for his freedom, he is estopped by the constitution . . . . The courts of Kansas will not suffer him to enter alive, and say that he is free." Worse yet, the "courts of the United States are closed against him, because of his African descent." Doolittle called the attention of Congressmen to the "numerous disabilities to which free persons of color of African descent are subjected, in many of the free states." Yet, in spite of his professed concern for black rights, and ignoring the denial of the elective franchise to free blacks within his own state, Doolittle referred to such black people as merely "strangers and sojourners among us."[201]

A few Republicans were critical of the Dred Scott decision, not like their more numerous party cohorts because of its assumed threat to the white man, but because of what it boded for black people. When Giddings assailed the decision, he did not agree with the Taney Court's interpretation of the Constitution, nor with the Court's claim that it was based on the beliefs of the Founding Fathers. Moreover, even if the decision had rested on the Constitution, that document did not and could not transcend the higher laws of God respecting the equality of all people.[202] William Parker Cutler, another Republican Congressman from Ohio, stated before the Presbyterian General Assembly in 1857, that the decision had "fixed the chains of slavery on millions of the human race." He believed that if the Court had addressed itself to the question "is it right to hold a man a slave because his ancestors were slaves," then that "decision must fall to the ground."[203]

While it may be true that a handful of Republicans favored a modicum of justice for blacks, they usually joined other Republicans in opposing equal social rights for them. Congressman John Farnsworth of Illinois thought that as far as certain basic political and economic rights were concerned, blacks should be the equals of whites. "When it comes to the question of his right to eat the fruits of the earth which his own hands have tilled, he is my equal . . . . When it comes to the question of protection of life . . . of the natural rights of man . . . he is my equal." As for social equality, however, Farnsworth had a different opinion. "When it comes to the question as to who shall sit at my table . . . or as to whom we shall marry . . . my taste revolts against such an equality."[204] In defending his call for separate schools-and by the same token anticipating the Jim Crow era-Harlan asked his legislative colleagues: "Who had proposed to make him [the black man] his [the white man's] equal in a social point of view? Nobody."[205] These Republicans did not seem to realize that economic, political and social rights were conjoined.

Some of the more tolerant Republicans were willing to grant a conditional equality. Giddings said that only "if a Negro had equal intelligence, morality and virtue," would he "favor giving him every right extended to whites."[206] How Giddings intended to measure these variables he never explained. While addressing the Democratic side of the House, Lovejoy, speaking for the party, stated that "we are not, not in the sense which you mean," in favor of social equality for blacks. Only in so far as political equality was at issue did Lovejoy believe that black people were "created equal," and even there he at times had reservations: "[W]e do not hold that they are socially equal, or that they are necessarily politically equal, or intellectually equal."[207]

More typically, others demonstrated little tolerance. Congressman Ephraim W. Farley of Maine would not concede any conditions toward black equality. "I never have believed," he proclaimed, "that the two races were destined . . . to live upon terms of equality, social or political . . . . "[208] Yet in the South, where there were few if any Republicans, social amenities between the races seemed more friendly than in the North. Impressionistic as his evidence may have been, Representative John Sherman of Ohio commented, as had Alexis DeTocqueville years earlier, that social relations "between the white and black races in the slave states . . . are often more kindly . . . than those existing between the same classes in the northern states."[209]

In addition to espousing justice for blacks in the North, some of these same Republicans also refused to side-step the issue of the immorality of holding blacks as chattels in the South. For one, Cutler, like the radical abolitionists, called the peculiar institution immoral and viewed slavery as a sin against God.[210] Owen Lovejoy took essentially the same position when, in 1859, he wrote that the "real question" in the slavery controversy, was simply "is slavery right or wrong?"[211] Giddings, perhaps more than any other politician, challenged the morality of the peculiar institution. As he had when a Free Soiler, Giddings connected the higher law doctrine of the radical abolitionists to what he believed to be the highest man-made law, the Declaration of Independence, and the principles for which it stood. He denied point blank that the framers of the Declaration believed that "'black men had no rights that white men were bound to respect.'" He thought this claim a "denial of the essential truths announced in the Declaration of Independence," a denial which could only be defended by a deliberate distortion of that document. As one of the leading members at the party's Philadelphia convention of 1856, Giddings expressed displeasure with the compromising posture of the party on the issue of slavery. Instead, he appealed to "God's higher law" and to the Declaration, with its major premise that all men are created equal before the law. He made his presence felt at that convention while serving on the platform committee; and his resolution extolling the ideal of equality, as stated in the Declaration, was ultimately written into the platform.

Two years later, when addressing Congress, Giddings took direct aim at slavery by equating it with a system of legalized murder which left the black man at the complete mercy of his master. "American infidels," he stated, "believe that no moral turpitude attaches to these statutory murders; while Christians hold that God's moral law remains unchanged by such human enactments: that the guilt of the murderer [the slaveholder] is in no degree modified by such statutes [that protect slavery]." In effect, Giddings made clear his belief that God would hold the slave master responsible for his actions against his black slaves, regardless of slave codes and other man-made laws protecting the master class. "All men," Giddings continued, "without respect to complexion or condition, hold from the Creator the right to live; who shall determine what portion of the community shall be slain? . . . [T]he [Chief] Executive [Buchanan] and his supporters say that white men may murder black men. The blacks deny this; God and Christianity and nature . . . all moral men deny it." When Giddings was not equating slavery with murder, he was at the very least equating it with mental and spiritual "torture;" because, under slavery the black man's "intellect shall be paralyzed, his soul enshrouded in ignorance and his moral nature brutalized." In short, it was the environment of slavery which explained any 'inferiority' which Negroes, as compared to Caucasians, may have manifested.[212] Contrary to those who believed in polygenism, Giddings here seemed to be saying that all men were essentially the same in endowments. If the black man was ignorant, immoral and brutal, it was the institution of slavery which made him so, not innate factors.

Given their belief in the higher law doctrine, these more liberal Republicans attacked the pragmatic and conservative course that their party was taking and called for a party based on moral principles, a party that would approach the standards of the radical abolitionists. George Julian was critical of those party members who were only concerned with making political capital out of the Kansas and Nebraska Act. In 1854 he complained that the "Anti-Nebraska excitement was the product of political, rather than moral causes; of transient influences, rather than deep-rooted convictions." The Indiana Congressman viewed the fusion movement, out of which the Republican Party was created, as a compromise of principle for political expediency. In a speech at Raysville, in 1857, he spoke of the "timid and halting policy of the Fusionists of the State during the past three years; of their insistence that theirs is a 'White Man's Party.'" He went on to note critically, that "great forbearance, moderation, and a studious deference to the constitutional rights of slavery have uniformly marked the policy of the Republican Party." He was also angered by the Philadelphia platform adopted for the 1856 presidential election, because of what he called its attack on abolitionism and its narrow antislavery base of non-extension. Julian's suspicions of his fellow Republicans carried over to the 1860 presidential nomination of Lincoln. He was opposed to Lincoln's nomination, because he believed Lincoln too conservative on the slavery question. Lincoln's political philosophy, he thought, differed little from that of the Democratic incumbent, James Buchanan.[213]

Giddings, too, like his son-in-law, George Julian, was often critical of his party. He was so upset by the 1860 platform committee in Chicago and its initial refusal (mainly at the urging of Benjamin Wade) to adopt again his resolution on the Declaration of Independence and equality for all mankind, that he stalked out of the convention hall. Although Giddings' resolution was later accepted by the platform committee, that concession did not alter his suspicions about Republican conservatism. Moreover, while most Republicans detested John Brown and avoided any association with him, Giddings considered him a friend, and on at least one occasion invited Brown to stay at his home. Giddings spoke on the same podium with Brown and before the Harper's Ferry raid contributed money to Brown's venture. In fact, Giddings was one of the few people to defend Brown after the raid; and, even though one Richmond, Virginia, newspaper had placed a ten thousand dollar price on his, Giddings', head because of his alleged implication in Brown's work, he did not seem to fear for his life. Since Giddings had once called the colonization scheme "immoral and utopian" and advocated the total and immediate abolition of slavery and not merely its non-extension, it came as no surprise that he viewed the Republican Party as both anti-republican and anti-Christian. One biographer notes that the "battle that he was to fight within the Republican Party between 1856 and 1860 was to demonstrate to Giddings' dismay, that though parties may be rallied by principles, they seldom are successfully run by them." Therefore, by 1860,

"Joshua Reed Giddings was again, as he had been throughout virtually his whole public life, in the minority, protesting against compromise of the principle of freedom."[214]

Chase, at times, also seemed unwilling to compromise his principles. "I rejoice heartily, most heartily, in your reelection," he wrote to the New Hampshire radical Congressman, John P. Hale, in 1858. "So [do] all of the Republicans in Ohio, except perhaps a few intensified fogies . . . . It is, I trust, a symbol that the genuine antislavery principle is not to be ignored" by the party. On principles and politics Chase wrote the following: "I have never sought to advance myself at the sacrifice of my principles, nor shall I do so."[215]

Chase's reputation for morality in politics attracted the support of William Henry Brisbane, former slaveholder turned Baptist minister and radical Republican. Brisbane strongly backed Chase's effort to secure the nomination as the party's presidential candidate in 1860. He saw Chase as an "earnest and zealous advocate of freedom," a man of "principles," when "nothing could be more unpopular, when indeed it seemed that he was casting away all the prospects of advancement." Brisbane believed that, in contrast to other Republicans, Chase was "too elevated [in character] to use the poor negro for a mere stepping stone to office." In particular, Brisbane was upset over some racialist editorials he had recently read in Ohio Republican newspapers. In attacking the black man, he said, they were in "very bad taste," and were "evidently designed" for the Republicans in "Missouri." If that was what Republicans had to resort to, to get elected, then, Brisbane thought, "it is better to be defeated with Chase . . . as our standard bearer, than to succeed in the election of one who bears no standard at all."[216]

Republican conservatism, as revealed in the remedies that most Republicans endorsed as proper for dealing with the issues of slavery and of blacks in America, was not only under fire from some within the party's ranks but from some without. Black leaders and radical abolitionists also drew the attention of their followers to the party's conservative bent; and again, as was true of the Free Soilers, an examination of the opinions of these outside critics will serve to throw additional light on the Republicans.

The suspicions of blacks about Republican motives were aroused early. Even though most black voters, in the few states where they were enfranchised, endorsed the Republican ticket in 1856, they held strong reservations about that party. For instance, the Cincinnati born black abolitionist, Peter Humphries Clark, who backed that party in 1856, quickly began to attack the orthodox elements within that organization. He noted that Republicans were more concerned with land speculation than with battling slavery.[217] A group of leading Boston blacks, including John S. Rock, George L. Ruffin and Coffin Pitts, met and passed a resolution which was critical of what they perceived as the racialism practiced by that party. Their resolution noted that the "resolve in the Republican platform endorsing the Kansas free state constitution, which prohibits colored men from going into that territory, and the determination of the Republican press to ignore the colored man's interest in the party, plainly shows us that it is not an anti-slavery party."[218]

Maturation of the Republican Party did nothing to erase black distrust. In 1858 a meeting of free blacks in New Bedford, Massachusetts, attended by such leaders as Charles L. Remond, Robert Morris, and Josiah Henson, charged that both Republicans and their Free Soil predecessors had been false to the interests of black people.[219] Two years later Robert Purvis, a black leader from Philadelphia, issued the following statement: "I could not be a member of the Republican party if I was so disposed . . . . I would not be a member of the Republican party if it was in my power. How could I, a colored man, join a party that styles itself emphatically the 'white man's party?' How could I, an abolitionist, belong to a party that is and must of necessity be a pro-slavery party?"[220] On July 4, 1860 H. Ford Douglass, a prominent black from Illinois, echoed similar sentiments at a radical abolitionist rally in Farmingham, Massachusetts. He asked his audience if "any man can tell me the difference between the anti-slavery of Abraham Lincoln and the anti-slavery of Henry Clay? Why there is no difference between them," Douglass declared. "Henry Clay was just as odious to the anti-slavery cause and [true] anti-slavery men as ever was John C. Calhoun." He noted that "Lincoln is . . . in favor of carrying out that infamous Fugitive Slave law [of 1850]," and had even "introduced into the District of Columbia a Fugitive Slave law" of his own. Moreover, Douglass related how he personally "went through the State of Illinois for the purpose of getting signers to a petition asking the Legislature to repeal the 'testimony law,' so as to permit colored men to testify [in court] against white men. I went to prominent Republicans, and among others to Abraham Lincoln and Lyman Trumbull, and neither of them dared to sign that petition."[221]

Blacks also attacked a policy dear to Republican hearts-colonization. For example, a convention of Massachusetts blacks evinced a "very decided feeling . . . against all colonization schemes to Liberia, Central America and elsewhere."[222] The Reverend Samuel E. Cornish of New York city, editor of one of the first black newspapers published in the United States, *The Colored American,* called for "emancipation without expatriation;" because he believed it was only in this way that black Americans would eventually achieve the "extirpation of prejudice" and the "enactment of equal laws."[223] Robert Purvis summed up black opposition to colonization perfectly when he proclaimed that he was "not a Republican. I can never join a party the leaders of which conspire to expel us from the country . . . ."[224]

White abolitionists, too, inveighed against the Republican Party. William Lloyd Garrison, who called colonizationists the "traducers of the free blacks," fully concurred with the views of his fellow black abolitionists. The "Republican party," he stated succinctly, "has only a geographical aversion to slavery . . . . It is a complexional party, exclusively for white men, not for all men, white or black."[225] Gerrit Smith, "denounced the Republican party as practicing 'shameful deceptions' and characterized it as a 'stupendous hypocrite and utter humbug.'" Smith viewed the party as a dishonest one, because its leaders refused to face head-on the issue of slavery. Indeed, the party "is the protector of slavery where it is, and wars upon it only where it is not," declared the New York abolitionist. That being the case, Smith believed that Republicans actually strengthened the pro-slavery opinion in the country and, conversely "demoralized" abolitionists like himself. As a result of his beliefs, Smith refused to support Republican homestead legislation, because such legislation "confine[d] the homestead privilege to white people, thus excluding blacks from the land, and virtually denying their right, as human beings, to the unrestricted gifts of providence."[226]

Keeping the above comments from black and white abolitionists in mind, one can see why in 1860 a number of leading black Americans found little difference between the positions of the two major parties on black rights and interests. Thomas Hamilton of New York city, founder and editor of the *Anglo-African,* said that both the Democrats and Republicans "entertain the same ideas . . . they differ only in regard to the way they shall go and the method of procedure." He noted that while the "Democratic party would make the white man the master and the black man the slave, and have them thus together occupy every foot of the American soil," the "Republican party . . . though with larger professions of humanity, is by far its [the black people's] more dangerous enemy. Under the guise of humanity, they do and say many things . . . but . . . their opposition to slavery means opposition to the black man, nothing else."[227]

Other black abolitionists joined Hamilton in assailing the Republican Party. H. Ford Douglass stated his opposition as follows: "I care nothing about that anti-slavery which wants to make the territories free, while it is unwilling to extend to me, as a man in the free states, all the rights of a man." Douglass' definition of a true antislavery party, one which could earn the respect and support of its assumed beneficiaries, black people, was one which endorsed both immediate abolition and equal civil rights for all citizens, regardless of skin color. Obviously the Republican Party fell far short of Douglass' criterion, and just as obviously Douglass was aware of this shortcoming. Therefore, he told fellow blacks that "no party is entitled to the sympathy of anti-slavery men, unless that party is willing to extend to the black man all the rights of a citizen."[228] In New York Frederick Douglass wrote that the Republican Party " . . . is simply opposed to allowing slavery to go where it is not at all likely to go . . . . " In fact, Frederick Douglass and other black leaders were so disappointed with Lincoln and his party in 1860, that they decided to support Gerrit Smith, who ran as an abolitionist candidate. The very presence of Smith in the campaign demonstrated that most true radicals saw little purpose in voting for Lincoln and his conservative Republican cohorts. At least with Smith as a candidate, those who wanted to base their votes on strict abolitionist principles could do so. Frederick Douglass came to the crux of the situation in 1860, when he declared that "ten thousand votes for Gerrit Smith at this juncture would do more . . . for the ultimate abolition of slavery in this country, than two million for Abraham Lincoln."[229]

Accordingly, between the party's founding and the election of 1860, Republican politicians and their constituents, with the exception of more liberal party members, consistently expressed the racist beliefs both of the learned community and the Free Soil Party. Black people were viewed as racially inferior to Caucasians, and many party members acted on that assumption when dealing with the black man and the issue of slavery. Blacks were excluded from the Western states and territories, often with the blessing and support of party politicians. A number of party members came out publicly against the granting of equal civil liberties to black Americans. Containing slavery meant also containing the black man, and the party openly played on white racial prejudice when calling for containment. The free West was to be white, and homestead legislation and the promotion of increased European immigration were, in part, designed to secure that goal. In fact, it was hoped that the United States would eventually be composed of an homogeneous white population and that gradual, compensated emancipation, along with natural black migration and black colonization, would secure that end. Such policies would leave the white man in complete control of the country's resources and, even perhaps, gain for him, through black colonization, the resources of the republics south of the United States. The party's political appeal, therefore, was economic and pragmatic, catering to white laboring and farm interests and, as such, party members generally not only eschewed the idealism of the abolitionists but on numerous occasions attacked their radicalism as well. A willingness, at least for the time being, to guarantee the existence of slavery in the South demonstrated, perhaps more than anything else, the conservative outlook of party members. In short, as black leaders, white abolitionists, and even several of the more liberal Republicans themselves had pointed out, there was little concern or room for the Negro in a party that labelled itself 'white.'

The impression that Republicans were essentially racists who were mainly dedicated to white interests was given a powerful boast between 1854 and 1860 by a coterie of influential Republican newspaper editors and popular writers. In the final analysis, much of the popularity and growth of this new sectional party between these years can probably be traced to the appeal to race made by these editors and writers.

CHAPTER 6

THE POPULARIZATION OF REPUBLICAN RACIALISM, 1854-1861

In our own humble way of thinking, we are frank to confess,
we do not believe in the unity of the races.

Hinton Rowan Helper, 1860

While Republican politicians and their followers made known the party's position on slavery and the black man through word of mouth, the brunt of the campaign to popularize Republican dogma and gain recruits for the new party rested on a number of leading party journalists and writers. Among the journalists were such people as Horace Greeley of the *New York Tribune,* Charles Henry Ray of the *Chicago Tribune* and B. Gratz Brown of the *Missouri Democrat,* the latter perhaps representing the most conservative wing of the party. Among the popular writers were George Weston, Thomas Ewbank, Frederick Law Olmsted and, most importantly, Hinton Rowan Helper. These writers and journalists, among others, served as both oracles and philosophers for the party. And, like the party's politicians, they seemed more intent on attacking the black man than attacking the institution of slavery; and, like their political cohorts, they helped to perpetuate the racial ideology of the learned community and the Free Soilers. Once again they proved that racist arguments could be utilized more advantageously to assail slavery rather than to defend it.

Because the written word represented the most important means of mass communication during the antebellum period, the contribution of the Republican writers and journalists proved crucial to the ultimate success of the party in the election of 1860. Helper was, undoubtedly, the most influential of these proselytes. He remains, as well, perhaps the best example of an American racist. A close friend of Greeley and an acquaintance of Sidney George Fisher, he enjoyed popularity among such leading Republican politicians as Chase, Seward, and Lincoln. One of the founders of the Republican Party, in 1856 he helped to create a party organization in Baltimore, Maryland. His major work, *The Impending Crisis of the South and How to Meet It,* caused a furor in Congress in 1859 when some sixty-eight Republican Congressmen, including John Sherman, Schuyler Colfax, Joshua Giddings, Benjamin Wade and Frank Blair, endorsed the book. Leading party editors, such as Horace Greeley and B. Gratz Brown, also endorsed Helper's book, and Brown published statistics from it in his *Missouri Democrat.* On the other hand, Southern members of Congress were highly critical of the book because of its pejorative picture of the South, and Northern Democrats attacked it because of its arraignment of their party. Besides castigating the South with its peculiar institution, and the Democratic Party for upholding that institution, however, Helper also castigated the black man. During the 1860 presidential campaign the party published a compendium of the *Impending Crisis.* More than one hundred and forty-two thousand copies were printed, a prodigious number for that period, and mostly on the presses of Greeley's *Tribune.* This book became the bible of the Republicans during their first successful presidential campaign in 1860, and its popularity in the North amid the party faithful is testimony to Helper's influence on the party.[1] In general, it can be said that other Republican writers viewed the black man, the South and the Democratic Party in the same denigrating light as did Helper and Republican and Free Soil politicians.

I

For yet another time blacks were portrayed as not only different from but inferior to Caucasians. Republican scribes depicted them as physically inferior and in some cases hideous. The New Yorker, Frederick Law Olmsted, Republican writer and friend of Horace Greeley and David Dudley Field, who travelled extensively in the South and wrote several famous books on his experiences, and who was later named head of the United States Sanitary Commission during the Civil War, referred to the "African peculiarity of feature" when describing blacks physically.[2] B. Gratz Brown was more specific when on several occasions, he wrote about the "holy terror of thick-lipped and woolly-headed Africans." Brown, as had others who utilized racial arguments, appeared to have a particular fascination for what he termed the "Negro's wool". In an article entitled "Africa and Curls," in which he implicitly also slurred lower class whites, the Missouri editor related a story about a black man who entered a country store and inquired about a bottle of "'Jaynes' Hair Tonic.'" When the clerk asked him why he needed it, the Negro allegedly replied "well now master, I likes de set of your curls . . . de fact is I must have somethin nuther of de kind, for I can't bar to have my har hanging down over my face like poor [white] folks." In another article, in which he drew a parallel between buffalo grass and the black man's hair, Brown noted that "its leaf has the fineness and spiral texture of a negro's hair."[3]

Helper, looking to emphasize other differences in the black physiognomy and being, and familiar with the work of the ethnological community, quoted writers such as Dr. Josiah Nott and Dr. Samuel Cartwright almost verbatim. He wrote of the Negro's "low and compressed forehead; his hard, thick skull; his small, backward-thrown brain; his short, crisp hair; his flat nose; his thick lips; his projecting, snout-like mouth; his strange, enuch-toned voice . . . [and] the malodorus exhalations from his person."[4] Even the black man's feet were apparently different; Charles Ray called attention to the South's need to order "nigger shoes" for its black population.[5] All of these characteristics, these writers insisted, separated the black from the white man and were indicative of the former's physical inferiority.

Blood, which had an especial attraction for the ethnological community, also captured the attention of Republican editors and writers. For example, Ray drew a distinction between the blood of the white man and that of the black man and referred to the latter as "savage blood."[6] Thomas Ewbank, who, besides being a Republican political economist was also an inventor, manufacturer and one of the founders of the American Ethnological Society, also made much of the alleged difference between "white and colored blood."[7]

Republican writers additionally argued that black people were mentally inferior to Caucasians. William H. Bailhache, editor of the *Illinois State Journal,* approached the subject obliquely. When he described white laborers as inherently "intelligent, free people" the implication would seem to have been that black workers were inherently unintelligent, unfree people.[8] Other Republican writers were more explicit. George M. Weston, a Republican political economist as was Ewbank, referred to black laborers as "an ignorant . . . population."[9] Their minds, Helper insisted, were "unlighted . . . [and] dark with ignorance."[10] Olmsted claimed that blacks appeared "very dull," in fact, "idiotic." They suffered from a "barbaric want of forethought." Then, quoting from Jefferson's *Notes on the State of Virginia,* Olmsted wrote of blacks that "'nature has been less bountiful to them in the endowments of the head,'" than it had to whites.[11] Richard Henry Dana Jr., who called blacks "an inferior race," assured his readers that an "intelligent Negro" was definitely the exception. Similar to Thomas Hart Benton, Dana claimed that even the Chinese, who intellectually were well below the white man, demonstrated "great superiority to the Negro [in] intelligence."[12]

A question among some of these Republican writers was whether or not the black race was permanently destined for abysmal ignorance. A few of them sometimes said no. Although there was, of course, no hope of the black man's ever reaching the pinnacle of white intelligence, his mind could be improved somewhat. The instrument for consummating this wonderful result was slavery. Under that institution, controlled and tutored by his white superior, the inferior black being would benefit, indeed already was benefitting, mentally and spiritually. Never mind that these same Republican writers disliked Southern slavery and, as will be seen, often alluded to its regressive labor force, its economic backwardness and, perhaps the worst to be feared, its commingling of the races, they, at times, as had some Free Soilers, and Republican politicians, could still see the institution as a school and civilizing force which somehow was functioning to uplift the black man. Therefore, even while he was supporting Frank Blair's efforts to separate the races in 1858, Greeley was insisting that black slaves "during their residence among us . . . have become imbued with American ideas." In fact they "have profited largely by the privileges of instruction, which they have enjoyed."[13] While promoting the cause of the emigration of blacks from the United States to Haiti, Brown claimed that the "American negro will have manifold advantages over the native [Haitian], because his training has been more thorough and effective." On another occasion, however, Brown's conclusion was that even a limited "intellectual development" of the black man would take at least a "hundred years." Only then would he begin to "have acquired ideas to which he is yet a stranger."[14] Olmsted, too, held mixed feelings on the benefits of slavery to the black man. Similar to Brown he did believe that American blacks would eventually become "civilized." Nevertheless, the New Yorker maintained that Negroes would never reach that level of civilization evinced by the "Teutons or Celts."[15]

More commonly, Republican writers were skeptical about or outrightly rejected the proposition that the black race exhibited any potential for intellectual improvement. George Templeton Strong, a well-known lawyer and author from New York city, brother-in-law of the writer Elias H. Derby and personal friend of Louis Agassiz, wrote about the "doubtful possibility of higher [mental] development for that race in the future."[16] And Ewbank, who, like the ethnologists, held that different physical traits among races were denotive of different mental traits and that, therefore, the "natural order of the races is indicated by the features, complexion, the hair, etc.," echoed the opinion of a number of Republican writers by asserting that the "distinguishing feature of the negro race is its mental inferiority." Not even education would help. The "development of high[er] intellectual endowments," declared this white writer, "is retarded" and "that which is innate in the [Negro] race, is not to be extirpated by external appliances."[17]

As some of these writers explained it, those who claimed that the Negro's mental capacity could be increased by training had been mislead. They had mistaken an ability to mimic or imitate for an ability to develop the intellect. In truth, the only thing the Negro was capable of was going through the motions of his white trainers; because of his innate ignorance he, like the monkey, merely aped his white superior and never internalized his lessons. As had the intelligentsia and some Free Soilers, several Republican writers adopted this theory. Negroes who seemed intelligent, argued Dana, only appeared that way, as they attempted to copy the actions of the white people among whom they lived.[18] Ewbank maintained that blacks belonged to a naturally imitative race; he wrote that while "we [whites] originate, he [the black] imitates. We excel in one, and he in the other."[19] The "negro is imitative in the extreme," insisted James Shepherd Pike, Washington, D.C. based journalist for the *New York Tribune.* "He can copy like a parrot or a monkey."[20] As it had for DeGobineau, this theory allowed Republican racialists to hold on to their belief that blacks were mentally inferior to whites in the face of evidence to the contrary provided by black scientists, writers, and statesmen.

Following the lead of the intellectuals, several Republican authors concluded that it was exactly because blacks were permanently inferior in both the physical and mental senses that they had been reduced to servitude. Physically speaking, wrote Ewbank, the Negro belonged to a race that was "peculiarly fitted, by low organizations, for the lowest kind of labor." Yet, even so, "were the negro not intellectually below the white man, it would be impossible to enslave him."[21] Dana and Greeley were in accord that the black man's ignorance accounted for his being held in slavery.[22] And, if Gratz Brown had no brief for that institution, he, like Samuel Cartwright, expressed the opinion that black people temperamentally were fitted for it.[23] Other Republicans followed the intelligentsia still further. Editor Ray implied an element of voluntarism by writing that Negroes, as members of the "degraded races," actually allowed themselves to be enslaved.[24] Helper, quoting from Jefferson's *Notes on the State of Virginia,* implied the same thing in his *Impending Crisis,* when he wrote of the "'degrading submissions,'" or the deference given to white authority by black people.[25] *The Philadelphia Daily News* implied an element of justice. Because the "African is naturally the inferior race . . . " concluded the Republican newspaper, "no injustice is done by keeping it in a subordinate condition."[26]

Reinforcing the black man's supposed aptitude for servitude were his supposed traits as a sambo. Here Republican propagandists joined intellectuals and Free Soilers in strengthening the stereotype. In doing so, they sometimes seemed to perceive slavery as little more than a nursery to care for childlike chattel. Weston portrayed blacks as sambos when he referred to them as a "singularly docile species" of mankind.[27] Dana wrote about "all the sensual and childlike tendencies of the [black] race." While travelling in Cuba, he described the black people he saw as typically sambo-like clowns, addicted to "flashy dresses, indolence and good-humor."[28] Olmsted expanded on this notion, adding that blacks had "greater vanity" than Teutons, and therefore "dressed with foppish extravagance," in "bright and strongly contrasting colours" and, "in the latest style of fashion." The black, according to this Republican writer, was merely a child, "an imperfect man, incapable of taking care of himself."[29] In at least one instance Strong depicted blacks as colossal buffoons and jesters, who were members of a "servile class."[30] The black sambo, declared Helper, loved "ease and sensuality."[31] Pike and Brown both proclaimed "Sambo" to be a member of an "ignorant and servile race" who was helpless without his white master to care for him.[32]

As these statements imply, sambo fell readily into bondage because of his lazy and indolent character. Temperamentally, he lacked energy and enterprise. However, if most Republican writers agreed that the terms 'lazy' and 'indolent' were apt, the degree of aptness was apparently arguable. Hence, while the *Philadelphia Daily News* described blacks as "not over fond of exercise"[33] and Dana drew attention to their "very tardy movements,"[34] Weston applied to them the term "idlers,"[35] Helper the term "proverbially indolent,"[36] and Ray referred to them still more disparagingly as simply "niggers who lie all day in the sun."[37] As to enterprise, the Reverend Robert J. Breckenridge of Kentucky, a lawyer and writer and Lincoln's chief political adviser in that state, depicted the black race as completely lacking that commendable quality, and doubted whether even the "invincible strength" of the white race would succeed in "carrying . . . forward . . . such a parasite . . . . "[38] Citing the "learned Dr. [Samuel] Cartwright" as a source, and adding his own opinions, Olmsted asserted that blacks were poor workers because of their "idleness" and "indolence." They only went "through the motions of labour" and therefore "cannot be depended upon a minute" when "out of sight." A la Jefferson, about the only area where blacks demonstrated any talent, claimed Olmsted, was "in music."[39] In an 1860 editorial for Greeley's *Tribune,* Pike reiterated the thought. Black people were members of a "feeble race, with none of the enterprise and hardihood of the natural born pioneer." They were the "fringes and parasites of an old civilization."[40]

If B. Gratz Brown is to be believed, blacks themselves could come to the conclusion that only slavery would indulge their propensity for sloth. Brown wrote of two black fugitives who, after living for a time in free Ohio, expressed a strong desire to return to their master in Missouri. Brown commented that "this preference for slavery is more astonishing . . . since a purse of fifty dollars was subscribed to start the negroes, if they would remain, and constant work at good wages was promised them. The negroes [however] expressed themselves delighted at getting off."[41]

Another part of sambo's mental fitness for slavery, according to Republicans, resulted from his being devoid of courage. As a 'natural' coward there was nothing he could do but accept the position in society assigned him by his courageous, white superior. Olmsted averred that blacks "recognize" this assumed superiority, and as a result "quail instinctively before their masters."[42] Helper proclaimed unequivocally that all blacks were "cowards."[43] Charles Ray referred to them as members of a "coward[ly] or down-trodden race."[44] To emphasize the point, Brown printed an article purporting to depict what happened when one black man from New Orleans challenged a second to a duel. Ridiculing the black dialect, Brown, in describing the "origin of the difficulty," wrote that "one of the parties . . . 'was crossed in lub by the oder, and dat him hona must hab satisfaction.'" Having met on the duelling field, however, the two men immediately began to concoct excuses to avoid a showdown. Finally, one of them yelled to the other: "'Nigger, is you satisfied?'" When the second man replied that he was, the first joined him in agreeing to leave the field of honor, noting, "'I's glad to get off so.'"[45]

Besides manifesting characteristics which had resulted in their enslavement, black people, according to Republican writers, manifested all of the characteristics of immorality. By nature blacks took to criminality, thievery, mendacity, drunkenness, uncleanliness, and licentiousness. Brown called blacks "criminal offscourings."[46] Pike wrote that "Sambo takes naturally to stealing."[47] Olmsted joined in and wrote that blacks "almost universally pilfer," but only "when they have a safe opportunity."[48] Helper and Dana agreed with Olmsted. To Helper Negroes were "proverbially . . . thievish;" to Dana they commonly practiced "theft." All three men also agreed that the word of blacks was not to be trusted. They had, said Helper, a "predisposition to fabricate falsehoods;" they were, said Dana, notorious liars through whom whites had but "a poor chance of getting at the truth." Black people, declared Olmsted, were known for their "duplicity," were, in his opinion, "proverbial" liars.[49]

Whitelaw Reid, a leading Republican newspaper editor from Ohio, received letters from his readers which complained that among the state's free black population existed much "'negro shiftlessness and dirt.'"[50] Though California's free black population was as yet small, Helper, after a visit to that state, declared the evidence to be conclusive: "like free negroes everywhere else," the blacks "inhabit the worst parts of the towns . . . and live commonly in characteristic filth and degradation." This renegade white Southerner further claimed that black people were inherently addicted to alcohol. Citing his black valet as typical, Helper insisted that the man "would get liquor to drink somehow; no matter in what shape it came, Ben must have liquor."[51] Olmsted concurred. A la Burmeister in respect to eating habits, Olmsted, too, averred that blacks "frequented" many "low eating and drinking shops." Blacks, he claimed, were "very fond of whiskey" and were "generally getting drunk" and as a result "making business for the police."[52] According to Helper and Olmsted black people were nothing more than drunken slobs.

Ray put more emphasis on the supposed licentious nature of blacks. They were, he assured his readers, no more than "sun-burnt heathens," simply "so many black bundles of wrong," who were useless except for "begetting their [own] kind."[53] Olmsted maintained that any money that the black man happened to receive, if not spent on alcohol, was "spent in . . . licentiousness and gambling." Morally, concluded this New York Republican, the average black was a "very bad creature."[54] Alluding to the presumably promiscuous behavior of black people, Dana asserted that "marriage by the church . . . is a restraint on the Negroes . . . to which it is not always easy to reconcile them."[55] The net result, wrote Helper, was that the myriad immoralities perpetrated by blacks were having a disastrous effect upon the moral character of the South. In comparing the Southern states, with their large black population, to the Northern states, with their large white population, Helper described the Southern states as poorer in "mind and morals" precisely because of their essentially black composition.[56]

If for a moment one could suspend judgement respecting facts, one might concede that to this point the Republican critics of the black personality had not entirely exceeded the limits of logic. In theory, at least, a cowardly, sambo-like clown could perhaps also be a thoroughly immoral being, although, arguably, some of the immoral characteristics attributed to him might in practice demand some courage. On the other hand, when the Republican critics insisted that this carefree sambo could suddenly climb out of his docile, non-violent shell and don the garb of a violently aggressive person, they did indeed exceed the limits of logic. Just as this contradiction had plagued the thinking of the intelligentsia and Free Soil and Republican politicians, so too did it that of Republican writers. To illustrate, Brown, who sometimes labelled black people harmless, "trifling negroes," at other times called them such things as "savage negroes," "untamed Africans," and "ferocious beings," altogether a "worthless and vicious" people.[57] Olmsted perpetuated this same contradiction. The shuffling, passive and obsequious sambo that he described in some places, in others was stereotyped in totally opposite terms. Suddenly the reader is faced with a black man who had a "stronger, dramatic and demonstrative character," one exhibiting "more excitability," than the supposedly more phlegmatic Caucasian. In fact, this newly transposed black man had "brutal propensities" and Olmsted warned whites of the "danger" from such a one.[58] Other writers wrote similarly about blacks. Dana, for instance, referred to their penchant for "violence," and Weston depicted them as wild and unruly, "looking merely to the animal enjoyment of life."[59]

Missouri editor Brown took the combined allegation of black immorality and aggressiveness in an obvious direction. In his report of the affair in which the two black men from New Orleans had avoided fighting a duel, Brown stated that the source of their dispute had been a black female. Apparently, black males were lustful creatures and, hitting on a sensitive topic for white males, Brown warned in another story that their lust was not confined to women of their own race. In this tale, he portrayed the black male as both a lecher after white women and a drunken wastrel. Brown told about a young, white woman in Massachusetts who promised a kiss to the first man who could catch her on ice skates. Obviously overlooking any moral implications attending the white woman's character, the editor went on to describe how, immediately upon hearing of her challenge, "an athletic negro . . . gave chase, and soon his arm encircled her waists [sic]. Her brother, however, averted the impending smack, by presenting the fellow with a five dollar bill." Not surprisingly, Brown ended his article with the comment: The "African started on a 'bender' with the funds."[60]

So, the honor of this particular white woman was presumably salvaged. Still, Republican writers warned, the outcome could be different; because the black male was ever ready to seize his opportunity. Since Olmsted proclaimed the Negro "more sensuous" than the Caucasian, though "less refined," the implications for white womanhood were clear.[61] An article written by Ray described the seduction of a white woman by a black man. The "result," the Chicago editor noted with obvious disapproval, "was a colored baby."[62]

A number of Republican writers, echoing their Free Soil predecessors, coupled the charge of blacks being aggressive and immoral to that of their being uncivilized and barbaric. Helper, for one, stated that the black race had yet to "take the initiatory step in the walks of civilized life."[63] Because of its barbaric nature, Breckenridge averred, the "black race has never had a nationality" of its own.[64] Indeed, 'barbaric' and 'barbarism' seemed to have been favorite epithets when whites characterized the black culture. After hearing a gang of slaves singing in the fields, Dana, who undoubtedly knew little of African culture, called their song nothing more than a "barbaric African chant . . . a barbaric tuneless intonation."[65]

Ray applied similar strictures to black speech, which he proclaimed a "barbarian guttural language." Blacks, themselves, he described as "savages from Africa" and the "barbarian hosts" of the Southern system of labor.[66] Pike, too, wrote of the "mass of black barbarism in the South;"[67] and Brown labelled every black man a "roaming barbarian."[68] Clearly to these Republican scribes the black man's 'barbarism' had preceded his enslavement. Ewbank asserted that one of the most obvious features of the history of the black race had been "its unbroken association with barbarism." The race had always been "immersed in barbarism."[69]

Whether his premise was that blacks were by nature slothful or vicious or both, it should arouse little wonder that the typical Republican writer portrayed them as inefficient, even useless, laborers. Black workers, according to Olmsted, "move very slowly and awkwardly" and were "dilatory in executing any orders." When they did do anything, it was marked by "carelessness." In fine, Olmsted pronounced blacks "far less adapted for steady, uninterrupted labour" than whites.[70] In his *Impending Crisis* Helper announced that since blacks were so "sluggish, awkward and careless in all their movements," it was not surprising that they could do "little more than half the amount of labor" that whites performed.[71] Dana also concluded that the nature of the race rendered it not "capable of efficient labor;"[72] and Ray described what labor it was able to perform as "rude and unproductive," while Strong did not see any value in black labor and declared it simply "worthless."[73]

In comparing what they contended was the agrarian and industrial backwardness of the South to the progressive economy of the North, several writers lay much of the responsibility at the feet of the South's black labor force. Here it is important again to remember that, though they might condemn slavery as an institution, these writers depicted blacks as inefficient workers not because they were slaves but because they were black. Southern slavery was economically regressive, Weston maintained, because of its inferior black laboring population.[74] After contrasting the value of agricultural and industrial production between several free and several slave states, Ray claimed that the difference in favor of the free states was due primarily to the "kind of labor or quality of labor" in the respective areas. The "decay of Virginia," he wrote, was "due to the tenacity with which she has clung to Negro slavery . . . [and] instead of the Virginia that might have been [had it relied on free white labor] . . . we have a decayed and indigent pride."[75] As had New York Free Soiler William Collins, Olmsted identified Southern economic decay with the issue of soil exhaustion, and tied both to the South's black labor force. While he described white laborers in the North as frugal and efficient, black laborers in the South "consume and waste as much as possible." To Olmsted slavery was not an economically viable institution because it had created within itself, in the form of black workers, the seeds of its own destruction. The New Yorker used numerous statistics to indicate the assumed superiority of the Northern economy and system of labor over that of the South.[76]

Helper dwelt constantly upon the "unprofitableness of slavery" and called this a "monstrous evil" for which he put considerable blame on the black man. Helper, too, tried to quantify the differences and much of the *Impending Crisis* is a compilation of distorted statistics to prove this point. If a statistic is perforce a random variable, Helper did not use statistics. Instead, he set about deliberately twisting and stacking his evidence, often by comparing the most productive free state for a given commodity, with the least productive slave state for that same commodity. As a result he could portray the South, with its largely black labor force, as a region which "lagged behind the North, woefully inert and inventionless," in fact the "cesspool of ignorance and degradation."[77]

Holding black labor responsible for the assumed economic backwardness of the South, Strong depicted it as a "nigger incubus 4,000,000 strong," which "weighed down, suffocated, and paralyzed" the Southern economy.[78] To Brown and Charles Nordhoff, a Republican journalist from New York city, black workers represented, at best, a "dismal" economic prospect. It was, Brown said, because so many of them were working as slaves that the Southern economy had become "almost desolate." Given that situation, he wanted to know "how . . . an institution [slavery] which . . . sows the seeds of weakness and decay . . . always maintains its clutch upon the power of the federal government?" The only hope that Brown could hold out for the South was that technology would one day eliminate inefficient black labor. Apparently convinced that blacks would be unable to adapt to the machine age, he wrote optimistically that "every machine is the auxiliary of free labor." To confirm Brown's statement, Nordhoff noted that black workers "cannot be trusted with machinery" because black labor was "improvident, wasteful, [and] unskillful."[79]

Ewbank, too, believed that technological and mechanical advancements would lead to the eventual displacement of the backward and inefficient slave. He insisted that "nothing is wanting but a proper combination of mechanical skill and when that is realized, slavery dies." The Republican essayist, echoing Eli Thayer, was certain that with the wider application of improved engineering designs to mechanical products, resources would be more fully utilized, and eventually "a piece of fuel costing less than the daily food of a negro will do more work in a day, than several negroes."[80]

II

Believing as they did that the black man was totally different in almost every conceivable respect, it was no surprise that Republican writers frequently subscribed to the polygenic theory of creation. They described the black man as a member of a race which had been created completely distinct from the Caucasian. Brown, for example, often thought and wrote in terms of "distinctions of race."[81] Breckenridge described the "distinctions of race, as an obstacle to indiscriminate abolition." To lend authority to his argument, this man of the cloth pointed out that "it has pleased God to create and to establish great diversities of race amongst men."[82] Ewbank, in particular, wrote of permanent "diversities of physical and mental structure," between blacks and whites. "Mankind is made up of races that vary in physical and mental structure," and blacks and whites represented the opposite poles in this regard. As had most ethnologists, Ewbank neatly placed these diverse races along a zoological chain, and confidently proclaimed that the "white race is the leading one. The others are stationary and always have been . . . [;] whatever the test is, the white man is acknowledged to stand at the head of the series, and the negro and kindred castes at the bottom." These latter he simply dismissed as "sub-races."[83]

Purporting to speak for the party as a whole, Helper flatly declared that Republicans "do not believe in the unity of the races." Sarcastically, he asserted that "nature has been pleased to do a trifle more for the Caucasian race than for the African." Moreover, he claimed that each race had its own system of thought; and, wherever the two races lived together in the same society, "there is no unity of thought, feeling or sentiment . . . no oneness of purpose, policy or action."[84] Such would always be the case, declared the *Philadelphia Daily News*. No race could change its way of thinking and habit of doing things, and this was just as true of the backward and barbaric black race, the members of which "to whites, however poor, . . . will always be negroes."[85]

Several Republican writers carried the arguments of polygenic creation and of racial distinctiveness to their furthest extreme. Analogous to the learned community and a number of Free Soilers, they likened the black men to animals, especially to the monkey or ape. Recall that it was supposedly his similarity to the last which enabled the black so easily to mimic the white man. In an 1857 editorial, Brown wrote of the "intrinsic superiority of the skilled labor of the free white man, over the animal force of the slave." In another article in which he related the story of a black slave named "Sawney," Brown came brutally to the point. Sawney's master gave him "permission to get a quarter's worth of zoology at a menagerie, at the same time hinting to him the striking affinity between the Simia and negro races. Our sable friend," Brown continued, "soon found himself . . . in front of a sedate looking baboon and eyeing the bipo-quadruped closely, soliloquised thus: 'folks sure's yer born; feet, hands, proper bad-looking countenance, just like nigger getting old, I reckon.' Then, as if seized with a bright idea, he extended his hand with a genuine Southern 'how ye do uncle.' The ape clasped the negro's hand and shook it long and cordially."[86]

Asserting that the black man was "nearly lost in the animal," Helper, like Brown, and a number of leading ethnologists, also compared the Negro to the monkey. When describing his black servant, Ben, who attended to him on his California tour, Helper wrote that, "Ben was about four feet six inches in height, very thin and very black; his grandfather must have been a chimpanzee, I felt quite sure of that, because his features were precisely those of an ancient baboon."[87] Strong described the actions of an "idiotic negro dwarf" he had seen in a New York city sideshow as "those of a nigger boy," whose "anatomical details" were "fearfully simian."[88] Ray picked up the cue. He as well implied a parallel between the black man and the monkey, and a lazy monkey at that. He claimed that "Cuffee has a right to eat bananas and sleep all day in the shade if he likes . . . he prefers that mode of life." Ray, however, could not always make up his mind about just which animal the black man reminded him. At one time he compared the black man to a mule, "who stands squarely upon his four feet," a "patient and steady . . . animal," who had a "simple taste." In keeping with the animal analogy Ray described the white master as the "patriarchal herdsman."[89]

III

It has, of course, been seen that the standard by which Republicans measured the black man's alleged imperfect humanity was the white man's alleged near perfect humanity. To emphasize the point, Republican writers gave equal time to extolling the complete superiority of the white race, but in particular of what they mistakenly called the Anglo-Saxon race, and its appointed destiny in North America. On this subject, their expressed sentiments were virtually identical to those of the intellectual and Free Soil communities. For instance, whereas Hinton Rowan Helper depicted blacks and dark skinned people generally as licentious and immoral, he identified Caucasians with "decency, virtue and justice."[90] Compared to the creative, aggressive white man, B. Gratz Brown claimed, the "slave never invents and never fights, and therefore in peace and war is inferior . . . . " The contrast between the races was even more vivid when the white man was Anglo-Saxon. The Anglo-Saxons, Brown wrote, evinced the "proud instincts of the superior race" and those peculiar, freedom-loving characteristics which made them unique among mankind.[91]

One trait which Republican writers enthusiastically attributed to the white man and which, they said, made him infinitely superior to the black man was an affinity for hard work. Contrasting energetic Caucasians with indolent sambos, Brown maintained that the former "work, toil, labor at all the avocations of life; they dig, spin, plow, ply the hammer and perform menial offices, but in none of them are they either slaves or [do they act] as slaves." Along with the white man's love for work, moreover, came other marvelous characteristics. "With free [white] labor," Brown continued, "you have enormous physical and mental power . . . arts, inventions, martial virtues . . . progress and the faculty of conquest." Because this was so and because black labor was "an inferior agent for tilling the earth, it should give way to free white labor, on the same principle that the sickle has given way to McCormick's reaper." Coming from a slave state, Brown seemed envious of the "white North" and continually compared the "superiority of white labor" in the North to the regressive character of black labor in the South.[92] Coming from a free state, Olmsted didn't have that problem. On the contrary, rather than sounding apologetic the New York reporter appeared haughty when he pronounced white laborers members of a "superior race," who formed an "ambitious and useful laboring population." Why was that, the reader might ask? Because, Olmsted replied, white workers had more "exact or analytic minds" than black workers.[93]

To Helper, one needed to search no further than the disparity in the working efficiency of the two races to explain why the North was more productive than the South. Because Northern society relied almost exclusively upon the "superior intelligence of the [white] laborers," it was "richer than the South in bone and sinew." The eventuality was that the "free states are worth at least thirty-four hundred million of dollars more than the slave states." Even so, Helper concluded, the South could be saved, might even "become a sort of garden spot, if it were worked by the hands of white men alone."[94]

It was only a short step from the conclusion that the Caucasian worker was far superior to the black worker-and, of course, to the Native American-to the conclusion that it was the manifest destiny of the Caucasian race to control the whole of North America. Bailhache was certain that the process was beginning in the South. There, "must African slave labor give way to free white labor."[95] "Negroes in the South," and even Native Americans, "must melt away before the white man" or be crushed by the "march of civilization," insisted Hinton Rowan Helper.[96] The next development, declared Pike, would see the Caucasian race extending its hegemony still further, because its "natural increase . . . on this continent demands the widest possible area for its expansion."[97] Brown agreed. "Free white labor . . . would advance to the accomplishment of its destiny . . . ." In an 1857 editorial, which he entitled "The Claims of White Labor," the influential Missouri newsman averred that the "white race is the true inheritor of this land," and that this inheritance was made obvious by the constantly "extending . . . area of free white labor."[98] In short, said Breckenridge, the Caucasians had before them "a glorious mission."[99]

By constant reference to the white man's manifest destiny, party writers, as had Free Soil and Republican politicians, were really calling for an homogeneous white population in the United States. In *The Land of Gold,* Helper saw little virtue in a racial melting pot, maintaining that different races could not live together in the United States. Applying this theory to the mixed population of California, he wrote that a "single glance at it will suffice to convince the most superficial observer, that its ingredients cannot be compounded into a harmonious, perfect and complete whole." Helper detested the fact that he saw in that state "all grades and conditions, all ages and sexes, all colors and custumes [sic], in short a complete human menagerie."[100]

The area of immediate concern and of most danger to white homogeneity was, of course, the South, where blacks and whites mingled freely. Unlike DeTocqueville, Olmsted was quite shaken and disturbed when he viewed, firsthand, this mingling process. To illustrate, he wrote as follows:

> I am struck with the close cohabitation and association of black and white-negro women are carrying black and white babies together in their arms; black and white children are playing together . . . black and white faces are constantly thrust together . . . . They all talked and laughed together . . . with a familiarity and closeness of intimacy that would have been noticed with astonishment, if not with manifest displeasure . . . at the North.

What further shocked Olmsted was that Southern whites were not apprehensive over this interracial contact. In fact one Southerner told the New York traveller that he was proud to ride in the same public conveyance with black people, and that that was the custom in the South.[101] This was quite a contrast to Olmsted's native New York city, where blacks were kept off of public vehicles, or worse, bodily removed if they attempted to board such. Under slavery, Jim Crow would have been difficult, if not impractical because, for example, each slave represented a large investment. However, after the Civil War and Reconstruction, the South, too, accepted segregation.

IV

Even though the term 'manifest destiny' would seem to define a foreordained result, Republican writers maintained that there was a major obstacle to its realization. That obstacle, naturally, was the black man. He stood in the way of the creation of an homogeneous and skilled white working society. He was the principal threat to white America's racial, economic and physical well-being.

Racially, Republicans alleged that through miscegenation the black man threatened the purity of the Caucasian population. As it did the politicians, the issue of miscegenation preoccupied a number of Republican editors and writers. They were troubled by the South's ambiguity of race. Henry D. Cooke, Republican editor of the *Ohio State Journal,* referred to what a number of his party termed as the bleaching process of slavery.[102] Ray likewise wrote about the Southern "effort to bleach the blacks," which, of course, was the same thing as "coloring the whites."[103]

Specifically, Ray noted that having white features in the South meant little, because "those who possessed straight hair and Anglo-Saxon features," were sometimes "set down as mulattoes," even though they were "as white-skinned as their owners." For instance, he described a case in Missouri where some recent German immigrants gave aid to a white girl, little dreaming that she was a fugitive slave. "These Germans supposed the girl to be free . . . because she was white," but apparently this fact was irrelevant in a slave state, where colors and races freely intermingled. Ray predicted that if miscegenation continued in the South at its present rate, "in the process of time, some one hundred and fifty or two hundred years hence, but few vestiges of the black race will remain among our posterity." The Chicago editor emphasized the "dreadfully fatal consequences to result from the wide-spread contamination of blood."[104] Brown held similar misgivings. In the Southern states, he warned, the "national [white] blood," was being tainted with the "produce of Ethiopian veins . . . . " Elaborating further on the "curse of mixed races" in that section, the St. Louis newspaperman called miscegenation a disease which produced "germs in the existing relations of the white and black races in the South."[105] Greeley blamed interracial coupling on slavery and Southern lewdness in general. He asserted that "debates on the propriety and profit of slavery, are very much like debates on the propriety and profit of brothel-keeping."[106] The analogy, of course, was not without substance. The only way to put an end to "amalgamation," declared Ray, was "by putting an end to slavery."[107]

To prove that miscegenation was leading to the disappearance of the white race in the South, Republican proselytizers cited statistics. Lyman Hall, editor of the *Portage County Democrat* of Ohio and a Republican despite his paper's name, claimed that the federal census of 1850 confirmed "in all its hideouness" the growing number of mulattoes in that section. "In the Southern states," he stated, "there are 348,974 mulattoes, while in the North there are but 58,877."[108] Ray expanded the number. Asserting that "we Northerners get sight of white fugitives often enough to understand whence 'physiological opinions' have their data," he wrote about "swarms" of mulattoes, "half a million or more . . . in the South" alone. "How is it," he asked rhetorically, "with that large class [of mulattoes], in whose veins the blood of the white preponderates?" Not well, he implied, because in the South "there are tens of thousands of men more than half white . . . and nearly all of their fathers claim to belong to the chivalry." "[N]early every Southern leader," the Chicago editor continued, "is a blood relation of negroes, either as parent, brother, uncle, cousin or nephew." "[W]hoever needs any confirmation of its truth has only to trace out the origin of the half dozen or more mulattoes nearest him."[109]

In the North the situation was apparently different. There, according to Bailhache, Republicans set the style by "abhorring any amalgamation with [between] the white and black races."[110] One reason for this abhorrence, averred Republican writers, was the belief, disseminated by the Northern scientists of the period, that miscegenation was an abnormal biological process. Lyman Hall labelled miscegenation an "unnatural custom" which could only occur via the "horrors of . . . sexual commerce" between the races.[111] Greeley explained the rarity of miscegenation in the North this way: blacks were members of a race "with whom we do not amalgamate kindly." The *Tribune* editor could happily report that "illicit [sic] intercourse between whites and blacks at the North is very far from common. It is to a great extent prevented by prejudices which do not prevail, at least generally, at the South."[112] Ray observed that the "birth of one [mulatto] in an antislavery community is as rare as that of an albino."[113]

Some writers, however, were less sanguine that the North's abhorrence of miscegenation would serve to keep the section racially pure. Notwithstanding that Republicans, following DeGobineau, were "in harmony with the great physical and physiological laws" which state that inevitably "deterioration is the consequence of the intermingling of the two [races]," Brown at times worried that the "Africanization of the North American continent is steadily progressing under the management of the slavery propaganda." In his eyes, apparently, it was this propaganda which had eventuated in the progressive state of Massachusetts passing a statute which allowed black children to attend white public schools. Brown expressed dismay that, as a result, the "blood of the Winthrops, the Otisses, the Lymans, the Endicotts, and the Elliots, is in a fair way to be amalgamated with the Sambos." Saying that he wished to "save posterity from the terrible curse of an adulteration and corruption of blood, and the progressive deterioration of body and mind," Brown wrote that already the North "would be startled at the . . . number of mulattoes" within its boundaries. He predicted that unless this insidious process was halted, the whole North eventually "is to be Africanized. Amalgamation has commenced [and] New England heads the column."[114]

For Brown, as for other writers, this racial deterioration would be one-sided, effecting only the white race. Even though the mulatto "mass would be impregnated by amalgamation, with many of the ideas and much of the energy of the white race," it would still represent an inferior species when compared to the pure Caucasian. Brown challenged his readers to "labor to restore the harmony of nature by separating the two [races] . . . instead of perpetuating the chaotic condition which prevails at present from their intermixture . . . . "[115] Ewbank joined Brown in insisting that the races must not be permitted "to commingle and be dissolved in a common stock." He claimed that "amalgamation of white and colored blood is bad enough on limited scales; were it possible to become general, the most disastrous and revolting results would follow; an ineradicable physical and mental leprosy would be entailed on the whole, and the beacon or standard of progress would vanish, for with the leading race it would be sunk out of sight in the mongrel."[116]

To illustrate to what depths racial mixing could supposedly lead, Republican writers, as had the ethnologists, held up as examples the populations in areas to the south and west of the United States. They viewed darker skinned peoples like the mestizo, for example, as racially inferior to the pure Caucasian, and countries, such as Mexico, with predominant mestizo populations, as nationally weak precisely because they were composed of Indian and Creole mixtures. When Brown wrote about what he called the mixed breeds of Spanish America, he depicted them as a people who were "incapable of sustaining law and order." He challenged his readers to "go to Brazil, and you will find a mongrel population, fluctuating beneath an imbecile and impoverished government."[117] "As yet, there has never been a civilized State within the [American] tropics," added Robert Breckenridge.[118]

Helper, in particular, held Latins and Mexicans in low esteem. Writing about Mexican women, he depicted them as lewd and immoral, and maintained that he had "never yet beheld one of them who, according to my standard of good looks, was really beautiful. Their pumpkin hues and slovenly deportment could never awaken any admiration in me," he insisted. "Nor are they particular," Helper continued, apparently equating the amount of clothing worn and the level of civilization, "to have their whole person clothed at the same time." Describing the inhabitants of Central America, he claimed that "it would be no easy task to find a more feeble and ineffective population . . . which now idles away a miserable existence in Nicaragua."[119]

Apart from the racial threat posed by blacks to Caucasian purity,

Republican minds also identified an economic threat posed by blacks to white laborers. There were so many black slaves in the South, wrote Horace Greeley, that "no demand exists for white labor."[120] This situation must be changed, Charles Ray insisted; the white laborer must be defended "from the necessity of working in competition or side by side with black slaves."[121] There was, declared William Bailhache, the simple fact that "free white labor and negro slave labor are incompatible."[122]

Even though B. Gratz Brown often viewed the black man as an ignorant worker, unable to do even unskilled tasks efficiently and therefore sure to be displaced by the white worker, he at times could express quite a different opinion. He could claim that black people, free or slave, could, indeed "compete against the white man . . . [and] blast the employment and lessen the earnings" of the latter, because they worked for less in the first instance and for nothing in the second. When it came to competition from skilled slave workers, of which there were a good number in the antebellum South, Brown could also be pessimistic. Whereas on several occasions he had depicted black labor as simply incapable of skilled endeavor and soon to be outmoded by technological advancements, in an 1858 editorial entitled "Negro Mechanics vs. Free White Mechanics," he asserted that skilled labor "competition between white and black laborers may be found in all the cities in the states where slavery flourishes." Turning to competition from the free black man, the Missouri editor told his readers that they could "go into any Southern city and . . . see [free] negroes engaged in all the mechanic arts, to the exclusion of free white laborers." Dividing the working classes by the denominator of skin color, he concluded that "free negro labor is . . . oppressive and irksome to the masses of our countrymen," and that all "negro labor, slave or free, is repulsive to the feelings and detrimental to the interests of our laboring classes." Because of its competition, "every white laboring man has been forced to flee for refuge and for work to the non-slaveholding states."[123]

Close to the assumed threat of economic conflict between black and white workers stood the fear that the continued presence of black people in a white society would lead to racial conflict. Pike, in fact, described the economic competition between "free [white] laborers" and a "degraded and servile [black] race" as the factor which would bring on "a conflict irrepressible."[124] Other writers seemed to base their predictions of racial strife on the simple assumption that the two races could not live peacefully together, because the black man was emotionally unstable. In the white mind, it will be recalled, docile sambo could suddenly become a violent firebrand. Breckenridge, for example, sounded an ominous warning: "twenty millions of us [whites]," and "four millions of blacks" were "fearfully combined" in the same society.[125] Although Olmsted perceived the dangers of insurrection greatest in those areas of the South where blacks greatly outnumbered whites, yet he asserted that "there is no part of the South where the slave population is felt to be quite safe from a contagion of insurrectionary excitement."[126] "Certain it is," stated Helper, "that the greater the diversity of colors and qualities of men, the greater will be the strife and conflict of feeling."[127]

To Republican propagandists, however, the white people of the South were oblivious to the danger, uncaring, in the words of Ray, that the "black population [was] outgrowing them and must sooner or later be numerous enough to overpower them and take possession of the soil." Indeed, warned Ray, citing statistics, the federal "Census of 1850 disclosed the fact that more than one-third of the population of the Southern states were negroes .... " Prophesizing "insurrection" and "doom," he added that, "no future event can be calculated on with more absolute certainty, than a mighty social convulsion in the southern half of the Union, unless some step is taken to check the increase of the servile race."[128] Should that step not be taken, warned Weston, the time would come when "whites must either exterminate the black race, or fly to save their own lives."[129] The similarly-minded Brown claimed that to find proof, one needed to look no further than the Haitian Revolution. In that convulsion, quite simply the "white race had disappeared." Apparently perceiving at least one Southern state as already approaching the point of combustion, Brown cautioned his readers that a "sable horde" would "carry fire and carnage throughout Georgia, exterminating all the whites."[130] Helper carried this same warning to all Southern whites, when he wrote of "a fate too horrible to contemplate . . . of barbarous massacre by the negroes."[131]

As these Republican writers saw it, then, the incidence of miscegenation, the extent of competition from black labor, and the potential for racial discord were directly proportional to the size of the black population. And the size of the black population was directly proportional to the birthrate among blacks and the efforts of the white South to increase that birthrate. The *Philadelphia Daily News* blamed the black race itself for its growth: "Negroes are a very prolific race, and their numbers in this country are increasing to such an extent as to excite serious apprehension for the future."[132] Pike also alluded to the "fecundity" of the African race;[133] and Helper described how this "dark population is growing upon us . . . [and] every new census is but gathering its appalling numbers."[134]

Other writers laid the blame for the increase in size of the black population at the feet of the master class. After all, under Southern slavery capital and labor were one and the same thing. Each black birth represented a significant increase to the slaveholder's net capital worth. Ray, citing Jefferson and his *Notes on Virginia,* accused the master class of working to "double and quadruple their stock of insurrection power by every means at their command."[135] Brown called the slaveholders' securing of more slaves, "their insane, suicidal policy."[136] According to these Republican critics, the slaveholders were seeking to sate their desire in several ways. First, and most effectively, they were deliberately breeding more slaves. The "past multiplication" of the number of black people in the South, Weston charged, "has been dictated by the interests of those who breed slaves."[137] In that section, the "breeding of slaves has become a science," wrote Ray; the Southern states were no more than "nigger-makers."[138] As an example of a slave-breeding state, Cooke singled out Virginia. The "export of colored laborers from that state to the planting states, amounts to twenty millions of dollars a year, being greater than the entire agricultural exports of Ohio."[139] Ray assailed the state, because it earned its "sustenance by slave-breeding." Virginia's raison d'eter in the Union was, in fact, to "extend the demand for negroes."[140]

Two other ways by which the master class supposedly aimed to increase the number of slaves were also pointed out by Ray. This Republican condemned the South's efforts to reopen the African slave trade; he declared that the slaveholders "desire annual recruits to the army of blacks, to bring back the hue that is fading out." Ray railed, as well, against the slaveholders because, they were trying to acquire foreign territory where the economy already depended upon slavery. He wrote that he was battling against the "acquisition of Cuba as a new slave state." The addition of such a "new mart" to the Union would merely give slaveholders additional incentive to breed "their one product, negro babies."[141] The inevitable result, according to Greeley, was that the Southern "community is thus more and more Africanized."[142] Though Pike, too, warned that if the process were not reversed an "Ethiopia in the South is inevitable," he seemed more troubled because the ultimate result would be the "Ethiopianizing of this [entire] continent."[143]

Viewing the Negro as racially, economically and physically menacing to white society, seeing his numbers on the rise, and being concerned that he would thwart the expansion of white people over the continent, Republican writers were apt to portray him and slavery, the system of which he was the integral part, as symbolic of evil, like the color black itself. One popular metaphor was to liken them both to a disease which threatened to infect Caucasian America. Some writers chose other figures of speech. Greeley, for example, referred to illegal slavers as the "Blackbird Fleet,"[144] implying that they were bringing in those undesirable birds which for many were a portend of evil. Helper called slavery a "black flag" and "an abomination and a curse" which wrought "horrid pollutions . . . . "[145]

The threat of the spread of slavery into the territories elicited a number of intriguing comparisons, each of which utilized the metaphor of race. The *Iowa State Register* of Des Moines said that to expand slavery would be to throw "a black pall over territory that belongs to free labor."[146] Referring to the "dark inspirations of the slavery propagandists," Brown warned that the "eclipse of freedom by the dark shadow of the institution [of slavery], would soon overspread all territories." To this editor, black people were the "'[Bohun] Upas' [a poisonous tree] of free society," who were "darkening the Heavens and withering the earth;" and he predicted how the "blighted fields of virtue and happiness would then be visible, in all their horror and desolation . . . consisting of the maximum of negroes and the minimum of whites."[147] All of this was in store unless, wrote Helper, white workers were sufficiently determined to "repulse and keep it [slavery] at a distance."[148] If they could accomplish this wonderful objective it would mean, in William Bailhache's colorful phrasing, the disappearance of the "black mists of the morning," which must "certainly disappear before the rising sun . . . [of] free white labor."[149]

V

Given the rapidly increasing number of black people in the South and the dangers which this increase was claimed to portend for the rest of the country, Republican writers, as had their political counterparts, portrayed the South as the black power. Out of step with the predominately white North, it supposedly favored the interests of the black man at the expense of the white man. Helper, who wrote of the South as an area which consisted mainly of little towns, or as he called them "niggervilles,"[150] clearly interpreted its pro-slavery sentiments as being pro-Negro, and was opposed to both. Strong derisively expressed this pro-black attitude of Southerners and the South in the lyrics of a song he wrote. To be sung to the tune of "Bonnets of Bonny Dundee," it noted how "each Southern Gent . . . loves Niggers," and how the region itself had a "love of buck-niggers," which love transcended all other interests.[151] The problem with Southerners, apparently, was their failure to make the proper distinctions of race.

Brown picked up this thought when he insisted that in the South "they set a far higher value upon the negro than the white man." Brown cited Southern journals to lend credence to his charge. The "Charleston Mercury," he wrote, "is in a terrible rage at the idea of white men [yeomen] taking [over] the country" by migrating and settling in every direction. In the South "white men . . . have no right to go anywhere, but to extend slavery. White men have no right to migrate, if their influx displaces slaves." Overlooking the fact that there were many black overseers, Brown continued: "White men are fit for nothing, but to be the overseers of negroes."[152]

As evidence that it catered to black people, Brown emphasized the point that the "South does not want white free labor. It does not suit her condition . . . . What she wants is negro slave labor, and that she must have." This preference explained why the South did "not desire emigration from Ireland and Germany," but rather "labor from the coast of Africa."

And it explained why in the South free white workers were not able to compete with slave labor. The South was purposely "endeavoring to perpetuate negro slavery . . . as an eternal drawback and competitor with the labor of a free white yeomanry." As a matter of fact, Brown told his subscribers, in some Southern states, "as in North Carolina, the slave owners combine against free white labor, and make it a point never to hire a white man, if they can find a black one." Similarly throughout the South slaveholders "in order to find them [their slaves] employment . . . underbid the free white mechanics, so that a man may hire a slave mechanic for a quarter less than a free white one;" and as a result, the "poor white mechanic starves." The South's ultimate objective, according to Brown, was, "by multiplying the labor of the slave," "to crush out" free labor and to "degrade and drive out [the] free white labor[er]."[153]

Taking Brown's home state as an example of the pervasiveness of pro-black sentiment in the South, Greeley concurred with the St. Louis editor's assessment. He labelled Missouri's society a "black barrier," which deterred "free [white] immigration . . . the life current of the State," from settling there.[154] The *Chicago Daily Democrat* saw the whites of all the free states as victims of this process; it described Southern slaveholders as "men, who have lauded it so long and so despotically over the freemen of the North."[155]

Even so, the most blatant proof of the South's diabolical intentions, insisted Republican writers, was to be found in its willingness not merely to accept racial amalgamation as a fact of life, but actually to promote it. This policy, according to Brown, involved a conspiracy, a "hideous intent," to spell the end of white racial superiority. In an 1857 editorial, entitled "The White Labor Question-Its Relation to National Affairs," he described the "day when Mr. Calhoun abandoned the tariff and adopted the negro." Brown claimed that white Southern slaveholders actually enjoyed the company of and intimate contact with black people.[156] Helper wrote in the same spirit that the Southern oligarchy, which was "filled with negro-nursed incumbents" to begin with, "has made it fashionable to 'have negroes around.'" So much was this the case that the "black veil through whose almost impenetrable meshes light seldom gleams, has long been pendent over their [white slaveholders'] eyes."[157] "What," Brown asked, "shall we say to this avowal, that they prefer to make 'companions and friends' of negro slaves, and that between them and their slaves exist 'ties and associations' so dear and sentimental, that no 'pecuniary wealth can tempt their severance?'" The Missouri editor wanted to know if the "most flagrant abolitionist ever suggested a nearer approach to 'negro equality' than this?"[158] Joseph Medill, owner of the *Chicago Tribune,* succinctly stated the attitude of Republican writers and publishers when, in depicting the 1860 presidential campaign in sectional and racial terms, he described it as the "fight of White Men against the Black Power."[159]

VI

Inextricably linked to the Republican claim that in the South black interests were given preference over white interests was the Republican claim that in the Democratic Party black interests were also given preference, and that this preference was manifested by both the Northern and the Southern wings of that party. Henry Cooke insisted that, should Northern voters support the Douglas Democrats, the effect would be tantamount to making "concessions to the negro sentiment" of the Southern Democrats.[160] Helper, like William Herndon, put it stronger: the Democrats collectively were the "Negro-driving Democracy."[161] In other words, the Democratic Party at the same time reflected and spoke for the South on this subject.

In making such charges, popular Republican writers and journalists repeated the opinions expressed by Republican and Free Soil politicians. To begin, the Democratic Party was obviously mesmerized by the black man. Charles Ray of the *Chicago Tribune* wrote that Democrats were "true nigger worshippers," so much so that they would readily consider dissolving the Union if "their affection for the African race is denied its gratification." Like the South, the party "sanctified niggers."[162] Gratz Brown joined the outcry: The "poor nigger Democracy," he announced, "were [sic] in a bad way;" having been "smitten with the negromania," they were reduced to "nigger-worshippers."[163] Holding the same sentiments as Brown, Strong renamed that party the "niggerocracy."[164] Horace Greeley accused the Democrats of forever "maundering and muddling about 'niggers,' 'niggers.'" This "Sham Democracy . . . seems incapable of letting the Black Race alone, whence result infinite confusions, hypocrisies, solecisms and mulattoes."[165]

This last, to be sure, trotted out yet again the hackneyed accusation of miscegenation. In reality, Ray charged, Democrats as "Amalgamationists" saw eye to eye with the South, and their emotional fixation on blacks was equally binding. The Chicagoan wondered just "how long it will take the process of amalgamation to fuse the whole negro race of the South, with the whole Democratic Party of the same section?" Democrats might tender lip service in opposing amalgamation, but he wrote sardonically, their way of preventing it was "by extending human slavery and all its temptations and opportunities." Constantly making references to the various schemes of the "Amalgamation Democracy," Ray claimed that the "ties of propinquity are multiplying every day between the Democracy and the blacks." Democrats "believe that the Union is in danger, and can only be saved by their process of amalgamation; and, as the fusion ceases when both races are free, it becomes necessary to enslave the blacks, in order to carry on the great Democratic work of saving the Union, by breeding mulattoes." In contrast to the Republicans who "at most, only propose to improve the political condition of the blacks . . . ," the editor charged that the "Democrats insist on improving the breed . . . . " Because of that party's supposed affinity for blacks, Ray, like Greeley, proposed that its name should be changed to the "Shamocratic Party." By the same token, he renamed the Republican Party the "Society for the Prevention of Amalgamation."[166]

The charge that the Democratic Party aped the South in fostering sexual unions between white people and black was, Republicans insisted, evidence that it also aped that section in its advocacy of equality for black people. "Is not a party thus mixed with and related to people of African descent practically in favor of negro equality?"[167] Ray asked. Under the leadership of that pro-slavery, pro-black Democracy which controlled the national government, wrote Brown, white workers were being "subjected to insulting comparisons, which place them upon the same level with the negro." In an 1859 editorial, "Land for the Landless," in which he promoted white homestead legislation, Brown wrote that administration Democrats "maintain that the fruitful bosom of the earth . . . is exclusively for those who own dollars and niggers." The Buchanan government was, he charged, "throwing its whole weight upon the side of negro equality."[168]

The Republican charge against the South that its preoccupation with black workers boded ill for white workers was also levelled at the Democracy. Once again class interests were subordinated to racial ones. The Democrat's "love for negroes," said Brown, "has superceded [sic] and driven out from his heart all regard for the rights and interests of the white . . . working and industrial classes." Under Buchanan, the Democrats were doing all in their power to arrest the "rightful ascendancy of white labor." In this endeavor, declared Brown, they were encouraged by all those pro-slavery, Democratic journalists, who would "supplant the white man" in the labor force, "by the introduction of the negro."[169]

Brown instanced his own state of Missouri as a place where the Democrats, supported by their "Negro [state] Legislature" and by their two leading St. Louis newspapers, those "Nigger Organs," the *Leader* and the *Republican,* were busily working to affect this result. The policy of both newspapers, Brown charged, was "to retain and multiply slaves . . . to the exclusion of the white population which swarms toward our state." The *Republican,* in particular, was "exerting all of its influence to degrade white labor and drive off white immigration." To this end, it was also "laboring to keep the free negroes here in Missouri." This newspaper's problem lay with its "inability to see through any other than African spectacles." As Brown often put it to his readers, the question was this: are you "in favor of encouraging the labor and skill and capital of your own race, or do you prefer . . . the employment of the negro race?" If the reader preferred the former, then only one conclusion was possible: The Democrats and their heirs and assigns must be driven from all political offices.[170]

According to Republican journalists, of course, the immediate arena in which the political contest between the Republican preference for white labor and the Democratic preference for black labor would be fought was the territories. There, said the Republican, California newspaper, the *Marysville Daily Herald,* the positions of the parties on the specific question of the extension of slavery would provide the acid test respecting their positions on the general question of "Niggerism." To make the point, the paper described a hypothetical conversation between a Democrat and a Republican. The former asked the latter why he called the Democratic Party the "nigger party" and received the following reply: "I call that the nigger party which labors to put niggers . . . into possession of every foot of territory that properly belongs to the free white citizens of the country . . . [and] to put down and drive out free white men, your brothers and mine . . . in order to put niggers in their places . . . . I am down on niggerism and opposed to any party which is its tool, and for this reason I oppose the Democratic [Party] as the only real nigger party."[171]

Perceiving the Democrats to be the vanguard of the Southern conspiracy to expand slavery, Republican writers called for a political fusion of all anti-extensionists to defeat the Democrats and therefore thwart the South's objective. In 1855 Pike declared that "it is a time when minor differences should be forgotten, and when all [anti-extensionists] should unite to complete the overthrow of those arch-traitors [to the white race], who, professing in their own language, . . . believe this to be a 'nigger era.'"[172] In Wisconsin, Republican journalists predicted that white voters felt so strongly about this Democratic treason against their race that they would make the 1856 presidential election a solemn referendum on the question of slavery in the territories. That election would decide for good "whether the territories would be reserved for free labor or Africanized."[173] Although the prediction was premature, it was to bear fruit in the subsequent presidential contest.

As it did to many Republican politicians, the Dred Scott decision of 1857 seemed to a number of Republican journalists additional evidence of the treason of the Democratic Party to the white race and of the control which the South exerted over that party. This decision by the Democratic dominated Court, some of the Republicans conjectured, would lead to a black inundation of the North. Others saw the decision as encouraging miscegenation and black equality or even black supremacy. Greeley was so worked up over the ruling, that he predicted "an invasion of the free states by slavery."[174] Bailhache claimed that "every reader can see for himself that the question of citizenship, as adjudicated in that case, has not the remotest connection with the negro's right to vote, hold office, or marry white women," which rights, he noted, still came under state jurisdiction. The question before the Court, Bailhache contended, "was not whether he [the black] was a full and complete citizen, with all the rights, privileges and immunities of a white citizen. Dred Scott did not claim that he was anything of the kind." The real point was that the Taney Court, by judicially overthrowing the Missouri Compromise of 1820, allowed slavery and with it the black man the license to expand. Bailhache was convinced that this decision "of the Locofoco party tends to produce and increase amalgamation and corruption of blood, while the policy of the Republican party prevents and restricts it."[175]

Brown, too, saw the Dred Scott decision as a Democratic plot to multiply and diffuse the black race over free states and territories at the expense of Caucasian laborers. He stated that the decision "is putting negroes above white men. The cause of free labor is ruthlessly sacrificed to that of slave labor; the American is forced out, that the African may be forced in. The white race is thus excluded by the Dred Scott decision, in order that the black race may have elbow-room to multiply." The effect of this decision is not merely "negro equality," which the regular Democratic "creed favors, it is negro supremacy."[176]

VII

The racial perceptions of many Republican journalists and popular writers can be seen as a coterminous voice with that articulated by the learned community, Free Soilers, and Republican politicians. Once more, the black man was assumed to be racially inferior to the Caucasian and especially to the Anglo-Saxon. Once more, miscegenation was seen as leading to the disappearance of the purity and hence superiority of the Caucasian race. Once more, the professed economic and political backwardness of the South with its growing mulatto population, and of the Latin American republics with their 'lesser breeds,' were cited as evidence of this process. And, once more, the dangers of slave insurrections and racial turmoil were foretold, if blacks remained in white society. Moreover, blacks, backward and unable to adapt to a technologically sophisticated industrial society, yet supported by the South and the pro-slavery Democrats, hindered the white man's progress and so-called manifest destiny. However, all this could change. With a shift in political power away from the predominant agricultural economy of the black South, represented by the Democratic Party, to the rising industrial economy of the white North, represented by the new Republican Party, blacks could not only be eliminated from the territories, but, ultimately, eliminated from American society. Just how Republican newspaper editors and popular writers would have the black man eliminated from American society will be considered in the next chapter.

CHAPTER 7

THE IMPENDING CRISIS AND HOW TO MEET IT

> Emancipation is a necessity, and the removal of the negro is
> also a necessity.

> B. Gratz Brown, 1858

To meet what they claimed were the threats posed by the black South and the black Democratic Party to the exclusive rights of white men, Republican journalists and popular writers offered the Republican Party and its program to their readers. Through newspapers, pamphlets, and books, the proselytizers sent out the word: Elect our party and it will administer the correct remedies to solve the assumed black problem.

These remedies were exclusion and containment to begin with, then, gradual, compensated emancipation coupled with elimination of black people from the United States by white labor competition, natural migration or colonization-these were the solutions embodied in the Republican policy to realize the manifest destiny of an homogeneous white nation. And they were solutions disseminated by most of the Republican journalists and writers, although a few of them could at times appear ambivalent on the subject and even occasionally espouse some measure of justice for blacks within the United States. Judging from their pronouncements, however, these few may not have been as racially liberal as the more enlightened of their political counterparts.

I

Before they could convince the Northern voter that their party offered the best antidotes for what they termed the 'black problem,' Republican writers had first to attract his attention. This they sought to do by claiming that only the Republican Party truly represented the interests of the white race. Illustrative of this claim were the statements of various propagandists. William Bailhache, editor of the *Illinois State Journal,* asserted that the Republican Party had a special mission to fulfill Henry Clay's aim to "exert . . . power in favor of white labor and intelligent enterprise."[1] Popular Republican writer Hinton Rowan Helper wrote that the party "espouse[d] the cause of the white man."[2] The only concern of Republicans, said the *Cincinnati Daily Commercial* during the 1860 campaign, involved the "interests of the free white man."[3] And during that same campaign Horace Greeley of the *New York Tribune,* identifying the party's cause with that of "free-labor citizens" who composed the "great intelligent middle class of farmers and artisans," asked his readers "in which class of states, the Free or the Slave states, does the white Caucasian race occupy . . . the more enviable position?" Obviously, the *Tribune* editor believed the free states, where the Republican Party-which he variously described as the "champions of the Caucasian race," the "white man's hope," and the "only safeguard free labor knew"-was fast gaining political hegemony.[4]

To emphasize to their readers the importance of race to the Republican position on the free labor issue, Republican writers, similar to Free Soil and Republican politicians, equated skin color with labor status. Ignoring, as they usually did, the economic interests of the large free black population in both the North and South, Republicans weakened working class unity. Charles Ray, editor of the *Chicago Tribune,* declared that since the "free laborers of the United States are white men [and] the slave laborers are colored men," Republicans would only promote the interests of the former class.[5] The editor of the *Missouri Democrat,* B. Gratz Brown, wrote in the same vein. Republican concern was for "white men, not negroes, freemen, not slaves." The principle at issue in the slavery question concerned not the rights and liberties of black people but the "rights and liberties of the free white working men of the country." This "free white labor question," stated Brown, was identical to the "Union question after all;" and the Republican Party would treat it so "in the coming time," because it would "agitate the rights of white men."[6]

By making continuous references to race when they considered the issue of slave labor opposing free labor, these Republican writers worked to attract the attention of white voters, including recent European immigrants. Washington, D.C. based journalist and writer James S. Pike equated the urgency of the labor question with the "urgency of the Negro question."[7] Greeley viewed the central issue of the 1860 election as the "'Nigger question;'" because the "interests and aspirations either of slave breeding or of free labor must and will be paramount in our national policy."[8] Ray, appealing directly to the racial aspirations of recently naturalized citizens, many of whom were jobless or in low paying jobs, wrote editorials with such titles as "Slaves Substituted for Irish."[9] Brown, too, acted to incite immigrant hostility toward blacks by appealing to white prejudice. He attacked one pro-slavery politician because the latter had had the audacity to "speak in the same breath of 'Germans and Irish, as well as negroes.'" Brown said that he was angry at "those [Democrats] whose leaders can compare them [European immigrants] with negroes." Wishing to appeal to all major Caucasian ethnic groups, and by the same token ignoring instances of Republican nativism, he wrote that Republicans, by contrast, were utterly opposed to the Democratic policy of expanding blacks and slavery "at the expense of white laboring men . . . of Americans, Germans, Irish and French, who work for their daily bread." Like Ray, seeking to emphasize the competition between black slaves and immigrant workers, Brown entitled one article "Turning Out Irishmen to Put in Negroes." In another, which he called "The Crusade Against White Labor," the St. Louis journalist stated that the "President [Franklin Pierce] proves to his own satisfaction, that it is cheaper to buy niggers, than employ 'filthy [white] operatives.'" Brown claimed that the "niggers" were being used "to supplant the Irish laborer on the railroad, and the

German on the farm, and the Yankee mechanic in the workshop." "This," Brown quipped, "is what high civilization demands. The African savage must be put in the place of the civilized white man."[10] To prevent such a fate, the voters, Ray insisted in 1858, must listen to the only true "White Man's Party," the Republican Party, one of whose leaders, Lincoln, was the "representative of the white man."[11]

It can be seen, then, that in arguing that only the Republican Party supported, in Brown's words, the "interest and prosperity of the white man in comparison with the negro, the Anglo-Saxon, in contrast with the African," Republican writers managed to make white and black interests appear to be at opposite poles and thereby to be mutually exclusive. As noted, they usually failed to include the one-half million free blacks in their definition of the working classes. In the process they diluted basic class interests with the poison of racial stereotyping, to the point that they pictured economic competition and racial competition as identical. "We [Republicans] take it," Brown averred, that "a [white] man may love his own race better than an inferior race, and may do all in his power to promote and multiply and extend the dominion of the former . . . ." Pictured was an ongoing "struggle between the races" for survival, and if the white man wanted to survive, he had best listen to the counsellors of the Republican Party.[12]

There were, however, other counsellors who also opposed slavery but who were not Republicans, counsellors who in fact attacked slavery with considerably more vehemence than did Republican Party leaders. These people were, of course, the radical abolitionists; and Republican writers went out of their way to convince their readers that it would be a mistake to support them. It would be a mistake, because they, like the Democrats, were only interested in promoting black interests. Where the Democrats would do it by extending slavery and the black population throughout the country, the abolitionists would do it by freeing the slaves. Olmsted, for one, disliked the idea of immediate emancipation as promulgated by the Garrisonians.[13] In his influential book, *The Impending Crisis,* Helper at the outset divorced himself and the Republican Party from the abolitionists. Unlike the latter, he maintained, with considerable understatement, that Republican "repugnance to the institution of slavery, springs from no one-sided idea, or sickly sentimentality" for the Negro.[14]

Claiming that the "abolitionists have never exhibited so much malignity towards any party, as towards the Republican party," and that Gerrit Smith and Wendell Phillips evinced especial hostility toward both the party and its candidate, Lincoln, B. Gratz Brown compared the radicals to the pro-slavery Southern extremists. Both were "enemies of the Union." Both were "for keeping up the [slavery] agitation and carrying it into all elections." "No two parties ever acted in more harmonious concert." Concluded Brown: "They are the two halves of a pair of shears, neither of which can cut without the other," and "they are both equally pestiferous."[15]

Republican author George Templeton Strong of New York was also convinced that the radical abolitionists, whom he variously dubbed "fanatics" and "Philo-Niggerites," "would sacrifice the Union" in order to aid the black slaves. Although it was important "that this, our republic, sanction and abet no wrong or injustice against Cuff and Dinah," the "system includes other elements beside Cuff and Dinah . . . ."[16] Put another way, the system also included white people and their interests were paramount. The Republican Party alone understood this; not the Democrats, not the abolitionists, only the Republicans.

In this way Republican writers and journalists, by conjuring up and emphasizing a "struggle between the races" and actively appealing to white fears, gained the audience to whom they could sell the Republican means for achieving a white America. At the same time, of course, they generated massive white enmity toward black people, with all that that portended.

II

These writers and journalists, just as Republican politicians, offered both short and long-term solutions to the 'problem' of the black presence. One short-term solution involved black exclusion. Republican writers wished to exclude black people completely from the North and West. Both Helper and Brown recommended this expedient as an initial step, until a permanent solution could be implemented. Helper told Southern slaveholders that whites in the free states and territories "do not want your negroes . . . . We would not give a handkerchief or a toothpick for all the slaves in the world."[17] Brown held up his home state as an example of what happened when slaves were present. He claimed that "as long as negroes [slaves] remain in the interior, their offshoot, in the shape of free negroes will infest our cities." "There is not a [white] man in Missouri," he declared, "but wants to get rid of the free negroes," and each therefore opposed the further "introduction of negro labor into this state." Brown also wrote a "protest against the employing of negro [slave] labor," in which he concluded that "even for the purpose of civilizing and Christianizing the African, we should not tolerate his presence," and advised his white readers to develop their racial prejudices; because "prejudices of color, rigidly applied, might exclude the negro, whether bond or free, from any portion of our virgin soil."[18]

One way to give practical application to Brown's call would be to encourage free Western homesteads for white settlers; and Republican writers supported this idea. Homestead legislation, they believed, would secure the West for the Caucasian race and exclude the black race. When Brown called for homestead legislation, he noted that if the federal government was prepared to make "large donations of public lands to railroad companies," it should also be prepared to make "similar donations for the purpose of extending the areas of white labor."[19] Republican writer and political economist Thomas Ewbank wanted homestead legislation because it would prevent what he termed an unnatural invasion of the West, "where the dark children of the sun are poured into the special homes of the white race."[20] Greeley believed he had found a cure for this supposed black threat; he wrote that white "homesteads would culminate in a practical restriction of slavery, by surrounding the South with a wall of non-slaveholding farmers."[21]

Accordingly, by specifying that homesteads should be for free whites, and not for free blacks, Republican journalists and writers would deny free blacks equal access, equal economic rights, to the Western territories. To make free blacks unwelcome in the free states as well, they sought there to deny them equal political rights. For example, major Republican newspapers in Iowa, such as the *Montezuma Weekly Republican,* the *Washington Press,* and the *Iowa Weekly Citizen,* opposed giving the elective franchise to free blacks.[22] Likewise the *Indianapolis Journal,* the foremost Republican newspaper in Indiana, opposed any idea of blacks receiving equal political rights with whites.[23] Back East, Greeley wrote that the aim of the Republican Party, "was not emancipation and the elevation of bondsmen to equal rights with persons of lighter complexion." Indeed, he labelled as "utterly false," any notion that Republicans had a "primary and overruling regard for the welfare or even the rights of negroes."[24] Pike agreed with his editor, asserting that black slaves "will not and cannot be emancipated and raised to the enjoyment of equal civil rights with the dominant and intelligent race; they will be driven out" instead.[25]

Republican writers took a similar tact respecting educational rights for free blacks. Richard Henry Dana's biographer notes that the famous New England writer and attorney "was not interested in legislation giving Negro children equality in the public schools."[26] As far as Brown was concerned, the Negro should "never be admitted to any social or political elevation above his present status." If black children were admitted to white public schools, the Missouri editor lamented, the "woolliest head and the thickest lips" would then have an "equal chance for education . . . with the whitest skin and the strongest Saxon." The Northern states would, he proclaimed, be "preferring a dissolution of the Union to negro equality." Only if the black man migrated to another country should he receive "actual equality with the rest of the population."[27]

The most effective way of checking the spread of the black man onto the virgin soil of the West, wrote Republican scribes, was by prohibiting the introduction of Southern slavery into the territories. Like their political counterparts and the earlier Free Soilers, these writers saw the containment of slavery, the chief source of free blacks, as the first step toward a white country. Containment would function as a perfect complement to white homestead legislation and black exclusion and, on a larger scale, serve the same end. Ewbank affirmed how it had been "a grave political error to break down the Missouri Compromise Line, and it is perhaps an equally grave one to delay its restoration."[28]

Republican arguments on behalf of containment divide themselves into two segments; the advocacy, itself, which emphasized the importance of the party to success, and the marvelous results that would eventuate. Republican writers consistently urged the containment of slavery and assured voters that their party stood firmly on that principle. Ray wrote about the commitment of Republicans to "confine the curse of slavery within its original limits."[29] In almost identical language Olmsted wished to see slavery "confined within its present limits."[30] Greeley declared that containment was the motive force behind the Republican Party.[31] If Brown called on all of his readers, whether they were "Americans, Whigs and [or] Democrats," to unite to "resist the extension of slavery," he could still maintain that Republicans stood foremost for the "localization of slavery."[32] In 1860 the *Hartford Evening Press,* in support of this Republican cause, appealed to the memory of Henry Clay, who, it said, had stated "he 'never, never, never' would vote to extend slavery into free territories."[33] William Bailhache likewise evoked the spirit of Clay. "[N]o position can be clearer," this Republican held, "than that advanced by Mr. Clay . . . that slavery must have a limit,"[34] and limitation was precisely the Republican goal.

According to Republican advocates three salutary results would follow the success of containment. First, asserted Pike, it would "confine the negro . . . . Hem him in. Coop him up. Slough him off." Republicans did not want to see the territories filled "with black . . . or inferior races."[35] The *Hartford Courant* maintained that "Republicans mean to preserve all of this country that they can, from the pestilential presence of the black man."[36] Ewbank guaranteed that with containment no more American territory would be occupied by an "inferior and foreign" black race, marked by "everlasting . . . degeneracy."[37] The Republican promise, then, as framed by Joseph Cover, one of the founders of the Wisconsin Republican Party and editor of the *Grant County Herald* was: "No slaveholders and no niggers in the territories . . . . Nigger slaves shall not be allowed to work among, associate, nor amalgamate with white people. Democrats must go to the old slave states if they want to own and live among niggers."[38] To Republican political economist George Weston the restricting of slavery would also halt an increase in the growth of the black population. The "further multiplication of the evil may be checked and finally prevented, by fixing its [slavery's] external limits."[39]

Secondly, it followed as a matter of course that the containment of slavery and blacks would make of the territories an exclusive white domain, would, in Pike's terms, "preserve just so much of North America as is possible to the white man."[40] This would be the result of a "proper" resolution to what Brown claimed was the "pressing question of American politics . . . . By the decision of no other question can the interests of the white races [sic] be so much effected . . . . Shall they have the exclusive occupation of the million and a half of square miles embraced in the territories of the Union, or shall they be excluded in whole or in part by the African?" Only the Republican Party had the correct answer. Declaring that the territories had not been "acquired by the blood of [or] treasure of negro slaves," the party, said Brown, answered that the black man had no right to be there; only the white man had that right.[41]

That this was the conclusion of the Republican Party, Greeley was certain. There might, he admitted, be a few "Republicans who are abolitionists;" there might be "others who anxiously desire and labor for the good of the slave; but there are many more than these whose main impulse is an ardent desire to secure the new territories to Free White Labor, with little or no regard for the interests of negroes, slave or free." And this largest group, explained the *Tribune* editor, represented the official position of the Republican Party, to wit, that "all the unoccupied territory of the United States . . . shall be reserved for the benefit and occupation of the white Caucasian race, a thing that cannot be except by the exclusion of slavery."[42] Although a Republican victory in achieving that objective would, said Bailhache, mean taking "direct issue with the self-styled Democratic Party,"[43] it would in the end, claimed Cover, guarantee that "white men . . . own and forever occupy the great West,"[44] would, declared Brown, mean the "triumph of a nation of white men . . . of our race, our migration, our civilized habits, and he [the Western settler] . . . with the blood of a white man in his heart."[45]

Thirdly, containment was at times seen by some Republicans as the beginning of the end of slavery itself. George Weston wrote of the restriction of slavery as holding out such a hope. Republicans, he said, must "surround" the slave states "with a cordon of free states . . . surround them with a circle of fire, to be gradually narrowed, until they perish in the flames."[46] Greeley, holding a similar opinion, stated that "to restrict slavery within its present limits, is to secure its speedy decline and ultimate extinction."[47]

In truth, though, most Republican writers, including Greeley himself at other times, accepted containment as only an initial step in solving what to their minds remained the conundrums posed by slavery and black people in North America. Looking for final solutions to these problems, they offered other ideas. One of these, the gradual, compensated emancipation of the slaves, was viewed by most as part of these solutions; but the question was, how were the blacks, once freed, to be eliminated from the country? The various ways in which the writers replied to this query were essentially the same as those settled on by the politicians within their own party and, earlier, by the Free Soilers and intelligentsia. Therefore, some thought that the free black's purported inability to labor efficiently would lead to his extinction; white workers would simply overwhelm him in the free labor market.

Strong confidently predicted that with "nigger emancipation . . . the downfall of the nigger-breeding (and mulatto breeding) aristocracy of those [slave] states must follow." Once blacks were exposed to a competitive labor economy, they would be helpless.[48] Henry Cooke, editor of the *Ohio State Journal,* took a similar position. Fending off predictions that freed Negroes would be able to compete with Northern white laborers, he asked: "Is there really any evidence that our [white] farming, mechanical and laboring classes are so inferior . . . that our people will be reduced to subjection by the same negroes which they maintain mastership of by superiority of character?"[49] Obviously Cooke thought not. Pike still more explicitly asserted that "under freedom, the blacks do not multiply as in slavery. The pickaninnies die off from want of care."[50]

Tying together the ideas of gradual emancipation and manifest destiny, Weston depicted history in terms of an inevitable process, something controlled by outside forces greater than man. Clearly if the process is inevitable man is denied free will. These outside or natural forces operated like the laws of physics, in that, given a certain set of factors the results were predetermined. Weston wrote that "when the white artisans and farmers want the room which the African occupies [slave states], they will take it, not by rude force, but by gentle and gradual and peaceful processes . . . . It is not more certain" Weston insisted, "that the native Indian recedes before the Anglo-Saxon, than that rude labor will recede before skilled labor; and slave labor, the slave being an African, can never be anything but labor of the rudest description." As a result of this rudeness, Weston prophesied the "extinction of the 'inferior' and 'feeble' races, in [the] presence of those which are more vigorous." He was certain that the "negro will disappear . . . at all events," and his disappearance would be "no catastrophe," but the result of what Weston called a natural process. However, the "system of slavery, which prevents this extinction, is no scheme of 'nature', but a violation of . . . natural laws," and therefore would have to be phased out.[51] A modern writer concludes that though Weston "implied the inferiority of the Negro," he "nevertheless demanded his freedom . . . and sought to prove that freedom . . . would not be ruinous as the South claimed. Freedom would be an economic asset, because it would increase the . . . opportunities for free white labor, and by implication, in the end ultimately eliminate the negro population."[52]

Although, as noted below, they argued for the theories of both natural migration and colonization, Brown and Helper sometimes seemed convinced that the competition of white workers would be sufficient to eliminate blacks from the American scene. Brown called for "gradual emancipation for the good of our state and city [St. Louis]." He admitted that the "extinction of slavery in Missouri may not do all that philanthropy wishes for the slave race, but that it will do much for the white race." Forgetting his earlier admonitions against the competition of free black labor, he observed that the gradual emancipation of the slaves would "accomplish with all rightful speed, the emancipation of the white race;" and he confidently predicted that "Missouri will be a free state during the present generation;" because white Missourians "will slough off the niggers in a few years." At that point, Brown declared, "white labor shall have gained the ascendancy, the respect, the developments that it needs," over the freed black man.[53] Like Brown, Helper also connected gradual emancipation to the "complete vindication of Free [white] Labor," which he was certain would result in a "total eclipse of the Black Orb." Perhaps more emphatically than most writers, he told Southern slaveholders that "you must emancipate them [the slaves] . . . or we [Republicans] will emancipate them for you."[54]

Some writers, including Brown and Helper, subscribed to the drainage theory of natural migration and its corollary, climatic determinism. These natural forces, they held, would empty the country of its unwanted black population. Wrote Brown: the "temperate latitudes are the natural inheritance of the white race, and the tropical latitudes of the black race."[55] Just as they joined the scientific community in ranking races according to physical beauty and mental capacity, so did these writers join them in stratifying races according to the geographic zones to which they were supposedly best adapted. Greeley, for one, wrote that black people had "constitutions suited to the climate" of tropical America.[56] Despite his belief in the traumatic effects on blacks of white labor competition, or perhaps in conjunction with such, Weston, too, had equatorial America in mind when he surmised that the Negro would eventually move to "regions more congenial to him."[57] Ray specifically spoke of the exclusive "adaptedness of Central and South America, in soil and climate, to the colored races and these races only."[58] When discussing that same region, Helper asserted that "white men may live upon its soil with an umbrella in one hand and a fan in the other, but they can never unfold or develop its resources," whereas darker skinned people apparently could.[59] According to Brown, tropical America was a "region . . . which can only be cultivated by negro labor." Describing this region as some sort of black man's Shangri-La, the Missouri editor boasted about the "salubrious and delicious climate of Mexico and of Central and South America," as a "congenial climate for the African race," in fact, the black man's "predestined inheritance."[60]

As had Weston, Ewbank also thought in terms of "climes congenial to negro constitutions." Indicative of his belief in polygenism, he insisted that the races were each created different, "to accord with the diverse conditions of the earth's great sections, each constituted to flourish best in climates akin to its native one." "As with animals," Ewbank maintained, "one race cannot perform the functions of the others" and "within certain parallels the white race will always flourish most, and so with the negro and intermediate races." He proclaimed it a basic law of nature, that the "black races [sic] deteriorate in vivacity and vigor as they recede from the tropics, while the physical and mental energies of white men diminish, as they penetrate them." In the final analysis "nature has therefore ordained a dividing line, or lines, between white and black" people.[61]

Since they elevated climatic determinism to the state of a natural law, a number of Republican writers claimed that simply freeing the black man from slavery would result in his migration and disappearance to the warmer tropical climes south of the United States. This belief in isothermal lines of migration was quite common in the antebellum period. Helper, for example, seemed to subscribe to the drainage theory when he wrote that the "time may come when negro slavery will no longer be profitable in the United States;" then, given emancipation, it would be "possible that the descendants of Ham may finally work their way beyond the present limits of our country." He added that "if negro slavery ever ceases to exist in the United States, Mexico, Central America and the countries still further south, will . . . become its outlets and receptacles." The United States, he presumed, "is too cold for negroes, and we [Republicans] long to see the day arrive when the latter shall have entirely receded from their uncongenial homes in America."[62]

Evidence of this natural black migration was to some authors already discernible in the movement of slavery itself to the deep South and Southwest. Weston stated that the "annexation of Texas was made palatable to the North, by the belief that the movement of slavery southward would thereby be hastened."[63] Brown pointed specifically to the decrease in black slaves in the Border states as illustrative of this southward shift of slavery and black people. He averred that the Southwest was fast becoming the center of the institution, and remained hopeful about the "gradual absorption of the African race into the commingled population of Mexico." The Missourian believed that when the "number of free blacks [were] augmented in the slaveholding states, they would be diffused gradually through Texas into Mexico and Central and Southern America, where nine-tenths of their present population are already of the colored races." With this southward shift of slavery and the increased manumission of blacks, Brown predicted that a "rapidly increasing portion of the African race will disappear from the limits of the Union."[64]

As with most Republicans who subscribed to natural migration, Brown assumed that these so-called lesser breeds in Central America and the Caribbean, being non-white themselves, would naturally welcome black Americans into their countries. In an 1858 editorial, entitled "Hayti

Inviting the Free Negroes of the United States," he asserted that he would "not be surprised to see an exodus of the free negroes of Canada and the United States to the West India islands at no distant day." Such an invitation would offer Southern slaveholders the perfect opportunity to free their slaves and "prove that they have some sympathy with the white working man." Brown then drew an analogy between the flow of the Mississippi River and the black man's southward migration. He wrote that the "current of the African emigration to the [deep] South is as palpable as that of the earth-bearing Father of Waters himself. [Given] the relative and absolute increase, in rapidly ascending ratios, of the black population . . . the corresponding diminution of the white population in that country follows. As the one goes in, the other goes out." Like Agassiz's, Brown's theory was closely linked to his belief in a natural "separation of the races, the black falling back on his native tropics, as the white advances." This natural migration and separation was the "only guarantee of . . . [Caucasian] physical purity."[65]

Still, Helper's and Brown's sometimes confidence in the theory of natural migration notwithstanding, they and other popular writers apparently were frequently impatient with the slow southward thrust of slavery and the progress of the black man's natural disappearance. They wanted to hasten the day when America would have an homogeneous white population. Just as had Free Soil and Republican politicians, they, therefore, opted for black colonization, and in some cases deportation, as the one sure way of solving the alleged black problem.

These writers, again in step with Free Soil and Republican politicians, looked back to Thomas Jefferson and Henry Clay for inspiration. To illustrate, when he described the black race's supposed inferiority as justification for colonization, Helper cited both Jefferson and Clay.[66] Ray wrote of "emancipation and deportation," which "in the language of Mr. Jefferson are the sole and sovereign cure[s] of the evil which threatens us."[67] Olmsted opted for gradual emancipation and colonization for the same reason, because, in his words, these were the "principles on which Jefferson desired to deal with slavery . . . . "[68] Indeed, it was because of Jefferson's espousal of colonization, that Brown referred to him as the "great founder of the Republican Party."[69]

The basic inducement employed by Republican propagandists to win adherents to colonization was, it goes without saying, racial. However, before stimulating their audiences by describing the specific racial bounties which, once blacks were settled abroad, would ostensibly bless white America, these writers titillated them with the immediate objectives of colonization. Accordingly, Weston, Helper, Pike, Brown and others emphasized that colonization would, most saliently, simply dispense with the presence of black people. While maintaining that the professed inferiority of the Negro would eventually result in his disappearance from the country, Weston, as had Henry Clay, was willing to "mitigate" the "evil" of an increasing black population by "some scheme of colonization at the general charge of the nation . . . . "[70] Helper, calling himself at once a "free soiler," an "emancipationist," and a "colonizationist," urged white Americans to support colonization to "rid ourselves . . . of the negroes," that most "undesirable population."[71] In early 1860, in an editorial for Greeley's *Tribune,* entitled "What We Shall Do with the Negro," Pike called for his "elimination . . . from our [sectional] controversy. But how," asked Pike, "is he to be got out? Only in one way. By dismissing him from among us, by a separation of the White and Black races," through colonization.[72] In another editorial, called "African Colonization vs. African Immigration," Brown counselled the exporting and not the importing of blacks. "[E]very [white] man who thinks his own race superior to the African race," Brown averred, should endorse colonization. Only colonization could avoid the terrible prospect of letting "all Africa loose upon the United States" and promise an homogeneous country.[73]

White homogeneity was an objective continually stressed by those Republican writers who promoted colonization. In 1858 Brown wrote that "we want first and foremost our own country . . . for free white men." Such "legislation as will involve their [blacks'] deportation" would ensure that "we shall have a homogeneous population. We shall have neither free negroes nor slaves, but only those of our own race, marching in the great march of civilization." In short, whites must "Americanize" the land, "not Africanize it."[74] In 1859 Ray was more terse than Brown but just as adamant: "[T]his Confederacy must be Anglo-Saxon or a failure. It must maintain its homogeneity of population."[75] It was to achieve that objective that Helper, exerting his considerable influence, demanded in his *Impending Crisis* that all white citizens support colonization.[76]

And the means to muster the energies of these citizens for that purpose, said Pike, was the Republican Party. Colonization, he pointed out, was merely the logical extension of that party's containment policy. The true "aim" of the Republican Party all along had been to "get rid of the negro population entirely . . . . [M]assing it within its present limits," through containment, was merely an initial step in its program.[77]

How, specifically, would white Americans benefit from the removal of blacks from the population? The Republican literati was no less verbose in answering that question than Republican politicians. First off, if containment alone would not accomplish it, colonization would surely lead to an end to slavery. Former North Carolinian Helper promised that by it we would not only "rid ourselves . . . of the negroes" but "of African slavery."[78] Missourian Brown pledged that colonization would "do away with the institution . . . of slavery . . . . " The "doctrine of the separation of the races" was, he stated, the "only antidote for the ills we have . . . the only solution of the slavery question." There simply was no other "remedy . . . but a grand policy of negro colonization."[79]

Other benefits would also accrue from the policy. Pike claimed that colonization was "all important as a means of promoting the national harmony and progress [of white Americans]."[80] One way in which white "harmony and progress" would be advanced, was through the elimination of the competition of black labor. Greeley, who supported Frank Blair's plans for colonization and, in typical Republican fashion ignored the interests of free black laborers, wrote approvingly of the Missouri Republicans that "it is not for freedom that they work, but for free labor; nor for that end even in its fullest sense, but for free white labor only. They would not purchase emancipation at the price of permitting the [free] negro to remain in Missouri."[81] Brown, too, noted that colonization would eliminate competition from black labor. He wrote that "if slave labor keeps wages down . . . and if free negro labor is offensive to our working men, there seems to be no remedy for either evil, except the removal of the negroes, bond and free, from this country." Using still stronger language, he proclaimed that "deportation will have thinned their [blacks'] ranks" and by doing so "emancipate the white man from the yoke of competition with the negro." By supporting the Republican policy of colonization "every [white] man who may feel an aversion to work beside slaves . . . may look forward to their ultimate removal."[82]

Another way in which Caucasian Americans would benefit from black colonization, according to these writers, was through the preservation of their allegedly pure-blooded racial lines. Brown considered colonization the "only practical, ultimate disposition of the negro race, that can or will avoid amalgamation" and thereby "preserve the purity of the white race." The noted Missouri editor asked his readers why, "if the National Democracy have such a horror of amalgamation, . . . do they not cooperate in the effort to send the negroes to Central America, and so preclude all possibility of amalgamation?" He insisted that only the "colonization of the negro . . . can abolish it and this the National Democracy are opposed to. To what party then, is the opprobrium of amalgamation attributable?"[83] Once black people were colonized, Greeley added, they would be "amid a population with which they could amalgamate," that is among what he and other Republicans assumed were lesser breeds.[84]

Black colonization would also be a boon to the white man, because it would clear the way for an increase in his numbers, something which these writers considered necessary if the country were to expand economically and technologically. For example, like fellow Missourian James Blair, Brown confidently predicted that colonization "shall rid our state of negroes" and thereafter "every man . . . may look forward to . . . the influx of free white labor."[85] Greeley, too, viewed colonization as part of a scheme for replacing deported black people with whites, or in his words "making room for the rapidly increasing white population" of the United States.[86]

With the removal of black slaves and free blacks and the increase in the number of white men, the threat or danger of slave insurrections and racial confrontations would also be eliminated. Brown claimed that colonization was the one sure way of "averting the castastrophies which their [blacks'] perpetual residence in the Southern states involves."[87]

Finally, when calling for black colonization Republican journalists, like Horace Greeley, hinted-although less broadly than Republican officeholders-that imperial largess might also come to white America. In 1858 the New York editor wrote that "Mr. [Frank] Blair . . . hit upon the true method, after all, of Americanizing Central America and the adjacent tropical regions." Ironically Greeley believed that ex-slaves would be the perfect people to "preach and practice democratic equality in Central America," and thereby draw this area closer to the United States both economically and politically.[88]

Besides benefitting the white people, Republican writers and journalists maintained that colonization would benefit black people. After all, at the very least, as Brown noted, he and his fellow Republicans only wished to help blacks to leave the country; they did not, as they might have, "advocate the extermination of the negro race in the United States."[89] Actually, claimed the writers, the black man would receive some very positive advantages from colonization. Again, as with party politicians, this claim may have been an attempt to garner black support for their scheme.

Be that as it may, one obvious way in which colonization would serve the black man was by encouraging his emancipation. These writers, as noted, thought that it would lead to an end to slavery and, therefore, black emancipation. Helper so argued.[90] So, too, did Brown. The latter asserted that historically "any scheme which has been glanced at to emancipate the slaves, has had their immediate expatriation as a leading feature . . . . To unshackle the slave is a problem easily solved; to dispose of him afterwards is rather an abstruse one, but not beyond the resources of enlightened statesmanship." The key lay in making the policy compulsory. Under Brown's plan there would be nothing voluntary, no choice by blacks themselves as to whether or not they would leave the country. He proclaimed that "emancipation is practicable only on the condition of the deportation of the emancipated class."[91]

Another way in which colonization would presumably serve the interest of blacks was climatically. Believing, as most of them did, in the theory of geographic determinism, Republican writers pronounced the United States too cold for black people. Greeley observed that colonization was a scheme which would "get rid of a population for . . . which the climate of the greater part of the United States is too cold . . . . ”[92] By promoting colonization, these Republicans were going to put the black man where he belonged, that is in a warmer, tropical climate. The "idea of negro colonization is taking deep hold of practical and enlightened minds," declared Brown, with the result being the anticipated "exodus of the negro to those latitudes which are [as] congenial to him, as they are unfriendly to the white." In fine, he thought that all Republicans "should labor to restore the harmony of nature by separating the two [races]" and sending blacks to their "natural" climatic zone.[93]

Not only would colonization serve the black man by freeing him from slavery and from the rigors of a cold and uncongenial climate, but, insisted party writers, it would also free him from the continued economic, social and political oppression which he would suffer by remaining in a predominantly white society. Brown likened the scheme to nothing less than the black man's salvation. The black man "must emigrate, if he would escape from membership in a pariah caste." In this way blacks would be freed from social and political ostracism at the hands of the "dominant race," because they would have "no superior, socially or politically."[94] Commenting on James Doolittle's 1859 Senate speech extolling colonization,[95] Brown added that, furthermore, the "African race will find its outlet from bondage, from admixture and from thriftlessness," by emigrating out of the country.[96]

Republican writers also had ideas about how emancipation and colonization were to be financed. Brown's scheme called for "gradual emancipation" along with "compensating the slaveholders." "[A]hundred million or two of dollars is no tax upon a nation for a national object," he assured his readers. With such tax monies in hand, the federal government would make "donations for accomplishing the emancipation of slaves" and presumably their deportation.[97] Obviously, if Brown ignored the rights of blacks when it came to their leaving the country involuntarily, he was scrupulous when it came to the property rights of white slaveholders. Helper, on the other hand, thought that the slaveholders themselves should bear the costs of freeing the black people and transporting them abroad. He devised a detailed, eleven-point program to abolish slavery, one part of which demanded a "tax of sixty dollars on every slaveholder for each and every Negro in his possession . . . between now [1857] and the 4th of July 1863, said money to be applied . . . to their colonization."[98] Apparently, Helper hoped that by Independence Day of 1863, all slaveholders would see the light, free their slaves and, financing the project out of the tax fund which they had subsidized out of their own pockets, remove them from the country.

Having decided upon separation, Republican writers, like Republican politicians, held mixed views on the proper location for the presumed salvation of black men. On one occasion Helper called for "their colonization in Central or South America," the location which most Republicans ultimately agreed upon. On another occasion, however, he demanded the "transportation of the blacks to Liberia." Evidently settling on the latter alternative, the noted Republican oracle recommended that the federal government use the tax money gathered from Southern slaveholders to "charter all the ocean steamers, packets and clipper ships . . . and keep them constantly plying between the ports of America and Africa."[99] Illinois editor Bailhache looked forward "to their [blacks'] future colonization in Liberia."[100] Greeley, on the other hand, wished that "all their [the South's] colored population" would be "transferred to Central America . . . . "[101] The leading Republican newspaper of Pennsylvania, the *Philadelphia Daily News,* suggested the resettlement of black Americans in Haiti, because the "climate [is] admirably adapted to the negro."[102] Brown, like Helper, was not quite sure just where to ship the black man. At one point he wrote that Republican policy "wisely designs to transfer the native negro population to . . . the inter-tropical belt" of Central American states. At another point the Caribbean looked more appropriate to Brown and, similar to the *Philadelphia Daily News,* he too promoted Haitian colonization, because "in Hayti he [the black man] will have no superior." Brown, however, was also ready to "suggest that our colored folks might be shipped to Liberia." He hoped that at least Missouri's slaves would be "manumitted and sent to Liberia."[103]

For Republicans who supported colonization as the final solution to a perceived menace, implementation seemed only to await the election of an administration controlled by their party. One Republican editor from Wisconsin, Christopher C. Sholes, was confident that with the election of Lincoln, hopes for black colonization would be fulfilled. Writing to his friend, Doolittle, during the 1860 presidential campaign, Sholes predicted Lincoln's election and noted that "before the close of the administration of Abraham Lincoln, we may expect to see a movement for a satisfactory solution and settlement of the great problem, how slavery is peacefully and satisfactorily to be disposed of. My views on this point accords [sic] with yours. Your plan [of colonization] is the only practicable one . . . [and] our next President . . . will be elected on a colonization platform."[104]

Actually, even before Lincoln assumed his presidential duties, a one-time Free Soil gun-runner and newspaper reporter for Greeley's *Tribune* in Kansas, James Redpath, had already formed the Haytian Emigration Bureau, which began by transporting a boat load of one hundred and eleven blacks to that island. To entice more prospective emigrants to this Northern private venture, Redpath employed several black recruiting agents, including James Holley, J. Dennis Harris and Samuel V. Berry. Though most free blacks would probably have opposed the work of the bureau had they known of it, Redpath persisted. He secured a commission from the Haitian government, which entitled him to conduct emigration operations for that government in the United States. In 1860 he opened his central emigration office in Boston, and from there published tracts painting a beautiful picture of the island and describing the assumed benefits of Haitian emigration to American-born blacks. All in all, Redpath's bureau netted some one thousand black colonists for this Haitian project, a good number of whom either died there or later returned to the United States. As unproductive, and in fact destructive of human life, as his scheme proved to be, Redpath's effort nevertheless served as a prototype for Lincoln's project at Ile a Vache, Haiti, several years later.[105]

III

With the goal of removing black people from the United States went, part and parcel, the goal of replacing them with white people. As has been seen, Eli Thayer, with his scheme of white colonization, was in the forefront of those who sought this objective; and some Republican editors and writers, Brown, Ray and Olmsted, to name three, joined Republican politicians in supporting the New Englander's project. On a number of occasions Brown endorsed "Mr. Thayer's plans," which "proposes [sic] the emigration [sic] of whites to these anarchic [slave] states."[106] Praising Thayer's efforts in Western Virginia, Olmsted depicted a simultaneous process, with whites moving in and blacks moving out. The New Yorker hoped that a "voluntary and spontaneous separation" of the races would be preceded by a flood wave "of whites to the slave districts."[107] Ray, too, backed Thayer's project. The Chicago newsman liked the idea that once the black workers were gone, "white laborers might be induced to immigrate" into the South. Southerners, for their own good, should work to "hasten the day in which a stream . . . of free white men shall begin to pour in upon them, stocking the labor market with intelligent industry."[108]

As Thayer's plans assumed tangible form, Brown expressed his admiration. The Missourian marvelled at the New Englander's "presumption of introducing white colonists into Virginia," because he, Brown, "would rather the negroes left the country than the whites." In one 1859 article describing Thayer's colony in Ceredo, Virginia, Brown preferred Thayer's method of "revolutionizing Virginia," to the more radical methods of John Brown, with his "miserable Harper's Ferry Raid." Editor Brown attacked the Southern Democratic press because, he said, it counselled "mobocratic resistance to any colonization or incoming of white men to the state of Virginia." He claimed that Southern slaveholders feared Thayer's efforts, because "if the scheme is successful, it may gradually drive out slavery and establish free labor in its stead."[109]

Turning his attention to prospects for his own state, where Thayer was also aiming to settle white colonists, Brown declared that "hundreds of thousands of families in the older states have now their eyes fixed upon Missouri . . . if only they can be confirmed in the faith that its future will be reserved to the industry of the white race." He was positive that a white "population would flow in from all sides, were the barrier of negro slavery . . . removed, and in place of 80,000 slaves, we should have 800,000 white men," or at the very least be able to "add three hundred thousand energetic white citizens to our state." Brown sarcastically labelled white colonization that "radical reform of substituting free for slave labor, white working men for black working men." To bolster his call for white colonization, Brown employed the familiar argument of soil depletion. According to this view, Negro laborers exhausted the land, and the only way to reclaim it was to "set on foot [the] . . . colonizing [of] white laborers upon the large tracts of exhausted land." Therefore, to achieve a white Missouri, and in fact a white America, the "deportation of negroes and an immigration of those who are bone of our bone and flesh of our flesh will be necessary."[110]

IV

Some Republican editors, just as some Free Soil and Republican politicians, were apt, however, to express viewpoints that were contradictory to those expressed by most of their fellow party editors. As early as 1854, editor Zebina Eastman of the *Free West,* one of the original founders of the Illinois Republican Party and perhaps reflecting his Liberty Party antecedents, recognized and criticized the conservative nature of the new political organization. "[I]n some respects," he wrote, "we are disappointed in the results . . . in the formation of the Republican party in this [Chicago] district. We have no sympathy with the timid, conservative policy which seemed to control the mass [of Republicans]."[111]

More significantly, several leading journalists, among whom were Greeley, Ray and Cooke, at various times supported basic political and economic rights for black Americans. Greeley evidently endorsed the elective franchise for free blacks, but in a condescending way. The "Negro," he asserted, "may . . . be inferior to the white man in many things, without at all invalidating his right to a voice in choosing the legislators and jurists by whom he is to be ruled and judged."[112] Ray appeared willing to grant blacks citizenship, when he assailed the Dred Scott decision, not, as many Republicans did, on its purported dangers to the white race, but rather as an example of the white man's "prejudice against color." He averred that such prejudice "is not only without the shadow of support from the Constitution of the United States, but is condemned by the increasing light of civilization . . . in the universal mind." By referring to the "universal mind," Ray may have been attacking polygenism, may have been acknowledging that if men thought and acted differently, it was because environmental factors were at work among them. In any event, he maintained that in the Constitution "distinction of color is no where recognized; that the conditions of citizenship are not even by implication made dependent upon nationality or blood."[113]

Others, like Henry Cooke, who attacked Republican homesteaders for thinking only in terms of white interests, appeared to be supporting at least one element of economic equality for black Americans. Eschewing the standard Republican practice of dividing the working classes along a color line, Cooke wrote that all "free laborers, both black and white, will look upon the acquisition of a homestead as one of the chief objects of life." In effect this editor seemed to recognize with the environmentalists that the needs of all working people, of whatever skin color, were essentially the same, and that all "free laborers, without regard to complexion, will devote part of their time to the accumulation of domestic comforts for their own families."[114]

Nevertheless, the nearest approach that most Republican writers made to showing concern for black Americans, was to assume toward them either a paternalistic or, in some cases, a romantic racial attitude. Ewbank, for instance, early adopted the concept of the 'white man's burden,' and seemed convinced that black people were simply "waiting for the strong race to help them up. The mission of the white race," he asserted, "is to extend civilization over the earth."[115] Reminiscent of the romantic racialists, Helper, as had Jefferson, pointed to what he thought was the black man's superior talent in music. Helper claimed that Ben, his valet, had a "very great proficiency" in that art. This, it should be added, was, according to Helper, the only activity in which blacks displayed any skill.[116]

V

With the significant exception of those represented by the people just noted, Republican writers and journalists generally exhibited the same conservatism toward the future of the black man and the resolution of the slavery question as did Republican political figures. The welfare of the Caucasian and not the black remained the primary concern; if a policy was seen to protect and benefit white interests it was considered good.

The attitudes of these writers toward slavery provide a case in point. For example, they were not often given to seeing the institution as doing a moral wrong to the slave. In fact, sometimes they could explicitly deny that it did. George Templeton Strong, for instance, "firmly believed that the relation of master and slave violates no moral law."[117] More commonly, the opinion was implied. Although he played a part as defense counsel in the Burns and Sims cases, Richard Henry Dana seemed more interested in the legal formalities-specifically whether due process was being observed-than in the profound moral issues involved. To Dana, the Fugitive Slave law of 1850 was reprehensible, not because of any moral considerations connected with its defense of human slavery, but because it did not provide, as the Constitution guaranteed, for a jury trial for fugitives. "If legally unimpeachable evidence against an escaped slave could be produced," his biographer writes, Dana "was willing to acquiesce in his return to slavery." In essence Dana concluded that the black man's rights "'are to be yielded to slavery.'"[118]

The Republican appeal to antislavery was therefore based on the rights of white people. Greeley identified the party's cause with that of "free [white] labor . . . middle class . . . citizens."[119] Charles Ray approved the character of the Republican antislavery appeal precisely because it was based on the exclusive rights of free white men.[120]

Expressing their desire to benefit white people, yet having respect for the niceties of due process and the Constitution, these disseminators of Republican dogma rather naturally saw no immediate urgency in abolishing slavery, and sought to apprise the slave states of that fact. Ostensibly, while speaking for the party, Greeley asked *Tribune* subscribers the following question: "did the Republican party propose to employ the power of the federal government to abolish slavery" at one fell swoop, as the radical abolitionists demanded? The New York editor's answer was, of course, that it did not.[121] The *Cincinnati Commercial* added its confirmation. In 1860 it denied that the Republican Party, upon taking office, had any plans immediately to abolish slavery. That institution was not something so horrible that it needed to be ended within a short time after the accession of the first Republican president. It could, the

Commercial gave assurances, be ended gradually and with due respect for the slaveholder's property interest in man.[122]

It was because of their conservative posture respecting slavery that Republican thinkers reacted with such consternation to John Brown's raid on Harper's Ferry. The event not only offended their political sensibilities but caused them concern that the voters would now associate the Republican Party with Brown's radicalism. Let the response of Joseph Medill of the *Chicago Tribune* serve as an illustration. Expressing his shock in a letter to Salmon P. Chase, Medill predicted that, as a result of Brown's action, "our party will suffer . . . . " A "vast number of our people are emigrants from slave states and you can hardly imagine the effect produced on their minds by the idea of negro stealing or a negro insurrection. It [radicalism] had killed Seward stone dead . . . . It is a terrible blow and throws our party on the defensive."[123]

The conviction of Republican publicists that, if it wanted to capture national office, their party must continue to project a conservative image on the questions of slavery and race, was evident through the election of 1860. Before switching his support to Lincoln, Horace Greeley, who represented Oregon at the Republican national convention, backed the conservative Edward Bates, for the presidential nomination. Greeley had nothing but praise for Bates and his Missouri Republicans and their "bold, manly, uncompromising position" on slavery; that is, he added with decided understatement, "they do not profess to be a philanthropic party . . . . They are not especially friends of the negro."[124]

To be sure, Bates did lose the nomination to Lincoln, but this fact did not indicate that the latter's ideas on issues differed markedly from those of the conservatives in his party. Two years earlier one of his critics had already confirmed the point. After hearing Lincoln speak in Charleston, Illinois, the journalist, Lyman Hall concluded that Lincoln "made color and race the ground of political proscription. He forsook principle and planted himself on low prejudice." In fine, Hall continued, "we thought a champion had been found . . . for human rights, for man as man, irrespective of . . . race . . . or other accidental circumstance . . . but we are disappointed . . . . Mr. Lincoln takes the same ground" as "Mr. Douglas."[125] Accordingly, conservative Republican writers and journalists, such as Medill, were delighted with Lincoln's nomination. They said they supported him since, as a Henry Clay Whig, he could win over conservative voters.[126] In substantiation of this conclusion, it perhaps only needs be added that Hinton Rowan Helper also preferred Lincoln as the candidate who could best appeal to "middling whites."[127]

VI

To recapitulate, most Republican writers and editors prided themselves and their party on their conservatism, in the sense that they promoted policies that championed the rights and interests of the nation's predominant white population and denied the rights and interests of the nation's black population. Just as Republican politicians did, these scribes urged exclusion and containment as immediate objectives and gradual emancipation with compensation as a future objective. If a handful of writers at times seemed ready to grant the freedman some basic legal rights, the rest argued that the country must eventually be rid of him. Some expected him to disappear through the workings of either geographic or economic determinism, but more seemed convinced that he would have to be physically removed to areas outside of the country; that only by colonization could the alleged black problem be eliminated from the United States once and for all. James Redpath, in fact, had started to carry out the latter policy, with his Haytian Emigration Bureau, but it would be under the Lincoln administration that the drive to colonize the black man enjoyed its greatest support. This support was based upon the same racial assumptions that had originally been set forth by the intelligentsia.

CHAPTER 8

REPUBLICANS, BLACKS AND THE CIVIL WAR

> Here . . . in Indiana we have a sufficient laboring population of white people for all the purposes of agriculture and other industry. In the organization of our state government we elected in favor of the white race by prohibiting the institution of slavery
>
> Albert G. Porter, 1862

With the victory of Abraham Lincoln in the 1860 presidential election, Republicans acquired national power for the first time. Voting followed sectional lines; Lincoln did not even appear on the ballot in the Southern states. Shortly after his election the states of the deep South made good their longtime threats and began to secede from the Union as the nation prepared for civil war. And, true to their conservative political philosophy, the Republicans, who dominated Congress after the majority of Democrats departed that body following secession, passed resolutions that 1) prohibited the introduction of slavery in any of the territories of the United States, and 2) guaranteed, at least for the immediate future, the inviolability of slavery within the slave states.[1]

More importantly, in seeking to explain why white Northerners and Southerners were determined to kill one another, many Republicans, in keeping with their racial beliefs, blamed the black man. They so magnified racial differences to the point that they proclaimed the very presence of a distinct and inferior black race, in a country which God had ordained should belong to the superior Caucasian race, caused whites above and below Mason's and Dixon's line to destroy each other. This line of argument could only increase white hatred for black people, which was directly manifested during the Civil War in a series of vicious white physical attacks on blacks in Northern cities. Furthermore, white Southerners-shortsighted, not as racially conscious as Northerners, and desiring to spread slavery and with it the black man into the virgin West-had provoked the conflict. For example, Postmaster General Montgomery Blair, who on numerous occasions referred to Caucasians as the "master race," stated baldy that the "real cause of the rebellion was the 'negro question and not the slavery question.'" In Blair's mind, it was "this antagonism of race which had led to our present calamities." In fact, in reference to the United States Blair asserted that the "essence of the contest is whether the white race shall have these lands or whether they shall be held by the black race."[2] Another Blair, Lincoln's spokesman in the House, Frank, used the same expression, i.e. "an antagonism of race," to assign causation.[3] A third Blair, Lincoln's influential political adviser, the aged Jacksonian Francis Preston Blair, agreed with his sons when he wrote that "it would be superfluous in the present attitude of the Gov't to argue the necessity of removing the element [blacks] that convulses its whole system."[4] "It is admitted on all hands," Lincoln's Commissioner of Emigration, the Reverend James Mitchell wrote to the president in 1862, "that our mixed and servile population constitute the root of those issues and quarrels" between the sections.[5] Reduced to its lowest common denominator the contest was, said Republican Senator Edgar Cowan of Pennsylvania, a racial one. In his words it was a "simple question between the white men and the negroes" over which would eventually control the government of the nation.[6] Lincoln reiterated Mitchell's and Cowan's sentiments when, in 1862, he personally told a group of black leaders that "but for your race among us, there could not be war."[7]

This mode of thinking only reinforced the conclusion that many Northern thinkers and political leaders had already reached: the United States must somehow be rid of the black presence. Obviously, various solutions had been contemplated since Jefferson's time. First, Southern slaveholders must be persuaded voluntarily to free their chattel. Secondly, and as a part of winning the slaveholders' acquiescence, the country must be rid of free blacks. A number of intelligentsia, who also doubled as Republicans, such as Dr. Julian Sturtevant of Illinois and Dr. Louis Agassiz of Massachusetts, assumed as late as 1863 that the problem would eventually solve itself, as blacks were eliminated in the marketplace by competing white workers (Sturtevant's prediction) or by blacks naturally migrating to warmer zones (Agassiz's prediction).[8]

Initially, a number of congressional Republicans seemed divided, some supporting Sturtevant's prediction, others Agassiz's, while still others appeared to combine the two. To illustrate, Representative George H. Yeaman of Kentucky echoed Sturtevant, claiming that after emancipation the black man "will enter the lists as a competitor, and as such will go down." Yeaman was confident that white men "will out-work him, out-thrive him, out-trade him, out-learn him, out-fight him [and] out-vote him . . . ."[9] On the other hand Representative William D. Kelley of Pennsylvania agreed with Agassiz, noting that Latin America beckoned the black man to come and seek his fortune.[10] Although Frank Blair was perhaps the major proponent of colonization in the House, ironically at times he claimed this unnecessary, because the black race naturally "gravitates to the tropics."[11] Representatives James W. Patterson of New Hampshire and John M. Broomall of Pennsylvania connected both Sturtevant's and Agassiz's projections. Quoting any number of ethnologists almost verbatim, Patterson claimed that the white man's "larger brain, stronger and more enduring muscles and . . . more active temperament" would "gradually push the weaker race from the continent" southward, to its natural home.[12] Broomall joined the two arguments, but in a slightly different fashion. Conceding black labor its worth, the Pennsylvanian stated that "one fact . . . ought to remove all fear of dangerous competition on the part of the negro," and that fact was that "He is a man of the tropics and is only kept in the temperate zone by force." Once slavery was terminated, blacks would move "constantly southward," into Latin America.[13] Most Republicans, however, including Sturtevant, Agassiz and some of the above, were ready to support a third remedy.

Into the second year of the war, the most touted Republican solution to the dual dilemmas posed by slavery and race was the same solution that many of the intelligentsia, Free Soilers and Republicans had recommended all along: gradual, compensated emancipation coupled with black colonization. Accordingly, various schemes for compensating slaveholders and financing colonization were introduced into Congress. One plan to reimburse slaveholders was proposed by Doolittle, in which one half the proceeds from the sale or lease of confiscated rebel estates would be returned to the slave states by the Treasury Department, to be used equally for compensating slaveholders and financing colonization.[14] Frank Blair proposed that newly emancipated blacks be put to work on public projects, in order to help cover the "expenses of their transportation" to another country.[15] Practically all Republicans, including the liberal Owen Lovejoy, backed some form of federal compensation for slaveholders.[16]

Once Southerners accepted compensation and colonization, the Union could be restored, black people would vanish, and best of all white men could get on with achieving their manifest destiny. Indeed, John Sherman worried that if blacks were not colonized somewhere, either out of the country or in parts of the South itself, Anglo-Saxon "nationality" would be "overthrown." On the other hand, and apparently in an effort to make the program attractive to its supposed beneficiaries, Sherman, Browning and Doolittle all noted how emigrating blacks would be spared white prejudice, Sherman specifically citing the black laws, North and South.[17] Rather than pursuing the morally sound and economically sensible course of removing these laws, and thereby removing the legal imprimatur for white prejudice, Sherman would remove black people. Fearing the presumed dangers to Anglo-Saxondom, the Lincoln administration and congressional Republicans forged ahead to implement the ambitious scheme.

In April 1862, under the chairmanship of Republican Congressman Albert S. White of Indiana, the House Committee on Emancipation and Colonization began work on a plan to bring about emancipation and to transport black Americans out of the country. Specifically, the republics to the south of the United States were being considered suitable sites. The Committee issued its report on July 16, 1862, noting that emancipation without "deportation and colonization . . . would oppress the nation with a helpless population." In calling for black colonization, the Committee report cited the long held Republican fears of miscegenation, labor competition and racial conflict. It dwelt upon the "opposition of a large portion of our people to the intermixture of the races." The report evinced concern that a sudden and immediate emancipation would "produce serious resistance on the side of the laborious interests of our own color and race." The White Committee also wrote about the "desperate desire" of black Americans for "that equality which . . . had [been] denied them" and that "by some bloody revolution they might possibly conquer [it] for themselves . . . ."[18]

To implement its plans, the Committee supplied financial details for compensating slaveholders. While receiving compensation from the federal government, slave owners would emancipate their chattels gradually, over a period of "twenty years." The White Committee completed its recommendations by proclaiming that Republican support for colonization was a matter of race: "this is a question of color, and is unaffected by the relation of master and slave." In that light, and indicative of the narrow Republican definition of the Caucasian race, the "Committee conclude that the highest interests of the white race, whether Anglo-Saxon, Celt or Scandinavin, require that the whole country should be held and occupied by those races [sic] alone."[19]

If colonization was supposed to be a voluntary program, at times it didn't appear that way. For instance, the White Committee Report left open the issue of deportation. Other leading Republicans seemed adamant in their support of forced emigration. David Wilmot was not reticent in recommending "compulsory emigration" for black Americans. Citing both Jefferson and Weston to back up his contention that colonization was both practical and possible, Doolittle calculated that if the federal government began an "annual deportation of 150,000" blacks, then the "last remnant . . . would be removed by the year 1907." Frank Blair had "not the least hesitation in . . . deporting these slaves when emancipated."[20]

During the same month that the White Committee began its work,

Congress, with overwhelming Republican backing, passed the District of Columbia Emancipation Act of April 16, 1862. Section eleven of this act provided Lincoln with both the legal foundation and financial means necessary to colonize blacks residing in the District; toward this measure, Congress appropriated $100,000.[21]

On July 12, 1862, Congress presented Lincoln with an additional $500,000 for colonization. Several days later it passed, again with overwhelming Republican support, including that of the radical Charles Sumner, a more sweeping statute, namely the Second Confiscation Act of July 17, 1862. Section twelve of this act provided Lincoln with a colonization rider which allowed him to transport out of the country all blacks living in those slave states which laid down their arms and accepted compensated emancipation. In this way Lincoln obtained a total of $600,000 with which to carry out colonization, a relatively large sum of money to begin what, at that point, was only an experiment.[22] What is amazing here is that so many Republican Congressmen seemed to assume, on little if any evidence, that the republics to the south of the United States would welcome and receive black American colonists. There is an arrogance here which, fueled by the Social Darwinism made popular by their party, later became obvious during the blatant imperialism of the Republican administrations of William McKinley and Theodore Roosevelt.

For his part Lincoln had begun, as early as December, 1861, to take action looking to black emigration. He ordered a naval expedition to Chiriqui (Panama) to investigate its suitability as a colony. Moreover, in both his first and second annual messages to Congress, Lincoln called for a concerted effort to achieve colonization, and his projection for total black removal was quite close to Doolittle's. In fact, in his second annual message the president asked for a Constitutional amendment to provide compensation for gradual emancipation to the "year of our Lord one thousand nine hundred," along with colonization and "deportation."[23]

Perhaps the climax of white arrogance and of Lincoln's effort to promote colonization occurred during his meeting with black leaders at the White House on August, 14, 1862. This meeting was significant in more than one respect. Arranged by James Mitchell, it was the first time that an American president had invited black Americans to the White

House. It was for the purpose of telling them, however, that they must leave the country. Lincoln began the meeting by noting that "you and we are different races," so much so, that he believed it impossible for blacks and whites to live together in the same community. Since he claimed that this commingling was the root cause of the Civil War, black people would have to go; as he told them in his much repeated remark, "it is better for us both . . . to be separated." Seemingly goading his visitors, Lincoln accused blacks of being "selfish" if they remained in the United States, where, he insisted, they were not wanted by the dominant white population. With apparent condescension, he declared that blacks "should sacrifice" their "present comfort, for the purpose of being as grand . . . as the white people." Lincoln also dealt with specifics. He told his black listeners that they need not go to Liberia, since he was thinking of a place closer to the United States, namely Central America. Then Lincoln came to the nub of why he had invited them: he wanted them to convince their own people to leave the country.[24]

The blacks who attended this White House meeting, including Frederick Douglass, later said that they were shocked at what they considered to be Lincoln's callousness. Nevertheless, being, in a sense, a captive audience, with the President of the United States doing all the talking as they listened in a state of disbelief, they said little in response. However, once word both of the meeting and of Lincoln's proposals became public knowledge, the reaction was swift and sure. For instance, Douglass attacked the whole idea of colonization, not only because he was opposed in principle, but because he saw the very promotion of the idea as a means of encouraging white hostility toward black people. He said that any thought of colonization was tantamount to "furnishing a weapon to all the ignorant and base, who need only the countenance of men in authority to commit all kinds of violence and outrage upon the colored people" in the free states.[25] In the same vein, Isaiah Wears, a black Philadelphian, maintained that "it is not the negro race that is the cause of the war; it is the unwillingness on the part of the American people to do the race simple justice . . . . The effect of this scheme of colonization, we fear, will be to arouse prejudice and to increase enmity against us."[26] A group of Long Island blacks came to the same conclusion regarding Lincoln's colonization policy; in their words such a policy only animated white people "who wish to insult and mob us," and therefore was a "mistaken policy."[27] Black leader Robert Purvis, like Wears also of Philadelphia, saw Republican colonization as driven by a pathological fear and animosity, by, in his words, an "insane and vulgar hate" of black people.[28] A meeting of blacks from that same city concurred with the sentiments of Wears and Purvis, and "pray[ed] for a more liberal and enlightened public policy."[29]

Other blacks also assailed Lincoln's proposals by invoking the environmentalist theory of universal manhood. They countered the polygenist idea of totally distinct races, which could not possibly live together, with that of the essential oneness of all mankind. A. P. Smith, a free black from New Jersey, asserted: "Let me tell you sir, President though you are, there is but one race of men on the face of the earth . . . physical differences no doubt there are, no two persons on earth are exactly alike in this respect; but what of that . . . ? Is our right to a home in this country less than your own, Mr. Lincoln?"[30] "We rejoice that we are colored Americans," wrote the above group of Long Island blacks when protesting the same meeting, "but deny that we are a 'different race of people,' as God has made of one blood all nations."[31] Robert Purvis summed up the anger that many blacks felt, when he wrote the following to an organizer of Lincoln's scheme, Senator Samuel C. Pomeroy of Kansas: "It is in vain [that] you talk to me about 'two races' and their 'mutual antagonism.'" As Smith had reminded Lincoln, Purvis reminded Pomeroy that there is just "one race and that is the human race." Obviously not the stereotypical sambo, Purvis was firm and to the point. "Sir," he continued, "we were born here and here we choose to remain . . . . Don't advise me to leave and don't add insult to injury by telling me it's for my own good. Of that I am to be the judge."[32]

These free blacks were not completely alone in their opposition to the Republican policy of colonization or in their espousal of the environmentalist concept of universal man. A few of the more liberal, broad-minded party members, such as Representatives Albert Gallatin Riddle of Ohio and William Boyd Allison of Iowa, along with Secretary of the Treasury Salmon P. Chase, were cool if not, at times, openly hostile to colonization, and essentially for the same reason. Riddle put his opposition to the scheme in this way: "It is idle to establish to me the inferiority of that sinless race-I see that they are men; useless, by curious physiological and ethnological disquisition, to affirm a difference between the African and Caucasian tribes-for I know that God created both."[33] Allison opposed colonization in analogous terms. The "colored man," said the Iowan, "is industrious, does acquire property, and appreciates with us the blessings of liberty . . . . "[34] Seeking to give Riddle's and Allison's thoughts practical application, Chase attacked Lincoln's colonization objectives. "How much better would be a manly protest against prejudice against color," he stated the day after the president's White House meeting with the black delegation. In lieu of colonization should come "a wise effort to give freemen homes in America."[35] Others, such as Representative Henry Winter Davis of Maryland, viewed colonization as historically absurd and impractical.[36]

In spite of the adverse reaction within the free black community of the North and by several Republican politicians, Lincoln and his supporters persevered in their efforts. With $600,000 already appropriated to begin the task, Lincoln and his new Secretary of the Interior, John P. Usher of Indiana, signed a contract, on December 31, 1862, with New York businessman Bernard Kock, a contract to transport blacks out of the country. The next day the president put his name to the final Emancipation Proclamation. The contract, which was later leased to two Wall Street investment brokers, Paul S. Forbes and Charles K. Tuckerman, culminated in the landing of the first black American colonists at Ile a Vache, Haiti, on June 1, 1863. The colonists, many from the Washington, D.C. area, were simply dumped there, with little planning and little of the promised supplies to sustain them. As a result this experiment proved to be a disaster, as some 108 of 435 black colonists died.[37]

Sometime in 1864, the Lincoln administration and its allies in Congress apparently abandoned the whole notion of colonization, although Frank Blair continued to back this policy by drawing analogies between Jefferson's idea and Lincoln's attempts to implement that idea. At the same time Senator James H. Lane of Kansas introduced an old idea, a bill for the internal colonization of blacks, this time in a portion of Texas which he hoped to see set aside for that purpose. Ironically, when promoting his plan, Lane described a different and certainly improved black man, all in an effort to make him appear a more viable emigrant. To illustrate, the black character was now "faithful, confiding, affectionate [and] industrious." Blacks were now "given to neatness and generally religious." Rather than being lazy and barbaric, blacks now exhibited "ambition" and even a "high civilization."[38] In fine, for some Republicans the idea of colonization died hard, but die it did. In May 1864, with opposition growing, Senator Morton S. Wilkinson of Minnesota introduced a resolution which led to the withdrawal of all congressional monies appropriated for the project.[39] Instead, Republicans reverted to the policy of containing black people in the South.

Had it then, all come merely to this? The rather feeble efforts of the American Colonization Society aside, had all of the proselytizing on behalf of colonization-by Jefferson and Clay, by scientists and intellectuals, and by Free Soil and Republican politicians, writers and journalists-finally come to no more than a single governmental attempt to settle a handful of blacks on one tiny island? Clearly the answer is yes. But why?

Some of the reasons are not far to seek. The initial experiment, to be sure, had failed; but there were more far ranging reasons. First, the loyal slave states, not to mention the slave states in secession, had rejected the Republican plan. Secondly, with few exceptions, free black Americans had also rejected the plan.[40] Thirdly, it was one matter for the government to allot $600,000 for an experiment in colonization and quite another, given the tremendous financial burden already imposed by the war, for it to shoulder additionally the enormous expenditures that a fully on-going project of colonization would entail. Lastly, securing the necessary shipping would be a problem, as the war preoccupied both merchant and naval vessels and Northern merchant shipping was being destroyed in record numbers by Confederate commerce raiders such as the C.S.S. *Alabama*.

In light of these obstacles, the reader might well ponder whether the idea of colonization had not been a chimera from the beginning; in other words, should not the obstacles been evident even back in Jefferson's day? After all, slaveholders, as a group, had never accepted the idea; free blacks, as a group, had never agreed to the proposal; and the cost, even without the added burden of war, had, as Thomas R. Dew pointed out in 1832, always been prohibitive.[41]

But if colonization was an unrealistic proposition from the outset, why had so many people persisted as its advocates? It would probably be asking too much for an historical study to give a satisfactory answer to such a question. Since self-proclaimed realistic people have throughout time frequently advocated unrealistic propositions, the question might better be left to the philosophers or psychologists. Be that as it may, one observation seems obvious: many Republican leaders and opinion makers of the 1850's had assumed that, under their guidance, the North and South would in good time be able to reach a resolution of the twin problems of slavery and race, one that would be beneficial to all white Americans. If their party, as a first step in this process, pledged to stop the further spread of slavery or black people, its promise not to violate slavery where it already existed would seem to have been tendered as proof that later steps to a final solution would be undertaken only with the cooperation of the South. The South thought differently.

The war, with its threat to the Union, forced the hand of Republican strategists. Now any answers to the lingering questions of slavery and race could only be addressed if they helped to answer what, to the Lincoln administration, was the more immediate and pressing question of preserving the Union. Consequently, after unsuccessfully seeking to win the slave states to its plan of gradual, compensated emancipation, and the slave states and free blacks to its plan of colonization, the government, after its single, half-hearted attempt to implement colonization, fell back on the original Free Soil expedient of containment,[42] but with an added feature pleasing to Northern blacks, abolitionists and European critics of the administration, emancipation. As well, Lincoln, in a consistent and familiar refrain for Republicans, also used emancipation to appeal to laboring whites, the major component of the Union war effort.

Several months after issuing his Preliminary Emancipation Proclamation, Lincoln, in his State of the Union address of December 1862, gave further indication of the new direction in which his administration was heading, when he remarked that "Emancipation, even without deportation, would probably enhance the wages of white labor."

Theoretically, with the end of slavery, employers, at least in the South, would have to bid for labor, thus raising wages in that section and, presumably, in the country as a whole. However, old ideas persisted, and he went on to insist that "with deportation, even to a limited extent, enhanced wages to white labor is mathematically certain." At the end of 1864 Lincoln called for increased European immigration, to replace the enormous manpower losses due to the war.[43] The president was joined by other Republicans, such as Representative Amassa Walker of Massachusetts. Walker declared that the elimination of slavery would reduce the increase in the black population, hence increasing employment opportunities for European immigrants. "The emancipationist," he contended, "demands the extinction of slavery because the interests of the white race require it."[44] Once again only white laboring interests were given consideration. Laboring free blacks, i.e. laborers per se, were ignored.

White interests in the North, however, had further demands. Emancipation without compensation[45] should be supplemented by efforts to keep blacks in the South. In that way the rest of the country would at least be preserved from the allegedly awful consequences which Republicans foresaw in a biracial society. Utilizing the learned community's arguments of climatic determinism and the sambo personality, some Republicans seemed to think that containment would be easy. Kelley of Pennsylvania thought that once emancipated, blacks would pose few problems. Citing Dr. Samuel G. Howe and the *American Freedmen's Inquiry Commission Report* as evidence, he noted that blacks were a "'docile and easily managed'" race. In any event blacks preferred the South, added Kelley, because of its "genial" climate.[46]

Other Republicans reassured themselves that freed blacks, of their own volition, would remain in the South. Representative William Davis of Pennsylvania based his prediction on the "fact" that the "black is not migratory," because he is too "feeble." Davis' Pennsylvania colleague, Samuel S. Blair, analogous to both Kelley and Davis, argued climatic determinism and promised Northern whites that blacks were "not nomadic," and therefore they need not worry. Another Pennsylvanian, Thaddeus Stevens, concurred, claiming that "If every southern slave were free, he would stay just where he is." Not only would blacks remain in the South but, because of its colder climate, thought Stevens, the "North would soon be drained of her African population."[47]

Just in case the black man was "migratory" however, the Baltimore and Ohio Railroad Company acted to retain escaping black contraband in Washington, D.C., refusing them passage northward.[48] In Congress, even liberals such as Julian of Indiana recommended that Northerners apply a dose of some of "our prejudices" to keep the Negro in his old home.[49] Trumbull of Illinois, his usual frank self, expressed the attitude of numerous Republicans on newly freed blacks in this way: "We do not want them."[50]

Not only would blacks be contained in the South, but some Republicans counseled their Caucasian constituents that emancipation would not bring about the feared equality of the races. On the contrary, it would bring about a white American. Representative Thomas T. Davis of New York said this because of his belief that the "distinction of races" was permanent.[51] Cowan and Broomall agreed, the latter stressing the "instinctive repulsion between distinct races."[52] Representative Glenni W. Scofield, also of Pennsylvania, confidently predicted that by simply emancipating the black slaves the "country will [eventually] become homogeneous."[53]

The Lincoln administration's shift in policy from emancipation and colonization to emancipation and containment was perhaps best demonstrated in 1864 and 1865 by the work of the Treasury Department in establishing Freedmen Labor Colonies in the South. These were created under the Department's *Rules and Regulations for Leasing Abandoned Plantations and Employing Freedmen* and, later, under the Freedmen's Bureau. In Congress this policy change was reflected in the comments of Representative Ithamar C. Sloan of Wisconsin. Referring to colonization as an "ignominious failure," Sloan called instead for the "simple, natural right of the blacks to own property and to enjoy the product of their own labor." Of course, the property that Sloan had in mind was that confiscated from ex-slaveholders as the war progressed. If blacks were to remain in the Union, as Sloan assumed, then the overwhelming majority would remain in the South.[54] Julian specifically offered the possibility of "homesteads of forty and eighty acres of land on the forfeited estates of rebels." It was hoped that this land, plus the "uncongenial climate" and the specter of "Anglo-Saxon domination" in the North, would act to keep blacks in the South.[55] Representative Cyrus Aldrich of Minnesota introduced a resolution to bolster black containment, by offering black union soldiers bounty lands in Florida after hostilities, also from confiscated estates.[56] In effect, containment would now be accomplished by various forms of internal colonization.

The Freedman's Bureau can be viewed as a major instrument of containment. However, several Republican Senators expressed reservations on the operations of the Bureau, and in particular its labor provisions and the pay of black workers. One Senator believed that the Bureau would "impose upon" blacks "a worse bondage than the masters of the South ever exercised over them . . . . " Another feared that the Bureau would "control and make money out of [the] . . . negroes." These concerns were not without merit. One problem was that the Commissioner of the Bureau was given enormous powers over its operations, without much outside control or input. Another problem was that the leasing provisions were vague, leaving open the option for white leasees, as well as black.[57]

Racialist considerations aside, there was another, more immediate factor that weighed heavily in favor of containment. By the time the final Emancipation Proclamation was issued on January 1, 1863, it was recognized by the Lincoln administration that the war would not be ended quickly, perhaps not even successfully. The Proclamation was a military necessity, a measure directed, in Lincoln's words, "toward ending the struggle." It would allow the administration to tap into a vast reserve of black manpower. Even here, Lincoln initially assigned blacks a secondary role, i.e. "to garrison forts, positions, stations and other places."[58] With Northern enlistments falling off, desertions increasing, and opposition to conscription growing in the white community, as evidenced by the massive draft riots in New York city, the Union forces needed an alternative source of manpower. Containment would insure the availability of black fighting men, a number of whom faced "compulsory enlistment." In turn, the military would act as an instrument for implementing containment. In fact, the Freedmen's Bureau was administered by military officers because it fell under the jurisdiction of the War Department.[59] By the end of the war approximately two hundred thousand black men had served in the Union Army and Navy.[60] However, while fighting for their freedom, blacks faced various forms of discrimination and experimentation.

Dr. Howe, Free Soiler and founding Republican, was one of the first to recommend the enlistment of black soldiers. Howe was a close friend of Louis Agassiz and a leading member of the United States Sanitary Commission, which commission preformed various "anthropological measurements" on black contrabands and soldiers. The war provided a perfect opportunity to test the theories of the intelligentsia by, for example, measuring the anatomies of black and white soldiers and comparing them. Howe was also an important member of the administration sponsored American Freedmen's Inquiry Commission, and both commissions were precursors of the Freedmen's Bureau. As was typical of most Free Soilers and Republicans, Howe's recommendation was freighted with racialist baggage. For instance, Howe could accept containment, as long as it was accompanied by the destruction of slavery. Similar to Patterson and Broomall, Howe apparently married the arguments of Agassiz and Sturtevant. Emancipation, Howe declared, would bring into play "natural laws, by the operation of which . . . the colored population will disappear from the Northern and Middle states, if not from the continent, before the more vigorous and prolific white race." That Howe was influenced by the teachings of Agassiz was obvious, not only in his use of expressions like "thermal laws," to describe this natural migration, but more importantly, during the time he served on these commissions he wrote to Agassiz for advice on black people.[61]

Representatives William McKee Dunn of Indiana and Lovejoy of Illinois likewise advocated the use of black troops, and this for selfish, racialist reasons, i.e. because they valued the life of a white man more than that of a black. And, recalling Nott and other members of the intelligentsia, the belief that blacks were immune to certain diseases once more surfaced. Even so, it wasn't enough that blacks would be sacrificed in a war that was not of their making, but what was worse, black troops would be segregated from white ones, would, through this and other forms of blatant discrimination, be made to feel the inferiority of which they were constantly accused. Dunn assured fellow Congressmen that black men would never be given command over white men, and that the two would be placed in separate regiments. Not wishing to put "niggers" in command of white soldiers, Lovejoy ridiculed the idea of a "'general Sambo, colonel Sambo, or captain Sambo.'" However, both Congressmen were mainly concerned with saving white lives, and said so explicitly. When speaking of Northern soldiers Dunn put the following question to fellow members: "Shall we not spare this precious white blood if we can find black men in the South . . . to take part in this contest?" Evidently Caucasian lives were "above price," while black lives were expendable. Moreover, Dunn continued, Northern white soldiers were more likely to perish from diseases like malaria in "Southern swamps and sickly locations," whereas blacks were ostensibly immune to such, because of "their peculiar physical adaptation." Lovejoy would gladly sacrifice black lives, if by doing so the Union Army "could save fifty thousand or one hundred thousand white loyal men."[62]

Numerous congressional Republicans joined Dunn and Lovejoy in seeking to preserve white lives at the expense of black ones. As had Dunn, Representative Cornelius Cole of California cited Southern diseases when urging black recruitment.[63] Some, similar to Lincoln, would assign to blacks the heavy labor jobs needed to maintain large armies in the field. Blacks would be utilized to do bull work, analogous to "mules" or "jackasses" said Zachariah Chandler.[64] Morton Wilkinson, Henry Wilson, Josiah Grinnell, Grimes, Harlan, Sherman, and Representative Carey Trimble of Ohio, to name a few, all saw an opportunity to spare white lives, and encouraged an accelerated recruitment effort.[65] Lane of Kansas asserted that he would "like to see every white man in the Army . . . returned to his family and his place filled by a negro" because, in classic understatement, he was "not so devoted" or "much the lover of the negro race . . . . "[66] Even the liberal and later Radical Republican Thaddeus Stevens recommended this policy in an effort to "stop the further effusion of white blood."[67] The implication was clear: blacks could be wasted because they were purportedly inferior.

Another factor that spurred the drive for black recruitment into the

Union Army was the belief that some blacks were already serving as soldiers in the Confederate Army. This belief was not exactly groundless. For example, free black regiments from New Orleans did serve in the Confederate cause. Dunn, for one, noted that "Negroes were in the ranks of the rebels, shooting down our soldiers . . . . "[68] John Sherman and Thaddeus Stevens said the same thing.[69] Ex-Michigan Senator, Republican Kinsley Scott Bingham wrote to Senator Jacob M. Howard that during the battle of First Bull Run, "Regiments of Negro slaves were employed to murder our men."[70]

Aside from being kept in segregated regiments, black troops faced other forms of discrimination. To illustrate, for most of the war pay scales for black troops were lower than those for whites. Moreover, deductions from their pay were made for family care and clothing allowances, but not from that of their white counterparts. Some Republican Congressmen, such as future President James A. Garfield, saw no reason to end this discrepancy in pay. Wilson of Massachusetts would continue this policy, stating that the Union forces could enlist "thousands of colored men at low rates of wages to do . . . ditching . . . . " Black troops, however, did more than "ditching." With less than a year to go in the war some black regiments, such as the famous 54th Massachusetts, which lost over half of its members in battle, hadn't received any pay at all. Worse, some loyal slaveholders in the Border states, Kentucky, for instance, received compensation of $300 per slave, for "volunteering" the services of their male bondsmen to Union military recruiters. Whereas a white enlistee would be awarded a federal bounty for signing up, and often state, county and local bounties as well, any bounty that a black soldier might have received went to his master. Aside from the slaveholders of Washington, D.C. who were officially compensated for their losses, in this way the Lincoln administration indirectly compensated other Border state slaveholders.[71]

In the face of such discrimination and poor treatment, black troops proved their bravery and, as indicated, sustained a disproportionate share of losses at such battles as Battery Wagner and Petersburg. Such service was bound to ameliorate, to some extent, the vicious prejudice that blacks suffered under. At the least it acted to dispel, in some minds, the myths spun by the intelligentsia, that blacks were members of a weak race of cowards and sambos. This prejudice which, "in the estimation of the ethnologist" held that the "negro cannot be made a soldier" was now, in the words of Maryland Republican, Representative John A. J. Creswell, proven to be "nonsense."[72]

Obviously some whites came away from the Civil War with a higher regard for black people than that which they held when the conflict commenced. Unfortunately some did not. With a plethora of racist literature to fall back on, literature emanating from most of the learned community, and more vicious tracts yet to be published once Reconstruction began, one need not wonder why some Republican politicians found it difficult to jettison some of their old beliefs. In early April 1865, several days before the surrender of General Robert E. Lee's Army of Northern Virginia, and his own assassination, Lincoln confided to General Benjamin F. Butler who, according to some historians was not a reliable witness, his fear for the country if the Negroes remained in it after the war. Lincoln then asked Butler if he thought that, by using the Navy and merchant marine which would be freed with the surrender of the Southern Confederacy, it would be possible to transport all the blacks out of the United States?[73] While the Civil War freed the black man from slavery, it did little to free him from the debilitating effects of white racialism. As numerous blacks pointed out, if anything, Republican policies during the war acted to exacerbate that racism around which their party evolved. That racism, in turn, was a product of the learned community, and was intensified with the growth of the Free Soil and Republican Parties.

Notes

NOTES—INTRODUCTION

1   James G. Blaine, *Twenty Years of Congress: from Lincoln to Garfield, with a Review of the Events which Led to the Political Revolution of 1860* (Norwich, Conn., 1884), vol. 1, 126, 130, 156-57, 169; Henry Wilson, *History of the Rise and Fall of the Slave Power in America* (N.Y., 1969, originally published in 1872), vol. 2, 522, 701-02, 704, vol. 3, 59; John A. Logan, *The Great Conspiracy: Its Origin and History* (N.Y., 1886), 47, 99-100, 170.

2   James Ford Rhodes, *History of the United States From the Compromise of 1850 to the Final Restoration of Home Rule at the South in 1877* (Norwood, Mass., 1907, originally published in 1892), vol. 1, 285, vol. 2, 430-35, 502; James Schouler, *History of the United States under the Constitution* (N.Y., 1891), vol. 5, 349, 356; John W. Burgess, *The Civil War and the Constitution, 1859-1865* (N.Y., 1901), vol. 1, 22-27, 60, 98-99; Arthur C. Cole, *The Irrepressible Conflict, 1850-1865* (N.Y., 1934), 276, 283, 304-05; Dwight L. Dumond, *Antislavery Origins of the Civil War in the United States* (Ann Arbor, Mich., 1966, originally published in 1939), 1, 3, 5, 24, 100, 107, 113-14, 121, 126, 130; Arthur Schlesinger, Jr., "The Causes of the Civil War: A Note on Historical Sentimentalism," *Partisan Review,* vol. 16, 1949, 968, 977-78. More recently Neo-Nationalism had been carried forward in some works which depict an abolitionized Lincoln, who, as president led a moral crusade against slavery. See, Harold M. Hyman, *A More Perfect Union, The Impact of the Civil War and Reconstruction on the Constitution* (N.Y., 1973), 210-11, 280-81; Lawanda Cox, *Lincoln and Black Freedom: A Study in Presidential Leadership* (Columbia, S.C., 1981), 3-25; Kenneth M. Stampp,

The Imperiled Union, Essays on the Background of the Civil War (N.Y., 1980), 123-35.

3   Charles A. and Mary R. Beard, *The Rise of American Civilization* (N.Y., 1947, originally published in 1927), 19, 21-23, 32-33, 39; Arthur Young Lloyd, *The Slavery Controversy, 1831-1860* (Chapel Hill, N.C., 1939), 272-75, 279, 282-84; Ulrich B. Phillips, *The Course of the South to Secession* (Gloucester, Mass., 1958, originally published in 1939), 157-62.

4   Avery O. Craven, *Civil War in the Making, 1815-1860* (Baton Rouge, La., 1968, originally published in 1959), 28-29, 30-32, 49; James G. Randall, *The Civil War and Reconstruction* (N.Y., 1937), 134, 146-47, 162-63, 173, 177, 181; Kenneth M. Stampp, *And the War Came, The North and the Secession Crisis, 1860-1861* (Ann Arbor, Mich., 1967, originally published in 1950), 148-50; George Fort Milton, *The Eve of Conflict, Stephen A. Douglas and the Needless War* (Cambridge, Mass., 1934), 173-74, 199, 208, 231, 241, 337-38.

5   Frederick J. Blue, *The Free Soilers, Third Party Politics, 1848-54* (Urbana, Ill., 1973), x, 20-21; James A. Rawley, *Race and Politics, Bleeding Kansas in the Coming of the Civil War* (Philadelphia, 1969), x; Chaplain W. Morrison, *Democratic Politics and Sectionalism, The Wilmot Proviso Controversy* (Chapel Hill, N.C., 1967), 67-70.

6   John Malvin, *North into Freedom*, Allan Peskin, ed. (Cleveland, 1966, originally published in 1879), introduction, 2; Eugene H. Berwanger, "Negrophobia in Northern Pro-slavery and Antislavery Thought," *Phylon*, vol. 33, 1972, 272; Berwanger, *The Frontier Against Slavery, Western Anti-Negro Prejudice and the Slavery Extension Controversy* (Urbana, Ill., 1971, originally published in 1967), 125; Ronald G. Walters, *The Anti-Slavery Appeal, American Abolitionism After 1830* (Baltimore, 1976), 15, 42.

7   Larry Gara, "Slavery and the Slave Power: A Crucial Distinction," *Civil War History*, vol. 15, 1969, 12, 16, 18.

8   Eric Foner, "Racial Attitudes of the New York Free Soilers," *New York History*, vol. 46, 1965, 315, 318; Foner, "Politics and Prejudice: The Free Soil Party and the Negro, 1849-1852," *Journal of Negro History* vol. 50, 1965, 243; Gerald Sorin, *Abolitionism, A New Perspective* (N.Y., 1972), 87.

9   George M. Fredrickson, "Toward a Social Interpretation of the Development of American Racism," as quoted in Nathan I. Huggins, Martin Kilson, and Daniel M. Fox, eds., *Key Issues in the Afro-American Experience* (N.Y.,

1971), 253; Fredrickson, *The Black Image in the White Mind* (N.Y., 1972), 140; Hinton Rowan Helper, *The Impending Crisis of the South and How to Meet It*, George M. Fredrickson, ed. (Cambridge, Mass., 1968), xliv-xlv.

10   For examples of this view see, Malcolm Moos, *The Republicans, A History of their Party* (N.Y., 1956), 31, 33-34, 69, 83; John M. Rozett, "Racism and Republican Emergence in Illinois, 1848-1860: A Re-Evaluation of Republican Negrophobia," *Civil War History*, vol. 22, 1976, 114; Roger A. Fischer, "The Republican Presidential Campaigns of 1856 and 1860: Analysis Through Artifacts," *Civil War History*, vol. 27, 1981, 123-37.

11   See, Lawanda Cox, *Lincoln and Black Freedom*, 3-32; Stephen B. Oates, *Abraham Lincoln, The Man Behind the Myths* (N.Y., 1984), 68-75, 100-119; Hans L. Trefousse, *Carl Schurz, A Biography* (Knoxville, Tenn., 1982), 59; Harold M. Hyman and William M. Wiecek, *Equal Justice Under Law, Constitutional Development, 1835-1875* (N.Y., 1982), 246-69, 275-77.

NOTES—CHAPTER 1

1   Frederick Merk, *Manifest Destiny and Mission in American History* (N.Y., 1963), 24-35, 50-60; Albert K. Weinberg, *Manifest Destiny, A Study of Nationalist Expansionism in American History* (Baltimore, 1935), 100-223; Norman A. Graebner, ed., *Manifest Destiny* (Indianapolis, 1968), xlvi-xlvii, lii-liii, 14-15, 22-23; Ray Allen Billington, *Westward Expansion, A History of the American Frontier* (N.Y., 1949), 572-73, 584-85.

2   William Stanton, *The Leopard's Spots, Scientific Attitudes Toward Race in America, 1815-1859* (Chicago, 1960), 24-26; Jacques Barzun, *Race: A Study in Superstition* (N.Y., 1965, originally published in 1937), 34-37; Herbert J. Seligmann, *Race Against Man* (N.Y., 1939), 6-41; Samuel Stanhope Smith, *An Essay on the Causes of the Variety of Complexion and Figure in the Human Species,* Winthrop D. Jordan, ed. (Cambridge, Mass., 1965), xxxii-xxxv. Jordan's edition, except for its introduction, is an exact replica of the second edition of Smith's book, which was published in 1810. Smith's work was first published in 1787.

3   For example, see speech of David Wilmot in the House of Representatives, 7/24/1850, as quoted in the *Congressional Globe,* Blair and Rives, Printers, Washington, D.C., 31st. Cong., 1st Session, Appendix, 940-43. For the

views of Horace Greeley, see the *New York Tribune*, New York, 7/16/1847. For the views of various Republican leaders, such as Representative Frank Blair of Missouri and Senator James R. Doolittle of Wisconsin, see the *Missouri Democrat*, St. Louis, 2/16/1859, 10/15/1859, 12/1/1859, 8/3/1860.

4   Winthrop D. Jordan, *White Over Black, American Attitudes Toward the Negro, 1550-1812* (Baltimore, 1969, originally published in 1968), 546-47. That Jefferson's theories were received and taken to heart by the predominate white community was recognized by David Walker, the free black publisher and printer of Boston. Walker noted that one of the major reasons which caused him to write his *Appeal to the Colored Citizens of the World* (Boston, 1829), was the great circulation and influence which Jefferson's *Notes on the State of Virginia* enjoyed among white Americans. Walker believed that Jefferson's remarks on black inferiority were a hindrance to the black man's fight to achieve equal social and political status within the United States. He wrote that it would take a long time for the black community to overcome the damage done by Jefferson's comments. See, Merril D. Peterson, *The Jefferson Image in the American Mind* (N.Y., 1960), 175-76. For a more detailed view of David Walker and early Pan-Africanism, see, Sterling Stuckey, *The Ideological Origins of Black Nationalism* (Boston, 1972), 7-117.

5   Philip S. Foner, *Basic Writings of Thomas Jefferson* (N.Y., 1950, originally published in 1944), 144-45. Jefferson's comments on the races in his *Notes on the State of Virginia*, are available from several different sources, including, Albert E. Bergh, ed., *The Writings of Thomas Jefferson* (Washington, D.C., 1907), vols. 1 and 2, 191-201, and William Peden, ed., *Notes on the State of Virginia* (Chapel Hill, N.C., 1955), 138.

6   Philip S. Foner, 145.

7   Ibid., 145-46.

8   Ibid., 147-48.

9   Ibid., 145, 148-49; John C. Miller, *The Wolf by the Ears, Thomas Jefferson and Slavery* (N.Y., 1977), 45-57. Miller's study is perhaps the best single work available on Jefferson's racial attitudes. See particularly chapters 6, 7, and 8.

10   Jordan, *White Over Black*, 432.

11   Bergh, 192.

12   Jefferson to Edward Coles, 8/25/1814, as quoted in Paul L. Ford, ed., *The*

Writings of Thomas Jefferson (N.Y., 1899), vol. 9, 477-79; Allen Johnson and Dumas Malone, eds., *Dictionary of American Biography* (N.Y., 1931), vol. 2, 296-97.

13   Philip S. Foner, 149; Jefferson to William Short, 1/18/1826, as quoted in Ford, 361-62. For further reading on Jefferson and the question of race, see, Jordan, *White Over Black*, 429-81, 546-47; Peterson, *Jefferson Image*, 167, 175-77; John Hope Franklin, *Racial Equality in America* (Chicago, 1976), 18-19; Gilbert Chinard, *Thomas Jefferson, the Apostle of Americanism* (Ann Arbor, Mich., 1957, originally published in 1929), 131-32; August Meier and Elliott Rudwick, *From Plantation to Ghetto* (N.Y., 1970, originally published in 1966), 48; Jacob E. Cooke, *Frederick Bancroft, Historian* (Norman, Okla., 1957), 171; Fredrickson, "Toward a Social Interpretation of the Development of American Racism," 252. Most of the blacks whom Jefferson observed were his own slaves, and slavery was not conducive to the development of literacy or artistic talents.

14   Herman Burmeister, *The Black Man, The Comparative Anatomy and Psychology of the African Negro* (N.Y., 1853), 6. See also, *Appleton's Cyclopedia of American Biography*, James G. Wilson and John Fiske, eds. (N.Y., 1888), vol. 1, 457. Burmeister travelled to South America and elsewhere to conduct his research. He was primarily interested in performing body measurements on the various races. Moreover, his work enjoyed worldwide popularity. For example, Burmeister's *Geschichte der Schopfung-Eine darstellung des Entwickelingsganges der Erde und Ihrer Bewohner* went through six editions, a number of which were published in the United States in the 1840's and 1850's.

15   Arthur DeGobineau, *The Inequality of Human Races* (Paris, France, 1853), 107; Stanton, 117, 174-75. Stanton's work is perhaps the best single study of the nineteenth century ethnologists. In 1856 DeGobineau's work was translated and published in the United States by Dr. Josiah Nott and Henry Holtz, a recent Swiss immigrant. DeGobineau cited the work of Dr. Samuel George Morton, as well as that of other American ethnologists. See, Barzun, 76. On DeGobineau's influence, see Jean Finot, *Race Prejudice* (London, England, 1906), 4-11.

16   James Hunt, *The Negro's Place in Nature* (N.Y., 1864), 10. Hunt cited other English physicians and anthropologists, such as Dr. Louis Buchner, Dr.

Pruner Bey, and Dr. R. Clarke, to lend support to his racist theories. See James Hunt, 22-26.

17   Alonzo Alvarez, *Progress and Intelligence of Americans* (Louisville, KY., 1863), 134, 145, 150-53. Wheat's work went through at least three editions.

18   Burmeister, 6-10.

19   DeGobineau, 107.

20   Alvarez, 149.

21   James Hunt, 7.

22   John H. Van Evrie, *White Supremacy and Negro Subordination* (N.Y., 1868, originally published in 1860), 93-95. Van Evrie published a newspaper, *The New York Day Book*, and a magazine, *The Old Guard*, which were the major organs of the New York City conservative anti-abolitionist Democratic Party.

23   Burmeister, 6, 12.

24   DeGobineau, 107.

25   Van Evrie, *White Supremacy*, 101.

26   Alvarez, 148.

27   Burmeister, 12.

28   Alvarez, 154.

29   Samuel Cartwright, "Slavery in the light of ethnology," as quoted in E.N. Elliott, *Cotton is King* (Augusta, Ga., 1860), 705; Cartwright, "Natural History of the Prognathous Species of Mankind," *New York Day Book*, 11/10/1857; Alvarez, 132, 154.

30   Alvarez, 154.

31   Ibid., 147-49.

32   Mrs. Henry Schoolcraft, *The Black Gauntlet: A Tale of Plantation Life in South Carolina* (Philadelphia, 1860), 49, 61; *Congressional Globe*, 35th Cong., 2nd. Session, 517.

33   James Hunt, 8.

34   Ibid., 10.

35   Burmeister, 16.

36   James Hunt, 25.

37   Josiah C. Nott and George R. Gliddon, *Types of Mankind: Or Ethnological Researches Based upon the Ancient Monuments, Paintings, Sculptures and Crania of Races, and upon their Natural, Geographical, Philological and*

Biblical History (Philadelphia, 1854), 68; Nott and Gliddon, *Indigenous Races of the Earth, or New Chapters of Ethnological Inquiry* (Philadelphia, 1857), 397. In the 1840's and 1850's Nott published a number of articles stressing racial differences. Most of his work appeared in various medical journals, such as the *American Journal of the Medical Sciences*. Nott often worked in conjunction with George R. Gliddon, the famous Egyptianologist and United States Ambassador to Cairo. *Types of Mankind* was dedicated to Samuel George Morton, the famous Philadelphia physician. For the most complete work on Nott see, Reginald Horsman, *Josiah Nott of Mobile, Southerner, Physician and Racial Theorist* (Baton Rouge, La., 1987).

38   Dr. Daniel Drake to Dr. John C. Warren, 1/4/1851, as quoted in *The National Intelligencer* (Washington, D.C.), 4/7/1851. Dr. John C. Warren was Professor of Medicine at Harvard. See, John D. Davies, *Phrenology, Fad and Science* (New Haven, Conn., 1955), 13, on the importance of Drake in American medicine. See also, Otto Juettner, *Daniel Drake and His Followers* (Cincinnati, Ohio, 1909), 7-84.

39   Samuel George Morton, *Crania Americana, or a Comparative View of the Skulls of Various Aboriginal Nations of North and South America* (Philadelphia, 1839), preface, iii, 1-4, 88, 253-60, 290; Morton, *Illustrated System of Human Anatomy, Special, General and Microscopic* (Philadelphia, 1849), 151; Stanton, 25, 28, 31-35, 41, 114-15; Davies, 147; Philip Borden, "Found Cumbering the Soil, Manifest Destiny and the Indian in the Nineteenth Century," as quoted in Gary B. Nash and Richard Weiss, eds., *The Great Fear, Race in the Minds of America* (N.Y., 1970), 93. The *Crania Americana* rapidly became a classic in its field. Much of the research for this book was based on Morton's large collection of skulls. He was the president of the Academy of Natural Sciences at Philadelphia, and may have been influenced by the work of Dr. Charles White of England. In 1799 White published his book, *The Regular Gradation of Man and in Different Animals and Vegetables*, in which he posited the theory that the European race stood the highest in the so-called chain of mankind, while the darker or black races stood lowest. White was probably the first writer to link black people to apes. He claimed that inferior anatomical differences were followed by inferior intellectual abilities. See, Samuel Smith, introduction.

40   Van Evrie, *Negroes and Negro Slavery: The First an Inferior Race, the Latter Its Normal Condition* (Baltimore, 1853), as quoted in Gilbert Osofsky,

ed., *The Burden of Race* (N.Y., 1967), 104-09. Apparently due to the demand for this work, Van Evrie reissued *Negroes and Negro Slavery* in 1861, and again in 1863. His second and more influential book, *White Supremacy and Negro Subordination*, went through at least two editions.

41   Nott and Gliddon, *Types of Mankind*, 67, 79, 89, 95-96, 403, 463, 465; Nott and Gliddon, *Indigenous Races*, 367; Stanton, 71, 148; Thomas F. Gossett, *Race, the History of an Idea in America* (Dallas, Tex., 1963), 64.

42   James Hunt, 8. In 1856 the French anthropologist, Gratiolet, originated the theory that the "cranial sutures of Negroes closed at an earlier period in individual growth than those of the white man, thus placing a rigid osseous limit on their mental growth." In 1863, James Hunt argued the same theory. See, George W. Stocking, *Race, Culture and Evolution* (N.Y., 1968), 55.

43   Burmeister, 10.

44   Sidney George Fisher, *The Trial of the Constitution* (Philadelphia, 1862), 274-75, 292-93, 297, 308, 331-33; Fisher, *The Laws of Race as Connected with Slavery* (Philadelphia, 1860), 10-15; *Dictionary of American Biography*, vol. 6, 410-11.

45   Alvarez, 140.

46   George Combe, *Notes on the United States of North America* (Philadelphia, 1841), vol. 1, 254; vol. 2, 63-64, 77-80, 112; Combe, *The Constitution of Man Considered in Relation to External Objects* (Hartford, Conn., 1842, originally published in 1839), 52-54; Morton, *Crania Americana*, 269-91; Davies, 20, 145; R.W. Haskins, *History and Progress of Phrenology* (Buffalo, N.Y., 1839), 87-97. On Phrenology in general, see, Orson S. Fowler, *Human Science or Phrenology* (Chicago, 1873). Combe, however, tended to discount the belief in distinct races or species, because such distinct species were usually unable to produce hybrids.

47   Nott and Gliddon, *Types of Mankind*, 67, 403, 460, 463.

48   James Hunt, 8.

49   Combe, *The Constitution of Man*, 156-61, 198-99; Davies, 143-48; Haskins, 12-17; Fowler, 164-65, 170-79, 219.

50   Cartwright, "Natural History of the Prognathous Species . . . ;" Cartwright, "Slavery in the light of ethnology," 707-12, 714-16. Cartwright wrote that "a perpendicular line, let fall from the forehead cuts off a large portion of the black man's face, throwing the mouth, the thick lips and the projecting teeth

anterior to the cranium." He wrote a number of essays on ethnology during the 1850's. Pieter Camper, the famous Dutch anatomist, began measuring facial angles in 1786, and believed that the "perfect angle," in the most "beautiful people," approached 100 degrees. Black people, according to Camper, fell far short of this ideal, and in fact were thought to be midway between the apes and the Europeans. See, Morton, *Crania Americana*, 250; Haskins, 13-20; Barzun, 35; Samuel Smith, xxxiv; Stanton, 25.

51 J. Aitken Meigs, "The Cranial Characteristics of the Races of Men," as quoted in Nott and Gliddon, *Indigenous Races*, 203, 222, 234, 325-26, 349.

52 James Hunt, 8-10.

53 Van Evrie, *White Supremacy*, introduction, 93-96. Van Evrie noted that there were "six distinct races of men, five of which are below the white or Caucasian race in the scale of the human creation, and the Negro is the lowest of all and inferior to all." The idea of a `chain of humanity' was basic to most racist thought.

54 Alvarez, 147.

55 Johann J.J. Von Tschudi, *Travels in Peru During the Years* 1838-1842 (London, England, 1847), 111.

56 Richard H. Colfax, *Evidence Against the Views of the Abolitionists, Consisting of Physical and Moral Proofs of the Natural Inferiority of the Negroes* (N.Y., 1833), 24-25.

57 Nott, "Dr. Nott's Reply to `C' . . . ," *Southern Quarterly Review*, vol. 8, 1845, 148-90; Nott and Gliddon, *Types of Mankind*, 96, 260.

58 Richard Colfax, 24.

59 Cartwright, "Slavery in the light of Ethnology," 698, 705.

60 Van Evrie, *White Supremacy*, 37.

61 Alvarez, 147-49.

62 James Hunt, 8-11.

63 Von Tschudi, 112.

64 DeGobineau, 205; Stanton, 117, 174-75. DeGobineau, as the title of his work makes clear, was a firm advocate of the theory of diverse races. He was one of the first proponents of what was later to become known as Social Darwinism. See DeGobineau, 39, 50, 107, 151, 205-06, 210.

65 Meigs, 222, 325-27.

66 DeGobineau, 107.

67   Alvarez, 132. There was hardly a part of the black man's physique, which escaped the scrutiny of white ethnologists. While Morton collected skulls, Peter A. Browne, a fellow Philadelphia naturalist, occupied himself in the collection of hair samples from all over the world. In 1852 Browne published his work, *The Classification of Mankind, by the Hair and Wool of their Heads, with the Nomenclature of Human Hybrids.* In his book, Browne claimed that the hair of the white man was more "perfect" than that of the black, because Caucasian hair contained a "central canal" for the "distribution of coloring matter," which canal was lacking in the hair of black people. No matter what part of the respective physical features of blacks and whites underwent 'scientific' analysis, the black man, it seemed, always came out second best. See Stanton, 152-53.

68   Gossett, 64-65; See also, Stanton, 162, 178, and Stocking 39.

69   Nott and Gliddon, *Types of Mankind*, front page and introduction, 52, 63, 67-68, 78-79, 95-96, 181, 260, 308, 403, 461-63, 465. See also, Stanton, 162, 178, and Stocking, 39.

70   Horsman, *Nott*, 115, 117; Louis Agassiz to Dr. S.G. Howe, 8/9,10/1863, as quoted in Elizabeth Cary Agassiz, ed., *Louis Agassiz, His Life and Correspondence* (Cambridge, Mass., 1885), vol. 2, 596, 605-06. See also, Edward Lurie, *Louis Agassiz, A Life in Science* (Chicago, 1960), 256-57, 260-61, 264, 305-06; Martin Duberman, *James Russell Lowell* (Cambridge, Mass., 1966), 187. Duberman referred to Agassiz, as the "most famous scientist of his day;" Nott and Gliddon, *Types of Mankind*, 78-79; Gossett, 59-60; Stanton, 103, 106-09. Agassiz, a Swiss immigrant, came to the United States in the 1830's, to work on the United States Coastal Survey. He was best known, however, for his work in zoology and glacialogy. Agassiz became famous as a lecturer at the Lowell Institute, in Boston, and as a professor at Harvard University. See Dirk J. Struik, *Yankee Science in the Making* (N.Y., 1968, originally published in 1948), 260, 272, 347-61.

71   Morton, *Crania Americana*, 7, 87.

72   DeGobineau, 50.

73   Cartwright, "Slavery in the light of ethnology," 698, 705.

74   Van Evrie, *White Supremacy*, 37, 48.

75   Burmeister, 16.

76   Richard Colfax, 26-29.

77   Burmeister, 15.

78   Cartwright, "Slavery in the light of ethnology," 698, 705, 720-23, 725-27; Cartwright, "Natural History of the Prognathous Species . . . . "

79   Schoolcraft, 49, 61.

80   Van Evrie, *White Supremacy*, 37, 48.

81   Fisher, *The Laws of Race*, 14-15.

82   Drake to Dr. John C. Warren, 12/31/1850, as quoted in *The National Intelligencer*, 4/5/1851.

83   Cartwright, "Slavery in the light of ethnology," 698, 705, 720-23, 725-27; Cartwright, "Natural History of the Prognathous Species . . . . "

84   James Hunt, 15-21; Burmeister, 17.

85   James Hunt, 15-21.

86   John W. Blassingame, *The Slave Community, Plantation Life in the Antebellum South* (N.Y., 1972), 132-44; Fredrickson, *The Black Image*, 111; Stanley M. Elkins, *Slavery, A Problem in American Institutional and Intellectual Life* (N.Y., 1963, originally published in 1959), 81-89.

87   Morton, *Crania Americana*, 87.

88   Burmeister, 14, 17.

89   Drake to Dr. John C. Warren, 12/26,31/1850, as quoted in *The National Intelligencer*, 4/3,5/1851.

90   Combe, *Notes on the United States*, vol. 1, 254; vol. 2, 63-64, 77-80, 112.

91   James Hunt, 19; Morton, *Crania Americana*, 87.

92   Cartwright, "Slavery in the light of ethnology," 720-21, 724-27.

93   Van Evrie, *Negroes and Negro Slavery*, 104-09.

94   James Hunt, 11.

95   DeGobineau, 205.

96   Burmeister, 16.

97   DeGobineau, 206.

98   James Hunt, 22.

99   Van Evrie, *White Supremacy*, 165.

100   Cartwright, "Slavery in the light of ethnology," 724-27.

101   One Dr. Mosely, as quoted in John Campbell, *Negro-Mania: Being an Examination of the Falsely Assumed Equality of the Various Races of Men* (Philadelphia, 1851), 132-33.

102   David Turnbull, *Travels in the West, Cuba, with Notices of Porto Rico and the*

Slave Trade (London, England, 1840), 171.

103   DeGobineau, 205-06.

104   James Hunt, 16, 22.

105   Mary L. Booth, "Emancipation and Colonization," *Brownson's Quarterly Review*, vol. 19, 1862, 220, 231-32. Booth, a native of New York City and a member of a prominent Irish-Catholic family, wrote the first major history of that city. During the Civil War she wrote (with William H. Seward's blessing) and translated propaganda and inspirational pieces, designed for distribution among Union soldiers. *Brownson's Quarterly Review* was the foremost Catholic journal in the country at that time. See, the *National Cyclopedia of American Biography*, James T. White and Company, publishers (N.Y., 1906), vol. 7, 321.

106   James Hunt, 16, 22.

107   Turnbull, 273.

108   Van Evrie, *White Supremacy*, 165.

109   James Hunt, 19; Drake to Dr. John C. Warren, 12/26,31/1850, as quoted in *The National Intelligencer*, 4/3,5/1851; Turnbull, 310; Morton, *Crania Americana*, 87; Cartwright, "Slavery in the light of ethnology," 725.

110   DeGobineau, 206.

111   Burmeister, 17.

112   James Hunt, 22.

113   Cartwright, "Slavery in the light of ethnology,", 724.

114   Burmeister, 16.

115   Cartwright, "Natural History of the Prognathous Species . . . ."

116   DeGobineau, 74-75.

117   Burmeister, 14.

118   Morton, *Crania Americana*, 88.

119   Van Evrie, *White Supremacy*, 138-39.

120   Von Tschudi, 111.

121   Drake to Dr. John C. Warren, 12/31/1850, as quoted in *The National Intelligencer*, 4/5/1851; James Hunt, 15.

122   Burmeister, 14.

123   DeGobineau, 205.

124   Van Evrie, *White Supremacy*, 241.

125   Alvarez, 132.

126   James Hunt, 13, 16.

127   Francis Pulszky, "Inconographic Researches on Human Races and Their
       Art," as quoted in Nott and Gliddon, *Indigenous Races*, 87, 124, 188.

128   Drake to Dr. John C. Warren, 12/31/1850, as quoted in *The National
       Intelligencer*, 4/5/1851.

129   Henry Barth, *Travels and Discoveries in North and Central Africa: Being a
       Journal of an Expedition Undertaken Under the Auspices of H.B.M.'s
       Government, in the Years 1849-1855* (London, England, 1857), vol. 1, xxii.

130   Richard Colfax, 26.

131   Julian M. Sturtevant, "The Destiny of the African Race in the United States,"
       Continental Monthly, vol. 3, 1863, 608; *National Cyclopedia*, vol. 13, 601.

132   DeGobineau, 179, 210.

133   Morton, *Crania Americana,* preface, iii, 1-4, 88; Agassiz to Dr. S.G. Howe,
       8/10/1863, as quoted in Elizabeth Cary Agassiz, vol. 2, 605-06; Lurie, 256-
       57, 260; Richard Colfax, 11, 22; James Hunt, 23; Alvarez, 124-32;
       DeGobineau, 117, 133, 179.

134   Van Evrie, *Negroes and Negro Slavery*, 105.

135   For examples of those who held the monogenic theory, see, James Cowles
       Prichard, *Researches into the Physical History of Mankind* (London, England,
       1841, originally published in 1836), vol. 1, 216, 336, 375-76. This work was
       dedicated to the German anthropologist, Dr. Johann Friedrich Blumenbach,
       and forms part of a five volume series which Prichard spent the better part of
       a lifetime researching. Prichard was a member of the Royal Academy of
       Medicine, Paris; the American Philosophical Society; and a corresponding
       member of the National Institute of France. He was also an honorary fellow
       of the King's and Queen's College of Physicians, Ireland. The British
       Association for the Advancement of Science, in its Report of its Seventeenth
       Meeting, entitled "Ethnology, or the Science of Races," supported Prichard's
       work. See, *The Edinburgh Review*, vol. 178, 1848, 433-36, 445-46, 452,
       457-58, 461-62, 469, 483-84; Moncure Daniel Conway, *Testimonies
       Concerning Slavery* (London, England, 1864), 5-7. Conway was a free
       thinker, and a founder of modern humanism. As a result of his experiences as
       a reporter during the Franco-Prussian War, he became one of the earliest
       advocates for a League of Nations, to maintain peace in the world. He
       detested war and slavery, because both were based on violence. Because of

his radical opinions, Conway was disliked by both conservative antislavery people and the Lincoln administration. In fact, as his biographer notes, the "abolitionists got in each other's way in denying any connection with Conway." Conway's writings fill eight pages of the *National Union Catalog Guide*, pre-1956 imprints. See, Conway, *Autobiography, Memories and Experiences of Moncure Daniel Conway* (Cambridge, Mass., 1904), vol. 1, 89-90, 94, 191, 314; Mary E. Burtis, *Moncure Conway, 1832-1907* (New Brunswick, N.J., 1952), 43-44, 48, 50, 61, 64, 69, 83-84, 91-92, 94, 104, 108, 115; Stocking, 40.

136 DeGobineau, 107, 151, 205.

137 Van Evrie, *White Supremacy,* 93.

138 DeGobineau, 179, 206-10.

139 Fisher, *The Laws of Race*, 10-11.

140 Theodore Parker to Francis Jackson, 11/24/1859, as quoted in John Weiss, *Life and Correspondence of Theodore Parker* (N.Y., 1864), vol. 2, 174-77; Parker, as quoted in Nott and Gliddon, *Types of Mankind*, 462; Parker, *The Slave Power*, James K. Hosmer, ed. (Boston, 1916), 122-23; Parker, *The World of Matter and the Spirit of Man* (Boston, 1907, originally published in 1857), vol. 6, 349-53; Octavius B. Frothingham, *Theodore Parker: A Biography* (Boston, 1874), 467; Tilden Edelstein, *Strange Enthusiasm, A Life of Thomas Wentworth Higginson* (New Haven, Conn., 1968), 210; Gossett, 181. For further reading on Parker and race, see, Weiss, vol. 2, 176, 204; Fredrickson, *The Black Image*, 100, 119-20, 157.

141 Alvarez, 142.

142 DeGobineau, 179, 206-10.

143 Parker to Francis Jackson, 11/24/1859, Parker to Govn. Fletcher, 11/27/ 1856, as quoted in Weiss, vol. 2, 174-77, 204; Parker, *The World of Matter*, 349-50; Edelstein, 210.

144 Nott and Gliddon, *Types of Mankind*, 67.

145 Drake to Dr. John C. Warren, 1/4/1851, as quoted in *The National Intelligencer*, 4/7/1851; Horace Bushnell, *A Discourse on the Slavery Question*, pamphlet, Hartford, Conn., 1839, 12, 14; Charles C. Cole, Jr., "Horace Bushnell and the Slavery Question," *New England Quarterly*, vol. 23, 1950, 29; Barbara M. Cross, *Horace Bushnell: Minister to a Changing America* (Chicago, 1958), 41, 49; Russel B. Nye, *Society and Culture in America, 1830-1860*

(N.Y., 1974), 300-01; Klaus J. Hansen, "The Millennium, the West, and Race in the Ante-bellum American Mind," *Western Historical Quarterly*, vol. 3, 1972, 376; Gossett, 180-81; Parker to Francis Jackson, 11/24/1859, Parker to S.P. Chase, 3/29/1858, as quoted in Weiss, vol. 2, 176, 229; Parker as quoted in Nott and Gliddon, *Types of Mankind*, 462; Parker, *The World of Matter*, 349-50; Parker, *The Slave Power*, 122-23; Parker, *The Rights of Man in America*, Frank B. Sanborn, ed. (Boston, 1911), 153-55, 195-200. Van Evrie strongly disagreed with the Anglo-Saxon supremacists, noting that "White men are white men." He described these supremacists as "ignorant and foolish people . . . ." See, Van Evrie, *White Supremacy*, 43.

146 Ralph Waldo Emerson, *The Works of Ralph Waldo Emerson* (N.Y., 1856), vol. 5, 49-51, 68; Ralph L. Rusk, *The Life of Ralph Waldo Emerson* (N.Y., 1949), 260, 293; Merk, *Manifest Destiny*, 40.

147 Louis F. Klipstein, "The Anglo-Saxon Race," *North American Review*, vol. 72, 1851, 35-42.

148 Parker, *The Slave Power*, 122-23; Parker, *The World of Matter*, 349-53; Frothingham, *Theodore Parker*, 467; Weiss, vol. 2, 176, 204; Gossett, 181; Nott and Gliddon, *Types of Mankind*, 462.

149 Emerson, 49-53, 68; Rusk, 260, 293; Merk, *Manifest Destiny*, 40.

150 Bushnell, 12, 14; Charles C. Cole, Jr., "Horace Bushnell," 29; Cross, 41, 49; Nye, 300-01; Hansen, 376; Gossett, 180-81.

151 Emerson, 49-53, 68; Rusk, 260, 293; Merk, *Manifest Destiny*, 40.

152 Bushnell, 12, 14; Charles C. Cole, Jr., "Horace Bushnell," 29.

153 Parker, *The Slave Power*, 122; Parker to S.P. Chase, 3/29/1858, as quoted in Weiss, vol. 2, 229; Gossett, 182-83; Drake to Dr. John C. Warren, 12/31/1850, as quoted in *The National Intelligencer*, 4/5/1851.

154 DeGobineau, 51, 210-11.

155 Fisher, *The Laws of Race*, 10-11, 14-15, 26-27.

156 Booth, 233-34.

157 Alvarez, 127.

158 Booth, 233-34.

159 Parker, as quoted in Gossett, 183.

160 Klipstein, 35-42. Klipstein was not against that racial mixing which was among equals—German, English, and Irish. Like many writers of the period, he used the term race incorrectly, i.e., to describe different ethnic groups. In

fact, he stated that "those nations that have wandered widest [Anglo-Saxons], and are most mixed, seem to be those possessed of the most forcible and progressive character." But, Klipstein cautioned, "this is true only when the mixture has been of families so nearly akin, that the descendants do not form a mongrel race, such as results from the mixture of black and white."

161   Sturtevant, 600-01, 603-04, 608; Gossett, 183; Klipstein, 40-42.

162   Drake to Dr. John C. Warren, 1/4/1851, as quoted in *The National Intelligencer*, 4/7/1851.

163   E.H. Derby, "Resources of the South," *Atlantic Monthly*, vol. 10, 1862, 508-09; *Dictionary of American Biography*, vol. 13, 569-71.

164   Van Evrie, *White Supremacy*, 152, 154, 161-62, 314.

165   Nott, "Statistics of Southern Slave Population," *DeBow's Review*, vol. 4, 1847, 277-85; Nott, "Nature and Destiny of the Negro," *DeBow's Review*, vol. 10, 1851, 330-31; Nott and Gliddon, *Types of Mankind*, 402, 465; Stanton, 72; S.J. Holmes, *The Negro's Struggle for Survival* (N.Y., 1966, originally published in 1937), 176.

166   Agassiz to Dr. S.G. Howe, 8/9,10/1863, as quoted in Elizabeth Cary Agassiz, vol. 2, 596, 605-06.

167   Drake to Dr. John C. Warren, 1/4/1851, as quoted in *The National Intelligencer*, 4/7/1851.

168   Nott, "Statistics of Southern Slave Population," 277-85; Nott, "Nature and Destiny of the Negro," 330-31; Nott and Gliddon, *Types of Mankind*, 402, 465; Stanton, 72; S.J. Holmes, 176; Agassiz to Dr. S.G. Howe, 8/9,10/1863, as quoted in Elizabeth Cary Agassiz, vol. 2, 596, 605-06.

169   Klipstein, 35-42.

170   Sturtevant, 600-01, 603-04, 608.

171   Fisher, *The Laws of Race*, 10-11, 14-15, 26-27.

172   Richard Colfax, 30-33.

173   Booth, 233-34; Parker, as quoted in Gossett, 183; Klipstein, 35-42.

174   Booth, 233-34.

175   Agassiz to Dr. S.G. Howe, 8/9,10/1863, as quoted in Elizabeth Cary Agassiz, vol. 2, 596, 602-03, 605-06.

176   Von Tschudi, 91.

177   Nott, "The Mulatto a Hybrid—Probable Extermination of the Two Races, if the Whites and Blacks are Allowed to Intermarry," *American Journal of the*

Medical Sciences, vol. 6, 1843, 252-56; Nott and Gliddon, *Indigenous Races*, 367.

178   Booth, 234.

179   Nott, "The Mulatto a Hybrid . . . ," 252-56. See also, Nott and Gliddon, *Indigenous Races*, 367; Nott, "Statistics of Southern Slave Population," 277-85; Nott, "Nature and Destiny of the Negro," 330-31.

180   Fisher, *The Laws of Race*, 26-27.

181   Van Evrie, *Negroes and Negro Slavery*, 107.

182   DeGobineau, 210-11.

183   Klipstein, 41.

184   Agassiz to Dr. S.G. Howe, 8/10/1863, as quoted in Elizabeth Cary Agassiz, vol. 2, 601.

185   Von Tschudi, 91, 114.

186   Jefferson to John Holmes, 4/22/1820, as quoted in Merril D. Peterson, ed., *Thomas Jefferson* (N.Y., 1975), 567-69.

187   Agassiz to Dr. S.G. Howe, 8/10/1863, as quoted in Elizabeth Cary Agassiz, vol. 2, 607; Parker to Francis Jackson, 11/24/1859, as quoted in Weiss, vol. 2, 174-77; Fisher, 33.

188   Drake to Dr. John C. Warren, 12/31/1850, as quoted in *The National Intelligencer*, 4/5/1851.

189   Ottis Clark Skipper, *J.D.B. DeBow, Magazinist of the Old South* (Athens, Georgia, 1958).

190   Charles Eliot Norton, book review of Sidney George Fisher's *The Laws of Race as Connected with Slavery*, *Atlantic Monthly*, vol. 7, 1861, 252-54.

191   Sturtevant, 606-09.

192   Parker to Francis Jackson, 11/24/1859, as quoted in Weiss, vol. 2, 176; Frothingham, *Theodore Parker*, 467, 473.

193   Sturtevant, 606-09. See also, Richard Hofstadter, *Social Darwinism in American Thought* (Boston, 1955, originally published in 1944), 5-7; Guion G. Johnson, "A History of Racial Ideologies in the United States," Schomberg Collection, New York Public Library, 1943, 164. Johnson's study was part of the Gunnar Myrdal Study, *An American Dilemma*, originally published in 1943. Sturtevant, along with DeGobineau, developed an early version of Social Darwinism, which, based as it was on racism, became popular during the Jim Crow era.

194   Drake to Dr. John C. Warren, 12/31/1850, 1/4/1851, as quoted in *The National*

Intelligencer, 4/5,7/1851.

195   Booth, 222-23, 226-27, 230-38. Booth's opinion is probably a fair representation of Irish-Catholic sentiment in the North. For further reading, see, *The Catholic Telegraph*, Cincinnati, Ohio, 7/8,15/1863; Bernard Mandel, *Labor: Free and Slave* (N.Y., 1955), 68; Charles H. Wesley, *Negro Labor in the United States, 1850-1925* (N.Y., 1927), 99-101; Henry C. Hubbart, *The Older Middle West, 1840-1880* (N.Y., 1936), 115; Sterling D. Spero and Abram L. Harris, *The Black Worker* (N.Y., 1931), 11-14, 187-98; Philip S. Foner and Ronald L. Lewis, eds., *The Black Worker to 1869* (Philadelphia, 1978), vol. 1, 268-79; Aaron M. Boom, "The Development of Sectional Attitudes in Wisconsin, 1848-1861," Ph.D. dissertation, University of Chicago, 1948, 213; Joseph George, Jr., "A Catholic Family Newspaper Views the Lincoln Administration: John Mullaly's Copperhead Weekly," *Civil War History*, vol. 24, 1978, 128-30; Larry Kincaid, "Two Steps Forward, One Step Back, Racial Attitudes During the Civil War and Reconstruction," as quoted in Nash and Weiss, 46-47. The Irish-Catholic urban element was especially antagonistic toward black people.

196   Richard Colfax, 30-33.

197   Drake to Dr. John C. Warren, 1/4/1851, as quoted in *The National Intelligencer*, 4/7/1851.

198   Norton, 254.

199   Derby, 508-09.

200   Nott and Gliddon, *Indigenous Races*, 366-67; Nott and Gliddon, *Types of Mankind*, 63.

201   Drake to Dr. John C. Warren, 1/4/1851, as quoted in *The National Intelligencer*, 4/7/1851.

202   Fisher, *The Laws of Race*, 36-38.

203   Alvarez, 146, 153.

204   Agassiz to Dr. S.G. Howe, 8/9,10/1863, as quoted in Elizabeth Cary Agassiz, vol. 2, 594-611, 615; Lurie, 143, 261; Nott and Gliddon, *Types of Mankind*, 78-79; Stanton, 190-91.

205   Van Evrie, *White Supremacy*, 199, 267.

206   Fredrickson, *The Black Image*, 101-02. See also, Carl N. Degler, "Racism in the United States: An Essay Review," *Journal of Southern History*, vol. 38, 1972, 101-08.

207   Bergh, 195.

208   Conway, *Testimonies Concerning Slavery*, 7, 70-71.

209   *Pennsylvania Freeman*, Philadelphia, 2/13/1845; *National Anti-Slavery Standard*, New York, 8/10/1848, 2/1/1849, 3/22/1849, 4/26/1849. Lowell was editor of the *Atlantic Monthly*, and a contributing editor to various antislavery publications. He was a corresponding editor to the *National Anti-Slavery Standard*, and the *Pennsylvania Freeman*.

210   Harriet Beecher Stowe, *Uncle Tom's Cabin or Life Among the Lowly*, (N.Y., 1962, originally published in 1852), 508. Part of the morality and innocence which Stowe attributed to blacks grew out of her depiction of them as docile sambos. See, William L. Van Deburg, *Slavery and Race in American Popular Culture* (Madison, Wis., 1984), 34-36.

211   Benjamin S. Hunt, *Remarks on Hayti as a Place of Settlement for Afric-Americans and on the Mulatto as a Race for the Tropics* (Philadelphia, 1860), 26-31.

212   Ibid.

213   Conway, *Testimonies Concerning Slavery*, 76. Another abolitionist who fully supported miscegenation, was the Reverend Gilbert Haven of Boston. When speaking about the abolition of slavery, Haven noted that "He [God] has emancipated them in order that He may thus reunite all mankind in one blessed brotherhood of blood and love." Far from viewing "black blood" as evil or inferior, Haven believed that "God intends to make that the choice blood of America. Not our proud Anglo-Saxon, not the Celtic, or German, or any other of the representative races, shall climb to the top of American society, but the African." Haven felt that the black man "has the most of Christ" and was "nearest God," because he demonstrated more "humility" than the white man. See, Gilbert Haven, *National Sermons* (Boston, 1869, originally published in 1863), 548-49.

214   *Pennsylvania Freeman*, 2/13/1845.

215   When describing the opposing agricultural systems of the North and South, Lowell personified the geographic sections in the following manner:

> On tother hand, his brother South
> Lived very much from hand to mouth,
> Played gentleman, nursed dainty hands,
> Borrowed North's money on his lands,

RACE AND THE RISE OF THE REPUBLICAN PARTY

And culled his morals and his graces

From cock-pits, bar-rooms, fights and races;

His sole work in the farming line

Was keeping droves of long-legged swine,

Which brought great bothers and expenses

To North in looking after fences,

And, when they happened to break through,

Cost him both time and temper too,

For South insisted it was plain

He ought to drive them home again

. . . Meanwhile, South's swine increasing fast,

His farm became too small at last

. . . He said one day to Brother North

. . . We soon shall need more land

. . . Poor North, whose Anglo-Saxon blood

Gave him a hankering after mud,

Wavered a moment, then consented,

And when the cash was paid, repented;

To make the new land worth a pin,

Thought he, it must be all fenced in

For, if South's swine once get the run on't

No kind of farming can be done on't . . .

Lowell not only equated black people with animals, but with the pig, an animal commonly held in low esteem. He later went on to describe how the South's swine ate, by "grunting, munching, rooting [and] shoving." See, James Russell Lowell, *The Poetical Works of James Russell Lowell* (Cambridge, Mass., 1890, originally published in 1848), 169; Duberman, *James Russell Lowell*, 78-79, 103, 185, 211, 217, 229, 234, 276, 357; *Appleton's Cyclopedia of American Biography*, vol. 4, 40-41. Lowell's *Biglow Papers* went through at least nine editions.

216   For an excellent discussion of the philosophy of the eighteenth century enlightenment, see June Barraclough, *Antoine-Nicolas DeCondorcet, Sketch for a Historical Picture of the Progress of the Human Mind* (London, England, 1955), 3-5, 7, 136-37, 147-51, 160-89, 194-99, 201-02. See also, Ernst

Cassirer, *The Philosophy of the Enlightenment* (Boston, 1955, originally published in 1932), 3-92; Pierre L. Van Den Berghe, *Race and Racism* (N.Y., 1967), 16.

217   Blumenbach, as quoted in Richard Colfax, 8-10; Prichard, vol. 1, 290-91; *Dictionary of Scientific Biography*, Charles C. Gillispie, ed. (N.Y., 1970), vol. 2, 203-04, 576-81; Jordan, *White Over Black*, 222-23, 285, 507; Seligmann, 6, 39-40; Barzun, 34-36, 44; Stocking, 30, 40. Blumenbach was impressed by a collection of poems by Phillis Wheately, the black poetess. Buffon, likewise supported the concept of monogenism.

218   Samuel Smith, xxxii, xliii, xliv, xlvi, 28-29, 33-36, 39-40, 47, 60-61, 125, 141, 152, 155-56, 160, 163-64, 184-85. Smith's ideas were attacked quite early by Dr. Charles Caldwell, in *Thoughts on the Original Unity of the Human Race* (N.Y., 1830). Caldwell, a Philadelphia physician, was the founder of two medical schools and a strong supporter of the polygenicists.

219   *National Anti-Slavery Standard*, 2/1/1849.

220   Rush, as quoted in Jordan, *White Over Black*, 283, 285-87, 448-49, 455, 517-22; Stanton, 12-13.

221   *National Anti-Slavery Standard*, 2/1/1849.

222   Samuel Smith, 55-56, 68-69, 72, 78; *National Anti-Slavery Standard*, 2/1/1849.

223   Samuel Smith, 100, 105.

224   Prichard, vol. 1, 164, 172, 216, 284-85, 290-91, 294, 335-36, 347, 371, 375-76. John Campbell, a prominent labor spokesman from Pennsylvania, noted that "the great advocate of the equality of races is Prichard." See, Campbell, *Negro-Mania*, 6, 77.

225   Blumenbach, as quoted in Prichard, vol. 1, 290-91.

226   Ibid., 164, 172, 216, 284-85, 290-91, 294, 335-36, 347, 371, 375-76.

227   Ibid., 164, 376.

228   *Dictionary of Scientific Biography*, vol. 2, 204.

229   Jordan, *White Over Black*, 283, 305-06, 344, 416-17, 440-41, 448-49.

230   Conway, *Testimonies Concerning Slavery*, 5-7, 60-61, 71.

231   Wilson Armistead, *A Tribute for the Negro* (Manchester, England, 1848), viii-xiv.

232   Samuel Smith, xliii-xlvi, 61, 72, 105, 125, 141, 152, 155-56, 160-64, 184-85.

233   Ibid., xliv.

234   Prichard, vol. 1, 284-85, 375-76; *Edinburgh Review*, vol. 178, 1848, 458-69.

235   Conway, *Testimonies Concerning Slavery*, 76.

236   Stocking, 40; Horsman, *Nott*, 117.

237   For example, Charles H. Wesley, in his article, "The Concept of the Inferiority of the Negro in American Thought," mentioned such popular racialists as Jared Sparks, John Campbell, and William J. Grayson, See, the *Journal of Negro History*, vol. 25, 1940, 546, 550-51, 554. Campbell attacked abolitionism and supported black colonization. In doing so, he held that "he [an abolitionist] would be a pure patriot and a philanthropist in every sense of the term, who could rid us of this intolerable curse [black people]; who could point out a plan by which this vicious, idle, lazy, mongrel race would be safely deposited in Liberia." Sounding like Wheat and Van Evrie, Campbell went on to state that the "destiny, constitution, intellect, civilization, and even diseases of the Negro, are all essentially different from the white," and added that "God himself has made the distinction, has made him inferior to the white." Therefore, Campbell concluded, "we [whites] must take efficient steps, ere long, to get rid of our Negroes, either by colonization or otherwise, but get rid of them we must." See, Campbell, *Negro-Mania*, 543-45.

NOTES—CHAPTER 2

1   *Tenth Annual Report of the American Colonization Society, 1827* (Washington, D.C., 1827), 21-22; Calvin Colton, *The Life, Correspondence and Speeches of Henry Clay* (N.Y., 1857), vol. 1, 191, 196-98; vol. 5, 330; George D. Prentice, *Biography of Henry Clay* (Hartford, Conn., 1831), 268-69; *Niles' Register*, vol. 73, 1847, 197-200; Samuel M. Schmucker, *The Life and Times of Henry Clay* (Philadelphia, 1860), 412, 417, 428; Daniel Mallory, ed., *The Life and Speeches of the Hon. Henry Clay* (N.Y., 1844), vol. 1, 519-27; Clement Eaton, *Henry Clay and the Art of American Politics* (Boston, 1957), 130-33. Colton was Clay's official biographer, chosen by Clay to be so.

2   Colton, *Life of Clay*, vol. 1, 191, 196-97; Prentice, 268; Eaton, 133; Schmucker, 417; Mallory, vol. 1, 519-27.

3   *Tenth Annual Report of the American Colonization Society, 1827*, 21-22; *Niles' Register*, vol. 73, 1847, 197-200; Joseph John Gurney, *Free and Friendly Remarks*, pamphlet, N.Y., 1839, 22; Colton, *Life of Clay*, vol. 1,

198; Thomas Hart Clay, *Henry Clay* (Philadelphia, 1910), 299-300; Albert B. Hart, *Slavery and Abolition, 1831-1841* (N.Y., 1906), 233.

4 Colton, *Life of Clay*, vol. 1, 196-98; Colton, *The Private Correspondence of Henry Clay* (N.Y., 1855), 476-77; Schmucker, 183-85; Thomas Clay, 296-300, 360; Joseph M. Rogers, *The True Henry Clay* (Philadelphia, 1904), 153-54; Glyndon G. Van Deusen, *The Life of Henry Clay* (Boston, 1937), 314, 318; Eaton, 130-32; Albert B. Hart, *Slavery and Abolition*, 266.

5 Colton, *Life of Clay*, vol. 1, 191-98; Colton, *Correspondence of Clay*, 476-77.

6 Henry Clay to Calvin Colton, 9/2/1843, as quoted in Colton, *Correspondence of Clay*, 476-77; *Dictionary of American Biography*, vol. 2, 320.

7 Colton, *Life of Clay*, vol. 1, 191-198; Schmucker, 209-10; Rogers, 154.

8 *The National Anti-Slavery Standard*, 3/22/1849; *New York Tribune*, 4/23/1847, 12/4/1847; *Niles' Register*, vol. 73, 1847, 197-200; Epes Sargent and Horace Greeley, *The Life and Public Services of Henry Clay* (Auburn, N.Y., 1852), 227, 285-90, 347; George R. Poage, *Henry Clay and the Whig Party* (Gloucester, Mass., 1965), 128; Thomas Clay, 113, 343; Schmucker, 216-19; William H. Hale, *Horace Greeley, Voice of the People* (N.Y., 1950), 140; Charles R. Hart, "Congressmen and the Expansion of Slavery into the Territories: A Study in Attitudes, 1846-1861," Ph.D. dissertation, University of Washington, 1965, 34; Frederick Merk, *Slavery and the Annexation of Texas* (N.Y., 1972), 68, 95-96; Parker, *The Slave Power*, 263. The idea of a demarcation line was first introduced into the Senate by Jesse Thomas of Illinois.

9 Schmucker, 216-19; Thomas Clay, 346-47. The natural limits thesis may, in fact, have had little validity, since, as some historians point out, slaves could and were employed in activities other than plantation agriculture. For example see, Harry V. Jaffa, *Crisis of the House Divided: An Interpretation of the Issues in the Lincoln-Douglas Debates* (N.Y., 1959), 388-99; Robert S. Starobin, *Industrial Slavery in the Old South* (N.Y., 1970), 13-33, 220-21. On the attitudes of Southern white immigrants in the new territories see, David S. Sparks, "The Birth of the Republican Party in Iowa, 1848-1860," Ph.D. dissertation, University of Chicago, 1951, 4; Berwanger, *The Frontier Against Slavery*, 11-12, 18-20.

10 Charles I. Foster, "The Colonization of Free Negroes in Liberia," *Journal of Negro History*, vol. 38, 1953, 47-48, 62; *The National Anti-Slavery Standard*,

3/22/1849; Joseph G. Rayback, *Free Soil, The Election of 1848* (Lexington, Ky., 1970), 23; Cooke, 175-79; Peter K. Opper, "The Mind of the White Participant in the African Colonization Movement, 1816-1840," Ph.D. dissertation, University of North Carolina, 1972, 159-220; Donald W. Riddle, *Congressman Abraham Lincoln* (Urbana, Ill, 1957), 103; Eli Seifman, "A History of the New York State Colonization Society," Ph.D. dissertation, New York University, 1966, 78-79. Two comprehensive studies on the subject of colonization are, P.J. Staudenraus, *The African Colonization Movement, 1816-1865* (N.Y., 1961), 25-27, 29-30, 52-53, 128-31, 134, 146-48, 172, 175, 186-87, 194, 198, 200, 211, 229-31 and, Early Lee Fox, *The American Colonization Society, 1817-1840* (Baltimore, 1919), 82, 85-86, 125, 129, 137, 140-41, 154-55, 174-75. Implicit in Clay's views on colonization, was the concern to preserve America for the white race. See, David M. Streifford, "The American Colonization Society: An Application of Republican Ideology to Early Antebellum Reform," *Journal of Southern History*, vol. 45, 1979, 201. In 1837 the American Colonization Society became a privately chartered antislavery organization, incorporated under the laws of Maryland, and run like any other business enterprise.

11   *Congressional Globe*, 25th Cong., 2nd. Session, Appendix, 55, 61-62; Fox, 82, 85-86, 123; Staudenraus, 52-53, 172, 175, 186-87; Betty Fladeland, *James Gillespie Birney: Slaveholder to Abolitionist* (Ithaca, N.Y., 1955), 53-54, 85-86; Bertram Wyatt-Brown, *Lewis Tappan and the Evangelical War Against Slavery* (N.Y., 1971), 84-86; Cooke, 175-79; Fredrickson, *The Black Image*, 25, 43-44; William Lloyd Garrison, *Thoughts on African Colonization* (Boston, 1832), 122.

12   Colton, *Life of Clay*, vol. 1, 196-99; Schmucker, 27, 426, 428; Thomas Clay, 296; Prentice, 266-69; Rogers, 154; Van Deusen, *Life of Clay*, 318; Mallory, vol. 1, 526. Liberia was created by the American Colonization Society with the help of the United States government in 1820, for the purpose of resettling black Americans.

13   Colton, *Life of Clay*, vol. 1, 196-98; Schmucker, 209-10.

14   *Thirty-Fourth Annual Report of the American Colonization Society, 1851* (Washington, D.C., 1851), 39; Colton, *Life of Clay*, vol. 4, 476-77; *Niles' Register*, vol. 73, 1847, 197-200; Eaton, 130; Mandel, 68. Much of Clay's political appeal in the 1844 presidential campaign was directed toward the

white laboring classes. A *Clay Minstrel* was published, with songs containing such appeals. See, Thomas Clay, 312-13.

15   Colton, *Life of Clay*, vol. 1, 196-99; Schmucker, 27, 426, 428; Thomas Clay, 296; Prentice, 266-69; Rogers, 154; Van Deusen, *Life of Clay*, 318; Mallory, vol. 1, 526.

16   *New York Tribune* 11/24/1847, 1/20/1848, 3/10/1849; Colton, *Life of Clay*, vol. 1, 188-89; vol. 5, 334-37; Schmucker, 205-15; Van Deusen, *Life of Clay*, 311-18; Thomas Clay, 340; Mallory, vol. 1, 515-27; Albert B. Hart, *Slavery and Abolition*, 314; Carl Schurz, *Life of Henry Clay* (Cambridge, Mass., 1892, originally published in 1887), vol. 1, 303.

17   Colton, *Life of Clay*, vol. 1, 188-89; vol. 5, 334-37; Schmucker, 205-15; Van Deusen, *Life of Clay*, 311-18; Thomas Clay, 340; Mallory, vol. 1, 515-57; Albert B. Hart, *Slavery and Abolition*, 314.

18   *New York Tribune*, 1/20/1848; Staudenraus, 32, 95, 188-89, 193, 245-49; Thomas R. Dew, *Review of the Debate in the Virginia Legislature of 1831 and 1832* (Richmond, Va., 1832), 46-130; Van Deusen, *Life of Clay*, 312-13; Louis R. Mehlinger, "The Attitude of the Free Negro Toward African Colonization," *Journal of Negro History*, vol. 1, 1916, 276-77, 283-86, 294, 301; Albert B. Hart, *Slavery and Abolition*, 314. Besides Liberia, several states, including New York, Pennsylvania and Maryland, had their own colonies on the west coast of Africa, which were the creation of the local or state chapters of the American Colonization Society, for the purpose of sending out the free blacks in these states. Basa Cove was the combined effort of the New York and Pennsylvania societies, while Cape Palmas belonged to the Maryland Society. See, Fox, 95-98.

19   Mallory, vol. 1, 520; Thomas Clay, 297, 300.

20   *National Era*, Washington, D.C., 10/21/1847; John H. Schroeder, *Mr. Polk's War, American Opposition and Dissent, 1846-1848* (Madison, Wis., 1973), 46-65; Alexander K. McClure, *Recollections of Half a Century* (Salem, Mass., 1902), 232-40; *The Liberty Press*, Utica, N.Y., 2/24/1848; Rawley, 147-48. Within a short time, the "Two Million Dollar Bill," became the "Three Million Dollar Bill," by which Polk asked Congress for military appropriations to wage war on Mexico. Although politicians such as Representative Jacob Brinkerhoff of Ohio and Senator James R. Doolittle of Wisconsin also brought the idea of the non-extension of slavery to national

political attention at about the same time David Wilmot did, Wilmot usually receives credit for popularizing the scheme. In fact the term "Brinkerhoff Proviso" was sometimes used in Congress. When the Republican Party was formed between 1854 and 1856, Wilmot joined the new party, and became chairman of the platform committee at the first national Republican presidential convention at Philadelphia in 1856. Like many Democrats, Wilmot was to play a leading role in the formation and policies of the new party. See, Charles Buxton Going, *David Wilmot, Free Soiler* (N.Y., 1924), 486; Michael F. Holt, *Forging a Majority, the Formation of the Republican Party in Pittsburgh, 1846-1860* (New Haven, Conn., 1969), 180; *Congressional Globe*, 30th Cong., 1st. Session, 332; William S. Myers, *The Republican Party, A History* (N.Y., 1968, originally published in 1928), 19.

21   *Congressional Globe*, 29th Cong., 2nd Session, 352-55; 30th Cong., 1st. Session, Appendix, 1076-80; Going, 174-75, 270; Rawley, 258. The use of symbolic expressions among Free Soilers was, in fact, quite common. The South was often depicted as the "dark land of slavery," and slavery itself was labelled the "black disease." Maps used at antislavery conventions often "portrayed the free states in immaculate white and the slave states in inky black." Black people were sometimes referred to as the "sable pall" or worse, the "black vomit." Such expressions offer a psychological clue to Anglo-Saxon racial attitudes in general, which saw the color black (and black people) as something evil, and hence to be avoided. Common Anglo-American terms, such as blackguard, blacklist, blackball and blacksheep, etc., all invoke evil or sinister connotations. It may be that American racialism can be found rooted in Anglo-Saxon culture. In all too many cases the very presence of the black man was regarded as something evil, dangerous, or simply degrading to Anglo-Americans. See, *Congressional Globe*, 29th Cong., 2nd. Session, 91, 175, 181, 272, 365, 427; Oliver C. Gardiner, *The Great Issue* (N.Y., 1848), 94-95; *New York Tribune*, 7/29/1848, 10/25/1849; Rayback, *Free Soil*, 212; Joel Kovel, *White Racism: A Psychohistory* (N.Y., 1971, originally published in 1970), 64-65; Gordon W. Allport, *The Nature of Prejudice* (N.Y., 1958, originally published in 1954), 177-78; Charles E. Silberman, *Crisis in Black and White* (N.Y., 1964), 114-15; Frantz Fanon, *Black Skin, White Masks* (N.Y., 1967), 188; Jordan, *White Over Black*, 3-43.

22   *Congressional Globe*, 29th Cong., 2nd. Session, 352-55; 30th Cong., 1st.

Session, Appendix, 1076-80; 31st. Cong., 1st. Session, Appendix, 940-43; Going, 174-75, 270.

23 *Congressional Globe*, 30th Cong., 1st. Session, Appendix, 1076-80; Darius Hall to Plimy Hall, 10/30/1848, Smelzer Family Papers, Olin Library, Cornell University; Going, 174-75; Eric Foner, "Racial Attitudes of the New York Free Soilers," *New York History*, vol. 46, 1965, 317-18; Osofsky, 117. Historian Catherine Newbold notes that in 1847, "Wilmot switched the emphasis [of antislavery] from territory free from slavery to territory free for white settlers." See, Catherine Newbold, "The Antislavery Background of the Principal State Department Appointees in the Lincoln Administration," Ph.D. dissertation, University of Michigan, 1962, 110; Richard R. Stenberg, "The Motivation of the Wilmot Proviso," *Mississippi Valley Historical Review*, vol. 18, 1932, 536.

24 *Congressional Globe*, 30th Cong., 1st. Session, Appendix, 1077, 1080; 31st Cong., 1st Session, Appendix, 943; Eric Foner, "Racial Attitudes of the New York Free Soilers," 317-18; Going, 174-75.

25 *Congressional Globe*, 29th Cong., 2nd. Session, 353-55; Going, 174-76, 345.

26 *Congressional Globe*, 31st Cong., 1st. Session, Appendix, 941; 29th Cong., 2nd. Session, 352-55; 30th Cong., 1st. Session, Appendix, 1076; Going, 165-66, 174.

27 *Congressional Globe*, 31st Cong., 1st. Session, Appendix, 941; 30th Cong., 1st. Session, Appendix, 1077. Wilmot, in referring to Thomas Jefferson, was comparing his proviso of 1846, to Jefferson's Northwest Ordinance of 1787. Wilmot saw himself as following directly in the antislavery, anti-extension footsteps of the Virginian. In 1847, while addressing the New York State Democratic Free Soil Convention at Herkimer, New York, Wilmot made the same comparison, a comparison that was very common among Free Soil politicians. See, Gardiner, 60-61.

28 *Congressional Globe*, 30th Cong., 1st. Session, Appendix pp. 792-93.

29 Ibid., 31st Cong., 1st. Session, Appendix, 511.

30 Ibid., 30th Cong., 1st. Session, 547, 2nd. Session, 354.

31 Ibid., 1st. Session, Appendix, 283.

32 Ibid., 2nd. Session, Appendix, 308.

33 Ibid., 1st. Session, Appendix, 834-41; *Speech of Horace Mann in the House of Representatives, June 30, 1848*, pamphlet, West Newton, Mass., 1848;

Congressional Globe, 32nd Cong., 1st. Session, Appendix, 1073; Horace Mann, *Slavery: Letters and Speeches* (Boston, 1851), 45, 54, 73-83, 128-35, 143-45, 154, 175.

34   Mann, *Slavery: Letters and Speeches*, 45, 54, 73-83, 128-35, 143-45, 154, 175.

35   Ibid.; *Congressional Globe*, 30th Cong., 1st. Session, Appendix, 834-41; 31st Cong., 1st. Session, Appendix, 223.

36   Lurie, 203; Richard Henry Dana Jr. Journal, 2/12/1843, 6/23,29/1849, 9/29/1853, 6/26/1860, Dana Papers, Massachusetts Historical Society; Samuel Shapiro, *Richard Henry Dana Jr., 1815-1882* (East Lansing, Mich., 1961), 23, 30-35, 56-57.

37   Blue, *The Free Soilers*, 68-69, 113-14, 125; *Congressional Globe*, 31st Cong., 1st. Session, 483.

38   *Congressional Globe*, 31st Cong., 1st. Session, Appendix, 254.

39   Ibid., 30th Cong., 1st. Session, 283.

40   *New York Tribune*, 1/10/1852, 12/28/1852, 1/10/1853, 5/14,24/1854; James S. Pike, *First Blows of the Civil War* (N.Y., 1879), 160-63, 198, 229, 235; Robert F. Durden, *James Shepherd Pike, Republicanism and the American Negro, 1850-1882* (Durham, N.C., 1957), preface, 3, 7, 9, 14-17; George Foster Talbot, "James Shepherd Pike," *Maine Historical Society Collections*, vol. 1, 1890, 235; Newbold, 205-06; William H. Hale, 154. During the 1850's Pike, as the Washington, D.C. correspondent for Greeley's *New York Tribune*, usually signed his editorials 'JSP.' See, Horace Greeley to Pike, 4/24,25,27,28/1850, 5/1,2,16/1850, James Shepherd Pike Papers, Folger Library, University of Maine.

41   *New York Tribune*, 1/10/1852, 12/28/1852, 1/10/1853, 5/14,24/1854; Pike, *First Blows*, 198, 229, 235; Durden, *James Shepherd Pike*, 3, 9, 15.

42   *The Liberty Press*, 2/17/1848. Another liberal free Soil Congressman from Massachusetts, ex-President of the United States, John Quincy Adams, also assumed black inferiority and concluded "that the intermarriage of black and white blood is a violation of the law of nature." See, John Quincy Adams, "The Character of Desdemona," *American Monthly Magazine*, vol. 1, 1836, 209-17.

43   William O. Lynch, "Antislavery Tendencies of the Democratic Party in the

Northwest, 1848-1850," *Mississippi Valley Historical Review*, vol. 11, 1924, 322, 324-25, 329.

44   Oliver Dyer, *Phonographic Report of the Proceedings of the National Free Soil Convention at Buffalo, N.Y. August 9th and 10th, 1848* (Buffalo, N.Y., 1848), 10-20. See also, Thomas V. Cooper and Hector T. Fenton, *American Politics* (Chicago, 1883), 30-32; Kirk H. Porter and Donald Bruce Johnson, *National Party Platforms, 1840-1956* (Urbana, Ill., 1956), 13-14.

45   Herbert D.A. Donovan, *The Barnburners* (N.Y., 1925), 86, 88, 106, 111-18; Myers, 24; James C.N. Paul, *Rift in the Democracy* (Philadelphia, 1951), 178; John D. Long, *The Republican Party: Its History, Principles and Policies* (N.Y., 1898), 29-30; John D. Hicks, "The Third Party Tradition in American Politics," *Mississippi Valley Historical Review*, vol. 20, 1933, 9-10; Sorin, 87; Wilfred E. Binkley, *American Political Parties* (N.Y., 1959, originally published in 1943), 208; Roy F. Nichols, *The Invention of the American Political Parties* (N.Y., 1967), 372-73; Joel H. Silbey, *The Shrine of Party* (Pittsburgh, 1967), 70; Herbert Agar, *The Price of Union* (Boston, 1950), 324-25; Edward M. Shepard, *Martin Van Buren* (Boston, 1899), 428-29; John Mayfield, *Rehearsal for Republicanism, Free Soil and the Politics of Anti-Slavery* (N.Y., 1980), 9-22, 118.

46   Gardiner, 52, 56; Eric Foner, "Racial Attitudes of the New York Free Soilers," 314; Morrison, 61. John Van Buren, like his father, was a member of the `Albany Regency' in the 1830's, and was elected state attorney general in 1845. See, *Dictionary of American Biography*, vol. 19, 151.

47   *The Liberty Press*, 8/31/1848.

48   *Congressional Globe*, 30th Cong., 1st Session, Appendix, 862, 865-66, 2nd. Session, 293; Gardiner, 161-64; *Niles' Register*, vol. 74, 1848, 9, 19; Henry H. Simms, *A Decade of Sectional Controversy, 1851-1861* (Chapel Hill, N.C., 1942), 135. Dix was one of the leading antislavery Democrats in New York state, and attended the 1848 Free Soil Party convention at Buffalo. During the Civil War, Lincoln commissioned him a major general, and after the war Dix was elected governor of New York, on the Republican ticket. See, *Dictionary of American Biography*, vol. 5, 326. The belief that the black population only increased under slavery and actually decreased under freedom, was quite common among political antislavery people.

49   *Congressional Globe*, 30th Cong., 1st. Session, Appendix, 862, 865-66,

2nd. Session, 293; Gardiner, 161-64; *Niles' Register*, vol. 74, 1848, 9, 19; Simms, 135.

50   *Congressional Globe*, 30th Cong., 1st. Session, Appendix, 862, 865-66, 2nd. Session, 293; Gardiner, 161-64.

51   *Congressional Globe*, 30th Cong., 1st. Session, Appendix, 581.

52   *Congressional Globe*, 29th Cong. 2nd. Session, 114-15; *The Radical Democracy of New York and the Independent Democracy*, pamphlet, Washington, D.C., 1852, n.a., 7; Blue, *The Free Soilers*, 86-88, 102; Donovan, 84-85; Eric Foner, "Racial Attitudes of the New York Free Soilers," 316-17; Rayback, *Free Soil*, 25. King, a one-time Jacksonian Democrat from northern New York, broke with the Polk administration Democrats in 1846, when he advised David Wilmot to issue his Proviso. King participated in the Buffalo Free Soil Convention of 1848, and fully supported Martin Van Buren's efforts during the campaign. He was elected to the United States House of Representatives as a Free Soiler in both 1848 and 1850. King was an early and enthusiastic supporter of the new Republican Party, and was seriously considered for the vice presidential slot on the party ticket in 1856. Between 1860 and 1864, King acted as chairman for the National Committee of the Republican Party. See, *Dictionary of American Biography*, vol. 10, 396-97.

53   *Congressional Globe*, 29th Cong., 2nd. Session, 114-15; *The Radical Democracy of New York and the Independent Democracy*, 7; Blue, *The Free Soilers*, 86-88, 102; Donovan, 84-85; Eric Foner, "Racial Attitudes of the New York Free Soilers," 316-17; Rayback, *Free Soil*, 25.

54   *Congressional Globe*, 30th Cong., 1st. Session, Appendix, 920-23.

55   *The Liberty Press*, 6/29/1848; *Congressional Globe*, 30th Cong., 2nd. Session, Appendix, 105.

56   George O. Rathbun, *The Free Soil Question and Its Importance to the Voters of the Free States* (N.Y., 1848), 63; Gardiner, 94-95; *Congressional Globe*, 29th Cong., 2nd. Session, 364-65; Eric Foner, "The Wilmot Proviso Revisited," *Journal of American History*, vol. 56, 1969-70, 277; Sorin, 87; *Biographical Directory of the American Congress, 1774-1971* (Government Printing Office, Washington, D.C., 1971), 1587.

57   Rathbun, 63; Gardiner, 94-95; *Congressional Globe*, 29th Cong., 2nd. Session, 364-65.

58   *Congressional Globe*, 29th Cong., 2nd Session, Appendix, 362.

59   Lewis Henry Morgan, *Ancient Society* (N.Y., 1907), 553; Morrison, 71. Morgan later served as a Republican in the New York State Assembly, between 1861 and 1868. Although Morgan was involved in politics, he was better known for his pioneering work on the Iroquois Confederacy. See, *Dictionary of American Biography*, vol. 13, 183-84.

60   *Congressional Globe*, 31st Cong., 1st. Session, Appendix, 261, 266.

61   Ibid., 563-64.

62   Ibid., 31st Cong., 1st. Session, 676; 32nd Cong., 1st. Session, 2255. One Massachusetts Conscious Whig and later Republican, Senator Timothy Davis, sought to oblige Dayton and offered an amendment to the 1850 Census bill, asking that census takers gather "medical and physiological information" on black Americans. See, *Congressional Globe*, 30th Cong., 2nd. Session, 627.

63   *Congressional Globe*, 32nd Cong., 2nd. Session, Appendix, 232-34.

64   W.L.G. Smith, *Fifty Years of Public Life, The Life and Times of Lewis Cass* (N.Y., 1856), 612-15; Frank B. Woodford, *Lewis Cass, The Last Jeffersonian* (New Brunswick, N.J., 1950), 245-47, 250-53.

65   Gardiner, 44.

66   Russell Jarvis, *Facts and Arguments Against the Election of General Cass by an Anti-Abolitionist* (N.Y., 1848), 58-63.

67   *New York Tribune*, 6/7/1848, 7/29/1848; Henry M. Field, *The Life of David Dudley Field* (N.Y., 1898), x, 115-16, 136; A.P. Sprague, *Speeches, Arguments and Miscellaneous Papers of David Dudley Field* (N.Y., 1884), vol. 2, 24; *Dictionary of American Biography*, vol. 6, 360-61. Field was one of the first to break with the administration Democrats over the issue of Texas annexation. He later became a Republican and a staunch supporter of Abraham Lincoln's nomination in 1860.

68   Lurie, 253; *New York Evening Post*, 4/12/1843, 12/24/1847, 4/20/1848, 6/12/1848, 7/17,18,19/1848, 10/3/1848, 11/24/1848, 10/18/1850, 5/23/1851, 7/30/1851, 9/8/1851; W.C. Bryant to Dear Brother, 2/7/1848, John Howard Bryant Papers, University of Southern California Library; Park Godwin, *A Biography of William Cullen Bryant* (N.Y., 1883), vol. 1, 413, 421-22; Charles H. Brown, *William Cullen Bryant* (N.Y., 1971), 214, 333, 339, 344; Merk, *Manifest Destiny*, 35-36, 40. In 1848 Bryant broke with the regular Democratic Party, by backing the Free Democratic presidential ticket of Martin Van Buren and Charles Francis Adams. In 1855 Bryant's *Evening Post*, which

had one of the largest circulations of any newspaper in the United States, came out in support of the new Republican Party. During the Civil War, Bryant was a faithful supporter and close friend of the Lincoln administration and opposed any compromise or armistice with the South. During Reconstruction, he became hostile toward the radical Republicans and favored many of Andrew Johnson's ideas on a quick and easy restoration of the Union. Bryant was in many respects typical of those Northern Free Democrats, who helped to create and formed the backbone of the early Republican Party, but later, during Reconstruction, began to drift back to their more conservative Democratic Party antecedents. See, Godwin, vol. 2, 43, 64, 80-81, 242; *The New York Evening Post, 1801-1925*, n.a. (Beck Printing Co., N.Y., 1925), 29; *Dictionary of American Biography*, vol. 3, 204.

69   *New York Evening Post*, 4/12/1843, 12/24/1847, 4/20/1848, 6/12/1848, 7/17,18,19/1848, 10/3/1848, 11/24/1848, 10/18/1850, 5/23/1851, 7/30/ 1851, 9/8/1851; W.C. Bryant to Dear Brother, 2/7/1848; Godwin, vol. 1, 413, 421-22; Charles H. Brown, 214, 333, 339, 344; Merk, *Manifest Destiny*, 35-36, 40.

70   *New York Evening Post*, 7/17,18,19/1848; Merk, *Manifest Destiny*, 35-36, 40; Godwin, vol. 1, 413-22.

71   *New York Evening Post*, 6/12/1848, 7/17,18,19/1848, 9/16/1848, 10/3/1848, 11/24/1848.

72   Ibid., 4/20/1848, 6/12/1848, 7/17,18,19/1848, 9/16/1848, 10/3/1848, 11/24/ 1848, 12/27/1848.

73   Ibid., 4/20/1848.

74   *New York Tribune*, 9/29/1847, 10/20/1847, 12/2/1847, 3/20/1850, 4/16/ 1850, 8/5/1850, 5/31/1853, 9/27/1853, 11/7/1853; Lurie, 142, 209; Donald C. Seitz, *Horace Greeley* (N.Y., 1970, originally published in 1926), 142; Van Deusen, *Horace Greeley, Nineteenth-Century Crusader* (Philadelphia, 1953), 113. Greeley gave strong support to John A. Dix's Senate speech of 1848, in which Dix, while espousing free soilism, castigated the black man. See note 48. In 1855, after the formation of the Republican Party, Greeley's *Tribune* became the leading organ of the new party. Before the advent of either the Free Soil or Republican Parties, Greeley was aligned politically with the antislavery Whigs of New York state. His two closest political allies were William Henry Seward and Thurlow Weed, and together they were often

referred to as the "triumvirate" of New York politics. Greeley was perhaps the leading Whig journalist in the United States during the 1840's, and was influential in getting the Whig economic program engrafted into the new Republican Party platforms. Henry Clay and the "American system" were foremost in his political philosophy. Although Greeley did not come out openly in support of Van Buren and Adams during the presidential election of 1848, he strongly suggested that all antislavery Whigs who were dissatisfied with the nomination of Zachary Taylor and Millard Fillmore, vote for the Barnburners or Free Democracy. Greeley noted that "we shall not probably act with them [Free Soil Whigs in the process of forming an independent third party] ... but it now seems to us that those Whigs who were determined to break with their party on the late nomination for President ... may better vote for Mr. Van Buren, than get up another candidate." Greeley asked his readers "why should not the Whig dissenters from General Taylor give their votes at once to Mr. Van Buren?" When writing to Schuyler Colfax of Indiana, Greeley noted that "I do like the principles he [Van Buren] now embodies; free soil and land reforms, and very probably the Free Soil party is the only live party around us." See, Greeley to Colfax, 9/15/1848, Greeley-Colfax correspondence, New York Public Library; *New York Tribune*, 12/4,21/1847, 2/16,17,18/1848, 6/2,24,26,29/1848, 3/10,31/1849; Horace Greeley, *Recollections of a Busy Life* (N.Y., 1868), 285; Francis N. Zabriskie, *Horace Greeley, the Editor* (N.Y., 1890), 206-07; Jeter A. Isley, *Horace Greeley and the Republican Party, 1853-1861* (Princeton, N.J., 1947), 213, 230, 293; Harlan H. Horner, *Lincoln and Greeley* (Urbana, Ill., 1953), 15, 114, 150; Whitelaw Reid, *Horace Greeley, A Biographical Sketch* (n.p., 1879), 11-12; Van Deusen, *Horace Greeley*, 30, 91-92, 108; Seitz, 217; Earle D. Ross, "Horace Greeley and the West," *Mississippi Valley Historical Review*, vol. 20, 1933, 64.

75 *New York Tribune*, 11/24/1847, 6/11/1849, 2/8/1850, 5/3,30/1850, 12/17, 26/1850; James Parton, *The Life of Horace Greeley* (Boston, 1872), 408-09; Isley, 33.

76 *New York Tribune*, 7/17/1847, 2/9/1850.

77 Ibid., 8/17/1847, 7/19,29/1848, 3/31/1849, 6/19/1849, 10/25/1849.

78 Ibid.

79 Ibid., 2/22/1847, 7/17/1847, 8/17/1847, 7/24/1848, 2/8/1850, 5/3/1850, 11/

26/1850; William M. Cornell, *The Life and Public Career of Hon. Horace Greeley* (Boston, 1872), 164-78.

80   *New York Tribune*, 11/28/1850, 12/17/1850.

81   Ibid.; Horace Greeley's proposed letter to be read by General Scott, Washington, D.C., 6/20/1852, Pike Papers; *National Anti-Slavery Standard*, 4/26/1849; Seitz, 149; Eric Foner, "Politics and Prejudice," 239.

82   *New York Tribune*, 7/21/1846, 5/5/1847, 12/4/1847, 3/10,31/1849, 1/31/1850, 2/1/1850, 8/5/1850; Greeley, *Recollections*, 285; Horace Greeley's proposed letter to be read by General Scott, Washington, D.C., 6/20/1852; Zabriskie, 206-07; Ross, 64; Horner, 66, 77-78.

83   *National Era*, 3/13,27/1851, 4/10,24/1851, 6/19,26/1851, 7/10/1851.

84   Ibid., 3/13/1851, 4/24/1851.

85   *Ithaca Journal*, Ithaca, N.Y., 8/30/1848, 9/27/1848.

86   *Buffalo Daily Republic*, Buffalo, N.Y., 8/11/1848.

87   *American Free Soil Almanac for 1849*, n.a. (Boston, 1849), 17.

88   *Boston Post*, 7/3,6,12,14,17,25/1848; *Boston Times*, 7/7/1848. Free Soil clubs and organizations were sometimes dubbed "Jeffersonian Leagues," in honor of Thomas Jefferson and the Northwest Ordinance of 1787. See, the *Ithaca Journal*, 7/26/1848; Rayback, *Free Soil*, 229, 249.

89   *Emancipator and Republican*, Boston, Mass., 7/25/1850; Lurie, 324, 331-33; *Congressional Globe*, 37th Cong., 3rd. Session, 762; Weiss, vol. 2, 210-12. Wilson is referring to the work of Dr. Charles Pickering, *The Races of Man: Their Geographical Distribution* (London, England, 1848).

90   *The Liberty Press*, 1/5/1848, 3/2/1848, 6/22/1848, 7/6,27/1848.

91   *Congressional Globe*, 30th Cong., 1st. Session, Appendix, 792-93.

92   *National Era*, 1/16/1851, 3/13/1851, 4/24/1851, 6/26/1851, 7/10,24/1851.

93   *Congressional Globe*, 30th Cong., 1st. Session, Appendix, 862, 865-66, 2nd. Session, 293; Morgan Dix, *Memoirs of John Adams Dix* (N.Y., 1883), vol. 1, 114-17; Gardiner, 161-64; Blue, *The Free Soilers*, 87-88.

94   *New York Evening Post*, 4/12/1843, 8/20/1844, 12/2/1847, 1/10/1848, 4/20/1848, 6/12/1848, 12/27/1848, 1/11/1849, 3/10/1849, 7/30/1851; Charles H. Brown, 214-15.

95   *New York Tribune*, 5/5/1847, 7/29/1848, 3/31/1849, 10/25/1849, 3/14/1854; Van Deusen, *Horace Greeley*, 90; Isley, 37, 41; Zabriskie, 206; William H. Hale, 133.

96 *National Era*, 1/16/1851, 4/24/1851, 6/26/1851, 7/10,24/1851.

97 Stanley Harrold, *Gamaliel Bailey and Antislavery Union* (Kent, Ohio, 1986), 107; Foster, 47-48.

98 Jarvis, 58-63.

99 *Congressional Globe*, 30th Cong., 1st. Session, Appendix, 862, 865-66, 2nd. Session, 293; Morgan Dix, vol. 1, 114-17; Gardiner, 161-64; Blue, *The Free Soilers*, 87-88.

100 *The Lockport Journal*, Lockport, NY, 1/7/1852; Eric Foner, *Free Soil, Free Labor, Free Men*, 268; *Congressional Globe*, 31st Cong., 1st. Session, 483.

101 *Congressional Globe*, 32nd Cong., 2nd. Session, Appendix, 232-34.

102 Ibid., 32nd Cong., 2nd. Session, 270; 31st Cong., 1st. Session, 1296.

103 *New York Evening Post*, 4/12/1843, 8/20/1844, 12/2/1847, 1/10/1848, 4/20/1848, 6/12/1848, 12/27/1848, 3/10/1849, 1/11/1849, 7/30/1851; Charles H. Brown, 214-15. On the idea of the Southern states as a tropical region and lush and easy provider of food, see, David Bertelson, *The Lazy South* (N.Y., 1967), 38-39, 68-69, 80, 179-80, 221.

104 *National Era*, 3/13,27/1851, 4/24/1851, 6/26/1851.

105 *New York Tribune*, 7/16/1847, 1/20/1848, 6/24,26/1848, 3/10/1849, 5/3, 30/1850, 8/5/1850; Greeley, *Recollections*, 285; Horner, 66; Ross, 64; Horace Greeley to W.C. Cowan, 1/20/1859, as quoted in Parton, *Life of Greeley*, 408-09.

106 *New York Tribune*, 7/16/1847, 1/20/1848, 6/24,26/1848, 3/10/1849, 5/3, 30/1850, 8/5/1850; Greeley, *Recollections*, 285; Horner, 66; Ross, 64. Few colonizationists ever bothered to ask black people how they felt about leaving the country. There was good reason for this, because the overwhelming majority of black Americans opposed the idea of colonization. See, Charles H. Bouyer to Samuel Wilkeson, 7/1/1840, American Colonization Society Papers, vol. 79, part 1, Library of Congress, Washington, D.C.; Reverend William McLain to Samuel Wilkeson, 8/12/1840, 10/2/1840, Wilkeson-Barringer Collection, Buffalo and Erie County Historical Society, Buffalo, N.Y.; Staudenraus, 32, 95, 188-89, 193; Seifman, 69-70; Cooke, 163; Leon F. Litwack, *North of Slavery, The Negro in the Free States, 1790-1860* (Chicago, 1971), 235, 259; Penelope Campbell, *Maryland in Africa* (Urbana, Ill., 1971), 39-40, 103-06; Theodore Draper, *The Rediscovery of Black Nationalism* (N.Y., 1970), 12, 17-18; Osofsky, 74-76; Werner T. Wickstrom,

"The American Colonization Society and Liberia," Ph.D. dissertation, Hartford Seminary, Hartford, Conn., 1958, 74-75; Mehlinger, 276-77, 283-86, 294, 301.

107 *New York Tribune*, 7/16/1847, 1/20/1848, 6/24,26/1848, 3/10/1849, 5/3, 30/ 1850, 8/5/1850; Greeley, *Recollections*, 285; Horner, 66; Ross, 64.

108 *New York Tribune*, 7/16/1847, 1/20/1848, 6/24,26/1848, 3/10/1849, 5/3, 30/ 1850, 8/5/1850.

109 Ibid., 11/24/1847, 5/3,30/1850, 12/6/1854.

110 Ibid., 7/17/1846, 10/3,28/1846, 8/5/1847, 9/29/1847, 4/21/1849, 3/20/1850, 11/27,28/1850.

111 Ibid., 7/21/1846, 9/29/1847, 11/2/1848, 8/9/1849. The black laws of Ohio, as in other states of the Northwest, were designed specifically for the purpose of keeping free blacks out of this area. See, Berwanger, *The Frontier Against Slavery*, 7-49; V. Jacque Voegeli, *Free But Not Equal, The Midwest and the Negro during the Civil War* (Chicago, 1967), 1-9; Theodore Clarke Smith, *The Liberty and Free Soil Parties in the Northwest* (N.Y., 1897), 7-8, 332-37; Malvin, 2-6; Hubbart, *The Older Middle West*, 46-51; Tom L. McLaughlin, "Popular Reactions to the Idea of Negro Equality in Twelve Non-Slaveholding States, 1846-1869: A Quantitative Analysis," Ph.D. dissertation, Washington State University, 1969, 20-59; Simms, 128-29; Frank U. Quillin, *The Color Line in Ohio* (N.Y., 1969, originally published in 1913), 22-24.

112 *New York Tribune*, 7/21/1846, 9/29/1847, 11/2/1848, 8/9/1849.

113 Ibid., 6/5,21/1847, 9/29/1847, 7/20/1849, 4/18/1855; Alexis DeTocqueville, *Democracy in America* (N.Y., 1969, originally published in 1848), 343. In describing the incident on the Broadway streetcar, Greeley noted that not only was the black man well dressed, but he also offered to pay the fare of all the other passengers in the car at the time, just to be allowed to ride and escape a heavy rainfall. Nothing, however, availed, as it was the practice among New York city streetcar drivers not to allow blacks a seat. One incident on a steamboat involved Henry Highland Garnet, the well-known black abolitionist. Garnet, in fact, suffered from such discrimination on a number of occasions. One such occurred on the Buffalo and Niagara Falls Railroad, in which he was ordered out of a car. "The conductor came back, and insultingly ordered me to leave the car," Garnet related, because "colored people cannot be permitted to ride

with the whites on this road." When Garnet refused to give up his seat, "the conductor . . . seized me violently by the throat, and choked me severely." See, *The Liberty Press*, 7/6/1848.

114   Fisher, *The Laws of Race*, 18-20, 23-27, 33, 36-38; Nicholas B. Wainwright, ed., *A Philadelphia Perspective, The Diary of Sidney George Fisher, Covering the Years 1834-1871* (Philadelphia, 1967), 267.

115   Fisher, *The Laws of Race*, 18-20, 23-27, 33, 36-38; Fisher, *Trial of the Constitution*, 273.

116   Fisher, *The Laws of Race*, 18-20, 23-27, 33, 36-38; Fisher, *Trial of the Constitution*, 275, 294.

117   Fisher, *The Laws of Race*, 18-20, 23-27, 33, 36-38.

118   Ibid.

119   Ibid.; Fisher, *Trial of the Constitution*, 274-75.

120   Aileen S. Kraditor, *Means and Ends in American Abolitionism, Garrison and His Critics on Strategy and Tactics, 1834-1850* (N.Y., 1967), 141-42, 152-53, 157, 170, 173, 180-82, 186, 215; Merton L. Dillon, *The Abolitionists, The Growth of a Dissenting Minority* (DeKalb, Ill., 1974), 130-31, 141, 144-46, 166; Walter M. Merrill, *Against Wind and Tide, A Biography of Wm. Lloyd Garrison* (Cambridge, Mass., 1971, originally published in 1963), 200-04, 208; Fladeland, 212, 255, 259, 261-62; William R. Brock, *Parties and Political Conscience: American Dilemmas, 1840-1850* (Millwood, N.Y., 1979), 224-25; Nye, *Society and Culture in America*, 65; Edgar E. Robinson, *The Evolution of American Political Parties* (N.Y., 1924), 126-27; Julian P. Bertz, "The Economic Background of the Liberty Party," *American Historical Review*, vol. 34, 1929, 257.

121   *Speech of Gerrit Smith at the National Convention of the Liberty Party, Buffalo, N.Y., October 20th., 1847*, pamphlet, Buffalo, N.Y., 1847, 4-8. After 1848, the Liberty Party had lost many of its members to the Free Soil Party. See, the *National Era*, 8/28/1848 and Ralph V. Harlow, *Gerrit Smith: Philanthropist and Reformer* (N.Y., 1939), 183-84.

122   Gerrit Smith, *Anti-Fugitive Slave Law Meeting, January 9, 1851*, pamphlet, Syracuse, N.Y., 1851; *The National Liberty Party Convention, September 30, 1852*, pamphlet, n.a., Auburn, N.Y., 1852; *Congressional Globe*, 33rd Cong., 1st. Session, Appendix, 529.

123   *North Star*, Rochester, N.Y., 9/1/1848.

124   *Colored National Convention, Cleveland, 1848*, pamphlet, n.a., Rochester, N.Y., 1848, 8.

125   Philip S. Foner, ed., *Life and Writings of Frederick Douglass* (N.Y., 1950), vol. 2, 175.

126   Robert P. Ludlum, "Joshua R. Giddings, Radical," *Mississippi Valley Historical Review*, vol. 23, 1936-37, 52, 58.

NOTES-CHAPTER 3

1   For three general studies that deal with Western opposition to the expansion of slavery, and the racial threat perceived in such, see: Berwanger, *The Frontier Against Slavery,* 1-6; Voegeli, *Free But Not Equal,* 1-9; Rawley, viii, x-xi, 12-13, 94-98. See also, David Davis to Judge W.P. Walker, 2/1845, David Davis Collection, Chicago Historical Society; Caleb B. Smith, Speech on the Slave Trade in Washington, D.C., 1/10/1849, as quoted in the *Congressional Globe,* 30th Cong., 2nd. Session, 215; David Wilmot, Speech on the Admission of California, 7/24/1850, as quoted in the *Congressional Globe,* 31st Cong., 1st. Session, 941; *The National Anti-Slavery Standard,* 8/10/1848; Helen M. Cavanagh, "Antislavery Sentiment and Politics in the Northwest, 1844-1860," Ph.D. dissertation, University of Chicago 1938, 46-47; Blue, *The Free Soilers,* 102; Osofsky, 118.

2   *Congressional Globe,* 29th Cong., 2nd. Session, 180-81; 33rd. Cong., 1st. Session, Appendix, 212-14, 219; Schuyler Colfax to William H. Seward, 12/6/1850, William Henry Seward Collection, University of Rochester Library. John Pettit represents an excellent example of the growing number of Free Democrats in the West.

3   Howard to John C. Vaughan and Thomas Brown, 7/9/1849, Jacob M. Howard Papers, Burton Historical Collection, Detroit Public Library. Howard addressed this letter to a group of Free Soilers in Cleveland, Ohio, who were celebrating the 52nd. anniversary of the passage of the Northwest Ordinance.

4   Ibid.

5   *Congressional Globe,* 30th Cong., 1st. Session, Appendix, 1160. On Corwin's early support for Free Soil principles, see Corwin to Thomas B.

Stevenson, 9/23/1847, 7/30/1848, Corwin Letters, Cincinnati Historical Society.

6   *Congressional Globe,* 33rd. Cong., 1st. Session, Appendix, 665.

7   Pattison to George W. Julian, 6/23/1850, George W. Julian Collection, Indiana State Library. Julian was Joshua R. Giddings' son-in-law.

8   *Alton Weekly Courier,* 7/1/1853, 8/19/1853.

9   *Congressional Globe,* 29th Cong., 2nd. Session, 180-81.

10 John Wentworth, *Congressional Reminiscences* (Chicago, 1882), 7, 25-35; Don E. Fehrenbacher, *Chicago Giant, A Biography of "Long John" Wentworth* (Madison, Wis., 1957), 69.

11 Wentworth, 7, 25-35.

12 *Congressional Globe,* 29th Cong., 2nd. Session, 180-81.

13 *Evansville Daily Journal,* Evansville, Indiana, 4/15/1853.

14 *Alton Weekly Courier,* 7/1/1853, 8/19/1853.

15 Cassius M. Clay, *The Life of Cassius Marcellus Clay, Memoirs, Writings and Speeches* (Cincinnati, 1886), 118; Horace Greeley, ed., *The Writings of Cassius Marcellus Clay, including Speeches and Addresses* (N.Y., 1848), 93. Clay's biographer, David L. Smiley, describes him as a man of "marked prejudices against the Negro." Cassius M. Clay was Henry Clay's cousin, and was a Clay Whig and political supporter of his namesake. He was later to be a strong backer of the Free Soil Party and to become a charter member of the Republican Party. Clay had no doubt that the "black is inferior [intellectually and physically] to the white." Smiley described Clay as a precursor of Hinton Rowan Helper, and noted that "Helper was only enlarging upon the work of Cassius M. Clay." See, Smiley, *Lion of White Hall, the Life of Cassius M. Clay* (Madison, Wis., 1962), 48, 66-69, 149-155, 168-170.

16 *Chicago Tribune,* 1/25,27/1854. Stewart and John L. Scripps were the founding editors of the original *Tribune,* and in the 1848 presidential election they gave their political support to Martin Van Buren and the Free Democrats. See, *The National Cyclopedia of American Biography,* vol. 7, 558.

17 Whipple, Southern Diary, vol. 9, 1843-1844, 59-76, Henry B. Whipple Papers, Minnesota Historical Society.

18 *Congressional Globe,* 31st Cong., 1st. Session, 1093.

19 John A. Kasson to Charles Kasson, 12/27/1842, 2/4/1843, Kasson Papers, Alderman Library Collection, University of Virginia.

20   William Salter, *Life of James W. Grimes* (N.Y., 1876), 48.

21   *Alton Weekly Courier,* 8/19/1853, 10/21/1853.

22   Greeley, *Writings of Clay,* 224; C.M. Clay to Salmon P. Chase, 12/21/1842, Salmon P. Chase Papers, Historical Society of Pennsylvania; C.M. Clay to Daniel Webster, 3/26/1850, as quoted in C.M. Clay, *Memoirs,* 201; Smiley, 56.

23   *Alton Weekly Courier,* 8/19/1853, 10/21/1853.

24   Benjamin Wade to Milton Sutliff, 2/13/1853, Milton Sutliff Papers, Western Reserve Historical Society Library, Cleveland, Ohio. During Reconstruction, Wade, while still living in Washington, D.C., wrote several letters to his wife Caroline, in which he seemed to express contempt for black workers. For example, after hiring a black woman as a servant, he complained that "for mere nigger power it will cost near five hundred dollars per year . . . . I wish we could get a white woman of the English or Northern European breed. I am getting sick of niggers." Several weeks later, Wade apparently fired his black servant Eliza, and hired a white woman in her place, and noted that "I think that she [white servant] is much stronger and more able than Eliza, and she seems to be of a more good and steady temperament. From the time I engaged her, she never . . . whiffled about as Eliza did." See, B.F. Wade to Caroline Wade, 3/9/1873, 4/26/1873, Benjamin F. Wade Papers, Library of Congress.

25   *Congressional Globe,* 30th Cong., 1st. Session, Appendix, 1158-64; Josiah Morrow, *Life and Speeches of Thomas Corwin* (Cincinnati, 1896), 351-53, 392-93, 457; Daryl Pendergraft, "Thomas Corwin and the Conservative Republican Reaction, 1858-1861," *Ohio State Archaeological and Historical Quarterly,* vol. 57, 1948, 17; Norman A. Graebner, "Thomas Corwin and the Election of 1848: A Study in Conservative Politics," *Journal of Southern History,* vol. 17, 1951, 164-70.

26   Greeley, *Writings of Clay,* 224.

27   Whipple, Southern Diary.

28   Schenck to Dear Daughters, 9/30/1851, Schenck Papers, Rutherford B. Hayes Library, Fremont, Ohio.

29   Lincoln to Mary Speed, 9/27/1841, as quoted in William P. Pickett, *The Negro Problem, Abraham Lincoln's Solution* (N.Y., 1969, originally published in 1909), 309-10.

30   Pattison to George W. Julian, 12/4/1852, Julian Collection.

31   Greeley, *Writings of Clay,* 347; *Alton Weekly Courier,* 7/1/1853.

32 *Congressional Globe,* 33rd. Cong., 1st. Session, 342, 1072, 1210, Appendix, 310-13, 664, 666; Albert G. Riddle, *The Life of Benjamin F. Wade* (Cleveland, 1886), 135.

33 *Congressional Globe,* 33rd. Cong., 1st. Session, 1072.

34 Ibid., 32nd Cong., 1st. Session, Appendix, 665, 739, 741, 775; Joshua R. Giddings to Joseph A. Giddings, 2/15/1844, Joshua R. Giddings Papers, Ohio Historical Society; Eric Foner, "Politics and Prejudice," 242, 244.

35 Schenck to Dear Daughters, 9/30/1851.

36 F.I. Herriott, "James W. Grimes Versus the Southrons," *Annals of Iowa,* vol. 5, 1926, 347-48; Wentworth, 7; *Congressional Globe,* 30th Cong., 1st. Session, Appendix, 1158-64.

37 Greeley, *Writings of Clay,* 531-32; C.M. Clay, *Memoirs,* 208.

38 Schenck to Dear Daughters, 9/30/1851.

39 *Congressional Globe,* 31st Cong., 1st. Session, Appendix, 729-34; Bingham to James G. Birney, 9/24/1848, James G. Birney Papers, Clements Library, University Of Michigan.

40 E. Wade to Albert Riddle, 2/3/1850, Albert Gallatin Riddle Collection, Western Reserve Historical Society Library.

41 B. Wade to Caroline Wade, 6/29/1851, 1/20/1852, Benjamin F. Wade Papers.

42 Pattison to George W. Julian, 12/4/1852.

43 *Congressional Globe,* 30th Cong., 1st. Session, 994.

44 Ibid., 1022-23.

45 Ibid., 33rd Cong., 1st. Session, Appendix, 661-68.

46 John Kirk to Calvin Kirk, 3/6,13/1853, 5/26/1853, John Kirk Papers, Chicago Historical Society.

47 *The True American,* Lexington, Ky., 1/14/1846, 2/11/1846; *Anti-Slavery Bugle,* Salem, Ohio, 5/4/1849. Clay founded *The True American* in 1845, as an antislavery organ. See, Smiley, 82-83. Clay insisted that "there is no question, but that the Caucasian or Pelasgian race of men is the first in mental and physical development." See, Greeley, *Writings of Clay,* 394.

48 *Congressional Globe,* 38th Cong., 2nd. Session, v; *Missouri Democrat,* 11/30/1854.

49 *Congressional Globe,* 33rd. Cong., 1st. Session, Appendix, 212-14, 219.

50 *Missouri Democrat* 7/12/1853.

51 Greeley, *Writings of Clay,* 206, 394, 531.

52   *Missouri Democrat,* 7/12/1853.

53   *Congressional Globe,* 33rd Cong., 1st. Session, Appendix, 447-48, 2nd. Session, Appendix, 251-52.

54   Ibid., 30th Cong., 1st. Session, Appendix, 1158-64; Morrow, *Thomas Corwin,* 351-53, 392-93, 457; Pendergraft, 17; Graebner, 164-70.

55   *Congressional Globe,* 30th Cong., 1st. Session, Appendix, 1158-64.

56   Ibid., 28th Cong., 1st. Session, 197, Appendix, 82-83.

57   *Chicago Democrat,* 2/15/1848, 3/7,21/1848, 4/11/1848, 1/2,16/1849, 2/9/1850, 11/2/1850.

58   *Western Citizen,* 5/23/1848, 4/30/1850, 12/10/1850; Edmund Fry to Eastman, 3/14/1852, Zebina Eastman Collection, Chicago Historical Society.

59   *Missouri Democrat,* 7/12/1853.

60   A.Y. Moore, *The Life of Schuyler Colfax* (Philadelphia, 1868), 72-88. Colfax was a strong and early supporter of Western free soilism. See, Colfax to Daniel D. Pratt, 7/15/1848, Daniel D. Pratt Collection, Indiana State Library.

61   *Congressional Globe,* 30th Cong., 1st. Session, Appendix, 1158-64.

62   Ibid., 29th Cong., 2nd. Session, 180-81.

63   Ibid., 30th Cong., 1st. Session, Appendix, 394-96.

64   Greeley, *Writings of Clay,* 119, 270; C.M. Clay, *Memoirs,* 208.

65   Whipple, Southern Diary.

66   *Western Citizen,* 12/19/1848. Eastman's paper exerted a considerable influence among the antislavery following in the Western states, first, as the Liberty Party organ of Illinois, then as a Free Soil Party organ. Joseph Medill and Company bought out the *Free West* on 7/12/1855, and it became merged, along with Wentworth's *Chicago Democrat,* and the original *Chicago Tribune,* into the new *Chicago Tribune.* In 1861 Eastman was appointed by Lincoln as United States Counsel to Bristol, England, were he served until 1869. See, Charles Williams to Eastman, 8/4/1847, Reverend Levi Spencer to Eastman, 8/31/1846, and Gamaliel Bailey to Eastman, 6/11/1847, Eastman Collection; John S. Wright, "The Background and Formation of the Republican Party in Illinois, 1846-1860," Ph.D. dissertation, University of Chicago, 1946, 17; Norman D. Harris, *The History of Negro Servitude in Illinois* (N.Y., 1969, originally published in 1904), 191; *A Memorial of Zebina Eastman by His Family,* n.d., Eastman Collection, 7, 9, 16; Zebina Eastman, *History of the Anti-Slavery Agitation and the growth of the Liberty and Republican Parties*

in the State of Illinois, pamphlet, Chicago, n.d., Eastman Collection, 139; *Free West,* 7/12/1855; Frank L. Mott, *American Journalism, A History: 1690-1960* (N.Y., 1964, originally published in 1941), 283-84; James M. Lee, *History of American Journalism* (Cambridge, Mass., 1917), 265-66; Philip Kinsley, *The Chicago Tribune* (N.Y., 1943), vol. 1, 33-36; Fehrenbacher, *Chicago Giant,* 73.

67   Joshua R. Giddings, *History of the Rebellion* (N.Y., 1864), 376.

68   Chase to Charles H. and John M. Langston, 11/11/1850, Salmon P. Chase Papers, Library of Congress; Rawley, 30; Eric Foner, "Politics and Prejudice," 242.

69   Gary R. Planck, "Abraham Lincoln and Black Colonization: Theory and Practice," *Lincoln Herald,* vol. 72, 1970, 61-64; George M. Fredrickson, "A Man but Not a Brother: Abraham Lincoln and Racial Equality," *Journal of Southern History,* vol. 41, 1975, 40-41, 47-48, 51-52, 54-55; *The Freeman,* New York city, 12/6/1884; *Illinois Daily Journal,* 8/30/1853; Don E. Fehrenbacher, "Only His Stepchildren: Lincoln and the Negro," *Civil War History,* vol. 20, 1974, 302-03, 305; Charles H. Wesley, "Lincoln's Plan for Colonizing the Emancipated Negroes," *Journal of Negro History,* vol. 4, 1919, 8-10; Earnest S. Cox, *Lincoln's Negro Policy* (Los Angeles, 1968, originally published in 1938), 7, 29, 38-39, 42-45, 56-57; John M. Rozett, "Racism and Republican Emergence in Illinois, 1848-1860: A Re-Evaluation of Republican Negrophobia," *Civil War History,* vol. 22, 1976, 106-08; Pickett, 310-13; Roy P. Basler, *The Collected Works of Abraham Lincoln* (New Brunswick, N.J., 1953), vol. 2, 268, vol. 3, 80-84, 145-46.

70   *Alton Weekly Courier,* 10/21/1853.

71   Greeley, *Writings of Clay,* 338, 363.

72   Rawley, 30.

73   *Chicago Tribune,* 1/25,27/1854.

74   *Congressional Globe,* 30th Cong., 1st. Session, 994.

75   Kinsley S. Bingham to Mary Bingham, 7/18/1848, 12/25/1848, Kinsley Scott Bingham Papers, Bentley Historical Library, University of Michigan; *Congressional Globe,* 30th Cong., 1st. Session, Appendix, 1108-09; 31st Cong., 1st Session, Appendix, 729-34. Historian Klaus J. Hansen noted, when discussing the ideological and psychological implications of Northwestern racism, that the North, unlike the South, could be "saved" for

white racial purity, if "a pure and undefiled race of pioneers would take possession of the West . . . . The presence of slavery, of blacks, of a transatlantic Africa in the West, would have made this impossible . . . . The Free Soiler, in his revulsion against the black man, was in fact recoiling from an inner self he was incapable of acknowledging." See, Hansen, 389-90.

76   Greeley, *Writings of Clay,* 180-81, 235. Even radical abolitionists, such as Charles Grandison Parsons and David Lee Child, and politicians most closely associated with abolitionism, such as Charles Sumner of Massachusetts, expressed concern over the growth of miscegenation in the South. See, Charles G. Parsons, *Inside View of Slavery: A Tour Among the Planters,* (Cleveland, 1855), vol. 1, 84; David Lee Child, *The Despotism of Freedom, or the Tyranny and Cruelty of American Republican Slave Masters,* (Boston, 1833), 54-55; Charles Sumner, *The Barbarism of Slavery: Speech of Hon. Charles Sumner, on the Bill for the Admission of Kansas as a Free State,* pamphlet, Washington, D.C., 1860, 27.

77   *Congressional Globe,* 32nd Cong., 1st. Session, Appendix, 772-75; Walter Buell, *Joshua R. Giddings* (Cleveland, 1882), 141.

78   Whipple, Southern Diary.

79   Chase to Edward S. Hamlin, 8/13/1852, Chase Papers, Library of Congress.

80   *Chicago Democrat,* 2/15/1848, 3/7,21/1848, 4/11/1848, 1/2,16/1849, 2/9/1850, 11/2/1850.

81   Kinsley S. Bingham to Mary Bingham, 7/18/1848, 12/25/1848, Bingham Papers.

82   *Congressional Globe,* 30th Cong., 1st. Session, Appendix, 1158-64. Senator James R. Doolittle, a Free Democrat from Wisconsin, and later an important backer of the Lincoln administration, was also concerned about the possibility of racial conflict. See, James L. Sellers, "James R. Doolittle," *Wisconsin Magazine of History*, vol. 17, 1933-34, 176; Leslie H. Fishel Jr., "Wisconsin and Negro Suffrage," *Wisconsin Magazine of History,* vol. 46, 1963, 180-96.

83   Greeley, *Writings of Clay,* 207, 327.

84   *Congressional Globe,* 32nd Cong., 2nd. Session, Appendix, 38-40.

85   Ibid., 33rd Cong., 1st. Session, Appendix, 453.

86   Jacob Brinkerhoff to Salmon P. Chase, 11/27/1847, Chase Papers, Historical Society of Pennsylvania; *Congressional Globe,* 28th Cong., 2nd. Session,

132; 29th Cong., 2nd. Session, 377-79; Eric Foner, "The Wilmot Proviso Revisited," 262; Morrison, 202. Chase held Brinkerhoff in high regard, and considered him a close friend. See, Chase to Edward S. Hamlin, 1/12/1850, Chase to Lewis D. Campbell, 5/25/1855, Chase to Eli Nichols, 11/9/1848, Chase Papers, Library of Congress.

87 *Chicago Democrat,* 2/15/1848, 3/7,21/1848, 4/11/1848, 1/2,16/1849, 2/9/1850, 11/2/1850.

88 *Congressional Globe,* 33rd Cong., 1st. Session, 339, Appendix, 313.

89 Lincoln's Speech at Peoria, Illinois, 10/16/1854, as quoted in Basler, vol. 2, 254-69.

90 *Congressional Globe,* 30th Cong., 1st. Session, 1022-23.

91 Herriott, 347-48.

92 *Congressional Globe,* 28th Cong., 2nd. Session, Appendix, 80.

93 Ibid., 29th Cong., 2nd. Session, 378.

94 Speech of Owen Lovejoy, as quoted in Joseph F. McGuire, "Owen Lovejoy, Congressman From the Prairie," M.S. thesis, Illinois State Normal University, 1950, 48.

95 Moore, 72-88.

96 Kinsley S. Bingham to Mary Bingham, 12/25/1848, Bingham Papers; *Congressional Globe,* 30th Cong., 1st. Session, Appendix, 1108-09; 31st Cong., 1st. Session, Appendix, 729-34.

97 *Congressional Globe,* 33rd. Cong., 1st. Session, 1592, Appendix, 212-14, 219.

98 Benton's speech, as quoted in Hinton Rowan Helper, *The Impending Crisis of the South and How to Meet It,* George M. Fredrickson, ed. (Cambridge, Mass., 1968), 208.

99 Greeley, *Writings of Clay,* 174, 187, 382; Clay to Daniel Webster, 4/3/1850, Clay to Reverend James C. Davis, 10/8/1857, as quoted in C.M. Clay, *Memoirs,* 204, 235.

100 *Congressional Globe,* 30th Cong., 1st. Session, 1022-23. In the same vein Bingham saw himself as a "representative of free white laboring men." See, Ibid., 31st Cong., 1st. Session, Appendix, 729-34.

101 Ibid., 33rd Cong., 1st. Session, Appendix, 447-48. Yates expressed concern over the probable increase in the number of black people, and its detrimental effects for white settlers, if Southern slavery should find its way into the free

territories. He worried over what he called the "nationalization" of slavery, and even the possible reopening of the African slave trade. See also, Ibid., 2nd. Session, Appendix, 251-52.

102   Herriott, 341-44.

103   *Congressional Globe,* 33rd Cong., 2nd. Session, Appendix, 42-46.

104   Lincoln's Speech at Peoria, Illinois, 10/16/1854, as quoted in Basler, vol. 2, 254-69; Pickett, 309-13. The Gott Resolution proposed to abolish the slave trade in Washington, D.C., by allowing the free blacks resident within the Capital to vote on the proposition. Lincoln voted against the resolution. Previously he had voted against the Palfrey bill, which would have abolished slavery altogether in the Capital. Moreover, Lincoln tended to ignore the issue of black kidnapping in Washington, D.C., and on one occasion voted to compensate a slaveholder whose slave was lost to the British during the War of 1812. In another instance, he acted as defense counsel for a Kentucky slaveholder, in which the slaveholder recovered a family of runaway slaves. See, Alfred G. Harris, "Lincoln and the Question of Slavery in the District of Columbia," *Lincoln Herald,* vol. 51, 1949, 18-20; Benjamin Quarles, *Lincoln and the Negro* (N.Y., 1962), 19, 23; Donald W. Riddle, *Congressman Abraham Lincoln,* (Urbana, Ill., 1957), 164, 166, 171, 174.

105   *Congressional Globe,* 30th Cong., 1st. Session, Appendix, 1072.

106   Ibid., 33rd Cong., 1st. Session, 1592, Appendix, 212-14, 219.

107   Ibid., 29th Cong., 2nd. Session, 377-79.

108   Clay to Salmon P. Chase, 12/21/1842, Chase Papers, Historical Society of Pennsylvania; Smiley, 58, 74.

109   *Congressional Globe,* 33rd Cong., 1st. Session, Appendix, 212-14, 219; 29th Cong., 2nd. Session, 180-81.

110   Ibid., 28th Cong., 1st. Session, 197.

111   Thomas Hart Benton, *Thirty Years View* (N.Y., 1856), 695; David Christy, *Pulpit Politics, or Ecclesiastical Legislation on Slavery, in its Disturbing Influences on the American Union* (Cincinnati, 1862), 465-68; Theodore Roosevelt, *Thomas Hart Benton* (Cambridge, Mass., 1886), 147, 260-61.

112   Colfax to William H. Seward, 3/26/1850, 3/15/1852, Seward Collection.

113   Pickett, 307-09; Quarles, *Lincoln,* 19-20, 29-30; Reinhard H. Luthin, "Abraham Lincoln Becomes a Republican," *Political Science Quarterly,* vol. 59, 1944, 420, 423; Fredrickson, "A Man but Not a Brother," 43-44.

114   B. Wade to Elisha Whittlesey, 7/3/1848, Elisha Whittlesey Papers, Western Reserve Historical Society Library; Corwin to Schenck, 2/13/1854, Schenck Papers; *Congressional Globe,* 30th Cong., 1st. Session, 1023; 33rd Cong., 1st. Session, Appendix, 310; Martin Erlich, "Benjamin Franklin Wade: The Road to Radical Republicanism," M.A. thesis, Wayne State University, 1954, 16; Kenneth B. Shover, "Maverick at Bay: Ben Wade's Senate Re-election Campaign, 1862-63," *Civil War History,* vol. 12, 1966, 24; Theodore Clarke Smith, *Parties and Slavery, 1850-1859* (N.Y., 1906), 18, 283; Albert B. Hart, *Salmon Portland Chase* (N.Y., 1899), 49; David Donald, ed., *Inside Lincoln's Cabinet, The Civil War Diaries of Salmon P. Chase* (N.Y., 1954), 19; Joseph B. Foraker, "Salmon P. Chase," *Ohio Archaeological and Historical Society Publications,* vol. 15, 1906, 314; Patrick W. Riddleberger, "The Radicals Abandonment of the Negro During Reconstruction," *Journal of Negro History,* vol. 45, 1960, 89; Sellers, 176; Theodore Calvin Pease and James G. Randall, eds., *The Diary of Orville Hickman Browning* (Springfield, Ill., 1925), vol. 1, xvi; *Quincy Whig,* Quincy, Ill., 10/29/1850; Maurice Baxter, *Orville H. Browning,* (Bloomington, Ind., 1957), 19-20; James A. Woodburn, "Henry Smith Lane," *Indiana Magazine of History,* vol. 27, 1931, 283; Walter Rice Sharp, "Henry Smith Lane and the Formation of the Republican Party in Indiana," *Mississippi Valley Historical Review,* vol. 7, 1920, 98-99.

115   Whipple, Southern Diary.

116   *Congressional Globe,* 29th Cong., 2nd. Session, 332-33; 30th Cong., 1st. Session, 712, Appendix, 394-96.

117   Ibid., 33rd Cong., 1st. Session, Appendix, 212-14, 219.

118   *Chicago Democrat,* 2/15/1848, 3/7,21/1848, 4/11/1848, 1/2,16/1849, 2/9/1850, 11/2/1850.

119   *Congressional Globe,* 32nd Cong., 2nd. Session, Appendix, 38-40.

120   Pease and Randall, vol. 1, xiv, xvi, xvii, 138-39; Baxter, 19-20, 66-67; *Sangamo Journal,* Springfield, Ill., 1/23/1845; *Quincy Whig,* 10/29/1850; *Illinois Daily Journal,* Springfield, Ill., 1/12,14,16,18/1854.

121   *Congressional Globe,* 33rd Cong., 1st. Session, Appendix, 447-48, 2nd Session, Appendix, 251-52.

122   Greeley, *Writings of Clay,* 206-07.

123   *Ashtabula Sentinel,* Ashtabula, Ohio, 8/5/1843, 9/2,9/1843; Joshua R. Giddings to Milton Sutliff, 6/11/1844, Sutliff Papers; Joshua R. Giddings,

Speeches in Congress (N.Y., 1868, originally published in 1853), 218, 302; Buell, 212-13; Willard D. Loomis, "The Anti-slavery Movement in Ashtabula County, Ohio, 1834-1854," M.S. thesis, Western Reserve University, 1936, 17, 68; Eric Foner, "Politics and Prejudice," 242-43; Wentworth, 25-35; Gamaliel Bailey to Zebina Eastman, 10/1/1849, Eastman Collection; Fehrenbacher, *Chicago Giant,* 69, 74, 104, 139; Woodburn, 283-85; Graham A. Barringer, "The Life and Times of Henry S. Lane," Ph.D. dissertation, Indiana University, 1927, 2-3, 13, 20, 25; Roger H. Van Bolt, "The Rise of the Republican Party in Indiana, 1855-1856," *Indiana Magazine of History,* vol. 51, 1955, 204, 207; *South Bend Register,* South Bend, Ind., 2/15/1849, 7/4/1850; Schuyler Colfax to Henry Clay, 5/29/1839, 7/17/1839, Schuyler Colfax Papers, Library of Congress; Willard H. Smith, *Schuyler Colfax* (Indianapolis, 1952), 25, 30, 32. Giddings' biographer, James Brewer Stewart, writes that "Giddings never once endorsed total Negro equality on either a national basis or throughout the free states . . . . He did view the black man in a paternalistic way . . . . His belief in the right of each state to regulate its own institutions led him to his program to denationalize slavery, but not to abolish it." See, Stewart, *Joshua R. Giddings and the Tactics of Radical Politics* (Cleveland, 1970), 199. Also, Giddings, at the 1852 presidential convention of the Free Democratic Party, could not bring himself to defend black equality, and instead, according to Charles Francis Adams' view of the affair, defended the platform's omission of such on the grounds of political expediency. See, Charles F. Adams to Charles Sumner, 8/15/1852, Charles Francis Adams Papers, Massachusetts Historical Society.

124   Franklin Johnson, *The Development of State Legislation Concerning the Free Negro* (N.Y., 1918), 96, 98-99, 102-03, 126, 128, 161-63, 206; John C. Hurd, *The Law of Freedom and Bondage in the United States* (Boston, 1862), vol. 2, 116-141, 176-77; Gilbert T. Stephenson, *Race Distinctions in American Law* (N.Y., 1969, originally published in 1910), 36-38, 165, 245, 282, 284. See also, Malvin, 2-6, 39, 67-68; Charles J. Wilson, "The Negro in Ohio," *Ohio Archaeological and Historical Publications,* vol. 39, 1930, 747, 752-56, 759-61, 764; James H. Radabaugh, "The Negro in Ohio," *Journal of Negro History,* vol. 31, 1946, 13-15; Francis P. Wisenburger, *The Passing of the Frontier, 1825-1850* (Columbus, Ohio, 1941), 41-45, 363; Frederick J. Blue, "The Ohio Free Soilers and Problems of Factionalism,"

Ohio History, vol. 76, 1967, 23-24; Philip S. Foner and Ronald L. Lewis, vol. 1, 152-54; Quillin, 22-25, 38-39; David A. Gerber, *Black Ohio and the Color Line, 1860-1915* (Urbana, Ill., 1976), 4-6; Charles T. Hickok, *The Negro in Ohio, 1802-1870* (Cleveland, 1896), 51, 70, 155; Leonard Erickson, "Politics and the Repeal of Ohio's Black Laws, 1837-1849," *Ohio History,* vol. 82, 1973, 154-162; George H. Porter, *Ohio Politics During the Civil War Period* (N.Y., 1968, originally published in 1911), 18-20; Hans L. Trefousse, "Ben Wade and the Negro," *Ohio Historical Quarterly,* vol. 68, 1959, 170; Reuben J. Scheeler, "The Struggle of the Negro in Ohio for Freedom," *Journal of Negro History,* vol. 31, 1946, 221-22; J.W. Schuckers, *The Life and Public Services of Salmon Portland Chase* (N.Y., 1874), 96-97; Albert B. Hart, *Chase,* 30-31.

125   Malvin, 39.

126   Hurd, vol. 2, 116-141, 176-77; Stephenson, 36-38, 165, 245, 282, 284; Franklin Johnson, 96, 98-99, 102-03, 126, 128, 161-63, 206; Emma Lou Thornbrough, *The Negro in Indiana Before 1900* (Indianapolis 1957), 55-56, 64-67, 73; Arvarh E. Strickland, "The Illinois Background of Lincoln's Attitude toward Slavery and the Negro," *Illinois State Historical Society Journal,* vol. 56, 1963, 482, 484-85, 488-89; Elmer Gertz, "The Black Laws of Illinois," *Illinois State Historical Society Journal,* vol. 56, 1963, 454-55, 457, 463, 466-67, 472; Mason M. Fishback, "Illinois Legislation on Slavery and Free Negroes, 1818-1865," *Transactions of the Illinois State Historical Society,* 1904, 414-32; George W. Julian, *Political Recollections, 1840 to 1872* (Miami, Fla., 1969, originally published in 1884), 116; Louis Pelzer, "The Negro and Slavery in Early Iowa," *Iowa Journal of History and Politics,* vol. 2, 1904, 471-73; Leola N. Bergmann, *The Negro in Iowa,* (Iowa City, Ia., 1969), 8-9, 11-15; Cavanagh, 62-63, 73; Hubbart, *The Older Middle West,* 45-51; Hubbart, "Pro-Southern Influences in the Free West," *Mississippi Valley Historical Review,* vol. 20, 1933, 48-49; Voegeli, *Free But Not Equal,* 1-9; Voegeli, "The Northwest and the Race Issue, 1861-1862," as quoted in Robert V. Haynes, *Blacks in White America Before 1865* (N.Y., 1972), 506-07; Berwanger, *The Frontier Against Slavery,* 20-25, 32-36, 42-45, 49; Ronald P. Formisano, "The Edge of Caste: Colored Suffrage in Michigan, 1827-1861," *Michigan History,* vol. 56, 1972, 28; Merk, *Manifest Destiny,* 38-39; Simms, 128-29; McLaughlin, "Popular Reactions," 20, 23-24, 27-59; Dillon,

The Abolitionists, 69. McLaughlin noted that "from Maine's entrance in the Union in 1819, until Nebraska was admitted in 1867, no new state was formed that allowed Negroes to vote." See, McLaughlin, "Grass-Roots Attitudes toward Black Rights in Twelve Non-slaveholding States, 1846-1869," *Mid-America,* vol. 56, 1974, 177-78; Thomas Stirton, "Party Disruptions and the Rise of the Slavery Extension Controversy, 1840-1846," Ph.D. dissertation, University of Chicago, 1926, 312. It may be true, that the black codes were not always enforced, because relatively small numbers of black people were resident in these states. On the other hand, there were cases, such as in Indiana and Illinois, where the codes were enforced. See, Malvin, 5-6.

127   *Congressional Globe,* 30th Cong., 1st. Session, Appendix, 1158-64, 2nd. Session, 215; 29th Cong., 2nd. Session, 180-81; 33rd Cong., 1st. Session, 339; Morrison, 201-02; William D. Foulke, *Life of Oliver P. Morton* (Indianapolis, 1899), 35; Quarles, *Lincoln,* 36-37; Greeley, *Writings of Clay,* 65, 71, 119; C.M. Clay, *A Review of the Late Canvass,* pamphlet, Lexington, Ky., 1840; Morton M. Rosenberg, *Iowa on the* Eve of the Civil War (Norman, Okla., 1972), 28.

128   *Chicago Democrat,* 2/15/1848, 3/7,21/1848, 4/11/1848, 1/2,16/1849, 2/9/1850, 11/2/1850.

129   *Congressional Globe,* 31st cong., 1st. Session, 1092-93.

130   Ibid., 30th Cong., 1st. Session, Appendix, 1158. Editor George Brown gave vent to similar fears, when he described Illinois as a "free white state" where existed, as in the states of the Northwest and in the Western territories, a "perfectly natural and might have been expected hostility . . . to free negroism." See, the *Alton Weekly Courier,* 3/18/1853, 4/1,8,15/1853, 12/9/1853. In the case of Oregon, Congress did restrict land titles to "white male citizens." See, *Congressional Globe,* 31st Cong., 1st. Session, 1547.

131   *Congressional Globe,* 30th Cong., 1st. Session, 1019.

132   Ibid., 2nd. Session, 215.

133   Brinkerhoff to Salmon P. Chase, 11/27/1847, Chase Papers, Historical Society of Pennsylvania.

134   Whipple, Southern Diary.

135   Baxter, 19-20.

136   Greeley, *Writings of Clay,* 120, 206-07.

137 *Congressional Globe,* 29th Cong., 2nd. Session, 180-81; 33rd Cong., 1st. Session, 1744. Howard felt this way also. See, Jacob M. Howard to John C. Vaughan and Thomas Brown, 7/9/1849, Howard Papers.

138 *Western Citizen,* 10/7/1851.

139 *Congressional Globe,* 33rd Cong., 1st. Session, Appendix, 212-14, 219.

140 Greeley, *Writings of Clay,* 71, 180-81, 248, 337.

141 *Alton Weekly Courier,* 3/4,18/1853.

142 *Missouri Democrat,* 7/12/1853.

143 *Western Citizen,* 5/23/1848, 4/30/1850, 12/10/1850.

144 William E. Smith, *The Francis Preston Blair Family in Politics* (N.Y., 1933), vol. 1, 151, 204, 240, 261, 263, 308-09, 369; Marvin R. Cain, *Lincoln's Attorney General, Edward Bates of Missouri* (Columbia, Mo., 1965), 46-47, 73-74, 77-79, 90, 98-100, 102-04; Leonard B. Wurthman Jr., "Frank Blair: Lincoln's Congressional Spokesman," *Missouri Historical Review,* vol. 64, 1970, 265-66; Charles Gibson, "Edward Bates," *Missouri Historical Society Collections,* vol. 2, 1900, 55; Edward Younger, *John A. Kasson* (Iowa City, Ia., 1955), 4-5, 53, 61-62, 65, 68; Reinhard H. Luthin, *The First Lincoln Campaign,* (Cambridge, Mass., 1944), 53-55. All three admired Henry Clay, but in 1848 Blair tried to emulate the New York Free Democrats, by starting his own Free Soil journal, the *Barnburner,* in St. Louis, the center of the Missouri antislavery movement. Brown became the famous Free Soil editor of the *Missouri Democrat,* in St. Louis, started from the defunct *Barnburner.* At the same time, free soilism was by no means dead in New York state. Between 1850 and 1856 it tended to take a more Whiggish tone, as Senator William H. Seward of New York came to the fore in the battle against slavery expansion. Eastern free soilism, however, did not appear to be anymore enlightened or advanced in racial attitudes, than that of the West. In 1853, when Seward spoke about the "destiny of America," he doubted whether the Caucasian and African races could ever combine into a nation that would be "at once aggressive and powerful . . . . Nor has the time yet come, if indeed it shall come within many hundred years, when Africa, emerging from her primeval barbarism, shall vindicate the equality of her sable races in the rights of human nature." Seward also referred to the "weaker races" of Spanish America, and asked if they could ever be "cured of the disease inherited from aboriginal and Spanish parentage." In effect, there

was no room for these people within the United States. See, Seward, *The Destiny of America,* pamphlet, Albany, N.Y., 1853, 6-7.

145 *Congressional Globe,* 30th Cong., 1st. Session, 994, Appendix, 1158-64; *Thirty-fourth Annual Report of the American Colonization Society,* Washington, D.C., 1851, 28; Morrow, 353, 392; Pendergraft, 6; Thomas D. Morris, *Free Men All, the Personal Liberty Laws of the North, 1780-1861* (Baltimore, 1974), 108.

146 Howard to John C. Vaughan and Thomas Brown, 7/9/1849, Howard Papers.

147 *Chicago Tribune,* 1/25,27/1854.

148 Planck, 61-64; Fehrenbacher, "Only His Stepchildren," 302-03, 307; George S. Boritt, "The Voyage to the Colony of Linconia," *Historian,* vol. 37, 1974-75, 619-22; Wesley, "Lincoln's Plan," 8-9; Rozett, 106-07.

149 Greeley, *Writings of Clay,* 62, 91, 235, 293, 327, 337, 339-40; *Western Citizen,* 12/23/1851; Clay to Daniel Webster, 4/3/1850, as quoted in C.M. Clay, *Memoirs,* 204; Smiley, 94, 101, 153.

150 Lyman Trumbull to Benjamin Trumbull, 11/12/1837, Lyman Trumbull Family Papers, Illinois State Historical Society; Arthur H. Robertson, "The Political Career of Lyman Trumbull," M.A. thesis, University of Chicago, 1910, 36-38; Berwanger, *The Frontier Against Slavery,* 124.

151 L. Kintner to Elisha Embree, 4/1/1849, Lucius C. Embree Collection, Indiana State Library.

152 A.L. Robinson to Julian, 8/28/1852, Julian Collection.

153 *Congressional Globe,* 31st Cong., 2nd. Session, Appendix, 309; Frederick J. Blue, *Salmon P. Chase, A Life in Politics* (Kent, Ohio, 1987), 27-28, 84; Chase to Frederick Douglass, 5/4/1850, Chase Papers, Historical Society of Pennsylvania.

154 Greeley, *Writings of Clay,* 62, 91, 235, 293, 327, 337, 339-40; Smiley, 94, 101, 153.

155 Lyman Trumbull to Benjamin Trumbull, 11/12/1837, Trumbull Papers, Illinois State Historical Society; Robertson, 36-38; Berwanger, *The Frontier Against Slavery,* 124.

156 Lincoln, "Eulogy on Henry Clay, July 6, 1852," as quoted in Basler, vol. 2, 130-32; John G. Nicolay and John Hay, *Complete Works of Abraham Lincoln* (Chicago, 1894), vol. 2, 172-77; Planck, 61-64; Fredrickson, "A Man but Not a Brother," 40-41, 47-48, 51-52, 54-55; Luthin, "Abraham Lincoln Becomes a

Republican," 420; *The Freeman,* 12/6/1884; *Illinois Daily Journal,* 8/30/1853; Marvin R. Cain, "Lincoln's Views on Slavery and the Negro: A Suggestion," *Historian,* vol. 26, 1964, 504; Brainerd Dyer, "The Persistence of the Idea of Negro Colonization," *Pacific Historical Review,* vol. 12, 1943, 58-59; Fehrenbacher, "Only His Stepchildren," 302-03, 305; Wesley, "Lincoln's Plan," 8-10; Cox, *Lincoln's Negro Policy,* 7, 29, 38-39, 42-45, 56-57; Quarles, *Lincoln,* 35-37; Pickett, 310-13; Rozett, 108; Charles A. Church, *History of the Republican Party in Illinois, 1854-1912* (Rockford, Ill., 1912), 50, 66.

157 *Journal of the House of Representatives of the State of Indiana,* 34th Session, 1849, 598-602; 35th Session, 1850, 39.

158 B. Wade to Elisha Whittlesey, 7/3/1848, Whittlesey Papers; *Western Citizen,* 1/20/1852; Erlich, 99-100.

159 C.M. Clay, *Memoirs,* 204.

160 Lincoln, "Eulogy on Henry Clay."

161 *Congressional Globe,* 33rd Cong., 1st. Session, 1592.

162 *Western Citizen,* 5/5/1849, 2/5/1850, 5/21/1850, 7/2/1850, 2/8,18/1851, 3/11/1851, 9/30/1851, 10/7,14/1851, 9/28/1852.

163 *The African Repository* (Washington, D.C.), vol. 24, 1848, 179-180; vol. 26, 1850, 111-12, 166-69, 362-63; *Thirty-fourth Annual Report of the American Colonization Society,* 1851, 10-11; *Western Citizen,* 2/3/1852; Edward W. Shunk, "Ohio in Africa," *Ohio State Archaeological and Historical Quarterly,* vol. 51, 1942, 79-84, 86; Cooke, 168-69; Weisenburger, 42-43, 365-67; Radabaugh, 15; Cox, *Lincoln's Negro Policy,* 26-27; Walter L. Fleming, "Deportation and Colonization: An Attempted Solution of the Race Problem," *Studies in Southern History and Politics* (N.Y., 1914), 5; Willard L. King, 51; Thornbrough, *The Negro in Indiana,* viii, 55, 73-75, 82-84, 89; Dwight L. Dumond, *Antislavery Origins of the Civil War in the United States,* (Ann Arbor, Mich., 1966, originally published in 1939), 14; Berwanger, *The Frontier Against Slavery,* 52-58; Quillin, 86; Simms, 140. The *African Repository* was the official journal of the American Colonization Society. David Christy, the famous Ohio colonizationist, considered mixed races sub-human, and viewed black people as ignorant barbarians. See, Christy, *Pulpit Politics,* 256-59, 662.

164 *Report of the Naval Committee to the House of Representatives, July 1850,* Washington, D.C., 1850, 54-55; *Journal of the House of Representatives of*

the State of Indiana, 35th Session, 1850, 39. For examples of separate state colonies, see, Fox, 95-98.

165   Willard L. King, 51.

166   Pease and Randall, vol. 1, xiv, xvi, xvii, 138-39; Baxter, 12-20, 66-67; *Sangamo Journal,* 1/23/1845; *Quincy Whig,* 10/29/1850; *Illinois Daily Journal,* 1/12,14,16,18/1854.

167   *Western Citizen,* 5/5/1849, 2/5/1850, 5/21/1850, 7/2/1850, 2/8,18/1851, 3/11/1851, 9/30/1851, 10/7,14/1851, 9/28/1852. Eastman came under attack from the free black community of Chicago, for his support of colonization. See, the *Western Citizen,* 7/2/1850.

168   James Brewer Stewart, 6-9, 30, 38; Pease and Randall, vol. 1, xiv, xvi, xvii, 138-39; Baxter, 19-20, 66-67; Loomis, 17; Eric Foner, "Politics and Prejudice," 242-43; McGuire, 29.

169   *Alton Weekly Courier,* 3/25/1853, 4/22/1853, 8/19/1853, 10/21/1853; Chase to Frederick Douglass, 5/4/1850, Chase Papers, Historical Society of Pennsylvania; Sellers, 176; Fishel, 180-96; Joseph M. Root to Joshua R. Giddings, 5/14/1864, Giddings Papers, Ohio Historical Society.

170   *Alton Weekly Courier,* 3/25/1853, 4/22/1853, 8/19/1853, 10/21/1853. Orris Crosby, a Free Soiler from Boone County, Illinois, seemed to synthesize the feelings of many party members on both containment and colonization, when he wrote that "[white] men in states, or even territories, will govern themselves. Slavery [however] cannot exist in our new territories nor in the Northern states. Negroes know enough to run away. They also know enough to make good and even pious Mexicans . . . but they never can be Americans." See, Orris Crosby to General Elijah Risley, 2/11/1850, Risley Letters, Olin Library, Cornell University.

171   *North Star,* Rochester, N.Y., 8/11,25/1848, 9/10,22/1848, 12/24/1848, 1/26/1849. Oliver Dyer, 21; Frederick Douglass, *Life and Times of Frederick Douglass, Written by Himself* (Boston, 1892), 275-78; *Proceedings of the Colored National Convention Held in Rochester, July, 6,7,8, 1853,* pamphlet, Rochester, N.Y., 1853, 53-55; Gerald Stanley, "Racism and the Early Republican Party: the 1856 Presidential Election in California," *Pacific Historical Review,* vol. 43, 1974, 171; Benjamin Quarles, *Frederick Douglass* (Washington, D.C., 1948), 143-46; Charles H. Wesley, "The Participation of Negroes in Anti-Slavery Political Parties," *Journal of Negro History,* vol. 29,

172   1944, 54-56, 64; Robert G. Weisbord, "The Back-to-Africa Idea," *History Today,* vol. 18, 1968, 31; Cooke, 163; Martin E. Dann, ed., *The Black Press, 1827-1890* (N.Y., 1971), 236, 255-57. Douglass edited the *North Star.*

172   Giddings Scrapbook, note of 9/22/1853, and Joshua R. Giddings to Maria Giddings, 5/10/1840, Giddings Papers, Ohio Historical Society.

173   Julian to Chicago free blacks, 9/17/1853, Julian Collection.

174   *Western Citizen,* 4/13/1852.

175   *Letter of Hon. S.P. Chase in Reply to Daniel O'Connell,* pamphlet, Cincinnati, 1843, 14.

176   George W. Julian, *Speeches on Political Questions* (Cambridge, Mass., 1872), 73, 76-77, 84, 96, 103-04, 113, 125; Grace Julian Clarke, *George W. Julian* (Indianapolis, 1923), 140, 142, 159-61.

177   Chase to John Hutchins, 10/15/1849, Chase Papers, Library of Congress; Robert B. Warden, *An Account of the Private Life and Public Services of Salmon Portland Chase* (Cincinnati, 1874), 322.

178   Julian, *Speeches on Political Questions,* 73, 125, 127, 159; *Congressional Globe,* 31st Cong., 1st. Session, Appendix, 573-79; Julian to Chicago free blacks, 9/17/1853; Clarke, 159; Patrick W. Riddleberger, *George Washington Julian, Radical Republican* (Indianapolis, 1966), 89-90; Riddleberger, "The Making of a Political Abolitionist: George W. Julian and the Free Soilers, 1848," *Indiana Magazine of History,* vol. 51, 1955, 234-35.

179   Julian, *Speeches on Political Questions,* 73.

180   Trefousse, "Ben Wade and the Negro," 162-63; Trefousse, *Benjamin Franklin Wade* (N.Y., 1963), 31-35, 45-46; Erlich, 19, 59; Weisenburger, 380; Morris, 90-91; Giddings, *Speeches in Congress,* 348, 361, 368, 379; Giddings, *History of the Rebellion,* 376, 403; *Cleveland Daily Herald,* 1/22/1848; Buell, 138-41; George W. Julian, *The Life of Joshua R. Giddings* (Chicago, 1892), 314, 319; James Brewer Stewart, 89-90; Chase to Edward S. Hamlin, 1/19,20,24/1849, Chase Papers, Library of Congress; Chase to Giddings, 3/6/1849, 4/4/1849 and Albert G. Riddle to Giddings, 1/15/1849, Giddings Papers, Ohio Historical Society; Christy, 437-38; Blue, "The Ohio Free Soilers and Problems of Factionalism," 18, 22-24; Franklin Johnson, 161-63; Schuckers, 96-97; Quillin, 39; Hickok, 51; Scheeler, 221-22; Albert B. Hart, *Chase,* 97.

181   Chase to Edward S. Hamlin, 1/19,20,24/1849; Chase to Giddings, 3/6/1849,

4/4/1849, Giddings Papers, Ohio Historical Society; Blue, "The Ohio Free Soilers and Problems of Factionalism," 18, 22-24; Franklin Johnson, 161-63; Schuckers, 96-97; Quillin, 39; Hickok, 51; Scheeler, 221-22; Albert B. Hart, *Chase*, 97. Chase was instrumental in writing various antislavery party platforms, such as the Liberty Party platform of 1843, and the Free Soil Party platform of 1848. See, Albert B. Hart, *Chase*, 59. Furthermore, Chase viewed both the Whig and the Democratic Parties as tools of the slaveholding interests, and although himself a Democrat, battled constantly during the antebellum period to reform that party. He was the major architect of both the Ohio Liberty Party and the Free Democratic movement in the West, which latter was the prototype of the nascent Republican Party. Chase wanted an independent political party based on the moral rejection of slavery. Black people recognized Chase's efforts in their behalf, and the blacks of Cincinnati presented him with a silver pitcher in 1845, as a "testimonial of gratitude to Salmon P. Chase . . . for his various public services in behalf of the oppressed and particularly for his eloquent advocacy of the rights of man." See, Chase to John P. Hale, 9/23/1847, 4/19/1848, 5/6/1848, 4/8/1851, 8/5/1852, Chase-Hale Correspondence, New Hampshire Historical Society; Chase to Milton Sutliff, 1/7/1851, Chase Papers, Library of Congress; Blue, "The Ohio Free Soilers and Problems of Factionalism," 24; Theodore Clarke Smith, *The Liberty and Free Soil Parties in the Northwest*, 167-69; Reinhard H. Luthin, "Salmon P. Chase's Political Career before the Civil War," *Mississippi Valley Historical Review*, vol. 29, 1943, 518-19, 521, 524; Weisenburger, 472; Erickson, 154-75; Schuckers, 78; Foraker, 314; Richard W. Solberg, "Joshua Giddings, Politician and Idealist," Ph.D. dissertation, University of Chicago, 1952, 267.

182   *Western Citizen*, 3/28/1848, 4/18/1848, 5/9,23/1848, 8/1/1848, 3/13/1849, 6/5/1849, 7/10/1849, 9/11/1849, 10/16/1849, 6/25/1850, 12/24/1850, 2/25/1851, 6/10/1851, 2/1,22/1853, 3/1,8,22/1853, 10/18/1853; *The Free West*, 12/1,8/1853; Willard L. King, 127.

183   Giddings to Maria Giddings, 1/2/1850, Giddings Papers, Library of Congress; Giddings Diary, 12/19,26/1849, and Giddings Scrapbook, note of 3/21/1842, Giddings Papers, Ohio Historical Society; Giddings, *Speeches in Congress*, 348, 361, 368, 379; Giddings, *History of the Rebellion*, 376, 403; *Congressional Globe*, 31st Cong., 1st. Session, 277; Charles Sumner to

Giddings, 10/18/1847, 11/1/1847, Giddings Papers, Ohio Historical Society; Solberg, 5-6, 167-70, 349-50, 377; Loomis, 45-46, 48; Benson J. Lossing, *A Biography of James A. Garfield* (N.Y., 1882), 260-61. Giddings, like Chase, was also the recipient of a testimonial from appreciative black people. See, Giddings to Wife, n.d., Giddings Papers, Library of Congress. Notwithstanding his censure and expulsion from the House of Representatives, Giddings was re-elected to his seat in Congress by a large majority of the voters in his district.

184 *Chicago Democrat,* 2/15/1848, 3/7,21/1848, 4/11/1848, 1/2,16/1849, 2/9/ 1850, 11/2/1850.

185 *Congressional Globe,* 33rd Cong., 1st. Session, 1072, 1210, Appendix, 664, 666; Malvin, 71.

186 *Congressional Globe,* 33rd Cong., 1st. Session, 504.

187 Ibid., 208.

188 Ibid., 339, 1744, 1832. Other Western Free Soilers who at times acted in defense of black political and economic rights included Schuyler Colfax, Austin Blair of Michigan, and Charles Durkee of Wisconsin. Both Blair and Durkee were especially strong advocates of equal treatment for black Americans. See, Colfax to William H. Seward, 12/6/1850, Seward Collection; *Report of the Debates and Proceedings of the Convention for the Revision of the Constitution of the State of Indiana, 1850,* Indianapolis, 1850, vol. 1, 456-57, 616-17; Moore, 48-51; *Detroit Advertiser,* 5/6/1846; Earl O. Smith, "The Public Life of Austin Blair, War Governor of Michigan," M.A. thesis, Wayne State University, 1934, 1, 12-13, 29, 88, 91-92; Jean Joy L. Fennimore, "Austin Blair: Political Idealist, 1845-1860," *Michigan History,* vol. 48, 1964, 130-66; Floyd B. Streeter, *Political Parties in Michigan, 1837-1860* (Lansing, Mich., 1918), 192; *Congressional Globe,* 32nd Cong., 1st. Session, Appendix, 887-91; Theodore Clarke Smith, "The Free Soil Party in Wisconsin," *Proceedings of the Wisconsin Historical Society,* vol. 42, 1894, 103, 106, 108, 116-17, 123, 136, 152-53; Kate Everest Levi, "The Wisconsin Press and Slavery," *Wisconsin Magazine of History,* vol. 9, 1925-26, 424; Boom 45-46.

189 Giddings Diary, 12/19,26/1849; Giddings, *Speeches in Congress,* 361; Giddings, *History of the Rebellion,* 376; Julian, *Giddings,* 314, 319; Solberg, 169-70, 349-50; Loomis, 45-46; Buell, 138-41; James Brewer Stewart, 89-

90; Alfred G. Harris, "Lincoln and the Question of Slavery in the District of Columbia," 18.

190 *Congressional Globe,* 33rd Cong., 1st. Session, 1072, 1210, Appendix, 664, 666.

191 Schuckers, 78-80.

192 *Western Citizen,* 10/16/1849.

193 *Congressional Globe,* 33rd Cong., 1st. Session, 1072, 1210, Appendix, 664, 666.

194 *Western Citizen,* 4/18/1848, 5/23/1848, 8/1/1848, 6/5/1849, 6/25/1850, 12/24/1850, 2/22/1853, 3/1,8,22/1853, 12/18/1853.

195 Giddings, *Speeches in Congress,* 379, 398-99, 433, 437, 484-85; Giddings, *History of the Rebellion,* 402-03; *Congressional Globe,* 31st Cong., 1st. Session, 277; 32nd Cong., 1st. Session, Appendix, 738-41; Julian, *Giddings,* 314, 319; Solberg, 5, 167-70, 349-50, 377; James Brewer Stewart, 89-90.

196 Schuckers, 52-65; Peter F. Walker, *Moral Choices* (Baton Rouge, La., 1978), 308-10, 328.

197 *Western Citizen,* 12/23/1851.

198 Owen Lovejoy, *The Supremacy of the Divine Law,* pamphlet, Chicago, 1843, 86-88; *Western Citizen,* 4/30/1850, 1/7/1851, 2/4/1851; Owen Lovejoy to Lewis Tappan, 2/4/1850, 8/18/1853, 4/3/1854, 8/27/1854, and Lovejoy to Henry Whipple, 8/20/1853, American Missionary Association Archives, Amistad Research Center, New Orleans; McGuire, 8, 14-15, 18, 20, 22, 34, 42; Ruth E. Haberkorn, "Owen Lovejoy in Princeton, Illinois," *Journal of the Illinois State Historical Society,* vol. 36, 1943, 284, 286, 291, 296-97, 302; Edward Magdol, *Owen Lovejoy: Abolitionist in Congress* (New Brunswick, N.J., 1967), 85. Historian Mark Krug, thought that while Lovejoy was antislavery, he was not an abolitionist. See, Krug, *Lyman Trumbull, Conservative Radical* (N.Y., 1965), 87.

199 Clarke, 146-48.

200 *Congressional Globe,* 31st Cong., 1st. Session, Appendix, 1587, 1621; Chase to Wife, 9/5/1850, Amistad Collection; Chase to Stanley Matthews, 2/26/1849, Chase Papers, Library of Congress; Chase to John P. Hale, 5/22/1848, Chase-Hale Correspondence; *Speech of Salmon P. Chase in the Case of the Colored Woman Matilda,* pamphlet, Cincinnati, 1837, 8-11, 29-31, 34-35; Schuckers, 42-43, 52-65; Warden 296-98, 305-06; Albert B. Hart,

Chase, 73-82; Donald, *Inside Lincoln's Cabinet,* 18; Frank W. Hale, "Salmon P. Chase: Rhetorician of Abolition," *Negro History Bulletin,* vol. 26, 1963, 168. The Matilda case was heard in the Ohio Supreme Court, whereas the Van Zandt case was carried to the United States Supreme Court. Van Zandt was charged with violating the federal Fugitive Slave law of 1793, by harboring and concealing a fugitive slave. In most of these cases, Chase argued that slavery was essentially a state institution, and since slavery was interdicted in the state of Ohio, due to the Northwest Ordinance of 1787, then fugitive slaves escaping to a free state, such as Ohio, were no longer slaves, but free persons. See, Hickok, 145.

201   *Western Citizen,* 5/2,15/1849, 10/8/1850, 3/12,19/1850, 4/19/1850, 5/21/1850, 6/11/1850, 8/27/1850, 11/15/1850, 2/11,25/1851, 6/3,10/1851, 9/23/1851, 5/11/1852, 6/23,27,29/1852, 8/17/1852, 9/7/1852, 10/5/1952; *The Free West,* 2/2,9,16,23/1854, 9/7,21,28/1854; John P. Hale to Eastman, 9/1/1847; Elihu B. Washburne to Eastman, 12/19/1854; *A Memorial of Zebina Eastman,* 10, 11, 15, and Eastman, *History of the Anti-slavery Agitation,* 139-41, Eastman Collection.

202   Malvin, 71; Giddings Scrapbook, note of 9/22/1853; Giddings, *Speeches in Congress,* 338-39, 341, 423, 432, 437-39, 450-51; *Congressional Globe,* 32nd Cong., 1st. Session, Appendix, 775; Solberg, 376.

203   Lovejoy, *The Supremacy of the Divine Law,* 86-88; McGuire, 8, 14-15, 18, 20, 22, 34, 42; Haberkorn, 284, 286, 291, 296-97.

204   Malvin, 71; Giddings Scrapbook, note of 9/22/1853; *Congressional Globe,* 32nd Cong., 1st. Session, Appendix, 775.

205   Chase to John P. Hale, 4/29/1848, Chase-Hale Correspondence; Schuckers, 78; Foraker, 314.

206   Giddings Diary, 12/19,26/1849; Giddings, *Speeches in Congress,* 361; Giddings, *History of the Rebellion,* 376; Julian, *Giddings,* 314, 319; Solberg, 169-70, 349-50; Loomis, 45-46; Buell, 138-41; James Brewer Stewart, 89-90; Alfred G. Harris, "Lincoln and the Question of Slavery in the District of Columbia," 18.

207   *Western Citizen,* 8/22/1848, 10/10/1848, 3/27/1849, 4/10/1849, 1/21/1851, 4/1/1851, 2/3/1852; *The Free West,* 1/11/1855. Eastman got his start in antislavery journalism in 1839, by working with Benjamin Lundy in publishing the *Genius of Universal Emancipation.* Lundy was an ardent

supporter of black colonization, who stressed the need for inter-American colonization projects, involving Haiti, Mexico, Canada, and Texas. Lundy feared the growing number of black people in the United States, and he predicted that unless blacks were removed from the presence of the predominately white population of the country, a bloody race war would result. See, Lawrence J. Friedman, *Inventors of the Promised Land* (N.Y., 1975), 226-29; *A Memorial of Zebina Eastman,* 7; Merton L. Dillon, *Benjamin Lundy and the Struggle for Negro Freedom* (Urbana, Ill., 1966), 258, 260.

208   Julian to Chicago free blacks, 9/17/1853; Julian, *Speeches on Political Questions,* 73, 76-77, 84, 96; Clarke, 66, 143.

209   *Letter of Hon. S.P. Chase in Reply to Daniel O'Connell,* 14.

210   *Western Citizen,* 9/11/1849, 2/26/1850, 6/22/1850, 1/28/1851, 7/29/1851, 8/5/1851, 1/6/1852; *The Free West,* 3/16/1854. In 1849 Eastman focused attention on differences between what he called political antislavery and abolitionism, when comparing antislavery speeches made by John Van Buren and Theodore Parker. Eastman drew an analogy by noting that "there is not only the moral distinction between chaff and wheat . . . but there is also a difference in the quality of wheat. The wheat in the Van Buren speech is by no means . . . chaff, or to be despised, but the wheat of the Parker speech is a more excellent article." Parker's speech was apparently motivated by a higher moral ideal, whereas Van Buren's was viewed by Eastman as simply that of a pragmatic politician. See, the *Western Citizen,* 9/11/1849.

211   *Congressional Globe,* 31st Cong., 1st. Session, 575, 578; Julian to William Lloyd Garrison, 11/18/1853, Julian Collection; Julian, *Speeches on Political Questions,* 84; Julian, *Political Recollections,* 38, 100-01. Julian, however much he may have admired the abolitionists, never actively joined an abolitionist society. See, Riddleberger, "The Making of a Political Abolitionist," 235.

212   Julian, *Speeches on Political Questions,* 76-77, 96, 103, 125; Clarke, 140.

213   Giddings Scrapbook, Address at Providence, R.I., 7/4/1854; *Congressional Globe,* 32nd Cong., 1st. Session, Appendix, 739, 741; Giddings, *Speeches in Congress,* 298-99, 398-99; Solberg, 52, 322; James Brewer Stewart, 226; Loomis, 10.

214   Chase to John P. Hale, 4/29/1848, Chase-Hale Correspondence.

215   *Congressional Globe,* 33rd Cong., 1st. Session, 339, 1744, 1832.

216 *Western Citizen,* 1/7/1851, 2/4/1851, 5/27/1851, 11/11/1851, 6/29/1852.

217 Julian to Chicago free blacks, 9/17/1853.

218 *Alton Weekly Courier,* 8/19/1853.

219 *Western Citizen,* 4/5/1853.

NOTES—CHAPTER 4

1 Eric Foner, *Free Soil, Free Labor, Free Men, The Ideology of the Republican Party before the Civil War* (N.Y., 1970), 60-61, 149-70; Blue, *The Free Soilers*, 169, 202-03, 232-33, 239-43, 254-56, 260-71; Morrison, 22-37, 46-50, 63-73, 149-60; Rawley, 12-13, 18-21, 30-31, 53-57, 71-73; Robert W. Johannsen, *Stephen A. Douglas* (N.Y., 1973), 200-03, 225-36, 251-53, 300-03.

2 *Congressional Globe*, 33rd Cong., 1st. Session, 280-82. The "Appeal" was also published in pamphlet form, and widely distributed throughout the free states. See, *Appeal of the Independent Democrats in Congress, to the People of the United States*, pamphlet, Washington, D.C., 1/19/1854. For further reading on the "Appeal" and its impact see, Blue, "The Ohio Free Soilers," 31; Eric Foner, *Free Soil, Free Labor, Free Men*, 94-95, 126; Julian, *The Life of Giddings*, 311; Cavanagh, 83.

3 *Chicago Tribune*, 5/7/1857.

4 *Congressional Globe*, 36th Cong., 2nd. Session, Appendix, 252.

5 *Missouri Democrat*, 8/30/1858; *Congressional Globe*, 36th Cong., 1st. Session, 39, 921.

6 John Sherman, *Recollections of Forty Years in the House, Senate and Cabinet* (Chicago, 1895), vol. 1, 141.

7 *Congressional Globe*, 35th Cong., 1st. Session, 445; 36th Cong., 1st. Session, 1166.

8 Foulke, 72. See also, Charles M. Walker, *Sketch of the Life, Character and Public Services of Oliver P. Morton* (Indianapolis, 1878), 23-25; Henry Smith Lane Speech at Indianapolis, Indiana, 7/13/1855, Henry Smith Lane Collection, Lilly Library, Indiana University; Van Bolt, 207. During the formation of the Republican Party in Indiana, the members called themselves the "People's Party," and many former Indiana Whigs, such as Lane, joined that party. Most of these early

Republicans were conservative on the slavery issue. See, Van Bolt, 204, 209; *Indianapolis Daily Journal*, 6/4,19,20,21,23/1856; Barringer, 2-3, 20, 24-25, 63; Sharp, 98, 104, 111; Foulke, 42.

9   Jesse K. Dubois to Trumbull, 4/4/1860, Lyman Trumbull Papers, Library of Congress.

10   *Congressional Globe*, 34th Cong., 3rd. Session, 13.

11   *Chicago Daily Democrat*, 5/13/1857.

12   *Congressional Globe*, 36th Cong., 2nd. Session, 100-04.

13   Ibid., Appendix, 86; Benjamin F. Shaw, "Owen Lovejoy, Constitutional Abolitionist and the Republican Party," *Transactions of the McLean County Historical Society*, vol. 3, 1900, 62, 67, 71; Edward Magdol, "Owen Lovejoy's Role in the Campaign of 1858," *Journal of the Illinois State Historical Society*, vol. 51, 1958, 410, 413.

14   Warden, 366-67; Chase to Hon. Henry Wilson, 12/13/1860, Chase Papers, Library of Congress; Peter F. Walker, *Moral Choices*, 311; Porter, 18; Donnal V. Smith, *Chase and Civil War Politics* (Columbus, Ohio, 1931), 5. In 1855 Chase was a personal friend of the conservative Blair family, and they were favorable to his nomination for the Republican Party presidential candidate in 1856. Francis Preston Blair Sr. of Maryland presided over the first National Republican Convention at Pittsburgh, on February 22, 1856. See, Reinhard H. Luthin, "Salmon P. Chase's Political Career before the Civil War," *Mississippi Valley Historical Review*, vol. 29, 1943, 524-26; Mary Karl George, *Zachariah Chandler* (East Lansing, Mich., 1969) 11.

15   J. McKibben to Trumbull, 12/26/1859, Trumbull Papers, Library of Congress.

16   Jeff L. Drigger to Trumbull, 2/26/1856, Trumbull Papers, Library of Congress. For similar sentiments see, H. Barber to Trumbull, 1/30/1856; G. T. Brown to Trumbull, 3/29/1856; Orville H. Browning to Trumbull, 5/19/1856, Trumbull Papers, Library of Congress.

17   Caleb B. Smith to Lincoln, 10/10/1860, David Davis Collection.

18   Edward Younger, *John A. Kasson* (Iowa City, Iowa, 1955), 95. See also, Sparks, "The Birth of the Republican Party in Iowa, 1848-1860," 248.

19   Henry B. Carrington, "Early History of the Republican Party in Ohio," *Ohio Archaeological and Historical Quarterly*, vol. 2, 1889, 327-31; Barringer, 66-67, 71-72; Going, 486.

20   *Letter of Francis P. Blair Esq. to the Republican Association of Washington,*

D.C., 12/10/1855, pamphlet, Washington, D.C., 1855, 1-8; Lewis Clephane, *Birth of the Republican Party* (Washington, D.C., 1889), 12-13; Elbert B. Smith, *Francis Preston Blair* (N.Y., 1980), 220-21, 265; Malcolm Moos, *The Republicans, A History of their Party* (N.Y., 1956), 22, 39, 42.

21   Moos, 42.

22   Frank Blair to Montgomery Blair, 10/15/1859, Blair Collection, State Historical Society of Missouri; William E. Smith, vol. 1, 372, 401, 439, 450, 456, 462, 479.

23   Baxter, 84-85; Pease and Randall, xviii, 237; Colfax to Alfred Wheeler, 1/13/1856, Schyler Colfax Papers, Library of Congress; Willard H. Smith, 115-17; Younger, 95; Sparks, "The Birth of the Republican Party in Iowa, 1848-1860," 248; Cain, *Lincoln's Attorney General*, 104-06.

24   Charles Zimmerman, "The Origin and Rise of the Republican Party in Indiana, from 1854 to 1860," *Indiana Magazine of History*, vol. 13, 1917, 393.

25   Paul Selby, *Genesis of the Republican Party in Illinois*, pamphlet, n.d., 6, Alfred Whital Stem Collection of Lincolniana, Library of Congress.

26   *Indianapolis Daily Journal*, 3/8/1860, 9/6,15,27,29/1860, 10/1,6,16/1860, 5/19/1860, 6/22/1860; Emma Lou Thornbrough, "The Race Issue in Indiana Politics during the Civil War," *Indiana Magazine of History*, vol. 47, 1951, 167-69, 175.

27   J.C. Sloe to Trumbull, 4/18/1856, Trumbull Papers, Library of Congress.

28   Shaw, 62, 67, 71.

29   *Congressional Globe*, 33rd Cong., 1st. Session, Appendix, 680.

30   Ibid., 34th Cong., 1st. Session, Appendix. 1187.

31   William E. Smith, vol. 1, 372.

32   *New York Tribune*, 10/25/1856.

33   Robert W. Johannsen, *Frontier Politics and the Sectional Conflict: The Pacific Northwest on the Eve of the Civil War* (Seattle, Wash., 1955), 24, 28-29, 34, 37-38, 46-47, 76-77, 91-93.

34   *Congressional Globe*, 35th Cong., 1st. Session, 774-75. Republicans James G. Blair of Missouri and Congressman David Kilgore of Indiana agreed with Tompkins. See, the *Chicago Tribune* 5/6/1857; *Congressional Globe*, 35th Cong., 1st. Session, 83. Historian Bernard Mandel writes that "while some of the Republicans expressed the hope that the triumph of free labor would also result in striking the shackles from the slaves, most of them made

no pretence of being concerned with the fate of the Negroes." Historian William E. Gienapp writes that "Republican strategists were acutely aware that concern for the welfare of blacks, free or slave, had never been a strong sentiment in the free states." See, Mandel, 149; Gienapp, "The Crime Against Sumner: The Caning of Charles Sumner and the Rise of the Republican Party," *Civil War History*, vol. 25, 1979, 231-34.

35   *Congressional Globe*, 36th Cong., 1st. Session, 73-74.

36   Sparks, "The Birth of the Republican Party in Iowa, 1848-1860," 252. Grimes was certain that "abolition sentiments . . . would assure Republican defeat in December."

37   *Congressional Globe*, 36th Cong., 1st. Session, 1629, 1632.

38   Wesley, "The Participation of Negroes in Anti-Slavery Political Parties," 72.

39   *Congressional Globe*, 36th Cong., 1st. Session, appendix, 135.

40   Sherman, vol. 1, 112, 141, 182, 234.

41   Eli Thayer, *The New England Emigrant Aid Company* (Worcester, Mass., 1887), 10-12, 20.

42   Woodburn, 283-85.

43   Willard L. King, 107, 158.

44   *New York Tribune*, 3/31/1849; Thayer, *The New England Emigrant Aid Company*, 10-12, 20.

45   *Missouri Democrat*, 1/10/1859.

46   *Illinois State Journal*, Springfield, Ill., 2/25/1857; *Chicago Tribune*, 2/21/1857.

47   *Missouri Democrat*, 12/21/1859.

48   *New York Evening Post*, 9/20/1856. See also, Tinsley Lee Spraggins, "Economic Aspects of Negro Colonization During the Civil War," Ph.D. dissertation, American University, Washington, D. C., 1957, 48; Elbert B. Smith, 233. Francis Preston Blair and the Blair family's influence and importance in the Lincoln administration remained strong, right through the war years. See, Francis P. Blair to Lincoln, 1/14/1861, Robert Todd Lincoln Collection, Library of Congress; A. Lincoln to M. Blair, 11/2/1863, Lincoln Papers, Illinois Survey Collection; *House Executive Document* No. 80, 38th Cong., 1st. Session, 1-3.

49   *Congressional Globe*, 35th Cong., 1st. Session, 8; Trumbull to J.B. Turner, 10/19/1857, Trumbull Papers, Illinois Survey Collection; *Missouri Democrat*,

7/4/1857, 8/18/1858. See also, Mandel, 149-50; Mildred C. Stoler, "Influence of the Democratic Element in the Republican Party of Illinois and Indiana, 1854-1860," Ph.D. Dissertation, Indiana University, 1938, 89, 93, 99; Arthur H. Robertson, "The Political Career of Lyman Trumbull," M.A. thesis, University of Chicago, 1910, 19, 36-38; Mark M. Krug, "Lyman Trumbull and the Real Issues in the Lincoln-Douglas Debates," *Illinois State Historical Society Journal*, vol., 57, 1964, 387.

50 *Missouri Democrat*, 11/20/1859. See also, Victor B. Howard, "Cassius Clay and the Origins of the Republican Party," *Filson Club History Quarterly,* vol. 45, 1971, 58-59, 61-64, 68; Smiley, 168-69.

51 Clay to Rev. James S. Davis, 10/8/1857, as quoted in C. M. Clay, Memoirs, 235.

52 *Congressional Globe*, 36th Cong., 1st. Session, 824, 912, 1618.

53 Rawley, 147.

54 *Congressional Globe*, 34th Cong., 1st. Session, 1520-21.

55 *Illinois State Journal*, 2/25/1857; *Chicago Tribune*, 2/21/1857.

56 *Congressional Globe*, 35th Cong., 1st. Session, 8; 34th Cong., 3rd. Session, Appendix, 91; Trumbull to J. B. Turner, 10/19/1857, Trumbull Papers, Illinois Survey Collection.

57 William H. Herndon to Trumbull, 4/24/1856, Trumbull Papers, Library of Congress.

58 Lincoln's Speech at Charleston, Illinois, 9/18/1858, as quoted in Basler, vol. 3, 145-79. See also, the *Portage County Democrat*, Ravenna, Ohio, 11/3/1858; Quarles, *Lincoln and the Negro*, 36; Rozett, 108; Gossett, 254; Cox, *Lincoln's Negro Policy*, 42-43; Cox, *The South's Part in Mongrelizing the Nation*, (Richmond, Va., 1926), 38.

59 *Congressional Globe*, 36th Cong., 1st. Session, 525.

60 C. M. Clay, *The Life of Cassius Marcellus Clay*, 83, 208.

61 Lincoln's Speech at Charleston, Ill., 9/18/1858, as quoted in Basler, vol. 3, 145-79.

62 *Missouri Democrat*, 8/18/1858.

63 *Congressional Globe*, 36th Cong., 1st. Session, 1585.

64 Ibid., 34th Cong., 1st. Session, Appendix, 274-75. See also, V. Jacque Voegeli, "The Northwest and the Race Issue, 1861-1862," *Mississippi Valley Historical Review,* vol. 50, 1963, 245.

65   *Congressional Globe*, 36th Cong., 1st. Session, Appendix, 270, 356-57.

66   Ibid., 35th Cong., 1st. Session, 1089, 2nd. Session, 1080-81.

67   *Missouri Democrat*, 10/15/1859.

68   Ibid., 11/13/1857.

69   *Congressional Globe*, 34th Cong., 1st. Session, Appendix, 868.

70   James Harlan, *Shall the Territories be Africanized?*, pamphlet, n.p., 1860, 6.

71   *Congressional Globe*, 36th Cong., 1st. Session, 1684.

72   Ibid., 35th Cong., 1st. Session, 293-98; 34th Cong., 1st. Session, Appendix, 791, 1203; 36th Cong., 2nd. Session, Appendix, 256. See also, Frank Blair, *Colonization and Commerce, An Address Before the Young Men's Mercantile Library Association of Cincinnati, Ohio*, pamphlet, Washington, D. C., 1859, 2; James D. McCabe Jr., *The Life and Public Services of Horatio Seymour, Together with a Complete and Authentic Life of Francis P. Blair Jr.* (N.Y., 1868), 312; William E. Smith, vol. 1, 443; Elbert B. Smith, 246.

73   *New York Herald*, 4/16/1860; *Congressional Globe*, 35th Cong., 2nd. Session, Appendix, 198. See also, Fredrickson, "A Man but Not a Brother," 51.

74   *Congressional Globe*, 34th Cong., 1st. Session, Appendix, 274-75. See also, Voegeli, "The Northwest and the Race Issue," 245.

75   *Congressional Globe*, 35th Cong., 2nd. Session, 944. See also, Samuel Nott, *Slavery and the Remedy* (N.Y., 1969, originally published in 1859), xxxi.

76   *Congressional Globe*, 35th Cong., 1st. Session, Appendix, 336.

77   Ibid., 34th Cong., 1st. Session, Appendix, 553-55; 35th Cong., 1st. Session, Appendix, 399.

78   *Missouri Democrat*, 7/7/1858.

79   *Colonization Society of Iowa Annual Report*, 1857, pamphlet, Iowa City, Iowa, 1857, 5, 7-10.

80   *Congressional Globe*, 36th Cong., 1st. Session, 225.

81   Ibid., 35th Cong., 2nd. Session, 1334-38.

82   Ibid., 34th Cong., 1st. Session, Appendix 274-75.

83   *Colonization Society of Iowa Annual Report*, 1857, 5, 7-10. Frank Blair insisted that "they [blacks] have not the energy, knowledge or means of the white man." See, *Missouri Democrat*, 12/1/1859.

84   *Congressional Globe*, 36th Cong., 1st. Session, 145-46.

85   Ibid., 33rd Cong., 2nd. Session, Appendix, 325.

86   *Missouri Democrat*, 8/2/1860.

87   *Congressional Globe*, 35th Cong., 2nd. Session, 265.

88   Ibid., 36th Cong., 1st. Session, Appendix, 45, 55-57.

89   *Missouri Democrat*, 7/23/1860.

90   *Congressional Globe*, 35th Cong., 1st. Session, 83.

91   Louis Krouskopf to Frederick Hassaurek, March, 1860, Frederick Hassaurek Collection, Ohio Historical Society.

92   *Congressional Globe*, 35th Cong., 1st. Session, 83.

93   Ibid., 2nd. Session, 944.

94   Ibid., 36th Cong., 1st. Session, Appendix, 45.

95   Ibid., 270, 356-57.

96   *Chicago Tribune*, 5/7/1857.

97   *Congressional Globe*, 35th Cong., 1st. Session, Appendix, 401.

98   *Missouri Democrat*, 1/10/1859.

99   Ibid., 11/13/1857.

100   *Congressional Globe*, 36th Cong., 1st. Session, 145-46.

101   Ibid., 34th Cong., 1st. Session, Appendix, 274-75.

102   Ibid., 36th Cong., 1st. Session, 1629, 1632, 1685.

103   Ibid., Appendix, 136, 149.

104   Ibid., 35th Cong., 2nd. Session, 985.

105   Ibid., 38th Cong., 1st. Session, 1979.

106   Cain, *Lincoln's Attorney General*, 99-100, 104-05, 212.

107   *Missouri Democrat*, 12/22/1859; A. Ballinger to Trumbull, 12/18/1860, Trumbull Papers, Library of Congress.

108   Frank Blair, *The Destiny of the Races of This Continent, An Address before the Mercantile Library Association*, Boston, pamphlet, Washington, D. C. 1859, 24-38; *Missouri Democrat*, 10/9/1860; Elbert B. Smith, 252.

109   *Congressional Globe*, 36th cong., 1st. Session, Appendix, 55-57.

110   Ibid., 369, 373-77; Riddle, *Life of Benjamin Wade*, 230-31. See also, Simms, 130.

111   *Missouri Democrat*, 11/13/1857.

112   Howard K. Beale, ed., *The Dairy of Edward Bates, 1859-1866* (Washington, D. C., 1933), 1, 14; Luthin, *The First Lincoln Campaign*, 59, 65.

113   Elias Nason and Thomas Russell, *The Life and Public Services of Henry Wilson* (N.Y., 1969, originally published in 1876), 278-79.

114 Frank Blair, *Colonization and Commerce*, 1-8. See also, the *Missouri Democrat*, 12/1/1859.

115 *Congressional Globe*, 36th Cong., 1st. Session, Appendix, 206.

116 Zachariah Chandler, An Outline Sketch of his Life and Public Services, published by the *Detroit Post and Tribune* office, Detroit, Mich., 1880, 122-23.

117 Hansen, 385-87, 389-90.

118 C. J. Warren, *Freedom's Songs for 1856* (N.Y., 1856), 20-21.

119 *Congressional Globe*, 35th Cong., 1st. Session, 1269.

120 Ibid., 34th Cong., 1st. Session, Appendix, 553-55, 2nd. Session, 86; 35th Cong., 1st. Session, Appendix, 399.

121 Ibid., 36th Cong., 1st. Session, 145-46.

122 Ibid., 35th Cong., 1st. Session, Appendix, 333.

123 *Missouri Democrat,* 4/8/1858, 10/9/1860.

124 Republicans often used the term Anglo-Saxon loosely. They did not necessarily mean just those Americans of English ancestry, as the term, in its strictest sense, would signify. For many, the term also meant German Americans, or Teutons (from whom the Anglo-Saxons supposedly originated), and Irish Americans, or Celts (believed to be closely related to the English). See, Klipstein, 35-42; Parker, *The World of Matter*, vol. 6, 349-50; Frothingham, *Parker*, 466-76; Haven, 548; Gossett, 181.

125 *Congressional Globe*, 34th Cong., 1st. Session, Appendix, 274-75; 36th Cong., 1st. Session, 1679-84.

126 Frank Blair, *Colonization and Commerce*, 1-8. See also, the *Missouri Democrat*, 12/1/1859; *Congressional Globe*, 35th Cong., 1st. Session, 296.

127 *Congressional Globe*, 34th cong., 1st. Session, Appendix, 274-75; 36th Cong., 1st. Session, 1679-84.

128 Frank Blair, *Colonization and Commerce*, 1-8; *Missouri Democrat*, 12/1/1859; *Congressional Globe*, 34th Cong., 1st. Session, Appendix, 274-75; 35th Cong., 1st. Session, 296; 36th Cong., 1st. Session, 1679-84.

129 *Zachariah Chandler, An Outline Sketch of his Life and Public Services*, 108, 112.

130 *New York Tribune*, 8/14/1858.

131 *Congressional Globe*, 36th Cong., 1st. Session, Appendix, 369.

132 Ibid., 36th Cong., 1st. Session, 405.

133   Thornbrough, *The Negro in Indiana*, 84-85, 90, 127, 181; Willis D. Boyd, "Negro Colonization in the National Crisis, 1860-1870," Ph.D. dissertation, University of California at Los Angeles, 1953, 144-46.

134   Frederic Bancroft, *Speeches, Correspondence and Political Papers of Carl Schurz* (N.Y., 1913), vol. 1, 54-57; Edward M. Burns, *The American Idea of Mission; Concepts of National Purpose and Destiny* (New Brunswick, N.J., 1957), 203. One of Schurz's political idols was Henry Clay, and Schurz published a biography of Clay in 1887. See, Carl Schurz, *Life of Henry Clay*, (Cambridge, Mass., 1892, originally published in 1887).

135   Boom, 176, 193, 208.

136   *Congressional Globe*, 35th Cong., 2nd. Session, 474.

137   Ibid., 36th Cong., 2nd. Session, 98-100.

138   Ibid., 35th Cong., 1st. Session, 294, 298.

139   *Missouri Democrat*, 7/23/1860.

140   Ibid., 12/1/1859; *Congressional Globe*, 36th Cong., 1st. Session, Appendix, 388; 35th Cong., 1st. Session, 480; Sherman, vol. 1, 150-51.

141   Thayer, *The New England Emigrant Aid Company,* 10-12, 20-25, 40-47; *Congressional Globe*, 35th Cong., 1st. Session, 227.

142   *Congressional Globe*, 35th Cong., 1st. Session, 1029.

143   Ibid., 34th Cong., 1st. Session, Appendix, 274-75; 36th Cong., 1st. Session, 1679-84.

144   Frederic Bancroft, vol. 1, 54-57.

145   *Missouri Democrat*, 3/21/1859; *Congressional Globe*, 35th Cong., 1st. Session, 964.

146   *Congressional Globe*, 35th Cong., 2nd. Session, 944; Samuel Nott, xxxi.

147   Ibid., 34th Cong., 3rd. Session, Appendix, 47.

148   Frank Blair, *Destiny of the Races*, 12-16.

149   W. D. Haley to Trumbull, 2/4/1856, Trumbull Papers, Library of Congress.

150   Thayer, *The New England Emigrant Aid Company,* 10-12, 20-25, 40-47; *Congressional Globe*, 35th Cong., 1st. Session, 227.

151   *Congressional Globe*, 34th Cong., 1st. Session, Appendix, 274-75.

152   Emerson D. Fite, *The Presidential Campaign of 1860* (N.Y., 1911), 227.

153   *Congressional Globe*, 34th Cong., 1st. Session, Appendix, 1187.

154   Ibid., 33rd Cong., 1st. Session, Appendix, 1007.

155   Ibid., 35th Cong., 1st. Session, Appendix, 171-72.

156   J. S. Cole to Trumbull, 12/27/1859, Trumbull Papers, Library of Congress.

157   *Congressional Globe*, 36th Cong., 1st. Session, 1584.

158   *Missouri Democrat*, 1/10/1859.

159   *Congressional Globe*, 38th Cong., 1st. Session, 1979.

160   Sherman, vol. 1, 150-51; *Congressional Globe*, 35th Cong., 1st. Session, 480.

161   F. W. Jones to Trumbull, 12/26/1860, Trumbull Papers, Library of Congress.

162   *Missouri Democrat*, 7/3/1860.

163   Louis Krouskopf to Frederick Hassaurek, March, 1860.

164   *Congressional Globe*, 36th Cong., 1st. Session, Appendix, 45.

165   Lincoln's Speech at Bloomington, Ill., 9/4/1858, as quoted in Basler, vol. 3,
       88-89.

166   *Congressional Globe*, 33rd Cong., 1st. Session, Appendix, 418; 34th Cong.,
       1st. Session, Appendix, 1173.

167   Ibid., 35th Cong., 2nd. Session, 967; *Missouri Democrat*, 3/21/1859.

168   *Zachariah Chandler, An Outline Sketch of his Life and Public Services*, 122-
       23.

169   *Congressional Globe*, 35th Cong., 2nd. Session, Appendix, 199.

170   Ibid., 34th Cong., 1st. Session, Appendix, 554.

171   James Hugo Johnston, *Race Relations in Virginia and Miscegenation in the
       South, 1776-1860* (Amherst, Mass., 1970), 180-84, 255-56; James Kinney,
       *Amalgamation! Race, Sex and Rhetoric in the Nineteenth Century American
       Novel*(Westport, Conn., 1985), 12.

172   A. Ballinger to Trumbull, 2/16/1860, Trumbull Papers, Library of Congress.

173   *Chicago Tribune*, 2/21/1857; *Illinois State Journal*, 2/25/1857.

174   C. M. Clay, *The Life of Cassius Marcellus Clay*, 208.

175   Robert F. Horowitz, *The Great Impeacher, A Political Biography of James
       M. Ashley* (N.Y., 1979), 36-37.

176   *Illinois State Journal*, 6/29/1857; *Missouri Democrat*, 9/20/1859.

177   *Illinois State Journal*, 6/29/1857.

178   Frank Blair, *Colonization and Commerce*, 1-8; *Congressional Globe*, 35th
       Cong., 1st. Session, 293-98.

179   William Kitchell to Trumbull, 1/1/1860, Trumbull Papers, Library of
       Congress.

180   Frank Blair, *Colonization and Commerce*, 1-8; Blair, *Destiny of the Races*,
       4, 6, 12-17, 22-25; *Congressional Globe*, 35th Cong., 1st. Session, 293-98.

181 *Congressional Globe*, 36th Cong., 1st. Session, 1906; Voegeli, "The Northwest and the Race Issue," 245.

182 *New York Herald,* 4/16/1860.

183 *Congressional Globe*, 36th Cong., 1st. Session, Appendix 369, 373-77.

184 Ibid., 424. Historian Joel Williamson notes the following: "During the decade of the 1850's slavery was becoming whiter, visibly so and with amazing rapidity." See, Joel Williamson, *New People, Miscegenation and Mulattoes in the United States* (N.Y., 1980), 63-67.

185 *Congressional Globe*, 34th Cong., 1st. Session, Appendix, 553-55.

186 Ibid., 35th Cong., 1st. Session, Appendix, 399.

187 Ibid., 36th Cong., 1st. Session, 1585.

188 Ibid., Appendix, 369, 373-77.

189 Ibid., 36th Cong., 1st. Session, 145-46.

190 Ibid., Appendix 369, 373-77.

191 *Missouri Democrat,* 8/18/1858.

192 Frank Blair, *Colonization and Commerce,* 1-8; Blair, *Destiny of the Races,* 4, 6, 12-17, 22-25, 27-28. See also, the *Missouri Democrat,* 2/7/1859, 12/1/1859.

193 *Missouri Democrat,* 11/20/1859.

194 Lincoln's Speech at Carlinville, Ill., 8/13/1858, and at Clinton, Ill., 9/2/1858, as quoted in Basler, vol. 3, 80, 84; *Illinois State Journal,* 6/29/1857; *Missouri Democrat,* 9/20/1859. See also, Rozett, 106-07; Ronald Takaki, "The Black Child Savage," in Nash and Weiss, 35.

195 *Congressional Globe,* 36th Cong., 1st. Session, Appendix, 417.

196 Ibid.

197 Ibid., 36th Cong., 1st. Session, 1906; Voegeli, "The Northwest and the Race Issue," 245.

198 *Congressional Globe*, 36th Cong., 1st. Session, Appendix, 417. For an excellent study of black slaveholders in the South, see, Carter Woodson, *Free Negro Owners of Slaves in the United States in 1830, Together with Absentee Ownership of Slaves in the United States in 1830* (Washington, D. C. 1924).

199 *Congressional Globe*, 36th Cong., 1st. Session, 1906; Voegeli, "The Northwest and the Race Issue," 245.

200 *New York Herald,* 4/16/1860.

201   *Congressional Globe*, 36th Cong., 1st. Session, Appendix, 369, 373-77.

202   Ibid., 34th Cong., 1st. Session, Appendix, 414.

203   Eli Thayer, *A History of the Kansas Crusade, Its Friends and Its Foes* (N.Y.,
      1889), 243.

204   *Congressional Globe*, 35th Cong., 1st. Session, 83.

205   Ibid., 33rd Cong., 1st. Session, Appendix, 157.

206   *Missouri Democrat*, 7/20/1859.

207   Ibid., 8/2/1860.

208   Henry Doolittle to Father, 1/25/1860, Doolittle Papers, Wisconsin State
      Historical Society.

209   *Congressional Globe*, 36th Cong., 1st. Session, Appendix, 369, 373-77.

210   Ibid., 424.

211   Henry Warren Lathrop, *The Life and Times of Samuel J. Kirkwood* (Iowa
      City, Iowa, 1893), 82-83.

212   Fite, 274.

213   Beale, 113, 191-92.

214   *Congressional Globe*, 35th Cong., 1st Session, 293-98; *Missouri Democrat*,
      10/9/1860; McCabe, 312.

215   *Congressional Globe*, 36th Cong., 1st. Session, 145-46; 35th Cong., 2nd.
      Session, 1354.

216   Ibid., 36th Cong., 2nd. Session, Appendix, 75-76.

217   Thayer, *The New England Emigrant Aid Company*, 10-12, 20-25, 40-47;
      Congressional Globe, 35th Cong., 1st. Session, 227.

218   *Congressional Globe*, 38th Cong., 1st. Session, 1979.

219   Beale, 113, 191-92; *Missouri Democrat*, 4/20/1859.

220   *New York Herald*, 4/16/1860; Sherman, vol. 1, 150-51; *Congressional Globe*,
      35th Cong., 1st. Session, 480.

221   *Congressional Globe*, 35th Cong., 1st. Session, 293-98.

222   Beale, 5; *Missouri Democrat*, 4/20/1859.

223   William Kitchell to Trumbull, 1/1/1860, Trumbull Papers, Library of
      Congress.

224   *Congressional Globe*, 36th Cong., 1st. Session, Appendix, 382.

225   Ibid., 1st. Session, 1632.

226   Ibid., 35th Cong., 2nd. Session, 1334-38.

227   Ibid., 1st. Session, 1089, 2nd. Session, 1080-91. While Republicans were

opposed to the acquisition of Cuba, some radical abolitionists were not. Gerrit Smith, for example, favored the annexation of Cuba, but not for the same reason slaveholders did. In fact, he thought such an acquisition would help to end slavery in the United States. One reason Smith advanced for his belief, was that with Cuba under United States control, the Navy could put an end to the illegal slave trade between that island and the Southern states. See, Octavius Brooks Frothingham, *Gerrit Smith, A Biography* (N.Y., 1901), 223-24, 307.

228 George B. Currey to Henry S. Lane, 2/2/1859, Lane Collection.

229 *Congressional Globe*, 36th Cong., 1st. Session, Appendix, 55-57.

230 Sparks, "The Birth of the Republican Party in Iowa, 1848-1860," 200-04.

231 *Congressional Globe*, 36th Cong., 1st. Session, 224-25, Appendix, 270, 356-57. On Southern attempts to reopen the slave trade see, Ronald T. Takaki, *A Pro-Slavery Crusade, The Agitation to Reopen the African Slave Trade* (N.Y., 1971), 230.

232 *Congressional Globe*, 36th Cong., 1st. Session, Appendix, 391.

233 Uriah Mills to Trumbull, 5/11/1856, Trumbull Papers, Library of Congress.

234 William H. Herndon to Trumbull, 7/12/1856, Trumbull Papers, Library of Congress.

235 *Congressional Globe*, 35th Cong., 2nd. Session, 1354. See also, Theodore Clarke Smith, *Parties and Slavery*, 242; Trefousse, *Benjamin Franklin Wade*, 112.

236 *Missouri Democrat*, 7/3/1860.

237 *Congressional Globe*, 36th Cong., 1st. Session, Appendix, 424.

238 *Missouri Democrat*, 10/15/1859, 10/9/1860. Frank Blair accused Southern Democrats of attempting to "hybridize our government . . . should Mr. Buchanan's scheme of amalgamation [through the expansion of slavery into the West] have a beginning." See, Frank Blair, *Destiny of the Races*, 17-20; *Missouri Democrat*, 2/7/1859.

239 *Chicago Tribune*, 4/24/1856.

240 Ibid., 4/3/1855, 7/18/1857.

241 Carl Schurz, *Judge Douglas, The Bill of Indictment, Speech Delivered at the Cooper Institute, New York, September 13, 1860*, pamphlet, Tribune Tract No. 9, N.Y., 1860; *Missouri Democrat*, 9/20/1860.

242 *Congressional Globe*, 35th Cong., 2nd. Session, 301.

243   William Kitchell to Trumbull, 5/25/1856, Trumbull Papers, Library of Congress.

244   Rawley, 167-68.

245   *Congressional Globe*, 36th Cong., 1st. Session, 267.

246   Ibid., Appendix, 424.

247   Ibid., 36th Cong., 1st. Session, 239.

248   William Windom to Alexander Ramsey, 12/9/1859, Alexander Ramsey Papers, Minnesota Historical Society.

249   J. B. Turner to Trumbull, 2/2/1860, Trumbull Papers, Library of Congress.

250   *Missouri Democrat*, 10/15/1859, 10/9/1860.

251   *Congressional Globe*, 35th Cong., 1st. Session, 854.

252   Nason and Russell, 277.

253   C. W. Gibson to Lane, 3/6/1860, Lane Collection.

254   John Kasson to Kirkwood, 7/18/1859, Kirkwood Papers.

255   *Congressional Globe*, 36th Cong., 1st. Session, Appendix, 206.

256   Barringer, 74-75.

257   *Congressional Globe*, 34th Cong., 1st. Session, Appendix, 688-90.

258   *Missouri Democrat*, 7/4/1857, 7/23/1860.

259   Ibid., 10/15/1859, 10/9/1860.

260   *Chicago Daily Democrat*, 11/13/1857.

261   J. T. Knox to Trumbull, 1/4/1858, Trumbull Papers, Library of Congress.

262   *Congressional Globe*, 34th Cong., 1st. Session, Appendix 647; 35th Cong., 1st. Session, 1219; *South Bend Register*, South Bend, Ind., 7/13/1856, 8/7/1856; Edward W. Martin, *The Life and Public Services of Schuyler Colfax* (N.Y., 1868), 320.

263   *Congressional Globe*, 35th Cong., 1st. Session, 774-75.

264   Ibid., 2nd. Session, 1268; 33rd Cong., 1st. Session, Appendix, 680.

265   *Missouri Democrat*, 7/4/1857, 7/23/1860. See also, *Chicago Tribune*, 4/3/1855, 7/2/1857; Frank Blair, *Destiny of the Races*, 27-28; *Congressional Globe*, 36th Cong., 1st Session, 60-61. John W. Geary, the Free Soil territorial governor of Kansas, could not have agreed more with Trumbull; he asserted that the white man, not the black, "should receive the especial protection and support of [the national] government" in Kansas. See, the *Missouri Democrat*, 1/21/1857.

266   Beale, xii; Cain, *Lincoln's Attorney General*, 99.

267 *Detroit Daily Advertiser*, 2/15/1858; Louis Pelzer, "History of Political Parties in Iowa from 1857 to 1860," *Iowa Journal of History and Politics*, vol. 7, 1909, 195-96; Pelzer, ``The Negro and Slavery in Early Iowa," 482; Sparks, ``The Birth of the Republican Party in Iowa, 1848-1860," 133, 142, 157-59.

268 *Congressional Globe*, 36th Cong., 1st. Session, Appendix, 56.

269 F. S. Rutherford to Trumbull, 12/7/1857, Trumbull Papers, Library of Congress.

270 *Congressional Globe*, 35th Cong., 1st. session, 1358.

271 *Missouri Democrat*, 8/18/1858.

272 Ibid., 4/8/1858.

273 Speech of Henry S. Lane, at Richmond, Wayne County, Indiana, 10/13/1859, Lane Collection.

274 Boom, 156.

275 Pelzer, "The Negro and Slavery in Early Iowa," 482.

276 *Missouri Democrat*, 7/4/1857, 8/18/1858.

277 *Illinois State Journal*, 6/29/1857; Lincoln's Speech at Charleston, Ill., 9/18/1858, as quoted in Basler, vol. 3, 145-79.

278 Formisano, 28, 34-39.

279 *Missouri Democrat*, 11/20/1859.

280 *Congressional Globe*, 34th Cong., 1st. Session, Appendix, 475.

281 *Missouri Democrat*, 8/18/1858, 7/23/1860.

282 *Congressional Globe*, 34th Cong. 1st. Session, Appendix, 129, 3rd. Session, Appendix, 91. For further insights into the conservative, racialist appeal of Indiana Republicans, see the *Indianapolis Daily Journal*, 3/8/1860, 5/19/1860, 6/22/1860, 9/6,15,27,29/1860, 10/1,6,16/1860.

283 *Chicago Tribune*, 4/15/1856.

284 Formisano, 28, 34-39.

285 *Congressional Globe*, 34th Cong., 1st. Session, Appendix, 365.

286 Stanley, 171, 173-74, 180, 182-84, 186-87; Boom, 136.

287 George P. Eisenmayer to Trumbull, 4/12/1856, Trumbull Papers, Library of Congress. See also, E. W. Downer to Trumbull, 8/5/1856; W. H. Gray to Trumbull, 9/12/1857; J. Miller to Trumbull, 9/12/1857; C. H. Kettler to Trumbull, 9/14/1857; E. J. Tishenor to Trumbull, 2/22/1858, Trumbull Papers, Library of Congress.

288   S. T. Glover to Browning, 6/13/1860, Orville Hickman Browning Letters, Illinois Survey Collection.

289   William H. Herndon to Trumbull, 2/15/1856. See also, 6/16/1856, 7/12/1856, 8/4,11/1856, 2/17/1857, 3/4/1857, 2/5,19/1858, 2/5,26/1859, Trumbull Papers, Library of Congress.

290   *Congressional Globe*, 35th Cong., 2nd. Session 1354.

291   Charles Billinghurst to Potter, 2/21/1860, John Fox Potter Collection, Wisconsin State Historical Society. In neighboring Minnesota, one local Republican wrote to Henry Sibley, a leading Republican politician from that state, asking for help, so that, by ridding his area of Democrats, "we could clean out Niggerism in Olmsted, 'root and branch.'" See, C. W. Cattom to Sibley, 9/8/1858, Henry M. Sibley Letters, Minnesota Historical Society.

292   *Detroit Daily Advertiser*, 11/3/1860.

293   Circular Letter, Republican Party, 9/3/1857, as quoted in William Salter, *Life of James W. Grimes* (N.Y., 1876), 101.

294   *Missouri Democrat*, 9/7/1860. See also, Jerome Dowd, *The Negro in American Life* (N.Y., 1926), 488; T. T. Munford, *Virginia's Attitude Towards Slavery and Secession* (N.Y., 1909), 167.

295   *Missouri Democrat*, 8/18/1858.

296   *Congressional Globe*, 36th Gong., 2nd. Session, Appendix, 256; Riddle, *Life of Benjamin Wade*, 230-31; Simms, 130; Robert F. Durden, "Ambiguities in the Antislavery Crusade of the Republican Party," as quoted in Martin Duberman, ed., *The Antislavery Vanguard, New Essays on the Abolitionists* (Princeton, N.J., 1965), 363-64.

297   *Missouri Democrat*, 7/20/1859, 12/1/1859; *Congressional Globe*, 35th Cong., 1st. Session, 293-98; Frank Blair to James R. Doolittle, 10/15/1859, Doolittle Papers, Library of Congress; McCabe, 303-04; William E. Smith, vol., 1, 450.

298   Nason and Russell, 279. See also, Richard H. Abbott, *Cobbler in Congress, The Life of Henry Wilson, 1812-1875* (Lexington, KY., 1972), 70.

299   *Congressional Globe*, 35th Cong., 1st. Session, 854.

300   Ibid., 33rd Cong., 1st. Session, Appendix, 579.

301   *Colonization Society of Iowa Annual Report*, 1857, 5, 7-10.

302   Fite, 274.

303   *Congressional Globe*, 36th Cong., 1st. Session, Appendix, 441.

304   *New York Herald*, 4/16/1860.

305   *Missouri Democrat*, 7/20/1859, 10/9/1860; Luthin, *The First Lincoln Campaign*, 53-54.

306   *Congressional Globe,* 36th Cong., 2nd. Session, Appendix, 275.

307   Ibid., 35th Cong., 1st. Session, 229.

308   *Missouri Democrat*, 1/21/1857.

309   *Congressional Globe*, 36th Cong., 1st. Session, 913.

310   F. R. Payne to Trumbull, 1/14/1860, Trumbull Papers, Library of Congress.

311   *Congressional Globe*, 36th Cong., 1st. Session, 145-46.

312   Ibid., Appendix, 270, 356-57.

313   Frank Blair, *Colonization and Commerce*, 1-8; *Missouri Democrat*, 8/2/ 1858, 10/9/1860. See also, McCabe, 311-17; William E. Smith, vol. 1, 308.

314   *Congressional Globe*, 35th Cong., 1st. Session, 1269.

315   Ibid., 34th Cong., 1st. Session, Appendix, 553-55; 35th Cong., 1st. Session, Appendix, 399.

316   *Chicago Tribune*, 5/7/1857; Rawley, 147.

317   *Chicago Tribune*, 4/3/1855, 7/2/1857; *Missouri Democrat*, 7/23/1860. See also, Frank Blair, *Destiny of the Races*, 27-28; *Congressional Globe*, 36th Cong., 1st. Session, 60-61.

318   Lincoln's Speech at Chicago, Ill., 7/10/1858, as quoted in Logan, 62-63; *Illinois State Journal*, 6/29/1857. See also, Lincoln's Speech at Bloomington, Ill., 9/4/1858, as quoted in Basler, vol. 3, 88-89; *Alton Weekly Courier*, 10/ 14/1858; John S. Wright, 221.

319   *Congressional Globe*, 36th Cong., 1st. Session, Appendix, 391.

320   *Missouri Democrat*, 9/7/1860; Dowd, 488; Munford, 167.

321   *Congressional Globe*, 35th Cong., 1st. Session, 293-98; *Missouri Democrat*,10/9/1860.

322   *Congressional Globe,* 35th Cong., 2nd. Session, 967.

323   Ibid., 36th Cong., 2nd. Session, Appendix, 68; 35th Cong., 1st. Session, 774-75.

324   *New York Herald*, 4/16/1860.

325   *Colonization Society of Iowa Annual Report*, 1857, 5, 7-10.

326   William Kitchell to Trumbull, 1/1/1860, Trumbull Papers, Library of Congress.

327   *Congressional Globe*, 36th Cong., 1st. Session, 60-61; *Missouri Democrat*, 8/30/1858.

NOTES—CHAPTER 5

1   *Congressional Globe*, 36th Cong., 1st. Session, 1629, 1632.

2   Hubbart, 114. As noted previously, the states of Ohio, Indiana and Illinois early on had black codes which, among other things denied blacks the right to vote.

3   McLaughlin, "Popular Reactions," 55, 59-60, 62, 79-80, 117-21.

4   Formisano, 28, 34-39.

5   Earl Spangler, *The Negro in Minnesota* (Minneapolis, Minn., 1961), 38.

6   William H. Herndon to Trumbull, 2/17/1857, 3/4/1857, Trumbull Papers, Library of Congress.

7   *Congressional Globe*, 35th Cong., 2nd. Session, 986.

8   V. W. Kingsley to Doolittle, 1/26/1860, James R. Doolittle Papers, New York Public Library.

9   *Congressional Globe*, 34th Cong., 1st. Session, Appendix, 868.

10   Ibid., 35th Cong., 2nd. Session, Appendix, 109.

11   Ibid., 36th Cong., 1st. Session, 1679-84, Appendix, 55-57. As noted, many fellow Republicans felt the same way as Harlan. In 1858, Lincoln specified what he meant by inequality: he stated that he was "not [now] nor ever . . . in favor of making voters or jurors of negroes, nor of qualifying them to hold office, nor to intermarry with white people." William W. Orme, another Illinois Republican, and a close friend of Lincoln and David Davis, rejected the Democratic charge "that the [Republican] party is in favor of negro equality." He called such allegations "simply absurd." Orme stated unequivocally, that "if the Republican party was in favor of negroes having equal rights with white men, it is a singular mode of bringing about that end, by prohibiting the intermingling of the two races." Trumbull asserted that "we [Republicans] deny to the negro equal political and civil rights." Finally, Edward Bates said that the very "idea of making the Negro the [political and social] equal of the white appalled him." See, Basler, vol. 3, 145-79; Speech of William W. Orme, 1860, William W. Orme Papers, Illinois Survey Collection; *Congressional Globe*, 36th Cong., 1st. Session, 39, 921; Beale, xii, 1, 141; Cain, *Lincoln's Attorney General*, 99-100, 104-05, 212; Luthin, *The First Lincoln Campaign*, 59, 65.

12   *Congressional Globe*, 35th Cong., 2nd. Session, 346.

13   Rawley, 167-68.

14   *Congressional Globe*, 35th Cong., 1st. Session, 2207.

15   Ibid., 1966; 36th Cong., 2nd. Session, 104, 1633; Riddle, *The Life of Benjamin Wade*, 230-31; Erlich, 143, 169. Using the example of Oregon, historian Robert W. Johannsen writes that the "people in Oregon had no desire to furnish a refuge for the Negro in any condition [slave or free]," because Oregonians were "intending to build up their state on a white basis." See, Johannsen, 24, 28-29, 34, 37-38, 46-47, 76-77, 91-93.

16   Sparks, "The Birth of the Republican Party in Iowa, 1848-1860," 173.

17   Thornbrough, "The Race Issue in Indiana Politics," 167-69, 175; Thornbrough, *The Negro in Indiana Before 1900*, 84-85, 90, 127, 181.

18   *Congressional Globe*, 36th Cong., 1st. Session, 1903.

19   A. Ballinger to Trumbull, 12/18/1860, Trumbull Papers, Library of Congress.

20   Orville Leston to Trumbull, 1857, Trumbull Papers, Library of Congress.

21   Speech of Lyman Trumbull at Chicago, 8/7/1858, as quoted in Frank Blair, *Destiny of the Races,* 29-30; *Congressional Globe*, 36th Cong., 1st. Session, 60-61; *Missouri Democrat*, 8/18/1858. See also, Stoler, 89, 93, 99; Krug, *Lyman Trumbull, Conservative Radical*, 152; John S. Wright, 237; Robertson, 19, 36-38.

22   *Congressional Globe*, 35th Cong., 1st. Session, 293-98; *Missouri Democrat*, 10/9/1860.

23   *Cincinnati Commercial*, 8/7/1858.

24   Speech of Henry Smith Lane at Indianapolis, Indiana, 7/13/1855; Speech of Henry Smith Lane at Richmond, Wayne County, Indiana, 10/13/1859, Lane Collection. See also, Van Bolt, 207.

25   *Missouri Democrat*, 2/27/1857; Elbert B. Smith, 240-42.

26   *Cadiz Republican*, Cadiz, Ohio, 1/18/1860.

27   Benton, 694-95. See also, Roosevelt, 147, 261, 295-99.

28   *Congressional Globe*, 35th Cong., 1st. Session, 445; 36th Cong., 1st. Session, 1166.

29   William R. Wilkinson to Trumbull, 9/8/1860, Trumbull Papers, Library of Congress.

30   *Congressional Globe*, 35th Cong., 1st. Session, 1044.

31   Ibid., 83.

32   A. Ballinger to Trumbull, 12/18/1860, Trumbull Papers, Library of Congress.

33 *Congressional Globe,* 36th Cong., 1st. Session, Appendix, 55-57. William Orme reasoned that "if we keep the negroes from the territories and don't suffer them to get in there among the white people, they can't be there to be on an equality with them." See Speech of William W. Orme, 1860, Orme Papers.

34 *Missouri Democrat,* 7/4/1857, 8/18/1858.

35 Jesse K. Dubois to Trumbull, 4/4/1860, Trumbull Papers, Library of Congress.

36 *Congressional Globe*, 36th Cong., 1st. Session, Appendix, 265.

37 Ibid., 35th Cong., 1st. Session, 1006.

38 Sparks, "The Birth of the Republican Party in Iowa, 1848-1860," 159, 173.

39 *Congressional Globe,* 36th Cong., 1st. Session, 1903; Stoler, 177.

40 Frank Blair, *Colonization and Commerce*, 1-8; *Missouri Democrat,* 8/2/1858, 10/9/1860. See also, McCabe, 311-17; William E. Smith, vol. 1, 308.

41 *Cincinnati Commercial*, 8/7/1858. See also, Pendergraft, 11-22.

42 Orville Leston to Trumbull, 1857, Trumbull Papers, Library of Congress.

43 Lincoln's Speech at Chicago, Illinois, 7/10/1858, as quoted in Logan, 62-63; *Illinois State Journal,* 6/29/1857; Lincoln's Speech at Bloomington, Illinois, 9/4/1858, and at Carlinville, Illinois, 8/13/1858, as quoted in Basler, vol. 3, 80-89; *Alton Weekly Courier,* 10/14/1858. See also, John S. Wright, 221. While speaking at Bloomington, Lincoln asked his audience "which party was practically in favor of amalgamation; we [Republicans] who wish to exclude negroes from the territory [Kansas], or those, who wished to mix them in with the whites there?"

44 *Congressional Globe*, 36th Cong., 1st. Session, Appendix, 136, 149.

45 Ibid., 35th Cong., 1st. Session, 8.

46 Ibid., 34th Cong., 1st. Session, Appendix, 432.

47 "Inaugural Address of Governor Walker," n.a., *Transactions of the Kansas State Historical Society*, vol. 5, 1889-1896, 339. See also, Berwanger, *The Frontier Against Slavery*, 105-16; Rawley, 95-98.

48 Doolittle to John Potter, 7/25/1859, Potter Papers.

49 *Congressional Globe*, 34th Cong., 1st. Session, Appendix, 1115.

50 Speech of Lyman Trumbull at Chicago, 8/7/1858, as quoted in Frank Blair, *Destiny of the Races*, 29-30; *Congressional Globe*, 36th Cong., 1st. Session, 60-61; *Missouri Democrat*, 8/18/1858.

51   Benjamin Wade to Orin Follett, 4/13/1856, Orin Follett Papers, Cincinnati Historical Society.

52   *Missouri Democrat*, 10/9/1860.

53   Speech of Henry Smith Lane at Richmond, Wayne County, Indiana, 10/13/1859.

54   Lincoln's Speech at Bloomington, Illinois, 9/4/1858, as quoted in Basler, vol., 3, 88-89.

55   *Letter of Francis P. Blair, Esq. to the Republican Association of Washington, D.C.,* 1-8; Moos, 22, 39, 42.

56   Thayer, *The New England Emigrant Aid Company*, 10-12, 20-25, 40-47; *Congressional Globe*, 35th Cong., 1st. Session, 227-29.

57   *Congressional Globe*, 36th Cong., 1st. Session, 1858.

58   Fite, 124-25, 156, 203, 227, 237-40. See also, J.E. Cairnes, *The Slave Power* (N.Y., 1862), 136.

59   Edward E. Dunbar to Doolittle, 1/5/1859, Doolittle Papers, Wisconsin State Historical Society.

60   *Congressional Globe*, 34th Cong., 3rd. Session, Appendix, 52.

61   *Missouri Democrat*, 9/7/1860.

62   Hawkins Taylor to Kirkwood, 7/21/1859, Samuel J. Kirkwood Papers, Iowa State Department of History and Archives, Des Moines, Iowa.

63   *Congressional Globe*, 36th Cong., 1st. Session, Appendix 55-57.

64   *New York Tribune*, 6/19/1860.

65   *Congressional Globe*, 34th Cong., 1st. Session, Appendix, 365.

66   Ibid., 35th Cong., 2nd. Session, 907, 1351; 36th Cong., 1st. Session, 1629, 1632, Appendix, 126; Doolittle to John Potter, 11/7/1860, Potter Papers; Doolittle to Trumbull, 11/10/1860, Trumbull Papers, Library of Congress; *Racine Advocate*, Racine, Wisconsin, 8/24/1859; *Missouri Democrat*, 3/21/1859, 8/3/1860.

67   *Congressional Globe*, 36th Cong., 1st. Session, Appendix, 215.

68   Ibid., 36th 1st. Session, 39, 921.

69   Ibid., 1873.

70   *Missouri Democrat*, 10/15/1859, 7/3/1860. See also, Cain, *Lincoln's Attorney General*, 99-100, 104-05, 212.

71   *Congressional Globe*, 35th Cong., 1st. Session, 774-75.

72   Ibid., 33rd Cong., 1st. Session, 280-82.

73   *Chicago Tribune*, 4/15/1856; *Missouri Democrat*, 8/3/1860.

74   *Chicago Tribune*, 5/7/1857; Rawley, 147.

75   J.M. Palmer to Trumbull, 12/9/1858, Trumbull Papers, Library of Congress.

76   *Congressional Globe*, 33rd. Cong., 1st. Session, Appendix, 1069.

77   Doolittle to Trumbull, 11/10/1860, Trumbull Papers, Library of Congress; *Congressional Globe*, 35th Cong., 2nd. Session, 1351; 36th Cong., 1st. Session, 1629, 1632; *Racine Advocate*, 8/24/1859; *Missouri Democrat*, 3/21/1859.

78   *Cass County Republican*, Dowagiac, Michigan, 5/31/1860; J. Elaine Thompson, "The Formative Period of the Republican Party in Michigan, 1854-1860," M.A. thesis, Wayne University, 1949, 45, 85-86; Leon F. Litwack, "The Federal Government and the Free Negro, 1790-1860," *Journal of Negro History*, vol. 43, 1958, 268-69.

79   *Missouri Democrat*, 7/26/1860.

80   Joseph G. Rayback, "The American Workingman and the Antislavery Crusade," *Journal of Economic History*, vol. 3, 1943, 162-63.

81   Boom, 176, 193, 208.

82   Francis and Theresa Pulszky, *White Red Black Sketches of Society in the United States* (N.Y., 1853), 196. One means of securing this white population for the West, was through the encouragement of European immigration. For instance, Michigan Republicans not only endorsed homestead legislation, but by appointing an "Agent of Immigration" for the state, whose job it was to "divert to the State the stream of European immigration," took a direct role in securing white immigrants to people Western homesteads. To help achieve that same end, Iowa Republicans called for more liberal naturalization laws. The Republican platform of 1860 called for the same thing. Minnesota Republicans, like Alexander Ramsey, made a special effort to appeal to the immigrant vote. See, Thompson, 85; Sparks, "The Birth of the Republican Party in Iowa, 1848-1860," 200-04; Fite, 240; John C. Haughland, "Alexander Ramsey and the Republican Party, 1855-1875: A Study in Personal Politics," Ph.D. Dissertation, University of Minnesota, 1961, 77-78.

83   *Congressional Globe*, 36th Cong., 1st. Session, Appendix, 57.

84   Ibid., 35th Cong., 2nd. Session, 1354.

85   Sparks, "The Birth of the Republican Party in Iowa, 1848-1860," 200-13.

86   *Missouri Democrat*, 7/20/1859.

87   *Congressional Globe*, 36th Cong., 1st. Session, Appendix, 55-57.

88   Rawley, 125.

89   McGuire, 65.

90   Isaac Lea to Trumbull, 12/26/1860, Trumbull Papers, Library of Congress; Sturtevant, 604-09; *National Cyclopedia*, vol. 13, 601.

91   *Congressional Globe*, 33rd Cong., 2nd. Session, Appendix, 235-37.

92   Ibid., 35th Cong., 1st. Session, Appendix, 298-301.

93   Ibid., 36th Cong., 1st. Session, Appendix, 132.

94   Ibid., 35th Cong., 1st. Session, 1089, 2nd. Session, 1080-81.

95   Lathrop, 82-83; Spraggins, 48.

96   *Congressional Globe*, 36th Cong., 2nd. Session, 104; Riddle, *The Life of Benjamin Wade*, 231-32.

97   Frank Blair, *Colonization and Commerce*, 1-8; Blair, *Destiny of the Races*, 6-7, 22-25; *Congressional Globe*, 35th cong., 1st. Session, 293-98.

98   Doolittle to Hannibal Hamlin, 8/20,29/1859, Hannibal Hamlin Papers, Folger Library, University of Maine; *Congressional Globe*, 35th Cong., 2nd. Session, 907, 967; 36th Cong., 1st. Session 1629, 1632; *Missouri Democrat*, 3/21/1859.

99   *Congressional Globe*, 35th Cong., 2nd. Session, 907, 967; *Missouri Democrat*, 3/21/1859.

100 Frank Blair, *Destiny of the Races*, 24-25; *Missouri Democrat*, 2/7/1859.

101 *Congressional Globe*, 35th Cong., 2nd. Session, 967; Doolittle to Dear Wife, 12/2/1860, Doolittle Papers, Wisconsin State Historical Society.

102 *Missouri Democrat*, 10/9/1860; Frank Blair, *Colonization and Commerce*, 1-8; *Blair, Destiny of the Races*, 4, 6, 12-17, 22-25; *Congressional Globe*, 35th Cong., 1st. Session, 293-98; Frank Blair to Doolittle, 10/15/1859, Doolittle Papers, Library of Congress. See also, *Missouri Democrat*, 1/20/1858, 2/7/1859, 10/9,15/1859, 12/1/1859, 7/16/1860; *Chicago Tribune*, 7/10/1858.

103 *Congressional Globe*, 36th Cong., 1st. Session, 58-61, 102.

104 Ibid., 2nd. Session, 104; Riddle, *The Life of Benjamin Wade*, 230-32.

105 Riddle, *The Life of Benjamin Wade*, 230-32.

106 *Congressional Globe*, 36th Cong., 1st. Session, Appendix, 369, 373-77.

107 Beale, xii. See also, Cain, *Lincoln's Attorney General*, 99.

108 *Congressional Globe*, 36th Cong., 1st. Session, 60-61.

109   Ibid., 1629, 1632; *Missouri Democrat*, 8/3/1860; Doolittle to Kirkwood, 11/9/1859, Kirkwood Papers.

110   Frank Blair, *Colonization and Commerce*, 1-8, *Missouri Democrat*, 10/15/1859, 12/1/1859, 10/9/1860; Frank Blair to Kirkwood, 11/3/1859, Kirkwood Papers.

111   *Colonization Society of Iowa Annual Report*, 1857, 5, 7-10.

112   *Missouri Democrat,* 7/26/1860.

113   *Congressional Globe*, 35th Cong., 2nd. Session, 907, 967, 1351; 36th Cong., 1st. Session, 1629, 1632; Doolittle to John Potter, 7/25/1859, 11/7/1860, Potter Papers. Even some Southern writers feared the increase of blacks in their region. See, William Henry Holcombe, *The Alternative: A Separate Nationality, or the Africanization of the South*, (New Orleans, 1860), 8-9.

114   *Chicago Tribune*, 5/6/1857.

115   Frank Blair, *Colonization and Commerce*, 1-8; Blair, *Destiny of the Races*, 4, 6, 12-17, 22-25.

116   *Missouri Democrat*, 12/21/1859; Beale, 113, 191-92; Cain, *Lincoln's Attorney General*, 78, 98-100, 104-05, 212. See also, Johannsen, 91-92; Boyd, "Negro Colonization in the National Crisis, 1860-1870," 27; Boyd, "The American Colonization Society and the Slave Recaptives of 1860-1861: An Early Example of United States-African Relations," *Journal of Negro History*, vol. 47, 1962, 109.

117   *Missouri Democrat*, 11/9/1857.

118   Dan E. Clark, *Samuel Jordan Kirkwood* (Iowa City, Iowa, 1917), 145; Lathrop, 82-83; Spraggins, 48. See also, Frank Blair to Doolittle, 11/3/1859, Doolittle Papers, Library of Congress; Doolittle to Kirkwood, 11/9/1859, Kirkwood Papers.

119   *Congressional Globe*, 36th Cong., 1st. Session, 734.

120   Ibid., Appendix, 178-80; Earle Field, "Charles B. Sedgwick's Letters from Washington, 1859-1861," *Mid-America*, vol. 49, 1967, 136.

121   *Missouri Democrat*, 10/15/1859. Blair told Southerners that "nobody will consent to emancipation, if the . . . negroes are to remain on our soil." See also, Frank Blair, *Colonization and Commerce*, 1-8; Blair, *Destiny of the Races*, 4, 6, 12-17, 22-25; *Congressional Globe*, 35th Cong., 1st. Session, 293-98; Frank Blair to Doolittle, 10/15/1859, Doolittle Papers, Library of Congress; *Chicago Tribune*, 7/10/1858.

122 *Congressional Globe,* 36th Cong., 2nd. Session, 104; Riddle, *The Life of Benjamin Wade*, 230-32.

123 James Mitchell, *Letter on the Relations of the White and African Races in the United States, showing the necessity of the colonization of the Latter addressed to the President of the U.S.,* pamphlet, Washington, D.C., 1862, 3; Boyd, "Negro Colonization in the National Crisis, 1860-1870," 144-46.

124 Doolittle to John Potter, 7/25/1859, 11/7/1860, Potter Papers. See also, *Congressional Globe,* 35th Cong., 2nd. Session, 907, 967, 1351; 36th Cong., 1st. Session, 1629, 1632; Doolittle to Hannibal Hamlin, 8/20,29/1859, Hamlin Papers; *Senate Executive Documents* No. 26, 35th Cong., 2nd, Session, 1-2; William E. Smith, vol. 1, 445-46; Sellers, 287-88.

125 *Illinois State Journal,* 6/29/1857; *Missouri Democrat,* 10/9/1860.

126 William Kitchell to Trumbull, 1/1/1860, 11/28/1860, Trumbull Papers, Library of Congress.

127 *Congressional Globe*, 36th Cong., 1st. Session, Appendix, 369, 373-77.

128 Frank Blair, *Colonization and Commerce*, 1-8; Frank Blair to Doolittle, 10/15/1859, Doolittle Papers, Library of Congress; *Congressional Globe*, 35th Cong., 1st. Session, 293-98.

129 Thornbrough, *The Negro in Indiana*, 84-85, 90, 127, 181.

130 *Chicago Tribune,* 5/6/1857.

131 Frank Blair, *Colonization and Commerce*, 1-8; Blair, *Destiny of the Races*, 6-7, 12-16, 22-25; *Missouri Democrat,* 10/15/1859.

132 *Congressional Globe*, 35th Cong., 1st. Session, 228-29. See also, Louis Filler, *The Crusade Against Slavery, 1830-1860* (New York, 1963, originally published in 1960), 239.

133 *Cadiz Republican*, 1/18/1860.

134 *Missouri Democrat,* 3/21/1859.

135 Doolittle to John Potter, 7/25/1859, 11/7/1860, Potter Papers.

136 *Congressional Globe*, 36th Cong., 1st. Session, 2011.

137 *Colonization Society of Iowa Annual Report*, 1857, 5, 7-10.

138 Trumbull as quoted in Frank Blair, *Destiny of the Races*, 27-28; *Congressional Globe*, 36th Cong., 1st. Session, 60-61; *Missouri Democrat,* 8/18/1858. See also, Krug, *Lyman Trumbull, Conservative Radical,* 152; John S. Wright, 237.

139 *Senate Executive Documents*, No. 26, 35th Cong., 2nd. Session, 1-2; Doolittle

to John Potter, 7/25/1859, 11/7/1860, Potter Papers; Doolittle to Trumbull, 11/10/1860, Trumbull Papers, Library of Congress; *Congressional Globe*, 35th Cong., 2nd. Session, 1351; 36th Cong., 1st. Session, 1629, 1632. See also, *Racine Advocate*, 8/24/1859; *Missouri Democrat*, 3/21/1859.

140   *Congressional Globe*, 36th Cong., 1st. Session, Appendix, 55-57.

141   Frank Blair, *Colonization and Commerce*, 1-8; *Congressional Globe*, 35th Cong., 1st. Session, 293-98; *Chicago Tribune*, 7/10/1858; *Missouri Democrat*, 1/20/1858, 2/7/1859, 10/9,15/1859, 12/1/1859.

142   *Missouri Democrat*, 12/21/1859; Beale, 113, 191-92; Cain, *Lincoln's Attorney General*, 78, 98-100, 104-05, 212.

143   *Congressional Globe*, 36th Cong., 1st. Session, Appendix, 149.

144   Ibid., 36th Cong., 1st. Session, 1629, 1632; Doolittle to John Potter, 7/25/ 1859, 11/7/1860, Potter Papers.

145   *Illinois State Journal*, 11/28/1857; Basler, vol. 2, 298-99. See also, Fredrickson, "A Man but not a Brother," 48-49, 51; Pickett, 314-15; Wesley, "Lincoln's Plan," 9.

146   Montgomery Blair to Doolittle, 11/11/1859, Doolittle Papers, Wisconsin State Historical Society. See also, *Missouri Democrat*, 2/27/1857; Luthin, *The First Lincoln Campaign*, 66; Elbert B. Smith, 240-42.

147   *Missouri Democrat,* 8/3/1860; Doolittle to Hannibal Hamlin, 8/20, 29/1859, Hamlin Papers.

148   Frank Blair, *Destiny of the Races*, 24-28; Elbert B. Smith, 252.

149   *Missouri Democrat,* 1/20/1858, 2/7/1859, 10/9,15/1859, 12/1/1859, 7/ 16/1860, 10/9/1860; *Chicago Tribune*, 7/10/1858. For further evidence of Blair's strong support for colonization, see: Frank Blair, *Destiny of the Races*, 4, 6, 12-17, 22-25; Blair, *Colonization and Commerce*, 1-8; *Congressional Globe*, 35th Cong., 1st. Session, 293-98; Fleming, 9-10; Cooke, 193-96; McCabe, 302-17; Elbert B. Smith, 246; William E. Smith, vol. 1, 446-49; Luthin, *The First Lincoln Campaign*, 53-54; Eric Foner, *Free Soil, Free Labor, Free Men*, 276; Leonard B. Wurthman Jr., "Frank Blair: Lincoln's Congressional Spokesman," *Missouri Historical Review*, vol. 64, 1970, 266-67; Carl Sandburg, *Lincoln, the War Years* (N.Y., 1939), vol. 1, 153; Daniel M. Grissom, "Personal Recollections of Distinguished Missourians-Frank Blair," *Missouri Historical Review*, vol. 20, 1926, 398.

150   D.C. Phillips to Trumbull, 12/11/1859. See also, H.C. Trinne to Trumbull, 12/15/1859, both in the Trumbull Papers, Library of Congress.

151   J. McKibben to Trumbull, 12/26/1859, Trumbull Papers, Library of Congress.

152   Rawley, 125.

153   Chase to Hon. Henry Wilson, 12/13/1860, Chase Papers, Library of Congress.

154   *Congressional Globe*, 36th Cong., 1st. Session, 60.

155   William Kitchell to Trumbull, 1/1/1860, 11/28/1860, Trumbull Papers, Library of Congress.

156   *Chicago Tribune*, 4/29/1857; Thayer, *The Kansas Crusade*, 31-32; *Congressional Globe*, 35th Cong., 1st. Session, 1342.

157   Montgomery Blair to Eli Thayer, 8/14/1860; Montgomery Blair to John D. Baldwin, 1860, Montgomery Blair Papers, Brown University Library.

158   *Congressional Globe*, 36th Cong., 1st. Session, Appendix, 150, 2nd. Session, 104. See also, Governor William Dennison to Wade, 11/30/1859, 2/6,21/1860, 5/12/1860, Benjamin F. Wade Papers.

159   Louis Krouskopf to Frederick Hassaurek, March, 1860, Hassaurek Collection.

160   G.C. Gillette to Charles Billinghurst, 3/27/1859, Charles Billinghurst Papers, Wisconsin State Historical Society.

161   Thornbrough, "The Race Issue in Indiana Politics during the Civil War," 167-69, 175.

162   *Congressional Globe*, 36th Cong., 1st. Session, Appendix, 55-57. Much of this promotion of colonization by the party, historian Brainerd Dyer notes, was reflected by increased contributions to the American Colonization Society. Dyer writes that during the late 1850's, when the party was actively propagating colonization, the "receipts of the Society were nearly a million dollars, a sum double that received during the preceding decade. The final year of the 1850's, the year of John Brown's raid, witnessed the contribution of one hundred and sixty thousand dollars, the largest amount contributed in any year." See, Dyer, 55.

163   *Colonization Society of Iowa Annual Report*, 1857, 5, 7-10.

164   Woodburn, 283-85; *Congressional Globe*, 36th Cong., 1st. Session, Appendix, 178-80.

165   Beale, 113, 191-92; *Missouri Democrat*, 12/21/1859.

166 *Congressional Globe*, 36th Cong., 1st. Session, 60-61; *Missouri Democrat*, 8/18/1858; Frank Blair, *Destiny of the Races*, 27-28.

167 Clark, 145; Lathrop, 82-83.

168 *Cadiz Republican*, 1/18/1860.

169 *Missouri Democrat*, 7/26/1860.

170 *Congressional Globe*, 35th Cong., 2nd. Session, 907, 967, 1351; 36th Cong., 1st. Session, 1629, 1632; *Senate Executive Documents*, No. 26, 35th Cong., 2nd. Session, 1-2; Doolittle to Trumbull, 11/10/1860, Trumbull Papers, Library of Congress. See also, Doolittle to Hannibal Hamlin, 8/20,29/1859, Hamlin Papers; *Missouri Democrat*, 3/21/1859, 8/3/1860; Racine Advocate, 8/24/1859.

171 *Missouri Democrat*, 10/15/1859, 12/1/1859, 10/9/1860; Frank Blair, *Colonization and Commerce*, 1-8; Frank Blair to Kirkwood, 11/3/1859, Kirkwood Papers.

172 William Dennison to Wade, 11/30/1859, 2/6,21/1860, Benjamin F. Wade Papers; *Congressional Globe*, 36th Cong., 1st. Session, Appendix, 150, 2nd. Session, 104; Riddle, *The Life of Benjamin Wade*, 230-32. See also, Trefousse, *Benjamin Franklin Wade*, 118; Erlich, 162-63; Margaret Shortreed, "The Anti-slavery Radicals, 1840-1868," *Past and Present*, vol. 16, 1959, 75. Other prominent Republicans who supported colonization included Governors William Bissell of Illinois and Alexander Randall of Wisconsin, and numerous congressional leaders, such as Henry Wilson and C.C. Washburn. See, Eric Foner, *Free Soil, Free Labor, Free Men*, 276.

173 *Congressional Globe*, 36th Cong., 1st. Session, 60-61.

174 Ibid., Appendix, 377.

175 Ibid., 55-57.

176 Ibid., 35th Cong., Senate Special Session, 1685; *Senate Executive Documents*, No. 26, 35th Cong., 2nd. Session, 1-2.

177 *Congressional Globe*, 36th Cong., 1st. Session, 60-61; *Missouri Democrat*, 8/18/1858.

178 *Congressional Globe,* 35th Cong., 1st. Session, 293-98.

179 Ibid., 36th Cong., 1st. Session, 2011.

180 *Illinois State Journal*, 2/25/1857; *Chicago Tribune*, 2/21/1857.

181 *Congressional Globe*, 34th Cong., 1st. Session, Appendix, 553-55; 35th Cong., 1st. Session, Appendix, 399.

182   Ibid., 36th Cong., 1st. Session, Appendix, 360.

183   Abbott, 70.

184   *Missouri Democrat*, 9/7/1860.

185   Frank Blair, *Destiny of the Races*, 4, 24.

186   *New York Herald*, 4/16/1860; *Congressional Globe*, 36th Cong., 2nd. Session,
       Appendix, 86.

187   *Congressional Globe*, 34th Cong., 1st. Session, Appendix, 274-75; 36th
       Cong., 1st. Session, 1679-84, Appendix, 55-57.

188   Solberg, 483-93. See also, Julian, *Giddings*, 420; Giddings to John P. Hale,
       7/12/1859, Hale-Giddings Correspondence, Dartmouth College Library.

189   McGuire, 57; Haberkorn, 301.

190   James Grimes to Wife, 6/24,27/1855, as quoted in Bergmann, 18-19;
       Younger, 4.

191   Vivian Thomas Messner, "The Public Life of Austin Blair," M.A. thesis,
       Wayne University, 1937, 218; Earl O. Smith, 29; Fennimore, 162; Formisano,
       35; Thompson, 17-18. Blair's proposal was passed. See, *Acts of the Legislature
       of the State of Michigan, Passed at the Regular Session of 1855* (Lansing,
       Mich., 1855), 414.

192   Benson J. Lossing, *A Biography of James A. Garfield* (N.Y., 1882),
       112-15.

193   *Ohio Executive Documents* (Columbus, Ohio, 1859), Part II, 52. See also,
       Porter, 28. The Ohio personal liberty law was enacted on April 17, 1857, and
       repealed on February 23, 1858. See. Stanley W. Campbell, *The Slave Catchers,
       Enforcement of the Fugitive Slave Law, 1850-1860* (Chapel Hill, N.C., 1968),
       171-85.

194   Martin, 320. Colfax apparently would grow more conservative because, as
       noted, in 1860 he was less concerned with black rights.

195   *Ohio Executive Documents*, 1859, Part II, 52; Porter, 28; Quillin, 98.

196   Julian, *Speeches on Political Questions*, 106, 109, 127, 134, 160; Grace
       Julian Clarke, 160-61, 169, 184.

197   *Congressional Globe*, 33rd. Cong., 1st. Session, 1057, 1071.

198   Ibid., 35th Cong., 2nd. Session, Appendix, 170-71.

199   Ibid., 1st. Session, Appendix, 93.

200   Martin, 302, 310.

201   *Congressional Globe*, 35th Cong., 1st. Session, 985; *Senate Executive*

Documents, No. 26, 35th Cong., 2nd. Session, 1-2; *Missouri Democrat*, 3/21/1859.

202 Giddings, *History of the Rebellion*, 402-03; Solberg, 452; *Congressional Globe,* 35th Cong., 1st. Session, 895-96.

203 Speech of William Parker Cutler before the Presbyterian General Assembly, Cleveland, Ohio, 1857, as quoted in Julia Perkins Cutler, *Life and Times of Ephraim Cutler* (Cincinnati, 1890), 321-26.

204 *Congressional Globe,* 36th Cong., 1st. Session, 239.

205 Ibid., 1679-84, Appendix, 55-57.

206 Solberg, 479.

207 *Congressional Globe*, 36th Cong., 2nd. Session, Appendix, 86.

208 Ibid., 33rd Cong., 1st. Session, Appendix, 680.

209 Ibid., 34th Cong., 3rd. Session, 54.

210 Speech of William Parker Cutler before the Presbyterian General Assembly, 321-26.

211 Owen Lovejoy to Lewis Tappan, 12/27/1859, American Missionary Association Archives.

212 *Congressional Globe*, 35th Cong., 1st. Session, 895-96; Giddings, *History of the Rebellion*, 402-03; Giddings Scrapbook, Giddings Collection, Ohio Historical Society; James Brewer Stewart, 258-71; Solberg, 435-36, 476; Buell, 204. See also, William S. Myers, *The Republican Party* (N.Y., 1927), 94-95; Frank Flower, *History of the Republican Party* (Springfield, Ill., 1884), 234.

213 Julian, *Speeches on Political Questions*, 106, 109, 127, 134, 160; Julian, *Political Recollections*, 181-89; Grace Julian Clarke, 160-61, 169, 184.

214 Giddings Scrapbook; Julian, *Giddings*, 370-74, 378-83; Solberg, 4-7, 435-38, 440-41, 472-76, 495-508, 515-17, 526-28, 536-37; James Brewer Stewart, 240, 254-56, 258-61, 271, 276; Buell, 200-01, 204. Stewart notes that by 1860, "Giddings' attempts to style himself a good Republican, while accounting to his conscience, were taking on ever greater tinges of unreality," because "his emphasis on justice had little influence on men who shared more fully than he, the nation's belief in Negro inferiority." See, Stewart, 226, 240.

215 Chase to John P. Hale, 6/17/1858, Chase-Hale Correspondence; Chase to Orin Follett, 1/1/1855, Orin Follett Papers.

216 Brisbane to Carl Schurz, 2/7/1859; Brisbane to Editor of the *Free Democrat*, 4/21/1859; Brisbane to Governor Chase, 6/22/1859, William Henry Brisbane Papers, Wisconsin State Historical Society.

217 C. Peter Ripley, ed., *The Black Abolitionist Papers* (Chapel Hill, N.C., 1986), vol. 2, 206.

218 *The Liberator*, Boston, Mass., 9/5/1856.

219 Herbert Aptheker, ed., *A Documentary History of the Negro People in the United States* (N.Y., 1969, originally published in 1951), 406-07.

220 *The Liberator*, 5/18/1860.

221 *Missouri Democrat*, 7/19/1860.

222 *New York Tribune*, 8/10/1858. See also, *Proceedings of the National Convention of Colored Men at Syracuse, N.Y., October 4,5,6,7, 1864*, pamphlet, Boston, Mass., 1864, 25-52; Dann, 236; McPherson, *The Negro's Civil War*, 77-97; McPherson, "Abolitionist and Negro opposition to Colonization During the Civil War," *Phylon*, vol. 26, 1965, 391-98.

223 *The Colored American*, New York, N.Y., 3/4/1837.

224 *The Liberator*, 5/18/1860.

225 William Lloyd Garrison, *Thoughts on African Colonization* (N.Y., 1969, originally published in 1832), 122, 131; Stanley, 171. See also, Walter M. Merrill, *Against Wind and Tide, A Biography of Wm. Lloyd Garrison* (Cambridge, Mass., 1971, originally published in 1963), 41, 59-60, 69-73, 138, 266; Betty Fladeland, *Men and Brothers, Anglo-American Antislavery Cooperation* (Urbana, Ill., 1972), 277; Dillon, *The Abolitionists*, 60-61; Dillon, *Benjamin Lundy*, 161.

226 *Portage County Democrat*, 11/24/1858; Gerrit Smith, *Letter From Gerrit Smith to Joshua R. Giddings, November 12, 1858*, pamphlet, Peterboro, N.Y., 1858; Frothingham, *Gerrit Smith*, 222.

227 *The Weekly Anglo-African*, New York, N.Y., 3/17/1860. See also, Howard H. Bell, "Negro Nationalism: A Factor in Emigration Projects, 1858-1861," *Journal of Negro History*, vol. 47, 1962, 49.

228 Speech of H. Ford Douglass, as quoted in *The Liberator*, 7/3/1860.

229 *Douglass' Monthly*, Rochester, N.Y., vol. 3, 10/1860, 338; Speech of Frederick Douglass, 8/29/1860, as quoted in McPherson, *The Negro's Civil War*, 8-9. See also, Wesley, "The Participation of Negroes in Anti-slavery Political Parties," 73.

NOTES—CHAPTER 6

1   Hinton Rowan Helper, *The Impending Crisis of the South and How to Meet It* (N.Y., 1860, originally published in 1857), 205-08, 213; Hugh C. Bailey, *Hinton Rowan Helper: Abolitionist-Racist,* (Montgomery, Ala., 1965), 15-17, 41, 45-46, 54, 134, 154-55; Joaquin Jose' Cardoso, "Hinton Rowan Helper: A Nineteenth Century Pilgrimage," Ph.D. dissertation, University of Wisconsin, 1967, 4, 58, 108, 197; Wainwright, 540-41; Hugh T. Lefler, "Hinton Rowan Helper Advocate of a 'White America,'" *Southern Sketches No. 1,* pamphlet, Charlottesville, Va., 1935, 5-7, 19, 22, 25; Gerald Gaither and John Muldowny, "Hinton Rowan Helper, Racist and Reformer: A Letter to Senator John Sherman of Ohio," *North Carolina Historical Review,* vol. 49, 1972, 377; *Congressional Globe,* 36th Cong., 1st. Session, 145-46; John Spencer Bassett, *Anti-Slavery Leaders of North Carolina* (Baltimore, 1898), 16-17; William E. Smith, vol. 1, 456; *Missouri Democrat,* 8/15/1859; Herman Von Holst, *The Constitutional and Political History of the United States* (Chicago, 1892), vol. 7, 13, 74-86.

2   Frederick Law Olmsted, *The Cotton Kingdom, A Traveller's Observations on Cotton and Slavery in the American Slave States* (N.Y., 1861), 37; *Dictionary of American Biography,* vol. 7, 24-28.

3   *Missouri Democrat,* 3/1/1856, 5/30/1857, 7/17/1858.

4   Hugh Bailey, 139-40; Helper, *The Impending Crisis,* 184, 302-03.

5   *Chicago Tribune,* 2/9/1855, 7/19,28/1859, 8/19/1859.

6   Ibid.

7   Thomas Ewbank, *Inorganic Forces Ordained to Supersede Human Slavery,* pamphlet, N.Y., 1860, 12, 16. Ewbank's work was read before the American Ethnological Society. See also, Fredrickson, *The Black Image,* 143; *Dictionary of American Biography,* vol. 3, 227-28.

8   *Illinois State Journal,* 2/25/1857.

9   George M. Weston, *The Progress of Slavery in the United States* (Washington, D.C., 1857), iv, 33-35, 130-31, 234-37. See also, Fredrickson, *The Black Image,* 154-55.

10   Helper, *The Impending Crisis,* 88, 113. Helper's hatred for the Negro knew no bounds, and shortly after the Civil War, he published two other works, which tore down the black man in every way conceivable. Helper's biographer,

when writing about one of these works, notes that the "Impending Crisis had been written, intentionally as preparation for Nojoque." *Nojoque, A Question For a Continent,* published in New York in 1867, is perhaps the most severe attack ever made by a Caucasian writer on the Negro race. The fact that this book came from the leading Republican political philosopher of the period is significant. A few examples from *Nojoque* will suffice to give the reader a sample of the character of Helper's work. The preface, for instance, contains the following: "Were I state here, frankly and categorically, that the primary object of this work is to write the negro out of America, and that the secondary object is to write him (and manifold millions of other black and bicolored caitiffs, little better than himself) out of existence, God's simple truth would be told." The very titles to his chapters are indicative of Helper's attitude. Chapter one is entitled "The Negro Anthropologically Considered; An Inferior fellow Done for." Chapter two is entitled "Black; A Thing of Ugliness, Disease and Death," while chapter five is headed "Removals, Banishments, Expulsions, Exterminations." Genocide was acceptable to Helper, in order to rid white society of black people. Helper's second postwar work, *The Negroes in Negroland,* published in New York in 1868, is more of the same thing, a diatribe, depicting black people in sub-human, animal terms. Near the end of this book, Helper wrote that "my opposition to slavery . . . looked to the ultimate whitening up of all the Southern states, and not to the spreading nor to the continuance of that foul blackness and discoloration of them, which then existed, [and] which still exists." See, Hugh Bailey, 134; Helper, *Nojoque,* preface, 14-15, 17, 64-67, 70-81, 155-57, 160-61, 184, 191, 218, 230-31, 237-38, 253, 294, 297, 373, 408, 416, 454-58; Helper, *Negroes in Negroland,* introduction, 7-172, 178-86, 223, 237-38, 250. Helper's heavy-handed racism, and nativism, drew fire from some Southern writers, such as John Gilmer, who attacked his anti-black and anti-Catholic views. See, John Gilmer, *War of Races* (Richmond, Va., 1867), 7-15.

11   Olmsted, *Cotton Kingdom,* xli, xlv, 32, 83, 565.

12   Richard Henry Dana Jr., *To Cuba and Back* (N.Y., 1859), 43, 59, 62, 65-66, 73, 104, 124, 126-27. Dana's book went through twelve editions. See, Shapiro, 110.

13   *New York Tribune,* 1/21/1858, 2/25/1858.

14   *Missouri Democrat,* 4/15/1859, 10/17/1860.

15   Olmsted, *A Journey in the Back Country* (N.Y., 1860), vi-ix; Olmsted, *Cotton Kingdom*, 466.

16   Allen Nevins and Milton H. Thomas, eds., *The Diary of George Templeton Strong* (N.Y., 1974), vol. 2, 304; *National Cyclopaedia of American Biography,* vol. 3, 523. At the outbreak of the Civil War, Strong was elected treasurer of the United States Sanitary Commission, under whose auspices various anthropometric measurements were conducted on Union troops of different races and ethnic origins.

17   Ewbank, 4-19, 26-31.

18   Dana, *To Cuba and Back,* 62.

19   Ewbank, 15.

20   James S. Pike, *The Prostrate State, South Carolina Under Negro Government* (N.Y., 1873), 18, 22, 29. See also, *New York Tribune,* 3/22/1855, 12/30/1859, 3/13/1860; Durden, *James Shepherd Pike,* 31.

21   Ewbank, 4-19, 26-31.

22   Dana, *To Cuba and Back*, 43, 59, 62, 65-66, 73, 104, 124, 126-27; *New York Tribune,* 3/13/1860, 12/17/1860.

23   *Missouri Democrat,* 4/25/1855, 7/31/1856, 5/2/1857.

24   *Chicago Tribune,* 12/29/1855.

25   Helper, *The Impending Crisis,* 195.

26   *Philadelphia Daily News*, 11/22/1860.

27   Weston, 244.

28   Dana, *To Cuba and Back,* 73, 127.

29   Olmsted, *Cotton Kingdom,* 37, 467, 565.

30   Nevins and Thomas, vol. 1, 199-200, vol. 2, 288.

31   Helper, *The Impending Crisis,* 88.

32   *New York Tribune,* 3/22/1855, 12/30/1859, 3/13/1860; Pike, *The Prostrate State,* 18, 22, 29; *Missouri Democrat,* 4/25/1855, 7/31/1856, 5/2/1857.

33   *Philadelphia Daily News,* 11/22/1860.

34   Dana, *To Cuba and Back,* 43, 62.

35   Weston, 234.

36   Helper, *The Impending Crisis,* 88, 380.

37   *Chicago Tribune,* 7/30/1859.

38   *Missouri Democrat,* 7/30/1855; *Dictionary of American Biography,* vol. 3, 10-11; *National Cyclopaedia of American Biography,* vol. 9, 242; *Appleton's*

Cyclopaedia of American Biography, vol. 1, 365. Breckenridge's name was sometimes spelled Breckinridge.

39　　Olmsted, *Cotton Kingdom*, 70, 95-97, 102-03, 467, 565.

40　　*New York Tribune,* 3/13/1860.

41　　*Missouri Democrat,* 3/26/1855. See also, *Missouri Democrat,* 3/27/1857, 4/14/1857, 4/15/1859.

42　　Olmsted, *Back Country,* 473.

43　　Helper, *The Impending Crisis,* 147.

44　　*Chicago Tribune,* 12/29/1855.

45　　*Missouri Democrat,* 2/21/1856.

46　　Ibid., 10/3/1857, 2/9,10/1859. When speaking of his own state, Brown noted how "Negroes are invited here from every jail yard in Virginia or Kentucky, no matter what crimes they may have committed."

47　　Pike, *The Prostrate State,* 29.

48　　Olmsted, *Cotton Kingdom,* 83.

49　　Hugh Bailey, 140; Dana, *To Cuba and Back,* 73, 124, See also, Hinton Rowan Helper, *The Land of Gold* (Baltimore, 1855), 266-67, 275; Helper, *The Impending Crisis,* 86-88; Olmsted, *Cotton Kingdom,* 82-83, 565; Olmsted, *Back Country,* 432.

50　　Royal Cortissoz, *The Life of Whitelaw Reid* (N.Y., 1921), vol. 1, 40-41. Before the Civil War Reid had an interest in and edited the *Xenia News* of Xenia, Ohio, During the war he edited the *Cincinnati Gazette* and, as a war correspondent, wrote articles for the *Cleveland Herald.* Reid was well acquainted with major Republican politicians, and after the conflict wrote a history of both the Civil War and Ohio's role in it. In 1868 he joined Greeley's *New York Tribune.* See, *Dictionary of American Biography,* vol. 15, 482-83.

51　　Helper, *Land of Gold,* 266-67, 275; Helper, *The Impending Crisis,* 86-88; Hugh Bailey, 140.

52　　Olmsted, *Cotton Kingdom*, 39, 76-77.

53　　*Chicago Tribune,* 2/15/1856, 7/30/1859.

54　　Olmsted, *Cotton Kingdom*, 77, 564.

55　　Dana, *To Cuba and Back,* 73, 124.

56　　Helper, *Land of Gold,* 266-67, 275; Helper, *The Impending Crisis,* 86-88; Hugh Bailey, 140.

57   *Missouri Democrat,* 12/3/1856, 2/28/1857, 4/1/1857, 10/3/1857, 2/9,10/ 1859, 10/17/1860.

58   Olmsted, *Cotton Kingdom*, 467, 565.

59   Dana, *To Cuba and Back,* 73, 124; Weston, 130.

60   *Missouri Democrat,* 10/3/1857, 2/9,10/1859.

61   Olmsted, *Cotton Kingdom,* 467.

62   *Chicago Tribune,* 2/15/1856, 7/30/1859.

63   Helper, *The Impending Crisis,* 182.

64   *Missouri Democrat,* 7/30/1855.

65   Dana, *To Cuba and Back,* 59.

66   *Chicago Tribune,* 6/26/1855, 8/10/1859.

67   *New York Tribune,* 3/13/1860.

68   *Missouri Democrat,* 10/17/1860. See also, *Missouri Democrat,* 12/3/1856, 2/28/1857, 4/1/1857.

69   Ewbank, 11-12.

70   Olmsted, *Cotton Kingdom*, 28, 102, 467.

71   Helper, *The Impending Crisis,* 88, 380.

72   Dana, *To Cuba and Back,* 43, 62.

73   *Chicago Tribune,* 3/3/1856; Nevins and Thomas, vol. 3, 66.

74   Weston, 34, 236, 242-43.

75   *Chicago Tribune,* 3/3/1856, 4/10/1857, 7/23/1857.

76   Olmsted, *Back Country,* 282, 374, 470-72; Broadus Mitchell, *Frederick Law Olmsted, A Critic of the Old South* (Baltimore, 1924), 106, 114-15, 138-39; Olmsted, *Cotton Kingdom,* 588-89.

77   Helper, *The Impending Crisis,* 44-45, 80-81, 85-86, 88, 91-92, 97, 113. On Helper and his use of statistics see Lefler, 27-30.

78   Nevins and Thomas, vol. 3, 60.

79   *Missouri Democrat,* 3/3,10/1857, 4/14/1857, 7/1/1858, 8/15/1859; Charles Nordhoff, *America for Free Working Men,* pamphlet, N.Y., 1865, 9, 30, 33; *Dictionary of American Biography,* vol. 7, 548.

80   Ewbank, 26-31.

81   *Missouri Democrat,* 10/3/1857.

82   Ibid., 7/30/1855.

83   Ewbank, 7-12.

84   Helper, *Land of Gold,* 39, 47, 96, 111; Helper, *The Impending Crisis,* 184.

85   *Philadelphia Daily News,* 11/22/1860.

86   *Missouri Democrat,* 5/29/1855, 3/3/1857.

87   Helper, *The Impending Crisis,* 88; Helper, *Land of Gold,* 257, 264, 268.

88   Nevins and Thomas, vol. 3, 12.

89   *Chicago Tribune,* 1/25/1855, 2/7/1855, 7/23/1857, 8/19/1859.

90   Helper, *Land of Gold,* 92-96, 111-13, 222, 268-73; Helper, *The Impending Crisis,* 44-45, 80-81, 85-86, 88, 91-92, 97, 113, 147. Since skin color was so important to Helper, as to other Republican writers, in measuring human worth, he equated California Indians with Negroes, and noted that "their skin is nearly as dark as that of the negro. Indeed they greatly resemble the African in color and general appearance." Moreover, being "inveterate gamblers," they, as blacks, were immoral. Helper confidently predicted that the California tribesmen would disappear before the white man, "like snow before a spring sun. They are too indolent to work, too cowardly to fight. When pinched by the severity of hunger, and unable to procure their customary filthy diet, they are driven to the settlements, where they steal if they can." All in all, Helper concluded, they were "filthy and abominable." Perhaps momentarily forgetting his equal abhorrence of black people, he wrote of these Indians that a "worse set of vagabonds cannot be found bearing the human form. They come into the world and go from it to as little purpose as other carnivorous animals. Their chief characteristics are indolence and gluttony." Not wishing to leave any non-white group out from his racial strictures, Helper also assailed certain Asian peoples; he referred to the Chinese living in California as "semi-barbarians." Unlike some Republicans, such as Thomas Hart Benton, who placed the Chinese above the black man, but below the Caucasian, Helper seemed to lump all darker skinned peoples together. Like blacks, the Chinese were "not desirable because . . . [they were] not useful." Furthermore, they were "full of duplicity, prevarication and pagan prejudices, and so enervated and lazy, that it is impossible for them to make true and estimable citizens." Besides, he insisted, "our population was already too heterogeneous before the Chinese came." See, Helper, *Land of Gold,* 92-96, 111-13, 222, 257-73; Helper, *The Impending Crisis,* 88.

91   *Missouri Democrat,* 2/28/1857, 10/17/1859. See also, *Missouri Democrat,* 4/25/1855, 7/31/1856, 12/3/1856, 4/1/1857, 5/2/1857, 1/14/1858, 8/27/1858, 10/17/1860.

92   Ibid., 4/25/1855, 7/31/1856, 12/3/1856, 2/28/1857, 3/3,10/1857, 4/1,14/

1857, 5/2/1857, 1/14/1858, 7/1/1858, 8/27/1858, 8/15/1859, 10/17/1859, 10/17/1860.

93   Olmsted, *Cotton Kingdom*, 466-67; Olmsted, *Back Country,* 304.

94   Helper, *The Impending Crisis,* 44-45, 80-81, 85-86, 88, 91-92, 97, 113, 147.

95   *Illinois State Journal,* 2/12/1857.

96   Helper, *Land of Gold,* 96, 272-73.

97   Durden, *James Shepherd Pike,* 31.

98   *Missouri Democrat,* 5/25,30/1857, 3/31/1858, 10/17/1860.

99   Ibid., 7/30/1855.

100   Helper, *Land of Gold,* 39, 47; Helper, *The Impending Crisis,* 97.

101   Olmsted, *Cotton Kingdom* 31-32, 132.

102   *Ohio State Journal*, Columbus, Ohio, 8/5/1859.

103   *Chicago Tribune,* 9/1/1857. See also, *Chicago Tribune,* 2/10/1855, 3/6/1855, 2/25/1856, 5/3/1856, 5/30/1857, 11/1/1858.

104   Ibid., 2/10/1855, 3/6/1855, 1/31/1856, 2/25/1856, 4/24/1856, 5/3/1856, 3/12/1857, 5/30/1857, 7/1,2,18/1857, 8/12/1857, 9/1/1857, 11/1/1858. In a recent study entitled "Miscegenation and the Free Negro in Antebellum 'Anglo' Alabama: A Reexamination of Southern Race Relations," historian Gary B. Mills found that in certain areas of Alabama, some of which have traditionally been labelled strong white supremacist counties, the occurrence of interracial marriages was not that uncommon, and that most of these marriages involved black males and white females. Therefore, when Ray and other Republican editors accused Southerners of tolerating such unions, there seems to be growing evidence that that was the case. See, *Journal of American History,* vol. 68, 1981, 16-34.

105   *Missouri Democrat,* 1/20/1858, 7/14/1859, 10/17/1859.

106   *New York Tribune,* 1/21/1858, 2/25/1858, 9/18/1858. See also, the *Missouri Democrat,* 3/1/1858.

107   *Chicago Tribune,* 7/1/1857. See also, *Chicago Tribune,* 2/10/1855, 1/31/1856, 4/24/1856, 3/12/1857, 7/2,18/1857, 8/12/1857, 9/1/1857.

108   *Portage County Democrat,* Ravenna, Ohio, 1/19/1859.

109   *Chicago Tribune,* 2/10/1855, 1/31/1856, 4/24/1856, 3/12/1857, 7/1,2,18/1857, 8/12/1857, 9/1/1857.

110   *Illinois State Journal,* 2/25/1857.

111   *Portage County Democrat,* 1/19/1859.

112   *New York Tribune,* 1/21/1858, 2/25/1858, 9/18/1858. See also, the *Missouri Democrat,* 3/1/1858.

113   *Chicago Tribune,* 4/24/1856.

114   *Missouri Democrat,* 4/25/1855, 2/12/1856, 1/20/1858, 8/27/1858, 7/14/1859, 8/13/1859, 10/17/1859, 10/17/1860.

115   Ibid.

116   Ewbank, 16.

117   *Missouri Democrat,* 2/24/1857, 10/17/1859.

118   Ibid., 7/30/1855.

119   Helper, *Land of Gold,* 92-96, 111-13, 222, 268-73.

120   *New York Tribune,* 12/17/1860.

121   *Chicago Tribune,* 2/25/1856. Charles Nordhoff noted that "Free labor is killed by such unnatural competition." See, Nordhoff, 11.

122   *Illinois State Journal,* 2/12/1857.

123   *Missouri Democrat,* 12/1/1856, 9/15/1857, 1/20/1858, 4/12/1858, 7/23/1858, 8/20/1858, 2/9/1859. For an excellent discussion of the role of blacks in Southern industry see, Robert S. Starobin, *Industrial Slavery in the Old South* (N.Y., 1970), 12-33, 148-63.

124   *New York Tribune,* 3/22/1855, 12/30/1859.

125   *Missouri Democrat,* 7/30/1855.

126   Olmsted, *Back Country* 376, 474.

127   Helper, *Land of Gold,* 96; Helper, *The Impending Crisis,* 128.

128   *Chicago Tribune,* 2/9/1855, 3/3/1856, 9/6/1856, 4/10/1857, 9/1/1857, 7/28/1859, 8/19/1859.

129   Weston, 236.

130   *Missouri Democrat,* 7/14/1859, 8/13/1859.

131   Helper, *Land of Gold,* 96; Helper, *The Impending Crisis,* 128.

132   *Philadelphia Daily News,* 11/22/1860.

133   *New York Tribune,* 12/18/1856, 1/30/1857, 3/13/1858; James S. Pike, *First Blows of the Civil War* (N.Y., 1879), 396-97; Durden, *James Shepherd Pike,* 25, 31.

134   Helper, *The Impending Crisis,* 91.

135   *Chicago Tribune,* 9/6/1856, 8/19/1859. See also, *Chicago Tribune,* 2/9/1855, 3/3/1856, 4/10/1857, 9/1/1857, 7/28/1859.

136   *Missouri Democrat,* 7/14/1859, 8/13/1859.

137　Weston, iv, 237.

138　*Chicago Tribune,* 8/12/1857, 7/28/1859. See also, *Chicago Tribune,* 2/9/ 1855, 1/9/1856, 2/18/1856, 7/2,18,23/1857, 8/19/1859.

139　*Ohio State Journal,* 8/10/1859.

140　*Chicago Tribune,* 7/23/1857. See also, *Chicago Tribune,* 2/9/1855, 1/9/1856, 2/18/1856, 7/2,18/1857, 8/12/1857, 7/28/1859, 8/19/1859. Gratz Brown referred to Virginia as the "mother of . . . niggers." See, *Missouri Democrat,* 11/19/1857.

141　*Chicago Tribune,* 2/9/1855, 1/9/1856, 2/18/1856, 7/2,18,23/1857, 8/12/1857, 7/28/1859, 8/19/1859.

142　*New York Tribune,* 12/17/1860.

143　Ibid., 12/18/1856, 1/30/1857, 3/13/1858. See also, Pike, *First Blows of* the *Civil War,* 396-97; Durden, *James Shepherd Pike,* 25, 31.

144　*New York Tribune,* 8/8/1860.

145　Helper, *The Impending Crisis,* 97, 175.

146　*Iowa State Register,* 12/12/1860.

147　*Missouri Democrat,* 10/28/1856, 8/27/1858, 7/14/1859.

148　Helper, *The Impending Crisis,* 97, 175.

149　*Illinois State Journal,* 2/12/1857.

150　Helper, *The Impending Crisis,* 42-44, 73, 83, 152-53, 159, 320, 380.

151　Nevins and Thomas, vol. 2, 297.

152　*Missouri Democrat,* 4/30/1857, 6/5/1857. See also, *Missouri Democrat,* 2/ 7/1855, 8/15/1855, 10/9/1856, 12/1/1856, 5/30/1857, 7/17,23/1858, 7/14/ 1859, 8/13/1859.

153　Ibid., 2/7/1855, 8/15/1855, 10/9/1856, 12/1/1856, 4/30/1857, 5/30/1857, 6/ 5/1857, 9/15/1857, 1/20/1858, 4/12/1858, 7/17,23/1858, 8/20/1858, 2/9/ 1859, 7/14/1859, 8/13/1859.

154　*New York Tribune,* 7/24/1858.

155　*Chicago Daily Democrat,* 10/31/1860.

156　*Missouri Democrat,* 2/7/1855, 4/25/1855, 8/15/1855, 2/12/1856, 10/9/1856, 12/1/1856, 4/30/1857, 5/30/1857, 6/5/1857, 7/17,23/1858, 8/27/1858, 7/14/ 1859, 8/13/1859, 10/17/1859.

157　Helper, *The Impending Crisis,* 42-44, 73, 83, 152-53, 159, 320, 380.

158　*Missouri Democrat,* 2/7/1855, 4/25/1855, 8/15/1855, 2/12/1856, 10/9/1856,

12/1/1856, 4/30/1857, 5/30/1857, 6/5/1857, 7/17,23/1858, 8/27/1858, 7/14/1859, 8/13/1859, 10/17/1859.

159   Joseph Medill to Joshua R. Giddings, 12/18/1856, Giddings Papers, Ohio Historical Society.

160   *Ohio State Journal,* 8/10/1859.

161   Helper, *The Impending Crisis,* 173. The Democracy, Helper maintained, was "unreservedly a sectional Nigger Party."

162   *Chicago Tribune,* 5/30/1857, 7/30/1859. See also, *Chicago Tribune,* 2/10/1855, 3/6/1855, 4/24/1855, 2/25/1856, 9/9/1856, 7/1,2,18/1857, 9/1/1857, 11/1/1858.

163   *Missouri Democrat,* 12/20/1856, 4/5/1857, 7/23/1858. See also, *Missouri Democrat,* 2/7/1855, 7/25,26,31/1856, 10/28/1856, 12/1,3/1856, 1/28/1857, 3/27/1857, 4/4,30/1857, 5/2,16,25/1857, 6/10/1857, 9/15/1857, 11/19/1857, 1/20,23/1858, 4/12/1858, 7/1/1858, 8/20/1858, 1/10/1859, 7/2,14,20/1859.

164   Nevins and Thomas, vol. 2, 304.

165   *New York Tribune,* 6/24/1857.

166   *Chicago Tribune,* 2/10/1855, 3/6/1855, 4/24/1855, 2/25/1856, 5/3/1856, 9/9/1856, 5/30/1857, 7/1,2,18/1857, 9/1/1857, 11/1/1858, 7/30/1859.

167   Ibid., 9/1/1857.

168   *Missouri Democrat,* 7/31/1856, 11/19/1857, 7/2/1859.

169   Ibid., 2/7/1855, 7/25,26,31/1856, 10/28/1856, 12/1,3,20/1856, 1/28/1857, 3/27/1857, 4/4,5,30/1857, 5/2,16,25/1857, 6/10/1857, 9/15/1857, 11/19/1857, 1/20,23/1858, 4/12/1858, 7/1,23/1858, 8/20/1858, 1/10/1859, 7/2,14,20/1859.

170   Ibid.

171   *Marysville Daily Herald,* Marysville, California, 9/27/1856.

172   *New York Tribune,* 3/22/1855, 12/30/1859.

173   Boom, 136.

174   Van Deusen, *Horace Greeley,* 220.

175   *Illinois State Journal,* 6/26/1857.

176   *Missouri Democrat,* 1/15/1858.

NOTES—CHAPTER 7

1   *Illinois State Journal,* 2/12/1857.

2   Helper, *The Impending Crisis,* 174.

3   *Cincinnati Daily Commercial,* 11/3/1860.

4   *New York Tribune,* 8/7/1858, 10/12/1858, 12/17/1860; Isley, 129-30.

5   *Chicago Tribune,* 2/25/1856.

6   *Missouri Democrat,* 3/27/1857, 5/30/1857, 9/15/1857, 11/14/1858. For similar views see also, *Missouri Democrat,* 2/7/1855, 7/25,26,31/1856, 10/28/1856, 12/1,3/1856, 1/28/1857, 4/4,5,30/1857, 5/2,16,25/1857, 6/10/1857, 1/14,20,22,23/1858, 4/12/1858, 7/1,23/1858, 8/20/1858, 1/10/1859, 7/14,20/1859. Brown did not support Fremont in the 1856 election, but instead reluctantly backed Buchanan, although his attitude on the slavery question clearly indicated that he belonged in the Republican camp. He became disillusioned with the regular Democrats shortly after the 1856 election, joined the Missouri Free Democrats, and from then on began to back the new Republican Party. In 1860 he came out strongly for Lincoln, See, *Missouri Democrat,* 10/25/1856, 3/23/1858, 10/17/1860.

7   *New York Tribune,* 3/13/1860,

8   Ibid., 7/4/1860.

9   *Chicago Tribune,* 2/10/1855, 3/6/1855, 2/25/1856, 5/3/1856, 5/30/1857, 7/1/1857, 11/1/1858.

10 *Missouri Democrat,* 2/7/1855, 7/25,26,31/1856, 10/28/1856, 12/1,3/1856, 3/27/1857, 4/4,5,30/1857, 5/2,16/1857, 6/10/1857, 9/15/1857, 1/20,22,23/1858, 4/12/1858, 7/1,23/1858, 8/20/1858, 1/10/1859, 7/14,20/1859.

11 *Chicago Tribune,* 11/1/1858. See also, 3/6/1855, 2/25/1856, 5/3/1856, 5/30/1857, 7/1/1857.

12 *Missouri Democrat,* 2/7/1855, 7/25,26,31/1856, 10/28/1856, 12/1,3/1856, 3/27/1857, 4/4,5,30/1857, 5/2,16/1857, 6/10/1857, 9/15/1857, 1/20,22,23/1858, 4/12/1858, 7/1,23/1858, 8/20/1858, 1/10/1859, 7/14,20/1859. To Brown's mind the intensity of this struggle between the races was such, that on several occasions he mentioned the possibility of whites "exterminating" blacks.

13 Broadus Mitchell, 71.

14 Helper, *The Impending Crisis,* 26.

15 *Missouri Democrat,* 2/23/1855, 3/27/1857, 9/15/1857, 7/27/1860. Brown particularly disliked the radical abolitionists in Massachusetts, referring to

them as the "freaks of philosophy at the North," and their movement as a "foolish and visionary fanaticism."

16 Nevins and Thomas, vol. 2, 240-41, 287, 302, 304-05, 477. To Strong, the question of the abolition of slavery was simply the "nigger question," and he variously referred to abolitionism as "niggerism," "niggerophily (or Philonigger-anthrophy)."

17 Helper, *The Impending Crisis,* 126-27.

18 *Missouri Democrat,* 10/25/1856, 12/1/1856, 2/13/1857, 5/25/1857, 7/27/ 1858, 2/9/1859.

19 Ibid., 9/14/1857.

20 Ewbank, 10-14.

21 Isley, 197.

22 *Montezuma Weekly Republican,* Iowa City, Iowa, 7/18/1857; *Washington Press,* Iowa City, Iowa, 7/1/1857; *Iowa Weekly Citizen,* Des Moines, Iowa, 9/2/1857.

23 *Indianapolis Journal,* 11/22/1860.

24 *New York Tribune,* 8/24/1856, 9/22,29/1856, 10/8,15,25/1856; Isley, 129-30.

25 *New York Tribune,* 1/31/1860, 2/1/1860.

26 Shapiro, 99.

27 *Missouri Democrat,* 4/25/1855, 8/15/1855, 10/3/1857, 4/15/1859, 9/11/1860.

28 Ewbank, 6-7, 13-14.

29 *Chicago Tribune,* 2/20/1855, 5/30/1857, 9/1/1857, 11/1/1858. Behind the "curse" of slavery expansion stood the Democrats, who, according to Ray, were "men who are engaged in the attempt to force slavery into new territory, excluding white men thereby." Ray asked his readers if the "labor of the free white men in the territories [shall] be put on a equality with the labor of the unpaid, unclothed . . . negro?" To Ray, the issue of slavery extension also involved the issue of miscegenation, and he declared that the "Republicans wish to keep the black and white races separate and unmixed."

30 Olmsted, *Back Country,* 372-73.

31 *New York Tribune,* 10/15/1856, 12/17/1860.

32 *Missouri Democrat,* 10/25/1856, 12/1,3/1856, 2/24/1857, 5/30/1857, 9/15/ 1857, 11/19/1857, 1/14/1858, 8/31/1858, 7/2/1859, 8/13,15/1859. Brown noted that the administration Democrats, "in favoring the extension of

slavery . . . favor the exclusion of white men, in order to put negroes in their places in all the new territories." The Democratic extremist in the South, the "fire-eater, wants to Africanize them [the territories]." The Republican Party, on the other hand, "contemplated the reservation of this entire continent, to the equatorial regions, for the white race . . . . " Brown thought it "wiser . . . to leave the negro in Africa, and appropriate our territories to our white brethren in Europe and America." If necessary, Republicans would "repel the black surge of slave labor to its native swamps [within the South]."

33 *Hartford Evening Press,* Hartford, Conn., 10/25,26/1860.

34 *Illinois State Journal,* 2/12,25/1857.

35 *New York Tribune,* 3/13/1860, 12/6/1860; Durden, *James Shepherd Pike,* 25, 30-31.

36 *Hartford Courant,* Hartford, Conn., as quoted in Rawley, 150-51.

37 Ewbank, 4, 13.

38 *Grant County Herald,* Lancaster, Wisconsin, 10/24/1857.

39 Weston, iv, 235.

40 *New York Tribune,* 3/13/1860, 12/6/1860; Durden, *James Shepherd Pike,* 25, 30-31.

41 *Missouri Democrat,* 10/25/1856, 12/1,3/1856, 2/24/1857, 5/30/1857, 9/15/ 1857, 11/19/1857, 1/14/1858, 8/31/1858, 7/2/1859, 8/13,15/1859.

42 *New York Tribune,* 10/15/1856, 12/17/1860. Greeley feared the expansion of slavery because; "wherever slavery is introduced, society settles down upon an African, instead of a Caucasian basis . . . [with] the whole system of society adapted to the capacities and requirements of negro slaves, rather than to those of white freemen."

43 *Illinois State Journal,* 2/12,25/1857. Bailhache insisted that either "the territories of the general government shall be reserved for white people, or be surrendered to the negroes."

44 *Grant County Herald,* 10/24/1857.

45 *Missouri Democrat,* 5/30/1857.

46 Weston, iv, 235.

47 *New York Tribune,* 10/15/1856, 12/17/1860.

48 Nevins and Thomas, vol. 2, 22, 287, 304-05.

49 *Ohio State Journal,* 8/5/1859.

50 Pike, *The Prostrate State,* 22.

51   Weston, 33-35, 130-31, 234-37.

52   Guion G. Johnson, "A History of Racial Ideologies in the United States," 164, Schomberg Collection, New York Public Library.

53   *Missouri Democrat,* 2/13,24/1857, 4/5/1857, 5/16/1857.

54   Helper, *The Impending Crisis,* 73, 81-82, 97, 112, 129.

55   *Missouri Democrat,* 10/3/1857, 7/14/1859, 10/17/1860.

56   *New York Tribune,* 1/21/1858, 2/25/1858.

57   Weston, 34.

58   *Chicago Tribune,* 8/19/1859.

59   Helper, *Land of Gold,* 221.

60   *Missouri Democrat,* 10/3/1857, 8/13/1859, 10/17/1859.

61   Ewbank, 7-9, 13.

62   Helper, *Land of Gold,* 221-22; Helper, *The Impending Crisis,* 298-99.

63   Weston, 35.

64   *Missouri Democrat,* 10/3/1857, 7/14/1859, 10/17/1860.

65   Ibid.

66   Helper, *The Impending Crisis,* 196-98, 205-06.

67   *Chicago Tribune,* 8/19/1859.

68   Olmsted, *Back Country,* viii-ix, 481.

69   *Missouri Democrat,* 2/2/1859.

70   Weston, 243.

71   Helper, *Land of Gold,* 39, 47; Helper, *The Impending Crisis,* 26, 97, 156, 182-83.

72   *New York Tribune,* 3/13/1860, 12/6/1860.

73   *Missouri Democrat,* 4/1/1857, 8/13/1859.

74   Ibid., 1/28/1857, 2/24/1857, 4/1,5/1857, 5/16/1857, 1/14,20/1858, 7/27/1858, 7/14/1859, 8/13/1859, 10/17/1859, 9/11/1860, 10/17/1860. See also, *Missouri Democrat,* 2/27/1857, 1/23/1858, 8/20,27/1858, 2/16/1859, 4/15/1859.

75   *Chicago Tribune,* 8/19/1859.

76   Helper, *Land of Gold,* 39, 47; Helper, *The Impending Crisis,* 26, 97, 156, 182-83.

77   *New York Tribune,* 3/13/1860, 12/6/1860.

78   Helper, *Land of Gold,* 39, 47; Helper *The Impending Crisis,* 26, 97, 156, 182-83.

79   *Missouri Democrat,* 7/27/1858, 8/13/1859, 10/17/1859. See also, *Missouri Democrat,* 1/28/1857, 2/24/1857, 2/27/1857, 4/1,5/1857, 5/16/1857, 1/14,20,23/1858, 8/20,27/1858, 2/16/1859, 4/15/1859, 7/14/1859, 9/11/1860, 10/17/1860.

80   *New York Tribune,* 3/13/1860, 12/6/1860.

81   Ibid., 1/21/1858, 2/25/1858, 8/7/1858; *Missouri Democrat,* 3/1/1858.

82   *Missouri Democrat,* 2/24/1857, 1/23/1858, 8/20/1858.

83   Ibid., 1/20,23/1858, 8/20/1858, 7/14/1859, 8/13/1859, 10/17/1859.

84   *New York Tribune,* 1/21/1858, 2/25/1858, 8/7/1858; *Missouri Democrat,* 3/1/1858.

85   *Missouri Democrat,* 1/28/1857, 4/1/1857.

86   *New York Tribune,* 1/21/1858, 2/25/1858, 8/7/1858; *Missouri Democrat,* 3/1/1858.

87   *Missouri Democrat,* 10/17/1860. See also, *Missouri Democrat,* 2/16/1859, 7/14/1859, 8/13/1859.

88   *New York Tribune,* 1/21/1858, 2/25/1858.

89   *Missouri Democrat,* 5/16/1857. See also, *Missouri Democrat,* 7/14/1859, 10/17/1859.

90   Helper, *The Impending Crisis,* 26, 156, 182-83.

91   *Missouri Democrat,* 1/28/1857, 2/24,27/1857, 4/5/1857, 1/23/1858, 8/20,27/1858, 7/14/1859, 9/11/1860.

92   *New York Tribune,* 1/21/1858, 2/25/1858, 8/7/1858; *Missouri Democrat,* 3/1/1858.

93   *Missouri Democrat,* 7/14/1859, 10/17/1859, 10/17/1860.

94   Ibid., 8/31/1858, 2/16/1859, 4/15/1859.

95   For Doolittle's Senate speech, see Chapter 5 notes 113, 139 & 170.

96   *Missouri Democrat,* 8/31/1858, 2/16/1859, 4/15/1859.

97   Ibid., 1/28/1857, 2/24,27/1857, 4/5/1857, 1/23/1858, 8/20,27/1858, 7/14/1859, 9/11/1860.

98   Helper, *The Impending Crisis,* 26, 156, 182-83.

99   Ibid.

100   *Illinois State Journal,* 1/28/1857, 4/9/1857.

101   *New York Tribune,* 1/21/1858, 2/25/1858, 8/7/1858; *Missouri Democrat,* 3/1/1858.

102   *Philadelphia Daily News,* 11/22/1860.

103 *Missouri Democrat,* 1/28/1857, 5/16/1857, 8/20,31/1858, 4/15/1859, 8/13/ 1859, 10/17/1859.

104 C.C. Sholes to Doolittle, 5/21/1860, Doolittle Papers, Wisconsin State Historical Society.

105 James Redpath, *A Guide to Hayti* (Boston, 1861), 1-11, 171-75; Willis D. Boyd, "James Redpath and American Negro Colonization in Haiti, 1860-1862," *Americas,* vol. 12, 1955, 172-82; Floyd J. Miller, *The Search For A Black Nationality, Black Emigration and Colonization, 1781-1863* (Urbana, Ill., 1975), 238, 241, 244-47; McPherson, *The Negro's Civil War,* 78-79, 88-89; Staudenraus, 244-45.

106 *Missouri Democrat,* 8/20/1858. Brown charged that if Southern Democrats had their way, Eli Thayer's efforts would be halted; because they wanted only "black slaves" to "come by the multitude, either artizans or mechanics . . . to compete with the sturdy toil of the white race." In the case of Virginia, "white men are not only to be repulsed, lest they may supercede [sic] slaves, but white men are to be driven out of Virginia, that slaves may take their places." In the case of his own state Brown wrote that "it is better for Missouri that she should be peopled by white men, than that she should be depleted by negroes." Besides being better workers, Brown concluded that "white men are a much better population [morally and intellectually] than negroes." See, *Missouri Democrat,* 10/9/1856, 1/28/1857, 4/14/1857, 5/16/1857, 6/5,10/1857, 9/15/ 1857, 1/20/1858, 3/31/1858, 7/1,27/1858, 3/16/1859, 11/25/1859.

107 Olmsted, *Back Country,* viii.

108 *Chicago Tribune,* 3/3/1856, 2/14/1857, 4/10/1857.

109 *Missouri Democrat,* 10/9/1856, 1/28/1857, 4/14/1857, 6/5,10/1857, 9/15/ 1857, 1/20/1858, 3/31/1858, 7/1,27/1858, 8/20/1858, 11/25/1859.

110 Ibid.

111 *Free West,* 9/21/1854.

112 *New York Tribune,* 6/24/1857.

113 *Chicago Tribune,* 4/10/1857.

114 *Ohio State Journal,* 8/11/1859.

115 Ewbank, 12.

116 Helper, *Land of Gold,* 265.

117 Nevins and Thomas, vol. 2, 304.

118   Shapiro, 89.

119   *New York Tribune,* 7/24/1858, 8/7/1858, 10/12/1858, 7/4/1860, 12/17/1860.

120   *Chicago Tribune,* 2/3,10/1857, 3/2/1857.

121   *New York Tribune,* 7/24/1858, 8/7/1858, 10/12/1858, 7/4/1860, 12/17/1860.

122   *Cincinnati Commercial,* 7/9/1860, 11/6/1860.

123   Joseph Medill to Chase, 10/30/1859, Chase Papers, Historical Society of Pennsylvania.

124   *New York Tribune,* 7/24/1858, 8/7/1858, 10/12/1858, 7/4/1860, 12/17/1860.

125   *Portage County Democrat,* 11/3/1858.

126   Joseph Medill to Chase, 10/30/1859, Chase Papers, Historical Society of Pennsylvania. See also, William E. Dodd, "The Fight for the Northwest, 1860," *American Historical Review,* vol. 16, 1911, 784-85.

127   Cardoso, 4, 58, 60, 88, 108, 110, 197. Even though he strongly supported a program of gradual emancipation and colonization, Helper nevertheless thought, according to Joaquin Cardoso, that a Republican triumph in 1860, "meant the beginning of an immediate crusade against . . . slavery . . . to be followed by a social assault against the Negro."

NOTES—CHAPTER 8

1   *Congressional Globe,* 36th Cong., 2nd. Session, Appendix, 1340, 1408; 37th Cong., 2nd. Session, 2618, Appendix, 93. For a good example of Republican conservatism at the beginning of the war, see Jacob M. Howard to Charles Jewett, 12/23/1861, Howard Papers.

2   Montgomery Blair, *Letter to the Meeting Held at the Cooper Institute, New York, March 6, 1862,* as quoted in Montgomery Blair, *Comments on the Policy Inaugurated by the President,* pamphlet, N.Y., 1863, 4-7, 16-20. For an example of white attacks on blacks during the Civil War see, Adrian Cook, *The Armies of the Streets: the New York City Draft Riots of 1863* (Lexington, Ky., 1974).

3   *Congressional Globe,* 37th Cong., 2nd. Session, 1632.

4   Francis Preston Blair to Lincoln, 11/16/1861, Richard W. Thompson Papers, Rutherford B. Hayes Library, Fremont, Ohio. For the influence of Blair senior on Lincoln see, Francis Preston Blair to Lincoln, 1/14/1861, David Davis Collection. See also, Elbert B. Smith, *Francis Preston Blair,* 266, 314-19.

5   James Mitchell, *Letter on the Relation of the White and African Races in the United States,* 3-12, 16, 24-26. See also, James Mitchell, *Report on Colonization and Emigration made to the Secretary of the Interior by the Agent of Emigration,* pamphlet, Washington, D.C., 1862, 5, 9-15, 17-20, 25-29; James Speed to James Harlan, 6/2/1865, Records of the Office of the Secretary of the Interior relating to the Suppression of the African Slave Trade and Negro Colonization, 1854-1872, United States Archives, Washington, D.C.

6   *Congressional Globe,* 37th Cong. 2nd. Session, 1052.

7   Lincoln's address to blacks of 8/14/1862, as quoted in Basler, vol. 5, 370-75. Lincoln clearly meant the black race. He told his listeners that the "colored race" was the "basis" of slavery, without which the "war could not have an existence." As an added insult he stated frankly that white soldiers, North and South, "do not care for you one way or the other."

8   Sturtevant, 606-09; Agassiz to Dr. S.G. Howe, 8/9,10/1863, as quoted in Elizabeth Cary Agassiz, vol. 2, 594-611.

9   *Congressional Globe,* 38th Cong., 1st. Session, 2010.

10   Ibid., 2nd. Session, 130, 287.

11   Ibid., 37th Cong., 2nd. Session, 1633-34.

12   Ibid., 38th Cong., 2nd. Session, 484.

13   Ibid., 1st. Session, 1769.

14   Ibid., 37th Cong., 2nd. Session, 2017-18. On a scheme to compensate Missouri slaveholders see, *Congressional Globe,* 37th Cong., 3rd. Session, 796.

15   *Congressional Globe,* 37th Cong., 2nd. Session, Appendix, 173.

16   Ibid., 3rd. Session, 24.

17   Ibid., 845, 2nd. Session, 83-84, 1492, 1520.

18   *House Report No. 148,* 37th Cong., 2nd. Session, 12-17, 32-33; *Congressional Globe,* 37th Cong., 2nd. Session, 1563, 3rd. Session, 1293; *House Journal,* 37th Cong., 2nd. Session, 542. Even though the war would seem to require full attention, the Republican fear of miscegenation would not subside. Scofield of Pennsylvania ignored the more urgent concern to address the House on the issue of the "practical amalgamation" that went on in the South. Republican Kelley, also of Pennsylvania, noted that the Democrat "has never seen the white northern man choose his companion from that

[black] race," and Republican Representative Thomas B. Shannon of California voiced similar sentiments. Even the liberal George Julian took up the time of Congress to condemn the "intimate relations" that existed between Southern whites and blacks, referring to this as the "most loathsome" example of "social equality" between the races. Facetiously he stated that "In some of the rebel states . . . the number of mulattoes is nearly equal to the number of Democratic voters." See, *Congressional Globe,* 38th Cong., 1st. Session, 773, 809, 2251, 2948.

19   *House Report No. 148,* 37th Cong., 2nd. Session, 12-17, 32-33; *Congressional Globe,* 37th Cong., 2nd. Session, 1563, 3rd. Session, 1293; *House Journal,* 37th Cong., 2nd. Session, 542.

20   *Congressional Globe,* 37th Cong., 2nd. Session, 1521, 2502, Appendix, 95-99.

21   *United States Statutes at Large,* George P. Sanger, ed. (Boston, 1863), vol. 12, 376-78; *Congressional Globe,* 37th Cong., 2nd. Session, 1191, 1266, 1286, 1319, 1333, 1371-72, 1522; Mitchell, *Report on Colonization and Emigration,* 5, 9-15, 17-20, 25-29. Of the 92 votes for the measure in the House, 84 were Republican, with only 8 Democrats voting for the bill. Of the 38 votes against the measure, 26 were Democrat and 12 were Republican. Of these 12 Republican votes against, however, 8 were Border or slave state Republicans. In the Senate, 29 of 29 yes votes were Republican. No Democrats voted for the bill. Of the 14 votes against the measure, 10 were Democrat, and 4 were Border state Republican. See, *Congressional Globe,* 37th Cong., 2nd. Session, 1526, 1648-49; *Biographical Directory of the American Congress,* 175-79.

22   *United States Statutes at Large,* vol. 12, 582, 589-92; *Congressional Globe,* 37th Cong., 2nd. Session, 1604, 3006, 3403. See also, Mitchell, *Report on Colonization and Emigration,* 5, 9-15, 17-20, 25-29. Of the 68 votes for the measure in the House, 67 were Republican, leaving only 1 Democrat voting for the bill. Of the 33 votes against the measure, 22 were Democrat. However, of the 11 Republicans who voted against the bill, 7 were Border state Republicans. In the Senate, 28 of the 28 yes votes were Republican. No Democrats voted for the bill. Of the 13 votes opposed, 8 were Democrat. Of the 5 Republican no votes, 2 were from Border state Republicans. See, *Congressional Globe,* 37th Cong., 2nd. Session, 3006, 3370; *Biographical*

Directory of the American Congress, 175-79. One Democratic Senator, William A. Richardson of Illinois, referred to Congress as a "lunatic asylum" because of its massive support for colonization, and to the scheme itself as "absurd and impossible." See, *Congressional Globe,* 37th Cong., 3rd. Session, 789.

23   Warren Beck, "The Chiriqui Improvement Company and Lincoln's plan to colonize slaves in Central America," M.A. thesis, Wayne State University, 1948, 38-39; *Congressional Globe,* 37th Cong., 2nd. Session, Appendix, 3, 3rd. Session, Appendix, 1-5. When writing on Lincoln and colonization, historian Frederick Bancroft noted that "Next to compensated emancipation, this was one of his favorite ideas." See, Bancroft, *The Life of William H. Seward* (N.Y., 1900), vol. 2, 345-46.

24   Basler, vol. 5, 370-75.

25   McPherson, *The Negro's Civil War,* 81-83, 88-89.

26   Ibid., 90-94.

27   *The Liberator,* 9/12/1862.

28   Robert Purvis to S.C. Pomeroy, 8/28/1862, as quoted in the *New York Tribune,* 9/20/1862.

29   *An Appeal from the Colored Men of Philadelphia to the President of the United States,* pamphlet, n.a., Philadelphia, 1862.

30   McPherson, *The Negro's Civil War,* 90-94.

31   *The Liberator,* 9/12/1862.

32   Robert Purvis to S.C. Pomeroy, 8/28/1862, as quoted in the *New York Tribune,* 9/20/1862. For further evidence of black opposition to colonization see, *Proceedings of the National convention of Colored Men at Syracuse, N.Y., October 4, 5, 6, 7, 1864,* 22-52; Staudenraus, 249; Beck, 3; Planck, 68-69; Paul J. Scheips, "Lincoln and the Chiriqui Colonization Project," *Journal of Negro History,* vol. 37, 1952, 451; Dann, 236; McPherson, "Abolitionist and Negro Opposition to Colonization," 391-98; Mehlinger, 276-301; Cooke, 163, 258. Secretary of the Interior John P. Usher noted, firstly the unwillingness of blacks to leave, and secondly the need for blacks in the Union forces as the major reasons for the administration abandoning colonization. See, Cooke, 258.

33   *Congressional Globe,* 37th Cong., 2nd. Session, 1641-42.

34   Ibid., 38th Cong., 1st. Session, 2116.

35   Diary of Salmon P. Chase, 8/15/1862, Chase Papers, Library of Congress.

36   *Congressional Globe,* 38th Cong., 1st. Session, Appendix, 45.

37   Forbes and Tuckerman to Usher, 4/6/1863; Usher to Forbes and Tuckerman, 4/30/1863; Usher to Robert Murray, 4/3/1863; Usher to John Cisco, 4/3/1863; Usher to Lyman Trumbull, 7/8/1862, Records of the Office of the Secretary of the Interior; Usher to Lincoln, 8/2/1862, Abraham Lincoln Collection, vol. 82, Library of Congress. On the poor condition and mistreatment of black colonists and loss of black lives see, Usher to Henry J. Raymond, 9/18/1863; Usher to D.C. Donnohue, 10/9,17/1863, 1/24/1864, 2/2/1864; D.C. Donnohue to Usher, 1/3,5/1864, 3/26/1864; Usher to Edwin M. Stanton, 2/1/1864; Usher to Tuckerman, 10/19/1863, 4/5/1864; Usher to Forbes and Tuckerman, 12/19/1863; James DeLong to Henry Conrad, 7/8,21,27/1863; James DeLong to D. C. Donnohue, 1/26/1864, Records of the Office of the Secretary of the Interior. Donnohue was a government investigator and agent sent to Haiti by Usher. DeLong was United States Counsel at Haiti. For an example of Lincoln's persistence in the Ile a Vache project see, Tuckerman to Usher, 10/20/1863, 1/9/1864, 1/13/1864, Records of the Office of the Secretary of the Interior.

38   *Congressional Globe,* 38th Cong., 1st. Session, 586, Appendix, 48.

39   Ibid., 1st. Session, 2218.

40   On the slave states' rejection of the plan see, Herman Belz, *Reconstructing the Union, Theory and Practice during the Civil War,* (Ithaca, N.Y., 1969), 103; James G. Randall, *Constitutional Problems Under Lincoln* (Urbana, Ill., 1964, originally published in 1926), 366-67; Randall, *Lincoln and the South* (Baton Rouge, La., 1946), 89-95; Peter J. Parish, *The American Civil War* (N.Y., 1975), 232; Voegeli, *Free But Not Equal,* 40. On black opposition to colonization see, Staudenraus, 32, 95, 188-89, 193; Cooke, 163; Litwack, *North of Slavery,* 235, 259; Penelope Campbell, 39-40, 103-06; Draper, 12, 17-18; Osofsky, 74-76; Mehlinger, 276-77, 283-86, 294, 301.

41   Thomas R. Dew, *Review of the Debate in the Virginia Legislature of 1831 and 1832* (Richmond, Va., 1832), as quoted in McKitrick, 27-29. Dew, professor of political economy at William and Mary College and a staunch pro-slavery advocate noted that "every plan of emancipation and deportation which we [Southerners] can possibly conceive is totally impracticable." See, Chancellor Harper, *The Pro-Slavery Argument: as Maintained by the most*

Distinguished Writers of the Southern States, including Chancellor Harper, Governor Hammond, Dr. Simms, and Professor Dew (Charleston, S.C., 1852), 292-93.

42   Historian V. Jacque Voegeli thoroughly covers Lincoln's plans for containment. See, Voegeli, *Free But Not Equal,* 86-88.

43   *Congressional Globe,* 37th Cong., 3rd. Session, Appendix, 4; 38th Cong., 2nd. Session, Appendix, 2.

44   Ibid., 37th Cong., 3rd. Session, 1084-85.

45   Slaveholders in the District of Columbia received $300 per slave. Lincoln was "gratified" that both "compensation and colonization" were incorporated into the D.C. Emancipation Act. See, Randall, *Lincoln and the South,* 89; Letter of Lincoln to Congress, 4/16/1862, as quoted in the *Congressional Globe,* 37th Cong., 2nd. Session, 1680, 3203, 3321; 38th Cong., 1st. Session, 2472, 2851; John W. Blassingame, "The Recruitment of Colored Troops in Kentucky, Maryland and Missouri, 1863-1865," *The Historian,* vol. 29, 1967, 536-37.

46   *Congressional Globe,* 38th Cong., 1st. Session, 774.

47   Ibid., 37th Cong., 2nd. Session, 44, 1107, 2301.

48   Ibid., 1644.

49   Ibid., 332.

50   Ibid., 1606.

51   Ibid., 38th Cong., 2nd. Session, 155.

52   Ibid., 1st. Session, 1769, 2140-41.

53   Ibid., 2nd. Session, 145.

54   Ibid., 1st. Session, 2235.

55   Ibid., 1185, 1188, 2251.

56   Ibid., 37th Cong., 3rd. Session, Appendix, 157, 281.

57   Ibid., 38th Cong., 1st. Session, 2933-34, 3263, 3331, 2nd. Session, 688, 983-84.

58   Nicolay and Hay, *Complete Works,* vol. 8, 112-15; *Congressional Globe,* 38th Cong., 1st. Session, 2802.

59   *Congressional Globe,* 38th Cong., 2nd. Session, 163, 610; Lincoln to Lt. Col. Glenn, 2/7/1865, as quoted in Basler, vol. 8, 266; W.E.B. DuBois, *Black Reconstruction in America, 1860-1880* (N.Y., 1968, originally published in 1935), 75-77; George R. Bentley, *A History of the Freedmen's Bureau* (Phila.,

1955), 17-19, 26-27. The military's role in containment was manifested in General Orders No. 64, issued on 8/29/1863, and No. 23, issued on 2/3/1864. Both orders were issued by Major General Nathaniel P. Banks. See, *Senate Executive Documents No. 29,* 38th Cong., 2nd. Session, 1-4; Nathaniel P. Banks, *Emancipated Labor in Louisiana,* pamphlet, n.p., 1864, 12-41; Jacob Dolson Cox, *Military Reminiscences of the Civil War,* (N.Y., 1900), vol. 2, 486; Bell Irwin Wiley, *Southern Negroes, 1861-1865* (New Haven, Conn., 1938), 184-90; Fred Harvey Harrington, *Fighting Politician, Major General N.P. Banks* (Phila., 1948), 104-09; Robert Dale Owen, James McKaye, Samuel G. Howe, *Preliminary Report touching the Condition and Management of Emancipated Refugees,* pamphlet, N.Y., 1863, 15-16, 22-26. Historian Stephen B. Oates notes that "In place of colonization, the Lincoln administration devised a refugee system, installed by the Army in the occupied South, which utilized Southern blacks in a variety of military and civilian pursuits. Although there were many faults with the system, it was based on sound Republican dogma: it kept Southern Negroes out of the North . . . . " See, Oates, "The Man of Our Redemption: Abraham Lincoln and the Emancipation of the Slaves," *Presidential Studies Quarterly,* vol. 9, 1979, 22.

60   Dudley T. Cornish, *The Sable Arm, Negro Troops in the Union Army, 1861-1865* (N.Y., 1966, originally published in 1956), 81-131; Joseph T. Wilson, *The Black Phalanx, A History of the Negro Soldiers of the United States in the Wars of 1775-1812, 1861-1865* (Hartford, Conn., 1888), 108-09, 123-25.

61   Haller, 20-23; Nevins and Thomas, vol. 2, 304; Frank B. Sanborn, *Dr. S.G. Howe, the Philanthropist* (N.Y., 1891), 251, 282-90; Elizabeth Cary Agassiz, vol. 2, 596-606.

62   *Congressional Globe,* 37th Cong., 3rd. Session, 600-05. Some congressional Republicans introduced resolutions demanding segregated units, with black troops under white officers. See, *Congressional Globe,* 38th Cong., 1st. Session, 604-05.

63   *Congressional Globe,* 38th Cong., 1st. Session, 742.

64   Ibid., 3349.

65   Ibid., 37th Cong., 2nd. Session, 3203, 3rd. Session, 77-78; 38th Cong., 1st. Session, 240, 242-43, 427, 1213, 2nd. Session. 335, 3199.

66   Ibid., 38th Cong., 1st. Session, 3487.

67   Ibid., 37th Cong., 3rd. Session, 79-80.

68   Ibid., 1255.

69   Ibid., 2nd. Session, 441, 3199.

70   Bingham to Howard, 7/26/1861, Howard Papers.

71   *Congressional Globe,* 37th Cong., 2nd. Session, 3203, 3321; 38th Cong., 1st. Session, 2472, 2851; Blassingame, "The Recruitment of Colored Troops," 536-37; Joseph T. Wilson, 116-23; Cornish, 188-89. On D.C. compensation see note 45.

72   *Congressional Globe,* 38th Cong., 2nd. Session, 122.

73   Benjamin F. Butler, *Autobiography and Personal Reminiscences* (Boston, 1892), 903-04. See also, Wesley, "Lincoln's Plan," 20; Fredrickson, "A Man but Not a Brother," 57; Boyd, "Negro Colonization in the National Crisis, 1860-1870," 166; Belz, 282-83; Howard P. Nash Jr., *Stormy Petrel: The Life and Times of General Benjamin F. Butler, 1818-1893* (Cranbury, N.J., 1969), 218-19; Cox, *Lincoln's Negro Policy,* 62-64; Pickett, 326-27; Scheips, 448-49. As noted, some historians discount Butler's statements, labelling him "wily," a person who was always engaged in "spinning designs," and therefore whose testimony was "dubious" at best. However, they fail to explain any possible motivation Butler may have had for lying in this matter. See, Sandburg, vol. 4, 26; Fehrenbacher, "Only His Stepchildren," 308. Like Lincoln, Mitchell also wanted to continue plans for black colonization in 1865. See, Mitchell, *Brief on Emigration and Colonization and Report in Answer to a resolution of the Senate,* pamphlet, Washington, D.C., 1865, 18.

BIBLIOGRAPHY

I. PRIMARY SOURCES

A. UNPUBLISHED: MANUSCRIPT COLLECTIONS

Charles Francis Adams Papers, Massachusetts Historical Society.

American Colonization Society Papers, Library of Congress.

Charles Billinghurst Papers, Wisconsin State Historical Society.

Kinsley Scott Bingham Papers, Bentley Historical Library, University of Michigan.

James G. Birney Papers, Clements Library, University of Michigan.

Blair Collection, State Historical Society of Missouri.

Montgomery Blair Papers, Brown University Library.

William Henry Brisbane Papers, Wisconsin State Historical Society.

Orville Hickman Browning Letters, Illinois Survey Collection, University of Illinois.

John Howard Bryant Papers, University of Southern California Library.

Salmon P. Chase Correspondence, American Missionary Association Archives, Amistad Research Center.

Salmon P. Chase Papers, Historical Society of Pennsylvania.

Salmon P. Chase Papers, Library of Congress.

Salmon P. Chase-John P. Hale Correspondence, New Hampshire Historical Society.

Schuyler Colfax Papers, Library of Congress.

Thomas Corwin Letters, Cincinnati Historical Society.

Orris Crosby Correspondence, Risley Letters, Olin Library, Cornell University.

Richard Henry Dana Papers, Massachusetts Historical Society.

David Davis Collection, Chicago Historical Society.

Ignatius Donnelly Papers, Minnesota Historical Society.

James R. Doolittle Papers, Library of Congress.

James R. Doolittle Papers, New York Public Library.

James R. Doolittle Papers, Wisconsin State Historical Society.

Zebina Eastman Collection, Chicago Historical Society.

Lucius C. Embree Collection, Indiana State Library.

Orin Follett Papers, Cincinnati Historical Society.

Joshua R. Giddings Papers, Ohio Historical Society.

Joshua R. Giddings Papers, Library of Congress.

Horace Greeley-Schuyler Colfax Correspondence, New York Public Library.

John P. Hale-Joshua R. Giddings Correspondence, Dartmouth College Library.

Darius Hall Correspondence, Smelzer Family Papers, Olin Library, Cornell University.

Hannibal Hamlin Papers, Folger Library, University of Maine.

Frederick Hassaurek Collection, Ohio Historical Society.

Jacob Merritt Howard Papers, Burton Historical Collection, Detroit Public Library.

George W. Julian Collection, Indiana State Library.

John A. Kasson Papers, Alderman Library Collection, University of Virginia.

John Kirk Letter Books, Chicago Historical Society.

Samuel J. Kirkwood Papers, Iowa State Department of History and Archives.

Henry Smith Lane Collection, Lilly Library, Indiana University.

Abraham Lincoln Papers, Illinois Survey Collection, University of Illinois.

Abraham Lincoln Collection, Library of Congress.

Robert Todd Lincoln Collection, Library of Congress.

Owen Lovejoy Correspondence, American Missionary Association Archives, Amistad Research Center.

William W. Orme Papers, Illinois Survey Collection, University of Illinois.

James Shepherd Pike Papers, Folger Library, University of Maine.

John Fox Potter Collection, Wisconsin State Historical Society.

Daniel D. Pratt Collection, Indiana State Library.

Alexander Ramsey Papers, Minnesota Historical Society.

Albert Gallatin Riddle Collection, Western Reserve Historical Society Library.

Robert C. Schenck Papers, Rutherford B. Hayes Library.

William Henry Seward Collection, University of Rochester Library.

Henry H. Sibley Letters, Minnesota Historical Society.

Milton Sutliff Papers, Western Reserve Historical Society Library.

Richard W. Thompson Papers, Rutherford B. Hayes Library.

Lyman Trumbull Family Papers, Illinois State Historical Society.

Lyman Trumbull Papers, Illinois Survey Collection, University of Illinois.

Lyman Trumbull Papers, Library of Congress.

Benjamin F. Wade Papers, Library of Congress.

Henry B. Whipple Papers, Minnesota Historical Society.

Elisha Whittlesey Papers, Western Reserve Historical Society Library.

Samuel Wilkeson Correspondence, Wilkeson-Barringer Collection, Buffalo and Erie County Historical Society.

B. PUBLISHED:

1. FEDERAL AND STATE GOVERNMENT REPORTS

Acts of the Legislature of the State of Michigan, Passed at the Regular Session of 1855. Lansing, Mich., 1855.

Biographical Directory of the American Congress, 1774-1971. Government Printing Office, Washington, D.C., 1971.

Congressional Globe. Blair and Rives, Printers, Washington, D.C., 25th Congress through 38th Congress.

House Journal. 37th Cong., 2nd. Session.

House Report No. 148. 37th Cong., 2nd. Session.

Journal of the House of Representatives of the State of Indiana. 34th Session, 1849; 35th Session, 1850.

Ohio Executive Documents. Columbus, Ohio, 1859, Part II.

Records of the Office of the Secretary of the Interior relating to the Suppression of the African Slave Trade and Negro Colonization, 1854-1872. United States Archives microfilm, 10 reels, Washington, D.C.

Report of the Debates and Proceedings of the Convention for the Revision of the Constitution of the State of Indiana, 1850. Indianapolis, 1850, vol. 1.

Report of the Naval Committee to the House of Representatives, July 1850. Washington, D.C., 1850.

Senate Executive Document, No. 26. 35th Cong., 2nd. Session.

Senate Executive Document, No. 29. 38th Cong., 2nd. Session.

United States Statutes at Large. Edited by George P. Sanger. Boston, 1863, 94 vols.

2. Newspapers

Alton Weekly Courier. Alton, Illinois.

Anti-Slavery Bugle. Salem, Ohio.

Ashtabula Sentinel. Ashtabula, Ohio.

Barnburner. St. Louis, Missouri.

Boston Post. Boston, Massachusetts.

Boston Times. Boston, Massachusetts.

Buffalo Daily Republic. Buffalo, New York.

Bureau County Republic. Princeton, Illinois.

Cadiz Republican. Cadiz, Ohio.

Cass County Republican. Dowagiac, Michigan.

Chicago Democrat. Chicago, Illinois.

Chicago Tribune. Chicago, Illinois.

Cincinnati Commercial. Cincinnati, Ohio.

Cleveland Daily Herald. Cleveland, Ohio.

Detroit Advertiser. Detroit, Michigan.

Douglass' Monthly. Rochester, New York.

Emancipator and Republican. Boston, Massachusetts.

Evansville Daily Journal. Evansville, Indiana.

Grant County Herald. Lancaster, Wisconsin.

Hartford Courant. Hartford, Connecticut.

Hartford Evening Press. Hartford, Connecticut.

Illinois Daily Journal. Springfield, Illinois.

Illinois State Journal. Springfield, Illinois.

Indianapolis Daily Journal. Indianapolis, Indiana.

Iowa State Register. Des Moines, Iowa.

Iowa Weekly Citizen. Des Moines, Iowa.

Ithaca Journal. Ithaca, New York.

Marysville Daily Herald. Marysville, California.

Missouri Democrat. St. Louis, Missouri.

Montezuma Weekly Republican. Iowa City, Iowa.

National Anti-Slavery Standard. New York, New York.

National Era. Washington, D.C.

National Republican. Washington, D.C.

New York Day Book. New York, New York.

New York Evening Post. New York, New York.

New York Herald. New York, New York.

New York Tribune. New York, New York.

North Star. Rochester, New York.

Ohio State Journal. Columbus, Ohio.

Pennsylvania Freeman. Philadelphia, Pennsylvania.

Philadelphia Daily News. Philadelphia, Pennsylvania.

Portage County Democrat. Ravenna, Ohio.

Quincy Whig. Quincy, Illinois.

Racine Advocate. Racine, Wisconsin.

Sandusky Commercial Register. Sandusky, Ohio.

Sangamo Journal. Springfield, Illinois.

South Bend Register. South Bend, Indiana.

The Catholic Telegraph. Cincinnati, Ohio.

The Colored American. New York, New York.

The Freeman. New York, New York.

The Free West. Chicago, Illinois.

The Liberator. Boston, Massachusetts.

The Liberty Press. Utica, New York.

The Lockport Journal. Lockport, New York.

The National Intelligencer. Washington, D.C.

The True American. Lexington, Kentucky.

The Weekly Anglo-African. New York, New York.

Washington Press. Iowa City, Iowa.

Western Citizen. Chicago, Illinois.

3. PAMPHLETS, JOURNALS, BOOKS, ARTICLES AND DOCUMENTARIES

Adams, John Quincy. "The Character of Desdemona." *American Monthly Magazine.* vol. 1, 1836, 209-17.

Alvarez, Alonzo. *Progress and Intelligence of Americans.* Louisville, Ky., 1863.

A Memorial of Zebina Eastman by His Family. Pamphlet, n.d., Eastman Collection.

American Free Soil Almanac for 1849. n.a., Boston, 1849.

An Appeal from the Colored Men of Philadelphia to the President of the United States. Pamphlet, n.a., Philadelphia, 1862.

Appeal of the Independent Democrats in Congress, to the People of the United States. Pamphlet, Washington, D.C., January 19, 1854.

Aptheker, Herbert, ed. *A Documentary History of the Negro People in the United States.* N.Y., 1969, originally published in 1951.

Armistead, Wilson. *A Tribute For the Negro.* Manchester, England, 1848.

Banks, Nathaniel P. *Emancipated Labor in Louisiana.* Pamphlet, n.p., 1864.

Barth, Henry. *Travels and Discoveries in North and Central Africa: Being a Journal of an Expedition undertaken under the Auspices of H.B.M.'s Government in the years 1849-1855.* London, England, 1857, 2 vols.

Blair, Frank. *Colonization and Commerce, An Address Before the Young Men's Mercantile Library Association of Cincinnati, Ohio.* Pamphlet, Washington, D.C., 1859.

_____. *The Destiny of the Races of This Continent, An Address before the Mercantile Library Association, Boston.* Pamphlet, Washington, D.C., 1859.

Blair, Montgomery. *Comments on the Policy Inaugurated by the President.* Pamphlet, N.Y., 1863.

Booth, Mary L. "Emancipation and Colonization." *Brownson's Quarterly Review,* vol. 19, 1862, 220-32.

Browne, Peter A. *The Classification of Mankind by the Hair and Wool of their Heads, with the Nomenclature of Human Hybrids.* Philadelphia, 1852.

Burmeister, Herman. *The Black Man, The Comparative Anatomy and Psychology of the African Negro.* N.Y., 1853.

Bushnell, Horace. *A Discourse on the Slavery Question.* Pamphlet, Hartford, Conn., 1839.

Cairnes, J.E. *The Slave Power.* N.Y., 1862.

Caldwell, Charles. *Thoughts on the Original Unity of the Human Race.* N.Y., 1830.

Campbell, John. *Negro-Mania: Being an Examination of the Falsely Assumed Equality of the Various Races of Men.* Philadelphia, 1851.

Cartwright, Samuel. "Natural History of the Prognathous Species of Mankind." Cited in *New York Day Book,* 11/10/1857.

_____. "Slavery in the light of ethnology." Cited in Elliott, *Cotton is King.* 698-727.

Child, David Lee. *The Despotism of Freedom, or the Tyranny and Cruelty of American Republican Slave Masters.* Boston, 1833.

Christy, David. *Pulpit Politics or Ecclesiastical Legislation on Slavery, in its Disturbing Influence on the American Union.* Cincinnati, 1862.

Clay, Cassius M. *A Review of the Late Canvass.* Pamphlet, Lexington, Ky., 1840.

Colfax, Richard H. *Evidence Against the Views of the Abolitionists, Consisting of Physical and Moral Proofs of the Natural Inferiority of the Negroes.* N.Y., 1833.

Colonization Society of Iowa Annual Report, 1857. Pamphlet, Iowa City, Iowa, 1857.

Colored National Convention, Cleveland, 1848. Pamphlet, n.a., Rochester, N.Y., 1848.

Combe, George. *A System of Phrenology.* Edinburgh, Scotland, 1843, 2 vols.

———. *Notes on the United States of North America.* Philadelphia, 1841, 2 vols.

———. *The Constitution of Man considered in Relation to External Objects.* Hartford, Conn., 1842.

Conway, Moncure Daniel. *Testimonies Concerning Slavery.* London, England, 1864.

Dana, Richard Henry. *To Cuba and Back.* N.Y., 1859.

DeGobineau, Arthur. *The Inequality of Human Races.* Paris, France, 1853.

Derby, E.H. "Resources of the South." *Atlantic Monthly,* vol. 10, 1862, 508-09.

DeTocqueville, Alexis. *Democracy in America.* N.Y., 1969, originally published in 1848.

Dew, Thomas R. *Review of the Debate in the Virginia Legislature of 1831 and 1832.* Richmond, Va., 1832.

Dyer, Oliver. *Phonographic Report of the Proceedings of the National Free Soil Convention at Buffalo, N.Y., August 9th and 10th, 1848.* Buffalo, N.Y., 1848.

Eastman, Zebina. *History of the Anti-Slavery Agitation and the growth of the Liberty and Republican Parties in the State of Illinois.* Pamphlet, Chicago, n.d., Eastman Collection.

Elliott, E.N. *Cotton is King.* Augusta, Ga., 1860.

Emerson, Ralph Waldo. *The Works of Ralph Waldo Emerson.* N.Y., 1856, 12 vols.

Ewbank, Thomas. *Inorganic Forces Ordained to Supersede Human Slavery.* Pamphlet, N.Y., 1860.

Fisher, Sidney George. *The Laws of Race as Connected with Slavery.* Philadelphia, 1860.

———. *The Trial of the Constitution.* Philadelphia, 1862.

Fowler, Orson S. *Human Science or Phrenology.* Chicago, 1873.

Gardiner, Oliver C. *The Great Issue.* N.Y., 1848.

Garrison, William Lloyd. *Thoughts on African Colonization.* Boston, 1832.

Giddings, Joshua R. *History of the Rebellion, Its Authors and Causes.* N.Y., 1864.

———. *Speeches in Congress.* N.Y., 1968, originally published in 1853.

Gilmer, John H. *War of Races.* Richmond, Va., 1867.

Gurney, Joseph John. *Free and Friendly Remarks.* Pamphlet, N.Y., 1839.

Harlan, James. *Shall the Territories be Africanized?* Pamphlet, n.p., 1860.

Harper, Chancellor. *The Pro-Slavery Argument; as Maintained by the most Distinguished Writers of the Southern States, including Chancellor Harper, Governor Hammond, Dr. Simms, and Professor Dew.* Charleston, S.C., 1852.

Haskins, R.W. *History and Progress of Phrenology.* Buffalo, N.Y., 1839.

Haven, Gilbert. *National Sermons.* Boston, 1869, originally published in 1863.

Helper, Hinton Rowan. *Nojoque, A Question For a Continent.* N.Y., 1867.

———. *The Impending Crisis of the South and How to Meet It.* N.Y., 1860, originally published in 1857.

———. *The Impending Crisis of the South and How to Meet It.* Edited by George M. Fredrickson, Cambridge, Mass., 1968, originally published in 1857.

———. *The Land of Gold.* Baltimore, 1855.

———. *The Negroes in Negroland.* N.Y., 1868.

Holcombe, William Henry. *The Alternative: A Separate nationality or the Africanization of the South.* New Orleans, 1860.

Hunt, Benjamin S. *Remarks on Haiti as a Place of Settlement for Afric-Americans and on the Mulatto as a Race for the Tropics.* Philadelphia, 1860.

Hunt, James. *The Negro's Place in Nature.* N.Y., 1864.

Hurd, John C. *The Law of Freedom and Bondage in the United States.* Boston, 1862, originally published in 1858.

"Inaugural Address of Governor Walker." n.a., *Transactions of the Kansas State Historical Society,* vol. 5, 1889-1896, 339.

Jarvis, Russell. *Facts and Arguments Against the Election of General Cass by an Anti-Abolitionist.* N.Y., 1848.

Johnson, Charles W. *Proceedings of the First three Republican National Conventions, 1856, 1860, and 1864.* Minneapolis, 1893.

Johnson, Guion G. "A History of Racial Ideologies in the United States." 1943, Schomberg Collection, New York Public Library microfilm, 1 reel.

Julian, George W. *Political Recollections, 1840 to 1872.* Miami, Fla., 1969, originally published in 1884.

_____. *Speeches on Political Questions.* Cambridge, Mass., 1872.

Klipstein, Louis F. "The Anglo-Saxon Race." *North American Review,* vol. 72, 1851, 35-42.

Letter of Francis P. Blair Esq. to the Republican Association of Washington, D.C., 12/10/1855. Pamphlet, Washington, D.C., 1855.

Letter of Hon. S.P. Chase in Reply to Daniel O'Connell. Pamphlet, Cincinnati, 1843.

Logan, John A. *The Great Conspiracy: Its Origins and History.* N.Y., 1886.

Lovejoy, Owen. *The Supremacy of the Divine Law.* Pamphlet, Chicago, 1843.

Lowell, James Russell. *The Poetical Works of James Russell Lowell.* Cambridge, Mass., 1890, originally published in 1848.

Malvin, John. *North into Freedom.* Edited by Allan Peskin, Cleveland, 1966, originally published in 1879.

Mann, Horace. *Slavery: Letters and Speeches.* Boston, 1851.

Meigs, J. Aitken. "The Cranial Characteristics of the Races of Men." Cited in Nott and Gliddon, *Indigenous Races,* 203-349.

Mitchell, James. *Brief on Emigration and Colonization and Report in Answer to a resolution of the Senate.* Pamphlet, Washington, D.C., 1865.

_____. *Letter on the Relation of the White and African Races in the United States, showing the necessity of the Colonization of the Latter, Addressed to the President of the U.S.* Pamphlet, Washington, D.C., 1862.

_____. *Report on Colonization and Emigration made to the Secretary of the Interior by the Agent of Emigration.* Pamphlet, Washington, D.C., 1862.

Morgan, Lewis Henry. *Ancient Society.* N.Y., 1907.

Morton, Samuel George. *Crania Americana, or a Comparative view of the skulls of Various Aboriginal Nations of North and South America.* Philadelphia, 1839.

_____. *Illustrated System of Human Anatomy, Special, General and Microscopic.* Philadelphia, 1849.

Nicolay, John G., and Hay, John. *Complete Works of Abraham Lincoln.* Chicago, 1894, originally published in 1890, 10 vols.

Niles' Weekly Register. Baltimore, vol. 73, 1847, vol. 74, 1848.

Nordhoff, Charles. *America for Free Working Men.* Pamphlet, N.Y. 1865.

Norton, Charles Eliot. Book review of Sidney George Fisher's *The Laws of Race as Connected with Slavery. Atlantic Monthly,* vol. 7, 1861, 252-54.

Nott, Josiah C. "Dr. Nott's Reply to 'C' . . . . " *Southern Quarterly Review,* vol. 8, 1845, 148-90.

_____. "Nature and Destiny of the Negro." *DeBow's Review,* vol. 10, 1851, 330-31.

_____. "Statistics of Southern Slave Population." *DeBow's Review,* vol. 4, 1847, 277-85.

_____. "The Mulatto a Hybrid—Probable Extermination of the Two Races, if the Whites and Blacks are allowed to Intermarry." *American Journal of the Medical Sciences,* vol. 6, 1843, 252-56.

Nott, Josiah C., and Gliddon, George R. *Indigenous Races of the Earth, or New Chapters of Ethnological Inquiry.* Philadelphia, 1857.

Nott, Josiah C., and Gliddon, George R. *Types of Mankind: or Ethnological Researches Based upon the Ancient Monuments, Paintings, Sculptures and Crania of Races, and Upon their Natural, Geographical, Philological and Biblical History.* Philadelphia, 1854.

Nott, Samuel. *Slavery and the Remedy.* N.Y., 1969, originally published in 1859.

Olmsted, Frederick Law. *A Journey in the Back Country.* N.Y., 1860.

_____. *The Cotton Kingdom, A Traveller's Observations on Cotton and Slavery in the American Slave States.* N.Y., 1861.

Owen, Robert Dale, McKaye, James, and Howe, Samuel G. *Preliminary Report touching the Condition and Management of Emancipated Refugees.* Pamphlet, N.Y., 1863.

Parker, Theodore. *The Rights of Man in America.* Edited by Frank B. Sanborn, Boston, 1911.

——. *The Slave Power.* Edited by James K. Hosmer, Boston, 1916.

——. *The World of Matter and the Spirit of Man.* Boston, 1907, originally published in 1857, 6 vols.

Parsons, Charles G. *Inside View of Slavery: A Tour Among the Planters.* Cleveland, 1855, 2 vols.

Peden, William, ed. *Notes on the State of Virginia.* Chapel Hill, N.C., 1955.

Pickering, Charles. *The Races of Man: Their Geographic Distribution.* London, England, 1848.

Pike, James S. *First Blows of the Civil War.* N.Y., 1879.

——. *The Prostrate State, South Carolina Under Negro Government.* N.Y., 1873.

Prichard, James Cowles. *Researches into the Physical History of Mankind.* London, England, 1841, originally published in 1836, 5 vols.

Proceedings of the Colored National Convention Held in Rochester, July 6,7,8, 1853. Pamphlet, n.a., Rochester, N.Y., 1853.

Proceedings of the National Convention of Colored Men at Syracuse, N.Y., October 4,5,6,7, 1864. Pamphlet, n.a., Boston, 1864.

Pulszky, Francis. "Inconographic Researches on Human Races and Their Art." Cited in Nott and Gliddon, *Indigenous Races,* 87-188.

Pulszky, Francis, and Theresa. *White Red Black Sketches of Society in the United States.* N.Y., 1853.

Rathbun, George O. *The Free Soil Question and Its Importance to the Voters of the Free States.* N.Y., 1848.

Redpath, James. *A Guide to Hayti.* Boston, 1861.

Report of the British Association for the Advancement of Science at its Seventeenth Meeting, entitled, "Ethnology, or the Science of Races." Cited in *The Edinburgh Review,* vol. 178, 1848, 433-84.

Ripley, Peter C., ed. *The Black Abolitionist Papers.* Chapel Hill, N.C., 1986, 2 vols.

Schoolcraft, Mrs. Henry. *The Black Gauntlet: A Tale of Plantation Life in South Carolina.* Philadelphia, 1860.

Schurz, Carl. *Judge Douglas, The Bill of Indictment, Speech Delivered at the Cooper Institute, New York, September 13, 1860.* Pamphlet, *Tribune Tracts No. 9,* N.Y., 1860.

Selby, Paul. *Genesis of the Republican Party in Illinois.* Pamphlet, n.d., Alfred Whital Stem Collection of Lincolniana, Library of Congress.

Seward, William Henry. *The Destiny of America.* Pamphlet, Albany, N.Y., 1853.

Smith, Gerrit. *Anti-Fugitive Slave Law Meeting, January 9, 1851.* Pamphlet, Syracuse, N.Y., 1851.

. *Letter From Gerrit Smith To Joshua R. Giddings, November 12, 1858.* Pamphlet, Peterboro, N.Y., 1858.

Smith, Stanhope. *An Essay on the Causes of the Variety of Complexion and Figure in the Human Species.* Edited by Winthrop D. Jordan, Cambridge, Mass., 1965, originally published in 1787.

Speech of Gerrit Smith at the National Convention of the Liberty Party, Buffalo, N.Y., October 20th., 1847. Pamphlet, Buffalo, N.Y., 1847.

Speech of Horace Mann in the House of Representatives, June 30, 1848. Pamphlet, West Newton, Mass., 1848.

Speech of Salmon P. Chase in the Case of the Colored Woman Matilda. Pamphlet, Cincinnati, 1837.

Sprague, A.P. *Speeches, Arguments and Miscellaneous Papers of David Dudley Field.* N.Y., 1884.

Stowe, Harriet Beecher. *Uncle Tom's Cabin or Life Among the Lowly.* N.Y., 1962, originally published in 1852.

Sturtevant, Julian M. "The Destiny of the African Race in the United States." *Continental Monthly,* vol. 3, 1863, 600-09.

Sumner, Charles. *The Barbarism of Slavery: Speech of Hon. Charles Sumner, on the Bill for the Admission of Kansas as a Free State.* Pamphlet, Washington, D.C., 1860.

Tenth Annual Report of the American Colonization Society, 1827. Washington, D.C., 1827.

Thirty-Fourth Annual Report of the American Colonization Society, 1851. Washington, D.C., 1851.

Thayer, Eli. *A History of the Kansas Crusade, Its Friends and Its Foes.* N.Y., 1889.

_____. *The New England Emigrant Aid Company.* Worcester, Mass., 1887.

The African Repository. Washington, D.C., 1848, vol. 24.

The National Liberty Party Convention, September 30, 1852. Pamphlet, n.a., Auburn, N.Y., 1852.

The Radical Democracy of New York and the Independent Democracy. Pamphlet, n.a., Washington, D.C., 1852.

Turnbull, David. *Travels in the West, Cuba, with Notices of Porto Rico and the Slave Trade.* London, England, 1840.

Van Evrie, John H. *Negroes and Negro Slavery: The First an Inferior Race, The Latter Its Normal Condition.* Baltimore, 1853.

_____. *White Supremacy and Negro Subordination.* N.Y., 1868, originally published in 1860.

Von Tschudi, Johann, J.J. *Travels in Peru During the Years 1838-1842.* London, England, 1847.

Walker, David. *Appeal to the Colored Citizens of the World.* Boston, 1829.

Warren, C.J. *Freedom's Songs for 1856.* N.Y., 1856.

Weston, George M. *The Progress of Slavery in the United States.* Washington, D.C., 1857.

White, Charles. *The Regular Gradation of Man and in Different Animals and Vegetables.* London, England, 1799.

Wilson, Henry. *History of the Rise and Fall of the Slave Power in America.* N.Y., 1969, originally published in 1872, 2 vols.

4. DIARIES, MEMOIRS, CORRESPONDENCE AND AUTOBIOGRAPHIES

Agassiz, Elizabeth Cary, ed. *Louis Agassiz, His Life and Correspondence.* Cambridge, Mass., 1885, 2 vols.

Bancroft, Frederic. *Speeches, Correspondence and Political Papers of Carl Schurz.* N.Y., 1913, 6 vols.

Basler, Roy P. *The Collected Works of Abraham Lincoln.* New Brunswick, N.J., 1953, 9 vols.

Beale, Howard K., ed. *The Diary of Edward Bates, 1859-1866.* Washington, D.C., 1933.

Benton, Thomas Hart. *Thirty Years View.* N.Y., 1856.

Bergh, Albert E., ed. *The Writings of Thomas Jefferson.* Washington, D.C., 1907, 20 vols.

Blaine, James G. *Twenty Years of Congress: from Lincoln to Garfield, with a Review of the Events which Led to the Political Revolution of 1860.* Norwich, Conn., 1884, 2 vols.

Butler, Benjamin F. *Autobiography and Personal Reminiscences.* Boston, 1892.

Clay, Cassius M. *The Life of Cassius Marcellus Clay, Memoirs, Writings and Speeches.* Cincinnati, 1886.

Colton, Calvin. *The Life, Correspondence and Speeches of Henry Clay.* N.Y., 1857, 6 vols.

_____. *The Private Correspondence of Henry Clay.* N.Y., 1855.

Conway, Moncure Daniel. *Autobiography, Memories and Experiences of Moncure Daniel Conway.* Cambridge, Mass., 1904, 2 vols.

Cox, Jacob Dolson. *Military Reminiscences of the Civil War.* N.Y., 1900, 2 vols.

Dix, Morgan. *Memoirs of John Adams Dix.* N.Y., 1883, 2 vols.

Donald, David, ed., *Inside Lincoln's Cabinet, The Civil War Diaries of Salmon P. Chase.* N.Y., 1954.

Douglass, Frederick. *Life and Times of Frederick Douglass, Written by Himself.* Boston, 1892.

Foner, Philip S., ed. *Basic Writings of Thomas Jefferson.* N.Y., 1950, originally published in 1944.

_____., ed. *Life and Writings of Frederick Douglass.* N.Y., 1950, 2 vols.

Ford, Paul L., ed. *The Writings of Thomas Jefferson.* N.Y., 1899, 10 vols.

Greeley, Horace. *Recollections of a Busy Life.* N.Y., 1868.

_____., ed. *The Writings of Cassius Marcellus Clay, including Speeches and Addresses.* N.Y., 1848.

Lincoln, Abraham. "Eulogy on Henry Clay, July 6, 1852." Cited in Basler, *Collected Works of Lincoln,* vol. 2, 130-32.

McClure, Alexander K. *Recollections of Half a Century.* Salem, Mass., 1902.

Nevins, Allan, and Thomas, Milton H., eds. *The Dairy of George Templeton Strong.* N.Y., 1974, 2 vols.

Pease, Theodore Calvin, and Randall, James G., eds. *The Diary of Orville Hickman Browning.* Springfield, Ill., 1925, 2 vols.

Sherman, John. *Recollections of Forty Years in the House, Senate and Cabinet.* Chicago, 1895, 2 vols.

Wainwright, Nicholas B., ed. *A Philadelphia Perspective, The Diary of Sidney George Fisher, Covering the Years 1834-1871.* Philadelphia, 1967.

Weiss, John. *Life and Correspondence of Theodore Parker.* N.Y., 1864, 2 vols.

Wentworth, John. *Congressional Reminiscences.* Chicago, 1882.

5. PERIOD BIOGRAPHIES WITH CONSIDERABLE PRIMARY MATERIAL

Adams, Charles F. *Richard Henry Dana: A Biography.* Boston, 1890, 2 vols.

Bancroft, Frederic. *The Life of William H. Seward.* N.Y., 1900, 2 vols.

Buell, Walter. *Joshua R. Giddings.* Cleveland, 1882.

Zachariah Chandler, An Outline Sketch of his Life and Public Services. Published by the *Detroit Post and Tribune* Office. Detroit, Mich., 1880.

Clarke, Grace Julian. *George W. Julian.* Indianapolis, 1923.

Clay, Thomas Hart. *Henry Clay.* Philadelphia, 1910.

Cornell, William M. *The Life and Public Career of Hon. Horace Greeley.* Boston, 1872.

Cutler, Julia Perkins. *Life and Times of Ephraim Cutler.* Cincinnati, 1890.

Field, Henry M. *The Life of David Dudley Field.* N.Y., 1898.

Foraker, Joseph B. "Salmon P. Chase." *Ohio Archaeological and Historical Society Publications,* vol. 15, 1906, 314.

Foulke, William D. *Life of Oliver P. Morton, Including his Important Speeches.* Indianapolis, 1899.

Frothingham, Octavius Brooks. *Gerrit Smith, A Biography.* N.Y., 1909.

_____. *Theodore Parker: A Biography.* Boston, 1874

Godwin, Park. *A Biography of William Cullen Bryant.* N.Y., 1883, 2 vols.

Gregory, James M. *Frederick Douglass the Orator.* N.Y., 1893.

Hamlin, Charles E. *The Life and Times of Hannibal Hamlin.* Cambridge, Mass., 1899.

Hart, Albert B. *Salmon Portland Chase.* N.Y., 1899.

Hollister, O.J. *Life of Schuyler Colfax.* N.Y., 1886.

Julian, George W. *The Life of Joshua R. Giddings.* Chicago, 1892.

Lathrop, Henry Warren. *The Life and times of Samuel J. Kirkwood.* Iowa City, Iowa, 1893.

Lossing, Benson J. *A Biography of James A. Garfield.* N.Y., 1882.

Mallory, Daniel, ed. *The Life and Speeches of the Hon. Henry Clay.* N.Y., 1844, 2 vols.

Martin, Edward W. *The Life and Public Services of Schuyler Colfax.* N.Y., 1868.

McCabe, James D. *The Life and Public Services of Horatio Seymour, Together with a Complete and Authentic Life of Francis P. Blair Jr.* N.Y., 1868.

Moore, A.Y. *The Life of Schuyler Colfax.* Philadelphia, 1868.

Morrow, Josiah. *Life and Speeches of Thomas Corwin.* Cincinnati, 1896.

Nason, Elias, and Russell, Thomas. *The Life and Public Services of Henry Wilson.* N.Y., 1969, originally published in 1876.

Parton, James. *The Life of Horace Greeley.* Boston, 1872.

Prentice, George D. *Biography of Henry Clay.* Hartford, Conn., 1831.

Reid, Whitelaw. *Horace Greeley, A Biographical Sketch.* n.p., 1879.

Riddle, Albert G. *The Life of Benjamin F. Wade.* Cleveland, 1886.

Roosevelt, Theodore. *Thomas Hart Benton.* Cambridge, Mass., 1886.

Salter, William. *Life of James W. Grimes.* N.Y., 1876.

Sanborn, Frank, B. *Dr. S.G. Howe, The Philanthropist.* N.Y., 1891.

Sargent, Epes, and Greeley, Horace. *The Life and Public Services of Henry Clay.* Auburn, N.Y., 1852.

Schmucker, Samuel M. *The Life and Times of Henry Clay.* Philadelphia, 1860.

Schuckers, J.W. *The Life and Public Services of Salmon Portland Chase.* N.Y., 1874.

Schurz, Carl. *Life of Henry Clay.* Cambridge, Mass., 1892.

Shaw, Benjamin F. "Owen Lovejoy, Constitutional Abolitionist and the

Republican Party." *Transactions of the McLean County Historical Society,* vol. 3, 1900, 62-71.

Shepard, Edward M. *Martin Van Buren.* Boston, 1899.

Smith W.L.G. *Fifty Years of Public Life, The Life and Times of Lewis Cass.* N.Y., 1856.

Talbot, George Foster. "James Shepherd Pike." *Maine Historical Society Collections,* vol. 1, 1890, 235.

Walker, Charles M. *Sketch of the Life, Character and Public Services of Oliver P. Morton.* Indianapolis, 1878.

Warden, Robert B. *An Account of the Private Life and Public Services of Salmon Portland Chase.* Cincinnati, 1874.

White, Horace. *The Life of Lyman Trumbull.* N.Y., 1913.

Zabriskie, Francis N. *Horace Greeley, the Editor.* N.Y., 1890.

II. SECONDARY SOURCES

A. UNPUBLISHED DOCTORAL DISSERTATIONS AND MASTERS THESES

Barringer, Graham A. "The Life and Times of Henry S. Lane." Ph.D. dissertation, Indiana University, 1927.

Beck, Warren. "The Chiriqui Improvement Company and Lincoln's plan to colonize slaves in Central America." M.A. thesis, Wayne State University, 1948.

Boom, Aaron M. "The Development of Sectional Attitudes in Wisconsin, 1848-1861." Ph.D. dissertation, University of Chicago, 1948.

Boyd, Willis D. "Negro Colonization in the National Crisis, 1860-1870." Ph.D. dissertation, University of California at Los Angeles, 1953.

Cardoso, Joaquin Jose'. "Hinton Rowan Helper: A Nineteenth Century Pilgrimage." Ph.D. dissertation, University of Wisconsin, 1967.

Cavanagh, Helen M. "Antislavery Sentiment and Politics in the

Northwest, 1844-1860." Ph.D. dissertation, University of Chicago, 1938.

Erlich, Martin. "Benjamin Franklin Wade: The Road to Radical Republicanism." M.A. thesis, Wayne State University, 1954.

Hart, Charles R. "Congressmen and the Expansion of Slavery into the Territories: A Study in Attitudes, 1846-1861." Ph.D. dissertation, University of Washington, 1965.

Haughland, John C. "Alexander Ramsey and the Republican Party, 1855-1875: A Study in Personal Politics." Ph.D. dissertation, University of Minnesota, 1961.

Loomis, Willard D. "The Anti-Slavery Movement in Ashtabula County, Ohio, 1834-1854." M.A. thesis, Western Reserve University, 1936.

McGuire, Joseph F. "Owen Lovejoy, Congressman From the Prairie." M.S. thesis, Illinois State Normal University, 1950.

McLaughlin, Tom L. "Popular Reactions to the Idea of Negro Equality in Twelve Non-slaveholding States, 1846-1869: A Quantitative Analysis." Ph.D. dissertation, Washington State University, 1969.

Messner, Vivian Thomas. "The Public Life of Austin Blair." M.A. thesis, Wayne University, 1937.

Newbold, Catherine. "The Antislavery Background of the Principal State Department Appointees in the Lincoln Administration." Ph.D. dissertation, University of Michigan, 1962.

Opper, Peter K. "The Mind of the White Participant in the African Colonization Movement, 1816-1840." Ph.D. dissertation, University of North Carolina, 1972.

Robertson, Arthur H. "The Political Career of Lyman Trumbull." M.A. thesis, University of Chicago, 1910.

Seifman, Eli. "A History of the New York State Colonization Society." Ph.D. dissertation, New York University, 1966.

Smith, Earl O. "The Public Life of Austin Blair, War Governor of Michigan." M.A. thesis, Wayne State University, 1934.

Solberg, Richard W. "Joshua Giddings, Politician and Idealist." Ph.D. dissertation, University of Chicago, 1952.

Sparks, David S. "The Birth of the Republican Party in Iowa, 1848-1860." Ph.D. dissertation, University of Chicago, 1951.

Spraggins, Tinsley Lee. "Economic Aspects of Negro Colonization During the Civil War." Ph.D. dissertation, American University, Washington, D.C., 1957.

Stirton, Thomas. "Party Disruptions and the Rise of the Slavery Extension Controversy, 1840-1846." Ph.D. dissertation, University of Chicago, 1926.

Stoler, Mildred C. "Influence of the Democratic Element in the Republican Party of Illinois and Indiana, 1854-1860." Ph.D. dissertation, Indiana University, 1938.

Thompson, J. Elaine. "The Formative Period of the Republican Party in Michigan, 1854-1860." M.A. thesis, Wayne University, 1949.

Wickstrom, Werner T. "The American Colonization Society and Liberia." Ph.D. dissertation, Hartford Seminary, 1958.

Wright, John S. "The Background and Formation of the Republican Party in Illinois, 1846-1860." Ph.D. dissertation, University of Chicago, 1946.

B. Biographies, Monographs and General Works

Abbott, Richard H. *Cobbler in Congress, The Life of Henry Wilson, 1812-1875.* Lexington, Ky., 1972.

Agar, Herbert. *The Price of Union.* Boston, 1950

Allport, Gordon W. *The Nature of Prejudice.* N.Y., 1958, originally published in 1954.

Appleton's Cyclopedia of American Biography. Edited by James Grant Wilson and John Fiske. N.Y., 1887, 6 vols.

Bailey, Hugh C. *Hinton Rowan Helper: Abolitionist-Racist.* Montgomery, Ala., 1965.

Barraclough, June. *Antione-Nicolas Decondorcet, Sketch for a Historical Picture of the Progress of the Human Mind.* London, England, 1955.

Bartlett, Irving H. *Wendell Phillips, Brahmin Radical.* Boston, 1961.

Barzun, Jacques. *Race: A Study in Superstition.* N.Y., 1965, originally published in 1937.

Bassett, John Spencer. *Anti-Slavery Leaders of North Carolina.* Baltimore, 1898.

Baxter, Maurice. *Orville H. Browning.* Bloomington, Ind., 1957.

Beard, Charles A., and Mary R. *The Rise of American Civilization.* N.Y., 1947, originally published in 1927.

Bell, Howard H. "Negro Nationalism: A Factor in Emigration Projects, 1858-1861." *Journal of Negro History,* vol. 47, 1962, 49.

Belz, Herman. *Reconstructing the Union, Theory and Policy during the Civil War.* Ithaca, N.Y., 1969.

Bentley, George R. *A History of the Freedmen's Bureau.* Philadelphia, 1955.

Bergmann, Leola N. *The Negro in Iowa.* Iowa City, Iowa, 1969.

Berlin, Ira. *Slaves Without Masters, The Free Negro in the Antebellum South.* N.Y., 1974.

Bertelson, David. *The Lazy South.* N.Y., 1967.

Bertz, Julian P. "The Economic Background of the Liberty Party." *American Historical Review*, vol. 34, 1929, 257.

Berwanger, Eugene H. "Negrophobia in Northern Pro-slavery and Antislavery Thought." *Phylon,* vol. 33, 1972, 272.

_____. *The Frontier Against Slavery, Western Anti-Negro Prejudice and the Slavery Extension Controversy.* Urbana, Ill., 1971, originally published in 1967.

Billington, Ray Allen. *Westward Expansion, A History of the American Frontier.* N.Y., 1949.

Binkley, Wilfred E. *American Political Parties.* N.Y., 1959, originally published in 1943.

Blassingame, John W. "The Recruitment of Colored Troops in Kentucky, Maryland and Missouri, 1863-1865." *The Historian*, vol. 29, 1967, 536-37.

_____. *The Slave Community, Plantation Life in the Antebellum South.* N.Y., 1972.

Blue, Frederick J. *Salmon P. Chase, A Life in Politics.* Kent, Ohio, 1987.

_____. *The Free Soilers, Third Party Politics, 1848-1854.* Urbana, Ill., 1973.

_____. "The Ohio Free Soilers and Problems of Factionalism." *Ohio History,* vol. 76, 1967, 23-24.

Borden, Philip. "Found Cumbering the Soil, Manifest Destiny and the

Indian in the Nineteenth Century." Cited in Nash and Weiss, *The Great Fear,* 93.

Boritt, George S. "The Voyage to the Colony of Linconia." *Historian,* vol. 37, 1974-75, 619-22.

Boyd, Willis D. "James Redpath and American Negro Colonization in Haiti, 1860-1862." *Americas,* vol. 12, 1955, 172-82.

_____. "The American Colonization Society and the Slave Recaptives of 1860-1861: An Early Example of United States-African Relations." *Journal of Negro History,* vol. 47, 1962, 109.

Brock, William R. *Parties and Political Conscience: American Dilemmas, 1840-1850.* Millwood, N.J., 1979.

Brown, Charles H. *William Cullen Bryant.* N.Y., 1971.

Burgess, John W. *The Civil War and the Constitution, 1859-1865.* N.Y., 1901, 2 vols.

Burns, Edward M. *The American Idea of Mission; Concepts of National Purpose and Destiny.* New Brunswick, N.J., 1957.

Burtis, Mary E. *Moncure Conway, 1832-1907.* New Brunswick, N.J., 1952.

Cain, Marvin R. *Lincoln's Attorney General, Edward Bates of Missouri.* Columbia, Mo., 1965.

_____. "Lincoln's Views on Slavery and the Negro: A Suggestion." *Historian,* vol. 26, 1964, 504.

Campbell, Penelope. *Maryland in Africa.* Urbana, Ill., 1971.

Campbell, Stanley. *The Slave Catchers, Enforcement of the Fugitive Slave Law, 1850-1860.* Chapel Hill, N.C., 1968.

Carrington, Henry B. "Early History of the Republican Party in Ohio." *Ohio Archaeological and Historical Quarterly,* vol. 2, 1889, 327-31.

Cassirer, Ernst. *The Philosophy of the Enlightenment.* Boston, 1955, originally published in 1932.

Chambers, William N. *Old Bullion Benton: Senator from the New West.* Boston, 1956.

Chinard, Gilbert. *Thomas Jefferson, the Apostle of Americanism.* Ann Arbor, Mich., 1957, originally published in 1929.

Church, Charles A. *History of the Republican Party in Illinois, 1854-1912.* Rockford, Ill., 1912.

Clark, Dan E. *Samuel Jordan Kirkwood*. Iowa City, Iowa, 1917.

Clephane, Lewis. *Birth of the Republican Party*. Washington, D.C., 1889.

Cleven, Andrew N. "Some Plans for Colonizing Liberated Negro Slaves in Hispanic America." *Journal of Negro History,* vol. 11, 1926, 35-49.

Cole, Arthur C. "President Lincoln and the Illinois Radical Republicans." *Mississippi Valley Historical Review,* vol. 4, 1917-1918, 419-20.

———. *The Irrepressible Conflict, 1850-1865*. N.Y., 1934.

Cole, Charles C. Jr. "Horace Bushnell and the Slavery Question." *New England Quarterly,* vol. 23, 1950, 29.

Cook, Adrian. *The Armies of the Streets: the New York City Draft Riots of 1863*. Lexington, Ky., 1974.

Cooke, Jacob E. *Frederic Bancroft, Historian*. Norman, Okla., 1957.

Cooper, Thomas V., and Fenton, Hector T. *American Politics*. Chicago, 1883.

Cornish, Dudley, T. *The Sable Arm, Negro Troops in the Union Army, 1861-1865*. N.Y., 1966, originally published in 1956.

Cortissoz, Royal. *The Life of Whitelaw Reid*. N.Y., 1921, 2 vols.

Cox, Earnest S. *Lincoln's Negro Policy*. Los Angeles, 1968, originally published in 1938.

———. *The South's Part in Mongrelizing the Nation*. Richmond, Va., 1926.

Cox, Lawanda. *Lincoln and Black Freedom: A Study in Presidential Leadership*. Columbia, S.C., 1981.

Crandall, Andrew Wallace. *The Early History of the Republican Party*. Boston, 1930.

Carven, Avery O. *Civil War in the Making, 1815-1860*. Baton Rouge, La., 1968, originally published in 1959.

Cross, Barbara M. *Horace Bushnell: Minister to a Changing America*. Chicago, 1958.

Curtis, Francis. *The Republican Party*. N.Y., 1904, 2 vols.

Dann, Martin E., ed. *The Black Press, 1827-1890*. N.Y., 1971.

Davies, John D. *Phrenology, Fad and Science*. New Haven, Conn., 1955.

Davis, David Brion. *The Problem of Slavery in Western Culture*. Ithaca, N.Y., 1966.

Degler, Carl N. "Racism in the United States: An Essay Review." *Journal of Southern History,* vol. 38, 1972, 101-08.

Dictionary of Scientific Biography. Edited by Charles C. Gillispie, N.Y., 1970, 14 vols.

Dillion, Merton L. *Benjamin Lundy and the Struggle for Negro Freedom.* Urbana, Ill., 1966.

———. *The Abolitionists, The Growth of a Dissenting Minority.* DeKalb, Ill., 1974.

Dodd, William E. "The Fight for the Northwest, 1860." *American Historical Review,* vol. 16, 1911, 784-85.

Donald, David. *Charles Sumner and the Coming of the Civil War.* N.Y., 1960.

———. *Lincoln Reconsidered.* N.Y., 1961, originally published in 1947.

Donovan, Herbert D.A. *The Barnburners.* N.Y., 1925

Dowd, Jerome. *The Negro In American Life.* N.Y., 1926.

Draper, Theodore. *The Rediscovery of Black Nationalism.* N.Y., 1970.

Duberman, Martin. *James Russell Lowell.* Cambridge, Mass., 1966.

———, ed. *The Antislavery Vanguard, New Essays on the Abolitionists.* Princeton, N.J., 1965.

Dubois, James T., and Mathews, Gertrude S. *Galusha A. Grow, Father of the Homestead Law.* N.Y., 1917.

DuBois, W.E.B. *Black Reconstruction in America, 1860-1880.* N.Y., 1968, originally published in 1935.

Dumond, Dwight L. *Antislavery Origins of the Civil War in the United States.* Ann Arbor, Mich., 1966, originally published in 1939.

Durden, Robert F. "Ambiguities in the Antislavery Crusade of the Republican Party." Cited in Duberman, *The Antislavery Vanguard,* 363-64.

———. *James Shepherd Pike, Republicanism and the American Negro, 1850-1882.* Durham, N.C., 1957.

Dyer, Brainerd. "The Persistence of the Idea of Negro Colonization." *Pacific Historical Review,* vol. 12, 1943, 58-59.

Eaton, Clement. *Henry Clay and the Art of American Politics.* Boston, 1957.

Edelstein, Tilden. *Strange Enthusiasm, A Life of Thomas Wentworth Higginson.* New Haven, Conn., 1968.

Elkins, Stanley M. *Slavery, A Problem in American Institutional and Intellectual Life.* N.Y., 1963, originally published in 1959.

Erickson, Leonard. "Politics and the Repeal of Ohio's Black Laws, 1837-1849." *Ohio History,* vol. 82, 1973, 154-62.

Fanon, Frantz. *Black Skin, White Masks.* N.Y., 1967.

Fehrenbacher, Don E. *Chicago Giant, a Biography of "Long John" Wentworth.* Madison, Wis., 1957.

_____. "Only His Stepchildren: Lincoln and the Negro." *Civil War History,* vol. 20, 1974, 302-05.

Fennimore, Jean Joy L. "Austin Blair: Political Idealist, 1845-1860." *Michigan History,* vol. 48, 1964, 130-66.

Field, Earle. "Charles B. Sedgwick's Letters from Washington, 1859-1861." *Mid-America,* vol. 49, 1967, 129-39.

Filler, Louis. *The Crusade Against Slavery, 1830-1860.* N.Y., 1963, originally published in 1960.

Finot, Jean. *Race Prejudice.* London, England, 1906.

Fischer, Roger A. "The Republican Presidential Campaigns of 1856 and 1860: Analysis Through Artifacts." *Civil War History,* vol. 27, 1981, 123-27.

Fishback, Mason, M. "Illinois Legislation on Slavery and Free Negroes, 1818-1865." *Transactions of the Illinois State Historical Society,* 1904, 414-32.

Fishel, Leslie H. Jr. "Wisconsin and Negro Suffrage." *Wisconsin Magazine of History,* vol. 46, 1963, 180-96.

Fite, Emerson D. *The Presidential Campaign of 1860.* N.Y., 1911.

Fladeland, Betty. *James Gillespie Birney: Slaveholder to Abolitionist.* Ithaca, N.Y., 1955.

_____. *Men and Brothers, Anglo-American Antislavery Cooperation.* Urbana, Ill., 1972.

Fleming, Walter L. "Deportation and Colonization: An Attempted Solution of the Race Problem." *Studies in Southern History and Politics.* N.Y., 1914, 5.

Flower, Frank. *History of the Republican Party.* Springfield, Ill., 1884.

Foner, Eric. *Free Soil, Free Labor, Free Men, The Ideology of the Republican Party before the Civil War.* N.Y., 1970.

_____. "Politics and Prejudice: The Free Soil Party and the Negro, 1849-1852." *Journal of Negro History,* vol. 50, 1965, 243.

_____. "Racial Attitudes of the New York Free Soilers." *New York History,* vol. 46, 1965, 315-18.

_____. "The Wilmot Proviso Revisited." *Journal of American History,* vol. 56, 1969-1970, 277.

Foner, Philip S., and Lewis, Ronald L., eds. *The Black Worker to 1869.* Philadelphia, 1978, 2 vols.

Formisano, Ronald P. "The Edge of Caste: Colored Suffrage in Michigan, 1827-1861." *Michigan History,* vol. 56, 1972, 28.

Foster, Charles I. "The Colonization of Free Negroes in Liberia." *Journal of Negro History,* vol. 38, 1953, 47-62.

Fox, Early Lee. *The American Colonization Society, 1817-1840.* Baltimore, 1919.

Franklin, John Hope. *From Slavery to Freedom, A History of Negro Americans.* N.Y., 1969, originally published in 1947.

_____. *Racial Equality in America.* Chicago, 1976.

Fredrickson, George M. "A Man but Not a Brother: Abraham Lincoln and Racial Equality." *Journal of Southern History,* vol. 41, 1975, 40-55.

_____. *The Black Image in the White Mind: The Debate on Afro-American Character and Destiny, 1817-1914.* N.Y., 1972.

_____. "Toward a Social Interpretation of the Development of American Racism." Cited in Huggins, Kilson, and Fox, *Key Issues in the Afro-American Experience,* 253.

Friedman, Lawrence J. *Inventors of the Promised Land.* N.Y., 1975.

Froman, Robert. *Racism.* N.Y., 1972.

Fuess, Claude M. *Carl Schurz: Reformer.* N.Y., 1932.

Gaither, Gerald, and Muldowny, John. "Hinton Rowan Helper, Racist and Reformer: A Letter to Senator John Serman of Ohio." *North Carolina Historical Review,* vol. 49, 1972, 377.

Gara, Larry. "Slavery and the Slave Power: A Crucial Distinction." *Civil War History,* vol. 15, 1969, 12-18.

Gatewood, Willard B. Jr. *Black Americans and the White Man's Burden, 1898-1903.* Urbana, Ill., 1975.

Genovese, Eugene D. *The Political Economy of Slavery.* N.Y., 1965.

George, Joseph Jr. "A Catholic Family Newspaper Views the Lincoln

Administration: John Mullaly's Copperhead Weekly." *Civil War History,* vol. 24, 1978, 128-30.

George, Mary Karl. *Zachariah Chandler.* East Lansing, Mich., 1969.

Gerber, David A. *Black Ohio and the Color Line, 1860-1915.* Urbana, Ill., 1976.

Gerteis, Louis S. *From Contraband to Freedman: Federal Policy toward Southern Blacks, 1861-1865.* Westport, Conn., 1973.

Gertz, Elmer. "The Black Laws of Illinois." *Illinois State Historical Society Journal,* vol. 56, 1963, 454-72.

Gibson, Charles. "Edward Bates." *Missouri Historical Society Collections,* vol. 2, 1900, 55.

Gienapp, William E. "The Crime Against Sumner: The Caning of Charles Sumner and the Rise of the Republican Party." *Civil War History,* vol. 25, 1979, 231-34.

Going, Charles Buxton. *David Wilmot, Free-Soiler.* N.Y., 1924.

Goldstein, Naomi. *The Roots of Prejudice against the Negro in the United States.* Boston, 1948.

Gossett, Thomas F. *Race, the History of an Idea in America.* Dallas, Tex., 1963.

Graebner, Norman A., ed. *Manifest Destiny.* Indianapolis, 1968.

———. "Thomas Corwin and the Election of 1848: A study in Conservative Politics." *Journal of Southern History,* vol. 17, 1951, 164-70.

Gravely, William. *Gilbert Haven, Methodist Abolitionist: A Study in Race, Religion and Reform, 1850-1880.* Nashville, Tenn., 1973.

Grissom, Daniel M. "Personal Recollections of Distinguished Missourians—Frank P. Blair." *Missouri Historical Review,* vol. 20, 1926, 398.

Haberkorn, Ruth E. "Owen Lovejoy in Princeton, Illinois." *Journal of the Illinois State Historical Society,* vol. 36, 1943, 284-302.

Hale, Frank W. "Salmon P. Chase: Rhetorician of Abolition." *Negro History Bulletin,* vol. 26, 1963, 168.

Hale, William H. *Horace Greeley, Voice of The People.* N.Y., 1950.

Haller, John S. *Outcasts from Evolution; Scientific Attitude of Racial Inferiority, 1859-1900.* Urbana, Ill., 1971.

Hansen, Klaus J. "The Millennium, the West and Race in the Ante-bellum

American Mind." *Western Historical Quarterly*, vol. 3, 1972, 388-90.

Harlow, Ralph V. *Gerrit Smith: Philanthropist and Reformer.* N.Y., 1939.

Harrington, Fred Harvey. *Fighting Politician, Major General N.P. Banks.* Philadelphia, 1948.

Harris, Alfred G. "Lincoln and the Question of Slavery in the District of Columbia." *Lincoln Herald,* vol. 51, 1949, 18-20.

Harris, Norman D. *The History of Negro Servitude in Illinois.* N.Y., 1969, originally published in 1904.

Harrold, Stanley. *Gamaliel Bailey and Antislavery Union.* Kent, Ohio, 1986.

Hart, Albert B. *Slavery and Abolition, 1831-1841.* N.Y., 1906.

Herriott, F.I. "James W. Grimes Versus The Southrons." *Annals of Iowa,* vol. 5, 1926, 347-48.

Hickok, Charles T. *The Negro in Ohio, 1802-1870.* Cleveland, 1896.

Hicks, John D. "The Third Party Tradition in American Politics." *Mississippi Valley Historical Review,* vol. 20, 1933, 9-10.

Hofstadter, Richard. *Social Darwinism in American Thought.* Boston, 1955, originally published in 1944.

Holmes, S.J. *The Negro's Struggle for Survival.* N.Y., 1966, originally published in 1937.

Holt, Edgar Allen. *Party Politics in Ohio, 1840-1850.* Columbus, Ohio, 1930.

Holt, Michael F. *Forging a Majority, the Formation of the Republican Party in Pittsburgh, 1846-1860.* New Haven, Conn., 1969.

Horner, Harlan H. *Lincoln and Greeley.* Urbana, Ill., 1953.

Horowitz, Robert. F. *The Great Impeacher, A Political Biography of James M. Ashley.* N.Y., 1979.

Horsman, Reginald. *Josiah Nott of Mobile, Southerner, Physician and Racial Theorist.* Baton Rouge, La., 1987.

_____. *Race and Manifest Destiny, The Origins of American Racial Anglo-Saxonism.* Cambridge, Mass., 1981.

Howard, Victor B. "Cassius Clay and the Origins of the Republican Party." *Filson Club History Quarterly,* vol. 45, 1971. 58-68.

_____. "The Illinois Republican Party." *Journal of the Illinois State Historical Society,* Vol. 64, 1971, 305-06.

Hubbart, Henry C. "Pro-Southern Influences in the Free West." *Mississippi Valley Historical Review,* vol. 20, 1933, 48-49.

_____. *The Older Middle West, 1840-1880.* N.Y., 1936.

Huggins, Nathan I., Kilson, Martin, and Fox, Daniel M., eds. *Key Issues in the Afro-American Experience.* N.Y., 1971.

Hyman, Harold M. *A More Perfect Union, The Impact of the Civil War and Reconstruction on the Constitution.* N.Y., 1973.

Hyman, Harold M, and Wiecek, William M. *Equal Justice Under Law, Constitutional Development, 1835-1875.* N.Y., 1982.

Isley, Jeter A. *Horace Greeley and the Republican Party, 1853-1861.* Princeton, N.J., 1947.

Jaffa, Harry V. *Crisis of the House Divided: An Interpretation of the Issues in the Lincoln-Douglas Debates.* N.Y., 1959.

Johannsen, Robert W. *Frontier Politics and the Sectional Conflict: The Pacific Northwest on the Eve of the Civil War.* Seattle, Wash., 1955.

Johnson, Allen, and Malone, Dumas, eds. *Dictionary of American Biography.* N.Y., 1931, 10 vols.

Johnson, Franklin. *The Development of State Legislation Concerning the Free Negro.* N.Y., 1918.

Johnson, Samuel A. "The Emigrant Aid Company in the Kansas Conflict." *Kansas Historical Quarterly,* vol. 6, 1937, 21-33.

Johnston, James Hugo. *Race Relations in Virginia and Miscegenation in the South, 1776-1860.* Amherst, Mass., 1970.

Jordan, Winthrop D. *White Over Black, American Attitudes Toward the Negro, 1550-1812.* Baltimore, 1969, originally published in 1968.

Juettner, Otto. *Daniel Drake and His Followers.* Cincinnati, 1909.

Kincaid, Larry. "Two Steps Forward, One Step Back, Racial Attitudes During the Civil War and Reconstruction." Cited in Nash and Weiss, *The Great Fear,* 46-47.

King, Willard L. *Lincoln's Manager, David Davis.* Chicago, 1960.

Kinney, James. *Amalgamation! Race, Sex and Rhetoric in the Nineteenth Century American Novel.* Westport, Conn., 1985.

Kinsely, Philip. *The Chicago Tribune.* N.Y., 1943, 2 vols.

Kovel, Joel. *White Racism: A Psychohistory.* N.Y., 1971, originally published in 1970.

Kraditor, Aileen S. *Means and Ends in American Abolitionism, Garrison and His Critics on Strategy and Tactics, 1834-1850.* N.Y., 1970, originally published in 1967.

Krug, Mark M. "Lyman Trumbull and the Real Issues in the Lincoln-Douglas Debates." *Illinois State Historical Society Journal,* vol. 57. 1964, 387.

———. *Lyman Trumbull, Conservative Radical.* N.Y., 1965.

Lee, James M. *History of American Journalism.* Cambridge, Mass., 1917.

Lefler, Hugh T. "Hinton Rowan Helper Advocate of a 'White America.'" *Southern Sketches No. 1.* Pamphlet, Charlottesville, Va., 1935, 5-25.

Levesque, George A. "Boston's Black Brahmin: Dr. John S. Rock." *Civil War History,* vol. 26, 1980, 341-42.

Levi, Kate Everest. "The Wisconsin Press and Slavery." *Wisconsin Magazine of History,* vol. 9, 1925-1926, 424.

Litwack, Leon F. *North of Slavery, The Negro in the Free States, 1790-1860.* Chicago, 1961.

———. "The Federal Government and the Free Negro, 1790-1860." *Journal of Negro History,* vol. 43, 1958, 268-69.

Lloyd, Arthur Young. *The Slavery Controversy, 1831-1860.* Chapel Hill, N.C., 1939.

Long, Byron R. "Joshua Giddings, A Champion of Political Freedom." *Ohio Archaeological and Historical Quarterly,* vol. 28, 1929, 31-53.

Long, John D. *The Republican Party: Its History, Principles and Policies.* N.Y., 1898.

Lovejoy, Arthur O. *The Great Chain of Being, A Study of the History of an Idea.* Cambridge, Mass., 1961, originally published in 1936.

Ludlum, Robert P. "Joshua R. Giddings, Radical." *Mississippi Valley Historical Review,* vol. 23, 1936-1937, 52-58.

Lurie, Edward. *Louis Agassiz, A Life in Science.* Chicago, 1960.

Luthin, Reinhard H. "Abraham Lincoln Becomes a Republican." *Political Science Quarterly,* vol. 59, 1944, 420-23.

———."Salmon P. Chase's Political Career before the Civil War." *Mississippi Valley Historical Review,* vol. 29, 1943, 518-26.

———. *The First Lincoln Campaign.* Cambridge, Mass., 1944.

Lynch, William O. "Antislavery Tendencies of the Democratic Party in the Northwest, 1848-1850." *Mississippi Valley Historical Review,* vol. 11, 1924, 322-29.

Magdol, Edward. *Owen Lovejoy: Abolitionist in Congress.* New Brunswick, N.J., 1967.

———. "Owen Lovejoy's Role in the Campaign of 1858." *Journal of the Illinois State Historical Society,* vol. 51, 1958, 410-13.

Mandel, Bernard. *Labor: Free and Slave.* N.Y., 1955.

Mayfield, John. *Rehearsal For Republicanism, Free Soil and the Politics of Anti-Slavery.* N.Y., 1980.

McKitrick, Eric L., ed. *Slavery Defended: the views of The Old South.* Englewood Cliffs, N.J., 1963.

McLaughlin, Tom L. "Grass-Roots Attitudes toward Black Rights in Twelve Non-slaveholding States, 1846-1869." *Mid-America,* vol. 56, 1974, 177-78.

McManus, Michael J. "Wisconsin Republicans and Negro Suffrage: Attitudes and Behavior, 1857." *Civil War History,* vol. 25, 1979, 41.

McPherson, James, M. "Abolitionist and Negro Opposition to Colonization During the Civil War." *Phylon,* vol. 26, 1965, 391-98.

———. *The Negro's Civil War.* N.Y., 1965.

Mehlinger, Louis R. "The Attitude of the Free Negro Toward African Colonization." *Journal of Negro History,* vol. 1, 1916, 276-301.

Meier, August, and Rudwick, Elliott. *From Plantation to Ghetto: An Interpretative History of American Negroes.* N.Y., 1970, originally published in 1966.

Merk, Frederick. *Manifest Destiny and Mission in American History.* N.Y., 1963.

———. *Slavery and the Annexation of Texas.* N.Y., 1972.

Merrill, Walter M. *Against Wind and Tide, A Biography of Wm. Lloyd Garrison.* Cambridge, Mass., 1971, originally published in 1963.

Miller, Floyd J. *The Search For a Black Nationality, Black Emigration and Colonization, 1787-1863.* Urbana, Ill., 1975.

Miller, John C. *The Wolf by the Ears, Thomas Jefferson and Slavery.* N.Y., 1977.

Mills, Gary B. "Miscegenation and the Free Negro in Antebellum 'Anglo'

Alabama: A Reexamination of Southern Race Relations." *Journal of American History,* vol. 68, 1981, 16-34.

Milton, George Fort. *The Eve of Conflict, Stephen A. Douglas and the Needless War.* Cambridge, Mass., 1934.

Mitchell, Broadus. *Frederick Law Olmsted, A Critic of the Old South.* Baltimore, 1924.

Moos, Malcolm. *The Republicans, A History of their Party.* N.Y., 1956.

Morris, Thomas D. *Free Men All, The Personal Liberty Laws of the North, 1780-1861.* Baltimore, 1974.

Morrison, Chaplain W. *Democratic Politics and Sectionalism, The Wilmot Proviso Controversy.* Chapel Hill, N.C., 1967.

Mott, Frank L. *American Journalism, A History: 1690-1960.* N.Y., 1964, originally published in 1941.

Mumford, T.T. *Virginia's Attitude Towards Slavery and Secession.* N.Y., 1909.

Myers, William S. *The Republican Party, A History.* N.Y., 1968, originally published in 1927.

Myrdal, Gunnar. *An American Dilemma, The Negro Problem and American Democracy.* N.Y., 1944, 2 vols.

Nash, Gary B., and Weiss, Richard, eds. *The Great Fear, Race in the Minds of America.* N.Y., 1970.

Nash, Howard P. Jr. *Stormy Petrel: The Life and Times of General Benjamin F. Butler, 1818-1893.* Cranbury, N.J., 1969.

National Cyclopedia of American Biography. James T. White and Company, publishers. N.Y., 1906, 60 vols.

Nichols, Roy Franklin. *The Invention of the American Political Parties.* N.Y., 1967.

Nye, Russel Blaine. *Fettered Freedom: Civil Liberties and the Slavery Controversy, 1830-1860.* Ann Arbor, Mich., 1949.

———. *Society and Culture in America, 1830-1860.* N.Y., 1974.

———. "The Slave Power Conspiracy, 1830-1860." *Science and Society,* vol. 10, 1946, 262-74.

Oates, Stephen B. *Abraham Lincoln, The Man Behind the Myths.* N.Y., 1984.

———. "The Man of Our Redemption: Abraham Lincoln and the

Emancipation of the black slaves." *Presidential Studies Quarterly*, vol. 9, 1979, 21-22.

_____. *To Purge This Land With Blood, A Biography of John Brown.* N.Y., 1972, originally published in 1970.

Olbrich, Emil. "The Development of Sentiment on Negro Suffrage to 1860." *Bulletin of the University of Wisconsin No. 477*, vol. 3, Madison, Wis., 1912.

Osofsky, Gilbert, ed. *The Burden of Race.* N.Y. 1967.

Parish, Peter, J. *The American Civil War.* N.Y., 1975.

Paul, James C.N. *Rift in the Democracy.* Philadelphia, 1951.

Pelzer, Louis. "History of Political Parties in Iowa from 1857 to 1860." *Iowa Journal of History and Politics,* vol. 7, 1909, 195-96.

_____. "The Negro and Slavery in Early Iowa." *Iowa Journal of History and Politics*, vol. 2, 1904, 471-73.

Pendergraft, Daryl. "Thomas Corwin and the Conservative Republican Reaction, 1858-1861." *Ohio State Archaeological and Historical Quarterly,* vol. 57, 1948, 17.

Peterson, Merril D. *The Jefferson Image in the American Mind.* N.Y., 1960.

_____., ed. *Thomas Jefferson.* N.Y., 1975.

Phillips, Ulrich B. *Life and Labor in the Old South.* N.Y., 1929.

_____. *The Course of the South to Secession.* Gloucester, Mass., 1958, originally published in 1939.

Pickett, William P. *The Negro Problem, Abraham Lincoln's Solution.* N.Y., 1969, originally published in 1909.

Planck, Gary R. "Abraham Lincoln and Black Colonization: Theory and Practice." *Lincoln Herald*, vol. 72, 1970, 61-64.

Poage, George R. *Henry Clay and the Whig Party.* Gloucester, Mass., 1965.

Porter, George H. *Ohio Politics During the Civil War Period.* N.Y., 1968, originally published in 1911.

Porter, Kirk H., and Johnson, Donald Bruce. *National Party Platforms, 1840-1956.* Urbana, Ill., 1956.

Pressly, Thomas J. *Americans Interpret Their Civil War.* N.Y., 1962.

Preston, Emmet D. "The Fugitive Slave Acts of Ohio." *Journal of Negro History,* vol. 28, 1943, 422-47.

Quarles, Benjamin. *Allies for Freedom: Blacks and John Brown.* N.Y., 1974.

———. *Frederick Douglass.* Washington, D.C., 1948

———. *Lincoln and the Negro.* N.Y., 1962.

Quillin, Frank U. *The Color Line in Ohio.* N.Y., 1969, originally published in 1913.

Radabaugh, James H. "The Negro in Ohio." *Journal of Negro History,* vol. 31, 1946, 13-15.

Ramsdell, Charles W. "The Natural Limits of Slavery Expansion." *Mississippi Valley Historical Review,* vol. 16, 1929, 151-71.

Randall, James G. *Constitutional Problems Under Lincoln.* Urbana, Ill., 1964, originally published in 1926.

———. *Lincoln and the South.* Baton Rouge, La., 1946.

———. *The Civil War and Reconstruction.* N.Y., 1937.

Rawley, James A. *Race and Politics, Bleeding Kansas in the Coming of the Civil War.* Philadelphia, 1969.

Rayback, Joseph. G. *Free Soil, the Election of 1848.* Lexington, Ky., 1970.

———. "The American Workingman and the Antislavery Crusade." *Journal of Economic History,* vol. 3, 1943, 162-63.

Rhodes, James Ford. *History of the United States From the Compromise of 1850 to the Final Restoration of Home Rule at the South in 1877.* Norwood, Mass., 1907, originally, published in 1892, 7 vols.

Riddle, Donald W. *Congressman Abraham Lincoln.* Urbana, Ill., 1957.

Riddleberger, Patrick W. *George Washington Julian, Radical Republican.* Indianapolis, 1966.

———. "The Making of a Political Abolitionist: George W. Julian and the Free Soilers, 1848." *Indiana Magazine of History,* vol. 51, 1955, 234-35.

———. "The Radicals Abandonment of the Negro During Reconstruction." *Journal of Negro History,* vol. 45, 1960, 89.

Robinson, Edgar E. *The Evolution of American Political Parties.* N.Y., 1924.

Rogers, Joseph M. *The True Henry Clay.* Philadelphia, 1904.

Rosenberg, Morton M. *Iowa on the Eve of the Civil War.* Norman, Okla., 1972.

Ross, Earle D. "Horace Greeley and the West." *Mississippi Valley Historical Review,* vol. 20, 1933, 64.

Rozett, John M. "Racism and Republican Emergence in Illinois, 1848-1860: A Re-Evaluation of Republican Negrophobia." *Civil War History,* vol. 22, 1976, 106-08.

Rozwenc, Edwin C., ed. *The Causes of the American Civil War.* Boston, 1961.

Rusk, Ralph L. *The Life of Ralph Waldo Emerson.* N.Y., 1949.

Sandburg, Carl. *Lincoln, the War Years.* N.Y., 1939, 4 vols.

Savage, W. Sherman. "The Contest over Slavery between Illinois and Missouri." *Journal of Negro History,* Vol. 28, 1943, 312.

Scheeler, Reuben J. "The Struggle of the Negro in Ohio for Freedom." *Journal of Negro History,* vol. 31, 1946, 221-22.

Scheips, Paul J. "Lincoln and the Chiriqui Colonization Project." *Journal of Negro History,* vol. 37, 1952, 448-49.

Schlessinger, Arthur Jr., ed. *History of U.S. Political Parties.* N.Y., 1973.

_____. "The Causes of the Civil War: A Note on Historical Sentimentalism." *Partisan Review,* vol. 16, 1949, 968-78.

Schlueter, Herman. *Lincoln, Labor, and Slavery.* N.Y., 1913.

Schouler, James. *History of the United States under the Constitution.* N.Y., 1891, 7 vols.

Schroeder, John H. *Mr. Polk's War, American Opposition and Dissent, 1846-1848.* Madison, Wis., 1973.

Seitz, Donald C. *Horace Greeley.* N.Y., 1970, originally published in 1926.

Seligmann, Herbert J. *Race Against Man.* N.Y., 1939.

Sellers, James L. "James R. Doolittle." *Wisconsin Magazine of History,* vol. 17, 1933-1934, 176.

Sewell, Richard H. *John P. Hale and the Politics of Abolition.* Cambridge, Mass., 1965.

_____. *Ballots For Freedom: Antislavery Politics in the United States, 1837-1860.* N.Y., 1976.

Shapiro, Samuel. *Richard Henry Dana Jr., 1815-1882.* East Lansing, Mich., 1961.

Sharp, Walter Rice. "Henry Smith Lane and the Formation of the

Republican Party in Indiana." *Mississippi Valley Historical Review,* vol. 7, 1920, 98-99.

Shortreed, Margaret. "The Anti-slavery Radicals, 1840-1868." *Past and Present,* vol. 16, 1959, 75.

Shover, Kennenth B. "Maverick at Bay: Ben Wade's Senate Re-Election Campaign, 1862-63." *Civil War History,* vol. 12, 1966, 24.

Shunk, Edward W. "Ohio in Africa." *Ohio State Archaeological and Historical Quarterly,* vol. 51, 1942, 79-84.

Silberman, Charles E. *Crisis in Black and White.* N.Y., 1964.

Silbey, Joel H. *The Shrine of Party.* Pittsburgh, 1967.

Simms, Henry H. *A Decade of Sectional Controversy, 1851-1861.* Chapel Hill, N.C., 1942.

Skipper, Ottis Clark. *J.D.B. DeBow, Magazinist of the Old South.* Athens, Ga., 1958.

Smalley, Eugene V. *A Brief History of the Republican Party.* N.Y., 1888.

Smiley, David L. "Cassius Clay and John G. Fee, A Study in Southern Antislavery Thought." *Journal of Negro History,* vol. 42, 1957, 201-13.

_____. *Lion of White Hall, The Life of Cassius M. Clay.* Madison, Wis., 1962.

Smith, Donnal V. *Chase and Civil War Politics.* Columbus, Ohio, 1931.

Smith, Elbert B. *Francis Preston Blair.* N.Y., 1980

_____. *The Death of Slavery, The United States, 1837-65.* Chicago, 1970, originally published in 1967.

Smith, Henry Nash. *Virgin Land, The American West as Symbol and Myth.* N.Y., 1970, originally published in 1950.

Smith, Theodore Clarke. *Parties and Slavery, 1850-1859.* N.Y., 1906.

_____. "The Free Soil Party in Wisconsin." *Proceedings of the Wisconsin Historical Society,* vol. 42, 1894, 103-53.

_____. *The Liberty and Free Soil Parties in the Northwest.* N.Y., 1897.

Smith, Willard H. *Schuyler Colfax.* Indianapolis, 1952.

Smith, William E. *The Francis Preston Blair Family in Politics.* N.Y., 1933, 2 vols.

Sorin, Gerald. *Abolitionism, A New Perspective.* N.Y., 1972.

Spangler, Earl. *The Negro In Minnesota.* Minneapolis, 1961.

Sparks, David S. "The Birth of the Republican Party in Iowa, 1854-1856." *Iowa Journal of History*, vol. 54, 1956, 1-22.

Spero, Sterling D., and Harris, Abram L. *The Black Worker.* N.Y., 1931.

Stampp, Kenneth M. *And the War Came, The North and the Secession Crisis, 1860-1861.* Ann Arbor, Mich., 1967, originally published in 1950.

_____. *The Imperiled Union, Essays on the Background of the Civil War.* N.Y., 1980.

Stanley, Gerald. "Racism and the Early Republican Party: the 1856 Presidential Election in California." *Pacific Historical Review,* vol. 43, 1974, 171.

Stanton, William. *The Leopard's Spots, Scientific Attitudes Toward Race in America, 1815-1859.* Chicago, 1960.

Starobin, Robert S. *Industrial Slavery in the Old South.* N.Y., 1970.

Staudenraus, P.J. *The African Colonization Movement, 1816-1865.* N.Y., 1961.

Stearn, Gerald Emanuel, and Fried, Albert, eds. *The Essential Lincoln.* N.Y., 1962.

Stenberg, Richard R. "The Motivation of the Wilmot Proviso." *Mississippi Valley Historical Review*, vol. 18, 1932, 536.

Stephenson, Gilbert T. *Race Distinctions in American Law.* N.Y., 1969, originally published in 1910.

Stewart, James Brewer. *Joshua R. Giddings and the Tactics of Radical Politics.* Cleveland, 1970.

Stocking, George W. *Race, Culture and Evolution.* N.Y., 1968.

Stoddard, Henry L. *Horace Greeley, Printer, Editor, Crusader.* N.Y., 1946.

Streeter, Floyd B. *Political Parties in Michigan, 1837-1860.* Lansing, Mich., 1918.

Streifford, David M. "The American Colonization Society: An Application of Republican Ideology to Early Antebellum Reform." *Journal of Southern History*, vol. 45, 1979, 201.

Strickland, Arvarh E. "The Illinois Background of Lincoln's Attitude toward Slavery and the Negro." *Illinois State Historical Society Journal,* vol. 56, 1963, 482-89.

Struik, Dirk J. *Yankee Science in the Making.* N.Y., 1968, originally published in 1948.

Stuckey, Sterling. *The Ideological Origins of Black Nationalism.* Boston, 1972.

Takaki, Ronald. *A Pro-Slavery Crusade: The Agitation to Reopen the African Slave Trade.* N.Y., 1971.

_____. "The Black Child Savage." Cited in Nash and Weiss, *The Great Fear,* 35.

Thomas, John L. *The Liberator, William Lloyd Garrison: A Biography.* Boston, 1963.

Thornbrough, Emma Lou. *The Negro in Indiana Before 1900.* Indianapolis, 1957.

_____. "The Race Issue in Indiana Politics during the Civil War." *Indiana Magazine of History,* vol. 47, 1951, 167-75.

Trefousse, Hans L. *Benjamin Franklin Wade.* N.Y., 1963.

_____. "Ben Wade and the Negro." *Ohio Historical Quarterly,* vol. 68, 1959, 170.

_____. *Carl Schurz, A Biography.* Knoxville, Tenn., 1982.

Turner, Frederick J. *The United States, 1830-1850: The Nation and Its Sections.* N.Y., 1935.

Van Bolt, Roger H. "The Rise of the Republican Party in Indiana, 1855-1856." *Indiana Magazine of History,* vol. 51, 1955, 204-07.

Van Deburg, William L. *Slavery and Race in American Popular Culture.* Madison, Wis., 1984.

Van Den Berghe, Pierre L. *Race and Racism.* N.Y., 1967.

Van Deusen, Glyndon G. *Horace Greeley, Nineteenth-Century Crusader.* Philadelphia, 1953.

_____. *The life of Henry Clay.* Boston, 1937.

Voegeli, V. Jacque. *Free But Not Equal, The Midwest and the Negro during the Civil War.* Chicago, 1976.

_____. "The Northwest and the Race Issue, 1861-1862." *Mississippi Valley Historical Review,* vol. 50, 1963, 245.

Von Holst, Herman. *The Constitutional and Political History of the United States.* Chicago, 1892, 8 vols.

Wade, Richard C. "The Negro in Cincinnati, 1800-1830." *Journal of Negro History,* vol. 39, 1954, 48.

Walker, Peter F. *Moral Choices.* Baton Rouge, La., 1978.

Walters, Ronald G. *The Anti-Slavery Appeal, American Abolitionism After 1830.* Baltimore, 1976.

Weinberg, Albert K. *Mainfest Destiny, A Study of Nationalist Expansionism in American History.* Baltimore, 1935.

Weisbord, Robert G. "The Back-to-Africa Idea." *History Today,* vol. 18, 1968, 31.

Wesley, Charles H. "Lincoln's Plan for Colonizing the Emancipated Negroes." *Journal of Negro History,* vol. 4, 1919, 8-10.

_____. *Negro Labor in the United States, 1850-1925.* N.Y., 1927.

_____. "The Concept of the Inferiority of the Negro in American Thought." *Journal of Negro History,* vol. 25, 1940, 546-54.

_____. "The Participation of Negroes in Anti-Slavery Political Parties." *Journal of Negro History,* vol. 29, 1944, 54-64.

Wiley, Bell Irwin. *Southern Negroes, 1861-1865.* New Haven, Conn., 1938.

Williamson, Joel. *New People, Miscegenation and Mulattoes in the United States.* N.Y., 1980.

Wilson, Charles J. "The Negro in Ohio." *Ohio Archaeological and Historical Publications,* vol. 39, 1930, 747-64.

Wilson, Joseph T. *The Black Phalanx, A History of the Negro Soldiers of the United States in the Wars of 1775-1812, 1861-1865.* Hartford, Conn., 1888.

Wisenburger, Francis P. *The Passing of the Frontier, 1825-1850.* Columbus, Ohio, 1941.

Wood, Forrest G. *Black Scare, The Racist Response to Emancipation and Reconstruction.* Los Angeles, Calif., 1968.

Woodburn, James A. "Henry Smith Lane." *Indiana Magazine of History,* vol. 27, 1931, 283.

Woodford, Frank B. *Lewis Cass, The Last Jeffersonian.* New Brunswick, N.J., 1950.

Woodson, Carter. *Free Negro Owners of Slaves in the United States in 1830, Together with Absentee Ownership of Slaves in the United States in 1830.* Washington, D.C., 1924.

Wurthman, Leonard B. Jr. "Frank Blair: Lincoln's Congressional Spokesman." *Missouri Historical Review,* vol. 64, 1970, 265-66.

Wyatt-Brown, Bertram. *Lewis Tappan and the Evangelical War Against Slavery.* N.Y., 1971.

Younger, Edward. *John A. Kasson.* Iowa City, Iowa, 1955.

Zimmerman, Charles. "The Origin and Rise of the Republican Party in Indiana, from 1854 to 1860." *Indiana Magazine of History,* vol. 13, 1917, 393.

INDEX